Tolley's
Venture Capital Tax Reliefs –
the VCT Scheme, the EIS & the CVS

Contributors

Howard Scott, BA (Oxon), FCA, CTA (Fellow) –
Tax Partner (Retired)

Robert Mitchell, LLB, ACA, CTA –
Tax Director

David Brookes, ACA –
Senior Tax Manager

Mark Casey, LLM (Cantab), CTA

Zigurds Kronbergs, MA, BSc, ARCS, ACA, FCCA

All with BDO Stoy Hayward LLP

LexisNexis™ UK

Members of the LexisNexis Group worldwide

United Kingdom	LexisNexis UK, a Division of Reed Elsevier (UK) Ltd, 4 Hill Street, EDINBURGH EH2 3JZ and Halsbury House, 35 Chancery Lane, LONDON WC2A 1EL
Argentina	LexisNexis Argentina, BUENOS AIRES
Australia	LexisNexis Butterworths, CHATSWOOD, New South Wales
Austria	LexisNexis Verlag ARD Orac GmbH & Co KG, VIENNA
Canada	LexisNexis Butterworths, MARKHAM, Ontario
Chile	LexisNexis Chile Ltda, SANTIAGO DE CHILE
Czech Republic	Nakladatelství Orac sro, PRAGUE
France	Editions du Juris-Classeur SA, PARIS
Germany	LexisNexis Deutschland GmbH, FRANKFURT and MUNSTER
Hong Kong	LexisNexis Butterworths, HONG KONG
Hungary	HVG-Orac, BUDAPEST
India	LexisNexis Butterworths, NEW DELHI
Ireland	LexisNexis, DUBLIN
Italy	Giuffrè Editore, MILAN
Malaysia	Malayan Law Journal Sdn Bhd, KUALA LUMPUR
New Zealand	LexisNexis Butterworths, WELLINGTON
Poland	Wydawnictwo Prawnicze LexisNexis, WARSAW
Singapore	LexisNexis Butterworths, SINGAPORE
South Africa	LexisNexis Butterworths, Durban
Switzerland	Stämpfli Verlag AG, BERNE
USA	LexisNexis, DAYTON, Ohio

Published by LexisNexis UK

A CIP Catalogue record for this book is available from the British Library.

ISBN 0 406 91992 5

Typeset by Phoenix Photosetting, Chatham, Kent
Printed and bound in England by Antony Rowe Ltd, Chippenham, Wilts

Visit LexisNexis UK at www.lexisnexis.co.uk

Foreword

Amid the excitement surrounding each year's crop of tax-avoidance techniques, it is often overlooked that there are, and have for many years been, many simpler tax incentives offered by governments to promote and expand small to medium-sized businesses.

These tax incentives aim to increase the flow of funds to such businesses by allowing high-net-worth individuals (and more recently, corporations) valuable tax reliefs on amounts invested as, broadly, ordinary shares in unquoted trading companies.

These reliefs will come into sharp focus over the next two years since the Venture Capital Trust scheme now permits individuals a 40% income tax credit on investments of up to £200,000 per person per tax year. This is a substantially increased contribution by the Exchequer when compared to the limits for earlier years. Although these enhanced reliefs are only scheduled to last until April 2006, it seems that some form of venture capital tax reliefs will always be around and they do have the enormous advantage of being relatively straightforward and, most significantly, capable of advance clearance with the Inland Revenue.

Aggressive tax-avoidance schemes have received a bad press from the Inland Revenue recently, culminating in a requirement for sponsors and others to notify the Inland Revenue of the more aggressive schemes.

Against such a background, the availability of EIS and VCT reliefs in a relatively straightforward format can be seen as a return to sanity.

Although the schemes are simple in concept and outline, they are detailed and tricky in their individual rules, conditions and requirements.

I very much welcome this timely new edition of Tolley's 'Venture Capital Tax Reliefs' written by the EIS/VCT team at BDO Stoy Hayward LLP.

They are building on the work of an illustrious predecessor, Mrs Mavis Seymour, who was very active in this area before her retirement. I believe this new book will prove to be of immense help to sponsors, investors and the management of the investee companies.

Martin Churchill – Editor, *Tax Efficient Review*.

15 June 2004

Acknowledgement

It will be clear from the list of contributors that the production of this book was a team effort by the EIS/VCT group at BDO Stoy Hayward LLP. We hope that this up to date publication will assist our colleagues in the profession, our clients and entrepreneurs to set up businesses with the benefit of these tax reliefs.

We have been helped in the production of this book by two earlier publications.

We would like to acknowledge these two earlier sources which were: 'Venture Capital Trusts and the Enterprise Investment Scheme' by Mavis Seymour, published by Butterworths 1995 (ISBN 0 406 05411 8) and 'The Enterprise Investment Scheme, Venture Capital Trusts and the Corporate Venturing Scheme' First Edition, published by Butterworth Tolley (ISBN 0 754 51459 5).

We have however endeavoured to build and expand on these earlier works and have introduced as many practical points from our own practice in these complex areas as we could.

Any comments and suggestions for improvement by readers are welcome.

Contents

Foreword		*iii*
Acknowledgement		*v*
Abbreviations		*ix*
Table of Cases		*xi*
Table of Statutes		*xiv*
Table of Statutory Instruments		*xxiii*
Part 1 Overviews		**1**
Chapter 1	Introduction	3
Chapter 2	The Venture Capital Trust Scheme	12
Chapter 3	The Enterprise Investment Scheme	16
Chapter 4	The Corporate Venturing Scheme	19
Part 2 Qualifying Conditions		**21**
Chapter 5	Qualifying Companies	23
Chapter 6	Qualifying Trades	111
Chapter 7	Qualifying Investors	151
Part 3 Investment Reliefs		**173**
Chapter 8	VCT Investment Relief	175
Chapter 9	EIS Investment Relief	184
Chapter 10	CVS Investment Relief	192
Part 4 Reduction or Withdrawal of Investment Reliefs		**197**
Chapter 11	Losing VCT Investment Relief	199
Chapter 12	Losing EIS Investment Relief	203
Chapter 13	Losing CVS Investment Relief	228
Part 5 Deferral Reliefs		**241**
Chapter 14	Reinvestment in VCT Companies	243
Chapter 15	Reinvestment in EIS Companies	255
Chapter 16	Reinvestment in CVS Companies	288
Part 6 Disposing of Investments		**297**
Chapter 17	Disposal of VCT Shares	299
Chapter 18	Disposal of EIS Shares	310
Chapter 19	Disposal of CVS Shares	329

Part 7 How the Reliefs Work **339**
Chapter 20 Giving and Withdrawing Investment Relief 341
Chapter 21 Overlaps with Other Investment Reliefs 363
Chapter 22 Giving and Withdrawing Capital Gains Reliefs 372
Chapter 23 Overlaps with Other Capital Gains Reliefs 380

Part 8 Administration **395**
Chapter 24 Claims, Approval and Clearances 397
Chapter 25 Information Powers and Requirements 428

Part 9 Practical Matters **437**
Chapter 26 Small Private Schemes 439
Chapter 27 Public Offers 460
Chapter 28 Exit Routes 475

Appendices
Appendix 1 Contents of a Shareholders' Agreement for the EIS Companies 483
Appendix 2 Checklist for directors of a VCT or EIS investee company 485
Appendix 3 Checklist for VCT or EIS investors 488
Appendix 4 Recognised Stock Exchanges 490
Appendix 5 Useful addresses 492
Appendix 6 IR Forms 494

Index 507

Abbreviations

AGM	annual general meeting
AIM	Alternative Investment Market
ARD	accounting reference date
BES	business enterprise scheme
BSS	business start-up scheme
CA 1985	Companies Act 1985
CVS	corporate venturing scheme
EGM	extraordinary general meeting
EIS	enterprise investment scheme
FA	Finance Act
FSA	Financial Services Authority
FSA 1986	Financial Services Act 1986
FSMA 2000	Financial Services and Markets Act 2000
IR	Inland Revenue
ITEPA 2000	Income Tax (Earnings and Pensions) Act 2003
PEP	personal equity plan
POS 1995	Public Offers of Securities Regulations 1995
RIR	rollover relief on reinvestment
SBIC	small business investment company (US)
SCEC	Small Companies Enterprise Centre
SI	statutory instrument
SMEs	small and medium-sized businesses
SPS	Savings and Pension Schemes office
SRO	self-regulating organisation
TA 1988	Income and Corporation Taxes Act 1988
TMA 1970	Taxes Management Act 1970
USM	Unlisted Securities Market
VCT	venture capital trust

Table of Cases

A

Ambrose Lake Tin and Copper Co, Re, Clarke's Case (1878) 8 Ch D 635, 47 LJ Ch 696, 26 WR 601, 38 LT 587, CA 8.1.5
A-G of the Duchy of Lancaster v G E Overton (Farms) Ltd [1982] Ch 277, [1982] 1 All ER 524, [1982] 2 WLR 397, 125 Sol Jo 828, CA 5.2.3.2

B

Barclays Bank plc v IRC [1994] STC 184, 67 TC 1, [1994] 2 BCLC 30, [1994] 11 LS Gaz R 36, 138 Sol Jo LB 25, CA; affd [1995] 1 AC 119, [1994] 3 All ER 1, [1994] 3 WLR 159, [1994] STC 580, 67 TC 1, [1994] 2 BCLC 239, [1994] 32 LS Gaz R 44, 138 Sol Jo LB 139, HL 8.1.5, 14.3.2
Birmingham and District Cattle By-Products Co Ltd v IRC (1919) 12 TC 92 . . . . . 6.8.2
Brown v Richardson [1997] STC (SCD) 233 . . . . . 6.1.4

C

Cannop Coal Co Ltd v IRC (1918) 12 TC 31 . . . . . 6.8.2
Castleton Management Services Ltd v Kirkwood [2001] STC (SCD) 95 . . . . . 6.5.10

D

Delian Enterprises v Ellis [1999] STC (SCD) 103 . . . . . 6.1.4

E

Eastham v Leigh, London and Provincial Properties Ltd [1971] Ch 871, [1971] 1 All ER 87, [1970] 3 WLR 848, 46 TC 687, 49 ATC 216, [1970] TR 203, 114 Sol Jo 808, 216 Estates Gazette 309; affd [1971] Ch 871, [1971] 2 All ER 887, [1971] 2 WLR 1149, 46 TC 687, 50 ATC 53, [1971] TR 33, 115 Sol Jo 266, 218 Estates Gazette 1413, CA 14.3.5

F

Fletcher (Inspector of Taxes) v Thompson [2002] EWHC 1552 (Admin), [2002] STC 1149, 74 TC 710, [2002] All ER (D) 265 (Jul) 12.5.12.2

G

Gardner (John) & Bowring, Hardy & Co Ltd v IRC (1930) 15 TC 602, Ct of Sess 5.3.4

H

Hall (George) & Sons v Platt (Inspector of Taxes) (1954) 35 TC 440, 33 ATC 340, 47 R & IT 713, [1954] TR 331, 164 Estates Gazette 497, L (TC) 1711 .... 5.3.4

I

IRC v Fraser (1942) 24 TC 498, 21 ATC 223, 1942 SC 493, 1942 SLT 280, Ct of Sess .. 6.3.3

J

Jerome v Kelly (Inspector of Taxes) [2002] EWCA Civ 1879, [2003] STC 206, [2003] 24 EG 163, [2003] 02 LS Gaz R 33, [2003] 03 EGCS 126, 147 Sol Jo LB 59, [2002] All ER (D) 365 (Dec); revsd [2004] UKHL 25, [2004] 2 All ER 835, [2004] 1 WLR 1409, [2004] STC 887, [2004] All ER (D) 168 (May) 14.3.5

Jones (Inspector of Taxes) v Nuttall (1926) 10 TC 346, 5 ATC 229, 70 Sol Jo 586, 42 TLR 384 .... 6.5.11

L

Lean and Dickson v Ball (1925) 10 TC 341, 1926 SC 15, Ct of Sess 6.5.11

Lord (Inspector of Taxes) v Tustain [1993] STC 755, 65 TC 761 .... 5.2.3.1, 21.8

Lyons v Cowcher (Inspector of Taxes) (1926) 10 TC 438 .... 7.6.2.9

M

Matrix-Securities Ltd v IRC [1994] 1 All ER 769, [1994] 1 WLR 334, [1994] STC 272, 66 TC 587, HL 24.6.5.1

Morden Rigg & Co and R B Eskrigge & Co v Monks (Inspector of Taxes) (1923) 8 TC 450, CA 5.3.4

N

Napier v Griffiths (Inspector of Taxes) [1991] STC 55n, 63 TC 745, CA 6.8.2

National Westminster Bank plc v IRC [1994] STC 184, 67 TC 1, [1994] 2 BCLC 30, [1994] 11 LS Gaz R 36, 138 Sol Jo LB 25, CA; affd [1995] 1 AC 119, [1994] 3 All ER 1, [1994] 3 WLR 159, [1994] STC 580, 67 TC 1, [1994] 2 BCLC 239, [1994] 32 LS Gaz R 44, 138 Sol Jo LB 139, HL 8.1.5, 14.3.2

P

Palser v Grinling, Property Holding Co Ltd v Mischeff [1948] AC 291, [1948] 1 All ER 1, [1948] LJR 600, 92 Sol Jo 53, 64 TLR 2, HL 5.2.3.2

Pepper (Inspector of Taxes) v Hart [1993] AC 593, [1993] 1 All ER 42, [1992] 3 WLR 1032, [1992] STC 898, 65 TC 421, [1993] ICR 291, [1993] IRLR 33, [1993] RVR 127, [1993] NLJR 17, HL 12.5.10.2

R

R v IRC, ex p Fulford-Dobson [1987] QB 978, [1987] 3 WLR 277, 60 TC 168, 131 Sol Jo 975, [1987] LS Gaz R 2197, [1987] STC 344 .... 6.9.4

R v IRC, ex p MFK Underwriting Agencies Ltd [1990] 1 All ER 91, [1990] 1 WLR 1545, [1989] STC 873, 62 TC 607, DC 24.6.5.1

R v Inspector of Taxes, ex p Clarke [1974] QB 220, [1972] 1 All ER 545, [1973] 3 WLR 673, 117 Sol Jo 815, 47 TC 691, 50 ATC 389, L (TC) 2431, CA 6.6.6

Reid v IRC (1947) 28 TC 451, [1947] TR 383, 1947 SC 707, 1948 SLT 119, Ct of Sess: 6.5.11

Rutledge v IRC (1929) 14 TC 490, 8 ATC 207, 1929 SC 379, 1929 SLT 296, Ct of Sess: 6.3.3

Ryall (Inspector of Taxes) v Hoare [1923] 2 KB 447, 8 TC 521, 2 ATC 137, 92 LJKB 1010, [1923] All ER Rep 528, 67 Sol Jo 750, 129 LT 505, 39 TLR 475 .... 7.6.2.9

S

Shepherd (Inspector of Taxes) v Law Land plc [1990] STC 795, 63 TC 692 .... 5.1.7
South Yorkshire Transport Ltd v Monopolies and Mergers Commission [1993] 1 All ER 289, [1993] NLJR 128, sub nom R v Monopolies and Mergers Commission, ex p South Yorkshire Transport Ltd [1993] 1 WLR 23, [1993] BCC 111, HL 5.2.3.2
Steele (Inspector of Taxes) v European Vinyls Corpn (Holdings) BV [1995] STC 31; on appeal sub nom Steele (Inspector of Taxes) v EVC International NV (formerly European Vinyls Corpn (Holdings) BV) [1996] STC 785, CA 5.1.6
Strange v Openshaw (Inspector of Taxes) [1983] STC 416, sub nom Openshaw v Strange 57 TC 544 .... 17.2.2, 18.2.2, 19.2.2

W

Walls v Livesey (Inspector of Taxes) [1995] STC (SCD) 12 .... 6.1.4
Wannell v Rothwell (Inspector of Taxes) [1996] STC 450, 68 TC 719 .... 6.1.4
Wild v Cannavan (Inspector of Taxes) [1997] STC 966, 70 TC 554, CA 24.8.3
Wisdom v Chamberlain (Inspector of Taxes) [1969] 1 All ER 332, [1969] 1 WLR 275, 45 TC 92, 112 Sol Jo 946, L (TC) 2292, sub nom Chamberlain (Inspector of Taxes) v Wisdom 47 ATC 358, [1968] TR 345, CA 6.3.3

Table of Statutes

Capital Allowances Act 2001
s 362(1) 6.5.11
Companies Act 1985
s 8 . . . . . . 26.6.9
28 . . . . . . 26.6.10
83 . . . . . . 27.4.10
101 . . . . . . 27.2.4
117 . . . . . . 12.8.5.1; 13.7.5; 15.11.3.1; 27.2.4
118 . . . . . . 27.2.4
121, 123 . . . . . . 26.6.14
224 . . . . . . 26.8.5
234A 26.8.6
233, 234 . . . . . . 26.8.4
244 . . . . . . 27.2.7
282 . . . . . . 27.2.6
(3) 26.6.11
286 . . . . . . 27.2.6
287 . . . . . . 26.6.7
288 . . . . . . 26.6.5
305 . . . . . . 26.6.11
348 . . . . . . 26.6.10
351 . . . . . . 26.6.6
352 . . . . . . 26.7.3
366A 26.8.1
369 . . . . . . 26.8.1, 26.8.2
378 . . . . . . 26.8.4
379A 26.8.1
Sch 24 . . . . . . 26.6.3
Finance Act 1995
s 71(2) 5.6.2.14
Finance Act 1998 . . . . . . 14.1.1
Sch 18
para 9 . . . . . . 24.10.3
55 . . . . . . 22.5.2; 24.10.3
57(2) 22.5.2
Finance Act 2000
s 63 . . . . . . 1.4.1
(4) 4.2
Sch 15 . . . . . . 1.4.1; 25.4.1
para 2(ca), (d) 5.16.1
3 . . . . . . 5.1.4; 6.1.3.3; 10.2.3; 13.2.1; 19.1.2; 20.6.2
5 . . . . . . 5.17.2

Finance Act 2000 – *contd*
Sch 15 – *contd*
para 6(1), (3) 5.17.3
7(1)–(6) 5.17.2
8(4), (5) 5.17.4
9(1), (4) 5.17.2
10(2)–(5) 5.17.5
11 . . . . . . 5.17.5; 21.7.3
(a) 5.16.6
12 . . . . . . 5.17.5
13 . . . . . . 5.17.6
14 . . . . . . 5.17.7; 10.2.4
16(1), (3), (5) 5.12.2
17 . . . . . . 5.10.1
(1) 5.1.10
(a) 5.15.1
(b) 5.1.7
(2) 5.15.1
(3) 5.1.8, 5.1.10, 5.15.1
18(1)–(3) 5.12.5
19(1)–(4) 5.12.3.2
20(1), (2) 5.16.1
21(1)(b) 6.1.4
(2)(a), (d) 5.16.2
(e) 5.16.1
(3) 5.16.6
(4)(a), (b) 5.16.6
(5) 5.16.7
21A(1), (2) 5.16.4
22 . . . . . . 5.13.2
23(1) 6.9.1
(2) 5.12.3
(3) 5.12.3, 5.16.2
(4) 5.12.3
(5) 5.12.3, 5.16.2; 6.8.1
(6) 5.12.3
(b) 5.12.3
(7) 5.12.3
(b) 5.16.4
(8) 5.12.3
(9)(a) 5.12.3
(11)(b) 5.16.7
24(1)–(4) 5.12.3.1
25(1)(a) 5.16.3; 6.4.1

Finance Act 2000 – *contd*
Sch 15 – *contd*
para 25(2) 5.12.3; 6.2.2, 6.6.1
proviso 6.6.6
(3) 5.12.3; 6.2.2
27(2), (3) 6.5.4.2
(5)(a)–(c) 6.5.4.3
(d)–(h) 6.5.4.4
28(2) 6.5.6.4
(3), (4) 6.5.6.7
(6) 6.5.6.5
29(2) 5.12.3; 6.5.8.1
(3)–(5) 6.5.8.1
32(2), (3) 6.5.14
33(1), (6) 6.5.15
35 . . . . 5.14.1; 10.1.2
(2) 5.14.2; 10.1.3
36 . . . . 6.2.1
(1)–(3), (5) 5.12.4
37(1)(a) 5.12.6.1
(b) 5.12.6.2
(c) 5.12.6.3
(2), (3) 5.12.6
(4) 5.12.6.1
(5) 5.12.6.2, 5.12.6.3
(6) 5.12.6.3
39 . . . . 20.3.2
(1) 10.2.1, 10.4; 20.3.4
(2) 10.3.2
40 . . . . 24.10.2
(7) 24.10.3
41(2), (3) 24.10.2
43 . . . . 24.10.6
44 . . . . 24.10.7
45(2)–(5) 10.3.3
46 . . . . 20.6.3; 23.8
47(5)–(7) 13.5
48 . . . . 13.2.1; 19.1.2; 20.6.2
49, 50 . . . . 13.4.3
53 . . . . 13.4.1
54(1) 13.6.1, 13.6.6
(c) 13.6.5
(2) 13.6.1
(3) 13.6.2
(3A) 13.6.3
(4) 13.6.5
55(1) 13.6.5
(2)–(4) 13.6.4
56(1) 13.7.2
(a)(ii) 13.7.2.1
(2) 13.7.3
(3) 13.7.2.1
(4)(a) 13.7.3
(b) 13.7.3.1
(5) 13.7.3.1
57(1)–(5) 13.7.4
58(5), (6) 13.7.5
(8) 13.7.2
59 . . . . 13.8.1; 19.2.2; 20.6.3.2
60(1) 20.6.4

Finance Act 2000 – *contd*
Sch 15 – *contd*
para 63 . . . . 20.7.4; 25.4.6
64 . . . . 25.4.2
65 . . . . 25.4.3
66 . . . . 25.4.4
67 . . . . 19.6.2
(1)(a) 19.8
68 . . . . 19.6.1, 19.6.4
(1) 22.8.1
69(1) 22.8.1
70 . . . . 21.7.2
(2) 22.8.1
71 . . . . 19.6.2
(1) 19.6.2.1
(3) 19.6.2
72 . . . . 22.8.1
73(1)(b) 16.3
(3) 16.3
74(1) 16.5.1
(2) 16.2.2, 16.5.1
(3) 16.5.1
75(2)–(4) 16.7.2
76(1) 16.6.2
(2) 16.6.5
(3)(a), (b) 16.6.3
(4) 16.6.4
78(1) 16.7.1
79(1) 16.7.3
(2) 16.7.3
(b) 16.7.3
(3) 16.7.3
(5) 16.7.4
80 . . . . 19.3.2
81 . . . . 19.3.2
(1) 19.3.3
(b) 19.3.4
(2) 19.3.5
(3) 19.3.3, 19.3.5
82 . . . . 19.3.2, 19.3.6
83 . . . . 19.3.2, 19.3.6.1
(1) 5.12.6.1; 23.8
84, 85 . . . . 23.8; 19.3.2, 19.3.6.1
86, 87 . . . . 19.3.2, 19.3.6.1
88 . . . . 19.3.2
89 . . . . 19.3.2
(1) 24.9.1
(2)–(4) 24.9.2
90(1) 24.9.2
(2) 24.9.2, 24.9.3
(3) 24.9.3
91(1) 24.9.2, 24.9.3
(2) 24.9.3
(3) 24.9.2
(4), (5) 24.9.4
92 . . . . 24.9.5
93(1) 19.4.1
(3) 19.4.2
(4) 19.4.3
94(1)–(3) 19.6.3

Finance Act 2000 – *contd*
Sch 15 – *contd*
para 96 .... 20.6.3
(1), (2) 19.2.1
97 .... 19.1.4
99 .... 4.2.3
102(1) 5.1.7, 5.12.3
Sch 16 .... 1.4.1
para 5(1), (3) 24.10.3
Sch 17
para 6 .... 5.1.3
Sch 18
para 4, 5 .... 6.5.8.2
Finance Act 2001 .... 7.6.1.5
Sch 15
para 28 .... 25.3.3
35(2), (3), (5) 25.3.3
40 .... 25.3.3
(2) 5.7.2
Sch 16
para 2 .... 5.2.5.5
Finance Act 2002
Sch 8 .... 5.17.6
para 1(1) 5.17.6
Sch 33
para 11 .... 5.6.2.6, 5.6.2.7
(3) 5.6.2.6, 5.6.2.7
Finance Act 2004 .... 1.10
s 89(1) 8.3.3; 20.2.5
Sch 18
para 1(7) 5.7.5.3
(8) 5.11.1
5 .... 5.7.3.2
6(1), (3) 12.5.6
17(1) 15.11.3.3
Sch 19
para 5 .... 22.3.2
7(1) 22.3.2
9 .... 5.5.3
(a) 5.5.4
11(a) 5.2.5.6, 5.2.5.7
(b) 5.2.5.6
(c) 5.2.5.8
12 .... 5.5.3
Sch 20
para 5(2)(a) 5.16.2
Financial Services and Markets Act 2000 .... 27.2.2, 27.4.1
s 15 .... 27.2.1
Hotel Proprietors Act 1956 .... 6.5.13
Income and Corporation Taxes Act 1988
s 11(1) 10.2.2
55 .... 6.3.10
130 .... 21.4.2, 21.7.3
208 .... 2.4
219 .... 28.5.3
(1) 28.5.6
254(1) 5.4.3
289(1)(a) 5.7.5.3; 9.2.5
Income and Corporation Taxes Act 1988 – *contd*
s 289(1)(aa) 5.7.5.3, 5.9.2; 9.2.5
(aza) 9.2.5
(b) 5.7.5, 5.7.5.3, 5.11.4; 6.2.1
(c), (d) 5.7.5
(1A) 5.7.5.2, 5.11.4
(1B), (1D), (1E) 5.7.3.2, 5.7.5.2
(2) 5.7.5.1, 5.11.4; 6.4.1
(a)(ii) 5.7.4, 5.7.5.1; 6.2.1, 6.8.1
(b) 5.13; 6.2.2, 6.6.1
(i) 6.6.6
(3) 5.7.5
(3A)(a), (b) 5.7.5.1
(6) 7.6.1.9; 9.2.7
(6ZA), (6ZB) 5.11.5.1
(7) 5.9.1; 9.12; 15.5.1, 15.7.5; 24.2.2; 26.1.5
(8)(b) 20.5.2.3
(8A) 5.7.5.3
(9) 5.11.1, 5.11.2.2
(12) 5.11.2.2
289A(1) 9.4; 20.2.7
(2) 9.3.3; 20.2.5
(a), (b) 9.3.5
(3) 9.4.1, 9.4.2.1
(4) 9.4.1
(5) 20.2.8
(6) 24.7.1
(7) 24.7.1, 24.8.1
(8) 24.7.2
290(1) 7.6.1.8
(2) 7.6.1.8; 9.3.1; 20.2.3
291 .... 15.8.11
(1)(a) 9.2.6
(b) 7.6.1.5; 12.3.1
(2) 7.6.2.2, 7.6.3.1
(3), (5) 7.6.2.6
(6) 12.5.2
291A(1) 7.6.2.9
(2) 7.6.2.9
(b) 7.6.2.9, 7.6.2.10
(3) 12.5.12.2
(a)–(e) 7.6.2.9; 12.5.7.2
(f) 7.6.2.9; 12.5.7.2
(i) 7.6.2.9
(4) 7.6.2.11
(5) 7.6.2.11
(a), (c) 7.6.2.11
291B(1) 7.6.3.1
(2) 7.6.3.1, 7.6.3.4
(3) 7.6.3.4
(4) 7.6.3.5
(5) 7.6.1.4
(5A) 7.6.3.2
(7) 7.6.3.3
(8) 7.6.3.1
(9) 7.6.3.3

Income and Corporation Taxes Act 1988 – *contd*

s 291B(10) 7.6.3.5
293(1A)(a) 5.7.2
(b) 5.7.2
(1B) 5.7.2
(2) 5.7.3.1; 6.9.1
(a) 5.7.3.1
(aa) 5.11.4
(3A)(a)–(c) 5.7.3.2
(3B) 5.7.3.2
(b) 5.7.3.2
(3C) 5.7.3.2
(a) 5.7.3.2
(3D)–(3F) 5.7.3.2
(4A), (4B) 5.7.3.2
(5), (6) 5.7.3.2
(6A) 5.8.1; 15.5.2
(6B)–(6D) 5.8.1
(8) 5.1.7
(a) 5.1.8, 5.11.1
(b) 5.1.10
(8A) 5.10.1
(8AA) 5.1.8, 5.1.10
(9)(d) 5.11.1
297(2) 6.5.1
(g) 6.5.15
(3)(a), (b) 6.5.4.2
(c) 6.5.4.4
(d)(i)–(iii) 6.5.4.3
(iv)–(vii) 6.5.4.4
(4) 5.7.3.2; 6.5.8.1, 6.5.8.2
(5) 5.7.3.2; 6.5.8.1
(5A)(a) 5.7.3.2; 6.5.8.1
(b) 5.7.3.2
(5B) 6.5.8.1
(5C) 6.5.8.1
(6) 6.5.6.4, 6.5.6.7
(7) 6.5.6.7
(8) 6.1.4
298(1) 6.5.15.1
(2) 6.5.15
(3) 6.3.2, 6.5.15
(5) 6.5.6.5, 6.5.8.2.1, 6.5.14
299(1) 18.7.1, 18.8.2; 20.5.2.3, 20.5.2.5
(a) 18.8.3; 20.5.2.5
(2) 18.7.1, 18.8.2; 20.5.2.5
(4) 18.8.6
(5) 18.2.2; 20.5.2.3
(5A) 18.2.2
(6) 18.4.2, 18.7.1; 20.5.2.5; 21.5
(6A) 18.4.3; 21.5
(6B)–(6D) 21.5
(8)(b) 18.2.2; 20.5.2.3
299A(1) 7.6.1.5; 12.4.2
(a) 12.4.1
(2) 12.4.1

Income and Corporation Taxes Act 1988 – *contd*

s 299A(3) 7.6.1.4; 12.4.1
299B 7.6.1.5
(1)(a) 5.7.6.1
(b) 5.7.6.2
(c) 5.7.6.3
(d) 5.7.6.4
(2) 5.7.6.1
(3) 5.7.6.2, 5.7.6.3
(4) 5.7.6.4
(6) 5.7.6
300(1BC) 12.6
(1C) 12.5.3.1
(1E) 12.5.10.2
(2) 12,5.3
(b) 12.5.6
(c) 12.5.7, 12.5.7.2
(d) 12.5.8
(e) 12.5.9
(g) 12.5.11.1
(h) 12.5.12.2
(i) 12.5.10.1
(3) 12.5.3, 12.5.12.1
(4)(a) 12.5.4.1, 12.5.6.1, 12.5.7.3
(b) 12.5.8.1
(c) 12.5.9.1
(d) 12.5.10.2
(e) 12.5.11.2
(f) 12.5.12.2
(g) 12.5.12.1
(5)(a) 12.5.5
(10) 12.5.10.2
300A(1) 12.7.1, 12.7.4
(2) 12.7.1
(4) 12.7.1
(5) 12.7.1
(6) 12.7.3
(8) 12.7.2
(9), (10) 12.7.4
301(3) 12.5.8
(5) 12.5.7.1
(6)(a) 12.5.1
(b) 12.5.3.1
(6A) 12.5.3.1
301A(1)–(4) 12.6
302(1)–(3) 7.6.4.1; 12.10.2
(4), (4A) 7.6.4.1, 7.6.4.2; 12.10.2
(4B) 7.6.4.2; 12.10.2
(5) 7.6.4.1; 12.10.2
303(1) 12.8.2
(1A), (1C) 12.8.3
(2) 12.8.4
(9) 12.8.5.1
(9A) 12.8.2
303A(1)–(3) 12.8.5.3
(4)–(6) 12.8.5.3
(7) 12.8.5.3

Income and Corporation Taxes Act 1988 – *contd*
s 303AA(1) 12.8.5.2
(4), (5) 12.8.5.2
304(1) 18.2.3
(2) 18.2.4.3
304A 18.8.6; 20.5.2.6
(1)(a) 5.10.1, 5.10.2
(b)–(d) 5.10.1
(e) 5.10.1, 5.10.2
(3), (4) 5.10.1, 5.10.2
(6) 5.10.1
304AA(1)(f) 5.10.2
305A 18.6.4; 21.2.3
306(1)(b) 24.8.10
(2) 24.5.6.3, 24.8.4
(3) 24.8.1
(3A) 24.8.1
(4) 24.8.6
(6) 24.8.3, 24.8.9
(7) 20.2.9
(8) 20.2.10
(9) 20.7.2
(10) 24.8.5
307(1) 20.5.5.1
(2) 20.5.5
(3) 20.5.4
(4) 6.9.7; 20.5.2.7
(5) 20.5.5
(6), (7) 20.7.3
308(2)(a), (d) 5.11.1
(3)(a) 5.11.5
(3A) 5.11.5
(4) 5.11.1, 5.11.6
310(1) 25.3.2
(2) 25.3.3
(2A) 25.3.2, 25.3.3
(3) 25.4.4
(4) 25.3.4
(5), (6) 7.6.1.4; 25.3.4
(7)–(9) 25.3.4
311(1) 9.2.6
(2) 7.6.1.2
(2A) 7.6.5; 9.4.2
(2B), (3) 7.6.5
(4), (5) 24.8.8
(6) 24.8.9
312(1) 5.1.3, 5.1.7, 5.1.8, 5.7.2, 5.7.5.2, 5.7.5.3, 5.9.1, 5.10.1; 6.7; 7.6.1.5, 7.6.2.3, 7.6.2.7; 9.1.2, 9.1.4; 12.3.1, 12.5.2; 26.2.1
(1A) 5.1.3; 7.6.1.4
(a) 7.6.2.6, 7.6.4.1; 12.3.1, 12.4.1, 12.5.3.1, 12.8.2; 15.2.2, 18.1.2; 26.1.4
(b) 5.1.3; 6.1.3.2; 12.3.1; 26.1.3
(1B), (1C) 5.7.2

Income and Corporation Taxes Act 1988 – *contd*
s 312(3) 20.5.2.4
(4) 7.6.4.1
344 6.5.15.1
(1) 7.6.4.2
(2) 6.5.15.1; 7.6.4.2
(3) 7.6.4.2
360 21.8.1; 26.3.7
(3A) 21.8.4
360A 21.8.1
363 21.8.1
414 2.2.1
415 2.2.1
416 5.1.10, 5.4.2, 5.10.1, 5.17.4
(2), (3) 5.1.8, 5.1.9, 5.16.1
(4) 5.1.8, 5.1.9.1, 5.16.1
(5), (6) 5.1.8, 5.1.9.2, 5.16.1
417(1), (2) 5.1.9.3
(3) 4.2.3; 7.3.4.1; 26.2.1
(a) 26.2.2, 26.2.3
(b) 26.2.5
(4) 4.2.3; 7.3.4.1; 26.2.1
(5) 6.5.15.1; 7.6.2.7
418 5.1.9.3
502(1) 6.7
503(1) 6.3.9
504(2)(a) 6.1.4
573 21.2.1; 22.8.1, 22.8.2
(1) 21.7.1
(2) 21.7.1; 22.8.2
(3) 21.7.1
(4A) 22.8.2
(5) 21.7.2
574 21.2.1; 22.7.1, 22.7.2
(1) 21.2.2, 21.3.1, 21.6.1, 21.6.2; 22.7.2
(3)(b) 21.3.2
(9) 21.2.2
575 21.2.2
(1) 18.6.4; 21.3.2
(2) 21.4.3
576 21.2.1
(1), (1A)–(1C) 21.5
(2) 21.3.3
(3) 22.7.2
(4), (4B) 21.4.2
(5) 21.4.2, 21.7.3
600G 4.2.3; 7.3.4.1
(1), (2) 26.2.5
824 20.7.5
826 20.7.7
832 21.3.1
(1) 5.6.2.7; 6.3.2, 6.5.11; 7.3.2; 8.1.4; 9.1.4, 10.2.2
837A(2), (4), (6) 6.6.3
838 5.5.2.1
(1)(a) 5.5.2.1, 5.10.1, 5.15.1

Income and Corporation Taxes Act 1988 – *contd*
s 839 . . . . . 5.1.6, 5.12.5, 5.17.2; 12.5.3.1; 25.3.2
(7) 5.1.6
840 . . . . . 5.1.8, 5.4.2, 5.10.1, 5.15.1; 7.6.3.5
841 . . . . . 5.2.2
842(1A) 5.6.2.9
(2)(b) 5.6.2.9
842AA(1) 2.2.1; 5.6.2; 24.2.7
(2) 2.2.1; 5.1.2, 5.6.2, 5.6.3
(a) 5.6.2.5
(b) 5.6.2.6
(c) 5.6.2.7
(d) 5.6.2.9
(e) 2.2.1; 5.6.2
(f) 5.6.2.13
(3) 5.1.2, 5.6.3; 24.2.3
(4) 5.6.3
(a) 24.2.4
(b) 24.2.4.2
(c) 24.2.4
(5) 5.6.2.11, 5.6.2.12
(5AA)–(5AC) 5.6.2.11
(5AD) 5.6.2.12
(5A), (5B) 5.6.2.6, 5.6.2.7
(6)(a)–(d) 24.4.2
(7) 24.4.3
(8) 20.4.3; 24.4.4
(9) 24.4.3.1
(10) 20.4.7.1
(11)(a) 5.6.2.9
(b) 5.6.2.13
(12) 5.4.5, 5.6.2.4
(14) 5.6.2.7; 24.2.2
Sch 15B
para 1(1) 7.3.1; 8.4
(2) 7.3.1; 8.2.5
(3) 7.5; 8.3.1
(4) 7.3.1; 8.2.1; 14.4.1
(5) 8.3.3
(6) 7.3.2; 20.2.8
(a) 20.2.8
(9) 8.2.7
2 . . . . . 7.4
(1) 7.3.4; 11.2.3
(a) 11.2.2
(2) 11.2.2
(3) 7.3.4, 7.3.4.1, 7.6.2.3; 8.2.3
(1) 17.1.3
(2) 20.4.1, 20.4.4
(3), (4) 20.4.2
(5) 17.2.5
(6) 17.2.6
(8)(a) 8.6.2.2; 17.4.2.2
(b) 17.4.2.1
(9) 17.2.3; 20.4.3
4(1) 20.4.7

Income and Corporation Taxes Act 1988 – *contd*
Sch 15B – *contd*
para 4(2) 20.4.2, 20.4.7, 20.5.5
(3) 20.4.6
6(1) 8.1.2; 17.1.5
(2) 7.3.2
7(1) 7.4
(3) 8.5.3
(a), (ia) 8.5.2
8(1) 8.6.1
(2) 8.6.2
(4) 8.6.3
(5) 8.6.2.2
(6)(a) 8.6.2.2
(b) 8.6.2.1
9(2) 8.2.6
Sch 18
para 1 . . . . . 5.5.2.2, 5.11.2.2
(1) 5.5.2.2, 5.11.2.2
3 . . . . . 5.5.2.2, 5.11.2.2
Sch 19
para 7(1) 5.2.3.1
Sch 28B 5.6.2.10; 24.5.6.3
para 1(2)(a) 5.6.3
(b) 5.6.2.6
(3) 5.2.5; 6.2.4
2(3) 5.2.2
(6) 5.2.2, 5.6.2.10
3 . . . . . 5.4.5
(2) 5.2.3
(aa) 5.5.4
(3) 5.2.4, 5.5.3, 5.5.4; 6.2.1, 6.4.1, 6.4.3, 6.9.1
(4) 5.2.4; 6.2.1, 6.8.1
(5) 6.2.1
(6) 5.5.4
(a)–(c) 5.2.3.2
(7) 5.2.3.2, 5.5.4
(8) 5.2.3.2
(a) 5.2.3.2
(9) 5.2.3.2
(b) 5.5.5.1
(10), (11) 5.2.3.2
4(1)(b) 6.2.2, 6.6.1
(f) 6.5.15
(2) 6.5.1
(3) 6.5.4.2
(c) 6.5.4.4
(4)(a)–(c) 6.5.4.3
(d)–(h) 6.5.4.4
(5) 6.5.8.1, 6.5.8.2
(6) 5.2.3.2; 6.5.8.1
(6A) 5.2.3.2; 6.5.8.1
(6B) 6.5.8.1
(6C) 5.2.3.2
(6D) 6.5.8.1
(7) 6.5.6.4, 6.5.6.7
(8) 6.5.6.7

Income and Corporation Taxes Act 1988 – *contd*
Sch 28B – *contd*
para 4(9) 61.4
5(1) 6.5.6.5, 6.5.8.2, 6.5.14
(2) 6.5.15.1
(3) 6.5.15
(4) 6.3.2, 6.5.15
(5) 6.5.15.1
5A 5.5.5.2
(2)(d) 5.5.4
(5) 5.5.2.2
6(1)(a) 5.2.5.3, 5.2.5.6, 5.2.5.7
(b) 5.2.5
(2)(a) 5.2.5.6
(b) 5.2.5.7
(2A) 5.2.5.7
(2AA) 5.2.5.6
(2AB)–(2AH) 5.2.5.4
(2B), (2C) 5.2.5.7
(3), (4) 5.2.5
7(1), (2) 5.3.1
(3) 5.3.2
(4) 5.3.4
(5) 5.3.1
(9), (10) 5.6.2.10
8(1)–(4) 5.3.5
9 .... 5.6.2.10
(1) 5.1.7, 5.4.1
10(3)(a) 5.5.3, 5.5.4
(c) 5.5.3
(ca) 5.5.2.1
(d) 5.5.3, 5.5.4
(e) 5.5.3
(4) 5.5.6
(5) 5.5.4, 5.5.7
10A(1)–(4) 5.6.2.4
10B 5.6.3
(1) 2.2.1; 5.6.2, 5.6.2.14
(2)(b) 5.6.2.14
(3), (4) 5.6.2.14
10D 5.4.6
10ZA 5.5.5.1
11 .... 5.2.3.1
11A 5.5.6
11B 5.6.2.12
(1), (2) 5.6.2.10
12(b) 5.3.5
13(2) 5.1.8
(3)(a) 5.4.3
(b) 5.4.4
(5), (6) 5.4.3
106(1) 5.4.5
(2), (3) 5.4.5
(4)–(8) 5.4.5
(10) 5.4.5
(13) 5.4.5
(14) 5.4.5
(15), (16) 5.4.5
(17) 5.4.5

Inheritance Tax Act 1984
s 23 .... 28.6.3
104 .... 28.6.4
Insolvency Act 1986
s 84 .... 28.3.5
Income Tax (Earnings and Pensions) Act 2003
s 232 .... 15.8.10
332 .... 12.5.12.2
Mineral Working (Offshore Installations) Act 1971 .... 6.5.6.5
Partnership Act 1890
s 1 .... 4.2.3; 7.3.4.1; 26.2.3
Patents Act 1977 .... 6.6.4
s 1 .... 6.6.4
(2)(b) 6.6.4
Petroleum Act 1998
Pt I (ss 1–9) 6.7
Petroleum Production Act (Northern Ireland) 1964 .... 6.7
Taxation of Chargeable Gains Act 1992 .... 19.1.4, 19.2.1
s 2A 23.7.2
10B 16.7.4
17(1)(a) 18.8.3
18(2) 18.8.4
(3) 18.6.2
21 .... 19.2.1
(2)(b) 17.2.1
22 .... 19.2.1
(2) 14.3.5
23 .... 19.2.1
24 .... 19.2.1
(1) 20.6.3
(2) 19.6.2; 20.6.3
28 .... 14.3.5
29 .... 21.3.3
30 .... 19.6.2.1; 21.3.3
58(1) 17.2.5; 18.2.3
60 .... 15.4.1.1
62 .... 17.2.4
(1) 18.2.4.4
100 .... 24.4.3.1
(1) 2.4
108(1) 17.4.1
116 .... 19.3.1
(10) 19.3.5; 23.8
(b) 15.3.1
127 .... 15.13.1, 15.13.3; 17.3.1, 17.3.4, 17.3.5; 18.3.1, 18.3.5; 19.3.1; 21.4.3; 23.8
128–130 .... 15.13.1; 17.3.5; 18.3.5
135, 136 .... 15.13.2; 17.3.7; 18.3.7
137(1) 5.10.1, 5.10.2
138 .... 5.10.1, 5.10.2
138A(1) 5.6.2.12
144(1), (2) 17.2.2; 18.2.2; 19.2.2
150A(1) 18.6.1

Taxation of Chargeable Gains Act 1992 – *contd*
s 150A(2) 18.1.2, 18.2.4.5, 18.5.1.1
(3) 18.2.3.1, 18.5.2
(aa) 18.5.2.1
(4) 18.4.2, 18.4.3
(5) 18.4.1
(6) 18.3.3, 18.3.4
(7) 18.3.5
(8), (8A)–(8D) 18.3.7
150B(1) 18.5.3
(3) 18.5.5
(4), (5) 18.5.4
151A(1) 17.5.1, 17.6.1, 17.7.1, 17.8.1
(2) 17.5.1
(4)(a) 17.4.2.2, 17.4.2.3
(b) 17.4.2.1
(5) 17.4.2, 17.4.2.3
151B(1) 17.4.1
(2) 17.3.4
(3) 17.3.3
(4) 17.3.5
(5) 17.3.7
(6) 24.4.5
(8)(a) 17.3.3.1
(b) 17.3.3.2
163 .... 23.5.1
165 .... 23.2.3, 23.2.4, 23.2.6, 23.3
(1) 23.2.6
(2)(b) 23.2.4
(4) 23.2.1, 23.2.3
(8)(a), (b) 23.2.4; 24.3.5.1
166 .... 23.2.1
169B 23.2.6, 23.3
170(2) 15.5.5, 15.5.6
192(2)(a) 23.8
241(3) 6.3.9
246 .... 14.3.5
253 .... 23.6.1; 25.6.3.7
(3) 23.6.2
(3A) 23.6.3
(4) 23.6.4
257 .... 28.6.2
260 .... 14.7.5; 15.7.5.1; 23.3, 23.2.6, 23.3.1, 23.4
(1) 23.3
(3) 23.2.1, 23.3
(6), (6A), (6B) 23.3
261 .... 23.2.1
272(1) 8.6.2.2
289B 23.7.3
Sch A1 .... 23.2.4; 24.3.5.1
para 10 .... 23.7.3
Sch 5B 15.5.5
para 1(1)(a) 15.4.1
(d) 15.4.2
(2) 15.5.1

Taxation of Chargeable Gains Act 1992 – *contd*
Sch 5B – *contd*
para 1(2)(a) 15.4.1
(4) 15.4.3
(5) 15.5.7
1A 15.7.5
2(1) 15.6.2
(2) 15.6.5
(3)(a), (b) 15.6.3
(4) 15.6.4
3(1) 28.1.4
(c), (d) 15.7.4
(e) 15.7.5
(3), (4) 15.7.4.1
(5) 15.7.6
4(1)(b) 15.7.2
(6) 15.7.2
5(1), (2) 15.7.3
7 .... 15.13.1
8(1)–(3), (5) 15.13.3
9(1) 15.13.2
10(1) 15.5.5
(2), (3) 15.5.6
(4) 15.5.5
11 .... 15.4.7
12(1), (2) 15.12
13(1) 15.8.1
(1B) 15.9
(2) 15.8.2
(c) 15.8.5
(e) 15.8.6
(3) 15.8.2, 15.8.6
(5) 15.8.11
(6) 15.8.13
(7) 15.8.10
(8) 15.8.6
(9)(a) 15.8.5, 15.8.6
(b) 15.8.8
(g), (h) 15.8.9
(10) 15.8.2.1
(11) 15.8.10.1
13A(1) 15.8.14
(a) 15.8.3.1
(3), (4) 15.9
(5)(a) 15.9
13B(1) 15.10.1, 15.10.4
(4), (5) 15.10.1
(6) 15.10.3
13C(2) 15.10.2
(4) 15.10.4
14(1) 15.11.2, 15.11.3.3
(2) 15.11.2.1, 15.11.3.3
(3), (4) 15.11.2, 15.11.3.3
(5) 15.11.3.1, 15.11.3.3
(6) 15.11.3.3
(a), (b) 15.11.3.3
(7) 15.11.2, 15.11.3.2, 15.11.3.3
14AA(1), (4), (5) 15.11.3.2

Taxation of Chargeable Gains Act 1992 – *contd*
Sch 5B – *contd*
para 15 .... 15.4.6
16(1) 25.3.2
(2) 25.3.3
(2A), (3A) 25.3.2, 25.3.3
(4), (4A) 25.3.3
(5)–(10) 25.3.4
17(1), (2), (4) 15.4.5
(5) 15.4.5
(b) 15.4.5
(6)–(8) 15.4.5
19(1) 15.4.7, 15.5.1, 15.6.3, 15.7.5
(2) 23.7.3
Sch 5BA
para 1 .... 23.7.3
2(4) 23.7.3
3(1), (2), (4) 23.7.3
5, 7 .... 23.7.3
Sch 5C
para 1(1) 14.4.1
(a), (b) 14.3.1; 15.3.1
(d) 14.4.2
(2) 14.5.1
(a) 14.3.4
(3) 14.3.2
(a) 22.3.2
(4) 14.4.3
2(1) 14.6.2
(b) 14.3.4
(2)(a) 14.6.5
(3) 14.6.3
(4) 14.6.4

Taxation of Chargeable Gains Act 1992 – *contd*
Sch 5B – *contd*
para 3(1) 14.7.1; 15.7.1; 28.1.4
(d), (e) 14.7.4
(g) 14.7.6
(3), (4) 14.7.4
(5) 14.7.7
(6) 17.2.3
4(1) 14.7.2
5 .... 14.7.3
6(3) 14.3.2
19(1) 15.2.2, 15.7.1
Sch 6
para 2(1) 23.5.6
Sch 7AC 19.5.1, 19.7
para 4 .... 5.2.5, 5.17.6
(1), (2), (4) 23.8
Taxes Management Act 1970
s 29 .... 24.8.10.1
34 .... 20.5.5
36(3) 24.8.10.1
42(1A) 24.5.3
(2) 22.3.3, 22.4.2
(3) 24.5.3
43 .... 24.5.3
43A(2) 24.8.10.1
59B(4) 22.3.3, 22.10.1
59D 20.7.4; 22.10.1
86(6) 20.7.1
87A 20.7.4; 25.4.6
95 .... 24.8.9; 25.3.5
98 .... 25.4.5
(1), (2) 25.3.5

Table of Statutory Instruments

Research and Development (Prescribed Activities) Regulations 2004, SI 2004/712 .... 6.6.2
reg 2 .... 6.6.3
Venture Capital Trust (Exchange of Shares and Securities) Regulations 2002, SI 2002/2661
reg 2(1) 5.6.2.12
3 .... 5.6.2.12
4, 5 .... 5.6.2.10, 5.6.2.12
6 .... 5.6.2.10, 5.6.2.12
7 .... 5.6.2.12
(3) 5.6.2.12
(5)–(9) 5.6.2.10
8(2) 5.6.2.12
(4)–(10) 5.6.2.10
9(2), (11) 5.6.2.12
(4)–(10) 5.6.2.10
Venture Capital Trust Regulations 1995, SI 1995/1979 .... 24.2.1
reg 3(3) 24.2.5.2

Venture Capital Trust Regulations 1995 – *contd*
reg 3(4) 24.2.5.1
(5) 24.2.5.3
4 .... 24.2.6; 25.2.2
5 .... 24.2.8; 25.2.2
6 .... 24.4.3
7 .... 24.2.8, 24.2.9
8 .... 24.4.1
(1)(a)–(d) 24.4.2
9 .... 24.5.1
(2), (3) 24.5.2
21A 24.3.6
22(2) 24.3.5
(4) 24.3.5.1
(5) 24.3.5.2
(6), (7) 24.3.5.3
23 .... 24.3.7
24 .... 25.2.4
25 .... 24.3.8; 25.2.4

Part 1

Overviews

Chapter 1

Introduction

1.1 Purpose and scope of this book

1.1.1 Guide to tax incentives

This book is a guide to the three main tax incentives that governments have introduced in the past decade to encourage outside investment in small and medium-sized unquoted trading companies. These incentives are the venture capital trust (VCT) scheme, the enterprise investment scheme (EIS), and the related tax relief for companies, the corporate venturing scheme (CVS). Directors of companies looking for finance, investors who wish to make tax-efficient investments, and sponsors and fund managers who organise the raising of capital will find the answers to many of their questions in this book.

For those readers who wish to have an overview of the reliefs, a brief outline of the rules of the scheme can be found in this chapter. Each of the next three chapters describes in more detail one of the schemes, starting with VCTs at **Chapter 2**. **Chapters 5** and **6** deal with the rules to be met by the company that provides a qualifying investment, and the conditions for qualifying investors are considered in **Chapter 7**. If the reader's main interest is to obtain up-front income tax relief on his or her investment, the reliefs are described and compared in **Chapters 8** and **9** (and in the case of corporate CVS investors, in **Chapter 10**). Where the reader is motivated by the need to defer a chargeable gain **Chapters 14, 15** and **16** look at each of the three deferral reliefs (VCT deferral relief, it must be noted, ceased to be available in respect of shares issued after 5 April 2004). **Chapters 11** to **13** consider the withdrawal of the reliefs and **Chapters 17** to **19** and **28** look at areas connected with the realisation of the investment. **Chapters 20** to **23** look at further tax reliefs that are available for those who wish to invest in unquoted trading companies and examine how the tax reliefs interact with each other. The administration of the schemes is covered in **Chapters 24** and **25**. For those who wish to find out more about setting up a private scheme, **Chapter 26** explains how this is done, and **Chapter 27** considers public share offers.

Worked examples are used to illustrate what the legislation means in practice, the opportunities there are and the pitfalls to be avoided. Where appropriate, extracts from Hansard are quoted to give a better understanding of the reasons for some of the rules. Insight into how the Inland Revenue deals with the same or similar rules, is given by reproducing extracts from the Inland Revenue's Venture Capital Schemes Manual, its statements of practice and by comments based on the practical experience of the authors.

1.1.2 A little history

The EIS, as originally introduced in 1994, built on its predecessors – the business start-up scheme (BSS) and the business expansion scheme (BES) – and was designed to address the problem encountered by small unquoted companies in attracting medium-term finance. This is often described as the equity gap. The EIS encouraged individuals to invest in higher-risk unquoted trading companies by offering a number of attractive tax reliefs. However, at that time there was no tax-efficient collective investment vehicle available.

This led, on 6 April 1995, to the introduction of a special tax-privileged investment vehicle, the VCT. The main advantages for investors are that it invests in a wide range of unquoted companies, thus spreading the risk, and is professionally managed.

Finally, and because EIS and VCT reliefs were only available to individuals, the CVS was introduced on 1 April 2000. Its aim (and it is still early days) is to encourage non-financial companies, including very large ones, to provide finance to the corporate business start-up sector, again, as with the EIS and VCT schemes, by giving tax incentives. The CVS, unlike the EIS and the VCT scheme, however, automatically expires on 1 April 2010. The CVS was modelled on similar schemes in the US.

1.2 A brief introduction to the three schemes

1.2.1 Venture capital trusts

When the VCT was introduced in 1995 as a new vehicle to encourage individuals to invest in unquoted companies the following statement was made:

> 'The Chancellor's intention is to put in place an effective set of measures to generate investment in the unquoted trading company sector. The aim, in particular, is to help provide more funds where they are most needed, among dynamic, innovative growing businesses.'
>
> (Inland Revenue Press Release of 29 November 1994)

1.2.2 Quoted investment trusts

By buying quoted shares in a VCT, which is a company broadly similar to an investment trust, individuals are able to invest in a range of investments. One of the conditions for approval is that VCTs must hold 70% of their assets in the form of investments in qualifying unquoted trading companies. Investment in one company or group of companies is limited to £1 million a year and such companies must not have assets in excess of £15 million before the VCT makes its investment. For VCT funds raised since July 1997, at least 10% of the value of each VCT investment must be in eligible shares. The definition of a qualifying company for VCT purposes is virtually the same as for the EIS and CVS reliefs.

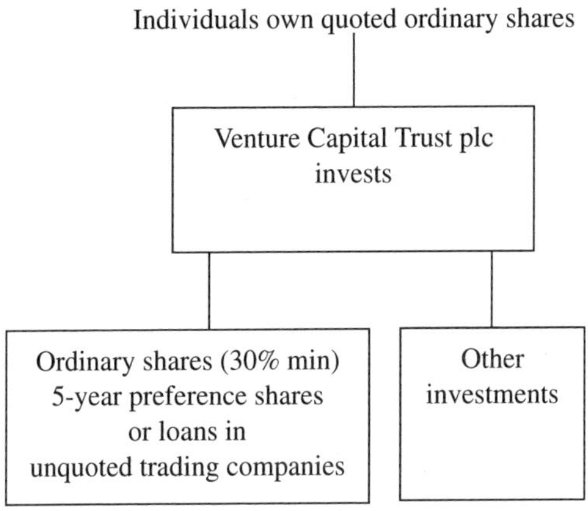

The conditions that a company has to meet to become a VCT can be found at **5.6**. The way in which a company actually obtains VCT approval is described at **24.2**.

1.2.3 Tax reliefs

The following types of tax relief are available:

(*a*) *Relief against income tax (investment relief)*. This is equal to 40% (20% before 6 April 2004 and again after 5 April 2006) of the amount subscribed for *new* ordinary shares in a VCT up to a maximum subscription of £200,000 per tax year **[see Chapter 8]**.

(*b*) *Relief against income tax (distribution relief)*. This is exemption from income tax on dividends in respect of ordinary shares in a VCT; this relief applies to shares acquired by purchase as well as to new shares acquired by subscription **[see Chapter 8]**.

(*c*) *Relief against capital gains tax (disposal relief)*. This is exemption from capital gains tax on disposal of ordinary shares in a VCT at any time. There is no tax relief of any kind if a loss arises on VCT shares **[see Chapter 17]**.

And, in respect of investment in VCT shares issued before 6 April 2004,

(*d*) *Relief against capital gains tax (deferral relief)*. This is the deferral of a charge to capital gains tax on a disposal of any asset where the disposal can be matched against an investment in a VCT that qualifies for investment relief **[see Chapter 14]**.

1.3 The enterprise investment scheme

1.3.1 Introduction

The EIS is the successor of the BES, which was introduced in 1983, itself to replace the earlier BES (introduced in 1981). In his November 1993 Budget the Chancellor (The Rt Hon Kenneth Clarke MP) said that the EIS would:

> 'Provide a targeted incentive for new equity investment in unquoted trading companies to help overcome the problems faced by such companies in raising small amounts of equity finance; and
>
> Encourage "business angels" (outside investors who introduce finance and expertise to a company) by enabling them to take an active part in the management of the company as paid directors without losing entitlement to relief.'
>
> (Inland Revenue Press Release of 29 November 1993)

When the EIS was debated in Standing Committee, the then Chief Secretary to the Treasury, Michael Portillo MP said:

> 'The scheme is worthwhile because we repeatedly hear – and I believe it – that it is difficult to attract small amounts of capital into small companies, which because they are small and relatively new are quite risky. The scheme is directed at their circumstances – it is directed towards the issue of new shares and towards attracting additional outside equity. Unlike the BES, it is based on relief at 20% and not at the marginal rate of tax. The investor has to believe that there is a good business reason for making the investment; he will not get a higher return just on the tax relief, even in the case of a company that is not successful.
>
> The underlying point is that if the British economy is to prosper on the basis of large and successful companies, those companies are likely to start as small and medium-sized companies that someone, along the way, had the vision to back. The scheme is geared towards that point.
>
> It is difficult to predict whether the money will be new or diverted from another source. However, a new tax relief is being introduced – the incentive does not otherwise exist. It can therefore be supposed that it will alter the behaviour of some people. It provides a mechanism that may attract money away from other forms of saving or may attract it away from spending. In any event, it may attract money to a section of the economy where it will be especially usefully deployed.'
>
> (Official Report SC A, 22 March 1994, col 776/777)

1.3.2 Tax reliefs

The following forms of tax relief are available:

(*a*) *Relief against income tax (investment relief)*. This is relief from income tax equal to 20% of the investment in new ordinary shares up to a maximum subscription of £200,000 per tax year **[see Chapter 9]**.

(*b*) *Relief against capital gains tax (disposal relief).* This is exemption from capital gains tax on a disposal of shares, provided that they have been held for at least three years (five years for shares issued before 6 April 2000) and the EIS investment relief has been given and not withdrawn **[see Chapter 18]**.

(*c*) *Relief against capital gains tax (deferral relief).* This is the deferment of a charge to capital gains tax on the disposal of any asset where the proceeds are reinvested in shares of an EIS company within the relevant time limits **[see Chapter 15]**.

(*d*) *Loss relief.* If EIS shares are disposed of at a loss, at any time, the loss can be set against either the investor's capital gains or his or her taxable income. If such a loss is incurred, the net cost to the investor is reduced to 48% of his or her investment after taking account of the investment and loss reliefs **[see Chapter 18]**.

1.4 The corporate venturing scheme

1.4.1 Introduction

The enterprise investment scheme and venture capital trust schemes have provided tax reliefs for investment in small higher-risk trading companies for many years. But both schemes are open only to individuals and no provision was made to encourage equity investment by non-financial companies. This omission was addressed with the introduction of the CVS by FA 2000, s 63 and Schs 15 and 16. The Government hopes that the scheme will lead to wider corporate venturing relationships similar to those that have proved successful in the US.

1.4.2 Tax reliefs

The following forms of relief are available:

(*a*) *Investment relief.* This is relief against corporation tax for qualifying subscriptions equal to 20% of the amount subscribed **[see Chapter 10]**.

(*b*) *Loss relief.* This is relief against company income for losses incurred on disposal of scheme shares **[see Chapter 19]**; and

(*c*) *Deferral relief.* This is relief postponing chargeable gains arising on scheme shares on their reinvestment into other scheme shares **[see Chapter 16]**.

1.5 Stringent conditions

Inevitably where public funds are made available in the form of tax relief, the level of control by the tax authorities designed to (a) prevent abuse and (b) target investment into the desired type of business is extensive.

The legislation includes anti-avoidance provisions to ensure that the reliefs provide a targeted incentive for new equity investment in unquoted trading companies. Thus the reliefs will be withdrawn if the investor disposes of his shares before the end of a specified period, or the investee company ceases to meet any of the qualifying conditions in its relevant period. In the case of the EIS and CVS, relief is also withdrawn where, for example, the investor receives value from the investee company in the period that starts one year before the share issue date and ends when the investor's holding period ends.

The stringency and non-commerciality of some of the EIS rules was commented on by the CBI in a report produced in December 1999 entitled *Why investors and companies do not use the scheme*. The report commented that the EIS was a prime example of a government initiative aimed at encouraging investment that is under-utilised due to its complex rules. The EIS rules were complicated, not understood by most people, and forbade many realistic and sensible commercial actions. The report recommended that the rules should be changed to become more flexible and commercial and that there should be a central unit within the Inland Revenue for administering the schemes. The latter proposal and a number of the other recommendations have been implemented and have markedly improved the operation and administration of the schemes.

Nevertheless, all three schemes contain complex and stringent conditions as to the investor, the investee company, and the nature of the investment. Many of these qualifying conditions are similar for all of the schemes. However, the differences are such that it would be impractical to attempt to cover the conditions for all three together and it has therefore been necessary to consider each of the three schemes separately.

The Inland Revenue publishes the following booklets on each of the three schemes:

IR 137	The Enterprise Investment Scheme
IR 169	Venture Capital Trusts
IR 2000	Corporate Venturing Scheme

1.6 A brief history of other venture capital reliefs

The EIS is the latest scheme to use tax reliefs as an incentive to encourage individuals to subscribe for equity in unquoted companies that carry on qualifying trades. A list of venture capital reliefs, both past and present, is set out below:

Year	*Scheme*
1980	Venture capital relief allowed individuals to claim income tax relief if losses were made on the disposal of shares in unquoted companies.
1981	The BSS allowed up-front income tax relief where investment was made in start-up companies.

1983	BSS became the Business Expansion Scheme (BES) and extended relief to investment in companies that were not start-ups.
1993	The entrepreneurs' rollover relief was introduced in March and was replaced in November by the rollover relief on reinvestment (RIR relief).
1994	The EIS was introduced to replace the BES.
1995	The VCT scheme was introduced.
1998	RIR was repealed on 5 April and relief for deferring gains became part of the EIS (deferral relief).
2000	The CVS was introduced.
2004	The annual investment maxima in the VCT and EIS were increased to £200,000; VCT deferral relief was withdrawn and the rate of income tax relief for the VCT was temporarily doubled to 40%.

1.7 Today's need for small business

In the recent past, reports on small and medium-sized businesses (SMEs) have been produced by many organisations, including the Confederation of British Industry and the Bank of England. The general conclusion is that SMEs still need to be encouraged. The Government has rightly pointed out that a large part of the future growth in the economy, and therefore in employment and wealth, will come from activity in the SME sector. Recent surveys have shown how important financing is to SMEs and also that the taxation rules play a crucial part in financing and investment decisions.

In the 2003 Budget, the Treasury announced the results of a review of the working of EIS. It noted that sums invested under the EIS exceeded £1,000 million per annum for the first time in 2000–01. It concluded that the scheme was 'reasonably effective'. However, it noted that the EIS lacked flexibility in certain areas, in particular its inability to accommodate certain structures used by business angels in the US.

Accordingly, the Government is exploring, by consultation, the scope for a variant of the US small business investment company (SBIC) to complement the EIS. The general model is to permit SBICs to raise funds not only from private sources but also in the form of 'soft' loans from the Government. The Chancellor's Pre-Budget Report of 10 December 2003 confirmed that spring 2004 would see the first launch of what are now to be called enterprise capital funds. At the time of going to press, no further details were available, however.

1.8 The Alternative Investment Market

Shareholders in unquoted companies, as opposed to quoted companies, have a problem of liquidity in that there is no market for their shares. However, there are several tax advantages that are available for shareholders in unquoted trading companies provided that other conditions are met.

In June 1995, the Stock Exchange launched the Alternative Investment Market (AIM) for small, young and growing companies, to replace the Unlisted Securities Market (USM) and the Stock Exchange Rule 4.2 dealing facility. In February 1995, the Inland Revenue announced that shares dealt in on AIM would be treated as unquoted shares for tax purposes.

Although the Official List requires companies to have a three-year track record of trading with the current management team, there are no such restrictions on joining AIM. There are likely to be higher risks in investing in AIM companies but also potentially higher returns. The introduction of AIM, together with the tax reliefs for the holders of unquoted shares, has made investment in unquoted shares more attractive.

1.8.1 Tax advantages for unquoted shares

Shares in most unquoted trading companies (not investment companies), including those who join AIM, have the following tax advantages, provided that other conditions are met:

(*a*) A company can receive an injection of new capital from:
  (1) individuals seeking the tax benefits available under EIS relief;
  (2) VCTs which may also make long-term loans;
  (3) another company, under the CVS.

(*b*) Where an individual shareholder in such a company sustains a loss on a disposal of shares for which he or she subscribed, the shareholder can elect for the loss to be relieved against his or her taxable income or capital gains.

(*c*) Individual shareholders who gift shares in such a company may claim the benefit of holdover relief and elect to defer any capital gain that arises at the time of the gift.

(*d*) Individual shareholders who have owned shares for two years in such companies may be entitled to inheritance tax business property relief. In general terms, a shareholder is entitled to the business property relief discount at 100%. This discount reduces the value on which inheritance tax is charged on a lifetime gift of shares or on death, to nil.

1.9 Outlook for investment in unquoted companies

The two incentives for individuals and certain trustees to invest in unquoted companies (the VCT scheme and the EIS) are similar but not identical and care must be taken to make the right choice. A comparative table of the reliefs may be seen at **5.18**.

1.10 Approach to this book

As will become apparent, almost every year brings changes to the legislation. Most of the changes have effect for shares issued or transactions occurring after a certain date, while a few 'wipe the slate clean'. There will therefore be investments in respect of which older rules still apply to a certain extent, at least until certain periods expire.

We have therefore taken the decision to impose a cut-off date, set at 6 April 1998. Only exceptionally do we describe rules that may still apply in respect of shares issued or transactions undertaken before that date. In respect of subsequent issues or transactions, the rules that are of current application or apply to the latest issues are always given prominence, and any departure from those rules in respect of earlier issues or transactions are described only to the extent that they differ from the former.

Citations of legislation are almost entirely those relating to the legislation in its current (latest) form, including all the changes made by FA 2004. Citations of repealed legislation are avoided where possible.

Chapter 2

The Venture Capital Trust Scheme

2.1 Introduction

The venture capital trust (VCT) scheme was born on 6 April 1995. It followed the release of a consultative document on venture capital trust companies, published by the Government in March 1994. Having taken into account some of the submissions made, the Chancellor of the Exchequer at the time, Kenneth Clarke, announced the introduction of the VCT scheme in his 1995 Budget speech on 29 November 1994.

Under the scheme, individual investors acquire shares, not directly in an investee company or indirectly in a number of investee companies via an EIS fund, as in the EIS **[see Chapter 3]**, but in a VCT, whose professional managers use the funds to make and manage investments in a range of 'small' unquoted companies. The individual investor obtains tax reliefs, similar to those available under the EIS scheme but at a higher rate (in the tax years 2004–05 and 2005–06 at least), for his or her investment **[see Chapter 8]**.

2.1.1 The nature of a VCT

A VCT is not a trust, but is a company, broadly similar to a quoted investment trust company, which has been approved by the Inland Revenue (on condition that it meet several requirements) and which subscribes for shares in, or lends money to, small unquoted companies. By contrast to the EIS and CVS, a loan where the borrower is not required to repay before five years have passed may be a qualifying investment under the VCT scheme.

Crucially, the shares in the VCT must be quoted on the Official List of the Stock Exchange, thus providing some liquidity to the owners of those shares.

2.1.2 A PEP for unquoted investments

A VCT investment provides individuals with the equivalent of the former personal equity plan (PEP) for a spread of investments in unquoted companies and allows tax reliefs in respect of investments of up to £200,000 per tax year. As with PEPs, an individual's capital gains on shares in the VCT and dividends from shares in the VCT are tax free **[see 2.3]**.

Trustees, companies and other bodies cannot receive these benefits.

2.1.3 Scope of this chapter

This chapter describes, in broad outline, the nature of a VCT's investments and the tax reliefs available to the investor, in this order:

(*a*) Conditions to be met by a VCT **[see 2.2]**
(*b*) An outline of VCT tax benefits for investors **[see 2.3]**
(*c*) Tax reliefs for the VCT itself **[see 2.4]**

2.2 Conditions to be met by a VCT

2.2.1 Introduction

As with other investment trust companies, a VCT must not be a close company, ie under the control of its directors or under the control of five or fewer shareholders and loan creditors (TA 1988, ss 842AA(1), 414, 415). Its shares must be quoted on the Stock Exchange (TA 1988, s 842AA(2)(e)), although it has until its second full accounting period to achieve a listing. The shares must not carry preferential rights and must be new on subscription. A VCT is a company that has satisfied the Inland Revenue that it has met certain conditions in its last completed accounting period and intends to meet them also in the current period and in subsequent periods.

To obtain approval, the VCT must satisfy the following conditions:

(*a*) the company's income in the period concerned must have been derived wholly or mainly from shares or securities;
(*b*) at least 70% by value of its investments must have been represented throughout the period by shares or securities comprised in 'qualifying holdings';
(*c*) at least 30% by value of its qualifying holdings must have been represented throughout the period by holdings of 'eligible shares';
(*d*) at no time in the period must the company's holding in any one company (other than another VCT) have exceeded 15% by value of its investments;
(*e*) the company must have distributed at least 85% of its income derived in the period from shares and securities;
(*f*) 'eligible shares' must comprise at least 10% by value of the totality of the shares or securities the company holds in any one investee company

(TA 1988, s 842AA(2); Sch 28B, para 10B(1) **[see 5.6.2]**).

The Inland Revenue may give provisional approval to a company that does not yet satisfy all these conditions, on the understanding that it will achieve full compliance gradually within a period of three years of raising its funds **[see 5.6.3]**. For the approval process, see **Chapter 24**. If the company fails to do so, the approval will be cancelled and any relief given will be withdrawn. Approval will also be withdrawn (although not necessarily retroactively) if a VCT subsequently ceases to satisfy these conditions.

2.2.2 Residence

A VCT need not be resident in the UK, but for practical reasons most are.

2.2.3 An exit route

The fact that a VCT is a quoted company gives the investor a secure exit route, which is a feature distinguishing VCTs from EIS companies and CVS companies. Initially, a VCT's share price is likely to be quoted at a discount to the underlying asset value of its portfolio, because of the cost of investigating and monitoring investments, the difficulty of valuing the VCT's underlying investments, and the lack of investors who would wish to sell within three years.

Dividends received from an investee company will be tax free to the VCT, but in practice dividends may not be paid that often, since funds are usually retained for reinvestment.

2.2.4 A comparison of VCTs and investment trusts

VCTs differ from approved investment trusts in the following two chief respects:

(*a*) a VCT need not be UK resident, although a non-resident VCT would be taxable on dividends from UK companies;
(*b*) a VCT is allowed to distribute its capital gains on the disposal of its investments, although in practice company law requirements may make this difficult.

2.3 Outline of VCT tax benefits for investors

2.3.1 Introduction

Where a company obtains VCT approval (full or provisional) there are tax benefits for both the investors **[see 2.3.2]** and the company **[see 2.4]**.

Except where mentioned below, the individual, the VCT and the investee company pay tax in the normal way. Stamp duty or stamp duty reserve tax is payable by the VCT when dealing in shares.

2.3.2 Tax benefits for subscribers

Four kinds of tax relief are, or have been, available to an investor in a VCT.

(*a*) 'Investment relief' for income tax on the amount subscribed for *new* shares in a VCT. The maximum amount that may be invested in any tax year by an individual is £200,000. Relief is currently given at 40% of the amount invested, but will revert to its former level of 20% from 6 April 2006. The 40% rate of relief is available for the two tax years 2004–05 and 2005–06 only. Full details may be found in **Chapter 8**.

(*b*) 'Distribution relief', in the form of an exemption from income tax on dividends from ordinary shares in a VCT within the limit for acquisitions given above, except that this relief is given for shares acquired by purchase (which do not qualify for the investment relief) as well as for those acquired by subscription. [**see 8.5**].

(*c*) Deferment of a charge to capital gains tax on a disposal of any asset where the disposal can be matched against an investment made before 6 April 2004 in a VCT which qualifies for investment relief, provided that the investment takes place within 12 months either side of the disposal giving rise to the gain. For this so-called 'deferral relief' **[see Chapter 14].**

(*d*) Exemption from capital gains tax on the disposal of ordinary shares in a VCT which, on acquisition, qualified for investment relief. Losses on disposals of VCT shares are not allowable losses **[see Chapter 17]**.

2.4 Tax reliefs for the VCT itself

Provided that a VCT is a UK-resident company, it will not pay corporation tax on dividends it receives from other UK-resident companies, under general principles (TA 1988, s 208). VCTs also enjoy the same exemption from corporation tax on capital gains that applies to authorised unit trusts and other approved investment trusts (TCGA 1992, s 100(1)). Although there will be some income that is taxable, such as interest received and income from overseas investments, after deducting the cost of managing the investments, there is unlikely to be much mainstream corporation tax payable.

Chapter 3

The Enterprise Investment Scheme

3.1 Introduction

3.1.1 Background

The enterprise investment scheme (EIS) was introduced in 1994 to encourage individuals to invest in unquoted trading companies by offering tax reliefs. Its origins go back to the business start-up scheme (BSS), introduced in 1981. This was renamed the business expansion scheme (BES) in 1983. The EIS replaced the BES from 1 January 1994.

3.1.2 Nature of the EIS

The aim of the EIS is to encourage investment in unquoted trading companies by giving tax reliefs to the investors.

Of the three venture capital schemes described in this book, the EIS is the most generous in terms of tax reliefs but its rules are the most complex and restrictive. The EIS is particularly suitable where the investment project is risky, as the maximum a higher-rate taxpayer can lose is 48% of his or her investment. It also allows individuals to be paid directors in the companies in which they invest and yet retain the tax reliefs, provided that certain conditions are met.

3.1.3 Scope of this chapter

This chapter will give an outline of how the EIS works **[see 3.2]**.

3.2 Outline of the EIS

3.2.1 The nature of the scheme

The EIS allows a company (a 'qualifying company') that meets certain conditions to raise funds by issuing full-risk ordinary shares to individual investors previously unconnected with the company.

EIS tax relief consists of four elements:

(*a*) *Investment (income tax) relief.* An investor can reduce his or her liability to income tax by an amount equal to 20% of the amount subscribed up to a maximum subscription of £200,000 per tax year, which represents a tax saving of as much as £40,000. This relief is normally given in the tax year in which the shares are issued, but in some cases a certain amount of relief can be carried back to the previous year **[see Chapter 9]**.

(*b*) *Deferral (capital gains) relief.* The investor can defer gains arising from the disposal of any asset or on the occasion on which previously deferred gains become chargeable by making an investment in the shares of an EIS company. The event giving rise to the gain must have occurred within the period beginning 12 months before the EIS investment and ending 36 months after the investment. This relief does not depend on obtaining EIS investment relief for the investment **[see Chapter 15]**.

(*c*) *Disposal relief.* Any gain realised on a disposal of EIS shares is tax free, provided that the shares qualified for EIS investment relief, which has not been withdrawn, and have been held for a minimum of three years or more **[see Chapter 18]**.

(*d*) *Loss relief.* If EIS shares are disposed of at a loss at any time, that loss can be set against either the investor's capital gains or his or her income in the year of disposal. If an investment is lost altogether, the net cost to the investor is reduced to 48% of the amount invested, after taking account of the investment and loss reliefs **[see Chapter 18]**.

A number of conditions, some quite complex, need to be met in order for a company and an individual investor to qualify. Broadly speaking, a qualifying individual **[see Chapter 7]** must make an investment by subscription for 'eligible shares' **[see 5.9.1]** of a qualifying company. The funds raised in this way must be used by the company, within certain time limits, for the purposes of a 'qualifying trade' carried on wholly or mainly in the UK, or to finance research and development towards the commencement of such a trade **[see Chapter 6]**. The types of trade that may be qualifying trades are restricted primarily so as to exclude those where the investors' capital is at low or negligible risk. In general, an individual who is or has been connected with the company or its trade within a certain time period does not qualify for investment or disposal relief. Investors seeking investment relief may become directors of the company, but must not receive remuneration for their services – except for certain professional advice etc – but an exception is made for 'business angels' who may receive reasonable directors' remuneration. There is a limit of £200,000 on the amount that an individual may invest in any year and a minimum investment of £500 in any one company. For the conditions to be satisfied by individual investors and the nature of their investments, see **Chapter 7**.

Although there is no statutory clearance procedure, the Inland Revenue is prepared to give an advance opinion on whether a company and its trade(s) should qualify under the EIS **[see Chapter 24]**.

There is a generous limit of £16m on the gross asset value that a company may have immediately after an EIS investment **[see 5.8.1]**.

Before the investor can claim EIS relief, the company must give him or her a certificate (Form EIS 3) attesting that the company has satisfied the conditions for relief. The company cannot issue that certificate until it has satisfied the Inland Revenue of that fact **[see Chapter 24]**.

Instead of investing directly in an EIS company, an individual may instead invest in an approved or unapproved EIS investment fund, which then makes investments in EIS companies on the investor's behalf **[see 7.6.5]**.

Investment relief is given for the year in which the investment is made, but is provisional in the sense that it may be withdrawn or reduced if a subsequent event takes place which contravenes the rules governing relief **[see Chapter 12]**. Up to £25,000 invested in the first six months of a tax year may be carried back for relief in the previous tax year **[see 9.4.1]**.

Trustees cannot claim investment relief (and therefore also disposal relief) on an investment in an EIS company but may be able to obtain deferral relief **[see Chapters 7 and 15]**.

Chapter 4

The Corporate Venturing Scheme

4.1 Introduction

The corporate venturing scheme (CVS) is the newest of the three venture capital schemes covered in this book. Whereas the VCT scheme and the EIS also both provide tax reliefs for investment in 'small' high-risk trading companies, they are open only to *individual* investors. Until the introduction of the CVS, there was no provision for equity investment in such companies by other *companies* not engaged in financial activities. The CVS plugs precisely this gap, and is modelled on similar schemes in the US.

It is fair to say that the CVS has not yet been widely adopted by UK companies, partly because it is relatively new (dating from 1 April 2000) and partly because it relates to a non-core investment activity for most companies. The general idea is to provide a tax incentive for large, well-established trading companies to assist smaller companies that might otherwise not be able to raise finance. It is not intended for use by financial companies.

4.1.1 Scope of this chapter

This chapter contains a brief outline of the CVS **[see 4.2]**.

4.2 An outline of the CVS

The scheme consists of a package of three separate reliefs:

(*a*) *investment relief* – relief against corporation tax for qualifying subscriptions **[see Chapter 10]**;
(*b*) *loss relief* – relief against company income for losses incurred on disposal of scheme shares **[see Chapter 19]**; and
(*c*) *deferral relief* – relief postponing chargeable gains on scheme shares on their reinvestment into other scheme shares **[see Chapter 16]**.

Unlike the VCT scheme and the EIS, the operation of the CVS is time-limited. The reliefs apply in respect of qualifying shares issued after 31 March 2000 and before 1 April 2010.

For all these reliefs, there are eligibility conditions in respect of the investing company, the issuing company and the investment. (FA 2000, s 63(4)).

Note that it is not possible, as it was in the VCT and still is in the EIS, to defer a gain on *any* asset by reinvestment in CVS shares; only a gain on other CVS shares may be deferred in this way.

Note also the nature of the investment relief, in the form of a corporation tax credit for the acquisition of a capital asset. The relief is capped at 20% of the amount invested, but the amount of the qualifying investment in any accounting period is without any ceiling.

4.2.1 The investor company

The investor company must not have an interest of more than 30% in the investee company during the 'qualification period' (normally three years from the issue of the shares). It must not control (as specially defined) the investee company; it must exist wholly for the purpose of carrying on a 'non-financial trade'; and the shares it acquires under the scheme must be its chargeable assets (as opposed to trading stock) immediately afterwards. For the conditions to be met by investor companies, see **5.17**.

4.2.2 The investee company

The conditions to be met by the investee company (the company issuing the shares) are similar to those for the VCT scheme, the EIS and, indeed, enterprise management incentives (EMIs). The company must be unquoted; 'independent' and have at least 20% of its ordinary share capital beneficially owned by 'independent individuals'; not be a member of certain partnerships or joint ventures with associated persons; have only 'qualifying subsidiaries'; satisfy the gross assets requirement (no more than £15 million before the issue and £16 million after the issue); and meet a trading activities requirement (qualifying and excluded trades for this purpose closely match those for EIS and VCT companies).

Conditions must also be satisfied regarding the investment itself. The investment must be by subscription for eligible shares, and the issuing company must intend to apply the proceeds for specific trading purposes. Furthermore, there must be no pre-arranged exits and there must be no tax avoidance motive. For the conditions to be met by investee companies, see **5.12** to **5.16**.

4.2.3 Withdrawal of relief

Investment relief may be withdrawn or restricted in certain circumstances, such as on the disposal of shares during the qualification period, and in other cases where there are certain receipts of value **[see Chapter 13]**.

Provision is made for company restructuring **[see 19.3]** and advance clearances, so that investment relief may not be withdrawn on company reorganisations, reconstructions and amalgamations **[see Chapter 24]**.

Part 2

Qualifying Conditions

Chapter 5

Qualifying Companies

5.1 Introduction

5.1.1 Scope of this chapter

The definitions of a qualifying (investee) company for all three reliefs discussed in this book are substantially similar, based as all three are on the template left by the BES. It therefore makes sense to examine them together in this chapter. However, because they differ in some details, in order to avoid confusion, we do not take a synoptic view, but discuss each of the definitions fully and in turn. A comparative table is provided in **5.18** so that the differences between the VCT and the EIS can be viewed at a glance – the CVS being somewhat separate, aimed as it is at corporate investors. The conditions to be met by investor companies in the VCT scheme and the CVS are somewhat different, of course. Those conditions are discussed immediately after the conditions for investee companies in both schemes.

The question of qualifying trades is dealt with separately in **Chapter 6**.

This chapter is therefore organised as follows:

(*a*) Further introductory information **[see 5.1.2ff]**
(*b*) Conditions to be met by VCT investee companies **[see 5.2]**
(*c*) Limits on investment in a VCT investee company **[see 5.3]**
(*d*) Investee companies: control of or by another company for the VCT scheme **[see 5.4]**
(*e*) Qualifying subsidiaries in the VCT scheme **[see 5.5]**
(*f*) Conditions to be met by VCT investor companies **[see 5.6]**
(*g*) Conditions to be met by EIS (investee) companies **[see 5.7]**
(*h*) Limits on investment in an EIS company **[see 5.8]**
(*i*) Share capital requirements for EIS companies **[see 5.9]**
(*j*) Control of or by another company for the EIS **[see 5.10]**
(*k*) Qualifying subsidiaries in the EIS **[see 5.11]**
(*l*) Conditions to be met by CVS investee companies **[see 5.12]**
(*m*) Limits on investment in a CVS investee company **[see 5.13]**
(*n*) Share capital requirements for CVS investee companies **[see 5.14]**

(*o*) Investee companies: control of or by another company for the CVS scheme **[see 5.15]**
(*p*) Qualifying subsidiaries in the CVS **[see 5.16]**
(*q*) Conditions to be met by CVS investor companies **[see 5.17]**
(*r*) Investee companies in the VCT scheme and the EIS: a comparative table **[see 5.18]**

5.1.2 Periods of restriction for a VCT company

A VCT investor company must have met the specified conditions in its last complete accounting period and must continue to meet them in the current accounting period (TA 1988, s 842AA(2), (3)). However, as will be seen later, in order to enable the earliest possible accreditation of a VCT investor company, it has an extended period of grace to achieve compliance with some of those conditions **[see further 5.6.3]**.

As regards VCT investee companies, there is, in contrast to the EIS and CVS, no specified period within which qualifying conditions must be met. In fact, these conditions must be met at all times. Indeed, as made plain in Parliament at the time the original legislation was being introduced, if any of the investee companies ceases to qualify at any time, approval of the VCT company could be forfeited if, as a result, it fails to meet any of the conditions in TA 1988, s 842AA(2), and there is no immediate replacement investee company.

5.1.3 Period of restriction for EIS companies

Whereas individual EIS investors are now faced with a confusing variety of periods within which they must satisfy the qualifying conditions **[see 7.6.1.6]**, for EIS investee companies, a single period continues to apply with respect to all qualifying conditions. The legislation refers to this period as the 'relevant period' and it runs as follows. It begins on the date on which the shares are issued ('the issue date') and ends immediately before the later of:

(*a*) the third anniversary of the issue date; and
(*b*) the third anniversary of the date on which the company began to carry on the trade.

This latter date is referred to in the legislation as the 'termination date' (TA 1988, s 312(1), (1A)(b)).

This period is sometimes referred to as 'the three-year period' or the 'relevant three-year period', although as can be seen, whereas its minimum length is three years, it can run for as long as five years (the qualifying trade must begin no later than two years after the shares are issued).

Example 5.1

The following dates relate to four EIS companies:

Company	*Trade Started*	*Shares Issued*	*Period for Conditions*
A	4.6.02	2.4.02	2.4.02–3.6.05
		5.3.03	5.3.03–4.3.06
B	1.1.02	3.4.02	3.4.02–2.4.05
		5.5.03	5.5.03–4.5.06
C	2.8.02	1.4.02	1.4.02–1.8.05
		2.1.03	2.1.03–1.1.06
D	3.1.03	3.9.01	3.9.01–2.1.06
		5.2.02	5.2.02–2.1.06

It should be noted that if the company carries on research and development, it must be doing so at the time of the issue date or begin to do so immediately afterwards (TA 1988, s 289(2)(b)), so that the relevant period will always end immediately before the third anniversary of the issue date.

It used to be the case that in practice, so it is understood, the Inland Revenue would calculate the relevant period so as to include the third anniversary. For example, if the period started on 5 March 2000 and the trade had already commenced, the relevant period would be treated as ending at midnight on 5 March 2003. However, this practice was only sustainable under the old definition of 'relevant period', which provided that the period ended 'three years after' the relevant date. The current definition, substituted by FA 2000, Sch 17, para 6, rendered that practice obsolete, as it provides that the period ends 'immediately before the termination date' (TA 1988, s 312(1A)). See now the Venture Capital Schemes Manual, para VCM 20600, which reproduces the phrase in the legislation. The new definition applies only to shares issued after 5 April 2000, however, so that in cases where the relevant period has yet to expire for shares issued before 6 April 2000 (which can only be where the qualifying trade was begun after the issue date), it could be the case that the old practice continues to be applied.

It should not be assumed that at the end of the relevant period tax relief cannot be withdrawn. There have been cases where the Inland Revenue's Special Compliance Office has examined the files of BES companies many years later. In one instance, it sought to withdraw BES relief given up to seven years earlier on the grounds that during the company's relevant period the rules were infringed.

5.1.4 Period of restriction for CVS companies

Under the CVS, both the investor company and the investee company must satisfy certain conditions throughout the 'qualification period'. This is defined to be the period beginning with the issue date of the relevant shares and ending immediately before the later of:

(*a*) the third anniversary of the issue date; and
(*b*) the third anniversary of the date on which the investee company or any of its qualifying 90% subsidiaries began to carry on a qualifying trade (where there is more than one such trade, the latest date on which such a trade began to be carried on)

(FA 2000, Sch 15, para 3).

For shares issued before 17 March 2004, the reference in point (*b*) above to 'qualifying 90% subsidiaries' should be read as a reference to 'qualifying subsidiaries'.

5.1.5 Residence requirements

It is not necessary for a qualifying company to be incorporated in the UK or be resident in the UK for the purposes of any of the three schemes.

Irrespective of where it is resident, a qualifying company or in the case of the VCT scheme and the CVS, the company issuing the shares to the VCT or CVS company must exist to carry on a trade wholly or mainly in the UK **[see 6.4]** either by itself or by one or more of its subsidiaries.

5.1.6 Connected persons

Common to all three schemes is the concept that during the issuing company's qualifying period it must not be under the control of another company. In all cases, persons connected with the person whose degree of control is being ascertained must be taken into account.

When looking at whether company A controls company B, the rights of any person who is connected with company A, such as its controlling shareholder (together with persons connected with that shareholder), are aggregated with those of company A. Brothers and sisters are connected persons for this purpose (TA 1988, s 839).

Example 5.2

Certain individuals wish to subscribe for 49% of the shares in Herbart Ltd with 51% being provided by John and his family. If John or his family subscribe for the shares, Herbart will be a qualifying company (provided all other conditions are satisfied), although John would not be entitled to EIS investment relief **[see 7.6.3]**. He would still qualify for deferral relief, however **[see Chapter 15]**. But if John subscribed for 50% of the shares and 1% was subscribed by Oldenburg Ltd, a company that he and his sister own, Herbart would not be a qualifying company as it would be under the control of Oldenburg Ltd and John, who is a person connected with Oldenburg.

Any two or more persons acting together to secure or exercise control of a company are treated in relation to that company as connected with one another and with any person acting on the directions of any of them to secure or exercise control of that company (TA 1988, s 839(7)).

In a relevant case two unconnected companies were held to have been acting together to exercise control over another company where they had entered into a shareholders' agreement (*Steele v European Vinyls Corpn (Holdings) BV* [1995] STC 31).

Example 5.3

Logos Ltd's share capital is owned 49% by Hippias Ltd and 2% by the managing director of Hippias. Logos would be treated as controlled by Hippias and its managing director acting together.

5.1.7 Existence of 'arrangements'

In all three schemes, in addition to the requirement that an investee company neither control nor be controlled by another company there is an additional requirement that there be no 'arrangements' in place for it to fall within the prohibition (TA 1988, s 293(8); TA 1988, Sch 28B, para 9(1); FA 2000, Sch 15, para 17(1)(b)).

Since 21 March 2000, there has been a statutory definition of 'arrangements' for the purposes of the EIS, VCT and the CVS. 'Arrangements' includes 'any scheme, agreement or understanding, whether or not legally enforceable' (TA 1988, s 312(1); FA 2000, Sch 15, para 102(1)). It was established in *Shepherd v Law Land plc* [1990] STC 795 that 'arrangements' includes option agreements, and it must extend, for example, to rights attaching to shares, debt-security agreements, shareholders' agreements and minutes of board meetings.

5.1.8 Control – an introduction

Just what control means in this context is unfortunately not uniform over the three schemes. Two different definitions of control are variously applied. Those definitions are the close-company definition found in TA 1988, s 416(2)–(6) ('the broader definition') and the definition in TA 1988, s 840 ('the narrower definition').

In the EIS, both definitions apply, depending on the context! To determine whether a company is under the control of another company (ie where the test is applied to a company that is potentially a subsidiary), the narrower definition has been used since 21 March 2000 (TA 1988, s 293(8AA)). By contrast, if one is considering a potential parent company, ie to determine whether a company controls another, the broader definition continues to be used (TA 1988, ss 293(8)(a), 312(1)). The rationale for this confusing change was never adequately explained.

In the VCT scheme, by contrast, control of one company by another is consistently determined by reference to the broader definition (TA 1988, Sch 28B, para 13(2)), with an important modification **[see 5.4.2]**.

The CVS also adopts differing definitions depending on the context. As regards the 'independence requirement', which concerns the prohibition of control by the investee company, the narrower definition is adopted (FA 2000, Sch 15, para 17(3)), whereas for the requirement that the investor company not control the investee company, the broader definition is used **[see 5.15** and **5.17]**.

5.1.9 The broader definition of control

The broader definition of control starts by referring generally to the ability of a person to control a company's affairs. This is followed by specific tests such as being entitled to the greater part of the company's shares, votes, distributable income, or assets in a winding-up:

> '(2) For the purposes of this Part, a person shall be taken to have control of a company if he exercises, or is able to exercise or is entitled to acquire, direct or indirect control over the company's affairs, and in particular, but without prejudice to the generality of the preceding words, if he possesses or is entitled to acquire—
>
> (*a*) the greater part of the share capital or issued share capital of the company or of the voting power in the company; or
>
> (*b*) such part of the issued share capital of the company as would, if the whole of the income of the company were in fact distributed among the participators (without regard to any rights which he or any other person has as a loan creditor), entitle him to receive the greater part of the amount so distributed; or
>
> (*c*) such rights as would, in the event of the winding up of the company or in any other circumstances, entitle him to receive the greater part of the assets of the company which would then be available for distribution among the participators.
>
> (3) Where two or more persons together satisfy any of the conditions of subsection (2) above, they shall be taken to have control of the company.'
>
> (TA 1988, s 416(2), (3))

5.1.9.1 *Entitlement to acquire*

When considering whether one company controls another, the 'controlling' company is treated as entitled to acquire anything that it is entitled to acquire at a future date or will at a future date be entitled to acquire (TA 1988, s 416(4)).

> *Example 5.4*
>
> Ghazali Ltd which owns 41% of the shares of Tus Ltd is granted options to acquire a further 10% of the shares in five years' time. At the date of the grant

Ghazali would be treated as controlling Tus, which would then not be a qualifying company.

5.1.9.2 *Rights of nominees and associates*

When considering the rights of a company (to see if it controls the investee company), one includes the rights of its nominees or associates (whether companies or individuals):

> '(5) For the purposes of subsections (2) and (3) above, there shall be attributed to any person any rights or powers of a nominee for him, that is to say, any rights or powers which another person possesses on his behalf or may be required to exercise on his direction or behalf.
> (6) For the purposes of subsections (2) and (3) above, there may also be attributed to any person all the rights and powers of any company of which he has, or he and associates of his have, control or any two or more such companies, or of any associate of his or of any two or more associates of his, including those attributed to a company or associate under subsection (5) above, but not those attributed to an associate under this subsection . . .'
>
> (TA 1988, s 416(5) and (6))

5.1.9.3 *Participators*

When considering whether a company is controlled by another company, one looks at all the rights the controlling company has as a 'participator', that is, a person who has an interest in the capital of the company either as a shareholder or as a loan creditor. The definition of 'participator' is as follows:

> '(1) For the purposes of this Part, a 'participator' is, in relation to any company, a person having a share or interest in the capital or income of the company, and, without prejudice to the generality of the preceding words, includes:
> (*a*) any person who possesses, or is entitled to acquire, share capital or voting rights in the company;
> (*b*) any loan creditor of the company;
> (*c*) any person who possesses, or is entitled to acquire, a right to receive or participate in distributions of the company (construing 'distributions' without regard to section 418) or any amounts payable by the company (in cash or in kind) to loan creditors by way of premium on redemption; and
> (*d*) any person who is entitled to secure that income or assets (whether present or future) of the company will be applied directly or indirectly for his benefit.
>
> In this subsection references to being entitled to do anything apply where a person is presently entitled to do it at a future date, or will at a future date be entitled to do it.

(2) The provisions of subsection (1) above are without prejudice to any particular provision of this Part requiring a participator in one company to be treated as being also a participator in another company.'

(TA 1988, s 417(1) and (2))

5.1.9.4 *Venture capital organisations etc*

It should be emphasised that to be under the control of another company a company must have a corporate shareholder, which could include a venture capital organisation, a corporate trustee, a bank or building society. The usual reason why a venture capital company is treated as controlling the investee company is that it holds shares that have a preferential right to dividends and/or to assets in a winding-up. For special provisions regarding VCTs see **5.4.2ff**.

The Inland Revenue does not take into account EIS funds (either approved or unapproved) **[see 7.6.5]** because the fund manager is acting as nominee for a large number of individual investors.

5.1.9.5 *Undertakings and underwriting*

When issuing a prospectus the attractiveness of the offer is enhanced by underwriting **[see 27.4.3]**. If the underwriter is a company, care must be taken to avoid the possibility that the investee company may come under the control of the underwriting company at a time when eligible shares are issued.

5.1.9.6 *Shares charged against loans*

Although the loan-linked investment provisions **[see 7.3.4 and 7.6.1.7]** will reduce the chances that shares may be charged against loans, this might still occur. Where shareholders of qualifying companies borrow on normal commercial terms, the bank may still take as part of its security, a charge against eligible shares. It is understood that the Inland Revenue would not treat the qualifying company as being under the control of the bank until it had called in over half of the shares in the company.

5.1.9.7 *Bona fide contingencies*

It might be thought that the grant of an option to acquire shares **[see 5.1.7]** would be disregarded if the exercise of the option was subject to a bona fide contingency. However, when looking at the words used to define 'control' of a company, it should be noted that their effect is not simply to include arrangements that will definitely result in the obtaining of control but also to include arrangements that *could* result in the control of a company. This means that a right to exercise an option, albeit contingent, could result in control and so must be taken into account.

5.1.9.8 *Management company*

It is the Inland Revenue's view that a normal management agreement **[see 6.3.12]**, of itself, is unlikely to put an investee company under the control of a management company.

5.1.10 The narrower definition of control

The narrower definition of control is that contained in TA 1988, s 840. In the context of control of one company by another it is applied:

(*a*) in the EIS for determining (since 21 March 2000 only) whether an investee company is under the control of another company (TA 1988, s 293(8)(b), (8AA));
(*b*) in the CVS for determining whether an investee company is under the control of another company (FA 2000, Sch 15, para 17(1), (3)).

It is worth reproducing the wording of the section in full (as far as relevant), as, in contrast to TA 1988, s 416, it is quite short:

> '. . . "control", in relation to a body corporate, means the power of a person to secure:
>
> (*a*) by means of the holding of shares or the possession of voting power in or in relation to that or any other body corporate; or
> (*b*) by virtue of any powers conferred by the articles of association or other document regulating that or any other body corporate,
>
> that the affairs of the first-mentioned body corporate are conducted in accordance with the wishes of that person . . .'

The chief difference between the broader and narrower definitions is clearly that the former includes the powers of loan creditors whereas the latter does not. It is worth noting, however, that the narrower definition does not restrict control by reference to shareholdings and rights in the company concerned; shareholdings, voting rights and powers conferred by documents of or in any company are included.

5.2 Conditions to be met by VCT investee companies

5.2.1 Introduction

A VCT investee company (ie a company in the shares of which the VCT investor company invests) must meet certain qualifying conditions. In brief, those conditions are that the company:

(*a*) be unquoted **[see 5.2.2]**;
(*b*) exist for a qualifying purpose **[see 5.2.3]**;

(*c*) if not already carrying on a qualifying trade, must begin one within 24 months of the share issue **[see 5.2.4]**;
(*d*) employ the funds raised in a qualifying trade to a prescribed extent within certain prescribed periods **[see 5.2.5]**; and
(*e*) not be controlled by another company nor itself control another company other than a qualifying subsidiary **[see 5.5]**.

5.2.2 The requirement to be unquoted

A VCT investee company must be an unquoted company. That is to say, a company none of whose shares, stocks, debentures or other securities are marketed to the general public. Shares etc are marketed to the general public if they are:

(*a*) listed on a recognised stock exchange;
(*b*) listed on a designated exchange in a country outside the UK;
(*c*) dealt in outside the UK by some designated means (TA 1988, Sch 28B, para 2(3)).

'Designated' here means designated by an order made by the Inland Revenue. This may designate an exchange by name or by a class framed by reference to any authority or approval given in a foreign country. **Appendix 4** provides a list of foreign stock exchanges that have been designated under TA 1988, s 841 for this and other purposes.

The Athens Stock Exchange	14 Jun 1993
The Australian Stock Exchange and any of its stock exchange subsidiaries	22 Sep 1988
The Cayman Islands Stock Exchange	4 Mar 2004
The Colombo Stock Exchange	21 Feb 1972
The Copenhagen Stock Exchange	22 Oct 1970
The Helsinki Stock Exchange	22 Oct 1970
The Johannesburg Stock Exchange	22 Oct 1970
The Korea Stock Exchange	10 Oct 1994
The Kuala Lumpur Stock Exchange	10 Oct 1994
The Mexico Stock Exchange	10 Oct 1994
The New Zealand Stock Exchange	22 Sep 1988
The Rio De Janeiro Stock Exchange	17 Aug 1995
The Sao Paulo Stock Exchange	11 Dec 1995
The Singapore Stock Exchange	30 Jun 1977
The Stockholm Stock Exchange	18 Jul 1985
The Stock Exchange of Thailand	10 Oct 1994
The Swiss Stock Exchange	12 May 1997

Any stock exchange in the following countries which is a stock exchange within the meaning of the law of the particular country relating to stock exchanges (or as specified below):

Austria	22 Oct 1970
Belgium	22 Oct 1970
Canada – Any stock exchange prescribed for the purposes of the Canadian Income Tax Act	22 Oct 1970
France	22 Oct 1970
Germany	5 Aug 1971
Guernsey	10 Dec 2002
Hong Kong – Any stock exchange which is recognised under Section 2A(1) of the Hong Kong Companies Ordinance	26 Feb 1971
Italy	3 May 1972
Ireland (Republic of)	22 Oct 1970
Japan	22 Oct 1970
Luxembourg	21 Feb 1972
Netherlands	22 Oct 1970
Norway	22 Oct 1970
Portugal	21 Feb 1972
Spain	5 Aug 1971
USA – Any exchange registered with the Securities and Exchange Commission of the United States as a National securities exchange	22 Oct 1970
USA – The NASDAQ Stock Market as maintained through the facilities of the National Association of Securities Dealers, Inc and its subsidiaries	10 Mar 1992

Although it is the case that most conditions relating to VCT investee companies must be satisfied at all times while the company remains part of the investor company's qualifying holdings, there is a period of grace to allow for subsequent expansion. Where a VCT's investment in unquoted companies includes a company that later obtains a quotation, that company is treated, in relation to shares or securities acquired by the VCT before that time, as continuing to be unquoted for a further five years (TA 1988, Sch 28B, para 2(6)).

5.2.3 The qualifying purpose

A VCT investee company may have only one of two purposes. It must either:

(*a*) exist 'wholly for the purpose of carrying on one or more qualifying trades, apart from purposes capable of having no significant effect (other than in relation to incidental matters) on the extent of the company's activities'; or

(*b*) be the parent company of a trading group

(TA 1988, Sch 28B, para 3(2)).

5.2.3.1 *The purposes for which a company exists*

Where the Inland Revenue considers companies are being set up primarily to obtain or enable venture capital relief of whatever sort, its opinion is that such factors as the lack of commerciality, together with, say, the existence of put and call options, can call into question whether it exists to carry on a qualifying trade at all. Guidance to staff as contained in the Venture Capital Schemes Manual in this connection insists on substance over form:

> 'The purposes for which a company exists fall to be ascertained primarily by reference to what, through its directors and employees, it actually does, and not, for example, by reference to the intentions of those who originally formed it. A new company whose directors are actively engaged in setting up a trade should not be regarded as failing to satisfy the rule merely because it is not yet trading and a large part of its funds is temporarily being held on deposit. However, the making of investments which are less easily realisable is likely to lead to the conclusion that the company exists for investment purposes, even if there is an intention to trade at a later date . . .
>
> The wording of the provision allows us to disregard any trivial or incidental activity.'
>
> (Venture Capital Schemes Manual, para VCM 15070)

As indicated in the above extract, it is not necessary to have a trade in place at the time of the subscription for shares in a new company. In the case of *Lord v Tustain* [1993] STC 755, which was concerned with close-company interest relief, it was necessary to consider the meaning of 'a trading company is any company which exists wholly or mainly for the purpose of carrying on a trade' (TA 1988, Sch 19, para 7(1) (now repealed)). Vinelott J said at 766:

> 'In my judgement, if a loan is made and shares are subscribed for to enable a company to acquire a trade at a time when the company is a shell it can fairly be said that the company exists for the purpose of carrying on that trade. The acquisition of the trade may then be said to be the means through which the purpose is achieved.'

Nevertheless, the intention to carry on a trade must be realised within two years of the issue date, or the investee company ceases to qualify **[see 5.2.4]**.

The words 'apart from purposes capable of having no significant effect (other than in relation to incidental matters)' were a new concept when they first appeared together with the VCT legislation in 1995. They have since been introduced into the EIS legislation also **[see 5.7.3.1]**. Although it is difficult to understand precisely what they mean, it would be prudent to assume that a company should do very little else apart from carry on a trade. Under the BES legislation a company had to exist 'wholly or substantially wholly for the purpose' of carrying on one or more qualifying trades. Although there was no definition of 'substantially wholly', in the Inland Revenue's opinion it meant very little short of wholly. That this continues to be the Inland Revenue's interpretation of the new words also is suggested by the reference in para VCM 15070 to the disregard (only) of 'trivial or incidental activity'. It has been suggested that a reason why a company was not expected to exist wholly to carry on a trade was that it also needed to exist to pay dividends to its shareholders.

Where a company is wound up or dissolved it will cease to exist to carry on a trade. This will not necessarily disqualify the company if certain conditions are met.

Those conditions are simply that:

(*a*) the winding-up is being carried out for bona fide commercial reasons and is not part of a tax avoidance scheme; and

(*b*) all the other conditions relating to the investee company remain satisfied.

(TA 1988, Sch 28B, para 11)

For shares or securities issued after 16 March 2004, an investee company that is carrying on or preparing to carry on a qualifying trade wholly or mainly in the UK or which satisfies one or other of the qualifying purposes continues to be regarded as doing so, notwithstanding that it is in administration or receivership if that would be the sole reason for its ceasing to qualify, provided that the administration or receivership order was made, and everything done as a consequence was done, for bona fide commercial reasons and not as part of a tax avoidance scheme (TA 1988, Sch 28B, para 11A). Virtually the same rule applied from 20 March 2000 and continues to apply to shares or securities issued before 17 March 2004. The difference is that the previous rule did not stipulate that the result of anything done as a consequence of the administration or receivership would be disregarded only if that were the *sole reason* for breach of the qualifying conditions. In theory, some other breach of the qualifying conditions could have occurred and been disregarded.

5.2.3.2 *Parent company of a trading group*

The second purpose for which a VCT investee company may exist is as the parent company of a trading group. This does not exclude the possibility that such a parent company can also carry on a qualifying trade **[see 5.2.5.3]**.

A parent company in this context is a company that has one or more subsidiaries, each of which is a qualifying subsidiary (TA 1988, Sch 28B, para 3(6)(a), (b)).

Qualifying subsidiaries are dealt with in **5.5**.

The requirement for there to be a trading group is met if the business of the group as a whole meets certain tests (TA 1988, Sch 28B, para 3(6)(c)).

In applying those tests, one has to consider the activities of the investee company and all of its subsidiaries as if those activities taken together constituted a single business. The tests are that neither the business nor a substantial part of it (see below for what is meant by 'substantial') must consist – with certain exceptions (see below) – of a non-qualifying trade **[see Chapter 6]** or of non-trading activities (TA 1988, Sch 28B, para 3(7)).

However, the following activities may be disregarded altogether when applying the tests:

(*a*) holding shares or securities in one or more qualifying subsidiaries or making loans to one or more qualifying subsidiaries;

(*b*) holding and managing property used by a group company (ie by the parent company or any of its qualifying subsidiaries) for the purpose of a qualifying trade or for research and development intended to lead to a qualifying trade of a group company;

(*c*) the making of loans by a qualifying subsidiary to the parent company;

(*d*) where a subsidiary is 'mainly trading', any incidental or insignificant non-trading activities

(TA 1988, Sch 28B, para 3(9), (10)).

A subsidiary is 'mainly trading' if it exists wholly for the purpose of carrying on one or more qualifying trades; it may within this condition have insignificant purposes that are not capable of having any significant effect (other than in relation to incidental matters) on the extent of its activities as a whole (TA 1988, Sch 28B, para 3(11)). This wording mirrors that discussed in **5.2.3.1** in relation to an investee company that is not the parent company of a trading group.

When applying the tests, two activities that are generally non-qualifying trades but in certain circumstances escape that definition are also excepted from falling foul of the trading-group rule.

The full description of these activities is contained in **Chapter 6**, but briefly they are:

(*a*) receiving royalties or licence fees wholly or substantially attributable to the exploitation of 'relevant intangible assets';

(*b*) the letting of ships (but not oil rigs or pleasure craft) on charter in certain circumstances

(TA 1988, Sch 28B, para 3(8)).

An intangible asset is relevant if its value has wholly or mostly been created by the company receiving the royalties or licence fees or by its parent company or a qualifying subsidiary (ie it is not an asset acquired from a third party) (TA 1988, Sch 28B, paras 3(8)(a), 4(6)). In this case, a parent company is a company having one or more 51% subsidiaries but which is not itself a 51% subsidiary (TA 1988, Sch 28B, para 4(6C)). In the case of intellectual property, creation must take place so that the right to exploit the property vests in the company (although it may also vest jointly in third parties) (TA 1988, Sch 28B, para 4(6A)).

For shares issued before 6 April 2000, there was a further activity that was disregarded, namely one that consisted to a substantial extent of receiving royalties or licence fees from films produced by the company receiving them, or from sound recordings or other products from such films, during the relevant period. The company had to be engaged throughout the relevant period in film production or distribution (of its own films).

The Inland Revenue interprets 'substantial' as meaning generally in excess of 20%. The Venture Capital Schemes Manual states, at para VCM 17040:

> 'Whether excluded activities amount in aggregate to "a substantial part" of a trade is a matter of fact, to be decided in the light of all the relevant circumstances . . . where judged by any measure which is reasonable in the circumstances of the case (normally turnover or capital employed), such activities account for less than 20 per cent of the activities of the trade as a whole, they are not regarded as amounting to a substantial part of the trade.'

This view is based on the decision in *A-G of the Duchy of Lancaster v GE Overton (Farms) Ltd* [1982] Ch 277. In that case, it was necessary for the court to decide whether a gold or silver object was treasure. For it to be treasure, it had to contain a substantial amount of gold or silver. Reference was made to an earlier case that had considered whether a substantial portion of rent was for furniture (*Palser v Grinling, Property Holding Co Ltd v Mischeff* [1948] 1 All ER 1). Although it was agreed that anything less than 20% could not be substantial, there was no suggestion that 20% or any higher percentage was substantial. More recently, the meaning of 'a substantial part of the UK' was discussed in *South Yorkshire Transport Ltd v Monopolies and Mergers Commission* [1993] 1 All ER 289.

As to the Inland Revenue's view of what a company exists for, see **5.2.3.1**.

5.2.4 Requirement to commence trade within 24 months

As we have seen in **5.2.3**, the investee company (or its qualifying subsidiary) need not be carrying on a qualifying trade at the time of the share issue. Nevertheless, at the time of that issue, the investee company or a 'relevant qualifying subsidiary' of that company must either:

(*a*) be carrying on a qualifying trade wholly or mainly in the UK; or
(*b*) be preparing to carry on a qualifying trade which it is the intention to carry on wholly or mainly in the UK

(TA 1988, Sch 28B, para 3(3)).

Where there is an intention to carry on a qualifying trade and that intention is abandoned at any time, the investee company ceases to be a qualifying company. Once the trade is begun, it must be carried on without interruption. If it is not begun within two years of the issue date, the company also ceases to qualify (TA 1988, Sch 28B, para 3(3), (4)).

For shares and securities issued after 16 March 2004, there is a significant relaxation of these requirements. While it is still the case that the trade must be begun within two years and be carried on without interruption subsequently, the identity of the company actually carrying on the trade may change. That is to say, the trade may be begun by one company and then be transferred to and carried on by another, provided that at all times the company carrying on the trade is either the investee company or a 'relevant qualifying subsidiary' of the investee company (TA 1988, Sch 28B, para 3(3), (4)). For shares and securities issued before 17 March 2004, it is the same company that must carry on the qualifying trade at all times.

For the meaning of 'relevant qualifying subsidiary', see **5.5**.

If it is a qualifying subsidiary that uses the VCT funds and carries on, or is intending to carry on, the qualifying trade, it must be a 90% subsidiary of the parent and not merely a 51% subsidiary (which is the holding threshold for qualifying subsidiaries in general) (TA 1988, Sch 28B, paras 3(3), (5A)). This means that whereas a parent company may have qualifying subsidiaries that are 51% subsidiaries and which are non-trading (as long as the group is still a trading group), any trading subsidiaries using the VCT funds must be 90% subsidiaries.

For the definition of qualifying subsidiaries, see **5.5**. For what is a qualifying trade, see **Chapter 6**.

5.2.5 The requirement to employ funds in a given way

To reinforce the rule that the issue of VCT shares must raise money for a qualifying activity, there are time limits for employing the money raised to a prescribed extent.

These rules have changed twice in recent years. The newest set of rules applies to shares and securities issued after 16 March 2004. For shares and securities issued on or before 16 March 2004, a different set of rules ('the intermediate rules') applies – but only since 7 March 2001; before that date a third set of rules ('the old rules') applied.

The newest rules, those relating to issues after 16 March 2004, are set out below, in sections **5.2.5.1** to **5.2.5.4**. The intermediate rules are explained in sections **5.2.5.5** to **5.2.5.8**. Finally, the old rules are discussed in **5.2.5.9**.

5.2.5.1 *The newest rules: general features*

The overarching rule is that all of the money invested by the VCT company in the relevant issue (the money raised by the issue of the holding that the VCT company has acquired as a result of its investment) must eventually be employed wholly for the purposes of the qualifying trade being or to be carried on by the investee company or a 'relevant' qualifying subsidiary (TA 1988,

Sch 28B, para 6(1)(b)). There is no requirement for the whole of the issue funds to be applied in this way – only those funds that constitute the VCT investment.

Example 5.5

Boethius Ltd issues 3 million £1 shares at par. A VCT company subscribes for 1 million of those shares. The £1 million VCT investment must be applied in the way indicated below, but the remaining £2 million raised may be applied in any way that Boethius Ltd wishes.

Employing money in preparing to carry on a trade is considered also to be employment for the purpose of a trade (TA 1988, Sch 28B, para 6(4)). Where an insignificant part of the money is employed for some other purpose, this is ignored (TA 1988, Sch 28B, para 6(3)).

The Inland Revenue has this to say in connection with what it means for money to be employed for a particular purpose:

'Money is most obviously "employed" when it is spent. However, money which is retained on current account may be regarded as employed for the purpose of the company's trade if its retention can reasonably be regarded as necessary or advisable for the purpose of financing current business requirements. But setting money aside to satisfy a contractual obligation which will become due at a later date does not constitute employment.

The company may choose to place the money to which the rule applies in a separate bank account so that it can keep track of how it is used. However, we do not insist on this. Any identification of money spent or otherwise employed which the company may wish to make and which is not inconsistent with the facts may be accepted, provided that the company accepts that it is committed irrevocably to that identification.

The initial employment of the money should be regarded as decisive. If, for example, the company uses the money it has raised to purchase gilt-edged securities with a view to selling them and using the proceeds in its trade later on, that money is employed when it is invested. If, by contrast, it places the money on deposit pending its use in the trade that money has not yet been employed. Lending the money free of interest to a subsidiary which is to use the money in its trade does not constitute employment.'

(Venture Capital Schemes Manual, para VCM 12080)

Using the proceeds of a VCT issue for the purposes of a trade includes repaying bank borrowings taken out for trading purposes (but not redeeming shares) and purchasing a trade. Normally, the proceeds cannot be used to acquire shares in another company. But where the intention is to purchase a trade, it is acceptable for this to be done by acquiring the shares and immediately transferring the assets of the new subsidiary to the investee company, leaving a dormant subsidiary. The Inland Revenue makes this proviso, however:

'Where the company (or a subsidiary) uses the money to acquire an existing trade, the qualifying business activity for which the money is employed is one of "preparing to carry on" that trade. The same applies where the company (or a subsidiary) employs the money in acquiring the share capital of a trading company with the object of enabling it to procure the transfer of the trade to itself, and the trade is duly transferred. This transfer is sometimes referred to as a "hive up" of the trade. However,

(*a*) where the "target company" also owns non-trading assets, the use of the money to acquire the share capital will not be employment *wholly* for the purpose of a qualifying . . . activity, whether or not those non-trading assets are also transferred; and

(*b*) any unnecessary delay in effecting the transfer of the trade will cast doubt on the company's claim to be an "active" company throughout the relevant period.'

(Venture Capital Schemes Manual, para VCM 12070)

Where the company to be acquired has subsidiaries, that company does not exist for a qualifying purpose. It may be possible to reorganise the group of companies before the acquisition.

A trading company that holds one or more investments will not qualify unless the value of those investments is insignificant, say less than 2% of the market value of the company's assets. For an asset to be an investment, there is normally the expectation of either income while it is held or gain on its eventual disposal. If, for example, a qualifying company and other traders hold shares in a company that exists to buy trade supplies in bulk for them to use, this is unlikely to be an investment.

If an investee parent company receives the proceeds of a share issue with a view to lending it down to its trading subsidiaries, care must be taken that the cash does not stay too long in the top company. In that situation, the Inland Revenue has argued that the parent company was holding an investment and was no longer a qualifying company.

Where an insignificant amount is used for a non-qualifying purpose, it does not require a separate holding to be deemed to exist corresponding to that amount (TA 1988, Sch 28B, para 6(3)). However, otherwise, where only part of the money invested by the VCT investor company is employed for a qualifying purpose, two separate holdings are deemed to exist, in proportion to the qualifying and non-qualifying use – one that is a qualifying holding and one that is not (TA 1988, Sch 28B, para 1(3)).

Not all the funds must be employed immediately, however. The money may be employed gradually over the course of two transitional periods.

5.2.5.2 *The first period*

The first transitional period lasts for 12 months from the 'trading time' (TA 1988, Sch 28B, para 6(2)(a)). The 'trading time' is the later of:

(*a*) the issue date; and
(*b*) the date on which the investee company or its relevant qualifying subsidiary begins to carry on the qualifying trade (which can be no later than 24 months after the issue date)

(TA 1988, Sch 28B, para 6(2AA)).

During the first period, the condition for employing the funds is that at least 80% of them must have been employed or must be intended for employment wholly for the purposes of the qualifying trade that the investee company or a relevant qualifying subsidiary is carrying on or intends to carry on (TA 1988, Sch 28B, para 6(1)(a), (2)(a)). However, where there is only intention, that intention must have been put into practice by the end of the period.

5.2.5.3 *The second period*

The second transitional period is the 12 months following the first period. Within this period, the balance (the remaining 20% or less) of the funds raised must be employed wholly for the purposes of the qualifying trade being carried on by the investee company or a relevant qualifying subsidiary (TA 1988, Sch 29B, para 6(1)(a)). For the sake of brevity, 'the investee company or a relevant qualifying subsidiary' will be abbreviated to 'qualifying trader company' from now on. This will be the shorthand phrase used to denote the company that is at any time qualified to prepare for or to carry on the qualifying trade.

5.2.5.4 *Partnerships, joint ventures and previous traders*

The basic rule is that both the qualifying trade and any preparations for such a trade must at all times after the issue date be carried on by a qualifying trader company (TA 1988, Sch 28B, para 6(2AB)). However, there are important relaxations of this rule.

Where preparations for a qualifying trade are being carried on at any time after the issue date by a qualifying trader company, the fact that the trade is already being carried on by a person other than a qualifying trader company does not of itself cause the basic rule to be breached. This is subject to the sole proviso that the other person may only carry on that trade before a qualifying trader company begins to carry it on (TA 1988, Sch 28B, para 6(2AC), (2AD)). Thus it is perfectly possible for another member of the group, say, such as a 51% subsidiary of the investee company, to be carrying on a trade and for the proceeds of the VCT issue to be applied within two years to be employed in that existing trade when it is transferred to a qualifying trader company.

What is more, the mere fact that the qualifying trader company is carrying on the qualifying trade in partnership or as a party to a joint venture does not cause the basic rule to be breached (TA 1988, Sch 28B, para 6(2AE)). As to what is a joint venture, **[see 5.3.4]**. Rules exist, however, to prevent the exploitation of partnerships or joint ventures to circumvent the investment limits **[see 5.3.3]**.

If the investee company or any other company is put into receivership, administration or liquidation (winding-up) or is dissolved without being wound up, and anything done as a consequence causes the qualifying trader company to cease to carry on the qualifying trade, then that in itself will not cause the basic rule to be breached, provided that:

(*a*) the thing done as a consequence of the receivership, administration, liquidation or dissolution was the sole cause of the cessation;

(*b*) after the cessation, the trade is carried on by a person who is not connected with the investee company and has not been so connected at any time in the year preceding the issue date; and

(*c*) either:

  (1) the entry into receivership or administration and everything done as a consequence or, as the case may be,

  (2) the winding-up or dissolution,

  is for bona fide commercial reasons and is not part of a tax avoidance scheme.

  (TA 1988, Sch 28B, para 6(2AF)–(2AH)).

It should be clearly understood that the main differences between the newest rules and the intermediate rules **[see 5.2.5.5 to 5.2.5.8]** are:

(*a*) the newest rules allow the identity of the company preparing to carry on and carrying on the qualifying trade to change, ie that different companies may be preparing to carry on or actually be carrying on the qualifying trade from time to time, provided that any such company ('the qualifying trader company' as it has been referred to here) is either the investee company or a relevant qualifying subsidiary. For what is a relevant qualifying subsidiary, see **5.5**. Under the intermediate rules, only a single company may carry on the trade or, having prepared to carry it on then do so;

(*b*) the newest rules also allow the qualifying trade to be an existing trade carried on by some other person before the qualifying trader company carries it on. This was not possible under the intermediate rules;

(*c*) the intermediate rules contain a further set of requirements to be met by the investee company and by the company carrying on the trade (whether or not that is the investee company) in every case where the investee company is the parent company of a trading group **[see 5.2.5.8]**. These requirements are missing from the newest rules.

5.2.5.5 *The intermediate rules: general features*

'The intermediate rules' is the name given here to the rules that apply in their full form as described below at any time after 6 March 2001, but only with respect to shares or securities issued before 17 March 2004 (FA 2001, Sch 16, para 2). Many of the provisions described apply, however, from an earlier date.

Both the overarching rule – that all of the money invested by the VCT company in the relevant issue must eventually be employed wholly for the purposes of the qualifying trade being carried on by the investee company or its qualifying subsidiary (TA 1988, Sch 28B, para 6(1(b)) – and the comments appearing in **5.2.5.1** are equally valid in respect of the intermediate rules.

5.2.5.6 *The intermediate rules: the first period*

The first transitional period lasts for 12 months from the 'trading time' (TA 1988, Sch 28B, para 6(2)(a)). The 'trading time' is the later of:

(*a*) the issue date; and
(*b*) the date on which the investee company or its qualifying subsidiary begins to carry on the qualifying trade (which can be no later than 24 months after the issue date)

(TA 1988, Sch 28B, para 6(2AA), before its amendment by FA 2004, Sch 19, para 11(b)).

During the first period, the condition for employing the funds is that the investee company or a qualifying subsidiary must either have employed at least 80% of the funds or intend to employ at least 80% of them wholly for the purposes of a qualifying trade that it is carrying on or intends to carry on (TA 1988, Sch 28B, para 6(1)(a), (2)(a), before amendment by FA 2004, Sch 19, para 11(a)).

5.2.5.7 *Intermediate rules: the second period*

The second transitional period is the 12 months following the first period. Within this period, the company or its qualifying subsidiary must employ the balance (the remaining 20% or less) of the funds raised wholly for the purposes of a qualifying trade (TA 1988, Sch 28B, para 6(1)(a), 2(b), before amendment by FA 2004, Sch 19, para 11(a)).

5.2.5.8 *Intermediate rules: additional requirements for parent investee companies*

Where the investee company is the parent of a trading group, whether or not it is also the company that is to carry on the qualifying trade, additional requirements must be satisfied by the company that carries on the trade ('the trader company').

Those requirements are that:

(*a*) the trader company exists wholly for the purpose of carrying on one or more qualifying trades; or
(*b*) it would do so if it were not for:

(1) holding shares or securities in qualifying subsidiaries (or in the case of such a subsidiary) in other qualifying subsidiaries, or
(2) making loans to qualifying subsidiaries or other qualifying subsidiaries, or
(3) holding or managing property used by the parent company or any of its qualifying subsidiaries for the purposes of a qualifying trade or research and development leading to a qualifying trade, or
(4) activities having no significant effect other than on incidental matters; or

(*c*) (where the trader company is a 90% qualifying subsidiary) the trader company exists wholly (apart from incidental or insignificant purposes) to hold or manage property as in point (*b*)(3) above; or has no profits liable to corporation tax and no part of its business consists in making investments

(TA 1988, Sch 28B, para 6(2A)–(2C); now repealed by FA 2004, Sch 19, para 11(c)).

5.2.5.9 *The old rules: the requirement to employ funds in a given way before 7 March 2001*

Before 7 March 2001, the rules for employing funds were a good deal stricter. From the time that the funds were raised (ie the issue date), all of them had to be wholly employed for the purpose of the trade or there had to be the intention that they be so employed. Such an intention had to be realised within 12 months of the issue date, or, if later, of the date trading was begun.

In other respects, the old rules were, for all significant purposes, identical to the intermediate rules.

5.3 Limits on investment in a VCT investee company

5.3.1 Maximum investment

The basic rule is that a VCT investee company can only receive up to £1 million of VCT funds in any tax year or specified period of six months (TA 1988, Sch 28B, para 7(1), (2)).

In deciding whether the VCT investment limit would be exceeded one does not simply look at the amount of the investment currently being raised from a particular VCT investor. It is necessary to consider what capital the company has raised from that VCT investor during the longer of the following periods:

(*a*) A period beginning with the start of the current tax year and ending with the date of the current VCT issue; and
(*b*) A date six months before the date of the current issue

(TA 1988, Sch 28B, para 7(5)).

Example 5.6

Tillich Ltd recently raised £1m by issuing shares to Paul VCT. The directors of Tillich wish to know when further shares can be issued to Paul.

Company	*(a) Last VCT issue*	*(b) End of tax year for (a)*	*(c) 6 months after (a)*	*(d) Earliest date of further VCT issue*
Tillich	11.8.03	5.4.04	10.2.04	6.4.04

5.3.2 VCT money raised

For VCT purposes, the maximum investment for the specified period is exceeded to the extent to which the total amount raised in that period from the issue of shares and securities by the investee company to a particular VCT investor, exceeds £1 million. Any excess over £1 million is treated as a separate non-qualifying holding of the investor. On a part disposal by the investor, the excess is treated as having been disposed of before the qualifying holding (TA 1988, Sch 28B, para 7(3)).

5.3.3 Fragmentation of activities

There are provisions to ensure that qualifying companies do not get round the limits by fragmenting their activities. Investment limits are reduced if, at the time the qualifying VCT investee company issues shares and securities to the VCT investor company, the investee company, or any of its qualifying subsidiaries, carries on any trade, or part of a trade, in partnership or as party to a joint venture with one or more persons and at least one of those persons is a company (TA 1988, Sch 28B, para 7(4)).

It should be noted that the other party must be, or must include, a company (individuals or trustees are ignored) but it need not be another qualifying company for this rule to apply.

The limit for the specified period is reduced by dividing it by the number of companies in the partnership or joint venture, whether or not they are qualifying companies. This provision applies even where the total amounts raised do not exceed the investment limit for the specified period.

Example 5.7

Rosmini plc is a company that has raised £600,000 of VCT capital for a dry cleaning service. Serbati Ltd is not a VCT investee company but is also in the laundry and dry cleaning business. If the facts are such that this relationship is considered by the Inland Revenue to be a joint venture, only £500,000 of the amount raised would attract VCT relief.

5.3.4 What is a joint venture?

Unfortunately the term joint venture is not defined in the legislation and, although there is some case law on the subject, there are differences of opinion as to its meaning. Essentially this is because a joint venture is not a distinct entity in its own right. A joint venture will normally take the form of a partnership or company with non-controlling shareholdings. What is meant here is presumably a collaborative effort that falls short of a partnership.

In the case of *George Hall & Sons v Platt* (1954) 35 TC 440 a farmer and a merchant agreed to grow crops on land that was occupied by the farmer. The farmer provided certain labour and the merchant provided seed, manure, harvesting and selling expenses, and accounts of the business reflected their equal interests. It was held that there was a partnership.

When the 1988 Finance Bill was published the following statement was made in an Inland Revenue press release concerning joint ventures in the context of assured tenancy companies:

> 'In general, where activities are planned or agreed jointly it is likely that there will be a joint venture. If, for example, two companies are jointly responsible for constructing a building and each subsequently owns and lets half of it, that is likely to constitute a joint venture. By contrast, if two companies merely employ the same firm of agents to manage their properties that is unlikely by itself to constitute a joint venture.'
>
> (Inland Revenue Press Release of 14 April 1988)

The Inland Revenue looks for certain features such as where two or more companies have the same directors or have a majority of the same shareholders, own adjacent properties, or negotiate jointly for the purchase or sale of property. However, the most important consideration is whether the boards of the companies act independently. Only where companies act jointly and share a significant amount of income or expenses is the Inland Revenue likely to contend that a joint venture exists.

The Inland Revenue's Inspector's Manual has this to say:

> 'The contention is sometimes advanced that an association between persons for a business purpose falls short of partnership in some way. Such an association is often called a "joint venture". On close examination many of these associations prove to be partnerships, despite the name applied to them. A 'joint venture' which is not a partnership is most likely to be found where parties already carrying on businesses of their own agree to co-operate in a single project but they do not agree to share net profits or losses. Where they do agree to share net profits or losses, it is likely that a partnership will result even where the parties are already engaged in their own businesses – *see Morden Rigg & Co and R B Eskrigge & Co v Monks* (8 TC 450) (Two companies purchased and sold cotton and shared profits. Agreement disclaimed that their relationship was one of partnership. Nevertheless held to be one); *John Gardner & Bowring, Hardy & Co v IRC*,

(15 TC 602) (Coal merchants entered into temporary and informal arrangements during strike for purchase and sale of coal. Profits divided equally. Held to be a partnership) . . .

But for a partnership to exist there must be a 'business'. And that business must be a business that is separate and distinct from any other business that the joint venturers may conduct on their own account. Such a situation occurs in a genuine share-farming agreement where a landowner and farmer combine, sharing their resources, with each party meeting their own expenses and taking a share of the produce.'

(para IM 324)

5.3.5 The gross asset limit

The value of the investee company's gross assets must not exceed £15 million immediately before the share issue concerned and £16 million immediately after the issue (TA 1988, Sch 28B, para 8(1)).

Where the investee company has qualifying subsidiaries, the limits are applied across the group consisting of the investee company and those subsidiaries, ignoring intra-group holdings and obligations (TA 1988, Sch 28B, para 8(2)–(4)).

The monetary limits can be altered by Treasury order (TA 1988, Sch 28B, para 12(b)).

The Inland Revenue considers the term 'gross assets' to mean the aggregate of the assets (being all forms of property that appear on the balance sheet) that would be shown in a balance sheet were one to be drawn up at the relevant time, without any deduction for liabilities. Such a balance sheet would be one drawn up in accordance with generally accepted accounting practice and on a consistent basis with that of previous periods. There is no requirement to value goodwill or other intangible assets if they would not have been included in the balance sheet. Where a balance sheet is not drawn up according to these principles at the relevant time, the latest balance sheet should be used and updated as precisely as possible. The assets immediately before the issue are not taken as including any advance payment received in respect of the issue (Inland Revenue Statement of Practice SP2/00).

5.4 Investee companies: control of or by another company for the VCT scheme

5.4.1 Introduction

The Government's aim in introducing the VCT relief for investors was to help small unquoted trading companies. So the rules are designed to prevent established groups of companies from benefiting. It is not surprising therefore to find excluded, companies that are, or could become, under the control of another company and companies that do, or could, control another company. Although it may have qualifying subsidiaries **[see 5.5]**, a VCT investee company must not at any time control (or together with any person connected with it control) another company or be under the control of another company (or another company and any other person connected with that other company).

Furthermore, there can be no arrangements in existence at any time by virtue of which the company could fall within the above prohibition (TA 1988, Sch 28B, para 9(1)).

Control of a qualifying company by an individual, trustee of a family trust or unit trust does not disqualify the company.

For the meaning of 'connected person', **[see 5.1.6]**.

5.4.2 The meaning of control

Control in this context is defined by the broader definition in TA 1988, s 416 **[see 5.1.9]**. However, that definition is subject to two important exceptions, namely that:

(*a*) rights in respect of certain fixed-rate preference shares; and
(*b*) rights of loan creditors

are ignored when considering whether a person controls a company (TA 1988, Sch 28B, para 13(3)).

In fact, the omission of loan creditors from the broader definition approximates it to the narrower definition of TA 1988, s 840 **[see 5.1.10]**.

5.4.3 The exclusion of fixed-rate preference shareholders

In determining whether a person controls a company with respect to the requirement that the investee company neither control nor be controlled by another company, certain fixed-rate preference shares that person or any other person holds (or is entitled to acquire) are left out of the equation (TA 1988, Sch 28B, para 13(3)(a)).

The shares in question must have all the following characteristics:

(*a*) they have been issued wholly for new consideration;
(*b*) they are not convertible into shares or securities of any other description;
(*c*) they do not confer the right to acquire any additional shares or securities (bonus issues);
(*d*) they carry no right to dividends other than dividends:
    (1) of a fixed amount or at a fixed rate expressed as a percentage of their nominal value, and
    (2) which, together with any sum paid on redemption, represent no more than a reasonable commercial return on the issue consideration;
(*e*) they do not at the time of asking carry any voting rights

(TA 1988, Sch 28B, para 13(5), (6)).

In fact, it is the norm for preference shares not to have voting rights except in certain specific situations, such as when the company defaults on preference dividend payments.

'New consideration' means essentially consideration that is genuinely external to the company (and therefore represents new capital). It specifically excludes consideration that stems directly or indirectly from the company's assets, such as capitalised distributions (TA 1988, s 254(1)).

The Inland Revenue takes a broad view of what is a reasonable commercial return (Venture Capital Schemes Manual, para VCM 62334).

5.4.4 The exclusion of loan creditors

In determining whether a person controls a company in respect of the requirement that the investee company neither control nor be controlled by another company, there are left out of account any rights that person or any other person holds (or is entitled to acquire) as a loan creditor of the company (TA 1988, Sch 28B, para 13(3)(b)).

5.4.5 Exception for restructuring

The rule that the investee company must not be under the control of another company is relaxed (at any time after 15 June 1999) where all the shares ('the old shares') of the investee company ('the old company') are acquired by a new company in the course of a restructuring meeting certain specified conditions (TA 1988, Sch 28B, para 10C(1)).

The conditions are that:

(*a*) the new company acquires all the shares of the old company;
(*b*) at the time of the issue, the new company has no issued share capital other than subscriber shares and new shares issued previously in exchange for old shares;
(*c*) the consideration for the old shares is wholly in the form of new shares in the new company;
(*d*) the consideration for the new shares consists wholly of old shares of the corresponding description;
(*e*) new shares of each description are issued to the holders of old shares of the corresponding description in proportion to their holdings;
(*f*) before the share exchange takes place, the Inland Revenue has given clearance that it is satisfied that the exchange will be carried out for bona fide commercial reasons and not as part of a tax avoidance scheme;
(*g*) the matching old shares were first issued to the VCT investor company, have been held by it ever since, and are kept by it until exchanged for the new shares.

'Shares' (except in the case of subscriber shares) includes 'securities'. Old shares match new shares, and vice versa, if the new shares are those given in exchange for those old shares.

(TA 1988, Sch 28B, para 10C(2), (3), (11), (14), (17)).

Where these conditions are satisfied, the following circumstances ensue:

(*a*) if the old company and the old shares satisfy the requirements relating to the investee company's business (in TA 1988, Sch 28B, para 3 – see **5.2.3** and **5.2.4**) immediately before the restructuring, then the matching new shares will also satisfy those requirements as long as the qualifying trade has been begun or is begun within two years of the issue of the old shares (TA 1988, Sch 28B, para 10C(4), (5));

(*b*) if the requirements relating to employment of the funds raised **[see 5.2.5]** are met by the old company and the old shares and the gross asset limit **[see 5.3.6]** has not been breached by the old company immediately before the restructuring, the requirements will continue to be met and the gross asset limit not exceeded in respect of the new shares to the same extent, unless the funds raised are not applied to the prescribed extent within the first and second periods mentioned in **5.2.5.1** and **5.2.5.2** (TA 1988, Sch 28B, para 10C(6), (7));

(*c*) in determining whether the £1 million maximum investment ceiling **[see 5.3.2]** has been breached in respect of investment in the new company, that invesment is deemed to be of the same amount as the investment in the matching old shares and made on the issue date of those old shares (TA 1988, Sch 28B, para 10C(8));

(*d*) if a valuation of the new shares is required to apply the 10% minimum eligible share content test **[see 5.6.2.14]**, they are deemed to have the value of the matching old shares at the time of their latest valuation (TA 1988, Sch 28B, para 10C(10)).

Where the old company has securities that are long-term (for a term of five years or more) loans (qualifying under TA 1988, s 842AA(12) – see **5.6.2.4**) and they are not exchangeable under the restructuring, the arrangements can still have the effect described, but the loan ceases to be a security of the old company (TA 1988, Sch 28B, para 10C(15), (16)).

If, after the restructuring begins, it is not completed or being completed, fails to satisfy the requirements described above, the new shares are deemed to satisfy none of the requirements (TA 1988, Sch 28B, para 10C(13)).

5.4.6 Exchange of convertible shares and securities

Another relaxation applies where the VCT company exercises (after 15 June 1999) a right of conversion attached to its holding of shares or securities. Provided that the convertible shares or securities were first issued to the VCT and that the right of conversion was attached to the shares or securities when they were issued and has not been varied, the same consequences ensue as under a restructuring as described in **5.4.5** (TA 1988, Sch 28B, para 10D).

5.5 Qualifying subsidiaries in the VCT scheme

5.5.1 Introduction

The exception to the rule that an investee company may not control any other companies is that it may have qualifying subsidiaries (TA 1988, Sch 28B, para 9(1)(a)).

There is a significant change in the shareholding condition for qualifying subsidiaries with respect to shares or securities issued after 16 March 2004.

5.5.2 Shares or securities issued after 16 March 2004

The shareholding condition is of two types. One relates to the qualifying subsidiaries an investee company may have in general; the second relates to the nature of the holding an investee company must have in a qualifying subsidiary that carries on the qualifying trade.

5.5.2.1 *Qualifying subsidiaries in general*

The subsidiary must be a '51% subsidiary' of the investee company (TA 1988, Sch 28B, para 10(3)(ca)). Broadly, a '51% subsidiary', is a company in which the company of which it is a subsidiary directly or indirectly owns more than 50% of the share capital (TA 1988, s 838(1)(a)). It is important to remember in this connection the other rules of TA 1988, s 838, namely that, broadly:

(*a*) ownership must be beneficial ownership (ie the qualifying company must not be a mere conduit for some ultimate other owner);

(*b*) ownership through a chain of two or more companies is computed in proportion to the holding of one company in the immediately inferior company. Thus, if company A owns 75% of company B and company B owns 80% of company C, company A is considered to own 75% × 80% = 60% of company C.

Further, no person other than the investee company or another of its subsidiaries may have control of the subsidiary, and nor must arrangements exist under which these conditions may be breached. Control in this context is that within the narrower definition **[see 5.1.10]** (TA 1988, Sch 28B, para 10(3)(d), (e)).

5.5.2.2 *Relevant qualifying subsidiaries*

However, any subsidiary that prepares to carry on or carries on the qualifying trade must be a 'relevant qualifying subsidiary' of the investee company **[see 5.2.4]**.

For a subsidiary to be a relevant qualifying subsidiary of its parent (investee) company, a number of conditions have to be satisfied. These are as follows:

(*a*) the investee company must possess at least 90% of the issued share capital of, and of the voting power in, the subsidiary;
(*b*) the investee company must be beneficially entitled to at least 90% of the distributable profits of the subsidiary;
(*c*) the investee company must be beneficially entitled to at least 90% of the assets available to equity holders of the subsidiary in the event of a winding-up of the company or in any other circumstances; and
(*d*) no person other than the investee company must have control of the subsidiary and there must be no arrangements in existence that would cause the foregoing conditions to be broken

(TA 1988, Sch 28, para 5A).

For control, the narrower definition **[see 5.1.10]** is applied.

The meaning of 'equity holder' and the measure of an equity holder's entitlement are both taken from the group relief provisions of TA 1988, Sch 18, paras 1 and 3 (TA 1988, Sch 28, para 5A(5)). There is no scope in this book to cover those definitions fully, but, essentially, an equity holder is analogous to a participator **[see 5.1.9.3]**, in that the definition encompasses both holders of ordinary share capital and loan creditors (other than in respect of normal commercial loans) (TA 1988, Sch 18, para 1(1)).

Example 5.8

Kapila Ltd raises £300,000 in May 2004 under the VCT scheme for a retail art supplies business. In February 2005, it sets up a subsidiary, Samkhya Ltd, to publish an art magazine, with an issued share capital of 100 £1 ordinary shares and loan capital. To give its publishing manager and its artistic director an incentive, Samkhya issues to both of them 18 £1 non-voting A ordinary shares for cash at par. Kapila has all the voting power in Samkhya, but in applying the test for a qualifying subsidiary, one looks at the entire issued share capital. Since Kapila owns 100 out of 136 shares, this equates to a holding of 73.5%, so Samkhya is a qualifying subsidiary and Kapila remains a qualifying holding of the VCT investor company.

However, Samkhya could at no time carry on the qualifying trade on which VCT relief depended, as it is not a relevant qualifying subsidiary (Kapila would have to have at least a 90% holding for that to be the case).

5.5.3 Shares or securities issued before 17 March 2004

Different conditions applied and continue to apply in respect of shares or securities issued before 17 March 2004. The principal difference is that a qualifying subsidiary had to be a '75% subsidiary', although it was still the case that a subsidiary carrying on the qualifying trade or preparing to carry it on had to be a 90% subsidiary.

The general shareholding condition is that for a subsidiary to be a qualifying subsidiary, the investee company or another of its subsidiaries must possess at least 75% of the subsidiary's issued share capital and of the voting power in the subsidiary. It or another subsidiary must also be entitled to at least 75% of the distributable profits and of the assets available to equity holders in the event of a winding-up or in any other circumstances (TA 1988, Sch 28B, para 10(3)(a)–(c), before amendment by FA 2004, Sch 19, para 12). For the meaning of equity holder, see **5.5.2**.

However, if it is a qualifying subsidiary that is to carry on the qualifying trade, the investee company must possess at least 90% of the issued share capital and voting power etc (ie the same conditions as described in the previous paragraph must be satisfied with respect to the investee company's entitlements, with the substitution of 90% for 75% (TA 1988, Sch 28B, para 3(3), before amendment by FA 2004, Sch 19, para 9).

A further condition is that there must be no person other than the investee company or another of its subsidiaries that has control of the qualifying subsidiary (again, the narrower definition of control – see **5.1.10** – is applied) and there must be no arrangements in existence that would cause these conditions to be broken (TA 1988, Sch 28B, para 10(3)(d), (e), before amendment by FA 2004, Sch 19, para 12).

Example 5.9

Take the same facts as in Example 5.8, but assume that Kapila raised the VCT funds in May 2003 and set up Samkhya in February 2004. In this case, the issue of 18 non-voting shares to the two directors causes Samkhya to lose the status of qualifying subsidiary (since Kapila's holding is below 75%), and hence Kapila is no longer a qualifying holding of the VCT investor company.

It is worth noting that for shares or securites issued before 17 March 2004, it is possible for another subsidiary to have control of the relevant qualifying subsidiary, whereas for shares or securities issued on or after 17 March 2004, only the investee company may have control **[see 5.5.2]**.

5.5.4 Subsubsidiaries

Can an investee company have qualifying subsubsidiaries; in other words, can a qualifying subsidiary be held through the medium of another subsidiary? For shares or securities issued after 16 March 2004, the answer seems to be 'yes' for qualifying subsidiaries generally, but not for relevant qualifying subsidiaries. That is to say, an investee company may have subsubsidiaries but the qualifying trade, if it is to be carried on by one or more subsidiaries, may only be carried on by a directly owned relevant qualifying subsidiary. For, although there is reference to:

(*a*) control of a subsidiary by another subsidiary (TA 1988, Sch 28B, para 10(3)(d), and
(*b*) disposal by a subsidiary of its interest in another subsidiary (TA 1988, Sch 28B, para 10(5).

it is clearly stated that a relevant qualifying subsidiary may only be controlled by the investee company (TA 1988, Sch 28B, para 5A(2)(d)).

On the other hand, in respect of shares and securities issued before 17 March 2004, the indicators point the other way, for there is also reference to the possession of not less than 75% of a subsidiary by another subsidiary (TA 1988, Sch 28B, para 10(3)(a), now repealed in respect of issues after 16 March 2004), and a relevant qualifying subsidiary is simply one in respect of which the definition is identical to that of a qualifying subsidiary, subject to the substitution of 90% for 75% (TA 1988, Sch 28B, para 3(3), before amendment by FA 2004, Sch 19, para 9(a)).

Before 27 November 1996, despite these positive indicators, the answer would have been 'no', as a qualifying subsidiary had itself to carry on a qualifying trade, hold or manage business property etc. However, since that date, there is no longer an explicit requirement relating to a qualifying subsidiary's activities.

Instead, the equivalent condition is expressed indirectly, in that an investee company, if it does not itself exist wholly for the purpose of carrying on one or more qualifying trades, must be the parent company of a trading group (TA 1988, Sch 28B, para 3(2)(aa)). This second requirement, it will be remembered **[see 5.2.3.2]**, necessitates looking at the activities of the parent company and its subsidiaries as a whole. For what constitutes a trading group, see **5.2.3.2**; for coverage of qualifying trades, see **Chapter 6**.

As long as there is at least one company in the group that carries on a qualifying trade wholly or mainly in the UK, for the purposes of which the VCT funds were raised (TA 1988, Sch 28B, para 3(3)), the others (including the parent company as the case may be) need not do so, as long as the group as a whole is a trading group (TA 1988, Sch 28B, para 3(6), (7)). This leaves one or more qualifying subsidiaries free, within those parameters, to act as intermediary holding companies for relevant qualifying subsidiaries, but only in respect of shares or securities issued before 17 March 2004.

5.5.5 Activities of qualifying subsidiaries

The second type of condition attaching to a qualifying subsidiary concerns the activities it is required to carry on. For the reasons given in **5.5.4**, there is no longer a requirement for every qualifying subsidiary to pursue or not to pursue particular activities.

It is instead necessary that an investee company, if it does not itself exist wholly for the purpose of carrying on one or more qualifying trades, be the parent company of a trading group.

It follows that some members of the group, provided that the group as a whole is still a trading group, may have activities that are not carried out wholly or mainly in the UK.

In that context and within those parameters, remarks made in 1994 by the Chief Secretary to the Treasury at the time, Michael Portillo MP, are still relevant. He was speaking about the EIS, but the same holds good for the VCT scheme:

> '. . . a company which attracts investment through the [VCT], but which happens to have a subsidiary which operates wholly or mainly abroad, will not be affected if the money is being attracted for the parent company. For that matter, a company which has a subsidiary doing its business wholly or mainly in the United Kingdom and which attracts investment into that subsidiary, is not affected by the fact that the same parent company may have another subsidiary which does its business wholly or mainly outside the United Kingdom.'
>
> (HC Official Report SC A, 22 March 1994, col 780)

Example 5.10

Spinoza is an unquoted Israeli company owned by six individuals. Its wholly owned subsidiaries in Israel and India manufacture industrial lighting units. It wishes to set up a UK subsidiary to assemble components made in India and market the finished product in Europe.

Spinoza can raise capital for its UK subsidiary by issuing eligible shares to a VCT investor with the necessary qualifying holdings. Although the activities of Spinoza and its other subsidiaries are carried on wholly outside the UK, it is still the parent company of a trading group, since its other subsidiaries are wholly owned (and are therefore qualifying subsidiaries) and their activities are not excluded activities. There is no requirement for the other subsidiaries to be carrying on their trades wholly or mainly in the UK.

5.5.5.1 *Property management*

A qualifying subsidiary can exist for the purpose of holding and managing property used by other members of the group for their trades or for research and development (TA 1988, Sch 28B, para 3(9)(b)). Such an activity is disregarded when considering whether the business of the group as a whole results in its being a trading group. Care must be taken that the property is acquired and used wholly for qualifying activities rather than partly for this purpose and partly for another purpose.

However, in respect of shares or securities issued after 16 March 2004, any 'property managing subsidiary' must be a relevant qualifying subsidiary of the investee company. A 'property managing subsidiary' is a qualifying subsidiary the business of which consists wholly or mainly in holding or managing land or any property deriving its value from land (TA 1988, Sch 28B, para 10ZA). In this case, the land involved is any land, and is not limited to land used for the purposes of a qualifying trade or of research and development.

For what is a relevant qualifying subsidiary, **[see 5.5.2.2]**.

5.5.5.2 *Dormant subsidiaries*

Provided that the investee company carries on a qualifying trade itself or the group is a trading group, one or more qualifying subsidiaries can be dormant.

Companies often keep dormant subsidiaries for commercial reasons, for example, because they wish to preserve the name.

5.5.6 Winding up a subsidiary

A qualifying subsidiary does not on that account cease to be a qualifying subsidiary while it or any other company is being wound up, provided that the winding-up is carried out for bona fide commercial reasons and is not part of a tax avoidance scheme (TA 1988, Sch 28B, para 10(4)). For shares or securities issued before 17 March 2004, there was no reference to the winding-up of any other company.

After 20 March 2000, a qualifying subsidiary that is carrying on or preparing to carry on a qualifying trade wholly or mainly in the UK continues to be regarded as doing so, notwithstanding that it is in administration or receivership, provided that:

(*a*) the administration or receivership order was made, and everything done as a consequence was done, for bona fide commercial reasons and is not part of a tax avoidance scheme; and
(*b*) it is only by reason of something done as a consequence of its being in administration or receivership that would otherwise cause it no longer to be regarded as doing so

(TA 1988, Sch 28B, para 11A).

For shares or securities issued before 17 March 2004, the act done as a consequence of the subsidiary's being in administration or receivership need not have been the *only* reason for failure to comply with the trading requirement for the exception to apply.

5.5.7 Sale of a subsidiary

An investee company (or another of its subsidiaries) is allowed to sell one or more of its qualifying subsidiaries if this is done for bona fide commercial reasons and not as part of a tax avoidance scheme. This is because a qualifying subsidiary remains a qualifying subsidiary notwithstanding that arrangements are in existence for the disposal of the entire holding in that subsidiary provided that the above conditions apply (TA 1988, Sch 28B, para 10(5)).

In each case, it would be necessary for the qualifying company to meet all the other conditions: for example, there must still be a qualifying trade being carried on by at least one company in the group.

5.5.8 Options to acquire shares

It is important to ensure that an investee company not take an option over the shares of a company that it intends to acquire, because at the time of granting the option there would be an arrangement whereby the investee company could control another company which is not at that time its qualifying subsidiary **[see 5.5.1]**.

Example 5.11

Carnap Ltd, which has been a qualifying company for two years, provides services for Schlick Ltd which carries on a qualifying trade. Carnap intends to offer to buy the shares in Schlick from its parent when they can agree the terms, but, in the meantime, the parent asks Carnap to grant it an unconditional option whereby in six months' time it could put its shares on to Carnap at market value. Such an option would disqualify Carnap as it has entered into an arrangement whereby it could control Schlick which is not at this stage a qualifying subsidiary.

5.5.9 Subscription for shares in a subsidiary

Subscriptions for shares in a subsidiary cannot qualify for VCT relief as the subsidiary must always be under the control of another company **[see 5.1.9]**.

5.6 Conditions to be met by VCT investor companies

5.6.1 Introduction

So far in this chapter, we have looked at the conditions that have to be satisfied by a VCT investee company, ie a company in which a venture capital trust can invest. In this section we consider the conditions that the investor company (the VCT itself) must satisfy. These concern both the nature and extent of the investor company's holding in any single investee company at any time as well as those relating to the nature and extent of its holdings as a whole.

5.6.2 Conditions for approval

Before an investor company can make investments under the VCT scheme, it must have obtained approval (this can either be full or provisional – see below and **5.6.3**) as a venture capital trust (VCT).

A VCT must be a company that is not a close company (TA 1988, s 842AA(1)). Secondly, each class of shares comprising its ordinary share capital must be listed in the Official List of the Stock Exchange (TA 1988, s 842AA(2)(e)). Those are the only two requirements relating to the company's status and composition. Before such a company can be approved as a VCT, however, it must satisfy a number of other detailed conditions relating to its investments. These conditions must have been satisfied during its most recent complete accounting period (TA 1988, s 842AA(2)), and the Inland Revenue must also be satisfied that they will be fulfilled during the current accounting period (TA 1988, s 842AA(3)).

The conditions are that:

(*a*) the company's income in the period concerned must have been derived wholly or mainly from shares or securities **[see 5.6.2.3 to 5.6.2.5]**;
(*b*) at least 70% by value of its investments must have been represented throughout the period by shares or securities comprised in 'qualifying holdings' **[see 5.6.2.6]**;
(*c*) at least 30% by value of its qualifying holdings must have been represented throughout the period by holdings of 'eligible shares' **[see 5.6.2.8]**;
(*d*) at no time in the period must the company's holding in any one company (other than another VCT) have exceeded 15% by value of its investments **[see 5.6.2.9]**;
(*e*) the company must have distributed at least 85% of its income derived in the period from shares and securities **[see 5.6.2.12]**;
(*f*) 'eligible shares' must comprise at least 10% by value of the totality of the shares or securities the company holds in any one investee company **[see 5.6.2.13]**

(TA 1988, s 842AA(2); Sch 28B, para 10B(1)).

For the periods in respect of which these conditions must be satisfied, see **5.6.3**.

5.6.2.1 *Stock Exchange listing requirements*

The Stock Exchange has decided that VCTs are not to be treated as investment trusts for the purposes of the Listing Rules (the Yellow Book) but has placed them in a separate category, the rules for which are contained in Chapter 26 of the Yellow Book. A brief summary of some of the rules is as follows:

(*a*) There is no requirement for a working capital statement, audited accounts, three-year records and continuity of management.
(*b*) A VCT is expected actively to manage its investments and have appropriate controls over them.
(*c*) A VCT is required to have an independent board, comprising a majority of directors who are not in the management team.
(*d*) The Stock Exchange needs to be satisfied that the managers have experience of managing similar types of investment for at least three years.

(*e*) The Stock Exchange requires a full risk statement to be included in the prospectus, including a statement as to the risk of loss of tax relief.

(*f*) Information cannot be included in the prospectus which appears to the Stock Exchange to promote the products and services of the investment managers. Investors looking for information showing the managers' track record are likely to be disappointed, therefore.

(*g*) The Stock Exchange has imposed an additional restriction, namely that property companies should not form more than 20% of a VCT's gross assets. The purpose of this restriction is to ensure that VCTs are not used as a back-door way of trying to list property companies.

(*h*) Where a VCT enters into a transaction with another fund managed by the same investment manager, this will be a related party transaction.

(*i*) Where the VCT invests alongside another fund managed by the same investment manager, this must be approved by the VCT's independent directors unless the investment is made either at the same time and on the same terms or in accordance with a pre-existing agreement between the VCT and the investment manager.

(*j*) If a VCT loses its tax status it must advise the Stock Exchange and dealing in its shares will normally be suspended.

5.6.2.2 *Investments*

A VCT is a company that holds and makes investments. Investments would normally include all assets capable of producing income or capital appreciation. These would include shares, options, warrants, units in unit trusts, corporate bonds, local-authority and government bonds, purchased bills of exchange, secondhand life insurance policies and interest-bearing bank accounts. Investments would not include current accounts, cash or foreign currency. However, there are restrictions on the types of investments that VCTs can hold **[see 5.6.2.3** to **5.6.2.5]**.

5.6.2.3 *Shares*

In this category of investments would be ordinary and preference shares and holdings in authorised unit trusts. To meet a further condition **[see 5.6.2.8]**, a significant proportion of the shares held by a VCT will have to be ordinary shares.

5.6.2.4 *Securities*

Securities have a special meaning in this context, as follows:

(*a*) they include a loan, whether secured or unsecured, provided that within five years of the time it is made, the company cannot be required to repay the loan, or to redeem or repurchase any stock or security relating to that loan;

(*b*) they do not include any stock or security relating to a loan that has been made to the company where the company can be required within five years to repay the loan or to redeem or repurchase the stock or security

(TA 1988, s 842AA(12)).

There is one exception to the five-year period stipulated by this rule. Where a loan is made on normal commercial terms that include a standard clause requiring repayment in the event of the borrower's default, this is permitted. However, if the default clause entitles the lender or anyone else to exercise an action that could cause the borrower to default, the Inland Revenue will not overlook it (Statement of Practice SP8/95).

A further condition relating to securities is that securities relating to a guaranteed loan cannot form part of a qualifying holding **[see 5.6.2.6]** (TA 1988, Sch 28B, para 10A(1)). A security relates to a guaranteed loan if there are arrangements in place for the investor company to receive anything directly or indirectly from a third party in the event of a failure by any person to comply with the terms of the loan or the terms of the security (TA 1988, Sch 28B, para 10A(2)). It is immaterial whether the arrangements apply to all cases of failure or only to some (TA 1988, Sch 28B, para 10A(3)). A third party here is any person other than the investee company or its subsidiaries (where it is the parent company of a trading group) (TA 1988, Sch 28B, para 10(4)).

5.6.2.5 *Wholly or mainly*

The first requirement for a VCT as listed in **5.6.2** is that, for the accounting period in question, the VCT company's income from its investments must have been derived wholly or mainly from shares or securities (TA 1988 s 842AA(2)(a)). The income to be considered is the VCT's gross statutory income, which does not include, for example, scrip dividends.

In this context, the Inland Revenue interprets 'wholly or mainly' to mean at least 70% (Venture Capital Schemes Manual, para VCM 60130), whereas in most other contexts, over 50% is considered to be sufficient.

The reason appears to be that the Inland Revenue sets the same 70% requirement for the approval of an investment trust (Statement of Practice SP14/91, para 17). It is worth noting that in the context of an investment trust, the Inland Revenue does not regard profit from a transaction in financial futures or options as derived from shares or securities.

5.6.2.6 *Proportion of qualifying holdings*

The second requirement for a VCT is that at least 70% by value of the VCT's investments, throughout the accounting period in question, must have consisted of shares and securities comprised in 'qualifying holdings' (TA 1988, s 842AA(2)(b)). For the time within which this requirement must be satisfied, see **5.6.3**.

A 'qualifying holding' is a holding of shares or securities in an investee company that satisfies the conditions discussed in sections **5.2** to **5.5**.

There is a further condition that the shares or securities be new, ie that they must have been issued first to the investor company; they must also have been held by the investor company continuously since the date of issue (TA 1988, Sch 28B, para 1(2)(b)). It is not a problem if the shares or securities subsequently become quoted **[see 5.2.2]**.

The purchase of existing shares and securities does not qualify.

There is a relaxation of the 70% requirement where an issue of ordinary shares has been made by the VCT on or after the date on which approval was given and there is a subsequent further issue of ordinary shares. The money raised by that further issue (and any money derived from the issue) is disregarded for the purpose of this test for the duration of up to three years – that is, in any accounting period ending within three years of the further issue (TA 1988, s 842AA(5A), (5B)).

This relaxation is subject to any regulations made under FA 2002, Sch 33, para 11, limiting the period of grace or disapplying the relaxation altogether. Such regulations would apply to shares issued after 16 April 2002 only (FA 2002, Sch 33, para 11(3)), but at the time of going to press, no such regulations had been made.

5.6.2.7 *Non-qualifying holdings*

Having invested 70% of the VCT's funds in qualifying holdings, VCT managers might be tempted to invest the remaining 30% of funds in (say) quoted shares and securities. However, it must be borne in mind that if any of the unquoted companies in the VCT's qualifying holdings fail to meet the scheme's conditions, the VCT approval could be forfeited and consequently investors could lose their tax reliefs. Sir George Young (then Financial Secretary to the Treasury) made this point during the Finance Bill 1995 debate.

> 'The trust would be well advised to keep its eyes on rather more than 70 per cent. because it must not fall below that percentage. To put it another way, the legislation gives the VCT a 30% leeway for when it buys and sells investments.'
>
> (HC Official Report, 25 January 1995, col 377)

Example 5.12

The Waissmann VCT at the end of its fourth accounting period was valued at £12 million. It held shares in Neurath Homes Ltd and Reichenbach Prints Ltd, which represented 7% and 6% of its qualifying holdings of £9 million. In the next month the Inland Revenue ascertained that a subsidiary of Neurath Homes had been dealing in land to a substantial extent (not a qualifying trade) and Reichenbach Prints had acquired 25% of the shares of another company. Unless Waissmann VCT has other investments in unquoted companies which can immediately replace the disqualified companies, the approved VCT status could be lost.

5.6.2.8 *Qualifying holdings of eligible shares*

The third requirement for a VCT's qualifying holdings is that at least 30% by value of the VCT's qualifying holdings throughout the accounting period in question must have been holdings of 'eligible shares' (TA 1988, s 842AA(2)(c)).

'Eligible shares' are shares comprised in a company's ordinary share capital which carry no present or future preferential right to dividends or to the company's assets on a winding-up, and no present or future right to be redeemed (TA 1988, s 842AA(14)). In this context, provided that the shareholder has a legal right, it does not matter whether that right is set out in the company's articles of association **[see 5.1.7]**, in a shareholders' agreement **[see 5.1.10]** or in another document.

The existence of pre-emption rights, the right of the company to purchase its own shares, or a formula setting out how a price will be calculated when shares are purchased from shareholders, will not of itself prevent shares from being eligible shares.

Ordinary share capital is all of a company's issued share capital, however it may be described, other than capital the holders of which have a right to a dividend at a fixed rate but have no other right to share in the profits of a company (eg preference shares, but not participating preference shares) (TA 1988, s 832(1)).

The split of 30% eligible shares and 70% other shares and securities does not apply to investments in each investee company singly but to the total of the VCT's qualifying holdings. Although a venture capital package normally includes a mixture of ordinary shares, preference shares and loans, the legislation allows a VCT to subscribe for eligible shares in one qualifying company and make a five-year loan to another, provided that, in respect of funds raised by the VCT since 2 July 1997, at least 10% by value of each investment made comprises eligible shares **[see 5.6.2.14]**.

There is a relaxation of the 30% requirement where an issue of ordinary shares has been made on or after the date on which approval was given and there is a subsequent further issue of ordinary shares by the VCT. The money raised by that further issue (and any money derived from the issue) is disregarded for the purpose of this test for the duration of up to three years – that is, in any accounting period ending within three years of the further issue (TA 1988, s 842AA(5A), (5B)).

This relaxation is subject to any regulations made under FA 2002, Sch 33, para 11, limiting the period of grace or disapplying the relaxation altogether. Such regulations would apply to shares issued after 16 April 2002 only (FA 2002, Sch 33, para 11(3)), but at the time of going to press, no such regulations had been made.

Provided that 30% of the qualifying holdings are in the form of eligible shares the VCT can invest by subscription in other types of ordinary shares or preference shares of the investee company.

Provided that the 30% test has been met, and at least 10% by value of each qualifying holding comprise eligible shares, the balance of investments in a qualifying holding could consist wholly or partly of securities. In general terms, securities for this purpose are corporate loans and loan stock that are capable of having a five-year life **[see 5.6.2.4]**.

5.6.2.9 *The 15% test*

The fourth requirement is that no holding by the VCT in any investee company may represent more than 15% by value of the VCT's investments throughout the accounting period in question. In applying this test any holding in another VCT or a company that would qualify as a VCT were its shares listed, is ignored (TA 1988, s 842AA(2)(d)).

Example 5.13

Wollheim VCT recently raised £6 million from offering its shares to the public and proposes to make the following investments in Richard Ltd. To subscribe £500,000 for ordinary shares and £350,000 for preference shares and to make it a five-year loan of £80,000. Assuming this holding is valued at £930,000 it would represent more than 15% of Wollheim VCT's total investments.

For this purpose, all holdings in companies that are members of a 51% group are treated as a single holding. Where the VCT is a member of a 51% group and is owed money by another member of the group, the debt is treated as a security held by the VCT investor company, and is included in applying the 15% test (TA 1988, s 842AA(11)(a); s 842(1A)).

The 15% test does not apply to a holding in a particular company which did not exceed 15% of the VCT's total investments at the time that it was made, provided that no additions have been made to that holding (TA 1988, s 842(2)(b)).

5.6.2.10 *Share exchanges where new shares fail to meet all the conditions*

There is some leeway when testing new shares or securities obtained in a share exchange for the necessary conditions. The new shares and securities must have been issued as part of a company reorganisation made for bona fide commercial reasons and not as part of a tax avoidance scheme. In these circumstances, new shares or securities not meeting some or all of the conditions are deemed to do so all the same (TA 1988, Sch 28B, para 11B(1)).

This tolerance may apply on the occasion of any company reorganisation or arrangement that takes place after 20 March 2000 and under which the original shareholder receives other shares or securities in the same or in another company. It does not matter whether the old shares or securities are transferred, cancelled or retained (TA 1988, Sch 28B, para 11B(2)).

The precise rules are set out in the VCT (Exchange of Shares and Securities) Regulations 2002, SI 2002/2661, dated 22 October 2002 but taking effect from 21 March 2000.

There are three types of share exchange that come within the regulations. In each case, it is envisaged that the VCT receives new shares or new securities in exchange for the old shares or old securities, with or without other consideration (SI 2002/2661, reg 3). The three types of exchange are:

(*a*) an exchange of shares or securities for those in the same company;
(*b*) an exchange of shares or securities for those in another company; or
(*c*) a scheme of reconstruction involving the issue of shares or securities

(SI 2002/2661, regs 4–6).

In the first type of exchange, new shares or securities ('the new holding') are issued to the VCT by the investee company in proportion to its existing holding (the exchange can be limited to one or more classes). Any new shares are issued solely in respect of old shares or old securities, but new securities may be issued solely in respect of old securities. Immediately after the exchange, the old shares or securities ('the old holding') are cancelled or extinguished. Issues of shares in return for convertible shares or securities are excluded (they are already covered under a separate rule – **[see 5.4.6]**). The issue does not have to be for a consideration, so bonus issues are included.

Where these circumstances apply, a number of deeming rules – similar to those applying on a restructuring – come into play:

(*a*) if the investee company, though no longer unquoted, is still regarded as unquoted because the five-year period of grace under TA 1988, Sch 28B, para 2(6) is still running, the same five-year period will run in respect of the new holding;
(*b*) if the employment of funds test **[see 5.2.5]** is met (or deemed to be met) and the gross asset limit **[see 5.3.6]** has not been breached (or deemed to be breached) by the investee company in respect of the old holding immediately before the exchange, the requirements will continue to be met and the gross asset limit not exceeded in respect of the new holding to the same extent, unless the funds raised are not applied to the prescribed extent within the first and second periods mentioned in **5.2.5.1** and **5.2.5.2**;
(*c*) in determining whether the annual (£1 million) investment limit **[see 5.3.1]** has been breached in respect of the investee company by the new holding, the investment in the new holding is deemed to be of the same amount as

the investment in the matching old holding and made on the issue date of the old holding

(SI 2002/2661, reg 7(5)–(8)).

Finally, during the period of the exchange (but for no longer than six months), the exchange is disregarded when applying the independence test (ie the prohibition of control of or by another company in TA 1988, Sch 28B, para 9 – **[see 5.4]**) (SI 2002/2661, reg 7(9), (10)).

The second type of exchange is one in which a company ('the new company') issues shares or securities ('the new holding') to the VCT in exchange for the VCT's shares or securities in the investee company ('the old holding'). Further requirements are that:

(*a*) either:
   (1) as a result of the exchange the new company holds more than 50% of the ordinary share capital of the investee company, or
   (2) the new company issues the new holding as part of a general offer made to members of the investee company or to a class of them, and made in the first instance on a condition which would result, if satisfied, in the new company's taking control of the investee company;

(*b*) the new shares are issued in exchange for old shares or old securities but any new securities are issued solely in return for old securities; and

(*c*) the exchange is not a restructuring falling within TA 1988, Sch 28B, para 10C **[see 5.4.5]**

(SI 2002/2661, reg 5).

In the circumstances described, the following deeming rules apply:

(*a*) during the period of the exchange, the new holding is deemed to satisfy all the requirements of TA 1988, Sch 28B, ie those relating to the investee company and the extent and nature of the VCT investor's holding in the investee company;

(*b*) before and during the exchange, the independence requirement in TA 1988, Sch 28B, para 9 and any arrangements leading to its breach **[see 5.4]** are ignored, to the extent they are incidental to the exchange;

(*c*) after the exchange, the new holding is treated at all times as satisfying the employment of funds test and the annual (£1 million) limit on investment;

(*d*) where, immediately after the exchange, any part of the new holding is quoted but otherwise satisfies all the requirements of TA 1988, Sch 28B other than those in paragraph (*c*) above, or is quoted and additionally fails one or more of the other requirements, it is nevertheless treated as meeting them for a limited period or earlier disposal by the VCT. The period in question is a period of two years beginning on the later of:
   (1) the first issue of the new holding to the VCT, and
   (2) the date on which all of the new holding becomes fully tradable;

(*e*) where, immediately after the exchange, any part of the new holding fails to satisfy any of the requirements of TA 1988, Sch 28B other than the requirement to be unquoted, the employment of funds test or the annual limit on investment, that part of the new holding is nevertheless treated as meeting the requirement(s) concerned for a limited period. The period in question begins on the date any part of the new holding is issued ('the first issue date') and, subject to any earlier disposal, ends three years later in the case of shares and five years later in the case of securities. However, if the shares or securities comprised in the holding become marketed to the general public, the period ends on the second anniversary of that time (or, if later, of the date on which the shares or securities become fully tradable)

(SI 2002/2661, reg 8(4)–(10)).

The third type of exchange envisaged by the regulations is one in which there is a scheme of reconstruction involving the issue of shares or securities. The precise circumstances are that:

(*a*) there is an agreement between the investee company and either:
   (1) the persons (including the VCT) holding shares or securities in the company, or
   (2) the persons (including the VCT) holding any one class (where there is more than one)

   concerning a scheme of reconstruction;
(*b*) under the arrangement, another company ('the new company') issues shares or securities to the relevant investors in the investee company in proportion to their existing holdings;
(*c*) the shares or securities ('the old holding') held by the investors are cancelled, redeemed or extinguished, or indeed retained;
(*d*) new shares are issued in respect of old shares or old securities, but new securities are issued solely in respect of old securities

(SI 2002/2661, reg 6).

In such circumstances, the following deeming rules apply:

(*a*) during the period of the reorganisation, the new holding is deemed to satisfy all the requirements of TA 1988, Sch 28B, ie those relating to the investee company and the extent and nature of the VCT investor's holding in the investee company;
(*b*) before and during the reorganisation, the independence requirement in TA 1988, Sch 28B, para 9 and any arrangements leading to its breach **[see 5.4]** are ignored, to the extent they are incidental to the exchange;
(*c*) after the reorganisation, the new holding is treated at all times as satisfying the employment of funds test and the annual (£1 million) limit on investment;
(*d*) where, immediately after the reorganisation, any part of the new holding is quoted but otherwise satisfies all the requirements of TA 1988, Sch 28B

other than those in paragraph (*c*) above, or is quoted and additionally fails one or more of the other requirements it is nevertheless treated as meeting them, for a limited period or until an earlier disposal by the VCT. The period in question is a period of two years beginning on the later of (1) the first issue of the new holding to the VCT and (2) the date on which all of the new holding becomes fully tradable;

(*f*) where, immediately after the exchange, any part of the new holding fails to satisfy any of the requirements of TA 1988, Sch 28B other than the requirement to be unquoted, the employment of funds test or the annual limit on investment, that part of the new holding is nevertheless treated as meeting the requirement(s) concerned for a limited period. The period in question begins on the date any part of the new holding is issued ('the first issue date') and, subject to any earlier disposal, ends three years later in the case of shares and five years later in the case of securities. However, if the shares or securities comprised in the holding become marketed to the general public, the period ends on the second anniversary of that time (or, if later, on the date on which the shares or securities become fully tradable

(SI 2000/2661, reg 9(4)–(10)).

5.6.2.11 *Valuation*

For the purposes of the 15% spread test **[see 5.6.2.9]** and the 70% qualifying holdings test **[see 5.6.2.6]**, the value of any holding of investments is the market value at the date it was acquired. This will usually be its cost. In subsequent years, the effect of an appreciation in value of the holding will be ignored unless:

(*a*) the investment is increased by a further holding of the same description; or

(*b*) any payment is made wholly or partly to discharge an obligation attached to the holding, which increases the value of the holding.

Where there is such an addition or payment, the value of the company's holding will be its market value immediately after the most recent addition or payment (TA 1988, s 842AA(5)). This could be a problem where an investment has increased in value but requires further capital.

Example 5.14

Hamilton VCT raised £12 million and invested £700,000 in William Ltd. Three years later William is worth £4 million and Hamilton's total investments are worth £25 million. William wishes to raise capital by means of a rights issue. Although Hamilton's VCT's holding in William at cost is within the 15% limit, it cannot take up the rights issue shares as this would trigger the revaluation of its holding and the 15% limit would be exceeded.

Where arrangements are in place for a restructuring of the investee company of the kind that represents an exception from the rule that the investee company must not be under the control of another company **[see 5.4.1]**, the value of the new shares is taken to be the value of the old shares at the time of their last valuation. This applies at the time when the new shares are issued and immediately after any subsequent addition to them under the arrangements in question. References to 'shares' include references to 'securities' (TA 1988, s 842AA(5AA), (5AB)).

Where the VCT exercises a right to conversion that it holds in respect of shares or securities that meet the conditions for an excepted restructuring **[see 5.4.5]**, the value of the new shares at the time of acquisition is similarly taken to be the same as the value of the convertible old shares or securities at the time of their last valuation (TA 1988, s 842AA(5AC)).

5.6.2.12 *Modifying the valuation on a share exchange*

A similar valuation rule applies on the occasion of a share exchange as part of a company reorganisation when the exchange is made for bona fide commercial reasons and not as part of a tax avoidance scheme. Where those conditions and further conditions set out in the VCT (Exchange of Shares and Securities) Regulations 2002, SI 2002/2661 are met, the value of the new shares, and of any old shares retained by the VCT is taken to be such that the 70% qualifying-holdings test **[see 5.6.2.6]**, the 30% eligible share test **[see 5.6.2.8]** and the 15% spread test **[see 5.6.2.9]** continue to be met (TA 1988, s 842AA(5AD); Sch 28B, para 11B).

These rules apply to exchanges occurring after 20 March 2000.

There are three types of share exchange that come within the regulations. In each case, it is envisaged that the VCT receives new shares or new securities in exchange for the old shares or old securities, with or without other consideration (SI 2002/2661, reg 3). The three types of exchange are:

(1) an exchange of shares or securities for those in the same company;
(2) an exchange of shares or securities for those in another company; or
(3) a scheme of reconstruction involving the issue of shares or securities

(SI 2002/261, regs 4–6).

The precise circumstances of these exchanges are described in **5.6.2.10**). For our purpose here, we are concerned with the valuation rule.

On the occasion of an exchange of shares or securities for those in the same company, when applying the three tests referred to earlier, the aggregate value of the new shares and new securities immediately after the exchange is given by the formula:

$$N_v = O_v \times \frac{N_{mv}}{N_{mv} + C}$$

N_v is the aggregate value of the new shares and new securities ('the new holding')
O_v is the aggregate value of the old shares and old securities ('the old holding') when last valued
N_{mv} is the aggregate market value of the new holding immediately after the exchange
C is the aggregate market value immediately after the exchange of:

(*a*) any monetary consideration;
(*b*) any monetary right (without a discount for postponement of the right to receive payment); and
(*c*) any other consideration except for the new holding

(SI 2002/2661, reg 7).

Clearly, therefore, where there is no consideration other than the new holding, its value is taken to be the same as the value of the old holding.

The valuation holds good until the new holding comes to be revalued because there is an addition of new investments of the same description or where a payment is made to release an obligation and thereby increase the value of the holding (the circumstances prescribed by TA 1988, s 842AA(5) – **[see 5.6.2.11]**).

Any part of the old holding that the VCT retains continues to be valued at its last valuation (apportioned where necessary) before the exchange, until it needs to be revalued in the circumstances described in the previous paragraph (SI 2002/2661, reg 7(3)).

If the share exchange is one in which the old holding is exchanged for shares and/or securities in another company, the same formula applies for valuing the new holding (SI 2002/2661, reg 8(2)).

In the third case, where there is a scheme of reconstruction involving the issue of shares or securities, the same formula is used to determine the aggregate value of the new shares and securities and any shares and securities of the transferor (target) company which the VCT has retained (either because they were not included in the reconstruction or were so included but were intended for retention), with the redesignation of two terms. In this instance:

N_v is the aggregate value being ascertained and
N_{mv} is the aggregate market value, immediately after the 'reorganisation period', of the new shares and new securities and the retained transferor company's shares or securities

(SI 2002/2661, reg 9(2)).

The reorganisation period is the period:

(*a*) beginning with the receipt as part of the scheme of reconstruction of shares or securities in the transferee (acquiring) company by the first shareholder or holder of securities to receive them; and
(*b*) ending when the last of the shares or securities of the transferee company are issued as part of the scheme

(SI 2002/2661, reg 9(11)).

Any shares or securities issued by virtue of an earn-out right are ignored for the purposes of (*b*). 'Earn-out right' has the meaning in TCGA 1992, s 138A(1) (SI 2002/2661, reg 2(1)).

5.6.2.13 *Income retention*

A fifth requirement for the VCT is that during the last complete accounting period in question it must have distributed at least 85% of the income derived in that period from shares and securities (TA 1988, s 842AA(2)(f)). To ascertain whether this condition has been met it will be necessary to look at the increase in the VCT's reserves of profits during the accounting period and then exclude profits and losses on the disposal of capital assets.

This rule is subject to two exceptions.

The first exception applies where the amount of income the company is required to retain in respect of the period by virtue of a restriction imposed by law exceeds 15% of the income the company derives from shares and securities (TA 1988, ss 842AA(11)(b), s 842(2A)).

However, the first exception does not apply in the following situation. Where the amount of income the company retains in respect of the accounting period exceeds the amount of income it is required to retain in respect of the period by virtue of a restriction imposed by law; and the amount of that excess or, where the company distributes income in respect of the period, that amount together with the amount of income which the company distributes, is at least £10,000. This figure is reduced proportionately where the period is less than 12 months (TA 1988, ss 842AA(11)(b), 842(2B)).

There is some doubt whether gross or net income is meant. The Inland Revenue's view is that 'the income retained must not exceed 15% of the gross income from shares and securities' (Venture Capital Schemes Manual, para VCM 60170). If this means the income before tax, it would be perverse, since the tax liability is not available for distribution. It would make more sense if by 'gross', the Manual means without deduction of expenses.

The second exception is that the 15% rule is not applied where the amount that the VCT would be required to distribute to comply with the rule is less than £15,000 (TA 1988, ss 842AA(11)(b), 842(2)(c)).

5.6.2.14 *Minimum eligible share content*

The sixth requirement is that the VCT's holding in any single investee company must comprise at least 10% by value of eligible shares (TA 1988, Sch 28B, para 10B(1)). 'Eligible shares' has the same meaning as in **5.6.2.8**.

For this purpose, the value of shares or securities at any time is their value immediately after a 'relevant event' occurring at that time. A 'relevant event' is:

(*a*) the VCT's acquisition of those shares or securities;
(*b*) the acquisition of other shares or securities of the same description (other than bonus issues) in the same investee company; or
(*c*) any payment discharging an obligation attaching to the VCT's holding so as to increase the value of the holding

(TA 1988, Sch 28B, para 10B(3)).

If no relevant event occurs at the time of valuation, the value is taken as the value of the shares or securities immediately after the last relevant event (TA 1988, Sch 28B, para 10B(2)(b)). At no time can the value of shares or securities be taken to be less than the consideration paid for them (TA 1988, Sch 28B, para 10B(4)).

Example 5.15

Lao-Tse is a VCT, which subscribes for 10,000 shares in a dot.com company, Confucius Ltd, for £90,000. At the same time, it makes a five-year loan to Confucius of £600,000. The total value of Lao-Tse's holding in Confucius is therefore £690,000 so that the 10% requirement is satisfied.

Confucius has three disastrous years, as a result of which its share price plummets, but no revaluation of the holding is necessary, as a relevant event has not occurred. Acute shortage of working capital leads Confucius to apply for, and Lao-Tse to grant, a further loan of £210,000. This is a relevant event, giving rise to a revaluation. The value of Lao-Tse's investments cannot be reduced below cost for this purpose, however, so that the aggregate value of its holding is now £900,000. The 10% requirement is just satisfied. Had Lao-Tse granted Confucius a loan of even £1 more than £210,000, the 10% requirement would not have been satisfied, and its holding in Confucius would have ceased to be a qualifying holding.

Any shares or securities acquired by money the VCT raised before 2 July 1997 can be ignored for the purposes of this rule (FA 1995, s 71(2)).

5.6.3 Gradual fulfilment of the conditions

We saw in **5.6.2** that all the conditions relating to the VCT investor company must have been satisfied in the most recent completed accounting period and during the current accounting period (TA 1988, s 842AA(2), (3)). However, it is recognised that many VCTs, especially new companies, will find it difficult to achieve the right levels of investment immediately, so the Inland Revenue is prepared to give provisional approval as the company gradually comes to satisfy the conditions.

Specifically, with reference to the conditions as listed in **5.6.2**:

(*a*) conditions (*a*), (*d*), (*e*) and the listing requirement must be satisfied by the end of the current accounting period or in the next period;
(*b*) conditions (*b*) and (*c*) must first be satisfied in respect of an accounting period beginning no later than three years after approval;
(*c*) condition (*f*) – that at least 10% of the VCT's investment in any one investee company be in the form of eligible shares – must be satisfied at all times

(TA 1988, s 842AA(4); Sch 28B, paras 1(2)(a), 10B).

For full details of the approval procedure, see **24.2.4**.

5.7 Conditions to be met by EIS (investee) companies

5.7.1 Introduction

An EIS investee company (from now on a 'qualifying company') must meet certain conditions throughout its relevant period **[see 5.1.3]**, but see the unquoted requirement **[5.7.2]** for an exception. Its directors need to be aware of those conditions **[see Appendix 2]** as any breach during that period would mean loss by EIS shareholders of all their tax reliefs.

In brief, a qualifying company must:

(*a*) be unquoted **[see 5.7.2]**;
(*b*) exist for a qualifying purpose **[see 5.7.3]**;
(*c*) employ the funds for its or its qualifying 90% subsidiaries' trades within 24 months **[see 5.7.4 and 5.7.5]**;
(*d*) not issue shares with 'pre-arranged exits' **[see 5.7.6]**; and
(*e*) not be controlled by another company or control another company other than a qualifying subsidiary **[see 5.10 and 5.11]**.

In addition, either the qualifying company or one or more of its qualifying subsidiaries must carry on a qualifying trade. Qualifying trades are discussed in **Chapter 6**.

5.7.2 The requirement to be unquoted

A qualifying company must be an unquoted company (TA 1988, s 293(1A)(a)) *at the beginning of its relevant period*, that is to say when the shares are issued. Since 7 March 2001, it is no longer necessary for the company to remain unquoted throughout the relevant period, as long as quotation is a result of subsequent growth or developments. There must be no arrangements in place at the issue date for the company to become quoted (see below).

This relaxation was introduced from 7 March 2001, in order to bring the EIS rules into line with those for the VCT scheme **[see 5.2.2]** and the CVS scheme **[see 5.12.2]**.

Readers should note that paragraph VCM 15020 of the Inland Revenue's Venture Capital Schemes Manual is not correct in this respect. It states that for shares issued before 7 March 2001 the company must remain unquoted throughout the relevant period. However, FA 2001, Sch 15, para 40(2) clearly provides that paragraph 12 of that Schedule, which changed the rule, applies not only to shares issued on or after 7 March 2001 but also to shares issued before that date, to which EIS relief was attributable immediately before that date.

Example 5.16

Ayer Ltd, an unquoted company, makes a qualifying EIS share issue on 1 April 2000, and begins trading on 1 May 2000. All EIS relief is intact as at 7 March 2001. Thanks to phenomenal growth, the directors decide to seek a listing on the Stock Exchange, which is granted on 2 February 2003. Although Ayer's relevant period does not end until 30 April 2003, investors do not lose their EIS relief as a result, since the new rule in section 293(1A) applies, by virtue of FA 2001, Sch 15, para 40(2).

What does 'unquoted' mean in this context? The primary definition is that none of the company's shares, stocks, debentures or other securities must be marketed to the general public (TA 1988, s 312(1)). This in turn means that those shares and securities must neither be listed on a recognised stock exchange nor on a designated foreign stock exchange, or be dealt in outside the UK by any means designated by the Inland Revenue (TA 1988, s 312(1B), (1C)). **Appendix 4** contains a list of recognised and designated stock exchanges and means of dealing. Securities traded on the Alternative Investment Market (AIM) or on OFEX are considered to be unquoted (Inland Revenue Press Release of 20 February 1995; Venture Capital Schemes Manual, para VCM 15020).

There must also be no arrangements in place for the qualifying company to cease to be an unquoted company or for it to become a subsidiary of another company by virtue of an exchange of shares with or without securities such that EIS relief continues **[see 5.10.2]** and nor for there to be arrangements in place for the new parent company to lose its unquoted status (TA 1988, s 293(1A)(b), (1B)). For the meaning of 'arrangements', see **5.1.7**.

5.7.3 The qualifying purpose

5.7.3.1 *Introduction*

An EIS company must exist chiefly to carry on a qualifying trade or hold shares in one or more qualifying subsidiaries that carry on such a trade. In fact, it may have only one of two purposes, namely:

(*a*) to exist wholly in order to carry on one or more qualifying trades or exist substantially wholly for that purpose; or
(*b*) to be the parent company of a trading group

(TA 1988, s 293(2)).

This must be so during the whole of the relevant period.

'Substantially wholly' here is shorthand for the legislative phrase that the company must exist wholly for the purpose of carrying on a qualifying trade or so exist apart from 'purposes capable of having no significant effect (other than in relation to incidental matters) on the extent of the company's activities' (TA 1988, s 293(2)(a)). The meaning of this phrase was discussed at **5.2.3.1**, but, essentially, only trivial and incidental activities will be overlooked (Venture Capital Schemes Manual, para VCM 15070).

5.7.3.2 *Parent company of a trading group*

The second purpose for which a qualifying company may exist is as the parent company of a trading group. This does not exclude the possibility that such a parent company can also carry on a qualifying trade.

A parent company in this context is a company that has one or more subsidiaries, each of which is a qualifying subsidiary (TA 1988, s 293(3A)(a), (b)).

Qualifying subsidiaries are dealt with in section **5.11**.

The requirement for there to be a trading group is met if the business of the group as a whole meets certain tests (TA 1988, s 293(3A)(c)).

In applying those tests, one has to consider the activities of the investing company and all of its subsidiaries as if those activities taken together constituted a single business. The tests are that neither the business nor a substantial part of it (see below for what is meant by 'substantial') must consist – with certain exceptions (see below) – of a non-qualifying trade **[see Chapter 6]** or of non-trading activities (TA 1988, s 293(3B)).

However, the following activities may be ignored altogether when applying the tests:

(*a*) holding shares or securities in one or more subsidiaries or making loans to one or more subsidiaries;
(*b*) holding and managing property used by a group company (ie by the parent company or any of its subsidiaries) for the purpose of a qualifying trade or for research and development intended for a qualifying trade of a group company;
(*c*) the making of loans by a subsidiary to the parent company;
(*d*) where a subsidiary is 'mainly trading', any incidental or insignificant non-trading activities

(TA 1988, s 293(3D), (3E)).

A subsidiary is 'mainly trading' if it exists wholly for the purpose of carrying on one or more qualifying trades; it may have insignificant purposes that are not capable of having any significant effect (other than in relation to incidental matters) on the extent of its activities as a whole (TA 1988, s 293(3F)). This wording mirrors that discussed in **5.2.3.1** in relation to a qualifying VCT investee company that is not the parent company of a trading group.

A non-trading activity (ie an activity carried on otherwise than in the course of a trade) that is permitted is research and development (TA 1988, s 293(3B)(b)). Before 7 March 2001, another was oil exploration. Since that date, oil exploration, if conducted with a view to commencing oil extraction, amounts to preparing to carry on a qualifying trade **[see 6.7]**.

When applying the tests, two activities that are generally non-qualifying trades but in certain circumstances escape that definition are also excepted from falling foul of the trading-group rule.

The full description of these activities is contained in **Chapter 6**, but briefly they are:

(*a*) receiving royalties or licence fees wholly or substantially attributable to the exploitation of 'relevant intangible assets'; and

(*b*) the letting of ships (but not oil rigs or pleasure craft) on charter in certain circumstances

(TA 1988, s 293(3C)).

An intangible asset is a relevant intangible asset if its value has wholly or mostly been created by the company receiving the royalties or licence fees or by its parent company or a qualifying subsidiary (ie it is not an asset acquired from a different third party) (TA 1988, ss 293(3C)(a), 297(4), (5)). In this case, a parent company is a company having one or more 51% subsidiaries but which is not itself a 51% subsidiary (TA 1988, s 297(5A)(b)). In the case of intellectual property, creation must take place in such a way that the right to exploit the property vests in the company (although it may also vest jointly in third parties) (TA 1988, s 297(5A)(a)).

For shares issued before 6 April 2000, the exception relating to royalties and licence fees was slightly more restrictive, as it required all the royalties or licence fees to be attributable to research and development that the company had carried out (and not merely to value that the company had wholly *or mostly* created).

For shares issued after 5 April 1998 and before 6 April 2000, there was a further activity that was overlooked, namely one that consisted to a substantial extent of receiving royalties or licence fees from films produced by the company receiving them, or from sound recordings or other products from such films, during the relevant period. The company had to be engaged throughout the relevant period in film production or distribution (of its own films).

The Inland Revenue interprets 'substantial' as meaning generally 20% or more **[see 5.2.3.2]**.

As to the Inland Revenue's view of what a company exists for, see **5.2.3.1**.

5.7.3.3 *Administration, receivership and liquidation*

Nothing done purely as a consequence of a company's being in administration or receivership (or purely as a consequence of a subsidiary's being in administration or receivership) causes it to lose its qualifying status, as long as it still exists for a qualifying purpose and provided that the administration or receivership and anything done as a consequence is carried out for bona fide commercial reasons and not as part of a tax avoidance scheme (TA 1988, s 293(4A)–(4B), as amended by FA 2004, Sch 18, para 5).

This new wording applies to shares issued after 16 March 2004. For shares issued after 20 March 2000 but before 17 March 2004, the conditions were slightly different. The exception applied to *anything* done as a consequence of the administration or receivership (and was not restricted to anything done *only* as a consequence of that state) and nor was there any reference to things done with reference to the administration or receivership of a subsidiary. Thus if a qualifying company's status changed as the result of actions undertaken during the course of a subsidiary's administration etc, there was no safeguard under this rule.

Before 21 March 2000, the Inland Revenue had previously indicated that it would not withdraw all the shareholders' EIS relief if the cessation by a receiver of the company's qualifying activities was followed without undue delay by a winding-up of the company under the conditions described below. The appointment of an administrative receiver has no effect on the company's status (*Tax Bulletin*, Issue 2, February 1992).

A company that is wound up or dissolved will cease to exist to carry on a trade. The same is true, in respect of shares issued after 16 March 2004, if any of the company's subsidiaries is wound up. If this occurs during the relevant period, EIS relief would be lost. However, EIS relief is preserved if:

(*a*) the winding-up or dissolution of the company or of its subsidiary (as the case may be) is being carried out for bona fide commercial reasons and not as part of a tax avoidance scheme; and

(*b*) the company would otherwise have continued to exist for a qualifying purpose

(TA 1988, s 293(5), (6)).

Before 21 March 2000, there was a further condition. The company's net assets (if there were any remaining) had to be distributed to members or dealt with as *bona vacantia* before the end of the relevant period; in the case of a winding-up, the period of compliance could be extended to run for three years from the beginning of the winding-up procedure.

A hive-down of the trade by a receiver to a newly formed subsidiary to preserve trading losses is apparently not acceptable to the Inland Revenue, presumably because it is tainted with tax avoidance motives. If a receiver is appointed, or such an appointment is imminent, therefore, consideration should be given to ways of preserving EIS relief. One possibility is to stop trading by means of a voluntary winding-up; alternatively, the EIS shares could be sold while the company still meets the EIS conditions.

5.7.4 The requirement to commence trade within 24 months

The qualifying company (or its qualifying 90% subsidiary) need not be carrying on a trade at the time of the share issue ('the issue date'). Nevertheless, at the issue date, the intention to carry on a trade must exist and that intention must be realised within two years of the issue date, or the company ceases to be a qualifying company (TA 1988, s 289(2)(a)(ii)) **[see 5.7.5]**.

For shares issued before 17 March 2004, for references to 'qualifying 90% subsidiary', read 'qualifying subsidiary'. For the meaning of these terms, see **5.11**.

5.7.5 The requirement to employ funds in a given way

To reinforce the requirement that the issue of EIS shares must raise money for a trade or purposes relating to a trade, there are rules providing for funds to be applied for prescribed purposes to a prescribed extent within a prescribed time.

These rules are that:

(*a*) the EIS shares, other than any of them that are bonus shares, must be issued in order to raise money for the purpose of a 'qualifying business activity' (for shares issued before 17 March 2004, it was necessary that both the EIS shares and all other shares in the same issue be issued in order to raise money for such an activity);

(*b*) at least 80% of the money raised by the issue of the EIS shares and any other eligible shares of the same class issued on the same day must be employed wholly for the purposes of a qualifying business activity within 12 months of the issue date. This period can be extended if the money has been raised wholly for the purposes of a qualifying trade, to end no later than 12 months after the trade has commenced; and

(*c*) all of the money must be employed for those purposes within a further 12 months

(TA 1988, s 289(1)(b)–(d), (3)).

For a discussion of what it means to employ money for a particular purpose, see **5.2.5**.

For the issue of bonus shares, see **5.7.5.3**.

5.7.5.1 *Qualifying business activity*

A company is carrying on a qualifying trade if at the issue date:

(*a*) it is carrying on a qualifying trade wholly or mainly in the UK or is preparing to carry on a qualifying trade that it intends to carry on wholly or mainly in the UK; or

(*b*) it is carrying on research and development or begins to carry on research and development immediately afterwards, from which the intention is to derive a qualifying trade to be carried on wholly or mainly in the UK.

The trade (or the research and development) may be carried on by the EIS company itself or by a 'qualifying 90% subsidiary' (TA 1988, s 289(2)). For shares issued before 17 March 2004, the subsidiary concerned could have been any qualifying subsidiary; for the distinction, see **5.11.1**.

As already noted (in **5.7.4**), if at the issue date, the qualifying trade has not yet been commenced, the qualifying company or the appropriate qualifying subsidiary must commence the trade within two years of the issue date (TA 1988, s 289(2)(a)(ii)). Once the trade has commenced, it must throughout the relevant period be carried on wholly or mainly in the UK.

Where the qualifying trade is being carried on or is to be carried on by a qualifying 90% subsidiary, any period in which it carried on that trade before it became a qualifying 90% subsidiary is disregarded in determining when the trade begins to be carried on for the purposes of the two-year rule (TA 1988, s 289(3A)(a)). In other words, if the trade is carried on by a company that only becomes a qualifying 90% subsidiary 26 months after the issue date, the two-year rule is not satisfied and the shares comprised in the issue are not eligible shares.

Similarly, in determining when a qualifying 90% subsidiary begins to carry on research and development, any period in which it did so before it became a qualifying 90% subsidiary is also disregarded (TA 1988, s 289(3A)(b)).

The rules discussed in the preceding two paragraphs apply in respect of shares issued after 16 March 2004 only.

5.7.5.2 *Companies that may carry on the qualifying business activity*

The qualifying trade (or the research and development) need not be carried on by the qualifying company; it may also be carried on by a 'qualifying 90% subsidiary' of that company. In either case, there are further conditions that must be satisfied throughout the relevant period with respect to the activities of the qualifying company or of any of its qualifying 90% subsidiaries concerned. Those conditions are that at no time must a person other than the qualifying company or a qualifying 90% subsidiary of that company carry on any of the following:

(*a*) the 'relevant qualifying trade';

(*b*) 'relevant preparation work'; or

(*c*) 'relevant research and development'

(TA 1988, s 289(1A)).

The 'relevant qualifying trade' is the qualifying trade that is the subject of the qualifying business activity. 'Relevant preparation work' is the preparations to carry on the qualifying trade undertaken by the company or a qualifying 90% subsidiary (where the qualifying trade is not actually being carried on at the issue date). The 'relevant research and development' is the research and development that the company or a qualifying 90% subsidiary are carrying on at the issue date or begin to carry on immediately afterwards **[see 5.7.5.1]** (TA 1988, s 289(1E)).

Where the qualifying company or a qualifying 90% subsidiary are carrying on relevant preparation work (ie preparing to carry on a qualifying trade), then the fact that a company other than the qualifying company or any subsidiary may have carried on the relevant qualifying trade at any time within the relevant period but before it begins to be carried on by the qualifying company or a qualifying 90% subsidiary (as the case may be) is ignored (TA 1988, s 289(1B)). What this means is that the qualifying business activity need not be carried on by the same company at all times. It is possible, for example, for the qualifying trade to be carried on by another company in the group (a 51% subsidiary, for example) but for the qualifying company then to issue EIS shares and apply the subscription monies to fund the carrying on of that trade by itself or by a qualifying 90% subsidiary.

If, during the relevant period, the relevant qualifying trade ceases to be carried on by the qualifying company or by any qualifying 90% subsidiary purely as the result of a winding-up or dissolution of the qualifying company or of any other company, or purely by reason of anything done as a consequence of the entry of the qualifying company or of any other company into administration or receivership, that fact alone will not necessarily mean that the qualifying conditions cease to be satisfied. The fact that the cessation has taken place and that the qualifying trade is subsequently carried on by another person ('the successor') will be disregarded provided that:

(*a*) the entry into administration or receivership and everything done as a consequence or the winding-up or dissolution (as the case may be) is for bona fide commercial purposes and is not part of a tax avoidance scheme; and
(*b*) the successor is not connected with the qualifying company at any time in the 'period of restriction'

(TA 1988, s 289(1C), (1D)).

The 'period of restriction' is the period beginning one year before the issue date and ending immediately before the third anniversary of the later of (1) the issue date and (2) the date on which the qualifying company or a qualifying 90% subsidiary begins to carry on the qualifying trade (TA 1988, s 312(1)).

This amount of flexibility exists in respect of shares issued after 16 March 2004. On or before that date, different rules applied, which required that the identity of the company carrying on the qualifying activity remained unchanged throughout the relevant period.

5.7.5.3 *Rules applying to shares issued before 17 March 2004*

These are as follows. The company that actually carries on the trade or the research and development ('the active company') must satisfy further conditions throughout the relevant period. These further conditions are that:

(*a*) where the active company was not the qualifying company, it had to be a 90% subsidiary of the qualifying company;
(*b*) the active company had to exist wholly or substantially wholly **[see 5.7.3.1]** to carry on one or more qualifying trades; or
(*c*) be such a company as in paragraph (*b*) but for the fact that its purposes included the holding of:
   (1) shares or securities in its subsidiaries,
   (2) the making of loans to its subsidiaries,
   (3) the holding and management of property used by the company or its subsidiaries to carry on one or more qualifying trades or research and development from which a qualifying trade was to be derived, or
   (4) in the case of a subsidiary, the making of loans to the parent; or
(*d*) in the case of a subsidiary, it existed wholly or substantially wholly **[see 5.7.3.1]** to hold or manage property used by the company or its subsidiaries to carry on one or more qualifying trades or research and development from which a qualifying trade was to be derived; or it was dormant. Dormant in this context meant that the company had no taxable profits and no part of its business consisted in the making of investments

It was also the case that a company was not regarded as failing to satisfy these conditions by reason of anything done as a consequence of its being in administration or receivership, provided that both the order to put it into administration or receivership and everything done as a consequence of its being in administration or receivership was for bona fide commercial reasons and not part of a tax avoidance scheme. Similarly, the fact that a company was put into liquidation or dissolved without being wound up before the end of the relevant period did not result in a breach of the qualifying conditions, provided that the winding-up or dissolution was done for bona fide commercial reasons and not as part of a tax avoidance scheme.

5.7.5.4 *Bonus shares and the fully paid up condition*

In order for shares to be qualifying shares, it has been necessary for them to be fully paid up and subscribed for wholly in cash. It was also necessary that all shares of the same class issued to the same investor on the same day (whether they were EIS shares or not) be fully paid up and that shares of the same class issued to other subscribers on the same day be fully paid up.

From 17 March 2004, however, this condition is relaxed. It is possible for the EIS investor and other subscribers also to receive bonus shares of the same class on the same day without jeopardising the EIS investor's eligibility for relief, provided that the EIS shares are still fully paid up and the investor subscribes for the EIS shares wholly in cash (TA 1988, s 289(1)(a)–(b)).

'Bonus shares' are any shares issued otherwise than for payment (whether that payment takes the form of cash or otherwise) (TA 1988, s 312(1)).

Shares (whenever issued) are not regarded as fully paid up for this purpose if there is an undertaking to pay cash at any future date for their acquisition (as for partly-paid shares) (TA 1988, s 289(8A); for shares issued before 17 March 2004, TA 1988, s 289(1)(aa) before amendment by FA 2004, Sch 18, para 1(7)).

5.7.6 Prohibition of pre-arranged exits

The issuing arrangements for the EIS shares must not include certain features that, broadly, provide for a means of releasing the investment or reducing the risk associated with making the investment.

Issuing arrangements are the arrangements under which the EIS shares are issued to the individual and any arrangements made before the issue date in connection with the issue (TA 1988, s 299B(6)).

There are four separate prohibited arrangements.

5.7.6.1 *Repurchase, exchange or other disposal*

There must be no issuing arrangements that provide for the EIS shares or any other shares or securities in or of the qualifying company to be repurchased from the investor, exchanged for other shares or otherwise disposed of. Excluded is an acquisition of the qualifying company's shares in circumstances such that relief continues in respect of the new shares (under TA 1988, s 304A – see **5.10.2**) (TA 1988, s 299B(1)(a), (2)).

5.7.6.2 *Arrangements to cease trading*

There must be no issuing arrangements that provide for the qualifying company or a connected person to cease trading. The trade does not have to be in existence at the issue date (TA 1988, s 299B(1)(b)). Excluded are arrangements that apply only in the event of a winding-up of the qualifying company, unless the issuing arrangements include arrangements providing for the winding-up or where the qualifying company is wound up otherwise than for bona fide commercial reasons (TA 1988, s 299B(3)).

5.7.6.3 *Arrangements for a disposal of assets*

There must be no issuing arrangements that provide for the disposal of all or a substantial part by value of the qualifying company's assets or those of a connected person. Again, excluded are arrangements that apply only in the event of a winding-up of the qualifying company, unless the issuing arrangements include arrangements providing for the winding-up or where the qualifying company is wound up otherwise than for bona fide commercial reasons (TA 1988, s 299B(1)(c), (3)).

'Substantial' means 20% or more **[see 5.2.3.2]**.

5.7.6.4 *Arrangements for insuring against loss*

Finally, it must not be the or a main purpose of the issuing arrangements to provide partial or complete protection for investors against the risks of the investment, by insurance, indemnity, guarantee or other means (such as schemes artificially to maintain the value of the shares) (TA 1988, s 299B(1)(d)). The Inland Revenue takes the view that normal warranties or indemnities given for the subscription are unlikely to infringe this requirement, although this depends on the circumstances (see, for example, IR 2000, p 30). Ordinary commercial arrangements such as insurance for the qualifying company and/or its qualifying subsidiaries against normal trading risks are excepted (TA 1988, s 299B(4)).

5.8 Limits on investment in a qualifying company

5.8.1 Maximum investment

Although there are limits on the amount any one individual may invest in EIS shares in any tax year if he or she wishes to obtain investment relief, there is no longer a limit of this description with respect to a qualifying company (the previous £1 million limit, which still exists for the VCT scheme – see **5.3.1** – was repealed for shares issued after 5 April 1998). Regard must still be had to the gross assets test, however **[see 5.8.2]**.

5.8.2 The gross assets test

EIS companies remain subject to a gross asset limit, however, restricting the EIS scheme to smaller companies. The gross assets of the qualifying company or of its group (itself and its qualifying subsidiaries) as the case may be, must not exceed £15 million before the issue of the shares and must not exceed £16 million immediately after the issue. Assets of group members which consist in rights against, or in shares in or securities of, another group member are disregarded (TA 1988, s 293(6A)–(6D)). For the meaning of gross assets, **[see 5.3.6]**.

5.9 Share capital requirements for qualifying companies

5.9.1 Eligible shares

Only 'eligible shares' qualify for EIS relief. Eligible shares are new ordinary shares that carry no present or future preferential right to dividends or to a company's assets on its winding-up and no present or future right to be redeemed (TA 1988, s 289(7)). In this context, provided that the shareholder has a legal right, it does not matter whether that right is set out in the company's articles of association **[see 5.1.10]**, in a shareholder's agreement **[see 5.1.7]** or in another document.

For the meaning of ordinary shares and the significance of pre-emption rights, see **5.6.2.8**. The remarks there apply equally to EIS shares.

These conditions must be observed throughout a period beginning with their issue and ending immediately before their 'termination date'. The termination date **[see 5.1.3]** is the later of:

(*a*) the third anniversary of the issue date; and
(*b*) the third anniversary of the date on which the company or a qualifying subsidiary began to carry on a qualifying trade financed by that issue

(TA 1988, s 312(1)).

This period is, of course, exactly coterminous with the 'relevant period'; that the legislation does not refer to it as such is probably an oversight.

5.9.2 Fully paid-up shares

It is no longer a condition of EIS relief (as it has never been of VCT relief) that all the qualifying company's shares must be fully paid up. Instead, all EIS shares must be fully paid up in respect of each investor if that investor is to obtain relief (TA 1988, s 289(1)(aa)) **[see 9.2.5]**.

5.10 EIS qualifying companies: control of or by another company

5.10.1 The independence requirement

As with the VCT scheme, there is an independence requirement for qualifying companies. A qualifying company must not at any time in the relevant period either:

(*a*) control (or together with a person connected with it control) any other company (other than its qualifying subsidiaries – see **5.11**); or (*b*) be under the control of another company (or of another company together with persons connected with that other company) without being a 51% subsidiary of that other company; or

(*c*) be a 51% subsidiary of another company

(TA 1988, s 293(8)).

Furthermore, there can be no arrangements in existence at any time in the relevant period with a view to bringing the company within the ambit of the proscribed situations listed above. For the meaning of arrangements, see **5.1.7**.

A '51% subsidiary' is a company in which another company, of which it is the subsidiary, directly or indirectly owns over 50% of the ordinary share capital (TA 1988, s 838(1)(a)).

Control here has two definitions. When testing whether the qualifying company exercises control over another company (potential parent), the broader definition in TA 1988, s 416 is used **[see 5.1.9]**; when testing whether it is under the control of another company (potential subsidiary) the narrower definition in TA 1988, s 840 **[see 5.1.10]** applies instead (TA 1988, ss 293(8), (8A), 312(1)). Before 21 March 2000, the broader definition applied in both cases (although the wording of the subsection was different). There is no clear reason why different definitions should be applied and it is likely to be solely an administrative convenience for the legislator. The use of the narrower definition in the potential subsidiary case mirrors the equivalent rule for the CVS (FA 2000, Sch 15, para 17 – see **5.15.1**), introduced at the same time. There is no requirement in the CVS, on the other hand, for the investee company not to control another, hence no change to the EIS rule.

For the role of connected persons in testing for control, see **5.1.6**.

There are two exceptions to the independence requirement. The first is that a qualifying company may have qualifying subsidiaries **[see 5.11]**. The second is where there is an acquisition in prescribed circumstances of the qualifying company's shares **[see 5.10.2]**.

5.10.2 Takeover of the qualifying company

The rule that the qualifying company may not be under the control of another company is relaxed where there is a takeover of the qualifying company by another company in prescribed circumstances involving the issue of the acquiring company's shares in exchange for those of the qualifying company.

The conditions for this treatment to apply relate not only to the form taken by the takeover but also to the acquiring and target companies. With respect to the takeover itself:

(*a*) the acquiring company must acquire all the shares and securities ('the old shares') in the qualifying EIS company ('the target company');

(*b*) the consideration for the acquisition must consist solely of shares and securities ('the old shares') in the acquiring company;

(*c*) where the old shares are of different descriptions, the new shares issued in exchange must be of the same description. Shares in the acquired company are of the same description as shares in the target company if they would be of the same class and carry the same rights if they were shares in the target company;
(*d*) the new shares (and securities, where appropriate) must be issued to each shareholder of the target company in proportion to that shareholder's holding in the target company

(TA 1988, s 304A(1)(a)–(d), (6)).

The acquiring company must be a new company, ie it must previously have issued only subscriber shares (TA 1988, s 304A(1)(a)).

As far as the target company is concerned, it must at some time previously have issued eligible EIS shares and issued a compliance certificate (EIS 3) in respect of those shares (TA 1988, s 304A(1)(e)). For the issue of EIS 3 certificates, **[see 24.8.7]**.

Finally, prior clearance must have been obtained from the Inland Revenue. It is not enough that all the conditions described above are satisfied; in the absence of a notice of approval from the Inland Revenue, there is no waiver of the normal rules, and the EIS investors in the target company will lose their relief. The Inland Revenue will not give its approval unless it is satisfied that the takeover (the exchange of shares) is taking place for bona fide commercial reasons and not as part of any tax avoidance scheme or arrangement in the sense of TCGA 1992, s 137(1) (TA 1988, s 304AA(1)(f)). That is to say, a clearance under TCGA 1992, s 138 for reconstructions will also serve as a clearance under this section.

Once all these hurdles have been cleared, the following consequences ensue:

(*a*) there is no disposal of the old shares and no acquisition of the new shares;
(*b*) the new shares are treated as issued to every shareholder at the time when the old shares were issued;
(*c*) the claim for EIS investment relief on the old shares is treated as if it had been made on the new shares and at the same time as that claim was made;
(*d*) the investor is treated as if he or she had received relief on the new shares in the same tax year as he or she in fact received relief on the old shares

(TA 1988, s 304A(3)).

The same consequences apply where the investor received his or her shares by a transfer from his or her spouse (for transfers between spouses, **[see 18.2.3]**). The investor is treated as if he or she had received relief on the new shares in the same tax year as the transferor spouse in fact received relief on the old shares (TA 1988, s 304A(4)).

If these rules apply to make the new shares stand in the shoes of the old, then there is also no disposal of the old shares for the purposes of deferral relief **[see 18.3.7]**.

5.11 Qualifying subsidiaries in the EIS

5.11.1 Introduction

The exception to the rule that a qualifying company may not control any other companies is that it may have qualifying subsidiaries (TA 1988, s 293(8)(a)). Two different types of condition must be satisfied in respect of qualifying subsidiaries. They relate on the one hand to the extent of the qualifying company's holding in the subsidiary and on the other hand to the activities of the subsidiary itself.

There is a significant change in the shareholding condition with respect to shares issued after 16 March 2004.

5.11.2 Shares issued after 16 March 2004

The shareholding condition is of two types. One relates to the qualifying subsidiaries a qualifying company may have in general; the second relates to the nature of the holding a qualifying company must have in a qualifying subsidiary that carries on the qualifying trade or qualifying research and development.

5.11.2.1 *Qualifying subsidiaries in general*

The qualifying company must directly or indirectly own more than 50% of the ordinary share capital of the subsidiary (TA 1988, s 308(2)(ca)). The general provisions of the Tax Acts relating to subsidiaries apply (TA 1988, s 308(5B)). This means, broadly, that:

(*a*) ownership must be beneficial ownership (ie the qualifying company must not be a mere conduit for some ultimate other owner);

(*b*) ownership through a chain of two or more companies is computed in proportion to the holding of one company in the immediately inferior company. Thus, if company A owns 75% of company B and company B owns 80% of company C, company A is considered to own 75% × 80% = 60% of company C.

Further, no person other than the qualifying company or another of its subsidiaries may have control of the subsidiary, and nor must arrangements exist under which these conditions may be breached. Control in this context is that within the narrower definition **[see 5.1.10]** (TA 1988, s 308(2)(d), (e)).

These conditions must be satisfied throughout the relevant period (TA 1988, s 308(1)).

5.11.2.2 *Qualifying 90% subsidiaries*

However, any subsidiary that carries on the qualifying trade or qualifying research and development must be a 'qualifying 90% subsidiary' of the qualifying company **[see 5.7.5.2]**.

For a subsidiary to be a qualifying 90% subsidiary of its parent company, a number of conditions have to be satisfied. These are that:

(*a*) the parent company must possess at least 90% of the issued share capital of and of the voting power in the subsidiary;
(*b*) the parent company must be beneficially entitled to at least 90% of the distributable profits of the subsidiary;
(*c*) the parent company must be beneficially entitled to at least 90% of the assets available to equity holders of the subsidiary in the event of a winding-up of the company or in any other circumstances; and
(*d*) no person other than the parent company must have control of the subsidiary and there must be no arrangements in existence that would cause the foregoing conditions to be broken

(TA 1988, s 289(9)).

For control, the narrower definition **[see 5.1.10]** is applied.

The meaning of 'equity holder' and the measure of an equity holder's entitlement are both taken from the group relief provisions of TA 1988, Sch 18, paras 1 and 3 (TA 1988, s 289(12)). There is no scope in this book to cover those definitions fully, but, essentially, an equity holder is analogous to a participator **[see 5.1.9.3]**, in that the definition encompasses both holders of ordinary share capital and loan creditors (other than in respect of normal commercial loans) (TA 1988, Sch 18, para 1(1)).

5.11.3 Shares issued before 17 March 2004

Different conditions applied and continue to apply for shares issued before 17 March 2004. The principal difference is that a qualifying subsidiary had to be a '75% subsidiary', although it was still the case that a subsidiary carrying on the qualifying trade had to be a 90% subsidiary. However, any subsidiary could carry on qualifying research and development; this activity was not limited to 90% subsidiaries.

The shareholding condition is that the qualifying company must have a holding of at least 75% in the subsidiary. This means an entitlement to no less than 75% of the issued share capital and of the voting power. It must also be entitled to the same minimum percentage of distributable profits and of the assets available to equity holders in the event of a hypothetical winding-up or in any other circumstances.

There is an important proviso here. If it is the subsidiary or subsidiaries that are to carry on the qualifying trade(s), and not the parent company, those subsidiaries must be 90% subsidiaries, not merely 75% subsidiaries.

For the meaning of 'equity holder' and the measure of entitlement, see **5.11.1.2**.

A further condition is that there must be no person other than the qualifying company or another of its qualifying subsidiaries that has control of the subsidiary (here the narrower definition of control – see **5.1.10** – is applied) and there must be no arrangements in existence that would cause the investee company to fail these conditions. Note that for shares issued after 16 March 2004, only the qualifying company may have control of a qualifying 90% subsidiary **[see further 5.11.4]**.

These conditions must be satisfied throughout the relevant period.

5.11.4 Subsubsidiaries

Can a qualifying company have qualifying subsubsidiaries? For shares issued after 16 March 2004, the answer seems to be yes for qualifying subsidiaries generally, but not for qualifying 90% subsidiaries. That is to say, a qualifying EIS company may have subsubsidiaries, but the qualifying trade, if it is to be carried on by one or more subsidiaries, may only be carried on by a directly owned qualifying 90% subsidiary. For, although there is reference to:

(*a*) control of a subsidiary by another subsidiary (TA 1988, s 308(2)(d)); and
(*b*) disposal by a subsidiary of its interest in another subsidiary (TA 1988, s 308(4)),

it is clearly stated that a qualifying 90% subsidiary may only be controlled by the qualifying company (TA 1988, s 293(9)(d)).

On the other hand, in respect of shares issued before 17 March 2004, the indicators point the other way, for there is also reference to the possession of not less than 75% of a subsidiary by another subsidiary (TA 1988, s 308(2)(a), now repealed in respect of issues after 16 March 2004), and a qualifying 90% subsidiary is simply one in respect of which the definition is identical to that of a qualifying subsidiary, subject to the substitution of 90% for 75% (TA 1988, s 289(9), before amendment by FA 2004, Sch 18, para 1(8)).

Before 27 November 1996, despite these positive indicators, the answer would have been 'no', as a qualifying subsidiary had itself to carry on a qualifying trade, hold or manage business property etc. However, since that date, there is no longer an explicit requirement relating to a qualifying subsidiary's activities.

Instead, the equivalent condition is expressed indirectly, in that a qualifying company, if it does not itself exist wholly for the purpose of carrying on one or more qualifying trades, must be the parent company of a trading group. This second requirement necessitates looking at the activities of the parent company and its subsidiaries as a whole. For what constitutes a trading group, see **5.7.3.2**; for coverage of qualifying trades, see **Chapter 6**.

As long as there is at least one company in the group that carries on a qualifying trade wholly or mainly in the UK, for the purposes of which the EIS funds were raised (TA 1988, s 289(1)(b), (1A), (2)), the others (including the parent company as the case may be) need not do so, as long as the group as a whole is a trading group (TA 1988, s 293(2)(aa)). This leaves one or more qualifying subsidiaries free, within those parameters, to act as intermediary holding companies for qualifying (90%) subsidiaries, but only in respect of share issues before 17 March 2004.

5.11.5 Trading wholly or mainly abroad

The second type of condition attaching to a qualifying subsidiary concerns the activities it is required to carry on. For the reasons given in **5.11.4**, there is no longer a requirement for every qualifying subsidiary to pursue or not to pursue particular activities.

It is instead necessary that a qualifying company, if it does not itself exist wholly for the purpose of carrying one or more qualifying trades, be the parent company of a trading group.

It follows that some members of the group, provided that the group as a whole is still a trading group, may have activities that are not carried out wholly or mainly in the UK.

In that context and within those parameters, remarks made in 1994 by the Chief Secretary to the Treasury at that time, Michael Portillo, are still relevant **[see 5.5.3]**.

5.11.5.1 *Property management*

If a qualifying company has at any time in the relevant period a subsidiary that is a 'property managing subsidiary', that subsidiary must be a qualifying 90% subsidiary (TA 1988, s 289(6ZA)). A 'property managing subsidiary' is a subsidiary whose business consists wholly or mainly in holding or managing land or property deriving its value from land (TA 1988, s 289(6ZB)).

This condition is imposed on shares issued after 16 March 2004 only. For shares whenever issued, property management can be disregarded in determining whether a group is a trading group **[see 5.7.3.2]**.

5.11.5.2 *Dormant subsidiaries*

Provided that the qualifying company carries on a qualifying trade or is the parent company of a trading group, it can have one or more dormant subsidiaries. A dormant subsidiary in this instance is one that has no profits for the purposes of corporation tax and no part of whose business consists in the making of investments. A dormant subsidiary need only be a 51% subsidiary (TA 1988, s 289(1A)(c), (1B)(b)).

5.11.5.3 *Winding up, administration and receivership*

A qualifying subsidiary remains a qualifying subsidiary while it or the qualifying company is being wound up, or dissolved without being wound up, provided that the winding-up or dissolution is carried out for bona fide commercial reasons and not as part of a tax avoidance scheme (TA 1988, s 308(3)(a)).

For shares issued before 17 March 2004, there was a further requirement, in that the subsidiary's net assets (if there were any remaining) had to be distributed to members or dealt with as *bona vacantia* before the end of the relevant period; in the case of a winding-up, the period of compliance could be extended to run for three years from the beginning of the winding-up procedure.

A similar relaxation is available for shares issued after 16 March 2004 when the subsidiary or any other company is in receivership or liquidation. Nothing done as a consequence of the subsidiary's or another company's being in administration or receivership will of itself cause the qualifying conditions to be broken, provided that the entry into administration or receivership and everything done as a consequence is for bona fide commercial reasons and is not part of a tax avoidance scheme (TA 1988, s 308(3A)).

5.11.6 Disposal of a subsidiary

A breach of the qualifying conditions does not necessarily take place for the sole reason that there are arrangements in place for the qualifying company or any of its other subsidiaries to dispose of the qualifying subsidiary, provided that the disposal is to take place for bona fide commercial reasons and is not part of a tax avoidance scheme (TA 1988, s 308(4)).

For shares issued before 17 March 2004, the rule was slightly different. There was no reference to arrangements and the disposal was to take place within the qualifying period. A breach of the qualifying conditions was not to occur by reason only of the disposal itself within the relevant period, with the same provisos as to commercial reasons and tax avoidance.

5.11.7 Options to acquire shares

It is important to ensure that a qualifying company does not take an option over the shares of a company that it intends to acquire (as a qualifying subsidiary), because at the time of granting the option, there would be an arrangement under which the qualifying company could control another company that is not at that time its qualifying subsidiary.

See further **5.5.8**.

5.11.8 Subscription for shares in a subsidiary

Subscriptions for shares in a subsidiary cannot qualify for EIS relief as the subsidiary must always be under the control of another company **[see 5.10.1]**.

5.12 Conditions to be met by CVS investee companies

5.12.1 Introduction

A qualifying CVS investee company (referred to in the legislation as the 'issuing company') must meet certain conditions. In brief, these conditions are that the company:

(*a*) be unquoted **[see 5.12.2]**;
(*b*) have a minimum percentage of ownership by independent individuals **[see 5.12.5]**;
(*c*) not be a member of certain partnerships or joint ventures **[see 5.12.3.2]**;
(*d*) not control or be controlled by another company (but it may have qualifying subsidiaries) **[see 5.15, 5.16]**;
(*e*) meet certain trading conditions **[see 5.12.3]**.

5.12.2 The requirement to be unquoted

A CVS investee company must be an unquoted company. That is to say, it must not, wherever it is resident, be:

(*a*) listed on a recognised stock exchange; or
(*b*) listed on a designated exchange in a country outside the UK; or
(*c*) dealt in outside the UK by any designated means

(FA 2000, Sch 15, para 16(1)).

Nor must arrangements exist for any such listing or dealing to take place. Further, unquoted status is deemed not to exist where there are arrangements for the investee company to become the wholly-owned subsidiary of another company by means of an exchange of shares, and for that other company's shares, debentures or other securities to become listed or dealt in as above (FA 2000, Sch 15, para 16(3)).

For a list of recognised stock exchanges, see **Appendix 4**.

What is important is that the company be unquoted at the issue date and not seek quotation thereafter. However, the fact that its shares are dealt in on a stock exchange that subsequently becomes recognised or designated will not make it lose qualifying status (FA 2000, Sch 15, para 16(5)).

5.12.3 Trading requirements

The investee company must throughout the qualification period **[see 5.1.4]** meet the 'trading activities requirement'. That requirement differs for 'single companies' as opposed to 'parent companies'. A 'single company' is a company that is not a 'parent company' or a 51% subsidiary of a parent company. A 'parent company' on the other hand, is a company that has one or more 51%

subsidiaries but is not itself a 51% subsidiary of another company (FA 2000, Sch 15, para 102(1)). For the meaning of '51% subsidiary', see **5.15.1**.

In the case of a single company, the trading activities requirement is that, disregarding any incidental purposes, the company exist wholly for the purpose of carrying on one or more qualifying trades and that it actually carry on such a trade or be preparing to do so (FA 2000, Sch 15, para 23(2)). However, the company must actually begin to carry on the trade within two years of the issue date (FA 2000, Sch 15, para 23(5)).

Incidental purposes are purposes having no significant effect on the extent of the company's activities, except in relation to incidental matters (FA 2000, Sch 15, para 23(9)(a)).

In the case of a parent company, the requirements will be familiar from the EIS and VCT legislation, but in the statute are more clearly expressed (the benefit of the 'rewrite' initiative). They are that:

(*a*) the business of the group as a whole not consist wholly or substantially in the carrying on of 'non-qualifying activities' (the double negative exists here presumably because a qualifying trade is defined by reference to what is not permitted); and
(*b*) the investee company or a 'qualifying 90% subsidiary' exist wholly for the purpose of carrying on one or more qualifying trades and actually be carrying on such a trade or be preparing to do so.

For what is a 'qualifying 90% subsidiary, see **5.16**.

As with the single company, that trade must be begun within two years of the issue date (FA 2000, Sch 15, para 23(3), (5)).

For shares issued before 17 March 2004, condition (*b*) was that 'at least one company (*in the group*) had to exist wholly for the purposes of carrying on one or more qualifying trades etc.

When considering the business of the group as a whole, the activities of the various group companies are taken together and regarded as one business (FA 2000, Sch 15, para 23(4)).

'Non-qualifying activities' are activities that are specifically excluded from being a qualifying trade and activities not carried on in the course of a trade. For what is a qualifying trade, see **Chapter 6**. There are two excluded activities that are not non-qualifying activities for this purpose, however – ie the investee company may carry them on without failing for that reason alone to satisfy the trading activities requirement. The two activities in question are:

(*a*) the letting of ships other than oil rigs or pleasure craft in certain circumstances **[see 6.5.6]**; and
(*b*) the receiving of royalties and licence fees wholly or substantially from the exploitation of intangible assets all or the greater part of the value of which has been created by the investee company, its parent company or a qualifying subsidiary **[see 6.5.8]**

(FA 2000, Sch 15, paras 23(8), 29(2)).

Certain activities, although not qualifying trades themselves, can be disregarded when considering the purpose for which a company exists. In the case of a single company, those activities are:

(*a*) property holding and management where the property is used by the company for the qualifying trade(s) it carries on; and
(*b*) holding qualifying shares, unless that amounts to a substantial part of the company's business

(FA 2000, Sch 15, para 23(6)).

In the case of a parent company, disregarded activities are:

(*a*) property holding and management where the property is used by a group company for the qualifying trade(s) it carries on;
(*b*) holding qualifying shares, unless that amounts to a substantial part of the company's business;
(*c*) holding shares in or securities of another group company or making loans to another group company; or
(*d*) incidental activities of a company that meets the trading activities requirement for a single company

(FA 2000, Sch 15, para 23(6)(b), (7)).

The Inland Revenue interprets 'substantial' as being 20% or more. See Venture Capital Schemes Manual, para VCM 17040 and **5.2.3.2**.

Research and development may also rank as a qualifying trade, provided that the intention is to benefit an existing qualifying trade carried on by the investee company or any qualifying 90% subsidiary (for shares issued before 17 March 2004, any other group company) or derive such a trade from it (FA 2000, Sch 15, para 25(2), (3)).

5.12.3.1 *Administration, receivership and liquidation*

Nothing done as a consequence of a company's being in administration or receivership causes it to fail to satisfy the trading activities requirement for that reason alone, provided that the administration or receivership and anything done as a consequence is carried out for bona fide commercial reasons and is not part of a tax avoidance scheme (FA 2000, Sch 15, para 24(1), (2)).

A company that is wound up or dissolved will cease to exist to carry on a trade. If this occurs during the qualification period, CVS relief would be lost. However, CVS relief is preserved if:

(*a*) the winding-up or dissolution is being carried out for bona fide commercial reasons and not as part of a tax avoidance scheme; and
(*b*) the company would otherwise have continued to satisfy the trading activities requirement

(FA 2000, Sch 15, para 24(3), (4)).

5.12.3.2 *The prohibition on trading in partnership etc*

Another requirement unique to the CVS, although it may be compared to the prohibition on parallel trades (these rules are now referred to as the 'replacement capital rules') in the EIS **[see 7.6.4]** is the prohibition on participating in a partnership or joint venture with certain associated persons.

In more detail, the requirement consists of the rule that, at no time in the qualification period, may an investee company or any of its qualifying subsidiaries either be a member of a prohibited partnership or be a party to a prohibited joint venture (FA 2000, Sch 15, para 19(1)). The purpose of the rule is to prevent an investee company from circumventing the trading activities requirement by use of a partnership or joint venture.

As regards partnerships, a prohibited partnership is one:

(*a*) that carries on or will carry on the qualifying trade by reference to which the investee company satisfies the trading requirement;
(*b*) that has at least one other company as a partner of the investee company; and
(*c*) where the same person(s) is/are the beneficial owner(s) of more than 75% of the issued share capital or the ordinary share capital of both the investee company and at least one of the other partner companies

(FA 2000, Sch 15, para 19(2), (4)).

Example 5.17

Fichte is an entrepreneur who has formed a company, Gartendingen Ltd, to manufacture and sell garden implements in partnership with his design and sales company, Gedanken Ltd, of which he is the sole shareholder. He also currently holds 85% of the shares in Gartendingen (the rest being held by outsiders) and wants to secure 10% equity investment from a CVS investor. CVS relief would not be available for the new shares, because after their issue, Fichte would still hold (85/110 =) 77.3% of the share capital of Gartendingen and its only qualifying trade is that carried out in partnership with Gedanken, where Fichte is the sole shareholder. As will be appreciated, there are various ways out of this dilemma (for Gartendingen to trade solely, for Fichte to reduce his 85% holding by a few percentage points (5% would be more than enough) before issuing the new shares etc).

A prohibited joint venture is one where:

(*a*) the investee company or its qualifying subsidiary carries on, or will carry on, the qualifying trade by reference to which it meets the trading activities requirement in its capacity as a party to the joint venture;
(*b*) at least one other party to the joint venture is another company; and
(*c*) the same person(s) is/are the beneficial owner(s) of more than 75% of the issued share capital or the ordinary share capital of both the investee company and at least one of the other parties to the joint venture

(FA 2000, Sch 15, para 19(3), (4)).

There is no definition of what constitutes a joint venture, although it is clearly an association between two or more parties formed to carry on a trade that falls short of a partnership. For a discussion of this point, see **5.3.4**.

5.12.4 Requirement to employ funds in a given way

As with the EIS and VCT scheme, the CVS investee company is obliged to put the funds raised by the issue of CVS shares to use in a prescribed way within a prescribed period.

The rule is that:

(*a*) all of the money raised by the issue of which the CVS shares form a part (and not just the money from the CVS shares themselves) must be employed in the way described below;
(*b*) at least 80% of the money raised by the issue must be employed wholly for the purposes of a qualifying trade (or research and development) by the investee company or a qualifying 90% subsidiary within 12 months of the issue date. This period can be extended if the trade in question had not yet begun at the time of the issue to end no later than 12 months after the trade has commenced; and
(*c*) all of the money must be employed for those purposes within a further 12 months.

Employing money for the purposes of a trade includes spending money on preparing to carry on the trade, except in the case of research and development (FA 2000, Sch 15, para 36(1)–(3)). For a discussion of what it means to employ money for a particular purpose, see **5.2.5**.

There is a special rule for situations where research and development counts as the qualifying trade. In such a case, the money may also be used for a trade that derives or benefits from the research and development (as will be evident from **5.12.3**) and is carried on by the investee company, its parent company or its qualifying 90% subsidiary. When the money is used in this way, there is an extra year's grace for employing all of it (ie three years, instead of the normal two) (FA 2000, Sch 15, para 36(5)).

For shares issued before 17 March 2004, for 'qualifying 90% subsidiary' read 'qualifying subsidiary'.

5.12.5 The individual-owners requirement

A requirement that is unique to the CVS is the rule that at least 20% of the investee company's ordinary share capital must throughout the qualification period be owned by one or more 'independent individuals' (FA 2000, Sch 15, para 18(1)).

An independent individual is one who, while he or she holds ordinary shares in the investee company is not a director or employee of that company or of any connected company, or the relative of such a director or employee. 'Relative' means a spouse, parent or remoter forebear or child or remoter issue (FA 2000,

Sch 15, para 18(2)). When an independent individual dies, shares forming part of his estate continue to be regarded as held by an independent individual while they remain in his or her estate (FA 2000, Sch 15, para 18(3)).

The definition of a connected person in TA 1988, s 839 applies (FA 2000, Sch 15, para 102(3)).

Example 5.18

Descartes Ltd issues 10,000 £1 shares under the CVS scheme to Diogenes Ltd. The other shareholders in Descartes are as follows:

10,000	Hector (director)
5,000	Patroclus (Hector's friend)
3,000	Cassandra (Patroclus's girlfriend)
10,000	Priam (Hector's father)
2,000	Various employees

Non-independent individuals are Hector (because he is a director), Priam (as Hector's relative) and the employees. Patroclus and Cassandra, although friends of Hector, are independent. Between them, they hold 8,000 shares out of the total 40,000, or 20%, so the individual-owners requirement is satisfied.

5.12.6 Prohibition of pre-arranged exits

The issuing arrangements for the CVS shares must not include certain features that, broadly, provide for a means of releasing the investment or reducing the risk associated with making the investment.

Issuing arrangements are the arrangements under which the CVS shares are issued; arrangements made before the issue date in connection with the issue; or, where information was provided to potential subscribers on pre-arranged exits, any arrangements made relating to the shares at the time of issue or afterwards but before the end of the qualification period. A pre-arranged exit is the possibility of making one of the prohibited arrangements before the end of the qualification period (FA 2000, Sch 15, para 37(2), (3)).

There are four separate prohibited arrangements.

5.12.6.1 *Repurchase, exchange or other disposal*

There must be no issuing arrangements that provide for the CVS shares or any other shares or securities in or of the investee company to be repurchased from the investor company, exchanged for other shares or otherwise disposed of. Excluded is an acquisition of the investee company's shares in circumstances such that no disposal is deemed to take place (under FA 2000, Sch 15, para 83(1) – see **19.3.6.1**) (FA 2000, Sch 15, para 37(1)(a), (4)).

5.12.6.2 *Arrangements to cease trading*

There must be no issuing arrangements that provide for the investee company or a connected person to cease trading. The trade does not have to be in existence at the issue date (FA 2000, Sch 15, para 37(1)(b)). Excluded are arrangements that apply only in the event of a winding-up of the investee company, unless the issuing arrangements include arrangements providing for the winding-up or where the investee company is wound up for non-commercial reasons (FA 2000, Sch 15, para 37(5)).

5.12.6.3 *Arrangements for a disposal of assets*

There must be no issuing arrangements that provide for the disposal of all or a substantial part by value of the investee company's assets or those of a connected person. Again, excluded are arrangements that apply only in the event of a winding-up of the investee company, unless the issuing arrangements include arrangements providing for the winding-up or where the investee company is wound up for non-commercial reasons (FA 2000, Sch 15, para 37(1)(c), (5)).

'Substantial' means 20% or more **[see 5.2.3.2]**.

5.12.6.4 *Arrangements for insuring against loss*

Finally, it must not be the or a main purpose of the issuing arrangements to provide partial or complete protection for investors against the risks of the investment, by insurance, indemnity, guarantee or other means (such as schemes artificially to maintain the value of the shares). The Inland Revenue takes the view that normal warranties or indemnities given for the subscription are unlikely to infringe this requirement, although this depends on the circumstances (IR Booklet IR2000, *The Corporate Venturing Scheme*, p 30). Ordinary commercial arrangements such as insurance for the investee company or for any group company against normal trading risks is excepted (FA 2000, Sch 15, para 37(6)).

5.13 Limits of investment in a CVS company

5.13.1 Maximum investment

There is no limit on the amount of CVS capital that an investee company may raise during any period. Like EIS and VCT investee companies, CVS investee companies are subject to the gross asset limit.

5.13.2 The gross asset limit

The gross assets of an investee company or of its group, as the case may be, must not exceed £15 million before the issue of the CVS shares and must not exceed £16 million after the issue. Assets of group members consisting in rights against or shares in or securities of another group company are disregarded (FA 2000, Sch 15, para 22).

For the meaning of 'gross assets', **see 5.3.5**.

5.14 Share capital requirements for CVS investee companies

5.14.1 Qualifying shares

CVS shares must be new ordinary shares that throughout the qualification period carry no present or future preferential right to dividends or to a company's assets on its winding-up and no present or future right to be redeemed (FA 2000, Sch 15, para 35).

In this context, provided that the shareholder has a legal right, it does not matter whether that right is set out in the company's articles of association [**see 5.1.10**], in a shareholder's agreement [**see 5.1.7**] or in another document.

For the meaning of ordinary shares and the significance of pre-emption rights and deferred shares, see **5.6.2.8**.

5.14.2 Fully paid-up shares

All CVS shares must be fully paid up at the issue date, but there is no requirement for all the investee company's shares to be fully paid up. An undertaking to pay cash to any person at a future date in respect of the share acquisition is not sufficient to make shares fully paid up (FA 2000, Sch 15, para 35(2)).

For shares issued before 17 March 2004, only an undertaking to pay cash to the *issuing company* was an insufficient condition for the shares to be fully paid-up.

5.15 CVS investee companies: control of or by another company

5.15.1 The independence requirement

As with the VCT scheme and the EIS, there is an independence requirement for CVS investee companies. An investee company must not any time in the qualification period either:

(*a*) be a 51% subsidiary of another company; or
(*b*) be under the control of another company (or of another company together with persons connected with that other company) without being a 51% subsidiary of that other company

(FA 2000, Sch 15, para 17(1)(a)).

Furthermore, there can be no arrangements in existence at any time in the qualification period with a view to bringing the company within the ambit of the proscribed situations listed above. For the meaning of arrangements, see **5.1.7**. However, arrangements providing for a takeover of the investee company in circumstances allowing for continuity of relief (under FA 2000, Sch 15, para 83(1) – see **19.3.6.1**) are disregarded (FA 2000, Sch 15, para 17(2)).

A '51% subsidiary' is a company in which another company, of which it is the subsidiary, directly or indirectly owns over 50% of the ordinary share capital (TA 1988, s 838(1)(a)).

The narrower definition of control, that provided by TA 1988, s 840 **[see 5.1.10]** applies here (FA 2000, Sch 15, para 17(3)).

The second arm of the independence requirement (the 'qualifying subsidiaries requirement') is that the investee company may have no subsidiaries that are not qualifying subsidiaries (FA 2000, Sch 15, para 20(1)). For qualifying subsidiaries, see **5.16**.

For the role of connected persons in testing for control, see **5.1.6**.

5.16 Qualifying subsidiaries in the CVS

5.16.1 Introduction

Where the investee company is not a single company, but a parent **[see 5.12.3]**, the only subsidiaries it may have during the qualification period and retain its qualifying status are qualifying subsidiaries (FA 2000, Sch 15, para 20(1)).

'Subsidiaries' in this connection are companies that the investee company controls, either alone or together with a connected person (FA 2000, Sch 15, para 20(2)). Control in this context has the wider sense of TA 1988, s 416(2)–(6) – see **5.1.9**.

For shares issued after 16 March 2004, a subsidiary is a qualifying subsidiary if it is a 51% subsidiary of the investee company and no person other than the investee company or another of its subsidiaries has control of that subsidiary. Here the narrower definition of control **[see 5.1.10]** is used (FA 2000, Sch 15, para 21(2)(ca), (d)).

For the definition of a 51% subsidiary, see **5.15.1**.

A further condition is that there must be no arrangements in existence that would cause these conditions to be broken (FA 2000, Sch 15, para 21(2)(e)).

For shares issued before 17 March 2004, a subsidiary is a qualifying subsidiary if the investee company or another of its subsidiaries possesses at least 75% of the issued share capital and at least 75% of the voting power. The investee company (or its subsidiary, as the case may be) must also be beneficially entitled to no less than 75% of the subsidiary's distributable profits and no less than 75% of its assets available to shareholders in the event of a winding-up of the subsidiary or in any other circumstances.

A further condition is that there must be no person other than the investee company or another of its qualifying subsidiaries that has control of the subsidiary (here the narrower definition of control – see **5.1.10** – is applied) and there must be no arrangements in existence that would cause these conditions to be broken.

5.16.1.1 *Qualifying 90% subsidiaries*

For shares issued after 16 March 2004, any subsidiary that carries on the qualifying trade or qualifying research and development must be a 'qualifying 90% subsidiary' of the investee company.

For a subsidiary to be a qualifying 90% subsidiary of its parent company, a number of conditions have to be satisfied. These are that:

(*a*) the parent company must possess at least 90% of the issued share capital of and of the voting power in the subsidiary;
(*b*) the parent company must be beneficially entitled to at least 90% of the distributable profits of the subsidiary;
(*c*) the parent company must be beneficially entitled to at least 90% of the assets available to the shareholders of the subsidiary in the event of a winding-up of the company or in any other circumstances; and
(*d*) no person other than the parent company must have control of the subsidiary and there must be no arrangements in existence that would cause the foregoing conditions to be broken.

(FA 2000, Sch 15, para 23(10)).

For control, the narrower definition **[see 5.1.10]** is applied.

5.16.2 Subsubsidiaries

Can an investee company have qualifying subsubsidiaries? For shares issued after 16 March 2004, the answer seems to be yes for qualifying subsidiaries generally, but not for qualifying 90% subsidiaries. That is to say, a CVS investee company may have subsubsidiaries, but the qualifying trade or research and development, if it is to be carried on by one or more subsidiaries, may only be carried on by a directly owned qualifying 90% subsidiary. For, although there is reference to:

(*a*) control of a subsidiary by another subsidiary (FA 2000, Sch 15, para 21(2)(d));
(*b*) a disposal by a subsidiary of its interest in another subsidiary (FA 2000, Sch 15, para 21(5)),

it is clearly stated that a qualifying 90% subsidiary may only be controlled by the investee company (FA 2000, Sch 15, para 23(10)). For shares issued before 17 March 2004, however, there was also the reference to the possession of not less than 75% of a qualifying subsidiary by another subsidiary (FA 2000, Sch 15, para 21(2)(a), repealed for shares issued after 16 March 2004 by FA 2004, Sch 20, para 5(2)(a)).

What is more, it was possible for any one or more companies in the group (which all had to be qualifying subsidiaries, of course) to carry on the qualifying trade. The answer in respect of these earlier shares, therefore, seems to be unequivocally 'yes'. Where the investee company is a parent company, there are two trading requirements. First, the business of the group as a whole must not consist wholly or substantially of non-qualifying activities; secondly, either the investee company or at least one group company must exist wholly for the purpose of carrying on one or more qualifying trades (FA 2000, Sch 15, para 23(3) before amendment by FA 2004, Sch 20, para 7(a)).

The first requirement, it will be remembered **[see 5.12.3]**, necessitates looking at the activities of the parent company and its subsidiaries as a whole. For coverage of qualifying trades, see **Chapter 6**.

5.16.3 Subsidiaries trading wholly or mainly abroad

A qualifying trade must be carried on wholly or mainly in the UK (FA 2000, Sch 15, para 25(1)(a)). For the reasons given in **5.16.2** above, however, there is no requirement for *every* qualifying subsidiary to carry on a qualifying trade, provided that either the investee company or a qualifying 90% subsidiary exists wholly for the purpose of doing so.

It follows that some members of the group, provided that the business of the group as a whole does not come to consist substantially of non-qualifying activities **[see 5.12.3]**, may have activities that are carried out wholly or mainly abroad. 'Substantially' means to the extent of at least 20% (Venture Capital Schemes Manual, para VCM 17040; see **5.2.3.2**).

See **5.5.5** for remarks made in Parliament in 1994, concerning the EIS, but equally applicable in this context to the CVS.

5.16.4 Property management

The holding and management of property used by a group company for the purposes of one or more qualifying trades carried on by a group company is an activity that is disregarded when determining whether the business of a group as a whole meets the trading activities requirement (FA 2000, Sch 15, para 23(7)(b)). It follows that a qualifying subsidiary may exist for this purpose without endangering its own or the group's qualifying status.

5.16.4.1 *Property managing subsidiaries*

If an investee company has at any time in the qualification period a subsidiary that is a 'property managing subsidiary', that subsidiary must be a qualifying

90% subsidiary (FA 2000, Sch 15, para 21A(1)). A 'property managing subsidiary' is a subsidiary whose business consists wholly or mainly in holding or managing land or property deriving its value from land (FA 2000, Sch 15, para 21A(2)).

This condition is imposed on shares issued after 16 March 2004 only.

5.16.5 Dormant subsidiaries

Provided that the investee company or a qualifying 90% subsidiary exists wholly for the purpose of carrying on a qualifying trade, and the business of the group as a whole meets the trading activities requirement, one or more qualifying subsidiaries may be dormant. This is equally true for shares issued before, as well as on or after, 17 March 2004.

5.16.6 Winding up a subsidiary

The fact that a qualifying subsidiary or a qualifying 90% subsidiary is being wound up or dissolved without being wound up – or indeed that any other company is undergoing a winding-up or dissolution – will not of itself cause the subsidiary to lose its qualifying status, provided that two conditions are satisfied:

(*a*) that the winding-up or dissolution is carried out for commercial reasons; and
(*b*) that it is not part of a tax avoidance scheme

(FA 2000, Sch 15, paras 21(3), (4)(b) and 11(a)).

Similarly, where a qualifying subsidiary or a qualifying 90% subsidiary (or another company entirely) is in administration or receivership, nothing done as a consequence of the administration or receivership will of itself cause the qualifying subsidiary or qualifying 90% subsidiary to lose its status as such, provided that the same two conditions are satisfied, namely:

(*a*) that the receivership or administration order was made and everything done as a consequence was done for commercial reasons; and
(*b*) is not part of a tax avoidance scheme

(FA 2000, Sch 15, paras 21(3), (4)(a) and 11(a)).

5.16.7 Sale of a subsidiary

An investee company (or another of its subsidiaries) is allowed to sell one or more of its qualifying subsidiaries if this is done for commercial reasons and is not to be part of a tax avoidance scheme. This is because a qualifying subsidiary does not lose its status as such merely because arrangements are in existence for the disposal of the entire holding in that subsidiary provided that the above conditions apply while the arrangements continue (FA 2000, Sch 15, para 21(5)).

For shares issued after 16 March 2004, similar provisions exist in respect of qualifying 90% subsidiaries. Namely, a qualifying 90% subsidiary does not lose its status as such purely by reason of the fact that arrangements are in existence for the investee company to dispose of its entire holding in the subsidiary, provided only that the disposal is to be undertaken for commercial reasons and is not to be part of a tax avoidance scheme (FA 2000, Sch 15, para 23(11)(b)).

5.17 Conditions to be met by CVS investor companies

5.17.1 Introduction

In marked contrast to the VCT scheme, the CVS demands that quite extensive conditions be satisfied by investor companies.

In summary, these are that:

(*a*) they not have a material interest in the investee company **[see 5.17.2]**;
(*b*) no reciprocal conditions be attached to their subscription **[see 5.17.3]**;
(*c*) they not control the investee company **[see 5.17.4]**;
(*d*) they exist wholly for the purpose of carrying on a non-financial activity **[see 5.17.5]**;
(*e*) the shares they hold in an investee company be their chargeable assets **[see 5.17.6]**; and
(*f*) their subscription for the investee company's shares not be part of a tax avoidance scheme **[see 5.17.7]**

(FA 2000, Sch 15, para 4).

5.17.1.1 *Residence*

There is no requirement for the CVS investor company to be UK resident. However, unless a non-resident company has a liability to UK corporation tax (which means that it must be carrying on a trade in the UK through a permanent establishment here), it will derive no benefit from the relief.

5.17.2 Prohibition of a material interest

At no time during the qualification period **[see 5.1.4]** must the investor company have a material interest in the investee company (FA 2000, Sch 15, para 5).

The definition of 'material interest' is borrowed from the EIS connectedness rule. The investor company has a material interest in the investee company if it directly or indirectly possesses or is entitled to acquire more than 30% of *either* the ordinary share capital of the investee company or of any 51% subsidiary of the investee company *or* of the voting power in the investee company or in any 51% subsidiary of the investee company (FA 2000, Sch 15, para 7(1), (6)). For what is a 51% subsidiary, see **5.15.1**.

In this case, 'ordinary share capital' includes, in addition to all of the company's issued share capital other than 'relevant preference shares', any loan capital that is directly or indirectly convertible into or carries the right to acquire share capital other than relevant preference shares (FA 2000, Sch 15, para 7(2)).

Loan capital includes debt incurred by the company for:

(*a*) any money borrowed or capital assets acquired;
(*b*) any right to receive income; or
(*c*) consideration substantially less at the time than the amount of the debt (including any premium)

(FA 2000, Sch 15, para 7(3)).

An example of (*b*) would be a contract with the investee company under which the investor company undertook to make annual payments to the investee company in return for a capital sum due at some later date.

An overdraft at the bank incurred in the ordinary course of the business is not loan capital (FA 2000, Sch 15, para 7(4)).

'Relevant preference shares' are defined by reference to four characteristics, so that they broadly include shares that have the characteristics of debt rather than equity. In this context, it is interesting to note that under International Accounting Standard (IAS) 32, which all EC listed companies will have to adopt in their consolidated accounts from 1 January 2005, preference shares as a whole are classed as debt. For CVS purposes, at any rate, relevant preference shares are shares:

(*a*) carrying no voting rights (at the time of testing, not necessarily for all time); and
(*b*) issued wholly for new consideration; and
(*c*) carrying no right either to conversion into shares or securities or to the acquisition of additional shares or securities; and
(*d*) carrying no right to dividends other than dividends of a pre-determined amount

(FA 2000, Sch 15, para 9(1)).

Dividends of a pre-determined amount can be of two kinds:

(*a*) of a fixed amount or at a fixed rate determined under the issue terms; or
(*b*) set at a percentage of the nominal value, but with a rate that fluctuates according to:

(1) a published rate of interest, or
(2) a rate of tax, or
(3) the retail prices index or any similar general index of prices published by or on behalf of a governmental authority of the country or countries in whose currency the shares are denominated, or
(4) a published index of share prices on a recognised stock exchange (eg the FTSE).

At the same time, the dividends must not depend to any extent on the results of the company's business or of any part of that business, or on the value of the company's assets. However, if the amount or rate of the dividends varies counter-cyclically with the results or asset values, that fact alone will not cause them to be viewed as dependent on those results or asset values (FA 2000, Sch 15, para 9(4)). By this is meant dividends whose rate or amount reduces in the event of an improvement in the results of the business or of an increase in the value of the company's assets, or increases in the event of a deterioration in the results of the business or of a decrease in the value of the assets.

Entitlement to acquire includes entitlement to acquire in future. In considering whether the investor company possesses or is entitled to acquire share capital or voting power, the rights and powers of any connected person must be taken into account; and where the investor company has any associates, the rights and powers of those associates are attributed to the investor company (FA 2000, Sch 15, para 7(1), (5)).

The definition of a connected person is that contained in TA 1988, s 839 **[see 5.1.6]**.

Wherever it occurs in relation to the CVS, the term 'associate' is defined as follows. A person who is associated with another person (B) is:

(*a*) a relative or partner (in the business, not the life, sense) of B;
(*b*) the trustee of any settlement of which B or any relative of B (living or dead) is or was a settlor;
(*c*) the trustee of any settlement containing a company's shares or obligations in which B has an interest;
(*d*) the personal representatives of a deceased person whose estate contains a company's shares or obligations in which B has an interest; and
(*e*) where B is a company, any other company with an interest in the shares or obligations referred to in (*c*) and (*d*)

'Relative' means a husband, wife, parent, remoter forebear (grandfather, grandmother etc), child or remoter issue (grandchild, great-grandchild and so on). It does not include collateral relatives (siblings, nieces, nephews, cousins etc) or in-laws (FA 2000, Sch 15, para 99; TA 1988, s 417(3), (4)). Therefore, neither a brother nor a mother-in-law is an associate, for example, nor is a life partner. But see the same definition for the purposes of the EIS **[7.6.2.3]**.

Whether a person is a partner depends on all the facts. A partnership is the relationship that subsists between persons carrying on a business in common with a view to profits (Partnership Act 1890, s 1). A person is likely to be treated as a partner where that person:

(*a*) is a member of the partnership by name (named on stationery etc);
(*b*) is entitled to a profit share; and
(*c*) is assessable to tax under Schedule D on a share of the profits of the partnership.

An individual is not normally treated as a partner if he or she is assessed to income tax on earnings (formerly, under Schedule E) and tax is deducted under PAYE.

Individuals who are simply directors and shareholders of the same company are not partners nor are individuals who simply own property as an investment, share profits and losses and are assessable to tax under Schedule A. However, if these individuals enter into a partnership agreement, agree to develop the property for sale, and use headed paper (or e-mail) describing themselves as partners, these would be strong indications that a partnership existed in law.

'Settlement' – and hence 'settlor' – are construed widely, under TA 1988, s 660G. The meaning of 'settlement' is not confined to a trust, but includes 'any disposition, trust, covenant, agreement, arrangement or transfer of assets'.

5.17.3 The prohibition of reciprocal arrangements

When an investor company subscribes for shares in the investee company, there must be no arrangements in place providing for any other person to subscribe for shares in another company in which the investor company or any other person who is a party to the arrangements has a material interest (FA 2000, Sch 15, para 6(1)). For what is a material interest, see **5.17.2**. For what are arrangements, see **5.1.7**.

Arrangements providing for the investee company to subscribe for any shares in any of its qualifying subsidiaries (whether or not they are qualifying subsidiaries at the time the arrangements are made) are ignored (FA 2000, Sch 15, para 6(3)).

Example 5.19

Empedocles is an inventor with a 60% stake in his company, Erasmus Ltd. A venture capital company, Epicurus plc, has agreed to subscribe £25,000 in new share capital in Erasmus, provided that Empedocles makes an equal equity investment in Engels Ltd, a company in which Epicurus has just acquired a 45% stake outside the CVS.

The investment by Epicurus plc in Erasmus Ltd does not qualify for the CVS, as it has a material interest in Engels Ltd, and the agreement with Empedocles is therefore a reciprocal arrangement.

5.17.4 The prohibition of control

The investor company must not at any time in the qualification period control the investee company. It is difficult to see how it could control the investee company without having a material interest in it **[see 5.17.2]**; nevertheless, both requirements stand side by side.

Here, 'control' has the wider definition of TA 1988, s 416 **[see 5.1.9]**, but with modifications.

The first modification is that the following considerations are disregarded:

(*a*) the investor company's or any other person's possession of, or entitlement to acquire, relevant preference shares in the investee company; and
(*b*) the investor company's or any other person's possession of, or entitlement to acquire, rights as a loan creditor of the investee company

(FA 2000, Sch 15, para 8(4)).

The second modification is that, where any rights or powers over or in the investee company or any of its subsidiaries are held by:

(*a*) a person connected with the investor company; or
(*b*) a director of the investor company or of any company connected with the investor company; or
(*c*) the husband, wife, parent or remoter forebear, child or remoter issue of a director within (*b*),

those rights and powers are attributed to the investor company (if they would not already be)

(FA 2000, Sch 15, para 8(5)).

5.17.5 The prohibition of financial activities

This condition is expressed in the alternative, depending on whether the investor company is a 'single company' or a 'group company'. A single company is a company that is neither a parent company nor a 51% subsidiary of another company. A parent company is a company that has one or more 51% subsidiaries and is not itself a 51% subsidiary of another company. A group company is a parent company or any of its 51% subsidiaries. For what is a 51% subsidiary, see **5.15.1**.

Where the investor company is a single company, it must, throughout the qualification period, exist wholly for the purpose of carrying on one or more non-financial trades. Incidental purposes may be disregarded (FA 2000, Sch 15, para 10(2)).

A non-financial trade is a trade that does not consist wholly or substantially in the carrying on of financial activities. Financial activities includes, but is not limited to:

(*a*) banking;
(*b*) money-lending;
(*c*) debt-factoring;
(*d*) finance-leasing;
(*e*) hire-purchase financing;
(*f*) insurance;
(*g*) dealing in shares, securities, currency, debts, or other financial assets;
(*h*) dealing in commodity or financial futures or options.

As might be expected, a trade must be carried on on a commercial basis and with a view to the realisation of profits (FA 2000, Sch 15, para 11).

In considering whether non-financial trades are being carried on, the following activities may be disregarded:

(*a*) the holding and managing of property used by the company for one or more non-financial trades that it carries on; and
(*b*) the holding of shares to which CVS investment relief is attributable, unless the holding of these shares amounts to a substantial part of the company's business

(FA 2000, Sch 15, para 10(5)).

Substantial means to the extent of 20% or more **[see 5.2.3.2]**. This second condition disqualifies a company whose main business is holding shares and in which the trading activity is peripheral; indeed, the trading activity must amount to more than 80% of the total.

If, on the other hand, the investor company is a group company, the non-financial requirement is satisfied if, throughout the qualification period:

(*a*) the group is a 'non-financial trading group' and
(*b*) the company either:
    (1) exists, apart from incidental purposes, wholly for the purpose of carrying on one or more non-financial trades or businesses other than trades, or
    (2) is the parent company of the group

(FA 2000, Sch 15, para 10(3), (4)).

A group is a 'non-financial trading group' unless the business of the group consists wholly or substantially in carrying on trades other than non-financial trades or businesses that are not trades. When considering what the business of the group is, one must look at the activities of all the group companies taken together as if they were one business.

In applying this test, the activities of any one group company may be disregarded to the extent that they consist of:

(*a*) the holding and managing of property used by a group company for one or more non-financial trades carried on by a group company; or (*b*) the holding of shares to which CVS investment relief is attributable, unless the holding of these shares amounts to a substantial part of the company's business; or

(*c*) the making of loans to another group company

(FA 2000, Sch 15, para 12).

5.17.6 Requirement as to chargeable assets

Immediately after the shares in the investee company have been issued to it, the investor company must hold them as chargeable assets, ie such that any gain arising on a disposal of those assets would be a chargeable gain (FA 2000, Sch 15, para 13).

The wording of this rule presents a potential difficulty in connection with the substantial-shareholdings exemption. If this condition needs only to be satisfied *immediately* after the shares are issued, and not necessarily at some future time, all well and good. However, if the shares *must remain* chargeable assets as here defined, this is unfortunate, as it appears to rule out shares that would form part of a substantial shareholding qualifying for an exemption on disposal under FA 2002, Sch 8. The substantial-shareholdings exemption provides that 'a gain accruing to a company . . . on a disposal of shares or an interest in shares in another company . . . is not a chargeable gain if the requirements of this Schedule are met' (FA 2002, Sch 8, para 1(1)). One requirement for the exemption is that the shares have been held uninterruptedly for at least 12 months in the 24 months preceding their disposal. Consider the case of an acquisition by a CVS investor company of 10% of an investee company's ordinary shares, within the criteria for the CVS. After one year has elapsed, these shares, provided the other requirements for the substantial-shareholdings exemption are met, qualify for that exemption on a hypothetical disposal. That makes them no longer a 'chargeable asset' within FA 2000, Sch 15, para 13. The implication is that, even if all the other requirements for CVS relief continue to be met, the holding ceases to qualify for CVS relief.

The fact that the amendments to the CVS rules contained in the substantial shareholdings legislation (TCGA 1992, Sch 7AC, para 4) do not touch on this issue **[see 23.8]** suggest either that it is not considered to be an obstacle or that it has not come to the attention of the Inland Revenue.

5.17.7 The prohibition relating to tax avoidance

The final requirement relating to the investor company is that it must subscribe for the shares for commercial reasons and not as part of a scheme or arrangement the purpose of which, or one of the main purposes of which, is tax avoidance (FA 2000, Sch 15, para 14).

5.18 A comparison of the VCT scheme and the EIS

The two incentives for individuals and certain trustees to invest in unquoted companies (the VCT scheme and the EIS) are similar but not identical, and care must be taken to make the right choice. A comparative table of the reliefs is shown below.

	VCT	*EIS full relief*	*EIS CGT deferral only*
Investment relief	40%[1]	20%	No
Subscription limit	£200,000	£200,000	None
Limit on tax relief per person per annum	£80,000[2]	£40,000	N/A
CGT deferral relief at 10% to 40%	No[3]	Yes	Yes
Time limit for reinvestment of gain:			
• before gain arises	(1 yr)	1 yr	1 yr
• after gain arises	(1 yr)	3 yrs	3 yrs
CGT-free increase in value of shares	Yes	Yes	No
Dividends tax free	Yes	No	No
Effective qualifying period – company's trade	Always	3 yrs	3 yrs
Effective qualifying period – disposal	3 yrs	At least 3 yrs	N/A
Loss relief	No	Yes	Yes
Can convert to investment company in future	No	Yes	Yes
Maximum shareholding	N/A	30%	100%
Available to trustees	No	No	Yes
Money received per trading company	£1m	Unlimited	Unlimited
Gross asset limit before/after investment	£15/16m	£15/16m	£15/16m

Notes

1 For investments made between 6 April 2004 and 5 April 2006 only. Previously and thereafter, 20%.

2 For 2004–05 and 2005–06 only. Thereafter it reverts to £40,000 (£200,000 × 20%).

3 Withdrawn where the VCT shares are issued (and therefore the investment made) after 5 April 2004.

Chapter 6

Qualifying Trades

6.1 Introduction

6.1.1 Certain types of trades

Although the purpose of all three schemes examined in this book is to encourage investment in unquoted trading companies, not all trading companies qualify. For example, it has been a fixed principle since the inception of the business start-up scheme (BSS) in 1981 that companies carrying on activities mainly of a financial or passive nature, should not benefit from the tax reliefs. Only companies or their subsidiaries carrying on qualifying trades are qualifying companies.

6.1.2 Scope of this chapter

This chapter is concerned with what is and what is not a qualifying trade and will examine the following areas:

(*a*) Use of money raised **[see 6.2]**
(*b*) What is meant by carrying on a qualifying trade **[see 6.3]**
(*c*) Where the trade must be carried on **[see 6.4]**
(*d*) Which activities are considered to be non-qualifying activities **[see 6.5]**
(*e*) Particular trades **[see 6.6]**
(*f*) Start of a qualifying trade **[see 6.7]**
(*g*) Cessation of a qualifying trade **[see 6.8]**

The meaning of a qualifying company was considered in **Chapter 5**, while **Chapter 7** deals with qualifying investors.

6.1.3 Periods of notification

6.1.3.1 *VCT companies*

All companies that represent a VCT's qualifying holdings **[see 5.6.2.6]** must meet the qualifying trade conditions at all times. There is no stipulated qualifying period for the VCT investee company, as there is under the EIS and CVS. If any of the investee companies ceases to carry on a qualifying trade it would cease to be part of the VCT's qualifying holdings. It follows that the VCT could lose its approval if it was not immediately able to replace that investment with another qualifying investment, and, as a consequence, does not meet the 70% qualifying holdings requirement **[see 5.6.2.6]**.

6.1.3.2 *EIS companies*

In the case of EIS relief, the conditions relating to a qualifying trade must be met during a period that starts with the issue of the EIS shares and ends on the later of (*a*) the third anniversary of the share issue and (*b*) the third anniversary of the commencement of the trade (TA 1988, s 312(1A)(b)).

6.1.3.3 *CVS companies*

CVS investee companies must carry on a qualifying trade throughout the 'qualification period'. This period runs from the issue date of the relevant shares and ends immediately before the later of:

(*a*) the third anniversary of the issue date; and

(*b*) the third anniversary of the date on which the investee company or any of its qualifying 90% subsidiaries began to carry on a qualifying trade (where there is more than one such trade, the date on which the later trade began to be carried on)

(FA 2000, Sch 15, para 3).

For shares issued before 17 March 2004, the reference in point (*b*) to 'qualifying 90% subsidiaries' should be read as a reference to 'qualifying subsidiaries'. **See also 5.1.4.**

6.1.4 Trade conducted on a commercial basis

For each of the schemes the qualifying trade must be conducted on a commercial basis and with a view to the realisation of profits (TA 1988, s 297 (8); TA 1988, Sch 28B, para 4(9); FA 2000, Sch 15, para 25(1)(b).

When considering whether a trade is conducted on a commercial basis it is sufficient that there is evidence to show that the intention was to make a profit. It is not relevant that there was actually a loss from the trading activity, or that there were tax deductions that reduced the corporation tax payable to zero.

The Inland Revenue had this to say about the requirement:

> 'There is no explicit time within which the profit must be made; so, provided that the prospect of a profit exists, the fact that it is distant is not a ground for refusing relief.

> If the trader is sustaining losses without a prospect of making a profit, he must have some other purpose. For example, it may be that the trade is a hobby or gives the trader personal enjoyment. Or that the trader is seeking to increase the value of a capital asset. There may be other such purposes, and it will usually be important to establish (by interview) what the particular taxpayer's purpose was.'
>
> (formerly Inspector's Manual, para IM3375)

This statement has not been reproduced in the new Business Income Manual, but there is no reason to believe the approach is any different.

The test is a subjective one. See, for example, *Walls v Livesey* [1995] STC (SCD) 12, which concerned similar wording in TA 1988, s 504(2)(a). In *Wannell v Rothwell* [1996] STC 450, an individual's speculative dealing in stocks and shares and commodity futures was held to be trading but not on a commercial basis. Other relevant recent cases are *Brown v Richardson* [1997] STC (SCD) 233 and *Delian Enterprises v Ellis* [1999] STC (SCD) 103.

6.2 Use of money raised

6.2.1 To carry on a trade

The proceeds of a VCT or EIS share issue must be used for the purposes of a trade that the qualifying company or a qualifying subsidiary is carrying on or intends to carry on wholly or mainly in the UK **[see 6.4]**. In both cases there is the proviso that the company must start trading within two years of the share issue date (TA 1988, s 289(1)(b), (2)(a) (ii); TA 1988, Sch 28B para 3(3), (4)).

For VCT relief, if within two years the intention to carry on a trade is abandoned, the company will cease to be a qualifying company. Furthermore, when a company starts to trade it must trade continuously thereafter (TA 1988, Sch 28B, para 3(5)). In the case of EIS relief, the trade must be carried on throughout the relevant period **[see 6.1.3.2]**.

Similar considerations apply for the CVS. The money raised by an issue of CVS shares must be applied within two years in a qualifying trade (FA 2000, Sch 15, para 36).

6.2.2 Qualifying non-trade activities

For the VCT, EIS and CVS reliefs, carrying on a qualifying trade is extended to research and development activities that will lead to a qualifying trade **[see 6.6]** (TA 1988, s 289(2) (b); TA 1988, Sch 28B para 4(1)(b); FA 2000, Sch 15, para 25(2),(3)). Before 7 March 2001, oil extraction was not a qualifying trade for the EIS, although it has always been a qualifying trade for the VCT scheme and the CVS (in the sense that it has not featured as an excluded activity). However, before 7 March 2001, oil *exploration*, although not a trade in itself, was a qualifying business activity for EIS relief. As with research and development, there had to be an intention that the exploration would lead to a qualifying trade **[see further 6.7]**.

6.2.3 How the funds are used

Using the proceeds of a VCT, EIS or VCS share issue for the purposes of a trade includes repaying bank borrowings used for trading purposes (but not redeeming shares) and purchasing a trade **[see further 5.2.5]**.

6.2.4 Management buy-outs

The issues discussed in **5.2.5** apply equally to a management buy-out. The Inland Revenue gave its view specifically on the application of the VCT scheme to management buy-outs in *Tax Bulletin*, Issue 18, August 1995:

> 'We have been asked in what circumstances it is possible for an acquisition of shares or securities in a company, which is to be used in a management buy-out, to give rise to a qualifying holding . . .
>
> There are many ways in which a buy-out might be organised . . . This article considers three basic outline scenarios. These are where a company is formed to acquire:
> - a trade
> - another company and its trade
> - a holding company with a number of trading subsidiaries
>
> and the funds obtained from the VCT are used by the company specifically to purchase the trade, company or group.
>
> In the first scenario, we will usually accept that the application of the funds to purchase the trade satisfies the requirement that the funds [be] employed for the purposes of the trade.
>
> The second scenario will often come about as the result of a refusal by the existing owners to sell the trade without selling the company. Our view is that, where shares are purchased, the money cannot normally be said to be employed for the purposes of a trade – rather it is employed in the making of an investment.
>
> However, if the trade is hived up to the acquiring company, leaving the acquired company as a dormant subsidiary, as soon as possible after the acquisition, we will usually accept that the funds have been employed for the purposes of the trade.
>
> In the third scenario, if all of the activities of the holding company and of *all* [original emphasis] of its subsidiaries are hived up to the acquiring company, we will usually accept that the funds have been employed for the purposes of the trade. To the extent that the trades are not hived up to the acquiring company, we consider the acquisition of the group is the making of an investment and not all the funds provided by the VCT are employed for the purposes of a trade or trades. Therefore, under TA 1988, Sch 28B, para 1(3) only part of the holding is a qualifying holding.'

Although parts of this statement have been reproduced in the Venture Capital Schemes Manual (para VCM 12070 – see **5.2.5**), neither the statement as a whole nor any direct reference to management buy-outs is made, hence we have reproduced the *Tax Bulletin* article in full.

It should also be borne in mind that the MBO managers will not be able to claim EIS relief if they invest in the new company alongside the VCT **[see 7.6.2.11]**.

6.2.5 Employment of funds

For the rules requiring the funds raised by new issues to be employed in qualifying activities, see, for the VCT scheme **5.2.5.1** to **5.2.5.3**; for the EIS, see **5.7.5**; for the CVS, see **5.12.4**.

6.2.6 Investments

A trading company that holds one or more investments will not qualify unless the value of those investments is insignificant, say less than 2% of the market value of the company's assets **[see further 5.2.5]**.

6.2.7 Parent companies and management charges

A parent company will often own such assets as patents, buildings, computers and vehicles and make a management charge to each subsidiary for providing management and services. To what extent would such a company be the parent company of a trading group (for VCT and EIS purposes) or the parent company of a group not wholly or substantially wholly carrying out non-qualifying activities (in the case of the CVS)?

Although the receipt of royalties or licence fees, the provision of legal or accountancy services and leasing are not qualifying trades, it is the activities of the group regarded as a single business entity that must be considered. Provided, therefore, that the 'tainted' activities of the parent company do not amount to a substantial proportion of the group's business as a whole, such activities should not prejudice the parent company's qualifying status.

Holding and managing property used for the purposes of the group's trade and making loans to subsidiaries are in any case specifically disregarded when applying these tests. In addition, the Inland Revenue has always regarded payment of directors' remuneration and statutory expenses and recovery of these through a management charge as acceptable activities for a parent company.

6.2.8 Deciding how much to raise

The Inland Revenue considers that a qualifying company should not raise more capital than it needs. This is a very simplistic approach for many reasons, including the following:

(*a*) Many new businesses fail because they underestimate the capital required. In the first couple of years they are sailing in unchartered waters, when anything that might go wrong often will go wrong. Depending on the business, it may take six months or more from starting the trade to attract a reasonable number of customers and begin to trade profitably. Accountants would advise their clients to err on the side of caution and underestimate the likely sales in the early years. If having taken advice on the capital it needs, the trade takes off at a faster rate, there is likely to be more cash available in the business. Accordingly, the directors should take care to ensure that the funds raised under the VCT scheme, EIS or CVS are employed in the trade within the 12–month and 24–month periods, rather than using the additional cash generated from trading.

(*b*) If the amount that can be raised is uncertain, the plans for using the capital will vary. For example, a company may require a minimum of £500,000 to start business in a small way, employing mainly part-time workers and renting a two-room office and workshop and hiring equipment and vehicles. If it can raise £1 million it would employ mainly full-time workers, take on a larger office and workshop and buy the equipment and vehicles. Having budgeted for amounts of £500,000 to £1 million, the amount actually raised may be £800,000, in which case some options are no longer available and there may be surplus cash.

(*c*) A company that says it can start a business with say £500,000 is likely to be viewed with suspicion. The investor may be concerned that the company will come back to the investors in six months' time looking for more capital. Potential investors are more likely to invest in a company that has a larger capital base.

(*d*) If it is necessary to raise money through a prospectus, many of the issue costs are fixed and the cost per £1 invested is greater if less than the £1 million is raised. As the average investor will be influenced by this, few sponsors will agree to sponsor an issue of less than £1 million. This is less of a problem now that the £1 million ceiling exists only for a VCT issue.

6.2.9 Cash deposits

Where a company has substantial cash, even if derived from such sources as borrowings, preference share capital or surplus income over expenditure, the Inland Revenue may argue that the company does not exist to carry on a trade. If the cash is held on deposit, other than on a temporary basis, it is the Inland Revenue's view that the company is holding the cash outside its trade, and is in effect making an investment. It should therefore be assumed that during the relevant qualifying period for EIS and CVS investee companies, or throughout, for VCT investee companies, the company will be under pressure from the Inland Revenue to use any cash it has, to pay a dividend or purchase a trading asset in order to avoid the withdrawal of tax relief **[see further 5.2.5]**.

6.3 Carrying on a qualifying trade

6.3.1 Introduction

An investee company or its qualifying subsidiary must not only exist to carry on a qualifying trade **[see 6.4** and **6.5]** it must actually carry on or be preparing to carry on a qualifying trade wholly or mainly in the UK **[see 6.4]**. The legislation does not say what is meant by a qualifying trade but provides that the trade, or a substantial part of it, must not consist of certain prohibited activities **[see 6.5]**.

6.3.2 Definition of 'trade'

The tax legislation is not very helpful in that it merely defines 'trade' as including every trade, manufacture, adventure or concern in the nature of trade (TA 1988, s 832 (1)). What is more, for VCT and EIS purposes, that part of the definition which relates to adventures or concerns in the nature of trade, is disregarded (TA 1988, s 298(3); TA 1988, Sch 28B, para 5(4)). This exclusion is omitted from the rules for the CVS, although given the totality of the other requirements, this is likely to be of little significance.

6.3.3 Case law on the meaning of 'trade'

Companies may acquire assets as investments, or for use in a trade, for resale, or for the shareholders' personal use. There is considerable case law on whether particular transactions amount to trading transactions. From these decisions useful guidelines have been established, which are known as the badges of trade. These are considered briefly in **6.3.4** to **6.3.9**.

Activities that have been held by the courts to be adventures in the nature of trade have tended to be isolated transactions:

(*a*) the purchase and sale of silver bullion (*Wisdom v Chamberlain* (1968) 45 TC 92, CA);
(*b*) the purchase and resale of whisky in bond (*IRC v Fraser* 1942 SC 493, 24 TC 498, Ct of Sess);
(*c*) the purchase and resale of a large quantity of toilet rolls (*Rutledge v IRC* 1929 SC 379, 14 TC 490).

6.3.4 Motive for acquisition and method of finance

In some cases the motive for acquiring the asset is evident from the surrounding facts and in other situations it can be inferred. For example, it would be difficult to argue that an asset had been bought by a company for use in its trade as opposed to being purchased for resale, if at the time it was acquired, the company did not have, or could not obtain, the means to finance it in the long term or pay for its upkeep.

6.3.5 Nature of the assets

The nature of the assets and how they have been used will usually indicate whether they were purchased with a view to resale. For example, if a company purchased a large plot of land, far in excess of what it could use for its trade and sold some of it, this is likely to be treated as a dealing transaction.

6.3.6 Period of ownership and reason for the sale

As a general rule, assets bought as investments or for use in the company's trade are held for a longer period than those purchased for resale. However, there will be cases where an asset was not purchased for resale but is sold to finance the acquisition or upkeep of the other assets or to provide working capital. Provided that there is evidence of the motive for the acquisition and also of how the asset has been used for the trade, this is unlikely to be taxed as a trading transaction.

6.3.7 Frequency of transactions

There is a presumption of trading if a company sells the same sort of asset on several occasions. However, the type of asset and the interval between sales would be relevant. For example, if a company operating shoe shops acquired four shop leases and assigned them at a profit all within a period of three years, there is an argument that it has been dealing in land. If, during the same period, the same company bought and sold shop furniture and equipment that it had used in the trade, that is unlikely to be treated as trading in furniture and equipment.

6.3.8 Making assets marketable

If there are activities to make the asset more marketable this would be seen as an indication of trading:

(*a*) Obtaining planning permission;
(*b*) Carrying out repairs and improvements;
(*c*) Splitting large quantities into smaller units;
(*d*) Incurring costs on packaging;
(*e*) Large-scale advertising;
(*f*) Opening a place of business.

6.3.9 Deemed trades

If an activity is deemed to be a trade for certain tax purposes, that does not necessarily mean it is a qualifying trade. For example, the commercial letting of furnished holiday accommodation is treated as a trade for the purposes of deducting expenses, loss relief and replacement of business asset rollover relief (TA 1988, s 503(1); TCGA 1992, s 241 (3)) but it is not a qualifying trade for the VCT, EIS or CVS reliefs.

6.3.10 Difficult areas

There will be some situations where it is important to review all the activities carried on by the company. Where relevant, reference could be made to case law including the badges of trade to consider the extent to which there are prohibited activites **[see 6.5]**.

> 'Concerns, such as quarries and gravel pits, whose profits arise out of land and which are brought into Case I by TA 1988, s 55 are not necessarily trades; each case must be considered on its merits.'
>
> (Venture Capital Schemes Manual, para VCM 17010).

6.3.11 Subcontracting

There is no restriction in the legislation on the engagement of subcontractors by a company. A qualifying company could therefore subcontract certain parts of its activities provided that it is left with sufficient activities to demonstrate that it exists to carry on a trade and is actually carrying on or preparing to carry on a trade.

6.3.12 Management agreements

Where companies carry on their trade by subcontracting the day-to-day management to a management company, there will be a management agreement. The inspector will want to see such an agreement to ensure that it is a genuine agreement for services and not, for example, an agreement allowing the use of the qualifying company's premises.

6.3.13 Trading in partnership

There are references in the VCT legislation to the carrying-on of a trade in partnership by a qualifying company, for example, where this may give rise to a reduction in the investment limit of £1 million **[see 5.3.5]**.

However, expect the inspector to examine closely the relationship between the qualifying company and the other partner, both initially and thereafter. If there is a trade carried on in partnership, ensure sufficient attention is given to the following:

(*a*) The company's contribution must not be passive, for example, simply lending money or letting its property or equipment be used. It must actively carry on the trade.

(*b*) There must not be a joint venture company, ie one owned equally by the parties for the purposes of the VCT scheme or the EIS. A VCT or EIS investee company must own more than 50% of the shares in its subsidiaries (in the case of shares – and for the VCT scheme also securities – issued before 17 March 2004, the ownership requirement was a minimum 75%) **[see 5.5 and 5.11]**. CVS investee companies must also have an interest of more than 50% in their qualifying subsidiaries.

(*c*) If an EIS investor is the partner of the company, or is an employee or paid director of the company's partner, he or she will not be eligible for EIS relief **[see 7.6.2.4]**.

For CVS investee companies, there is the requirement that neither they nor their qualifying subsidiaries carry on their qualifying trade in a partnership or joint venture with another company with which they are under joint 75% control **[see 5.12.3.2]**.

6.4 Where the trade must be carried on

6.4.1 Wholly or mainly in the UK

For all three schemes, a qualifying investee company or its 90% qualifying subsidiary must use the funds raised for a trade it carries on or intends to carry on wholly or mainly in the UK (TA 1988, s 289 (2); TA 1988, Sch 28B, para 3(3); FA 2000, Sch 15, para 25(1)(a)). When asked whether these rules (at that time, in respect of the EIS only) were acceptable to the European Commission, the Chief Secretary to the Treasury at the time, Mr Michael Portillo, said:

> '. . . where the United Kingdom taxpayer gives a subsidy under tax legislation such as this, it is to be expected that a benefit will arise to the United Kingdom from the concession in the form of profits and the creation of prosperity . . . whereas the BES required companies to be resident and registered in the United Kingdom, there is no parallel provision in the schedule . . . I am clear that it is not state aid. It is a tax concession for individuals. State aid is quite different because it involves the transfer of moneys through subsidies from Government to companies. The Commission would, however, be interested in restrictions on the residency [sic] and registration of companies and I have every confidence that the Commission will recognise that, within national tax legislation, it is legitimate to direct benefit to the country within which the tax regime applies.'
>
> (Official Report SC A, 22 March 1994, col 781)

The UK for this purpose includes the territorial sea – that is, waters within 12 miles of the coast. It does not include the Channel Islands or the Isle of Man.

6.4.2 Criteria used

Whether a company is trading wholly or mainly in the UK is a question of fact. The Inland Revenue has given its view of the question in Statement of Practice SP3/00, which is reproduced in full below:

'*Location of activity*

1 The provisions for—
- the enterprise investment scheme;
- venture capital trusts;
- the corporate venturing scheme;
- enterprise management incentives; and
- capital gains tax reinvestment relief (which is not available for investments made after 5 April 1998)

each include the requirement that a company's trade should, at a certain time or for a certain period, be "carried on wholly or mainly in the United Kingdom". This statement explains the way in which the Inland Revenue applies this condition in those contexts.

2 The way in which the requirement is applied in any particular case will depend on the relevant facts and circumstances. A company may at any given time carry on some of the activities of the trade outside the UK and yet satisfy the requirement if the major part of the trade, that is over half of the trading activity, taken as a whole, is at that time carried on within the UK.

3 In considering whether the requirement is satisfied, the Inland Revenue will take into account the totality of the activities of the trade. For example, [it] will consider where the capital assets of the trade are held, where any purchasing, processing, manufacturing and selling is done, and where the company's employees and other agents are engaged in its trading operations. For trades involving the provision of services, the location of the activities giving rise to the services and the location where they are delivered will both be relevant.

4 No one factor is in itself likely to be decisive in any particular case. In particular, the Inland Revenue will not regard a company's activities as not being carried on in the UK solely because—
- the goods or services which it manufactures or provides are exported or supplied to overseas customers;
- its raw materials are purchased from abroad; or
- its raw materials or products are stored abroad.

5 In the case of a trade consisting of ship chartering, the trade will be considered to satisfy the requirement if all the charters are entered into in the UK and the provision of the crews and the management of the ships while under charter take place mainly in the UK. If these conditions are not met the test may still be satisfied, but this will depend on all the facts and circumstances of the case.

6 The corresponding requirements in certain of the schemes mentioned in relation to research and development . . . are applied in a similar way.'

6.4.3 Groups of companies

It is possible to raise money for a group of companies that includes one or more subsidiaries not trading wholly or mainly in the UK. This is because, when deciding whether it is trading wholly or mainly in the UK, the group is considered as a whole. However, the rules for applying the funds raised effectively limit their application to trades carried on wholly or mainly in the UK.

Under the CVS, all of the funds raised by an issue must be applied for the purpose of a qualifying trade or for research and development carried on wholly or mainly in the UK (FA 2000, Sch 15, para 36). Under the EIS, for shares issued before 17 March 2004, the share issue must actually be made in order to raise money for the purposes of a qualifying business activity (a qualifying trade or qualifying research and development) and all of the funds raised by an issue must actually be applied for the purposes of that activity within two years. With shares issued after 16 March 2004, however, the position is slightly different. Some of the shares comprised in the issue may be bonus shares **[see 5.7.5.3]**. For all that, since bonus shares do not themselves give rise to funds, it is still the case that all the funds raised by the issue must be applied for the purposes of a qualifying business activity. To apply some of the funds raised towards a foreign trade is still, therefore, not permissible. Of course, if venture scheme capital is raised for a qualifying activity, capital from within the group may be released for financing the foreign trade.

In the VCT scheme, whereas VCT funds must still be applied to a qualifying trade wholly or mainly in the UK (TA 1988, Sch 28B, para 3(3)) it is possible to issue shares partly for a qualifying purpose and partly for other purposes, so an issue of one million £1 shares at par, for example, could be split between £600,000 (say) VCT shares for a UK trade and £400,000 for a foreign trade outside a venture capital scheme.

Example 6.1

Hume Ltd makes leather furniture in the UK and has started exporting its products to continental Europe. It wishes to raise £400,000 to extend its premises in the UK and £500,000 for its wholly-owned German subsidiary, Hegel GmbH, for it to acquire showrooms in Stuttgart and Dresden.

If £900,000 is raised by a share issue, EIS or CVS relief would not be available, as the proceeds of the issue must be used to fund trades carried on wholly or mainly in the UK. However, if subscriptions totalling £400,000 were made under the VCT scheme, the remaining funds from the issue could be used in Germany, although they would not form part of the qualifying holding for the VCT investor.

6.5 Excluded activities

6.5.1 List of excluded activities

The following is the list of activities that must not form a substantial part of the investee company's trade:

(*a*) dealing in land **[see 6.5.2]**;
(*b*) dealing in commodities or futures or in shares, securities or other financial instruments **[see 6.5.3]**;

(*c*) dealing in goods otherwise than in the course of an ordinary trade of wholesale or retail distribution **[see 6.5.4]**;
(*d*) banking, insurance, money-lending, debt-factoring, hire-purchase financing or other financial activities **[see 6.5.5]**;
(*e*) letting ships on charter **[see 6.5.6]**;
(*f*) leasing or letting assets on hire **[see 6.5.7]**;
(*g*) receiving royalties or licence fees **[see 6.5.8 and 6.5.9]**;
(*h*) providing legal or accountancy services **[see 6.5.10]**;
(*i*) property development **[see 6.5.2]**;
(*j*) farming or market gardening **[see 6.5.11]**;
(*k*) holding, managing or occupying woodlands; any other forestry activities; timber production **[see 6.5.12]**;
(*l*) operating or managing hotels or comparable establishments, or managing property used as a hotel or comparable establishment **[see 6.5.13]**;
(*m*) operating or managing nursing homes or residential-care homes, or managing property used as a nursing home or residential-care home **[see 6.5.14]**;
(*n*) providing services or facilities for any trade carried on by another person (other than a company of which the company providing the services or facilities is the subsidiary) which consists, to a substantial extent of activities listed above; and in which a controlling interest is held by a person who also has a controlling interest in the trade carried on by the company **[see 6.5.15]** (TA 1988, s 297(2); Sch 28B, para 4(2) and FA 2000, Sch 15, para 33).

Until 7 March 2001, the list of excluded activities for an EIS qualifying company also included oil extraction activities **[see 6.7]**.

The Inland Revenue interprets 'substantial' as meaning 20% or more – or, more often as more than 20% (see, for example, IR169, *Venture Capital Trusts*, p 6). See Venture Capital Schemes Manual, para VCM 17040, and for a fuller discussion, **5.2.3.2**.

The inspector is likely to look to see if this condition has been breached at provisional clearance, when EIS tax certificates are applied for and thereafter as each set of the company's accounts is received.

6.5.2 Dealing in land

Dealing in land is the activity of acquiring land with the intention of selling it at a profit. The sale of property in the same state as it was acquired, ignoring any changes of planning permission, is a dealing transaction. It is no less dealing if the property is made more attractive to the purchaser by the carrying-out of repairs and renovations.

It is no longer necessary to distinguish between dealing in land on the one hand and property development on the other, as property development is now also an excluded activity. Before 17 March 1998, property development was not an excluded activity for either the EIS or the VCT scheme. It has always been an excluded activity for the CVS.

6.5.3 Dealing in commodities etc

A trade must not consist to a substantial extent of dealing in commodities, futures, shares, securities and other financial instruments. It is understood this last item was included to cover such activities as dealing in second-hand life-assurance policies.

The Inland Revenue explains its approach to dealing in commodities as follows:

> 'The dictionary meanings of "commodities" and "goods" are rather similar, but it can be inferred from the use of the words in adjacent paragraphs [in the legislation] that they are intended to have distinct meanings here. The distinction is most easily conveyed by means of an example; sugar is a commodity, but a bag of sugar is goods.
>
> Dealing in commodities covers any dealing done on a commodities market. Inspectors should not contend that dealing done in any other way comes under this heading without first consulting Revenue Policy, Business Tax (EIS). A manufacturing trade in which a "commodity" is used in the manufacturing process is not regarded as disqualified merely because the company carrying it on buys in the commodity markets and has dealings in the futures markets to even out price fluctuations.'
>
> (Venture Capital Schemes Manual, para VCM 17060)

6.5.4 Wholesale and retail distribution

6.5.4.1 *Dealing in goods*

Dealing in goods, as such, is an excluded activity. However, straightforward wholesale or retail trades should have no difficulty in being qualifying trades for scheme purposes.

However, if there is a proposal to raise capital for a wholesale or retail trade, directors and advisers should consider the rules set out in **6.5.4.2** to **6.5.4.4**. This will enable them where possible to make any modifications to the way in which they carry on, or intend to carry on, their business.

The legislation starts by defining a trade of wholesale and retail distribution and then sets out criteria for deciding whether a trade is ordinary.

According to the Inland Revenue, 'goods' is regarded as having a very wide meaning in this context, covering virtually any tangible asset other than those mentioned in other paragraphs in the list of excluded activities.

6.5.4.2 *Ordinary wholesale and retail distribution*

A trade of wholesale distribution is one in which the goods are offered for sale and sold to persons for resale by them, or for processing and resale by them, to members of the general public for their use or consumption. This definition has the effect of excluding the wholesaler who sells to other wholesalers.

A trade of retail distribution is one in which the goods are offered for sale and sold to members of the general public for their use or consumption (TA 1988, s 297(3)(a), (b); TA 1988, Sch 28B, para 4(3); FA 2000, Sch 15B, para 27(2), (3)).

Having defined wholesale and retail distribution the legislation goes on to describe what is 'ordinary' by listing features that indicate whether the trade is ordinary or not. Not all of the listed features will always be relevant, and the presence or absence of a particular feature is not conclusive.

6.5.4.3 *Features that indicate an ordinary trade*

The legislation lists features that are present in many ordinary trades:

(*a*) buying in bulk and selling small amounts;
(*b*) buying in one market and selling in another, for example, buying from a manufacturer and selling to the general public;
(*c*) the employing of staff and incurring of expenses, such as packaging, transport and rent, in addition to the cost of the goods. In the case of a company, these must be in addition to any remuneration paid to a person connected with it

(TA 1988, s 297(3)(d)(i)–(iii); TA 1988, Sch 28B, para 4(4)(a)–(c); FA 2000, Sch 15, para 27(5)(a)–(c)).

6.5.4.4 *Features that indicate the trade is not ordinary*

The following five features suggest a trade is not ordinary:

(*a*) The trader buys from or sells to someone with whom he is connected.
(*b*) Purchases are made specifically for a customer.
(*c*) Goods are held for a period that is longer than normal, which may suggest that they are appreciating in value.
(*d*) The trade is not carried on at a normal place of business, for example, a person may be selling goods from his own home rather than from a shop.
(*e*) The trader sells stock which he does not take delivery of

(TA 1988, s 297(3)(d)(iv)–(viii); TA 1988, Sch 28B, para 4(4)(d)–(h); FA 2000, Sch 15, para 27(5)(d)–(h)).

The third of these 'non-ordinary' indicia is expanded on by the legislation, in the case of the VCT scheme and the EIS, to provide that:

> 'a trade is not an ordinary trade of wholesale or retail distribution if:
> (i) it consists to a substantial extent of dealing in goods of a kind which are collected or held as an investment or of that activity and any other activity of a kind falling within [the excluded activities list], taken together; and

(ii) a substantial proportion of those goods are held by the company for a period which is significantly longer than the period for which a vendor would reasonably be expected to hold them while endeavouring to dispose of them at their market value.'

(TA 1988, s 297(3)(c); TA 1988, Sch 28B, para 4(3)(c))

This provision is not present in the CVS legislation, but it is not thought that its omission makes any significant case for arguing the contrary.

The sort of goods this provision has in mind are fine wines, works of art, antiques and vintage cars (see Venture Capital Schemes Manual, para VCM 17090).

The Inland Revenue will check to see whether there is a substantial proportion of the stock which is not being actively marketed at a realistic price.

Inspectors are instructed not to object to a trade on the grounds that the type of goods is such that only a small and specialised group of people is likely to be interested in using or consuming them (Venture Capital Schemes Manual, para VCM 17080).

6.5.5 Banking, insurance etc and other financial activities

The reference in the exclusion to 'other financial activities' is apparently there to cover activities such as assuming or bearing the customer's financial risk. The giving of financial advice is not intended to fall within this exclusion. See Venture Capital Schemes Manual, para VCM 17100.

6.5.6 Shipping and ship chartering

Shipping companies that carry on their trade in the UK qualify but those that charter their ships will not qualify unless they meet certain conditions.

There are two kinds of ship chartering.

6.5.6.1 *The time charter*

This is where the shipowner lets the ship for a fixed period of time. The ship, with the crew and equipment, is let for a fixed cost. Usually, the charterer decides on the route and the cargo to be carried, and is responsible for the operating expenses such as fuel, pilotage and port dues. The navigation and technical operation of the ship remains the responsibility of the owner.

6.5.6.2 *The voyage charter (the 'spot market')*

This is where a shipowner agrees to carry cargo from one port to another. Most of the costs are met by the owner and freight is usually paid per unit of cargo or as a lump sum irrespective of the quantity.

6.5.6.3 *Comparative advantages*

Time charters give the shipowner security of income over a period, whereas the profitability of voyage charters depends on a high utilisation of the ship. In either case there are brokers who bring both parties together.

Cargo carried tends to fall into two categories:

(*a*) dry cargo such as grain, aggregate, fertilisers, coal, chemicals and heavy engineering products; and
(*b*) clean petroleum products and liquid chemicals such as petrol, aviation spirit and naphtha.

6.5.6.4 *Permissible ship chartering*

Ship chartering is permitted if the following conditions are met and other lettings and activities are not carried on to any substantial extent:

(*a*) The investee company must be the beneficial owner of each ship. This means that the ship cannot be owned by someone else and chartered to the investee company, nor can it be bought by the investee company on hire-purchase or on conditional sale terms. The ships can be new or second-hand and do not have to be built in the UK. Oil rigs and pleasure craft **[see 6.5.6.5]** are not ships for this purpose.
(*b*) The investee company must be solely responsible for marketing its chartering services.
(*c*) The investee company can only have ships that are registered in the UK **[see 6.5.6.6]**. The Channel Islands and the Isle of Man are not part of the UK for this purpose.
(*d*) The investee company must meet certain conditions concerning the conduct of its trade **[see 6.5.6.7]**.

(TA 1988, s 297(6); TA 1988, Sch 28B, para 4(7); FA 2000, Sch 15, para 28(2)).

6.5.6.5 *Oil rigs and pleasure craft*

An oil rig is defined as any ship that is an offshore installation for the purposes of the Mineral Working (Offshore Installations) Act 1971. A pleasure craft means any ship of a kind primarily used for sport or recreation such as a yacht (TA 1988, s 298(5); TA 1988, Sch 28B, para 5(1); FA 2000, Sch 15, para 28(6)). It is the Inland Revenue's opinion that a cruise liner is a ship used by the operator primarily to transport passengers.

6.5.6.6 *UK registration of ship*

There are conditions to be met if a ship is to be UK registered. For example, senior members of the crew must have British nationality or hold certificates issued by certain other countries. The rest of the crew can be of any nationality but each should hold an able seaman's certificate.

6.5.6.7 *Charter conditions*

The conditions relating to chartering are as follows:

(*a*) The qualifying company cannot let its ship out on charter for a period in excess of 12 months or have an option whereby it could extend the period. However, the lessee (the charterer) can be granted an option, exercisable during or at the end of the 12-month period, should the lessee wish to extend the period.

(*b*) The letting agreement must be a bargain at arm's length between unconnected persons unless the agreement is between members of the same group and either one party is the parent and carrying on a qualifying trade and the other is its qualifying subsidiary or both parties are qualifying subsidiaries of the same parent.

(*c*) The qualifying company must be responsible for making the management decisions (other than those concerning husbandry) and defraying expenses (other than those directly incidental to a particular voyage or to the employment of the ship for that period).

(*d*) There must be no arrangements for another person to be responsible for these matters.

(TA 1988, s 297(6), (7); TA 1988, Sch 28B, para 4(7), (8); FA 2000, Sch 15, para 28(3), (4)).

In 1986 Mr Norman Lamont, then Financial Secretary to the Treasury, explained the background to this condition (in respect of the BES):

> 'It has been put to us that EIS companies would be put at a considerable disadvantage if they were unable to make use of some of the services of a specialist ship manager. It has been argued that obtaining crews would be difficult and that stores and repairs would be costly to obtain . . . we propose to allow a company to use an agent to undertake certain functions. These are what are known in the trade as husbandry and they include the supply of crew and provisions. But the company would retain responsibility for the commercial management of the ship, for example bunkerage and the loading and unloading of cargo.'
>
> (HC Official Report, 17 July 1986, col 1271)

6.5.6.8 *Trading wholly or mainly in the UK*

In all three schemes, the money raised must be applied in a trade carried on wholly or mainly in the UK **[see 6.4]**. How this condition is applied to ship chartering by the Inland Revenue is explained in SP 3/00 **[see 6.4.2]**.

6.5.7 Leasing and letting assets on hire

The reason given by the Financial Secretary to the Treasury in 1984 for excluding leasing was as follows:

> 'A company that acquires assets and leases them to someone else will itself usually have relatively little direct economic activity, compared to the company that employs those assets in its own trade. And, in the case of finance leasing, the company's operation will be almost exclusively of a financial nature and one where, by virtue of the lease itself, the risk will have been largely, if not entirely, laid off. In short the operations of such a company will in this sense be essentially of a passive and financial nature, and as such not the kind of active and high-risk operation for which the scheme was intended.'
>
> (HC Official Report, 11 July 1984, col 1131)

Leasing covers any trading activity that consists in allowing the customer the use of the trader's property. Examples are car hire, television rental and the use of warehousing or safe-deposit facilities. It is restricted to cases where, subject to reasonable conditions imposed by the trader, the customer is free to use the property as his own. In cases where the customer is not free to use the property as his own – for example, what is essentially a taxi service, or the storage of articles by the trader in warehouses or safes – the person using the property is the trader, not the customer. This is not regarded as leasing.

Car hire was touched on in an article in the Inland Revenue's *Tax Bulletin*, Issue 54, August 2001. It confirmed the advice just given, characterising it as the difference between providing a transportation service for customers (which is not letting an asset on hire) and providing a transportation facility for use by the customer (which is). A taxi service, for example, was likely to be a transportation service. By contrast, the provision of chauffeured car hire was likely to be a transportation facility. The fact that the customer does not personally drive the car does not necessarily mean that he or she is not the person using the car. It is the true nature of the contract between the parties that is decisive, not the label.

According to the Inland Revenue, the leasing of land will not normally be part of a trade at all. See further below.

6.5.8 Royalties and licence fees for intellectual property

A qualifying trade may not normally consist substantially of receiving royalties or licence fees. Royalties or licence fees are typically received where property rights of certain kinds, such as copyright or design rights, are exploited by granting permission to another person to make use of that property. For example, a publisher who acquires rights over a book might exploit them by granting another publisher the right to publish a paperback edition in exchange for royalties based on sales. However, there will be cases – such as the retailing of CDs

– where, although the sales are made under licence, the receipts are nevertheless not royalties but consideration for the supply of goods.

6.5.8.1 *Shares issued from 6 April 2000*

However, for shares issued after 5 April 2000, there is an important exception from the general exclusion, which concerns royalties or licence fees for the use of intellectual property. A trade is not to be regarded as failing to qualify if, at some time during the relevant period (in the case of the EIS and CVS) or at any time (in the case of the VCT scheme) it consists to a substantial extent of receiving royalties or licence fees from the exploitation of 'relevant intangible assets'. It may even qualify if it receives royalties or licence fees in respect of other assets, as long as those 'tainted' royalties etc do not form a substantial part in terms of value (TA 1988, s 297(4); TA 1988, Sch 28B, para 4(5); FA 2000, Sch 15, para 29(2)).

A 'relevant intangible asset' is one the whole or greater part of which (in terms of value) has been created by:

(*a*) the company carrying on the trade; or
(*b*) the parent company of a subsidiary carrying on the trade; or
(*c*) a qualifying subsidiary of the parent company

In the case of conditions (*b*) and (*c*), the relevant company had to be in the relationship described throughout the period during which it created the intangible asset. So a subsidiary acquired after the asset had been created would not qualify, for example (TA 1988, s 297(5); TA 1988, Sch 28B, para 4(6); FA 2000, Sch 15, para 29(3)).

An 'intangible asset' is any asset that falls to be treated as such according to generally accepted accounting practice (GAAP) (TA 1988, s 297(5B); TA 1988, Sch 28B, para 4(6B); FA 2000, Sch 15, para 29(4)). In this context, UK GAAP is contained in Financial Reporting Standard 10 (FRS 10), which defines intangible assets as being 'non-financial fixed assets that do not have physical substance but are identifiable and are controlled by the [company] through custody or legal rights'. Examples include:

(*a*) patents
(*b*) trademarks
(*c*) copyrights
(*d*) registered designs and design rights
(*e*) database rights
(*f*) computer software
(*g*) licences (eg mobile phone licences, IRUs, airline routes)
(*h*) brands
(*i*) domain names
(*j*) know-how
(*k*) trade secrets

(*l*) customer lists
(*m*) franchise rights
(*n*) information or techniques having economic value
(*o*) certain rights in respect of plant varieties

Goodwill is not an intangible asset. See also HM Treasury's Explanatory Notes to the Finance Bill 2002, in relation to clause 83 (later section 84) and Sch 29.

Intellectual property is a subset of intangible assets. For the purposes of venture capital schemes, it is defined as being:

(*a*) any patent, trademark, registered design, copyright, design right, performer's right or plant-breeder's right; or
(*b*) any rights under the law of any country or territory outside the UK which correspond or are similar to the above

(TA 1988, s 297(5C); TA 1988, Sch 28B, para 4(6D); FA 2002, Sch 15, para 29(5)).

In the case of an intangible asset that is intellectual property, it needs only to have been created in circumstances such that the right to exploit it vests in the company that created it (alone or jointly with other parties) (TA 1988, s 297(5A)(a); TA 1988, Sch 28B, para 4(6A); FA 2000, Sch 15, para 29(5)). This allows for the situation where the property was created as part of a collaborative project with a third party or an employee (see Venture Capital Schemes Manual, para VCM 17310).

6.5.8.2 *Shares issued before 6 April 2000*

This exception for royalties or licence fees from intangible assets was introduced by FA 2000, Sch 18, paras 4 and 5, and applies only in respect of shares that were issued after 5 April 2000. Where still relevant, the following discussion concerns the exceptions applying to shares issued on or before that date under the VCT scheme or the EIS. The CVS only came into being on 6 April 2000, so what follows is of no application to it.

Before that time, there was a much more limited exception for the receipt of royalties or licence fees. This was restricted to royalties receivable in connection with research and development on the one hand and film production on the other. For research and development, see **6.6.4**. For film production, see **6.5.8.2.1**.

6.5.8.2.1 FILM PRODUCTION

The exception for royalties or licence fees from film production was worded as follows:

> 'A trade shall not be treated as failing to comply [with the conditions for a qualifying trade] by reason only of its consisting, to a substantial extent, in the receiving of royalties or licence fees if:

(*a*) the company carrying on the trade is engaged in:
  (i) the production of films; or
  (ii) the production of films and the distribution of films produced by it in the relevant period/since the issue

and

(*b*) all royalties and licence fees received by it are in respect of films produced by it in that period/since the issue of the relevant holding, in respect of sound recordings in relation to such films or in respect of other products arising from such films.'

(TA 1988, s 297(4) and TA 1988, Sch 28B, para 4(5), as originally enacted; now repealed)

An explanation of the particular facets of the film industry as they relate to venture capital schemes follows.

Film production companies did not raise much money under the BES or initially under the EIS because there were problems in trying to work within the rules of the EIS (and VCT scheme) and in attracting investors. Producing a film appears to the investor to be a very expensive single project and thus a risky form of investment. However, in the last few years of the BES some very low budget films were made with most of the directors, producers, actors and suppliers agreeing not to be paid until the film made a profit. In other cases, films were only made once specific contracts were in place with third parties who agreed to repay the cost of making the film and to share the royalties. The ability to obtain loss relief under the EIS was an additional incentive.

Making a film consists of four stages:

(*a*) The development of a film package; when:
  (1) a script is written for a screen play;
  (2) a producer acquires the underlying rights to the project;
  (3) a director and leading actors are approached; and
  (4) a production manager is engaged to prepare a production budget and a shooting schedule.

(*b*) The pre-production stage, when locations are found, sets are designed and built, costumes are designed and made, the director and cast are engaged.

(*c*) The production stage when the filming of the picture takes place.

(*d*) The post-production stage, when the film is edited, the sound is added and the master prints prepared.

When the film package has been developed, finance is sought to shoot the film. The money comes from a group of equity investors, distributors and broadcasters. If the film is a success, equity investors are repaid their investment plus interest, and share in the net profits. Distributors either advance cash or guarantee to pay a lump sum on delivery of the film in exchange for certain distribution rights. Similarly, broadcasters either advance cash against broadcasting rights or provide licensing agreements.

The distributor's guarantee and the broadcaster's licensing agreement can be discounted with a film financing institution. Cash from these sources is used to provide the funds for the production stage.

Film production companies receive most of their income from royalties and licence fees on the sale of television, video and theatrical rights, sound recordings and other products. As we have seen, under the rules of the VCT scheme and the EIS such activities should not form a substantial part of the company's trade **[see 6.5.1]**. However, an exception was made for film companies. This was the case even where only one film was produced by the company during its relevant period.

The definitions of 'film' and 'sound recording' remain in the legislation:

> ' "film" means an original master negative of a film, an original master film disc or an original master film tape;
>
> "sound recording", in relation to a film, means its sound track, original master audio disc or an original master audio tape.'
>
> (TA 1988, s 298(5); TA 1988, Sch 28B, para 5(1))

The wording differs slightly between the two schemes.

Any attempt by the investee company to produce a film in partnership or as a party to a joint venture with another company in order to overcome the problem of financing the film production stage would breach the rules of the VCT scheme **[see 5.3.4]**. Depending on how much was raised from investors seeking tax reliefs, the effect could be that each shareholder would receive tax relief on part only of his investment.

If money (equity and loans) is introduced into the qualifying company from different sources to help finance the film production, it is necessary to ensure that the qualifying company does not inadvertently fall under the control of another company **[see 5.4]**. If this were to happen the shareholders would lose all their tax relief.

Since the introduction of the general exception for the receipt of royalties from the exploitation of intangible property **[see 6.5.8.1]**, the special provisions for film production companies became superfluous.

6.5.9 Licence fees – land and buildings

A similar problem is encountered by companies carrying on a trade that involves access by customers to the business premises. A licence is a permission to enter upon another person's land for an agreed purpose. It justifies what would otherwise be trespass and the existence of consideration makes it a contractual licence.

In active trades, which involve an element of allowing access to customers, the Inland Revenue had in the past adopted a very narrow interpretation of the legislation. However, more recently the Inland Revenue has adopted a different approach. It accepts that there are many situations where the grant of the right to use the property is incidental to a trade of supplying services; for example, in return for payment for a cinema ticket the proprietor undertakes not just to admit the customer and provide a seat but to show a film. In such cases it is considered that there is not a distinct activity of receiving licence fees.

See *Tax Bulletin*, Issue 54, August 2001. For leisure and sports facilities, **[see 6.5.9.2]**

6.5.9.1 *Upkeep of the property*

Another factor the Inland Revenue is now willing to take into account is the cost of keeping the property in a good condition. It accepts that in some cases where licence fees are received, although there is no direct provision of services to customers, continuous work is required to keep the property in a fit state for use by them. The question to be considered in any particular case is whether such work is, or is not, greater in amount than the work involved in obtaining the fees. It is therefore important when applying for provisional clearances to give details as to how many people will be employed. See again *Tax Bulletin*, Issue 54.

6.5.9.2 *Sports facilities*

The provision of sports facilities could mean different things. At one extreme, the activity of letting tennis courts to the general public by the hour (assuming it to be part of a trade) involves the simple receipt of a fee in return for the right to enter on to the land and is an excluded activity. But where the payment is consideration for the active provision of services by the trader it is not a licence fee of that kind. For example, the Inland Revenue accepts that receipts from admission to an actively supervised gymnasium or health club with trainers in attendance to advise on personal fitness programmes and the use of equipment are not licence fees.

Admission to facilities, such as sports facilities, is often provided to club members. If the membership subscription is in effect a season ticket it makes no difference to the status of the payment as a licence fee. Where, however, there is a genuine club of a kind that facilitates social contact between members, membership subscriptions will not be licence fees. However, the proprietor of such a club might also receive fees from members' guests or visitors, and reduced fees from members. In these cases it will be necessary to consider the principles set out in **6.5.9** to establish whether the fees are to be regarded as licence fees or not.

A leisure or sports facility starts its trade when it opens its doors to the public. Where an investee company has to build or substantially refurbish the property before it can start the trade, it is preparing to carry on a trade, and has a maximum of two years in which to do so.

6.5.10 Legal and accountancy services

In *Castleton Management Services Ltd v Kirkwood* [2001] STC (SCD) 95, the company was incorporated in 1994 and agreed in June 1995 to supply printing, postage, stationery, technical accountancy and taxation literature, and the services of accounting and taxation personnel to an accountancy firm. Subsequently, the employees of the accountancy firm became employees of the taxpayer company, which continued to provide services, including the services of the staff concerned to the accountants. Some time later, the company made a share issue to five subscribers for a total of £299,000, and wished to certify the issue as one qualifying for EIS relief. The Inland Revenue refused under this heading. The company contended that it was supplying staff and not accountancy services. The Special Commissioner rejected the contention and dismissed the appeal, on the grounds that the purported difference 'between the provision of the services of accountants and the provision of accountancy services is in fact a distinction without a difference'. The accountancy firm's clients would have detected no change in the relationship between themselves and the firm following the interposition of the taxpayer company. The supply of the services of accountants to an accountancy firm had to be viewed as the supply of accountancy services and thus an excluded activity.

6.5.11 Farming and market gardening

Farming is not defined for the purposes of the venture capital schemes but the Taxes Act 1988 provides the following definition:

> ' "farm land" means land in the United Kingdom wholly or mainly occupied for the purposes of husbandry, but excluding any dwelling or domestic offices, and excluding market garden land, and "farming" shall be construed accordingly.'
>
> (TA 1988, s 832(1))

There are occasions when what appears to be husbandry is its fact a trade. For example, fish farming is not regarded by the Inland Revenue as husbandry if the fish are fed artificially on pelleted food. Similarly, it is its view that husbandry does not include battery-hen or intensive pig-farming if the animals are kept indoors and have food brought to them.

However, for the purposes of agricultural buildings allowances, husbandry includes 'any method of intensive rearing of livestock or fish on a commercial basis for the production of food for human consumption' (CAA 2001, s 362(1)).

In essence, the position is that, according to established case law (*Lean and Dickson v Ball* (1925) 10 TC 341; *Jones v Nuttall* (1926) 10 TC 346; *Reid v IRC* (1947) 28 TC 451), intensive farming of the kind described is not husbandry, hence the need specifically to extend the meaning for the purposes of CAA 2001. See Inspector's Manual, para IM2260a.

Market gardening is also defined in TA 1988, s 832(1), as follows:

> ' "market garden land" means land in the UK occupied as a nursery or garden for the sale of the produce (other than land used for the growth of hops) and "market gardening" shall be construed accordingly.'

6.5.12 Forestry and timber production

'Holding, managing or occupying woodlands, and any other forestry activities and timber production' are excluded activities. There is no definition in the Tax Acts of woodlands or forestry. The *Concise Oxford Dictionary* defines 'woodlands' as 'wooded country' and 'forestry' as 'the science and art of managing forests'. The Venture Capital Schemes Manual has this to say:

> 'The exclusions concerned with woodlands, forestry and timber production cover everything from the planting of trees to the harvesting of timber, to the extent that they constitute or are part of a trade. They apply whether or not the company owns the woodland. The processing of raw timber is not covered.'
>
> (Para VCM 17150)

6.5.13 Hotels and similar establishments

A hotel is defined in the Hotel Proprietors Act 1956 as 'an establishment held out by the proprietor as offering food, drink and, if so required, sleeping accommodation, without special contract, to any traveller presenting himself who appears able and willing to pay a reasonable sum for the service and facilities provided and who is in a fit state to be received'.

The exclusion extends to the operation or management of establishments similar to hotels. These are guest houses and hostels or other establishments run mainly to provide overnight accommodation (TA 1988, s 298(5A)). They do not, therefore, include prisons, nursing homes and residential care homes (which have a separate exclusion), or boarding schools. Whether or not food is provided is irrelevant.

However, the exclusion does not apply if the company has no estate or interest in, and is not in occupation of, the building.

See also Venture Capital Schemes Manual, para VCM 17160.

6.5.14 Nursing homes and residential care homes

Operating or managing nursing homes or residential care homes, or managing property used as a nursing home or residential care home is an excluded activity.

A nursing home is defined as 'any establishment which exists wholly or mainly for the provision of nursing care for persons suffering from sickness, injury or infirmity or for women who are pregnant or have given birth to children'. A residential care home is 'any establishment which exists wholly or mainly for the provision of residential accommodation, together with board and personal care, for persons in need of personal care by reason of old age, mental or physical disabilities, past or present dependence on alcohol or drugs or any past illnesses or past or present mental disorders' (TA 1988, s 298(5); TA 1988, Sch 28B, para 5(1); FA 2000, Sch 15, para 32(2), (3)).

As with hotels and guest houses, the exclusion does not operate unless the company has an estate or interest in the home or occupies it.

6.5.15 Providing services to excluded trades

An investee company is not carrying on a qualifying trade if it provides services or facilities to a person carrying on an excluded activity and there is a person who, alone or with his associates, has a controlling interest in both trades (TA 1988, ss 297(2)(g), 298(2); TA 1988, Sch 28B, paras 4(1)(f), 5(3); FA 2000, Sch 15, para 33(1), (6)). In this context, the person carrying on the non-qualifying activity can be engaged in any business, profession or vocation (TA 1988, s 298(3); TA 1988, Sch 28B, para 5(4); FA 2000, Sch 15, para 33(6)(b)). The intention is to prevent the circumvention of the prohibited activities by setting up a company to provide all or part of the services. For example, accountancy is a non-qualifying activity. Under this provision, if a company were set up to supply services such as typing, filing etc to an accountancy partnership, its shareholders would not be able to claim VCT or EIS relief if that company was controlled by the spouses of the partners. This provision does not prevent a subsidiary from supplying services to its parent, however.

6.5.15.1 *Meaning of 'control of trade'*

For these purposes, if the trade is carried on by a company, a person is treated as having a controlling interest in that trade if:

(*a*) he or she controls the company; or

(*b*) the company is a close company and he or she or an associate of that person is a director of the company and is either:

   (1) the beneficial owner of, or

   (2) able, directly or through the medium of other companies or by any other indirect means, to control more than 30% of the ordinary share capital of the company; or

(*c*) not less than half of the trade could, in accordance with the ownership rules for company reconstructions (TA 1988, s 344(2)), be regarded as belonging to that person;

and, in any other case, if he or she is entitled to not less than half of the assets used for, or of the income arising from, the trade (TA 1988, s 298(1)); TA 1988, Sch 28B, para 5(2)).

A director in this context includes a person occupying the position of director by whatever name called, and certain managers (TA 1988, s 417(5); TA 1988, Sch 28B, para 5(5)).

6.5.15.2 *Ownership of half the trade*

It is possible, by reference to the attributive ownership rules of TA 1988, s 344, for a person to have a controlling interest in a trade without controlling the company. The Venture Capital Schemes Manual has the following example:

> 'Suppose A holds 25% of the ordinary share capital of Y Ltd, the remaining 75% being held by X Ltd. A also holds 40% of the share capital of X Ltd. In these circumstances, A does not control Y Ltd within the section 416 definition of the term. However, A does own more than half the trade of Y Ltd, because section 344(2)(b) enables a proportion of X Ltd's 75% holding in Y Ltd to be attributed to [A] even though he does not control X Ltd. [A] thus owns 25% + 30% (40% of 75%) of Y's trade.'
>
> (para VCM 17250)

NB: the example as reproduced in the Manual erroneously introduces another person, B, into the picture, where A is meant.

6.6 Research and development

6.6.1 Introduction

Although carrying on research and development is not in itself a trade, it is nevertheless treated in the VCT scheme and the CVS as if it were a qualifying trade, provided that it is being carried on with a view to deriving a qualifying trade from its results to be carried on wholly or mainly in the UK (TA 1988, Sch 28B, para 4(1)(b); FA 2000, Sch 15, para 25(2)). Under the EIS also, carrying on research and development from which it is intended that a qualifying trade to be carried on wholly or mainly in the UK will be derived, is a 'qualifying business activity' that may be funded by the issue of EIS shares (TA 1988, s 289(2)(b)). The EIS, unlike the other two schemes, also stipulates that the research and development be itself carried on wholly or mainly in the UK. It is not possible, however, for a company to qualify if it is simply engaged in providing research and development services for other companies or institutions.

6.6.2 What is meant by research and development

Within the period covered in this book, the definition of research and development for tax purposes has changed twice. The latest change has effect as far as all three schemes are concerned with respect to shares issued after 5 April 2004 (Research and Development (Prescribed Activities) Regulations 2004, SI 2004/712). This latest definition will be referred to in the text that follows as 'the new definition'. For shares issued between 6 April 2000 and 5 April 2004, a different definition ('the 2000 definition') applied and continues to apply. For VCT and EIS shares issued before 6 April 2000, yet another definition ('the old definition') applies.

The 2004 Guidelines and further information may be found at www.dti.gov.uk/support/rd_guidelines.htm.

6.6.3 The new definition

By 'research and development' is meant those activities that are treated as such by generally accepted accounting practice, excluding oil and gas exploration and appraisal (TA 1988, s 837A(2), (6)). The Treasury may, however, specifically exclude or include certain items, by order.

The Treasury is given the power to make regulations to supplement or amend the GAAP definition by issuing guidelines (TA 1988, s 837A(4)). The latest version of those guidelines is *Guidelines on the meaning of research and development for tax purposes* issued by the Secretary of State for Trade and Industry on 5 March 2004. Activities that are treated as research and development under those Guidelines are regarded as research and development for tax purposes; equally, activities not so treated are not regarded as research and development for tax purposes (Research and Development (Prescribed Activities) Regulations 2004, SI 2004/712, reg 2).

Generally accepted accounting practice in the UK is currently contained in Statement of Standard Accounting Practice (SSAP 13), *Accounting for Research and Development*.

It would be beyond the scope of this book to reproduce or provide commentary on the entire contents of the Guidelines or indeed of SSAP 13, but a few important points can be highlighted here.

SSAP 13 limits itself to spending in the fields of science and technology and divides research and development into three broad categories:

(*a*) pure (or basic) research;
(*b*) applied research;
(*c*) development.

6.6.3.1 *Pure or basic research*

This is 'experimental or theoretical work undertaken primarily to acquire new scientific or technical knowledge for its own sake rather than directed towards any specific aim or application'.

6.6.3.2 *Applied research*

This is 'original or critical investigation undertaken in order to gain new scientific or technical knowledge and directed towards a specific practical aim or objective.'

6.6.3.3 *Development*

'Use of scientific or technical knowledge in order to produce new or substantially improved materials, devices, products or services, to instal new processes or systems prior to the commencement of commercial production or commercial applications, or to improving substantially those already produced or installed.'

According to SSAP 13, the chief feature that distinguishes research and development activity from non-research activity is the presence in the former of an appreciable amount of innovation. If the activity departs from routine and breaks new ground, it should normally be included in research and development; if it follows an established pattern, it is not normally included in research and development.

6.6.3.4 *The DTI Guidelines*

The DTI Guidelines state that for tax purposes research and development takes place when a 'project' seeks to achieve an 'advance in science or technology'. Activities that 'directly contribute' to achieving such an advance through the resolution of 'scientific or technological uncertainty' are research and development. Certain 'qualifying indirect activities' related to such projects are research and development also. But indirect activities other than qualifying indirect activities are not research and development.

An 'advance in science or technology' is an advance in overall knowledge or capability in a field of science or technology (rather than a company's own state of knowledge or capability alone). A 'project' consists of a number of activities conducted to a method or plan in order to achieve an advance in science or technology. The project should encompass all the activities that collectively serve to resolve the scientific or technological uncertainty associated with achieving the advance. A project may itself be part of a larger commercial project, but those parts of that larger project that do not address scientific or technological uncertainty do not for that reason become research and development.

Activities that 'directly contribute' to achieving an advance in science or technology are activities that singly or together attempt to resolve an element of the scientific or technological uncertainty associated with achieving the advance. They include:

(*a*) activities to create or adapt software, materials or equipment needed to resolve the scientific or technological uncertainty, provided that the software, material or equipment is created or adapted solely for use in research and development;

(*b*) scientific or technological planning activities; and

(*c*) scientific or technological design, testing and analysis undertaken to resolve the scientific or technological uncertainty.

Actvitities that do not directly contribute to the resolution of scientific or technological uncertainty include:

(*a*) the range of commercial and financial steps necessary for innovation and for the successful development and marketing of a new or appreciably improved process, material, device, product or service;

(*b*) work to develop non-scientific or non-technological aspects of a new or appreciably improved process, material, device, product or service;

(*c*) the production and distribution of goods and services;

(*d*) administration and other supporting services;

(*e*) general supporting services (such as transport, storage, cleaning, repair, maintenance and security).

For qualifying indirect activities, see below.

Scientific or technological uncertainty exists when knowledge of whether something is scientifically possible or technologically feasible, or how to achieve it in practice, is not readily available or deducible by a competent professional working in the field. It will often arise from turning something that has already been established as scientifically feasible into a cost-effective, reliable and reproducible process, material, device, product or service. System uncertainty is included in this definition. It is scientific or technological uncertainty that results from the complexity of a system rather than uncertainty about how its individual components behave. In electronic devices, for example, whereas the characteristics of individual components or chips may be fixed, there can still be uncertainty about the best way to combine those components to achieve an overall effect.

Unlike the 2000 Guidelines, the 2004 Guidelines do not contain a list drawn from SSAP 13 of various activities that would normally be included in, and a list of activities that would normally be excluded from, research and development. For such lists, see **6.6.4.5**.

The 2004 Guidelines do, however, contain a list of 'Qualifying indirect activities'. These are:

(*a*) scientific and technical information services, insofar as they are conducted for the purpose of research and development support (such as the preparation of the original report of research and development findings);

(*b*) indirect supporting activities such as maintenance, security, administration and clerical activities, and finance and personnel activities, insofar as undertaken for research and development;

(*c*) certain ancillary activities essential to the undertaking of qualifying research and development (eg taking on and paying staff, leasing laboratories and maintaining research and development equipment including computers used for research and development purposes);
(*d*) training required to support a research and development project directly;
(*e*) research by students and researchers carried out at universities;
(*f*) research (including related data collection) to devise new scientific or technological testing methods, survey methods or sampling methodologies;
(*g*) feasibility studies to inform the strategic direction of a specific research and development activity.

6.6.4 The 2000 definition

The 2000 definition relied on the Research and Development (Prescribed Activities) Regulations 2000, SI 2000/2081 and the previous DTI Guidelines issued on 28 July 2000.

Those Guidelines, which do not differ markedly from the new 2004 Guidelines nevertheless contained lists giving examples of qualifying and non-qualifying activities which are not reproduced in the 2004 Guidelines.

6.6.4.1 *Activities normally constituting research and development*

(*a*) Experimental, theoretical or other work aimed at the discovery of new knowledge or the advancement of existing knowledge;
(*b*) searching for applications of that knowledge;
(*c*) formulation and design of possible applications for such work;
(*d*) testing in search for, or evaluation of, product, service or process alternatives;
(*e*) design, construction and testing of pre-production prototypes and models and development batches;
(*f*) design of products, services, processes or systems involving new technology or substantially improving those already produced or installed;
(*g*) construction and operation of pilot plants.

6.6.4.2 *Activities normally excluded from research and development*

(*a*) Testing analysis either of equipment or product for purposes of quality or quantity control;
(*b*) periodic alterations to existing products, services or processes even though these may represent some improvement;
(*c*) operational research not tied to a specific research and development activity;
(*d*) the cost of corrective action in connection with breakdowns during commercial production;
(*e*) legal and administrative work in connection with patent applications, records and litigation, and the sale or licensing of patents;

(*f*) activity, including design and construction engineering, relating to the construction, relocation, rearrangement or start-up of facilities or equipment other than facilities or equipment whose sole use is for a particular research and development project;
(*g*) market research.

6.6.4.3 *Further excluded activities*

The 2000 Guidelines also gave a further list of activities that would normally be excluded from the definition of research and development, unless they were included in the list above as an integral part of a larger research and development project:

(*a*) general education and training;
(*b*) scientific and technical information services;
(*c*) general-purpose data collection;
(*d*) calibration of standards and routine testing and analysis of materials, components, products and processes;
(*e*) the acquisition of rights in, or arising from, research and development;
(*f*) routine computer maintenance or software development;
(*g*) specialised (routine) medical care;
(*h*) policy studies.

6.6.4 The old definition

For the purposes only of VCT and EIS shares issued before 6 April 2000, the old definition continues to apply, although in practice there is likely to be little significant difference.

Under that definition, research and development was any activity that was intended to result in a patentable invention (within the meaning of the Patents Act 1977) or in a computer program.

Under Patents Act 1977, s 1 the main requirements are that:

(*a*) the invention is new;
(*b*) it involves an inventive step; and
(*c*) it is capable of industrial application.

Although computer programs are excluded under Patents Act 1977, s 1(2)(b), they were specifically included in the above definition.

6.6.5 Can subcontractors be used?

In 1985 John Moore, then Financial Secretary to the Treasury, made the following comment with regard to the BES:

> '. . . an R and D company which satisfies the conditions in clause 42 will not cease to qualify merely because it contracts out some of its R and D activities, provided that it can demonstrate that it intends to derive and carry on a qualifying trade from those activities . . . if, for example, a company had substantial R and D activities of its own and also retained full control over the rights in activities that were contracted out, it would qualify.'
>
> (HC Official Report SC B, 4 June 1985, col 329)

6.6.6 Requirement to start immediately

A further condition attached to research and development under the EIS scheme is that, if the company is not already carrying it on when the shares are issued, it begin to do so immediately afterwards (TA 1988, s 289(2)(b)(i))).

The word 'immediately' was said to mean 'with all reasonable speed considering the circumstances' in the decision in *R v Inspector of Taxes, ex p Clarke* (1971) 47 TC 691. In 1985 John Moore, then Financial Secretary to the Treasury, declined to accept any particular definition but instead explained why there was a requirement that the research and development start as soon as the shares are issued:

> 'Under the normal rules for BES companies, a company is allowed up to two years from the issue of BES shares in which to commence its qualifying trade . . . Investors cannot claim their relief until the company has started trading and carried on the trade for four months . . . this provides an incentive for companies to start trading as soon as possible. It avoids the possibility that investors might get relief even though, for a period, their investment was held by the company on risk-free deposit pending the start of trading . . .
>
> Investors have no guarantee that an R and D company will be able to start trading within the two year time limit . . . To overcome this problem clause 42 provides special treatment for R and D companies. Investors in these companies will be able to claim their relief even though the company will be engaged in what would normally for other BES companies be regarded as pre-trading activities. Moreover, the relevant period for R and D companies will be a maximum of three years, compared with five. . . . Given this special treatment it seems reasonable to require that the company should make a start on its R and D activities as soon as the BES shares have been issued.'
>
> (HC Official Report SC B, 4 June 1985, col 332)

The treatment of research and development in this sense is a hotchpotch. By the time the VCT scheme was enacted, it was no longer felt necessary to insist on an immediate beginning to the research and development. However, in the CVS there is the provision that, although carrying on research and development with a view to a trade in mind is considered to be carrying on a trade, preparing to carry on research and development does not count as preparing to carry on a trade (FA 2000, Sch 15, para 25(2), proviso). There is no equivalent of this provision in the VCT legislation.

6.6.7 Royalties and licence fees from research and development

As we have seen, generally, an investee company does not qualify under any of the schemes if it receives royalties or licence fees to any substantial extent. There is a general exception to this rule where the royalties or licence fees are received largely in respect of intangible assets that the company or a member of its group has created **[see 6.6.3]**.

For the VCT scheme and the EIS only, there was, and is, a narrower exception for shares issued before 6 April 2000. A company receiving substantial amounts in royalties or licence fees was not, for that reason only, to be regarded as carrying out excluded activities if:

(*a*) it was engaged in research and development (in the case of the EIS, throughout the period of restriction); and
(*b*) all of its income from royalties or licence fees (in the case of the EIS, in the period of restriction) related to research and development that the company had carried out.

A company that is continuously occupied in developing new computer programs or updating old ones benefited from this exception. However, the conditions were very narrowly worded and excluded many computer software companies.

Example 6.2

Iconoclast Ltd is a company set up by Hobbes to market a newly developed software package for dentists. In 1997 Hobbes purchased the UK rights to a computer program. Subsequently he upgraded it, added new features and tailored it specifically for dentists. In January 2000 it was predicted that 40% of the company's income would come from licence fees from the program that Hobbes developed. Iconoclast decided to make a share issue on 1 April 2000. Unfortunately as the development was carried out by Hobbes and not by the company the investors were not eligible for EIS relief.

In this case, it would have been of no assistance to Hobbes to wait a week and issue the shares on 8 April, by which time the new general exception applied. Because the intangible asset (the program) was created not by Iconoclast or any group member, but by Hobbes, the company is still not a qualifying investee company for any of the three schemes. If the program had been intellectual property, which it is not, Hobbes could have secured relief since the right to exploit it has vested in the company **[see 6.5.8.1]**.

6.6.7.1 *Computer software sales*

Because computer software can only be protected by copyright it is only ever sold under the terms of a software licence agreement. Where a company is creating and selling software it will wish to preserve its property rights by making its 'sales' by way of granting licences. The Inland Revenue accepts that this should not be treated as a receipt of licence fees.

However, where a further charge is made based on the ongoing use of the software, this is regarded by the Inland Revenue as licence fee income and must therefore not amount to a substantial part of the company's activities.

Example 6.3

Herder Ltd develops and sells computer software on the following basis. £30,000 is payable on delivery which includes the installation and a week's training for the client's staff. Thereafter, there is a charge of £100 per member of staff who has used the software in the last four months. The latter charge is regarded as licence-fee income and must not amount to a substantial part of the company's activities if Herder Ltd is to be a qualifying company.

6.7 Oil exploration and extraction

'Oil' is defined as any substance won or capable of being won under the authority of a licence granted under either the Petroleum Act 1998, Part I or the Petroleum Production Act (Northern Ireland) 1964, other than methane gas won in the course of operations for making and keeping mines safe (TA 1988, s 502(1)).

'Oil extraction' consists of activities carried out in the UK or in a designated area of the Continental Shelf, including searching for, extracting, transporting, storing and carrying out the initial treatment of the oil (TA 1988, s 502(1)).

Since 7 March 2001, oil extraction has been a qualifying trade for the purposes of the EIS. It has always been a qualifying trade for the purposes of the VCT scheme and the CVS.

Oil exploration was defined in TA 1988, s 312(1) as searching for oil. Although not itself a trade, it was under certain conditions treated before 7 March 2001 as a 'qualifying business activity' for the purposes of the EIS.

The conditions for it to be so treated were as follows:

(*a*) the exploration had to be carried on by either the investee company or any subsidiary;

(*b*) it had to be carried on wholly or mainly in the UK – whereas this included UK territorial waters, it did not include the UK Continental Shelf (see Inland Revenue Press Release of 19 May 1986);

(*c*) there had to be an intention to derive a qualifying trade from the exploration to be carried on wholly or mainly in the UK. For this purpose, oil extraction did count as a qualifying trade;

(*d*) the exploration had either to be carried on at the issue date or begun immediately afterwards;

(*e*) the investee company or its subsidiary had to hold an oil exploration licence for the area concerned, issued either to it or to its subsidiary, for at least three years from the issue date;

(*f*) at the issue date, neither the investee company nor any of its subsidiaries was permitted to hold an appraisal or development licence for that area.

Once the investee company or any subsidiary had issued its shares and had an exploration licence for an area, it could, within the following three years, apply for and be issued with an appraisal or development licence for that area. This was treated as an extension of the exploration licence and as such did not disqualify the company.

Once, with effect from 7 March 2001, oil extraction was admitted as a qualifying trade for the EIS, the special provisions on oil exploration became redundant, and they were repealed. If the company carrying out the exploration intends to carry on a qualifying trade (oil extraction) derived from the exploration, the exploration activity will be a qualifying business activity, since it consists of preparing to carry on a trade. If the exploration is not intended to lead to a trade of oil extraction, it is not and nor would it under the old rules have been a qualifying activity.

6.8 Starting a qualifying trade

6.8.1 How soon need the trade start?

For all three schemes, a company preparing to carry on a qualifying trade at the time of the share issue must actually begin trading within 24 months of the issue date (TA 1988, s 289(2)(a)(ii); TA 1988, Sch 28B, para 3(4); FA 2000, Sch 15, para 23(5)).

6.8.2 When does a trade start?

The Inland Revenue usually applies the decision in *Birmingham and District Cattle By-Products Co Ltd v IRC* (1919) 12 TC 92. In this case the purchase of a factory, the appointment of the works manager and the purchase of raw materials were seen as preparations for the start of a trade. It was decided that the trade started when the manufacturing process commenced. In general terms, this means that a trade starts when the company is in a position to sell its goods and services to its customers.

Examples of when a trade starts are as follows:

(*a*) when a hospital is in the position to admit its first patient;
(*b*) when a school is able to give classes to its first pupil;
(*c*) when a hairdressing salon opens its doors to the public;
(*d*) when land is acquired with planning permission to develop it, in the case of a property developer.

The start of a trade is a question of fact for the Commissioners to decide (*Cannop Coal Co Ltd v IRC* (1918) 12 TC 31). See also *Napier v Griffiths* (1991) 63 TC 745 and the Inland Revenue's Business Income Manual, para BIM 70505.

6.8.3 Starting non-qualifying activities

An investee company or its subsidiary company could fail to qualify if it starts its business by carrying on a non-qualifying activity, for example, if it uses the cash raised to make investments pending the purchase of trading assets. However, where a trading activity is not in the prohibited category but is either insignificant or is not the trade for which the capital was raised, the inspector may simply not accept that the qualifying trade has started.

6.9 Cessation of a qualifying trade

6.9.1 Breach of the conditions

If during the investee company's relevant period or, for the VCT scheme, at any time it or its subsidiary ceases to carry on a qualifying trade, the company could be disqualified and all the shareholders' tax reliefs lost (TA 1988, s 293(2); TA 1988, Sch 28B, para 3(3); FA 2000, Sch 15, para 23(1)). It is therefore important, where the company intends to change its qualifying trade, to ensure that the second trade starts before the first trade ends, to be absolutely certain that relief will not be lost.

Having said that, the Inland Revenue is prepared to overlook a small period of time where there is a gap between trading, while one trade has ceased and another is about to begin, or there is an interruption in operations due to external causes:

> 'The cessation of trading, other than an involuntary and temporary cessation caused by some eventuality such as a fire, will normally mean that a company ceases to exist for the purpose of carrying on a trade. But there is no reason why the company should not dispose of one trade and begin another, provided the interval between the two activities is brief.'
>
> (Venture Capital Schemes Manual, para VCM 15070)

6.9.2 Winding up the company

Winding up a company before it has carried on its qualifying activities for the requisite period (or, for the VCT scheme, at any time during the life of the relief in respect of those shares) need not cause the investors' tax reliefs to be withdrawn if certain conditions are met **[see 6.9.4]**.

6.9.3 Appointment of an administrative receiver

The appointment of an administrative receiver has no effect as such on the company's status. It is not the same as commencing proceedings for a winding-up (IR *Tax Bulletin*, Issue 2, February 1992).

6.9.4 Appointment of a receiver to realise assets

With effect from 21 March 2000, for the VCT scheme and the EIS, and from inception for the CVS, any failure to satisfy a requirement which is due entirely to the fact that the company or any other company has been put into administration or receivership is disregarded, provided that everything done as a consequence is done for commercial reasons and not as part of a tax avoidance scheme **[see 5.2.3.1, 5.7.3.3 and 5.12.3.1]**.

Before that date, it was not the Inland Revenue's practice to withdraw the shareholders' tax reliefs if the cessation of the company's qualifying activities by a receiver was followed without undue delay by the winding-up of the company in accordance with the conditions set out immediately below. Those conditions were as follows:

(*a*) The company had to cease its qualifying trade or activities by reason of being wound up or dissolved. The winding-up could not simply follow the cessation of trade, it had to cause the cessation.

(*b*) The winding-up or dissolution had to take place for bona fide commercial reasons and not as part of a scheme or arrangement where the main purpose or one of the main purposes was to avoid tax.

(*c*) For EIS companies, there was a further condition, namely that any net assets had to be distributed to their members (or dealt with as *bona vacantia*) before the end of the period of restriction (the relevant period) or three years from the commencement of the winding-up, if later.

Any delay had therefore to be avoided.

The hive-down of the trade by a receiver to a newly formed subsidiary to preserve trading losses is not acceptable to the Inland Revenue. This is presumably because it taints cessation with tax-avoidance motives (*R v Inspector of Taxes, Reading, ex p Fulford-Dobson* [1987] STC 344). However, a scheme of reconstruction involving an exchange of the company's shares for shares in a new company may preserve the relief **[see 5.10.2]**.

6.9.5 Disposal to preserve tax relief

Where it is clear that the investment is lost, another course of action is to sell the shares in question while the company still qualifies. The shareholder, the sponsor or EIS fund manager should try to persuade someone, perhaps the founder, to purchase all the qualifying shares for a nominal sum in order to preserve the shareholders' tax reliefs.

6.9.6 Proceeds from a liquidation

Although the liquidation of a company during the investor's relevant period **[see 7.6.1.6]** would not of itself cause all the EIS investment relief to be withdrawn, relief will be withdrawn by reference to the amount that a shareholder receives in the liquidation in respect of his or her ordinary shares **[see 12.5.12.1]**.

6.9.7 Events subsequent to disposal

The reason that it is important to dispose of EIS shares is that if, after the disposal, the company ceases to trade, a shareholder's EIS relief cannot be withdrawn provided that he or she is no longer connected with the company (TA 1988, s 307 (4)).

Chapter 7

Qualifying Investors

7.1 Introduction

In the previous two chapters, we have looked at the conditions that an investee company must meet **[Chapter 5]** and at the trades that an investee company or its subsidiaries must carry on **[Chapter 6]** in order for relief under any of the three schemes considered in this book to be available or preserved. In this chapter, we shall look at the rules that individual investors must follow, both with regard to themselves and to their investment, if they are to be able successfully to claim relief under the VCT scheme or the EIS. The CVS, of course, is designed for corporate investors, and the conditions that have to be met by CVS investor companies have already been examined in **5.17**, and will not be repeated here.

7.2 Scope of this chapter

(*a*) Rules relating to investment relief for investors in a VCT **[see 7.3]**
(*b*) Rules relating to distribution relief for investors in a VCT **[see 7.4]**
(*c*) The maximum investment in a VCT **[see 7.5]**
(*d*) Qualifying conditions for investors in the EIS:
  (1) general rules relating to investors **[see 7.6.1]**
  (2) employees, directors and business angels **[see 7.6.2]**
  (3) individuals with a significant interest in the company **[see 7.6.3]**
  (4) replacement capital **[see 7.6.4]**
  (5) investment through approved EIS funds **[see 7.6.5]**

7.3 Rules relating to investment relief for investors in a VCT

7.3.1 Introduction

In contrast to the EIS, there are few conditions attaching to an individual investor in a VCT scheme. The nature of the VCT, as a vehicle for collective investment, makes the complicated EIS provisions designed to exclude persons with a significant interest in the investee company unnecessary.

An individual aged 18 or more who subscribes in cash on his or her own behalf for new 'eligible shares' **[see 7.3.2]** in a VCT can claim relief from income tax in respect of his or her investment for the tax year in which the shares are issued (TA 1988, Sch 15B, para 1(1), (2), (4)). For details of the relief, see **Chapter 8**.

7.3.2 Eligible shares

'Eligible shares' are new 'ordinary shares' issued by a VCT which carry no present or future preferential rights to dividends, or to a company's assets on a winding-up and no present or future right to be redeemed (TA 1988, Sch 15B, para 1(6)). These conditions must be satisfied for a minimum of three years from the date on which the shares are issued ('the issue date') or three years from the beginning of the qualifying trade, if later. For shares issued before 6 April 2000, the conditions had to be satisfied for at least five years after the later of the issue date and the start of the qualifying trade.

'Ordinary shares' are shares forming part of the company's 'ordinary share capital' (TA 1988, Sch 15B, para 6(2)). Ordinary share capital in turn means all the issued share capital (irrespective of its description or name) of the company, other than capital whose holders have a right to a dividend at a fixed rate but have no other right to share in the profits of the company (TA 1988, s 832(1)).

7.3.3 Prohibition on tax avoidance

No relief is due unless the individual subscribes for the shares, and the shares are issued, for genuine commercial reasons and not as part of a tax avoidance scheme. Clearly, knowing that the investment will qualify for tax relief is not considered to be taking part in tax avoidance.

7.3.4 Prohibition on loan-linked investments

No relief is given where the investor (or an associate of his – see **7.3.4.1**) has obtained a loan during the 'relevant period' which would not have been made, or would not have been made on the same terms, if the investor had not subscribed for the shares in the VCT (or been proposing to do so) (TA 1988, Sch 15B, para 2(1)). A loan for this purpose includes the giving of credit or the assumption of a debt.

The 'relevant period' begins on the later of:

(*a*) the incorporation of the VCT company and
(*b*) the day two years before the issue date

and ends immediately before the third anniversary of the issue date (TA 1988, Sch 15B, para 2(3)). The maximum length of the period is thus five years.

Not all loans made to acquire shares fall foul of this rule. The test is whether the lender has made the loan on terms that are influenced by the fact that the borrower or an associate is contemplating the investment.

In considering a particular loan, the Inland Revenue's primary concern is the reason why the lender made the loan rather than why the borrower applied for it. This means that the relief may not be denied solely because the loan is used to finance the acquisition, provided that the loan is not made on the security of the VCT shares. Thus a loan from a bank for the purpose of the investment would not prevent the giving of relief if the bank would have made a loan on the same terms to a borrower who was intending to use it for a different purpose.

The Inland Revenue also has regard to:

(*a*) the qualifying conditions imposed on the borrower;
(*b*) the existence or not of incentives or benefits offered to the borrower;
(*c*) the time allowed for repayment;
(*d*) the amount of interest charged;
(*e*) the timing of interest payments; and
(*f*) the nature of the security pledged

(Inland Revenue Statement of Practice SP 6/98).

7.3.4.1 *Meaning of 'associate'*

An associate is:

(*a*) any partner (ie a business, not a life partner) or 'relative' of the investor;
(*b*) the trustee of any settlement of which the investor or any living or deceased 'relative' is or was a settlor;
(*c*) the trustee of any settlement containing a company's shares or obligations in which the investor has an interest; and
(*d*) the personal representative of a deceased person whose estate contains a company's shares or obligations in which the investor has an interest.

'Relative' means a husband, wife, parent, remoter forebear (grandfather, grandmother etc), child or remoter issue (grandchild, great-grandchild and so on). It does not include collateral relatives (siblings, nieces, nephews, cousins etc) or in-laws (TA 1988, Sch 15B, para 2(3); TA 1988, s 417(3), (4)). Therefore, neither a brother nor a mother-in-law is an associate, for example, nor is a life partner.

Whether a person is a partner depends on all the facts. A partnership is the relationship that subsists between persons carrying on a business in common with a view to profits (Partnership Act 1890, s 1). A person is likely to be treated as a partner where:

(*a*) he is a member of the partnership by name (named on stationery etc);
(*b*) he is entitled to a profit share; and
(*c*) he is assessable to tax under Schedule D on a share of the profits of the partnership.

An individual is not normally treated as a partner if he or she is assessed to income tax on earnings (formerly, under Schedule E) and tax is deducted under PAYE.

Individuals who are simply directors and shareholders of the same company are not partners nor are individuals who simply own property as an investment, share profits and losses and are assessable to tax under Schedule A. However, if these individuals enter into a partnership agreement, agree to develop the property for sale, and use headed paper (or e-mail) describing themselves as partners, these would be strong indications that a partnership existed in law.

'Settlement' – and hence 'settlor' – are construed widely, under TA 1988, s 660G. The meaning of 'settlement' is not confined to a trust, but includes 'any disposition, trust, covenant, agreement, arrangement or transfer of assets'.

7.4 Rules relating to distribution relief for investors in a VCT

A 'relevant distribution' by a VCT is exempt from income tax if it is beneficially owned by a 'qualifying investor' (TA 1988, Sch 15B, para 7(1)).

For the meaning of 'relevant distribution' and details of the relief, **[see Chapter 8]**.

A 'qualifying investor' is an individual aged 18 or over who is beneficially entitled to the distribution in question because he or she holds the shares in respect of which the distribution is made either in his or her own right or beneficially through a nominee. A nominee for this purpose includes the trustees of a bare trust of which the investor is the only beneficiary (TA 1988, Sch 15B, para 2).

For distribution relief, it is not necessary for the shares to have been obtained by subscription, nor need they have qualified for VCT investment relief. Shares acquired by purchase or gift qualify equally.

7.5 Maximum investment in a VCT

In any one tax year, an individual may claim tax relief on an investment amounting to no more than £200,000 (TA 1988, Sch 15B, para 1(3)). Before 6 April 2004, the limit was £100,000. The same limit, and not a separate £200,000, applies to distribution relief. Thus, if an individual subscribes for £180,000 of VCT shares in any one tax year, purchases of no more than £20,000 could additionally obtain distribution relief.

For the procedure where the maximum is exceeded, see **8.6**.

7.6 Qualifying conditions for investors in the EIS

7.6.1 General rules relating to investors

To obtain EIS relief a qualifying individual must have made one or more qualifying investments. A qualifying investment is one where an individual has subscribed in full for eligible shares in a qualifying company **[see Chapter 5]** or where a nominee such as the manager of an approved EIS fund **[see 7.6.5]** has subscribed on the individual's behalf. The individual must not be connected with the company **[see 7.6.2]**.

Trustees and companies do not qualify for EIS investment relief, but trustees may obtain deferral relief by reinvesting into EIS companies **[see Chapter 15]**.

7.6.1.1 *Residence*

UK residence is not a condition for EIS investment relief. However, gains can only be deferred by EIS investors who are resident and ordinarily resident in the UK (or treated as UK-resident under the terms of a double tax treaty), since they would otherwise not be within the charge to Capital Gains Tax **[see 15.4.2]**.

7.6.1.2 *Shares in joint names*

Although an individual must subscribe for shares on his or her own behalf this does not prevent the issue of shares in joint names. Where two or more subscribers apply jointly for shares in an EIS company, the shares are held on bare trust for them and each is treated as having subscribed on his or her own behalf for an equal amount of the subscription (TA 1988, s 311(2)). If a potential shareholder is short of capital, a joint application may be the answer.

Example 7.1

David and Stephen agree to subscribe £50,000 jointly for a 30% interest in an unquoted trading company. Although David contributes £40,000 and Stephen £10,000, each will receive up to 20% tax relief on £25,000.

7.6.1.3 *Outside investors*

It was thought that those individuals that were already connected with the company such as existing shareholders with significant holdings, partners of the company, the company's employees and paid directors and their associates, did not need encouragement to invest. However, the EIS rules do allow an outside investor or an existing unpaid director to make an EIS investment and then become a paid director **[see 7.6.2.11]**.

7.6.1.4 *Reciprocal arrangements*

No relief is available to an individual who enters into reciprocal arrangements to obtain EIS relief. The situation envisaged is where an individual would not qualify for EIS relief if he or she invested in a company (the first company). The individual therefore enters into an agreement to invest in a second company in respect of which he or she would qualify, but as part of the arrangement, another person agrees to invest in the first company (TA 1988, s 291B(5)). It is worth noting that the other party referred to in this section could be a trustee or a company. If the inspector has reason to believe that a claimant is party to such an arrangement any person concerned can be required to provide information about it (TA 1988, s 310(5), (6)).

Example 7.2

David is looking for an EIS investor to subscribe for shares in his company H Ltd and Simone is looking for an EIS investor for her company, DB Ltd. If Hildegard (David's mother) agrees to invest in DB, provided Jean-Paul (Simone's husband) invests in H, this would be a reciprocal arrangement. As a result, neither Hildegard nor Jean-Paul would be able to claim EIS relief.

7.6.1.5 Guaranteed exit arrangements

An individual will not be entitled to EIS relief if he or she subscribes for shares under arrangements with a view to:

(*a*) the repurchase, exchange or disposal of any other description of those or any other shares or securities in the company; or
(*b*) the cessation of any trade carried on by the company or by a person connected with the company; or
(*c*) the disposal of all or a substantial part of the assets of the company or of a person connected with the company; or
(*d*) the provision of partial or complete protection against the risks attached to making the investment (whether by a form of insurance, indemnity, guarantee etc or otherwise)

(TA 1988, s 299B).

Normal arrangements for the winding-up of the company in the event of insolvency etc, of the kind that might be found in a company's Articles of Association are exempt from this rule.

The arrangements in (*a*) do not include arrangements for the takeover of the EIS company by a new acquiring company in the circumstances described in **5.10.2**).

The arrangements in (*d*) do not include arrangements which are confined to the provision of such protection against the risks arising in the course of carrying on its business as the company might be expected to provide in normal commercial circumstances (TA 1988, s 299B(4)).

7.6.1.6 *Periods of restriction*

To obtain and preserve EIS relief, the investor must meet certain conditions throughout a specified period. This period varies according to the purpose to which it relates.

In order to qualify for relief, the investor must not be connected to the company for a period that:

(*a*) begins two years before the shares are issued; and
(*b*) ends immediately before the 'termination date'

(TA 1988, s 291(1)(b)).

The termination date in relation to any shares is the later of:

(*a*) the third anniversary of the issue date; and
(*b*) the third anniversary of the date on which the trade that the share issue was intended to finance commenced

(TA 1988, s 312(1)).

The minimum length of this period is thus five years.

Before the amendments made by FA 2001, this period was known as the 'designated period', but had the same beginning and end dates.

To determine when shares have been issued, see **8.1.5**.

For the period during which the investor must not dispose of the shares if relief is not to be withdrawn, see **18.1.2**. For the period during which the investor must not receive value if relief is not to be withdrawn, see **12.5.2**.

7.6.1.7 *Prohibition on loan-linked investments*

No relief is given where the investor (or an associate of his – see **7.6.2.3**) has obtained a loan during the 'relevant period' which would not have been made, or would not have been made on the same terms, if the investor had not subscribed for the shares in the investee company (or been proposing to do so) (TA 1988, s 299A(1)). A loan for this purpose includes the giving of credit or the assumption of a debt.

The 'relevant period' begins on the later of:

(*a*) the incorporation of the investee company and
(*b*) the day two years before the issue date

and ends immediately before the later of:

(*a*) the third anniversary of the issue date and
(*b*) the third anniversary of the date on which the qualifying trade began

(TA 1988, ss 299A(3), 312(1), (1A)(1)).

The maximum length of the period is thus five years.

Not all loans made to acquire shares fall foul of this rule. The test is whether the lender has made the loan on terms that are influenced by the fact that the borrower or an associate is contemplating the investment.

In considering a particular loan, the Inland Revenue's primary concern is the reason why the lender made the loan rather than why the borrower applied for it. This means that the relief may not be denied solely because the loan is used to finance the acquisition, provided that the loan is not made on the security of the EIS shares. Thus a loan from a bank for the purpose of the investment would not prevent the giving of relief if the bank would have made a loan on the same terms to a borrower who was intending to use it for a different purpose.

The Inland Revenue also has regard to:

(*a*) the qualifying conditions imposed on the borrower;
(*b*) the existence or not of incentives or benefits offered to the borrower;
(*c*) the time allowed for repayment;
(*d*) the amount of interest charged;
(*e*) the timing of interest payments; and
(*f*) the nature of the security pledged

(Inland Revenue Statement of Practice SP 6/98).

7.6.1.8 *Minimum and maximum subscriptions*

Unlike the VCT scheme, the EIS requires a minimum investment in any one company in any one tax year of £500 (TA 1988, s 290(1)). An exception is made for investments through an approved EIS fund **[see 7.6.5]**.

The maximum investment qualifying for relief in any one tax year, spread over no matter how many companies, is £200,000 (TA 1988, s 290(2)). Before 6 April 2004, the limit was £150,000.

For what happens when the limit is exceeded, **see 9.5**.

Example 7.3

Immanuel invests the following amounts in new EIS shares by subscription in the calendar years 2004 and 2005.

Date	*Company*	*Shares*	*Amount (£)*	*Comments*
02.05.04	A Ltd	300	450	NQ*
15.08.04	B Ltd	25,000	50,000	Q
01.10.04	C Ltd	40,000	60,000	Q
24.12.04	A Ltd	300	450	NQ*
01.02.05	D Ltd	75,000	80,000	Q
01.04.05	B Ltd	15,000	15,000	Q/NQ**

Q = qualifying; NQ = not qualifying

* Taken individually, neither of these subscriptions qualifies, because they are both for less than £500. However, since the total subscribed to A Ltd for shares issued in 2004–05 is more than £500, the total investment qualifies for relief.

** This subscription takes the total invested and qualifying for relief in 2004–05 over the £200,000 limit. £9,100 will qualify for relief and the remaining £5,900 will not. Immanuel could, however, elect to carry back up to half of his qualifying subscriptions made before 6 October 2004 to 2003–04 (provided the *£150,000* limit for that year is not exceeded as a result). This would allow all of the £15,000 subscribed in B Ltd on 1 April 2005 to qualify in 2004–05 **[see further 9.4.1]**.

7.6.1.9 *The prohibition on tax avoidance*

No relief is due unless the individual subscribes for the shares, and the shares are issued, for genuine commercial reasons and not as part of a tax avoidance scheme (TA 1988, s 289(6)). Clearly, knowing that the investment will qualify for tax relief is not considered to be taking part in avoidance.

7.6.2 The prohibition on connected persons

7.6.2.1 *Introduction*

An individual investor cannot qualify for EIS investment or disposal relief if he or she is connected to the investee company at any time during the period of restriction, for which **[see 7.6.1.6]**.

The minimum length of the period of restriction is five years, as we have seen, and, since the qualifying trade must begin no later than two years after the issue date, the maximum length is seven years.

For shares issued after 5 April 1998 and before 6 April 2000, a different period of restriction applied. This was the so-called seven-year period, which began two years before the issue date and ended immediately before the fifth anniversary of the issue date.

The rest of this section looks at how an individual may be 'connected' to the investee company.

7.6.2.2 *Preliminary definition of connection*

The legislation provides that an individual is connected with the investee company if he or she, or an associate of the individual:

(*a*) is an employee of the investee company or of a subsidiary of the investee company; or
(*b*) is an employee of a partner of the investee company or of a subsidiary of the investee company; or
(*c*) is a partner of the investee company or of a subsidiary of the investee company; or
(*d*) is a director of the investee company or of a subsidiary of the investee company; or
(*e*) is a director of a company that is a partner of the investee company or of a subsidiary of the investee company; or
(*f*) has a significant interest in the investee company or in any subsidiary of the investee company

(TA 1988, s 291(2)).

There are certain exceptions for directors **[see 7.6.2.9]**.

7.6.2.3 *The meaning of 'associate'*

In order to avoid unnecessary duplication, the definition of 'associate' for EIS purposes is not repeated here, as it is identical to that applying for the purposes of the VCT scheme. Readers should therefore refer to **7.3.4.1**, replacing the statutory reference there to TA 1988, Sch 15B, para 2(3) by one to TA 1988, s 312(1).

7.6.2.4 *Employees and partners*

To qualify for EIS investment or disposal relief neither the individual, nor any associate of the individual, can at any time in the period of restriction (for which **[see 7.6.1.6]**) be employed by the company, its subsidiary, or partner. Neither can the individual enter into a partnership with the company or any subsidiary. This can be a trap for the unwary as the period of restriction starts two years before the EIS share issue.

Example 7.4

Fiona subscribes £5,000 for ordinary shares in Pygmalion Press Ltd, a company with a subsidiary, Berkeley Books Ltd. A year earlier Berkeley Books employed Fiona's mother on a part-time basis. As Fiona's associate (her mother) was an employee of the company's subsidiary, Fiona would not be eligible for EIS invesment or disposal relief.

7.6.2.5 *Company secretaries*

It is the Inland Revenue's view that a company secretary who receives no payment, has no benefits-in-kind or employment contract and carries out only those duties attributable to a company secretary, will not be an employee of the company for EIS purposes.

7.6.2.6 *Meaning of 'subsidiary'*

In deciding whether an individual is connected with a company, the meaning of 'subsidiary' must be watched, and it is important to realise that a subsidiary for these purposes has previously extended beyond those that are qualifying subsidiaries **[see 5.11]**.

In respect of shares issued before 17 March 2004, a company is a subsidiary of the investee company if it is a '51% subsidiary' of the investee company at any time in the 'relevant period'. The 'relevant period' is the period that begins on the later of:

(*a*) the incorporation of the company and
(*b*) the date two years before the issue date

and ends immediately before the later of:

(*a*) the third anniversary of the issue date and
(*b*) the third anniversary of the day on which the qualifying trade began

(TA 1988, ss 291(3), (5) and 312(1A)(a)).

It can be seen immediately that this is not necessarily the same period as that during which the investor must not be a connected person, and the two tests are applied independently. It does not matter, therefore, whether or not the subsidiary is a subsidiary during the time that the investor is a director, employee, or partner.

Example 7.5

Lacan is a founder member and director of Néant Ltd, an ice-cream manufacturer, which was incorporated on 1 March 2001 and began trading on 25 April 2001. Lacan resigns from the board and leaves the company on 1 March 2003. On 1 January 2004, Néant Ltd is taken over by Signifier Ltd, a larger rival and a long-standing manufacturer. On 12 June 2004, Signifier makes a new share issue under the EIS and Lacan wishes to subscribe. Will he qualify for EIS relief?

The relevant period during which Néant may not be a subsidiary of Signifier is the period from 12 June 2002 (two years before the issue date as incorporation (of Signifier) took place many years earlier) until 12 June 2007 (the third anniversary of the issue date, as the qualifying trade is already being carried on). The period during which Lacan may not be a director of Signifier or of a subsidiary also begins on 12 June 2002 (two years before the issue date) and ends on 12 June 2007 (three years after the issue date, for the same reason as above). He was a director for part of this period (from 12 June 2002 until 1 March 2003). Lacan is therefore not eligible for EIS investment or disposal relief on the 12 June 2004 issue even though he was a director only before Néant became a subsidiary.

7.6.2.7 *Meaning of 'director'*

For these purposes, an individual is a 'director' of a company not only where he or she has that position, however called, but also if he or she is any person on whose directions or instructions the actual directors are accustomed to act. Such people exercising a dominant influence on a company without formally being members of the board are often called 'shadow directors'. Also included is any individual who plays a part in the management of the business and who has, either alone or with any associates, direct or indirect control over 20% or more of the company's ordinary share capital (TA 1988, ss 312(1) and 417(5)).

7.6.2.8 *Meaning of 'associate'*

See **7.3.4.1** for the definition of this term.

7.6.2.9 *The exception for 'unpaid' directors*

Although an individual's possession of a directorship or shadow directorship of the investee company or of a subsidiary normally makes him or her a connected person and hence ineligible for EIS investment or disposal relief, there is an exception for 'unpaid' directors. 'Unpaid' means in receipt of no payments that are not qualifying payments.

This exception allows an investor who chooses not to be involved in the day-to-day management of the business but still wishes to be an unpaid director in order to veto any decision that would cause his or her relief to be withdrawn not to become ineligible.

Such a person is not connected with the investee company just because he or she, or an associate, is a director of that or another company. However, in the following situations the investor (or an associate, or a partnership of which the investor or an associate is a member) would be treated as connected with the company:

(*a*) Where the investor receives a payment other than a 'qualifying payment' (see below) from the investee company or a 'related person' (see below) during the period of restriction **[see 7.6.1.6]**.

(*b*) Where the investor is entitled to receive such a payment in respect of that period or any part of it.

(TA 1988, s 291A(1)).

It should be emphasised that EIS investment relief will be totally withdrawn if an unpaid director receives, or is entitled to receive, a payment that is not permitted, however small. For this purpose any payment includes a payment made to the individual indirectly or to the individual's order or benefit (TA 1988, s 291A(2)(b)).

A 'related person' in relation to an investee company means any of the following persons:

(*a*) Any company of which the individual or the individual's associate is a director, being a company which is:
  (1) a subsidiary of the investee company;
  (2) a partner of the investee company;
  (3) a partner of any of the investee company's subsidiaries or

(*b*) Any person connected with the investee company **[see 7.6.2.1 to 7.6.2.8]** or any of the companies just described

(TA 1988, s 291A(2)).

Example 7.6

Jeremy controls Panopticon Ltd, which issued shares under the EIS. Jeremy's friend Martin invested £50,000 and claimed EIS investment relief. While one of the directors was off sick for six months Martin helped Jeremy manage the company and Jeremy paid Martin £10,000 from his own bank account. Martin will lose all his EIS investment relief because he has received a payment from a related person.

An individual may be a director and still receive a payment from the company or a related person without ceasing to qualify, however, if the payment falls within the list of acceptable payments ('qualifying payments') described below.

(a) *Director's travelling expenses*

An unpaid director may receive any payment or reimbursement of travelling or other expenses wholly, exclusively and necessarily incurred by the director or an associate in the performance of his or her duties as a director of the company (TA 1988, s 291A (3)(a)).

(b) *Interest and dividends*

An EIS investor may receive interest that represents no more than a reasonable commercial return on money lent to the investee company or to a related person. Furthermore, any dividend or other distribution that does not exceed a normal return on the investment can be received (TA 1988, s 291A(3)(b) and (c)).

(c) *Payment for goods*

A director may receive payment for the supply of goods which does not exceed their market value (TA 1988, s 291A(3)(d)).

(d) *Rent*

Rent may be received by a director for any property occupied by the investee company or a related person which does not exceed a reasonable and commercial rent for the property (TA 1988, s 291A(3)(e)).

(e) *Payment for certain services*

An unpaid director may receive any reasonable and necessary remuneration that:

(*a*) is paid for services rendered to the investee company in the course of a trade or profession; and
(*b*) is taken into account in computing the profits and gains of the trade or profession under Case I or II of Schedule D or would be so taken into account if it fell in a period on the basis of which those profits or gains are assessed under that Schedule (TA 1988, s 291A(3)(f)).

For EIS relief there is a further restriction – the services must not be secretarial or managerial services or services of a kind provided by the person to whom they are rendered (TA 1988, s 291A(3)(f)(i)).

The following are examples of payments to be avoided, being payments from the company or a related person to a director or associate:

(*a*) Consideration for the purchase of a building even at market value. The director is not within the exemption for selling goods, as a building is not moveable property.
(*b*) Payments that are assessable under Schedule D Case VI, for example, for guaranteeing an overdraft (*Ryall v Hoare* (1923) 8 TC 521) or for underwriting the share issue (*Lyons v Cowcher* (1926) 10 TC 438).

7.6.2.10 *Directors' companies*

An investee company may agree to pay another company for the services of an unpaid director. The charging company could be owned by the sponsor or be the director's service company. Could such a director or an associate invest in the investee company and claim EIS investment and disposal relief? If the individual is a paid director who meets the conditions in **7.6.2.11** this should not be a problem. But if he or she is an unpaid director and is either a shareholder in the charging company or receives cash or other value from that company then it could be said that he or she is receiving 'a payment made to him indirectly or to his order or for his benefit' (TA 1988, s 291A(2)(b)).

7.6.2.11 *Business angels*

The general rule is that paid directors are not eligible for EIS investment or disposal relief because of their connection with the company **[see 7.6.2.2]**. However, an exception is made for business angels, who are outside investors who introduce finance and expertise to a company. Such an individual is allowed to claim EIS relief on his or her investment and receive reasonable remuneration provided that, at the time eligible shares are first issued to that person, he or she has not previously been connected with the company or its trade.

Such an individual must be issued with eligible shares at a time when the individual (or an associate) has never been:

(*a*) connected with the investee company; or
(*b*) an employee of any person who previously carried on the trade or part of the trade carried on by the investee company or by a subsidiary.

For this purpose, the trade previously carried on includes any business, profession or vocation (TA 1988, s 291A(5)). An individual who is an unpaid director would be connected with the company at the time of his or her investment if during the period of restriction the investor had received, or was entitled to receive, a payment from the company which was not specifically permitted **[see 7.6.2.9]**.

Example 7.7

On 1 June 2003, Marilyn subscribes £100,000 for a 20% interest in Misfit Ltd. Her husband Arthur then joins the board of Misfit and becomes entitled to a modest salary. As Arthur has had no previous connection with Misfit, Marilyn is able to claim EIS investment and disposal relief.

If further shares are subscribed for by the paid director (or his or her associate), those shares will be eligible for relief provided that they are issued before the end of the third anniversary of the latest issue of eligible shares which satisfied the above conditions or, if later, the third anniversary of the commencement of the trade (TA 1988, s 291A(5) (c)).

Example 7.8

Continuing the above example, Arthur subscribes for further shares in Misfit two years later. Assuming the acquisition does not mean that his interest in the company (together with his wife's), exceeds 30%, he should be able to claim EIS investment and disposal relief. This is because on the first issue of shares he and his wife were not connected with the company and three years have not elapsed since that issue. Any shares issued to Arthur after 31 May 2006 would not be eligible for EIS investment or disposal relief.

For shares issued before 6 April 2000, a different period during which further shares could be issued applied. That period was five years after the issue date of the latest eligible shares.

A director's remuneration (leaving out of account any reasonable and necessary payment as described in **7.6.2.9**) must be reasonable for his or her services to the company (TA 1988, s 291A(5)(a)). Remuneration for this purpose includes benefits-in-kind (TA 1988, s 291A(4)).

If the Inland Revenue can successfully contend that the business angel is receiving excessive remuneration, he or she will lose all his or her EIS tax reliefs. This poses a problem for the company's and the business angel's advisers as they will be unable to give the angel an assurance that his or her remuneration will not be challenged. It is most unlikely that the inspector will indicate at provisional clearance or at EIS 1 stage whether the remuneration is considered to be excessive. The responsibility therefore rests with the business angel to ensure that he or she only takes reasonable remuneration as it is his or her tax relief that is at stake.

During the Finance Bill 1994 debate on the EIS, it was made clear by the Chief Secretary to the Treasury, Mr Michael Portillo, that the director's remuneration must not be linked to the amount of his or her investment.

'We intend that business angels should not only be non-executive directors, but should participate in the management of the company and be, if necessary, the managing director or the finance director. As such, they will be remunerated reasonably for their services . . . Presumably there would be other directors. There might be directors who have not made such an investment. A comparison would have to be made in those circumstances. The remuneration that the director receives is not in respect of the capital that he has invested. It is in respect of the service that he renders to the company. It could, therefore, be reasonable for a managing director or a finance director to be paid more than other directors. The Revenue would want to see, in relation to the scale, success and profits of the company and the remuneration of other directors, that the remuneration clearly related to the contribution made by that individual to the company through his expertise. The Revenue would not want it to be a second reward for the capital that he invested.'

When asked about someone who introduces a new range of contacts that results in a great deal of new business for the company, the Minister said

'In those circumstances, I imagine that the company would operate a recognisable bonus scheme. The remuneration must relate to the benefit that is brought to the company by the individual's business and managerial acumen; it must not be a reward for his capital. His capital is rewarded by the gains that he may make, and he is given an incentive to invest the capital by all the provisions of the EIS. We are not looking for him to be doubly rewarded for that, but he may be rewarded for the extra benefits that he brings, which may be of great importance to the company. That is why the EIS is being set up in such a way that it will invite people to form an association with a company'

(HC Official Report SC A, 22 March 1994, col 786).

Example 7.9

Banich has been asked to join the board of Metrics BV, a company intending to manufacture electronic measuring instruments in the UK. The ordinary share capital is owned £80,000 by Dialectics NV, and nine individuals including Banich have subscribed £100,000 each and intend to claim EIS relief. If the Inland Revenue can show that Banich's proposed remuneration of £60,000 a year is excessive considering his services to the company, he will lose his initial investment relief of £20,000 plus the opportunity of a tax-free gain.

As an individual cannot become a paid director if he was an employee of a person who previously carried on the company's trade (see above), management buy-outs are at a disadvantage compared to management buy-ins. This was a policy decision **[see 7.6.2.4]**.

Example 7.10

Montaigne Ltd has been set up by its founders to take over the business of Tower Ltd. The finance for the purchase will be by way of bank loans, institutional money and ordinary shares subscribed by the founders. If Montaigne's founders had not previously been connected with Tower Ltd they could claim EIS relief on their shares and be paid directors. This may enable them to increase their investment. If, on the other hand, they had been employees of Tower Ltd neither EIS investment nor EIS disposal relief would be available.

Although the intention may generally have been that business angels would be taken on by existing companies that are in need of expertise and new capital, directors of new companies are not excluded. It would therefore be acceptable for a small group of individuals to set up a new company, be paid reasonable remuneration for the services they provide to the company and claim EIS investment relief for their investment. However, care must be taken that they are not already connected with the company or its trade **[see 7.6.2.2]**.

7.6.3 Individuals with a significant interest in the company

7.6.3.1 *Introduction*

An individual investor is also connected with the investee company if he or she or any associate has a significant interest in the company (TA 1988, s 291(2)).

An individual has a significant interest in the investee company if he or she directly or indirectly possesses or is entitled to acquire more than 30% of any of the following:

(*a*) the issued share capital of the company or of any of its subsidiaries;
(*b*) the loan capital and issued share capital of the company or any of its subsidiaries;
(*c*) the voting power in the company or in any of its subsidiaries;
(*d*) the rights to the assets of the company or of any of its subsidiaries available to equity holders in the event of a winding-up

(TA 1988, s 291B(1), (2)).

Since the test involves direct and indirect entitlement, it enables the Inland Revenue to look through intermediate entities to the ultimate owner.

Example 7.11

Søren owns 22% of the issued share capital of Whippet Ltd. Another 20% is owned by Venstre Ltd, in which Søren holds 45% of the capital. Søren's direct holding in Whippet is 22% and his indirect holding is 45% × 20% = 9%. Since 22% + 9% = 31%, Søren would not be entitled to EIS relief for any shares issue by Whippet.

As in the prohibition on employments and some directorships, 'subsidiary' means any 51% subsidiary at any time in the 'relevant period' **[see 7.6.2.6]**. For the meaning of '51% subsidiary', **see 5.15.1**.

For this purpose an individual is entitled to acquire anything that he or she is entitled to acquire at a future date or will at a future date be entitled to acquire. This includes an individual who has been granted share options unless the exercise of the options is subject to a genuine contingency. There is also attributed to any person any rights or powers of any other person who is an associate **[see 7.3.4.1]** (TA 1988, s 291B(8)). The right to acquire has to exist in relation to *issued* share capital. An individual who is entitled to receive share capital to be issued at some time in the future does not have such a right.

7.6.3.2 *Subscriber shares*

If an individual who intends to be an EIS investor is the sole subscriber or one of fewer than four subscribers to the company, he or she would be connected to the company by virtue of having 100%, 50% or 33.3% of the shares, respectively, and so be disqualified. This problem is dealt with by TA 1988, s 291B(5A), which provides that the individual's ownership of the subscriber shares will be ignored until the company issues further shares, provided that it neither carries on a trade nor makes preparations to carry on a trade in the meantime.

7.6.3.3 *Loan capital*

For these purposes, loan capital includes any debt incurred by the company:

(*a*) for any money borrowed or capital assets acquired by the company;
(*b*) for any right to receive income created in favour of the company; or
(*c*) for consideration the value of which to the company was (at the time when the debt was incurred) substantially less than the amount of the debt (including any premium on it) (TA 1988, s 291B(7)).

It therefore includes loans from all sources and overpayments. It does not include bank overdrafts, normal hire-purchase debts or finance leases.

In determining whether an individual is connected with a company, a bank overdraft is not treated as loan capital provided that the debt arose in the ordinary course of the bank's business (TA 1988, s 291B(9)).

When EIS shareholders' interests are close to 30% they need to be monitored on a regular basis. Provided that the EIS shareholder made the loan to the company after the EIS share issue, consideration should be given to repaying part of that loan whenever part of the bank loan is to be repaid. In respect of shares issued before 17 March 2004, this would not have been appropriate where the shareholder's loan was made before the EIS share issue, as a repayment would have been treated as value received **[see 12.5.6]**.

Example 7.12

The share and loan capital of Principia Ltd is as follows:

	Issue date		*Two years later*	
	Shares	*Loans*	*Shares*	*Loans*
	£	£	£	£
Denis	45		45	
John Stuart	25	15	25	15
Friedrich	10		10	
George	20		20	
Bank loan		20		5
Total	**100**	**35**	**100**	**20**

Initially, John Stuart owns 25% of the company's share capital and 29.63% (40/135) of the combined share and loan capital. As a result of Principia's repayment of part of the bank loan in the following two years, John Stuart's interest increases to 33.33% (40/120) and all of his EIS investment and disposal relief is lost.

In deciding whether a person is connected with a company, guarantees are not taken into account. Therefore if an investee company requires further finance, it may be appropriate for a shareholder to act as guarantor for the company's loan, rather than actually lend money to the company. It must, however, be borne in mind that if the guarantee is called upon, the shareholder would become the company's creditor and, in that situation, could be entitled to more than 30% of the company's assets.

If a loss is made on a loan to a trader or as a result of meeting a guarantee of such a loan, capital loss relief is normally available **[see 23.6]**.

7.6.3.4 *Rights in a winding-up*

Assuming a hypothetical winding-up of the company at any time, an EIS shareholder must not have rights to more than 30% of the company's (or subsidiary's) assets that would then be available for distribution to the company's equity holders. For this purpose the persons who are equity holders exclude those who have made normal commercial loans (TA 1988, s 291B(2) and (3)).

Example 7.13

Sheila subscribes for 28% of Gish Ltd which owns 90% of Greta Ltd. Sheila also owns 6% of Greta Ltd in her own right. Sheila is not eligible for EIS investment or disposal relief as she has rights in a winding up of Greta to more than 30% of its assets and Greta is a subsidiary of Gish, the investee company. Sheila is entitled to 25.2% (28% × 90%) of Greta's assets indirectly and 6% directly.

7.6.3.5 *Ability to control the company or a subsidiary*

Even if an individual does not have a significant interest in the investee company or any of its subsidiaries under the above tests, he or she is still disqualified if, through other means, he or she can control the investee company or a subsidiary (TA 1988, s 291B(4)). Control for this purpose is subject to the narrower definition **[see 5.1.10]** so that it means the power of a person to secure:

(*a*) by means of the holding of shares or the possession of voting power in or in relation to that company or any other company; or
(*b*) by virtue of any powers conferred by the articles of association or other documents regulating that company or any other company

that the affairs of the first-mentioned company are conducted in accordance with the wishes of that person, and, in relation to a partnership, means the right to a share of more than one-half of the assets, or of more than one-half of the income, of the partnership (TA 1988, ss 291B(10) and 840).

This provision is also subject to the exception for subscriber shares **[see 7.6.3.2]**.

7.6.4 Replacement capital

7.6.4.1 *Introduction*

There are provisions designed to ensure that neither EIS investment nor EIS disposal relief is available to anyone who directly or indirectly owned the business before it became owned by the investee company. Although this part of the legislation (which goes under the title of 'replacement capital') refers to the withdrawal of relief, it also has the effect that where relief has not been given, it will be denied (TA 1988, s 312(4)).

An individual is not entitled to either EIS investment or EIS disposal relief if he or she alone or as part of a group of persons controls or has controlled a company; and

(*a*) the shares in that company or
(*b*) its trade or trading assets

are acquired at any time during the 'relevant period' by the EIS company or any of its subsidiaries. In deciding whether an individual controls a company for this purpose, the interests, rights and powers of his or her associates **[see 7.3.4.1]** are aggregated with the individual's (TA 1988, s 302(1) to (5)). In the case of investors who are paid directors, account is taken of previous control of the trade at any time, not just within the relevant period (TA 1988, s 302(4A)). This change was made to be consistent with the business angel rules **[see 7.6.2.11]**.

In this instance, the 'relevant period' is the period beginning with the later of:

(*a*) the company's incorporation and
(*b*) two years before the issue of the shares

and ending immediately before the later of:

(*a*) the third anniversary of the issue and
(*b*) the third anniversary of the date on which the company began to carry on the trade financed by the share issue

(TA 1988, ss 302(5), 312(1A)(a))

Example 7.14

Bertrand, Freddie, Martin, Jeremy and Nicole are in partnership selling video recorders. Subsequently Bertrand, Freddie, Martin and Renée set up a new company Vidrec Ltd and each of them subscribes £50,000 for 25% of the issued share capital. Vidrec intends to buy the partnership business.

Bertrand, Freddie, and Martin are members of a group that controls the trade that Vidrec intends to take over and are part of a different group that controls Vidrec's trade. If the sale goes ahead Bertrand, Freddie and Martin will not be eligible for EIS investment or disposal relief on their investment in Vidrec.

7.6.4.2 *Ownership of a trade*

Where a trade is carried on by two persons it belongs to them in the same proportion as they share the trading profits. If it is carried on by trustees it belongs to those who are entitled to the income from the trust. Where a trade is carried on by a company it belongs to the persons who own the ordinary share capital in proportion to their shareholdings (TA 1988, ss 302(4) and 344(1)–(3)).

A subsidiary for these purposes is a company that would be a qualifying subsidiary if its 'relevant period' were the period in **7.6.4.1**.

Where the investor is a director of the investee company (or of a partner or subsidiary company) and is entitled to receive reasonable remuneration, his or her control of the company that previously carried on the trade acquired by the investee company is tested over the whole of the time before the end of the relevant period (TA 1988, s 302(4A), (4B)).

7.6.5 Approved EIS funds

An approved EIS fund is a collective investment vehicle that meets certain guidelines that have been issued by the Inland Revenue. It is similar in some ways to a unit trust or VCT.

When an individual invests through an approved EIS fund, he or she receives a tax-relief certificate from the fund manager **[see 24.8]**. The individual can then claim income tax relief by reference to the date the fund closed, provided that 90% of the money raised is used to subscribe for qualifying shares within the following six months (TA 1988, s 311(2A), (2B)). However, the dates on which the shares are issued are still used to determine the periods of restriction for the individual and the company **[see 7.6.1.6** and **5.7.2]**. As the individual is acquiring an interest in a range of companies, he or she is also allowed to invest less than £500 in any one qualifying company (TA 1988, s 311(3)).

Example 7.15

Voltaire invests £2,000 in the Candide EIS Fund, which closes on 26 March 2004. The managers of the fund subscribe for the following shares on his behalf:

2004	*Company*	*Shares*	*Subscribed*
		No	£
4 April	Cunégonde Ltd	200	300
6 May	Pangloss Ltd	150	150
11 May	Issachar Ltd	400	400
23 June	Cacambo Ltd	200	500
13 July	Vanderdendur Ltd	150	450
9 August	Pacauette Ltd	200	200

If Voltaire had invested in these companies directly he would only have been entitled to EIS relief on the shares in Cacambo as the other subscriptions would have been too small.

Part 3

Investment Reliefs

Chapter 8

VCT Investment Relief

8.1 Introduction

Individuals who subscribe for eligible shares in a venture capital trust (VCT) company may claim an initial income tax relief (the 'investment relief') provided that they satisfy the conditions described in **Chapter 7** and the VCT company and the companies in which it invests satisfy the conditions in **Chapters 5** and **6**. The relief is only available where ordinary shares are subscribed for, not where they are purchased. The maximum income tax saving in any one tax year is £80,000 (40% of the share subscription limit of £200,000). This 'double' relief is available for two tax years only – 2004–05 and 2005–06. After 5 April 2006, the amount of relief reverts to 20%, but the increased investment limit of £200,000 remains in force. Before 6 April 2004, the maximum investment in any one tax year was £100,000. The same reliefs are available to a spouse. A second kind of relief, 'distribution relief', is available for purchased shares as well as for subscription shares. **See 8.5**.

8.1.1 Scope of this chapter

This chapter considers the following areas:

(*a*) Further introductory items **[see 8.1.2ff]**
(*b*) Entitlement to claim the relief **[see 8.2]**
(*c*) Amount of the relief **[see 8.3]**
(*d*) When the relief is given **[see 8.4]**
(*e*) The distribution relief **[see 8.5]**
(*f*) What happens when a person's investments exceed the £200,000 limit **[see 8.6]**.

8.1.2 Eligible shares

Eligible shares are new ordinary shares that, throughout the period of three years beginning with the date on which they are issued ('the period of restriction'), carry no present or future preferential right to dividends or to a company's assets on its winding up and no present or future right to be redeemed (TA 1988, Sch 15B, para 6(1)).

For shares issued before 6 April 2000, the period of restriction was five years, not three.

8.1.3 Pre-emption rights etc

The existence of pre-emption rights, the right of the company to purchase its own shares **[see 28.5]**, or a formula setting out how a price will be calculated when shares are purchased from shareholders, will not, of itself, prevent shares from being eligible shares.

8.1.4 Ordinary shares

Ordinary shares are all of a company's issued shares, however they are described, other than capital the holders of which have a right to a dividend at a fixed rate but have no other right to share in the profits of the company (TA 1988, s 832(1)). In other words, provided that preference shares are able to participate in surplus profits, they can be ordinary shares even though they cannot be eligible shares.

8.1.5 When shares are issued

In *National Westminster Bank plc v IRC; Barclays Bank plc v IRC* [1994] STC 184, the court was asked to decide whether BES shares had been issued by midnight of 15 March 1993. On 16 March 1993 the Chancellor had announced that for shares issued on or after that day there would be no entitlement to BES relief if the shareholder received a loan linked to his investment **[see 7.6.1.7]**. The banks in question had raised BES funds a week or more before the Budget, had allotted the shares, informed the subscribers that they had been successful, and given instructions for the name of the nominee company to be entered in the BES company's members' register. However, by midnight on 15 March 1993 this entry had not been made in the register.

The Inland Revenue submitted that the shares were not issued until the nominee company's name was entered in the register of members. The Inland Revenue lost at the High Court, where it was held that the shares had been issued before 16 March as the company was at that time irrevocably bound to complete the formalities and the taxpayer was bound to submit to their completion.

The Court of Appeal found in favour of the Inland Revenue, however. In a majority decision, the House of Lords dismissed the taxpayers' appeals, emphasising the difference between allotment and registration. It was said that an allotment created an enforceable contract for the issue of shares and conferred a right to be registered. It was registration that completed the process of issuing the shares. Until registration, the individual to whom the shares had been allotted was neither a member nor a shareholder (*Re Ambrose Lake Tin and Copper Co, Clarke's Case* (1878) 8 Ch D 635). On the facts of the case, the issue of shares could only take place after registration, which in all cases had taken place after 15 March 1993.

8.2 Entitlement to claim the relief

8.2.1 Individuals

The investment relief can only be claimed by individuals, not by trustees or companies. Furthermore, an individual cannot claim VCT investment relief unless he or she is at least 18 years of age (TA 1988, Sch 15B, para 1(4)).

8.2.2 Residence

The VCT investment relief can be claimed by an individual wherever he or she is resident. The Chief Secretary to the Treasury, then Mr Michael Portillo, when asked in 1994 whether EIS relief for non-residents was in the public interest, replied (the same holds good for the VCT scheme):

> 'The fact that the person is not resident is of no particular concern; he has a source of taxable income and he is choosing to offset part of his tax liability in the United Kingdom by investing in the scheme. Under the scheme, he receives tax relief only at 20 per cent and not at his marginal rate of tax, assuming that it is higher. Therefore he does not escape tax liability in the United Kingdom, nor is he induced to make the investment only for tax-driven reasons, because the investment will still have to make sense to him, as relief is being given at only 20 per cent and not at his marginal rate'.
>
> (HC Official Report SC A, 22 March 1994, col 788).

By contrast, the VCT deferral relief **[see Chapter 14]** could only be claimed by an individual who was UK-resident or ordinarily resident during his or her relevant period. For the effect of an individual change of country of residence for tax purposes after making a VCT (or EIS) investment **see 14.7.4 and 15.7.4**.

8.2.3 Individual's period of restriction

To be eligible for the investment relief and retain it, an individual must meet certain conditions during a period (known as the 'relevant period'), which starts with the later of (*a*) the date of incorporation of the company and (*b*) two years before the shares are issued, and ends immediately before the third anniversary of the share issue (TA 1988, Sch 15B, para 2(3)).

For shares issued before 6 April 2000, the relevant period ended five years after the issue date.

8.2.4 More than one share issue

Every time a VCT issues shares to individual investors a new relevant period commences for those shares.

8.2.5 Subscription for shares

The individual must subscribe on his or her own behalf for eligible shares **[see 7.3.2]** in a VCT (the investor company) (TA 1988, Sch 15B, para 1(2)).

8.2.6 Nominees and joint ownership

Although VCT shareholders must subscribe on their own behalf, the shares can be subscribed for by a nominee and shares can be owned jointly. However, in connection with tax-free dividends (the distribution relief – **[see 8.5]**), the VCT legislation refers to a nominee as including the trustees of a bare trust of which the individual is the only beneficiary (TA 1988, Sch 15B, para 9(2)).

8.2.7 Bona fide commercial subscription

An individual is not entitled to investment relief unless the shares are both subscribed for and issued for bona fide commercial purposes and not as part of a scheme or arrangement the main purpose of which, or one of the main purposes of which, is the avoidance of tax (TA 1988, Sch 15B, para 1(9)).

8.2.8 Loan-linked investments

It is a condition of obtaining (and retaining) the investment relief that the subscription must not have been linked with the obtaining of a loan on favourable terms. This condition is fully explained in **7.3.4**.

8.3 Amount of the relief

8.3.1 Annual limit on the subscription

The maximum amount of subscriptions in a tax year which attracts the investment relief is £200,000 for qualifying investments (TA 1988, Sch 15B, para 1(3)). Before 6 April 2004, the maximum was £100,000. For details of what happens when this limit is exceeded **[see 8.6]**.

Example 8.1

Ludwig's share transactions in a company that became a VCT at 20 October 2003 are as follows.

Date	*Transaction*	*Shares* No 000	*Cost* £000
Nov 2003	Subscription	60	60
Mar 2004	Purchase of shares	10	9
Oct 2004	Subscription	80	80
Jan 2005	Subscription	200	220

In 2003–04 Ludwig would be entitled to investment relief of £12,000 on his £60,000 subscription but not on his purchase.

In 2004–05 Ludwig would be entitled to investment relief of £80,000 made up as follows: £32,000 on his £80,000 subscription and £48,000 on £120,000 of his £220,000 subscription. The remaining £100,000 (being in excess of the £200,000 limit for the year) does not qualify for relief.

8.3.2 Minimum investment

The VCT legislation does not provide for a minimum subscription. However, VCTs may impose a minimum subscription of say £2,000 for administrative reasons.

8.3.3 Relief at one of two rates of tax

For shares issued (and therefore investments made) after 5 April 2004 and before 6 April 2006 (ie in the two tax years 2004–05 and 2005–06), individuals are able to obtain relief at the higher rate of income tax on the total of the amounts they have subscribed for eligible shares in a tax year or, if it is smaller, that amount which reduces the individual's liability to income tax for that year to nil (TA 1988, Sch 15B, para 1(5), as amended by FA 2004, s 94(1)).

For shares issued before 6 April 2004 and again for those issued after 5 April 2006, relief is given at the lower rate of income tax.

In 2004–05, the higher rate of income tax is 40% and the lower rate is 20%. These rates have remained unchanged since 1992–93.

The investment reliefs are given before other reliefs and VCT investment relief is given before other reliefs, including the EIS relief. For details on giving effect to the VCT investment relief in calculating the individual's tax liability see **Chapter 20**.

8.3.4 Attribution of VCT initial relief to shares

In contrast to the situation with EIS **[see Chapter 9]** there is no attribution of VCT investment relief to individual shares.

8.4 When the relief is given

An individual can elect to claim VCT investment relief on all or any of his or her subscriptions for eligible shares up to £200,000 in a tax year. VCT investment relief is not attributed to each share as is the case for EIS. Effect is given to VCT investment relief in the tax year in which the shares are issued, provided that the company has received VCT approval for that year (TA 1988, Sch 15B, para 1(1)). Again, unlike the EIS rules **[see 9.4.1]**, there can be no carry-back of VCT investment relief.

8.5 VCT distribution relief

8.5.1 Introduction

As was mentioned in **8.1**, there is a second form of income tax relief for investors in a VCT. This relief ('distribution relief') takes the form of an exemption from income tax on dividends received from a VCT.

8.5.2 Qualifying conditions

The qualifying conditions for distribution relief were outlined in **7.4**. For distribution relief, it is not necessary for the shares to have been obtained by subscription, nor indeed need they have qualified for VCT investment relief. Shares purchased or acquired by gift qualify equally.

It is a further condition of relief that the shares have been acquired for bona fide commercial purposes and not as part of a tax avoidance scheme (TA 1988, Sch 15B, para 7(3)(a)(ia)). This condition did not apply to acquisitions made before 9 March 1999.

8.5.3 Relevant distributions

The relief is given in respect of 'relevant distributions'. Relevant distributions are distributions by a VCT company which consist of a dividend (including a capital dividend) in respect of the company's ordinary shares paid in respect of (not necessarily during) an accounting period in which the company is a VCT. The investor must also have acquired the shares at a time when the company is a VCT (TA 1988, Sch 15B, para 7(3)).

8.5.4 The permitted maximum

The £200,000 permitted maximum investment in any tax year (£100,000 in tax years before 2004–05 and also in tax years after 2005–06) applies equally and jointly to the distribution relief as to the investment relief. This means that shares acquired by subscription and qualifying for investment relief and shares acquired by other means and qualifying for distribution relief but not for investment relief are aggregated in testing whether the maximum has been exceeded.

Example 8.2

If we return to the facts in Example 8.1, and assume Ludwig made a further purchase of shares in December 2004, we see that his pattern of acquisitions in the VCT company (which became a VCT at 20 October 2003) were as follows:

Date	*Transaction*	*No of shares (000)*	*Cost (£000)*
Nov 2003	Subscription	60	60
Mar 2004	Purchase	10	9
Total (2003–04)		**70**	**69**
Oct 2004	Subscription	80	80
Dec 2004	Purchase	20	18
Jan 2005	Subscription	200	220
Total (2004–05)		**300**	**318**

In 2003–04, the purchase of 10,000 shares for £9,000 does not qualify for investment relief but it would qualify for distribution relief. The £100,000 permitted maximum is not exceeded.

In 2004–05, Ludwig's purchase of a further 20,000 shares does not qualify for investment relief, but does qualify for distribution relief and counts towards the permitted maximum for both forms of relief. Accordingly, of the January 2005 subscription, only £102,000 of the investment qualifies for investment relief, whereas in Example 8.1, without the additional purchase, £120,000 qualified for investment relief.

8.6 Exceeding the £200,000 limit

8.6.1 Introduction

There will be occasions where investors in a particular tax year acquire VCT shares in excess of their £200,000 limit, either because of a misunderstanding of the rules or for commercial reasons.

Where, in a tax year, the value of an individual's acquisitions of VCT shares is more than £200,000 (£100,000 before the tax year 2004–05 and again in tax years after 2005–06), it is necessary to determine which shares represent the qualifying investment and which represent the excess (TA 1988, Sch 15B, para 8(1)). This is important for determining the shares on which investment relief should be given **[see 8.3.1]** or withdrawn **[see 17.4]**, whether the qualifying investment has been made within the period allowed **[see 14.3.2]** so that a gain can be deferred (but only in respect of investments made before 6 April 2004 **[see Chapter 14]**), and the extent to which an individual's dividends on his or her VCT shares should qualify for distribution relief **[see 8.5]**.

8.6.2 Acquisitions to be considered

The acquisitions of VCT shares to be considered in a tax year are all shares acquired as follows:

- shares acquired by the individual in question or by the individual's nominee;
- ordinary shares that were acquired when the company was a VCT

(TA 1988, Sch 15B, para 8(2)).

8.6.2.1 *VCT shares acquired on the same day*

Where eligible shares are acquired on the same day, investment relief is given on £200,000. Where different descriptions of shares in a single VCT are acquired on the same day, the qualifying investment and the excess is determined by apportioning the acquisitions by reference to their values (TA 1988, Sch 15B, para 8(6)(b)).

Example 8.3

On 14 May 2004 George subscribes £200,000 for A shares and £50,000 for B shares in a VCT. George can claim VCT investment relief on £160,000 (200/250 × £200,000) of the A shares and £40,000 (50/250 × £200,000) of the B shares.

8.6.2.2 *VCT shares acquired at different times*

Where shares are acquired at different times in the tax year, the shares representing the excess over £200,000 are identified as those that are acquired later (TA 1988, Sch 15B, paras 3(8)(a), 8(6)(a)). Although an individual must make a claim for VCT relief where he or she acquires more than the maximum VCT investment of £200,000 in a tax year, the individual is unable to choose on which of the VCT shares he or she can claim the relief.

Example 8.4

Freddie subscribes £100,000 for shares in Language VCT on 4 May 2003 and £100,000 for shares in Truth VCT on 23 March 2004. Freddie can claim VCT investment relief on all of the Language VCT shares but on none of the Truth VCT shares. This would be a problem if he was hoping to use his 23 March 2004 investment to defer a gain of £30,000 that arose on a disposal on 10 May 2004.

8.6.2.3 *Market value*

In determining the value of the shares acquired, the capital gains tax definition of market value applies (TA 1988, Sch 15B, para 8(5)). This is defined as the price that the shares in question might reasonably be expected to fetch on a sale in the open market (TCGA 1992, s 272(1)).

Example 8.5

Reece makes the following acquisitions of shares in VCTs:

1 May 2004	Subscription for 60,000 shares in Importance plc	£120,000
1 August 2004	Subscription for 30,000 shares in Being plc	£60,000
1 August 2004	Purchase of 40,000 shares in Importance plc	£100,000

The acquisition on 1 May 2004 is within the permitted maximum. Of the acquisitions on 1 August 2004, £80,000 exceeds the permitted maximum, and the excess is apportioned as to £30,000 (60/160 × £80,000) to the shares in Being and £50,000 (100/160 × £80,000) to the shares in Importance. This means that Reece will be able to claim investment relief and distribution relief in respect of £30,000 (£60,000 – £30,000) of the Being shares and distribution relief in respect of £50,000 (£100,000 – £50,000) of the Importance purchase as well as both reliefs for all of the 1 May subscription.

8.6.3 Share exchanges and reconstructions

A special rule applies where an investor holds ordinary shares in a VCT which, when acquired, did not exceed the permitted maximum, and in consequence of a scheme of reconstruction acquires new ordinary shares that are, for capital gains purposes, treated as the same assets as the original shares. Such new shares:

(*a*) are not taken into account in calculating whether other shares acquired in the same year exceed the permitted maximum; and

(*b*) are themselves treated as being within the permitted maximum, except that where part of the original shares was in excess of the permitted maximum, an appropriate proportion of the new shares is also treated as being in excess of the permitted maximum

(TA 1988, Sch 15B, para 8(4)).

Chapter 9

EIS Investment Relief

9.1 Introduction

A qualifying individual investor may claim income tax relief ('investment relief') on amounts that he or she subscribes for eligible shares in a qualifying company. The conditions that a qualifying individual must satisfy in respect of himself or herself and in respect of the investment are explained in **Chapter 7**. The conditions that must be satisfied by an EIS investee company (a 'qualifying company') are detailed in **Chapters 5** and **6**.

Investment relief is available only where the individual subscribes for shares, not for shares acquired by some other means, such as purchase or gift.

The maximum amount of relief obtainable in any tax year after 2003–04 is £40,000 (20% of the maximum qualifying subscription, namely £200,000). See **9.3.1** and **9.3.2** for the annual maxima and minima. In 2003–04 and earlier years, the maximum relief in any one year was £30,000 (20% of £150,000).

There is no 'distribution relief', as there is with the VCT scheme, so dividends from EIS investee companies are not exempt from income tax.

9.1.1 Scope of this chapter

This chapter considers the following areas:

(*a*) Further introductory items **[see 9.1.2–9.1.6]**
(*b*) Entitlement to claim the relief **[see 9.2]**
(*c*) Amount of the relief **[see 9.3]**
(*d*) When the relief is given **[see 9.4]**
(*e*) What happens when an individual's investments exceed the £200,000 limit **[see 9.5]**

9.1.2 Eligible shares

Eligible shares are new ordinary shares that, throughout the period beginning with the issue of the shares and ending on the later of:

(*a*) the third anniversary of the issue date and
(*b*) the third anniversary of the date on which the qualifying trade **[see Chapter 6]** began,

carry no present or future preferential right to dividends or to a company's assets on its winding-up and no present or future right to be redeemed (TA 1988, ss 289(7), 312(1)).

9.1.3 Pre-emption rights etc

The existence of pre-emption rights, the right of the company to purchase its own shares **[see 28.5]**, or a formula setting out how a price will be calculated when shares are purchased from shareholders, will not, of itself, prevent shares from being eligible shares.

9.1.4 Ordinary shares

Ordinary shares are all of a company's issued shares, however they are described, other than capital the holders of which have a right to a dividend at a fixed rate but have no other rights to share in the profits of the company (TA 1988, ss 312(1) and 832(1)).

9.1.5 When shares are issued

Shares are issued only once they have been fully registered **[see 8.1.5]**.

9.2 Entitlement to claim the relief

9.2.1 Individuals

EIS investment relief may only be claimed by individuals, not by trustees or companies. There is, however, no minimum age, as there is for the VCT scheme and the CVS, for investors.

9.2.2 Residence

There is no need for an individual to be UK-resident or ordinarily resident in order to claim the relief, although it will, of course, be of use only to an individual having a liability to UK income tax. For the rationale of not limiting the relief to UK residents, see the remarks of the Chief Secretary to the Treasury in the House of Commons in March 1994, reproduced in **8.2.2**.

For the effect of an individual's change of residence after making an EIS investment, see **15.7.4**.

9.2.3 Individual's period of restriction

To be eligible for the investment relief and to retain it, an individual must meet certain conditions during different periods of restriction. These periods are discussed in the appropriate section of the book. Thus, the period during which the individual must not be connected with the qualifying company is set out in **7.6.1.6**. For the period during which the individual must not receive 'value', **[see 12.5.2]**.

9.2.4 Several share issues

Every time that an EIS company issues shares to individual investors, a new period of restriction commences in respect of those shares. This can lead to complications when considering exit routes for EIS shareholders **[see Chapter 28]**.

9.2.5 Subscriptions for shares

The individual must subscribe in cash on his or her own behalf for eligible shares in an EIS company (TA 1988, s 289(1)(a)) and the EIS shares must be fully paid up at the issue date (TA 1988, s 289(1)(aa)).

However, where shares are issued after 16 March 2004, the fact that the investor may receive bonus shares of the same class on the same day does not prevent that investor from obtaining relief in respect of the shares for which he or she has subscribed in cash (TA 1988, s 289(1)(a), (1)(aza)).

9.2.6 Nominees and joint ownership

Although EIS shareholders must subscribe for shares on their own behalf, the shares can be subscribed for by a nominee (TA 1988, ss 291(1)(a) and 311(1)) and shares can be owned jointly **[see 7.6.1.2]**.

9.2.7 Bona fide commercial subscription

An individual is not entitled to investment relief unless the shares are both subscribed for and issued for bona fide commercial purposes and not as part of a scheme or arrangement the main purpose of which, or one of the main purposes of which, is the avoidance of tax (TA 1988, s 289(6)).

9.2.8 Loan-linked investments

It is a condition for obtaining (and retaining) the investment relief that the subscription not be linked with the obtaining of a loan on favourable terms. This condition is fully explained in **7.6.1.6**.

9.3 Amount of the relief

9.3.1 Annual limit on the subscription

The maximum amount of subscriptions in a tax year which attracts the investment relief is £200,000 (TA 1988, s 290(2)). For 2003–04 and earlier years, the maximum subscription was £150,000. The limit is applied to amounts subscribed in any tax year, regardless of when the shares may be issued. For details of what happens when this limit is exceeded, see **9.5**.

9.3.2 Minimum investment

Unless the investor uses the medium of an approved EIS investment fund, the minimum subscription in any one company in any one tax year qualifying for relief is £500. In the reverse of the rule for the maximum, what matters is what is subscribed for issues made in any one year, regardless of the amount actually subscribed in that year.

Example 9.1

Gwyneth subscribes £400 for shares in Shakespeare Ltd on 1 April 2004; the shares are issued on 7 April 2004. She subscribes a further £400 in the same company on 1 October 2004 for an issue on the same date. Gwyneth qualifies for relief in respect of the £800 invested in Shakespeare's issues in 2004–05, even though she actually subscribed less than £500 in both 2003–04 and 2004–05.

It is also possible to subscribe more than one amount of less than £500 in a given tax year in respect of issues by the same company and qualify for relief, if the aggregate amount subscribed for shares issued in the particular tax year is £500 or more. **See 7.6.1.8**.

9.3.3 Relief at the lower rate of tax

The individual obtains relief at the lower rate of income tax (currently 20%) on the total of the amount he or she has subscribed for eligible shares in the tax year, or, if it is smaller, the amount that reduces his or her income tax liability for that year to nil (TA 1988, s 289A(2)). For the order of set-off of various reliefs, see **Chapter 20**.

9.3.4 Restriction of investment relief

Investment relief may need to be restricted because one or more qualifying conditions have been breached, for example:

(*a*) where qualifying investments exceed £200,000 **[see 9.5]** or
(*b*) where the company has redeemed some of its share capital in the year before the issue **[see 12.5.4]**

9.3.5 Attribution of relief to shares

When EIS relief has been claimed on an issue of shares, it is apportioned over the number of shares in the issue. This is relevant if the investment relief has to be restricted, is later reduced or has to be withdrawn.

For reductions and withdrawals, see **Chapters 12** and **15**. For restriction caused by excessive investment, see **9.5.**

The general rule for attribution is that where investment relief is obtained in a tax year in respect of a single issue of shares, it is attributed pro rata to the shares in that issue (TA 1988, s 289B(2)(a)). Where investment relief has been obtained in respect of two or more issues, the relief for the year is apportioned between those issues in proportion to the amount subscribed and then attributed to those issues accordingly (TA 1988, s 289B(2)(b)). This means that if the total of two or more subscriptions for eligible shares in a tax year exceeds the permitted maximum, the excess is apportioned between all the subscriptions, not just attributed to the last subscription, as is the case for the VCT scheme, as illustrated by Example 8.2 in **8.5.4**. For how this works in practice, see Example 9.7 in **9.5**.

If after an original issue of EIS shares, the investee company makes a bonus issue, the attribution made in respect of the original issue is amended by treating the original issue as including the bonus issue and attributing the relief to each of the shares in the combined holding.

Example 9.2

Bernard subscribes for the following eligible shares:

1.7.04	10,000 ordinary shares in Making Sense Ltd @ £1	£10,000
1.12.04	20,000 ordinary shares in Morality Ltd @ £1.50	£30,000

Bernard's investment relief for 2004–05 is £8,000 (20% of £40,000), which is apportioned as to (10/40 × £8,000) = £2,000 (20p per share) to the Making Sense shares and (30/40 × £8,000) = £6,000 (30p per share) to the Morality shares.
On 1 October 2005, Morality Ltd makes a bonus issue of one new ordinary share for every four ordinary shares held, so that Bernard receives 5,000 bonus shares. The bonus shares are treated as part of the original holding, so that the relief of £6,000 is now attributable to 25,000 shares (24p per share). The original attribution to the Making Sense shares is not affected.

9.4 When the relief is given

An individual may elect to claim EIS investment relief on all or any of his or her qualifying subscriptions for eligible shares, up to an amount of £200,000 per year, as we have seen. Effect is given to EIS investment relief in the year in which the shares are issued (TA 1988, s 289A(1)). This is the case even if the subscriptions are paid in a different year, as illustrated by Example 9.1 in **9.3.2**. Accordingly, it is important to ensure that shares are issued in the same tax year as the subscription is made.

There are two exceptions to this general rule. The first is where the individual makes a claim to carry back some of the relief to the previous tax year **[see 9.4.1]** and the second is where investment is made through an approved EIS fund **[see 9.4.2]**.

9.4.1 Carry-back of EIS relief

Where taxable income is not known until after the end of the tax year, it is too late for most tax planning exercises, but it could still be worth investing under the EIS and making a carry-back claim.

Where EIS shares are issued before 6 October in a tax year, the individual may claim to carry back part of his or her subscription to the previous tax year. The shares that are the subject of the carry-back claim are treated as issued in the previous year and attract tax relief at the rate applicable in that earlier year. The maximum amount of subscriptions that can be carried back is one-half of each qualifying subscription, subject to an overall limit of £25,000. The amount carried back, taken together with the actual qualifying subscriptions in the earlier year, must not exceed £200,000 in 2004–05 or later years but £150,000 in 2003–04 and earlier years (TA 1988, s 289A (3), (4)).

The claim cannot be revoked.

Example 9.3

On 31 January 2004, Willard subscribes £140,000 for eligible shares in Stimulus Ltd and claims relief for 2003–04. On 31 July 2004, he subscribes £40,000 for eligible shares in Word Ltd. In his self-assessment return for 2004–05, he claims relief on £40,000 and asks for part of the relief to be given for 2003–04. The amount available for carry-back would normally be £20,000 (half of the subscription of £40,000), but the maximum he can claim for 2003–04 is £150,000, so only £10,000 can be carried back.

Example 9.4

Amanda, who subscribes £35,000 for 17,500 shares in August wishes to make the maximum carry-back claim. The maximum subscription that can be treated as relating to shares issued in the previous tax year is the smaller of (a) and (b) below:

(a) £17,500 being 8,750 shares (half the shares issued) at £2 a share;
(b) £25,000 being 12,500 shares at £2.

Example 9.5

On 5 September 2004 Joanne subscribes £60,000 for 80,000 eligible shares. Joanne can claim under the EIS to carry back up to £25,000 of her subscription. If she claims the maximum amount, 33,333 (25/60ths of £80,000) of her shares will be treated as issued in 2003–04.

9.4.2 Investment through approved EIS funds

Where an investment is made through an approved EIS fund **[see 7.6.5]**, the investment relief is given as if the shares were issued on the date on which the fund closes, provided that 90% or more of the total amount invested is subscribed for eligible shares issued within six months starting from the date the fund closes (TA 1988, s 311 (2A)).

Example 9.6

Edmund invests £20,000 in the Husserl EIS approved fund, which closes on 3 October 2004. More than 90% of the money raised is subscribed for EIS shares in the following six months. Edmund is treated as having shares issued to him on 3 October 2004. If he wishes, he can elect to treat half of the shares he subscribed for as issued in 2003–04.

9.4.2.1 *Attribution of relief carried back to shares*

When relief is carried back, the relevant shares are treated as if they had been issued in the previous year, and are therefore included in the shares to which the total relief in that year is attributed (TA 1988, s 289A(3)).

9.5 Exceeding the investment limit

There will be occasions where investors acquire EIS shares in excess of the permitted maximum in a particular year, either because of a misunderstanding of the rules or through commercial necessity.

We have already seen how relief is attributed to shares for EIS purposes **[see 9.3.5]**. On the occasion of an investment of more than the permitted maximum, the rules work like this.

Example 9.7

Hypatia's pattern of investment in EIS issues in 2004–05 is as follows:

Date	*Investee company*	*No of shares*	*Amount invested*
1.7.04	Theon Ltd	10,000	£20,000
11.11.04	Alexandria Group Ltd	35,000	£140,000
2.1.05	Theon Ltd	20,000	£40,000
31.3.05	Neoplatonism Ltd	4,000	£16,000
Total		**69,000**	**£216,000**

Hypatia has invested £16,000 over the limit (the entire late subscription to Neoplatonism Ltd). As Hypatia made no EIS investments in 2003–04, she can elect to carry back one-half of the amount subscribed to Theon Ltd in July 2004 back to 2003–04. The amount carried back is £10,000, attributed to 5,000 shares. That leaves an excess of £6,000. Instead of being attributed entirely to the Neoplatonism subscription, it is apportioned over all the subscriptions in 2004–05 (except the amount carried back) in this manner (to the nearest £):

1.7.04	(10,000/206,000) × £6,000	=	£291
11.11.04	(140,000/206,000) × £6,000	=	£4,078
2.1.05	(40,000/206,000) × £6,000	=	£1,165
31.3.05	(16,000/206,000) × £6,000	=	£466

This leaves the following picture for 2004–05:

Date	*Company*	*No of shares*	*Amount subscribed*	*Amount on which relief given*
1.7.04	Theon Ltd	5,000	£10,000	£9,709
11.11.04	Alexandria Group Ltd	35,000	£140,000	£135,922
2.1.05	Theon Ltd	20,000	£40,000	£38,835
31.3.05	Neoplatonism Ltd	4,000	£16,000	£15,534
Total		**64,000**	**£206,000**	**£200,000**

Chapter 10

CVS Investment Relief

10.1 Introduction

A company that makes a qualifying investment in a CVS investee company may claim corporation tax relief ('investment relief') on amounts that it subscribes for eligible shares in that company. The conditions that must be satisfied by the investor company and by its investments are described in **5.17**. The conditions that must be satisfied by the investee company are described in **Chapters 5** and **6.**

Investment relief is available only where the investor company subscribes for shares, and not where it acquires them by other means, such as purchase or transfer.

There is no 'distribution relief', as there is with the VCT scheme, so in the event that the investee company is non-resident, dividends from it will be taxable, subject to double tax relief for foreign withholding tax and, where appropriate, for foreign underlying tax. Dividends from UK investee companies would be exempt from corporation tax in any case.

10.1.1 Scope of this chapter

This chapter considers the following areas:

(*a*) Further introductory items **[see 10.1.2 and 10.1.3]**
(*b*) Entitlement to claim the relief **[see 10.2]**
(*c*) Amount of the relief **[see 10.3]**
(*d*) When the relief is given **[see 10.4]**

10.1.2 Eligible shares

Eligible shares are new ordinary shares that throughout the 'qualification period' carry no present or future preferential right to dividends or to a company's assets on its winding-up and no present or future right to be redeemed (FA 2000, Sch 15, para 35).

In this context, provided that the shareholder has a legal right, it does not matter whether that right is set out in the company's Articles of Association in a shareholder's agreement or in another document **[see 5.1.7]**.

For the meaning of ordinary shares, **see 8.1.4** and for the significance of pre-emption rights and deferred shares, **see 8.1.3** and **8.1.5**, respectively. These matters apply equally as regards the CVS.

10.1.3 Fully paid-up shares

All CVS shares must be fully paid up at the issue date, but there is no requirement for all the investee company's shares to be fully paid up. An undertaking to pay cash to the investee company (and, for shares issued after 16 March 2004, any other person in respect of the acquisition) at a future date is not sufficient to make shares fully paid up (FA 2000, Sch 15, para 35(2)).

10.2 Entitlement to claim the relief

10.2.1 Companies

Since the CVS is intended for corporate investors only, investment relief may be claimed by companies only (FA 2000, Sch 15, para 39(1)).

10.2.2 Residence

There is no requirement on the investor company to be UK-resident. For the relief to be of any use to a non-resident company, of course, it must have a liability to UK corporation tax, which in turn means in the case of a non-resident company that it must be carrying on a trade in the UK through a UK permanent establishment (TA 1988, s 11(1)).

A 'company' is 'any body corporate or unincorporated association but does not include a partnership, a local authority or a local authority association' (TA 1988, s 832(1)). Some forms of foreign legal entity that are recognised as corporations in their state of residence may not be so regarded by the Inland Revenue, and vice versa.

10.2.3 The qualification period and the period of restriction

The qualifying conditions described in **Chapters 5 and 6** must be satisfied throughout the 'qualification period'. This is the period that begins on the issue date and ends on the later of (*a*) the date immediately before the third anniversary of the issue date and (*b*) the date immediately before the third anniversary of the commencement of the qualifying trade (FA 2000, Sch 15, para 3).

However, when it comes to a receipt of 'value' by the investor company, which is an occasion for the reduction or withdrawal of relief, a different period ('the period of restriction') applies **[see 13.2.1]**.

10.2.4 Bona fide commercial subscription

The subscription by the investor company for shares must be made for 'commercial reasons' and not as part of a tax avoidance scheme (FA 2000, Sch 15, para 14).

10.3 Amount of the relief

10.3.1 No limit on the subscription

By contrast with both the VCT scheme and the EIS, in the CVS there is no maximum on the amount of subscriptions that may qualify for investment relief in any accounting period. For that matter, there is no minimum subscription either.

However, the relief obtained is limited by the amount of the investor company's liability to corporation tax in that period **[see 10.3.2]**.

10.3.2 Relief at a fixed rate

The relief is given in the form of a reduction in the investor company's liability to corporation tax, not as a deduction in computing the taxable profits. This puts it fully in line with the VCT and EIS investment reliefs.

The amount of the reduction is computed as 20% of the qualifying investment(s) in the accounting period concerned, limited by the company's corporation tax liability (ie it cannot create a loss) (FA 2000, Sch 15, para 39(2)). The 20% rate corresponds to the 20% applying for the EIS relief, but no longer corresponds to the small companies rate of corporation tax, which it did originally.

10.3.3 Attribution of relief

The rules for attributing the relief to particular shares and share issues are similar to those for the EIS **[see 9.3.5]**.

Where relief is successfully claimed in respect of two or more issues in any accounting period, the relief is attributed to the shares in proportion to the amounts subscribed (FA 2000, Sch 15, para 45(2)).

Example 10.1

Berkeley plc makes two CVS investments in its accounting period, the year ended 31 December 2004. They are:

25.7.04	Hylas Ltd	20,000 shares	£100,000
28.12.04	Philonous Ltd	15,000 shares	£75,000

Berkeley obtains the maximum relief (20% × £175,000) = £35,000 for the investments. It is apportioned as to (100/175) × £35,000 = £20,000 to the Hylas shares and (75/175) × £35,000 = £15,000 to the Philonous shares.

Where there is a bonus issue, the bonus shares are deemed to have been comprised in the original holding and the relief attributed to the original holding is attributed proportionately also to the bonus shares (FA 2000, Sch 15, para 45(3)–(5)).

Example 10.2

Taking the facts of Example 10.1, suppose that Hylas Ltd makes a 2:5 bonus issue on 1 January 2005. The relief attributed to the Hylas shares was £20,000 (or £1 per share). The bonus issue increases the holding to 28,000 shares, diluting the relief to 71.4p per share.

These rules enable relief that needs to be reduced or withdrawn in full in the event of a breach of the qualifying conditions to be attributed to the appropriate shares.

10.4 When the relief is given

A CVS investor company receives relief in respect of the shares *issued* to it in the accounting period concerned, regardless of when the subscription is actually made (FA 2000, Sch 15, para 39(1)).

As to when shares are issued, see **8.1.5**.

10.4.1 Carry-back not available

There is no carry-back or carry-forward of CVS investment relief. Any relief that is restricted by reference to the company's liability to corporation tax is 'lost'.

Part 4

Reduction or Withdrawal of Investment Reliefs

Chapter 11

Losing VCT Investment Relief

11.1 Introduction and background

11.1.1 Introduction

The Government considers that the VCT, EIS and CVS reliefs are very generous. While wishing to encourage investment in unquoted trading companies, it did and does not want to see any of these reliefs abused. Accordingly, for each relief there is a period or periods during which certain conditions have to be met. If either the investor or the investee company fails to meet these conditions during the specified period(s), tax relief may be reduced or withdrawn.

In the EIS and CVS, there are also rules penalising the investor who receives 'value' from the investee company after claiming and receiving relief. The VCT scheme contains no similar rules, but in common with the others denies or withdraws relief where the investment is or becomes linked with the receipt of a loan on favourable terms ('loan-linked investments'). In all three schemes, relief is withdrawn if the shares are disposed of within a specified period of time. Disposal of venture capital investments, and its consequences, is dealt with in **Chapters 17, 18** and **19**.

This chapter (for the VCT scheme) and **Chapters 12** and **13** (for the EIS and CVS, respectively) explain the situations in which relief is lost (without there being a disposal of the investment) for each of the schemes in turn. It should be borne in mind that on some occasions, relief is withdrawn entirely and on others reduced (ie partially withdrawn). For the sake of convenience, we shall refer to 'withdrawal' when we mean entire withdrawal and to 'reduction' when we mean a partial withdrawal of relief. Where either or both is in point, we shall refer to a 'loss' of relief.

For an explanation of the mechanism for withdrawing or reducing relief, as opposed to the occasions causing withdrawal or reduction, see **Chapter 20**.

11.1.2 Scope of this chapter

This chapter is concerned with the following areas:

(*a*) Occasions on which relief may be lost **[see 11.1.3]**
(*b*) Loan-linked investments **[see 11.2]**
(*c*) Breach of qualifying conditions **[see 11.3]**

11.1.3 Occasions for loss of relief

Perhaps because of the indirect method of investment, the VCT scheme has the least number of and the least complicated provisions dealing with loss of relief. There are only three separate occasions on which VCT relief, once given, may be lost. They are:

(*a*) on the receipt of a favourable loan (a 'linked loan') – see **11.2**
(*b*) on a breach of the qualifying conditions – see **11.3**; and
(*c*) on an early disposal of the investment – see **Chapter 17**.

11.2 The receipt of a linked loan

11.2.1 Background

Investments linked to the receipt by the investor of a loan became so popular and expensive to the Treasury in the days of the BES that they were stopped in the March 1993 Budget. All three schemes featured in this book contain a rule that the tax relief is withdrawn if such loans are made at any time in the restricted period.

11.2.2 The restricted period

As was explained in **7.3.4**, it is impossible for an investor to receive VCT relief if at the time the shares are issued or in the intervening period before the claim to relief is made, he or she has received a 'linked loan'. However, once relief has been given, it may still be withdrawn if such a loan is received after the claim has been made and accepted. The period (referred to in the legislation as the 'relevant period') during which there is a prohibition on such loans is the period beginning on the later of:

(*a*) the incorporation of the VCT company (the investor company) and
(*b*) the day two years before the issue date

and ending immediately before the third anniversary of the issue date (TA 1988, Sch 15B, para 2(3)). The maximum length of the period is thus five years.

For shares issued before 6 April 2000, the period ended five years after the issue date; hence the maximum length of the period was seven years. Some such periods will therefore still be current.

Example 11.1

Quine makes the following investments in VCT companies:

1 March 2000	25,000 shares in Akron plc	£75,000
1 May 2000	10,000 shares in Orman plc	£15,000

Akron plc was incorporated on 1 January 1996 whereas Orman plc was not incorporated until 25 August 1999.

The periods during which Quine may not receive linked loans with respect to Akron and Orman are therefore:

Akron:	1 March 1998 to 28 February 2005
Orman:	25 August 1999 to 30 April 2003

A 'loan' for this purpose includes the giving of credit and the assumption of a debt (TA 1988, Sch 15B, para 2(2)). The loan may be made by any person, not necessarily the VCT company or any person connected with it (TA 1988, Sch 15B, para 2(1)(a)).

For the circumstances in which a loan is considered to be linked to the investment, see **7.3.4**.

11.2.3 Consequence of receiving a linked loan

If the investor receives a linked loan at any time during the restricted period, investment relief in respect of those shares is withdrawn, as he or she ceases to be entitled to the relief (TA 1988, Sch 15B, para 2(1)). The amount or duration of the loan is irrelevant. Accordingly, the same consequences follow as on any other breach of the qualifying conditions **[see 11.3]**.

A withdrawal of investment relief on the grounds that a linked loan has been received has no effect on the availability of distribution relief, however. Provided that the company is still a VCT, that the holding was acquired within the annual permitted maximum by the investor when the company was a VCT, and is paid out of profits earned while the company was a VCT, distribution relief remains available.

11.3 Breach of the qualifying conditions

11.3.1 No limit to the restricted period

There must be no breach of the qualifying conditions with respect to the investor **[see Chapter 7]**, the investee company **[see Chapters 5 and 6]** or the investment itself **[see Chapter 7 also]**.

There is no finite period during which these conditions must be satisfied. Relief will be lost if they are broken at any time, subject to limited exceptions.

11.3.2 Consequence of a breach

Subject to the exceptions referred to in **20.4**, a breach of the qualifying conditions leads to a loss of entitlement to the investment relief, and hence to its withdrawal.

Chapter 12

Losing EIS Investment Relief

12.1 Introduction and background

12.1.1 Introduction

As explained in **11.1.1**, there are various events that can give rise to a loss of EIS investment relief. Those events will be discussed in this chapter, with the exception of an early disposal of EIS shares, which is covered, together with all disposals of EIS shares and their consequences, in **Chapter 18**.

For an explanation of the terms 'loss', 'reduction' and 'withdrawal' of relief as they are used in this chapter, see **11.1.1**.

12.1.2 Scope of this chapter

This chapter is concerned with the following areas:

(*a*) Occasions for loss of investment relief **[see 12.2]**
(*b*) Breach of the qualifying conditions **[see 12.3]**
(*c*) Loan-linked investment **[see 12.4]**
(*d*) The receipt of value **[see 12.5]**
(*e*) The exception for receipts of insignificant value **[see 12.6]**
(*f*) The exception for return of replacement value **[see 12.7]**
(*g*) Value received by other shareholders **[see 12.8]**
(*h*) The former rules for receipts of value by other members generally **[see 12.9]**
(*i*) The receipt of replacement capital **[see 12.10]**

12.2 Occasions giving rise to loss of investment relief

A loss of EIS investment relief may be caused by the occurrence during a specified period of any of the following events:

(*a*) breach of the qualifying conditions in respect of investors, investee companies or the investment itself **[see 12.3]**;

(*b*) a disposal by the investor of some or all of the EIS shares **[see Chapter 18]**;
(*c*) the receipt of a 'linked loan' by the investor **[see 12.4]**;
(*d*) the receipt of 'value' by the investor from the company **[see 12.5 to 12.7]**;
(*e*) the receipt of 'value' by other shareholders **[see 12.8 to 12.9]**;
(*f*) the receipt by the investor of 'replacement capital' **[see 12.10]**.

12.2.1 Restricted periods

The periods during the currency of which these events cause relief to be reduced (to nil where appropriate) or withdrawn vary from one event to another. See under the relevant provision for details.

12.3 Breach of the qualifying conditions

12.3.1 The restricted period

There must be no breach of the qualifying conditions, whether with respect to the individual investor **[see Chapter 7]**, the investee company **[see Chapters 5 and 6]** or with respect to the investment itself **[see also Chapter 7]**.

However, there is potential for considerable confusion in the proliferation of 'restricted periods'. Generally speaking, the restricted period in relation to the investor and breach of the qualifying conditions is one of two differing periods. For example, the period during which an investor may not be connected with the company is the period that begins two years before the shares are issued and ends immediately before the later of:

(*a*) the third anniversary of the issue date and
(*b*) the third anniversary of the date on which the trade that the share issue was intended to finance commenced

(TA 1988, ss 291(1)(b), 312(1)).

Other conditions, however, have to be satisfied during the so-called 'relevant period', which is the period that begins on the later of:

(*a*) the date of incorporation of the company and
(*b*) two years before the date on which the qualifying trade begins

and ends immediately before the later of:

(*a*) the third anniversary of the issue date and
(*b*) the third anniversary of the date on which the trade that the share issue was intended to finance commenced

(TA 1988, s 312(1A)(a)).

Reference must be had to where the particular condition is covered to find which restricted period is the one applying to that condition.

The picture is relatively simpler when it comes to the restricted period during which the investee company must satisfy the qualifying conditions. That period is generally the period that begins with the issue of the shares and ends immediately before the later of:

(*a*) the third anniversary of the issue date and
(*b*) the third anniversary of the date on which the trade that the share issue was intended to finance commenced

(TA 1988, s 312(1A)(b)).

12.3.2 Consequence of a breach of the qualifying conditions

A breach of the qualifying conditions results in a loss of entitlement to relief, so that any relief given is withdrawn.

12.4 The receipt of a linked loan

12.4.1 The restricted period

As was explained in **7.6.1.7**, it is impossible for an investor to receive EIS relief if at the time the shares are issued or in the intervening period before the claim to relief is made, he or she has received a 'linked loan'. However, once relief has been given, it may still be withdrawn if such a loan is received after the claim has been made and accepted. The period (referred to in the legislation as the 'relevant period') during which there is a prohibition on such loans is the period beginning on the later of:

(*a*) the incorporation of the EIS company and
(*b*) the day two years before the issue date

and ending immediately before the later of:

(*a*) the third anniversary of the issue date and
(*b*) the third anniversary of the date on which the trade that the share issue was intended to finance commenced

(TA 1988, ss 299A(3), 312(1A)(a)). The maximum length of the period is thus five years.

For shares issued before 6 April 2000, the period ended five years after the issue date; hence the maximum length of the period was seven years. Some such periods will therefore still be current.

Example 12.1

Anderson makes the following investments in EIS companies:

1 March 2000	25,000 shares in Sydney Ltd	£50,000
15 June 2000	10,000 shares in John Ltd	£10,000

Sydney Ltd was incorporated on 1 January 1996 whereas John Ltd was not incorporated until 3 February 2000.

The periods during which Anderson may not receive linked loans with respect to Sydney and John are therefore:

Sydney:	1 March 1998 to 28 February 2005
John:	3 February 2000 to 14 June 2003

A 'loan' for this purpose includes the giving of credit and the assumption of a debt (TA 1988, s 299A(2)). The loan may be made by any person, not necessarily the EIS company or any person connected with it (TA 1988, s 299A(1)(a)).

For the circumstances in which a loan is considered to be linked to the investment, see **7.6.1.7**.

12.4.2 Consequence of receiving a linked loan

If the investor receives a linked loan at any time during the restricted period, investment relief in respect of those shares is withdrawn, as he or she ceases to become entitled to the relief (TA 1988, 299A(1)). The amount or duration of the loan is irrelevant. Accordingly, the same consequences follow as on any other breach of the qualifying conditions **[see 12.3]**.

12.5 The receipt of value

12.5.1 Introduction

The rules against receipts of 'value' are primarily designed to prevent an investor in EIS shares from having access to the capital invested by direct or indirect means. They work by causing investment relief to be reduced or withdrawn.

The value-received rules for EIS are very widely drawn. They do not simply relate to payments received by the investor and his or her associates from the company but also from a person connected with the company, and beyond that to value received by other members of the investee company **[see further 12.5.3 and 12.8.1]**.

When considering whether an individual has received value, any reference to a payment or transfer to an individual includes a reference to a payment or transfer made to that individual indirectly or to or for his or her order or benefit (TA 1988, s 301(6)(a)).

After 6 March 2001, relief is not withdrawn or reduced if the value received is 'insignificant' **[see 12.6]** or if 'replacement value' is returned to the company within certain time limits **[see 12.7]**.

12.5.2 The restricted period

The period during which value must not be received (known in the legislation as 'the period of restriction') is the period beginning one year before the issue date and ending immediately before the later of:

(*a*) the third anniversary of the issue date and
(*b*) the third anniversary of the date on which the qualifying trade began

(TA 1988, s 312(1)).

Before 7 March 2001, a different period (and a different name – the 'designated period') applied. That period was identical to the period of restriction, except that it began *two* years before the issue date (TA 1988, s 291(6), now repealed).

12.5.3 The meaning of value and when it is received

Value is received when, during the period of restriction, any of the following events occurs:

(*a*) the company repays, redeems or repurchases any of its share capital or other securities which belong to the investor **[see 12.5.4]**;
(*b*) a person connected with the company purchases any of the company's shares or securities belonging to the investor **[see 12.5.5]**;
(*c*) the company or a person connected with the company makes a payment to the investor for giving up his or her right to any of the company's share capital or securities on their cancellation;
(*d*) the company makes a payment to the investor for giving up his or her right to a debt other than an ordinary trade debt or a debt for reimbursement of travelling expenses or reasonable remuneration for services **[see 12.5.7]**;
(*e*) the company releases or waives the investor's liability to the company or discharges the investor's liability to a third person **[see 12.5.8]**;
(*f*) the company makes the investor a loan, unless it is repaid in full before the issue of the EIS shares **[see 12.5.9]**;
(*g*) the company provides the investor with a benefit or facility **[see 12.5.10]**;
(*h*) the company transfers assets to, or receives assets from, the investor otherwise than at market value **[see 12.5.11]**;
(*i*) the company makes a payment to the investor in connection with the winding-up of the company **[see 12.5.12.1]**;
(*j*) the company makes any other payment other than those that are qualifying payments **[see 12.5.12.2]**; or

(*k*) the investor receives in respect of ordinary shares a payment or asset in a winding-up of the company in circumstances where it does not cease to be a qualifying company

(TA 1988, s 300(2), (3)).

Where the EIS shares were issued before 17 March 2004, value was also received by an investor if the company repaid a debt owed to him or her, and incurred before the investor subscribed for the shares. However, where the shares concerned are issued after 16 March 2004, a loan repayment only constitutes value if the loan was associated with the acquisition and the debt was incurred before the subscription **[see fully 12.5.6]**.

12.5.3.1 *Associates and connected persons*

For the purposes of the value-received rules, an investor is treated as receiving value whenever an associate of his or hers receives value (TA 1988, s 301(6)(b)). For the meaning of 'associate', see **7.3.4.1**. An investor is also treated as receiving value from a company if he or she receives value from a person connected with the company. For this purpose, the connection subsists for the duration of the 'relevant period', whether or not the connection exists at the time the individual receives the value (TA 1988, s 300(1C)).

The 'relevant period' here means the period beginning on the later of:

(*a*) the date of incorporation of the company and
(*b*) two years before the date on which the shares were issued.

and ending immediately before the later of:

(*a*) the third anniversary of the issue date and
(*b*) the third anniversary of the date on which the trade that the share issue was intended to finance commenced

(TA 1988, ss 300(1C), 301(6A), 312(1A)(a)).

The definition of 'connected person', except where there is a specific rule to the contrary, is that found in TA 1988, s 839. For an explanation of what this means, see **5.1.6**.

12.5.4 Repayment, repurchase or redemption of any shares or securities

Where an investor holds shares or securities in an EIS company, he or she is treated as receiving value from the company if the company repays, repurchases or redeems any of the investor's shares or securities during the period of restriction [for which **see 12.5.2**]. There is no restriction on the type of share or security that is purchased or redeemed; for example, it includes the redemption of preference shares or debentures held by the investor and is not limited to the investor's EIS shares.

12.5.4.1 *Amount of value received*

The value received on the occasion of a repayment, repurchase or redemption is the greater of the amount received and the market value of the shares or securities concerned (TA 1988, s 300(4)(a)).

Example 12.2

In June 2004, Baader and Ficino each hold 2,000 £1 redeemable preference shares in Figline Ltd, in which Passmore holds 96% of the ordinary shares. In July 2004, Baader and Ficino each subscribe £10,000 for ordinary shares in Figline. They each receive £2,000 of EIS investment relief. The company redeems Baader's preference shares in May 2005 at £1.20, which is their market value.

Baader is treated as receiving value of 2,000 × £1.20 = £2,400. As a result, his relief is reduced by £2,400 @ 20% = £480.

12.5.5 Purchase of shares or securities by connected person

The second occasion on which value is received in the list in **12.5.3** (see paragraph (*b*)) is on the purchase by a person connected with the company of any shares and securities in the investee company held by the investor or an associate of the investor (TA 1988, s 300(5)(a)). Here, 'connected person' means a person connected with the investee company for EIS purposes (ie a director, employee, person with an interest of more than 30% etc – see **7.6.2**).

12.5.5.1 *Amount of value received*

The value received is again said to be the greater of the amount received and the market value of the shares or securities.

Example 12.3

Take the facts of Example 12.2, but suppose that instead of undergoing redemption, Baader's shares are sold to Passmore in June 2006 for their market value at that time of £2,500. Passmore is connected with the company, and hence Baader loses £500 of his relief.

Example 12.4

The issued share capital of LCD Ltd comprises 100,000 £1 ordinary shares. Lucy holds 60,000 while Cameron and Drew both hold 20,000. Cameron and Drew sell their shares at par to Lucy. The following day, they subscribe for a further 50,000 shares each at par. LCD has obtained £100,000 of new equity capital, but £40,000 has effectively come from Lucy. Cameron and Drew both qualify for EIS investment relief but since they have received value before their subscription, their relief is limited in both cases to 20% of (£50,000–£20,000).

12.5.6 Repayment of investor's loan

As the aim of the EIS is to raise additional capital, one can understand why there has been a rule that prevents an individual who is already the company's loan creditor from having his or her loan converted into shares of that company and receiving EIS relief. However, there has always been a good case for saying that the aim of the EIS would still be served if relief had been available when an unsecured loan was converted into ordinary shares in the borrowing company. The effect would be to substitute a situation where the lender could demand repayment from the company at any time, leaving it in a precarious position, for what would have been a minimum three-year equity investment.

Be that as it may, the situation as respects shares issued before 17 March 2004 is that where the company repays any debt owed to the investor, the investor is treated as receiving value from the company. However, any debt incurred by the company on or after the date on which the individual acquired his or her shares, assuming it was not consideration for the extinguishment of an earlier debt, is ignored (TA 1988, s 300(2)(b)).

However, the force of this argument has finally been recognised and FA 2004 has removed the penalty for repayments of loans not connected with the acquisition of the shares.

As respects EIS shares issued after 16 March 2004, there is a receipt of value only where the company repays a debt to the investor that it incurred 'in pursuance of any arrangements for or in connection with the acquisition of the shares in respect of which the relief is claimed' (TA 1988, s 300(2)(b), as substituted by FA 2004, Sch 18, para 6(1)). Even where the loan and the acquisition are connected, there is still no receipt of value where the loan was incurred *after* the issue date and was not consideration for extinguishment of an earlier loan.

There is a transitional provision. The old rule continues to apply where a debt incurred before 17 March 2004 is repaid if the investor subscribed for the shares before that date also and the subscription took place on the same day or before the loan was made (FA 2004, Sch 18, para 6(3)).

12.5.6.1 *Amount of value received*

When an investor's debt is repaid, and value is deemed to have been received, the amount of that value is the greater of the payment received and the market value of the debt (TA 1988, s 300(4)(a)).

Example 12.5

Erigena Ltd, a company owned by John Scotus, is short of cash. In February 2002, John Scotus, who has not been able to draw his own salary for several months, borrows £10,000 from Adam and the company borrows £9,000 from Dugald to pay its employees' wages for one month. On 1 March 2003, Adam and

Dugald both agree to subscribe £40,000 for a 20% interest in the company. Both receive £8,000 in EIS investment relief (£40,000 @ 20%). In March 2004, John Scotus repays Adam's loan. As Adam is now an EIS investor in Erigena and John Scotus is connected with Erigena, this is repayment of a loan incurred before the subscription and therefore a receipt of value. Adam's relief is reduced by £10,000 @ 20% = £2,000. Dugald's loan is repaid by the company on 1 January 2006, and his relief is reduced by £9,000 @ 20% = £1,800 accordingly. If he and the company had agreed to delay the repayment by just two months, the period of restriction would have ended, and there would have been no reduction of Dugald's relief.

Since the shares were issued before 17 March 2004, it does not matter that the loan was not originally made as a condition for the share issue, or was not otherwise connected with the issue. Nor for the same reason would it have made any difference to Adam if John Scotus had repaid the loan in April 2004, say. If, however, the share issue by Erigena to which Adam and Dugald both subscribed had taken place at any time after 16 March 2004, neither the repayment received by Adam nor that received by Dugald would have been deemed to be a receipt of value.

12.5.6.2 *Loan sandwich*

Where an individual wishes to acquire shares and lend money to the company, it has hitherto been important that he or she make the loan after the share acquisition so that it can be repaid if the individual so wishes within the period of restriction without a clawback of relief.

There has been a pitfall for EIS investors because the EIS period of restriction commences before the shares are issued **[see 12.5.2]**. What could happen is that within a year of making the loan, the shareholder subscribes for more shares in the company and finds that the loan is sandwiched between the two share issues. In such a case the loan could not be repaid until the end of the period of restriction for the second share issue. If it was repaid before then, the investor has not been eligible for all or part of his or her EIS relief on the second share issue.

Example 12.6

Madhva subscribes £10,000 for ordinary shares in Udipi Ltd on 1 March 2003 and receives £2,000 EIS relief. Six months later a cash shortage arises. Madhva agrees to lend £5,000 to the company. A year later the company wishes to expand into a different market and existing shareholders are asked to subscribe for more shares. If Madhva were to subscribe for more shares (which are issued before 17 March 2004) and receive EIS relief he would be locking in his £5,000 loan for another three years.

The position changes for shares issued after 16 March 2004, as we have seen in **12.5.6**. The existence of a 'loan sandwich' no longer prevents repayment of the loan before the end of the period of restriction for the second issue, because there is no receipt of value as a result, provided that there is no connection between the loan and the share issue. It does not matter if the first issue predates 17 March 2004, as the loan repayment takes place after that issue and so does not in any way constitute a receipt of value.

Example 12.7

If the second issue of shares by Udipi Ltd in Example 12.6 takes place after 16 March 2004, Madhva's loan is not locked in and he may receive a repayment at any time without losing EIS investment relief.

12.5.7 Payment for giving up right to a debt

The investor is treated as receiving value if the company pays him or her for giving up his or her right to any debt (with three exceptions) on its extinguishment. The exceptions are:

(*a*) a debt that is an ordinary trade debt **[see 12.5.7.1]**;
(*b*) allowable travelling expenses **[see 12.5.7.2]**; and
(*c*) payments for services and other payments **[see 12.5.7.2]**

(TA 1988, 300(2)(c)).

12.5.7.1 *Meaning of 'an ordinary trade debt'*

An ordinary trade debt means any debt for goods or services supplied in the ordinary course of a trade or business where the credit given does not exceed six months and is not longer than that normally given to the customers of the person carrying on the trade or business (TA 1988, s 301(5)).

Where the company owes money to the investor, it would be an ordinary trade debt if, for example, the investor is in business as a designer and has provided the company with designs on normal credit terms.

12.5.7.2 *Debts for travelling expenses and services*

The second class of exception relates to amounts owed to the investor or the investor's associate by way of:

(*a*) travelling or other expenses incurred wholly, exclusively and necessarily by him or her or by the associate in fulfilling that individual's duties as a director of the company; and (*b*) any reasonable and necessary remuneration for services rendered to the investee company or a related person for business or professional services (excluding secretarial or managerial services) and taken or liable to be taken into account in computing that individual's Schedule D Case I or II profit

(TA 1988, ss 300(2)(c) and 291A(3)(a), (f)).

12.5.7.3 *Amount of value received*

When an investor receives payment for giving up his or her right to a debt, he or she is deemed to receive value of an amount equal to the greater of the payment received and the market value of the debt (TA 1988, s 300(4)(a)).

12.5.8 Release of investor's liabilities

An EIS investor is treated as having received value if the company:

(*a*) releases or waives any liability he or she has to the company; or
(*b*) discharges, or undertakes to discharge, any liability that the investor has to a third person

(TA 1988, s 300(2)(d)).

A company is treated as having released or waived a liability if the liability is not discharged within 12 months of the time when it ought to have been discharged (TA 1988, s 301(3)). There is no exception for ordinary trade debts, such as the investor may have if he or she was in business and had bought goods for resale on normal credit terms from the company.

12.5.8.1 *Amount of value received*

For EIS purposes, the value received is taken to be the amount of the liability (TA 1988, s 300(4)(b)).

Example 12.8

Cate subscribes £10,000 for ordinary shares in Lothlorien Ltd and receives £2,000 EIS relief. Two years later the company's accounts shows that she owes the company £1,500 for a computer that she purchased 14 months earlier on one month's credit. Cate would be treated as having received value of £1,500 from the company and would lose £300 (£1,500 × 20%) of her relief.

Example 12.9

Thomas subscribes £10,000 for ordinary shares in Reid Ltd and receives £2,000 EIS relief. A year later the company agrees to pay Thomas's liability of £4,000 to the local builder who had repaired his house. Thomas would be treated as having received £4,000 from the company and would lose £800 (£4,000 × 20%) of his relief.

12.5.9 Loans to investors

An investor who has acquired eligible shares and obtained EIS relief is not allowed to have access to that money by borrowing from the company or by assigning his or her third-party debts to the company. Any money that the investor borrows from, or any debt that he or she incurs with, the company is treated as value received unless it is repaid in full before the shares are acquired (TA 1988, s 300(2)(e)).

12.5.9.1 *Amount of value received*

The amount of the value received for EIS purposes is the amount of the loan or advance reduced by any repayment made before the issue of shares in respect of which relief is claimed (TA 1988, s 300(4)(c)).

Example 12.10

On 1 January 2005 Kate borrows £6,000 from Sensibility Ltd repayable in equal amounts on 1 March, 1 April and 1 May 2005 pending the settlement of her father's estate. On 25 April 2005, she subscribes £10,000 for shares in Sensibility and claims EIS relief. As she owes £2,000 to Sensibility, Kate will be treated as having subscribed only £8,000 and her initial relief will be £1,600.

12.5.10 Provision of benefits or facilities

12.5.10.1 *Introduction*

The value-received provision that has the widest scope is that where the company provides the investor with a benefit or facility (TA 1988, s 300(2)(f)). Examples of benefits or facilities are:

(*a*) where an investor can have the free use of real property, vehicles or equipment;
(*b*) where investors are entitled to discounts when purchasing the company's goods and services;
(*c*) where the effect of an action by the company increases the value of shares of a company in which the investor has an interest; and
(*d*) where an investor is granted an option to acquire shares at below the market value at the date of exercise.

12.5.10.2 *Amount of value received*

Where a benefit or facility is provided for an EIS investor the value received, for the purposes of withdrawing investment relief, is the cost to the company of providing the benefit less any consideration given by the investor (TA 1988, s 300(4)(d)).

It is necessary to decide what is meant by the 'cost to the company'. It could be the marginal cost, the average cost or the income forgone. In connection with benefits-in-kind, the House of Lords decided in *Pepper v Hart* [1992] STC 898 that 'cost to the company' meant the marginal cost rather than the average cost. Therefore, if a discount on products and services merely means that the company makes a smaller profit it can be argued that there is no cost to the company. Similarly, there is no cost to a company in granting an option to acquire its shares.

Example 12.11

Angelina is an EIS investor and unpaid director of Croft Ltd and has subscribed £100,000 for ordinary shares in the company. The company has granted Angelina an option to acquire a further 5% of the company's share capital exercisable on the sixth anniversary of the share issue, at a price of £1 a share, provided that the asset value of the company has grown by at least 50%. Angelina will not lose any EIS relief as there is no cost to the company in granting the option. However, she has a 'securities option', potentially subject to income tax under ITEPA 2003, Part 7, Chapter 5!

No value is received if the benefit or facility is provided as part of the reasonable remuneration of a director (TA 1988, s 300(10), (1E)).

12.5.11 Transfers of assets

12.5.11.1 *Consideration other than at market value*

This rule catches transactions in which the investor receives value either by transferring assets to the company at an overvalue (so that he or she receives more in consideration from the company than the asset is worth) or conversely where the company transfers assets to the investor at an undervalue (so that the investor pays less consideration than the asset is worth) (TA 1988, s 300(2)(g)).

12.5.11.2 *Amount of value received*

For EIS purposes, the value received, as might be expected, is the difference between the market value of the asset and the consideration (if any) given for it (TA 1988, s 300(4)(e)).

Example 12.12

Ramanuja subscribes £50,000 for ordinary shares in Trivandrum Ltd, and claims £10,000 EIS investment relief. Just over a year later, he sells a car to the company for £3,000, when its market value is no more than £1,800. As the company has paid £1,200 over the car's market value, Ramanuja loses EIS relief of £1,200 @ 20% = £240.

12.5.12 Various other payments

12.5.12.1 *Payments on a winding-up*

An EIS investor is deemed to receive value from the company if he or she receives a payment or an asset in respect of his or her ordinary shares on the occasion of a bona fide winding-up or dissolution of the company which does not of itself cause a breach of the qualifying conditions (TA 1988, s 300(3)).

The amount of value received on such an occasion is the amount of the payment or the market value of the asset, as appropriate (TA 1988, s 300(4)(g)).

Example 12.13

Lisa subscribes £25,000 for ordinary shares in Friends Ltd and receives £5,000 EIS investment relief. After 18 months, it becomes apparent that there is very little demand for the company's product and it is decided to wind the company up. Lisa accepts office furniture worth £2,000 as her share of the company's assets.

Lisa has received value of £2,000 and will lose £400 of her relief. She will, however be able to obtain loss relief on the disposal of her shares **[see Chapter 18]**.

12.5.12.2 *Payments other than directors' qualifying payments*

An investor receives value whenever he or she receives any other so far unspecified payment from the company, other than the following, which are qualifying payments that a director may receive without being disqualified as a connected person:

(*a*) reimbursement of travelling and other expenses incurred wholly, necessarily and exclusively (and hence deductible from taxable earnings under ITEPA 2003, s 332) as a director of the company;
(*b*) interest that represents no more than a reasonable commercial rate of return;
(*c*) a dividend or distribution that represents no more than a normal return on the investment;
(*d*) a payment for goods at no more than market value;

(*e*) a reasonable commercial rent for property occupied by the company or by a related person;

(*f*) reasonable remuneration for professional or trade services

(TA 1988, s 291A(3)); or

(*g*) discharge of an ordinary trade debt

(TA 1988, s 300(2)(h)).

The value received where none of these exceptions applies is the amount of the payment (TA 1988, s 300(4)(f)).

This category includes directors' remuneration from connected companies. In *Fletcher v Thompson* [2002] STC 1149, two brothers invested over several years in several companies that were letting property under assured tenancies. They claimed and obtained BES income tax relief (analogous to EIS investment relief). The inspector later withdrew the relief on the grounds that the individuals had received 'value' under TA 1988, s 300(2)(h), namely in respect of 'any other payment except a payment of the kind mentioned in any of the paragraphs of section 291A(3) or a payment in discharge of an ordinary trade debt' (ie the payments considered in this section). The wording of the legislation was in every material way the same for the BES as it now is for the EIS.

Here, the value came from directors' remuneration paid to the brothers not from the BES companies but from a building company that they controlled between them and was for services rendered to that company. However, the brothers also controlled the BES companies between them and those companies and the building company were thus connected persons as being under common control under the definition in TA 1988, s 839. As already noted **[see 12.5.1]**, value received from a person connected with the EIS company is equally liable to cause reduction or withdrawal of investment relief.

The taxpayers argued, first, that the remuneration was a benefit **[see 12.5.10]** for which they had given full consideration; secondly that, if it did fall within the category of 'other payments' that it was paid in discharge of an ordinary trade debt. The High Court dismissed both of these contentions.

The conclusion is that payments from a company under common control, even if they are made for full consideration and have no connection with the EIS investee company, may nevertheless constitute value, unless they fall within one of the specific exclusions discussed immediately above. This decision does not, however, affect those directors who receive remuneration from the EIS company only. They can still obtain EIS investment relief where they meet the conditions of the business angel provisions **[see 7.6.11]**.

12.6 Exception for insignificant value

Where value is received after 6 March 2001, it does not cause investment relief to be lost if the value is 'insignificant'. Amounts are insignificant in all cases where they are no greater than £1,000. Amounts that are greater than £1,000 may still be insignificant if they are considered to be such relative to the individual's original subscription (TA 1988, s 301A(1)–(3)).

No guidance is given as to what 'insignificant' may be in this second instance, where no numerical or percentage value is indicated. HM Treasury's Explanatory Notes to the Finance Bill 2001 are of no help. The Inland Revenue's view, as set out in the Venture Capital Schemes Manual, is that this second arm is practically of no application. It states:

> 'Our view is that for the purpose of the second category above "insignificant" must be given its normal dictionary meaning of "trifling" or "completely unimportant". Thus in most cases it is very unlikely to cover any amount in excess of £1,000.'
>
> (para VCM 26310)

Yet it cannot have been the intention of the legislator to include a provision of little or no application. It is clear that some sort of meaningful comparison has to be made, whereas if something is '*completely* unimportant' it belies comparison. The relevant definitions in the *Concise Oxford Dictionary* (5th edition, 1964), for example, are 'unimportant, trifling'. The issue has not been tested in the courts, but it is difficult from a common-sense point of view, for example, to regard, say, value of less than £3,000 when compared to the maximum investment of £200,000 as anything other than insignificant.

Be that as it may, there are provisions to ensure that no amount, however small, is insignificant if there are arrangements in place at any time in the 12 months preceding the share issue for the investor or an associate to receive or become entitled to receive any value during the period of restriction from the investee company or a connected person (TA 1988, s 301A(3), (4)).

To prevent a dripfeed of insignificant amounts, there is also a rule aggregating various receipts of value within the period of restriction. This rule provides that where an investor receives value and has previously received one or more insignificant amounts of value during the period of restriction, and the aggregate of those previous receipts and the latest receipt is not insignificant, the investor is treated as having received the aggregate amount at this latest time. Amounts that have previously been aggregated under this rule are disregarded (TA 1988, s 300(1BC)).

Example 12.14

On 2 February 2003, Romola subscribes £10,000 for 5,000 ordinary shares in Dodie Ltd, which begins trading on 1 July 2003. During the course of 2005, she receives two items of equipment from the company, worth respectively £300 and £400, for which she pays a nominal £5 each. In May 2006, Dodie gives her, free of charge, a second-hand laptop worth £750. The first two receipts were insignificant, but she is now treated as receiving value of (£300 + £400 + £750 – £10) = £1,440, causing relief of £288 to be lost. If the laptop had been transferred to her three months later, the period of restriction would have expired (on 30 June 2006) and no loss of relief would have occurred.

Before 7 March 2001, no amount of value, however small, was disregarded.

12.7 The exception for return of replacement value

12.7.1 Introduction

A second exception that applies where value is received after 6 March 2001 is for occasions when the value given is returned or replaced (hence the name 'replacement value').

The exception applies where:

(*a*) the person from whom the value ('the original value') was received ('the original supplier') receives value in return ('the replacement value') from the person who received the original value ('the original recipient') by way of a 'qualifying receipt';
(*b*) the replacement value is at least equal to the original value; and
(*c*) the replacement value is given before or after the original value, subject to certain conditions **[see 12.7.2]**

(TA 1988, s 300A(1), (2)).

Where the exception applies, the receipt of the original value is disregarded and no investment relief is lost as a result.

A receipt is a qualifying receipt if it arises as a result of:

(*a*) any one, or any combination of, the following:
 (1) a payment (other than an 'excepted payment') by the original recipient to the original supplier,
 (2) the acquisition of an asset by the original recipient from the original supplier for a consideration exceeding market value,
 (3) the disposal of an asset by the original recipient to the original supplier for no consideration or for a consideration less than its market value;

 or
(*b*) where the receipt of the original value arose as a result of the release or waiver of any liability of the investor to the company or of an undertaking to discharge the investor's liability to a third party **[see 12.5.8]**, the reversal of that event; or
(*c*) where the receipt of the original value arose as a result of the purchase by a party connected to the company of any of the investor's share capital or securities or of the payment by such a connected person to the investor in return for the latter's giving up any right in relation to the company's capital or securities **[see 12.5.5]**, a repurchase by the original recipient of the

shares or securities in question or the reacquisition by the original recipient of the right in question for consideration of not less than the market value of the shares, securities or right

(TA 1988, s 300A(4)).

An excepted payment (as in point (a)(1) above) is broadly the type of payment disregarded as a receipt of value in the first place; namely:

(*a*) a payment for any goods, services or facilities provided whether in the course of trade or otherwise by the original supplier or any person who is an associate of or connected with the original supplier at any time in the period of restriction, of an amount that is reasonable in relation to their market value;
(*b*) a payment of interest at no more than a reasonable commercial rate of return on a loan made to the original recipient or to a person who is an associate of the original recipient at any time in the period of restriction;
(*c*) a payment of no more than market value for the acquisition of an asset;
(*d*) a payment not exceeding a reasonable and commercial rent for property occupied by the original recipient or by any person who is an associate of the original recipient at any time during the period of restriction;
(*e*) a payment in discharge of an ordinary trade debt;
(*f*) a payment for any shares or securities of the company in any circumstances other than those in point (*a*)(2) above

(TA 1988, s 300A(5)).

12.7.2 Time restraints on a receipt of replacement value

The receipt of replacement value may take place either before or after the original receipt (TA 1988, s 300A(8)). However, certain time limits are put in place.

Where the replacement value is received before the original receipt, it must be provided within the period of restriction (ie no earlier than one year before the issue of the shares).

Where the replacement value is received after the original receipt, it must be provided as soon as is 'reasonably practicable' in the circumstances.

Where the original receipt of value is the subject of appeal proceedings, the replacement value must be provided within 60 days of the conclusion of the appeal.

Unless the replacement value is received within these time limits, it is disregarded and the original receipt of value stands, with the consequential loss of relief.

12.7.3 The amount of replacement value

The amount of the replacement value deemed to be received depends on the nature of the qualifying receipt.

Where the receipt is one of those enumerated in point (*a*) in **12.7.1**, the amount is the aggregate of the payment and the difference between the market value of any asset mentioned in point (*a*)(1) or (*a*)(2) and the consideration received.

Where the receipt is of the kind mentioned in point (*b*) in **12.7.1**, the amount of replacement value is equal to the amount of the original value.

Where the receipt is of the kind mentioned in point (*c*) in **12.7.1**, the amount of replacement value is the amount of consideration received by the original supplier (TA 1988, s 300A(6)).

Unless the replacement value is at least equal to the original value, it is disregarded and does not reduce the loss of investment relief caused by the receipt of the original value.

12.7.4 The effect of replacement value

Where replacement value is received and the conditions described in **12.7.1** and **12.7.2** are satisfied, the receipt of the original value is disregarded, and no loss of relief results (TA 1988, s 300A(1)).

However, if the replacement value is provided by a subscription for new shares by the investor or an associate, no investment relief is granted for those shares or for any other shares in the same issue (TA 1988, s 300A(9), (10)).

12.8 Value received by other shareholders

12.8.1 Introduction

The provisions on receipt of value are so widely drawn that an investor may be deemed to receive value even where the value is actually received by another shareholder, who is not an EIS investor. The reason goes back to the purpose of the EIS, which is to encourage individuals to provide unquoted companies with *additional* capital. It was never the intention to give tax reliefs for a capital injection that simply replaces capital that has or will be withdrawn by other shareholders. In other words, the company should be using the EIS capital it receives for its trading activities.

12.8.2 Repayment of capital to other shareholders

An EIS investor can lose all or part of his or her EIS relief if, at any time during the period of restriction **[see 12.5.2]**, the company or any subsidiary repays, redeems or repurchases the share capital of another shareholder or makes any payment to that person for giving up his right to capital on its cancellation (TA 1988, s 303(1)).

A 'subsidiary' here means any company that is a 51% subsidiary of the investee company at any time during not the period of restriction **[see 12.5.2]** but the so-called 'relevant period' defined in TA 1988, s 312(1A)(a) **[see 12.5.3.1]**) (TA 1988, s 303(9A)).

This provision differs from that applying to the investors themselves **[see 12.5.4]** in that it does not cover the purchase of shares by a person who is connected with the company for EIS purposes **[see 12.5.5]**. However, this condition is particularly harsh where the repayment occurs in a subsidiary of the investee company before it became a subsidiary.

Example 12.15

Garai Ltd raises £1 million of EIS capital on 1 April 2002. Daniel Ltd is a successful company in the same business with a 90% dormant subsidiary, Deronda Ltd. In October 2004 it is proposed that Garai buy the shares in Daniel. It comes to light that in May 2003 Deronda had purchased some of its own shares for £100,000.

In this situation, EIS shareholders in Garai would lose part of their investment relief because of Deronda's share purchase within the restricted period (1 April 2001 to 31 March 2005). The shares in Deronda should therefore be sold before Daniel is acquired.

12.8.2.1 *Repayments received before 7 March 2001*

Where repayments were received before 7 March 2001, different restricted periods applied.

In respect of EIS shares issued after 5 April 2000 but before 7 March 2001, the restricted period (known then as 'the designated period') began a year earlier than the current restricted period, ie two years before the issue date, but ended coterminously with the current period (ie immediately before the later of (*a*) the third anniversary of the issue date and (*b*) the third anniversary of the commencement of the qualifying trade).

For shares issued after 5 April 1998 but before 6 April 2000, there was yet a different restricted period (known as 'the seven-year period'). This was the period that began two years before the issue date and ended five years after the issue date.

Regardless of when the shares were issued, however, if the repayment falls after 6 March 2001, the current restricted period applies.

12.8.3 Effect of a repayment of share capital

Where another shareholder who does not as a result of the repayment himself lose EIS investment relief, EIS deferral relief or CVS investment relief (or would have done so if the amount received were not insignificant) has his share capital repaid, the EIS shareholders' entitlement to EIS relief is reduced. The reduction is an amount equal to tax at the lower rate for the tax year in which the relief was given applied to the amount received by the other shareholder (TA 1988, s 303(1A), (1C)).

Example 12.16

Keira obtains £8,000 EIS relief (£40,000 × 20%), when she subscribes for £1 ordinary shares in Zhivago Ltd. The shares are held as follows:

	£1 ord shares		*£1 redeemable preference shares*
	No	*Subscribed*	*at par*
	(000)	£(000)	(000)
Boris	15	15	12
Yuri	10	15	
Keira	20	40	
Julie	35	70	
	80	140	

If the company redeems Boris's preference shares for £12,000, Keira would lose relief of £2,400 (£12,000 × 20%).

12.8.4 Loss of relief by more than one investor

Where EIS investment relief is to be lost by more than one EIS shareholder in the above circumstances, it is reduced in proportion to their qualifying investments (TA 1988, s 303(2)).

Example 12.17

Take the same facts as Example 12.16 except that Yuri also obtains EIS relief of £3,000 (20% × £15,000). The deemed value received of £12,000 would be apportioned according to the relative qualifying subscriptions of Yuri and Keira. Yuri would lose relief of £655 ((15,000/55,000) × £12,000 × 20%) and Keira would lose relief of £1,745 ((40,000/55,000) × £12,000 × 20%).

12.8.5 Exceptions

There are three exceptions to the rule.

12.8.5.1 *Exception for minimal capital requirements*

The first exception is for payments that are made to satisfy Companies Act requirements. Where shares are issued in order to satisfy the minimum capital requirements for a public company under Companies Act 1985, s 117, and then redeemed within 12 months of issue, the redemption is ignored for these purposes (TA 1988, s 303(9)).

12.8.5.2 *Insignificant repayments*

The second exception has applied since 7 March 2001 only. A repayment is disregarded where the greater of:

(*a*) the amount received by the other member and
(*b*) the market value immediately before the repayment is made of the shares to which it relates

is 'insignificant' in relation to the market value immediately after the repayment of the remaining issued share capital of the investee company (or of the subsidiary, where appropriate) (TA 1988, s 303AA(1)).

Again, no definition of 'insignificant' is given nor is there a monetary amount specified, as there is in relation to value received by investors **[see 12.6]**, but attention must again be drawn to the highly restrictive interpretation put on the term by the Inland Revenue (see Venture Capital Schemes Manual, para VCM 26420) and the commentary in **12.6** as to the unlikelihood that this could have been the intention.

As with the rule in **12.6**, insignificant repayments are not disregarded where there are arrangements in place at any time in the 12 months preceding the share issue for the repayment to be made or for any person to become entitled to such a repayment (TA 1988, s 303AA(4), (5)).

12.8.5.3 *Restriction on loss of EIS relief where CVS relief lost*

Shares issued by an investee company between 1 April 2000 and 31 March 2010 may also be qualifying shares under the CVS scheme. That scheme also contains rules **[see Chapter 13]** reducing or withdrawing investment relief on the receipt of value. In order to prevent a double loss of relief in a company that has both EIS and CVS investors, there is a rule restricting the loss of EIS relief in such circumstances.

More precisely, where:

(*a*) there is a repayment, redemption or repurchase of share capital from any other shareholder other than a CVS shareholder and the EIS investor(s) affected under the conditions described in **12.8.1** to **12.8.4**, such that the EIS investor(s) otherwise stand to lose(s) relief; and
(*b*) an amount of CVS investment relief has been lost by the CVS shareholder(s) as a result of the same repayment **[see 13.4.3]**

there is no loss of EIS relief if the result of the formula X – 5Y, where X is the amount of the repayment and Y is the amount of CVS investment relief lost, is £1,000 or less (TA 1988, s 303A(1)–(3)).

Where the amount by which the repayment exceeds five times the CVS relief withdrawn is more than £1,000 (ie X – 5Y > £1,000), the amount received for the purposes of the EIS rule is taken to be X – 5Y, and not X (TA 1988, s 303A(7)).

Example 12.18

The shareholdings in Symposium Ltd are distributed as follows:

Shareholder	*Shares*	*Amount subscribed*
Plato	5,000	£10,000
Socrates	8,000	£16,000
Phaedon plc	20,000	£35,000
Others	37,000	£59,000
Total	**70,000**	**£120,000**

Plato is an EIS investor, who has received EIS investment relief of £2,000. Phaedon plc is a CVS investor, which has received CVS investment relief of £7,000. The other shareholders also hold £10,000 of preference shares. Within the restricted periods for both the EIS shares and the CVS shares, those preference shares are redeemed for their market value at the time of £12,000. As a result, Phaedon loses £12,000 × 20% = £2,400 of CVS investment relief and Plato stands to lose all of his EIS investment relief (since £12,000 is greater than £10,000).

The formula X – 5Y, however, yields the result £12,000 – £12,000 = £nil, which is not greater than £1,000. Therefore, the repayment is disregarded for EIS purposes, and Plato loses none of his relief.

It will be quickly seen that, unless the CVS investor's investment relief was originally restricted because of an insufficient corporation tax liability (or for some other reason such as an earlier receipt of value), or is reduced rather than withdrawn, X will always equal 5Y and no EIS relief will be lost.

As with the exceptions for insignificance **[see 12.6 and 12.8.5.2]**, this exception does not operate if in the 12 months preceding the issue of the EIS shares, there were arrangements in place for a repayment to be made to a non-EIS, non-CVS shareholder by the investee company or by a subsidiary or for any person to be entitled to such a repayment (TA 1988, s 303A(4)–(6)).

Where the repayment is made after 6 March 2001, the above rules come into play even when no CVS relief was actually lost because the amount of the repayment was insignificant.

12.9 The former rules for receipt of value of all kinds by other members

12.9.1 Introduction

Before 7 March 2001, the receipt of value by members other than EIS investors by means other than a repayment of share capital also had consequences, which could lead to a total withdrawal of EIS investment relief. This was because the receipt of any such value caused there to be a recalculation of EIS investors' interests in the investee company.

12.9.2 How the former rules worked

The former rules applied whenever value in its widest sense was received from the company or any subsidiary. For this purpose, the circumstances when value was received and the quantum of the value were the same as those set out above, except that in **12.7** payments were only included where they were made for less than full consideration.

For this purpose a person was treated as entitled to receive anything that he was entitled to receive at a future date or would at a future date have been entitled to receive.

If a non-EIS shareholder received value from the company it was necessary to adjust the company's issued ordinary share capital by the amount of the value received for the purpose of recomputing the shareholders' interests in the company.

The adjustment was made to the non-EIS shareholder's issued ordinary share capital by applying the following fraction:

$$\frac{S - V}{S}$$

where S = the amount subscribed for the shares and
where V = the value received by the owners of those shares.

This could have the effect of taking EIS shareholders' interest over 30% with the result that they lost all their EIS relief through no fault of their own.

Example 12.19

Take the facts in Example 12.16 except that Julie receives a benefit valued at £35,000.

The formula $\frac{\text{S £70,000} - \text{V £35,000}}{\text{S £70,000}}$ produces a fraction of one-half.

After halving Julie's share capital the shareholdings would be:

	(000)	%
Boris	15	24
Yuri	10	16
Keira	20	32
Julie	17.5	28
	62.5	100

All of Keira's EIS investment relief would be lost, as following the adjustment of Julie's shareholding she would have more than a 30% interest in the company.

12.10 The receipt of replacement capital

12.10.1 Introduction

There are rules designed to ensure that EIS investment relief is withdrawn from any EIS investor who directly or indirectly owned a business before it came under the ownership of the investee company. These rules go under the name of 'replacement capital'.

12.10.2 How the rules work

An EIS investor loses all his or her investment relief where he or she alone or as part of a group of persons controls or has controlled a company and either the shares in that company or that company's trade or trading assets are acquired at any time during the restricted period by the EIS investee company or any of its subsidiaries.

In deciding whether an individual controls a company for this purpose, the interests, rights and powers of any of that individual's associates are aggregated with his or hers. In the case of investors who are paid directors, account is taken of previous control of the trade at any time, not just during the restricted period (TA 1988, s 302(1)–(5)).

For a full explanation of the rules, see **7.6.4**, as they apply equally to prevent the giving of EIS investment relief.

Chapter 13

Losing CVS Investment Relief

13.1 Introduction and background

13.1.1 Introduction

As explained in **11.1**, in relation to the VCT scheme, various events during a specified period of time following a CVS investment can cause a loss of investment relief. Those events will be discussed in this chapter, with the exception of an early disposal of CVS shares, which is covered, together with all disposals of CVS shares and their consequences, in **Chapter 19**.

For an explanation of the terms 'loss', 'reduction' and 'withdrawal' of relief as they are used in this chapter, and in **Chapters 11** and **12**, see **11.1.1**.

13.1.2 Scope of this chapter

This chapter is concerned with the following areas:

(*a*) Occasions for loss of investment relief **[see 13.2]**
(*b*) Breach of the qualifying conditions **[see 13.3]**
(*c*) The receipt of value **[see 13.4]**
(*d*) The exception for receipts of insignificant value **[see 13.5]**
(*e*) The exception for return of replacement value **[see 13.6]**
(*f*) The receipt of value by other shareholders **[see 13.7]**
(*g*) The grant of options over CVS shares **[see 13.8]**

13.2 Occasions giving rise to loss of investment relief

A loss of CVS investment relief may be caused by the occurrence during a specified period of any of the following events:

(*a*) a breach of the qualifying conditions in respect of investor companies, investee companies or the investment itself **[see 13.3]**;
(*b*) a disposal by the investor company of some or all of the CVS shares **[see Chapter 19]**;

(*c*) the receipt of 'value' by the corporate investor from the company **[see 13.4 to 13.6]**;
(*d*) the receipt of 'value' by other shareholders **[see 13.7]**; or
(*e*) the grant of options over the CVS shares **[see 13.8]**.

13.2.1 Restricted periods

There are, by contrast with the EIS provisions, only two different restricted periods, during the currency of which events can occur to cause loss of investment relief.

They are the 'qualification period', which is the single period during which the qualifying conditions for investors, investees and the investment have to be met **[see Chapters 5 to 6]**. To recapitulate, the qualification period is the period that begins on the issue date of the shares and ends immediately before the later of:

(*a*) the third anniversary of the issue date and
(*b*) the third anniversary of the date on which the qualifying trade began

(FA 2000, Sch 15, para 3).

When it comes to the receipt of value **[see 13.4]**, however, a second period, known as 'the period of restriction', comes into play. The period of restriction begins one year before the issue date and ends at the same time as the qualification period, ie immediately before the later of:

(*a*) the third anniversary of the issue date and
(*b*) the third anniversary of the date on which the qualifying trade began

(FA 2000, Sch 15, para 48).

Since the qualification period invariably starts on the issue date, the period of restriction is simply one year longer, to encompass the year before the shares are issued.

In this chapter, the terms 'qualification period' and 'the period of restriction' will be used where that period specifically is meant; where either or both periods are intended, we shall use the generic term 'restricted period', used elsewhere in this book.

13.3 Breach of the qualifying conditions

There must be no breach of the qualifying conditions, whether with respect to the investor company **[see 5.17]**, the investee company **[see Chapters 5 and 6]** or with respect to the investment itself **[see also Chapter 5]** at any time during the qualification period **[see 13.2.1]**.

13.3.1 Consequence of a breach of the qualifying conditions

A breach of the qualifying conditions results in a loss of entitlement to relief, so that any relief already given is withdrawn.

13.4 The receipt of value

13.4.1 Introduction

The rules against receipts of 'value' are primarily designed to prevent an investor in CVS shares from having access by direct or indirect means to the capital invested. They work, as we have seen with the EIS rules, by causing relief to be reduced or withdrawn.

The value-received rules for the CVS, although they are based on the EIS rules, are not quite so widely drawn. Nevertheless, they also apply not only to payments received by the investor company and its connected persons from the investee company and its connected persons, but also to value received by other members of the investee company.

When considering whether an investor company has received value, any reference to the investor company includes references to any person who is during the period of restriction **[see 13.2.1]** connected with the investor company. Likewise, any reference to the investee company includes a reference to any person who is during the period of restriction connected with the investee company (FA 2000, Sch 15, para 53).

Relief is not reduced or withdrawn if the amount of value received is 'insignificant' **[see 13.6 and 13.7]**.

13.4.2 The restricted period

The period during which value must not be received if it is not to cause loss of relief is the period of restriction **[see 13.2.1]**.

13.4.3 The meaning of 'value' and when it is received

There are nine circumstances in which the investor company is deemed to receive value. They will be familiar from the EIS value-received rules, and are set out below in tabular form, together with the amount of value treated as received on each occasion.

	Triggering event	*Amount of value received*
1	Repayment, redemption or repurchase of its share capital or securities owned by the investor company, or payment to the investor company for giving up its right to any of the investee company's share capital or for any security on its cancellation or extinguishment	The greater of the payment received and the market value of the shares or securities
2	Repayment of a debt owed to the investor company as part of any arrangement for acquiring the shares, provided that it was incurred before the issue date or was incurred in consideration for the extinguishment of a debt predating the issue	The greater of the payment received and the market value of the debt
3	Payment to the investor company for surrendering its rights to payment of any debt on its extinguishment	The greater of the payment received and the market value of the debt
4	Release or waiver of any liability of the investor company to the investee company or discharge of or undertaking to discharge any liability of the investor company to a third party (includes circumstances where the debt is not repaid within 12 months of the date when it should have been discharged)	The amount of the liability
5	Making of a loan or advance to the investor company, which remains unpaid at the issue date, including debts due from the investor company assigned to the investee company by a third party. Excludes ordinary trade debts	The amount of the loan or advance, less the amount of any 'related payment' made before the issue date
6	Provision to the directors or employees of the investor company or any of their associates of a benefit or facility. Does not apply to 'qualifying payments'	The cost to the investee company of the provision, less any consideration given for it by the recipient or an associate
7	Disposal at an undervalue or gratuitously of an asset to the investor company	The difference between the market value of the asset and any consideration given for it

8	Acquisition at an overvalue of any asset from the investor company	The difference between the market value of the asset and the consideration paid for it
9	Any other payment to the investor company except for a 'qualifying payment'	The amount of the payment

For these purposes, references in the table to a debt or liability exclude any debt or liability that could be discharged by a 'qualifying payment' made by the debtor. References to a payment or a disposal made to a person include payments or disposals made indirectly to that person or to his order or benefit. The provision of a benefit or facility does not include provision made such that if a payment equal in value to the benefit had been made instead, the payment would have been a 'qualifying payment'.

An 'ordinary trade debt' is a debt for goods or services supplied in the ordinary course of business where any credit given is for no longer than six months and is no longer than is normally given to customers by the supplier.

A 'qualifying payment' (see occasions 6 and 9 in the table, and above) is any of the following:

(*a*) a payment by any person for goods, services or facilities provided by the investor company, whether or not in the course of trade, which is reasonable in relation to their market value;
(*b*) a payment by any person of interest representing no more than a reasonable commercial return on money lent to that person;
(*c*) a payment by any company of a dividend or other distribution representing no more than a normal return on any investment in shares or securities of that company;
(*d*) a payment of no more than market value for the acquisition of an asset;
(*e*) a payment by any person of rent for the occupation of property, which is no more than a reasonable and commercial rent for that property;
(*f*) a payment in discharge of an ordinary trade debt

(FA 2000, Sch 15, paras 49, 50).

All the above transactions when made with a person are understood also to mean made with a person connected at any time in the period of restriction with the first person (the connection need not exist at the time of the transaction).

Example 13.1

In December 2003, Ricoeur plc, which already holds 10,000 redeemable preference shares in Valence Ltd, which has been trading for several years, agrees to subscribe £50,000 for ordinary shares at par in the company and claims CVS investment relief, of £10,000 (£50,000 @ 20%). In February 2005, Valence redeems the preference shares at their market value of £1.20.

The period of restriction for the CVS issue runs from December 2002 to December 2006. As a result of the redemption, Ricoeur loses relief of ((10,000 × £1.20) × 20%) = £2,400.

13.5 Exception for receipts of insignificant value

The receipt of value does not cause investment relief to be lost if the value is 'insignificant'. Amounts are insignificant in all cases where they are no greater than £1,000. Amounts that are greater than £1,000 may still be insignificant if they are considered to be such relative to the investor company's original subscription (FA 2000, Sch 15, para 47(7)).

No statutory definition or guidance is given for the meaning of 'insignificant' in this second instance. For a discussion and criticism of the Inland Revenue's narrow interpretation, see **12.6**. The relevant paragraph of the Venture Capital Schemes Manual, repeating its interpretation for the purposes of the CVS, is para VCM 50630.

There are provisions to ensure that no amount, however small, is insignificant if there are arrangements in place at any time in the 12 months preceding the share issue for the investor company or a connected person to receive or become entitled to receive any value during the period of restriction from the investee company or a connected person (FA 2000, Sch 15, para 47(6)).

To prevent a dripfeed of insignificant amounts, there is also a rule aggregating various receipts of value within the period of restriction. This rule provides that where an investor company receives value and has previously received one or more insignificant amounts of value during the period of restriction, and the aggregate of those previous receipts and the latest receipt is not insignificant, the investor company is treated as having received the aggregate amount at this latest time. Amounts that have previously been aggregated under this rule are disregarded (FA 2000, Sch 15, para 47(5)).

13.6 The exception for return of replacement value

13.6.1 Introduction

A second exception that applies where value is received is for occasions when the value given is returned or replaced (hence the name 'replacement value').

The exception applies where:

(*a*) the person from whom the value ('the original value') was received ('the original supplier') receives value in return ('the replacement value') from the person who received the original value ('the original recipient') by way of a 'qualifying receipt';

(*b*) the replacement value is at least equal to the original value; and (*c*) the replacement value is given before or after the original value, subject to certain conditions **[see 13.6.2]**

(FA 2000, Sch 15, para 54(1), (2)).

Where the exception applies, the receipt of the original value is disregarded and no investment relief is lost as a result.

13.6.2 Definition of qualifying receipt

A receipt is a qualifying receipt if it arises as a result of:

(*a*) any one, or any combination of, the following:
  - (1) a payment (other than an 'excepted payment') by the original recipient to the original supplier,
  - (2) the acquisition of an asset by the original recipient from the original supplier for a consideration exceeding market value,
  - (3) the disposal of an asset by the original recipient to the original supplier for no consideration or for a consideration less than its market value;

  or

(*b*) where the receipt of the original value arose as a result of the release or waiver of any liability of the investor company to the investee company or of an undertaking to discharge the investor company's liability to a third party (see item 4 of the table in **13.4.4**), the reversal of that event

(FA 2000, Sch 15, para 54(3)).

13.6.3 Definition of 'excepted payment'

An excepted payment (as in point (*a*)(1) of **13.6.2**) is broadly the type of payment disregarded as a receipt of value in the first place; namely:

(*a*) a payment for any goods, services or facilities provided whether in the course of trade or otherwise by the original supplier or any person who is an associate of or connected with the original supplier at any time in the period of restriction, of an amount that is reasonable in relation to their market value;

(*b*) a payment of interest at no more than a reasonable commercial rate of return on a loan made to the original recipient or to a person who is an associate of or connected with the original recipient at any time in the period of restriction;

(*c*) a payment not exceeding a reasonable and commercial rent for property occupied by the original recipient or by any person who is an associate of or connected with the original recipient at any time during the period of restriction;

(*d*) a payment by any company of a dividend or other distribution representing no more than a normal return on any investment in shares or securities of that company;

(*e*) a payment of no more than market value for the acquisition of an asset;
(*f*) a payment in discharge of an ordinary trade debt;
(*g*) a payment for any shares or securities of the company in any circumstances other than those in point (*a*)(2) above

(FA 2000, Sch 15, para 54(3A)).

These definitions of 'qualifying receipt' and 'excepted payment' apply to value received and shares issued after 6 March 2001. For value received before 7 March 2001 and shares issued in the period 6 April 2000 to 6 March 2001, a qualifying receipt could arise by reason of events in point (*a*)(1) or (*a*)(2) in **13.6.2** only where the original receipt of value was item 7 or item 8 in the table in **13.4.3**; and an excepted payment was either a qualifying payment (see points (*a*)–(*f*) following the table in **13.4.3**) or a payment for shares and securities within para (*g*) immediately above.

13.6.4 Time restraints on a receipt of replacement value

The receipt of replacement value may take place either before or after the original receipt (FA 2000, Sch 15, para 55(2)). However, certain time limits are put in place.

Where the replacement value is received before the original receipt, it must be provided within the period of restriction (ie no earlier than one year before the issue of the shares).

Where the replacement value is received after the original receipt, it must be provided without there being an 'unreasonable delay'.

Where the original receipt of value is the subject of appeal proceedings, the replacement value must be provided within 60 days of the conclusion of the appeal.

Unless the replacement value is received within these time limits, it is disregarded and the original receipt of value stands, with the consequential loss of relief.

Where the replacement value consists of, or includes, a subscription for shares by the investor company (or any person connected with it at any time in the period of restriction for the original shares), the subscriber is eligible neither for CVS investment relief nor for EIS investment relief (nor, for that matter, for EIS deferral relief) for that subscription or in respect of any shares in that issue (FA 2000, Sch 15, para 55(3), (4)).

13.6.5 The amount of replacement value

The amount of the replacement value deemed to be received depends on the nature of the qualifying receipt.

Where the receipt is one of those enumerated in point (*a*) in **13.6.2**, the amount is the aggregate of the payment and the difference between the market value of any asset mentioned in point (*a*)(2) or (*a*)(3) and the consideration received.

Where the receipt is of the kind mentioned in point (*b*) in **13.6.2**, the amount of replacement value is equal to the amount of the original value (FA 2000, Sch 15, para 54(4)).

Unless the replacement value is at least equal to the original value, it is disregarded and does not reduce the loss of investment relief caused by the receipt of the original value (FA 2000, Sch 15, para 54(1)(c)). Any single occasion on which replacement value is received may be applied to prevent loss of investment relief once only (FA 2000, Sch 15, para 55(1)).

13.6.6 The effect of replacement value

Where replacement value is received and the conditions described in **13.6.2** to **13.6.4** are satisfied, the receipt of the original value is disregarded, and no loss of relief results (FA 2000, Sch 15, para 54(1)).

13.7 Value received by other shareholders

13.7.1 Introduction

The provisions on receipt of value are widely drawn, in that an investor company may be deemed to receive value even where the value is actually received by another shareholder who is not a CVS investor.

The CVS rules in this respect mirror the EIS rules relating to value received after 6 March 2001 and in respect of shares issued after 6 March 2001 **[see 12.8]** and affect only the repayment of share capital and not other receipts of value.

13.7.2 Repayment of capital to other shareholders

A CVS investor company can lose all or part of its CVS investment relief if, at any time in the period of restriction **[see 13.2.1]**, the investee company or any subsidiary repays, redeems or repurchases the share capital of certain other shareholders **[see 13.7.2.1]** or makes any payment to that person for giving up his right to capital on its cancellation (FA 2000, Sch 15, para 56(1)).

A 'subsidiary' here means any company that is a 51% subsidiary of the investee company at any time during the period of restriction (FA 2000, Sch 15, para 58(8)). As will be appreciated, this rule can cause investment relief to be lost even where the repayment occurs in a subsidiary of the investee company at a time before it became such a subsidiary.

Example 13.2

Mansfield Ltd raises £1 million of CVS capital on 1 April 2002. Jayne Ltd is a successful company in the same line of business with a 90% dormant subsidiary, Vera Ltd. In October 2004, it is proposed that Mansfield buy the shares in Jayne. It comes to light that in May 2003, Vera had purchased some of its own shares for £100,000.

In this situation, since the repurchase took place within the period of restriction for the CVS issue (1 April 2001 to 31 March 2005), the CVS investors would lose part of their investment relief, even though they had no control whatsoever over the repayment. The shares in Vera should therefore have been sold before Jayne is acquired (a due diligence investigation should have uncovered these facts!).

13.7.2.1 *Other shareholders to whom repayments can cause loss of relief*

It is not all other shareholders to whom a repayment of capital may cause CVS investment relief to be lost. The shareholders excluded from this rule are:

(*a*) other CVS investor companies payment to whom would cause them to lose CVS investment relief on the grounds of an early disposal of shares or of a receipt of value; and
(*b*) EIS investors payment to whom would cause them to lose EIS investment relief on the grounds of an early disposal of shares or of a receipt of value or would cause a deferred gain under EIS deferral relief to crystallise
(*c*) or in either case would have done so were it not 'insignificant'

(FA 2000, Sch 15, para 56(1)(a)(ii), (3)).

The rule in point (*c*) applies only after 6 March 2001 or with respect to shares issued after that date.

13.7.3 Effect of a repayment of share capital to other members

Where another shareholder who is not excluded from these rules as explained in **13.7.2.1** receives value in the form of a repayment of capital as described in **13.7.2**, the CVS investor company's investment relief is lost, to the extent of 20% of the amount of value received by the other shareholder, up to the limit of the original relief (FA 2000, Sch 15, para 56(2), (4)(a)).

Example 13.3

Claudette plc obtains £56,000 of CVS relief (£280,000 @ 20%) when it subscribes for £5 ordinary shares in Colbert Ltd. Share ownership in Colbert Ltd is as follows:

	£5 ordinary shares		*£10 redeemable preference shares at par*
	No (000)	*Amount subscribed (£000)*	*No (000)*
Claudette plc	56	280	
Chauchoin Ltd	98	490	
Lily	42	210	3
Tovarich plc	29	145	
Total	**225**	**1,125**	**3**

Lily is not an EIS investor and Chauchoin Ltd and Tovarich plc are not CVS investors.

If the company redeems Lily's preference shares at par (which is their market value) within the period of restriction for Claudette Ltd's CVS shares, Claudette will lose investment relief to the extent of £6,000 (£30,000 @ 20%). Since the amount of value received by Lily (£30,000) is only 2.7% of Colbert Ltd's remaining issued share capital, it is an open question whether this amount is insignificant in comparison, so that Claudette should not lose relief at all **[see 13.7.4]**.

13.7.3.1 *Loss of relief by more than one CVS investor*

Where CVS investment relief is to be lost by more than one CVS investor company as a result of the same repayment of capital to another shareholder, the reduction is applied in proportion to their qualifying investments (FA 2000, Sch 15, para 56(4)(b), (5)).

Example 13.4

Take the facts of Example 13.3, but this time assume that Tovarich Ltd is also a CVS investor. The £30,000 value received by Lily is apportioned between Claudette plc and Tovarich plc in the ratio 280 : 145 so that the relief lost by Claudette plc is (£30,000 × 280/425 × 20%) = £3,953 and by Tovarich plc is (£30,000 × 145/425 × 20%) = £2,047. See **13.7.4** for the insignificance argument.

13.7.4 Exception for insignificant value received

As with value received by the CVS investor itself, and indeed, as with EIS relief, value received by another shareholder is ignored for these purposes if it is insignificant. Here, no monetary value is denoted. Instead, a repayment of capital will be insignificant if the greater of (*a*) the payment received and (*b*) the market value of the capital in respect of which it is made is insignificant in comparison to the market value of the investee company's (or the subsidiary's, as the case may be) remaining issued share capital (assuming that the capital relating to the repayment is cancelled) (FA 2000, Sch 15, para 57(1)–(3)).

Attention must again be drawn to the highly restrictive interpretation put on the term by the Inland Revenue (see Venture Capital Schemes Manual, para VCM 50630) and the commentary in **12.6** as to the unlikelihood that this could have been the intention of the legislation.

As with the rule in **13.5**, insignificant repayments are not disregarded where there are arrangements in place at any time in the 12 months preceding the CVS share issue for the repayment to be made or for any person to become entitled to such a repayment (FA 2000, Sch 15, para 57(4), (5)).

13.7.5 Exception for company law requirements

A second exception is for payments that are made to satisfy Companies Act requirements. Where shares are issued in order to satisfy the minimum capital requirements for a public company under Companies Act 1985, s 117, and then redeemed within 12 months of issue, the redemption is ignored for these purposes (FA 2000, Sch 15, para 58(5), (6)).

13.8 The grant of options over the shares

13.8.1 Put and call options and withdrawal of relief

Another event that will cause the withdrawal of CVS investment relief is the grant during the *qualification period* (NB: not the period of restriction) by a third party of a put option (binding the grantor to buy shares) or by the investor company of a call option (binding the grantor to sell shares) over any CVS shares (FA 2000, Sch 15, para 59).

Part 5

Deferral Reliefs

Chapter 14

Reinvestment in VCT Companies

14.1 Introduction and background

14.1.1 Background to deferment

So far in this book, after introducing the main features of the VCT scheme, the EIS and the CVS **[Chapters 2 to 4]**, we have looked at the qualifying conditions for obtaining VCT, EIS and CVS reliefs **[Chapters 5 to 7]**, and at how the investment reliefs are given **[Chapters 8 to 10]** and how they may be reduced or withdrawn **[Chapters 11 to 13]**. Now it is time to examine the second chief relief associated with venture capital investment, and that is the ability to defer capital gains by investing into EIS or CVS companies. These reliefs run parallel to the investment reliefs, and the one does not displace the other. Before 6 April 2004, the same relief also applied to reinvestment in VCT companies.

First, a note about history. The ability to defer gains by investing into EIS companies has been available since 29 November 1994 (it was not an original feature of the EIS nor at all of its predecessors, the BES and the BSS). The parallel ability to defer gains by investing into VCT companies has been available since its introduction on 6 April 1995. Finally, the ability to defer gains by investing into CVS companies has also been available since the inception of that scheme on 6 April 2000. Since 6 April 2004, however, gains can no longer be deferred by investing in VCT companies. The Chancellor balanced this withdrawal of relief by doubling the investment relief available for VCT investments for a temporary period of two years, ending on 5 April 2006. However, because a one-year window remains for VCT deferral relief (for matching with shares issued as late as 5 April 2004), finally closing after 5 April 2005, and gains that have been deferred by investment in VCT shares remain liable to clawback, the subject is treated in full in this chapter.

A relief that has come and gone is the 'reinvestment rollover relief' (RIR), which was introduced on 29 November 1993, as the replacement for a more narrowly targeted scheme, the entrepreneurs' rollover relief, which lasted for all of eight months (from 15 March 1993). RIR allowed the taxpayer to roll over any gain into an investment into qualifying unquoted companies. The investee companies had to carry on qualifying trades and meet other conditions closely similar to those applying in the EIS, but the investment did not have to be a subscription and there was no bar on the taxpayer's being connected to the investee company. Indeed, shares for which EIS or VCT relief had been obtained were expressly excluded. RIR thus existed side by side with the reliefs for EIS and VCT for just about four years, until RIR was abolished by FA 1998 and merged with the EIS relief.

It is interesting to note that the EIS relief (like the former VCT relief) allows the gain on any asset to be deferred, whereas the CVS relief applies to gains arising from the disposal of CVS shares only.

As with the investment reliefs, the 'deferral' (sic) relief for each scheme will be dealt with in separate chapters, although they share many features in common, subject to the additional complexity inherent in the EIS deferral relief.

14.1.2 Scope of this chapter

This chapter deals with the following topics:

(*a*) A summary of VCT deferral relief **[see 14.2]**
(*b*) Which gains could be deferred? **[see 14.3]**
(*c*) Who could claim VCT deferral relief? **[see 14.4]**
(*d*) What were qualifying investments? **[see 14.5]**
(*e*) How much of the gain could be deferred? **[see 14.6]**
(*f*) When does the gain crystallise? **[see 14.7]**

14.2 A summary of the former VCT deferral relief

VCT deferral relief allowed a chargeable gain made by an individual ('the investor') **[see 14.4]** to be deferred if, within the 'qualifying time' **[see 14.3]** the investor made a 'qualifying investment' (broadly into VCT shares on which VCT investment relief is available and given) **[see 14.5]**. The gain was deferred to the extent that it was matched by the qualifying investment. As in all rollover reliefs, the qualifying investment could be made within a certain time preceding the accrual of the gain as well as within a certain time afterwards. The deferred gain crystallises (becomes taxable) when there is a 'chargeable event' in relation to the investment, but could be deferred again if matched with a further qualifying investment. There can be no qualifying investment in VCT shares issued after 5 April 2004.

14.2.1 Deferred gains, indexation and taper relief

It is important to realise that VCT deferral relief is not like CGT rollover reliefs in that the deferred gain is not rolled over into the cost of the replacement asset (VCT shares) but stands deferred unless and until a chargeable event occurs **[see 14.7]**, when it becomes immediately assessable in its original amount.

There is thus no question of indexation or taper relief during the period of deferment. For the interaction of taper relief and the VCT reliefs generally, **see Chapter 23**.

14.3 Which gains could be deferred?

14.3.1 The types of eligible gain

There were two main types of gain that could be deferred:

(*a*) the chargeable gain arising on the disposal (after 5 April 1995) or deemed disposal of any asset; and
(*b*) a gain that had already been deferred under either VCT deferral relief or EIS deferral relief and then came back into charge whether because of a disposal or on the occurrence of some other chargeable event

(TCGA 1992, Sch 5C, para 1(1)(a), (b)).

14.3.2 Period for making qualifying investments

The time allowed for making the qualifying investment on which the claim to defer the gain could be based was known as the 'qualifying time'. That time was the period beginning 12 months before and ending 12 months after the gain arose (the date on which it arose was referred to as 'the accrual time'). The Inland Revenue had the power to allow an extension of the period at either end. This power, incidentally, could only be exercised at higher levels, as it was not devolved to area inspectors (Venture Capital Schemes Manual, para VCM 68050) (TCGA 1992, Sch 5C, para 1(3)).

A qualifying investment was made on the date that the shares were issued. As the question of when shares are issued was decided in *National Westminster Bank plc v IRC; Barclays Bank plc v IRC* [1994] STC 184 **[see 8.1.5]**, the reference in the capital gains tax legislation to the treatment of shares comprised in a letter of allotment as issued was disapplied (TCGA 1992, Sch 5C, para 6(3).

It follows that no qualifying investment can be made after 5 April 2004.

14.3.3 The deferral relief window

VCT deferral relief has, as we have seen, been abolished for shares issued after 5 April 2004. However, because the qualifying time runs for one year either side of the gain to be deferred, there is a window that remains open for gains made in the year up to 5 April 2005. Gains made after 5 April 2004 but within 12 months of a VCT investment made before 6 April 2004 may still be deferred. The window finally closes only after 5 April 2005, since such a gain cannot be matched with an investment made before 6 April 2004.

Example 14.1

Ayer makes a gain of £50,000 on 1 May 2004 and a further gain of £25,000 on 31 March 2005. If he wishes to defer those gains by making a qualifying VCT investment or investments, he must do so within the qualifying time for the gain in question.

The qualifying time for the gain on 1 May 2004 runs from 1 May 2003 to 1 May 2005. The qualifying time for the gain made on 31 March 2005 runs from 31 March 2004 to 31 March 2005.

Deferral relief is not available for shares issued (and hence investments made) after 5 April 2004.

It follows that the effective qualifying time for the 1 May 2004 gain is the period from 1 May 2003 to 5 April 2004 (any qualifying investment made in that period may be matched against the gain).

Similarly, the effective qualifying time for the 31 March 2005 gain is the period from 31 March 2004 to 5 April 2004 (five days only).

14.3.4 Limits on the gain deferred

When making VCT qualifying investments, the amount of gain that could be deferred could not exceed the qualifying expenditure on which the investment relief was given (TCGA 1992, Sch 5C, para 2(1)(b)).

There was also, although it was nowhere explicit in the legislation, an upper limit of £100,000 on the amount of the qualifying investment that could be made in any tax year. This was so because a qualifying investment could only be one in respect of which the investor was given VCT investment relief (TCGA 1992, Sch 5C, para 1(2)(a)).

Where the accrual time was 6 April, there were two tax years in which VCT investments could be made; if the accrual time was any other date, the number of tax years to choose from was three.

Example 14.2

Chrysippus disposes of a property on 24 June 2002, realising a gain of £465,000. If he wishes to defer the gain by making qualifying VCT investments, he can also do so partially.

The qualifying time is the period from 24 June 2001 to 24 June 2003, so the maximum that can be invested in VCT shares is:

24 June 2001 to 5 April 2002	2001–02	£100,000
6 April 2002 to 5 April 2003	2002–03	£100,000
6 April 2003 to 24 June 2003	2003–04	£100,000
Total		**£300,000**

However, it is open to Chrysippus to make qualifying EIS investments also for which the qualifying time ends two years later (24 June 2005) – see **Chapter 15**.

If Chrysippus disposes of another property on 24 June 2003, however, his qualifying time would begin on 24 June 2003 but end on 5 April 2004, after which new investments can no longer be matched with gains.

What mattered was that the investment relief for the qualifying investment was given. The fact that the amount of investment relief that the investor actually received was restricted because his or her income tax liability was insufficient, was irrelevant. Thus, in Example 14.2, if Chrysippus's liability to income tax in 2002–03 was only (say) £10,000, so that his VCT investment relief was limited to half the investment (£50,000 @ 20%), the full £100,000 invested could still qualify to match the gain. See Venture Capital Schemes Manual, para VCM 68030.

14.3.5 Date of disposal

Usually the date of disposal is the date of the contract even if the asset is conveyed, delivered or transferred at a later date. However, if the contract is conditional or subject to the exercise of an option, the disposal will not occur until the conditions are met (TCGA 1992, s 28).

A conditional contract is one subject to a condition precedent, ie where the non-fulfilment would prevent the contract from taking effect (*Eastham v Leigh, London and Provincial Properties Ltd* (1971) 46 TC 687). The time of the disposal of an asset is also the time of the acquisition of the asset by the new owner.

Normally where compensation is receivable, the time of disposal is the time the sum is actually received (TCGA 1992, s 22(2)). In the case of land that is compulsorily acquired, the disposal occurs at the time the compensation is agreed or otherwise determined at first instance, or if earlier, the time when the authority lawfully enters on the land (TCGA 1992, s 246).

In *Jerome v Kelly* [2004] UKHL 25, [2004] STC 887, the House of Lords held that where the owner of an asset contracts to dispose of it, and the contract is subsequently completed, the disposal for CGT purposes takes place when the contractual obligation is performed and not when it is created. This means that where the asset is transferred to a third party after the contract is made but before it is completed, it is the third party that makes the disposal, not the original owner.

14.4 Entitlement to claim a deferment

14.4.1 Claimants

The investor claiming VCT deferral relief had to be an individual (TCGA 1992, Sch 5C, para 1(1)) and there was the added condition that he or she had to be at least 18 years of age (TA 1988, Sch 15B, para 1(4)), for otherwise the investor could not make a qualifying investment in VCT shares. For the conditions that investors must meet for VCT investment relief generally, see **Chapter 7**.

14.4.2 UK residence

The investor had to be resident or ordinarily resident in the UK at the time when he or she made the qualifying investment and at the time the gain arose (TCGA 1992, Sch 5C, para 1(1)(d)).

14.4.3 Dual residence

The investor was not treated as meeting the UK residence condition if:

(*a*) though resident or ordinarily resident in the UK at the time of the qualifying investment, he or she was regarded for the purposes of any double taxation treaty as resident outside the UK; and

(*b*) ignoring the capital gains exemption on VCT shares, the treaty would have had the effect that he or she would not have been liable in the UK to tax on a gain arising on a disposal, immediately after the acquisition, of the shares acquired in making that investment

(TCGA 1992, Sch 5C, para 1(4)).

This situation arose where the investor was resident in the UK under UK domestic law (say, because he was physically present in the UK for more than 183 days in the tax year concerned) but also resident in some other jurisdiction under that jurisdiction's domestic law concerning residence. In such cases, if the other jurisdiction had a tax treaty with the UK, there would normally be a 'tie-breaker' article to determine for treaty purposes whether the investor was UK-resident or resident in the other jurisdiction.

Tax treaties also contain provisions conferring the right to tax any particular type of income or capital gain on either or both treaty partners. In the case of capital gains made by a non-resident of the UK, the treaty could well provide that the gain be taxable only by the treaty partner. This rule had in mind the situation where the particular treaty concerned denied the UK the right to tax the gain arising on any disposal of the VCT shares acquired.

14.5 Qualifying investments

14.5.1 The meaning of 'qualifying investment'

The investor made a qualifying VCT investment if:

(*a*) he or she subscribed for any shares in one or more qualifying companies and was given VCT investment relief in respect of them;

(*b*) those shares were issued at the qualifying time (and in any case before 6 April 2004) **[see 14.3.2]**; and
(*c*) where the time of the share issue was before the accrual time **[see 14.3.2]** those shares were still held by the investor at the accrual time (TCGA 1992, Sch 5C, para 1(2)).

Example 14.3

Rita subscribes £50,000 for VCT shares in September 2003 and receives VCT investment relief in December 2003. On 4 August 2004 she realises a £50,000 gain on the sale of a property and claims to defer the gain. If she still owns her VCT shares on 4 August 2004 she will be able to defer the gain, as the investment was made before 6 April 2004.

14.5.2 Qualifying companies

For the conditions that an investee company must meet in order that a qualifying VCT investment can be made, see **Chapters 5** and **6**.

14.6 Deferring gains

14.6.1 Introduction

A claim for VCT deferral relief could be made in respect of either a gain arising on the disposal of an asset or one that had occurred through the crystallisation of a previously deferred gain. In this section both types of gain will be referred to as the 'original gain'.

14.6.2 Amount of the gain that could be deferred

The amount of the gain that could be deferred was so much of the investor's 'unused qualifying expenditure' **[see 14.6.3]** on the shares:

(*a*) as was specified in the claim; and
(*b*) did not exceed so much of the original gain as was unmatched **[see 14.6.4]**.

The amount of the specified expenditure was set against a corresponding amount of the original gain (TCGA 1992, Sch 5C, para 2(1)).

14.6.2.1 *What is meant by the chargeable gain?*

Given the existence of indexation, taper relief, loss relief and so on, it is important to know exactly what is meant by the 'chargeable gain' in these circumstances. The gain that was eligible for deferment was the gain that remained after mandatory deductions such as indexation (and for gains made before 6 April 2003, retirement relief) but before taper relief or any relief for losses brought forward. Taper relief and loss relief are applicable only when and if any part of the gain remains in charge or the deferred gain crystallises without being deferred further.

14.6.3 Unused qualifying expenditure

Qualifying expenditure was expenditure on investment into VCT shares for which VCT investment relief was given, and it was unused to the extent that it had not already been set against the whole or any part of a chargeable gain (TCGA 1992, Sch 5C, para 2(3)).

Example 14.4

Donald disposes of a property on 9 July 2003 and realises a gain of £65,000. In November 2003 he subscribes £100,000 for VCT shares and obtains VCT investment relief. Donald claims to defer his £65,000 gain. Before he makes his VCT claim his unused qualifying expenditure is £100,000 and after the claim it is £35,000.

14.6.4 Unmatched gain

The unmatched gain is that part of the original gain which has not already been deferred by making a qualifying VCT or EIS investment (TCGA 1992, Sch 5C, para 2(4)).

Example 14.5

Oakeshott disposes of a property on 28 December 2003 and realises a gain of £135,000. In March 2004 he subscribes £80,000 for a qualifying investment and receives VCT relief. Oakeshott claims to defer £80,000 of his £135,000 gain. Before he makes the claim his unmatched gain is £135,000 and after the claim it is £55,000.

14.6.5 Expenditure on which investment relief is given

The investor's qualifying expenditure on shares was a sum equal to the amount on which the VCT investment relief was given. Where the amount of qualifying expenditure was set against the whole or a part of the original gain, that part of the gain was treated as if it had not accrued at the time of the disposal or crystallisation (the accrual time). Instead, the deferred gain was treated as accruing on the occurrence of a chargeable event **[see 14.7.1]** such as a disposal of the shares or a breach of the VCT rules (TCGA 1992, Sch 5C, para 2(2)(a)).

14.7 When gains crystallise

14.7.1 Introduction

A chargeable gain that has been deferred on making a successful claim for VCT deferral relief crystallises (ie is brought back into charge) on the occurrence of any of the following 'chargeable events' (TCGA 1992, Sch 5C, para 3(1)):

(*a*) a disposal by the investor of the acquired shares at any time. Where the shares have been transferred within marriage to the investor's spouse, the chargeable event is a disposal by the transferee spouse to a third party. For disposals of VCT shares, **[see Chapter 17]**;

(*b*) a scheme of reconstruction under which the acquired shares (if they qualify for investment relief but not for CGT disposal relief **[see Chapter 17]**) are exchanged for other shares or securities not qualifying for VCT relief **[see 17.3.7]**;

(*c*) a cessation of UK residence within three years of the investment by the investor or, where the acquired shares have been transferred within marriage to the investor's spouse, a cessation of UK residence by the transferee spouse within three years of the investment **[see 14.7.4]**;

(*d*) the withdrawal of qualifying VCT status from the investee company (other than by a retroactive cancellation of a provisional approval) **[see 14.7.5]**; or

(*e*) a loss of VCT investment relief on the shares in circumstances other than any in points (*a*) to (*d*) above **[see 14.7.6]**

(TCGA 1992, Sch 5C, para 3(1)).

By 'acquired shares' are meant the shares acquired as a result of the qualifying investment.

14.7.2 Gain accruing on a chargeable event

When the first chargeable event in relation to the shares occurs, the deferred chargeable gain is treated as accruing at the time of that event. The amount of the chargeable gain is equal to so much of the original gain as has been deferred by application of the qualifying investments (TCGA 1992, Sch 5C, para 4(1)).

14.7.3 Person chargeable on crystallisation

The deferred chargeable gain based on the investment in qualifying shares does not always accrue to the person who received the VCT investment relief on the shares. It could accrue to the spouse to whom the shares have been transferred, for example. Depending on what the chargeable event is, the gain accrues to the person who:

(*a*) becomes a non-resident while holding the shares;
(*b*) disposes of the shares (includes share exchanges);
(*c*) holds the shares when the withdrawal of VCT approval takes effect or circumstances arise in respect of which the relief is withdrawn or reduced;

where:

(1) the person holding the shares at a particular time is treated as the person to whom any chargeable gain accrues; and
(2) at that time, some of those shares are held by the investor and others are held by the investor's spouse or former spouse, the amount of the chargeable gain accruing is computed separately in relation to the investor and the spouse without reference to the shares held by the other

(TCGA 1992, Sch 5C, para 5).

14.7.4 Cessation of UK residence

To have obtained and to retain a deferral of a gain on a VCT investment the investor must have been and remain UK-resident or ordinarily resident and not be dual-resident **[see 14.4.2 and 14.4.3]**. There is a chargeable event where, within the 'relevant period' of three years from acquiring the shares:

(*a*) the investor still owns the shares but is no longer UK-resident; or
(*b*) the investor's spouse owns the shares and is no longer UK-resident

(TCGA 1992, Sch 5C, para 3(1)(d), (e)).

In the case of shares issued before 6 April 2000, the relevant period was five years. It may still be running, therefore, for such shares if there has been no previous chargeable event.

14.7.4.1 *Working abroad temporarily*

There is an exception for employees seconded abroad or working abroad temporarily. The deferred gain does not crystallise in relation to any shares if:

(*a*) the reason why the person in question has ceased to be UK-resident is that he or she works in an employment or office, all the duties of which are performed outside the UK; and
(*b*) the person again becomes UK-resident or ordinarily resident within the period of three years from the time when he or she became non-resident, without having meanwhile disposed of any of the shares

(TCGA 1992, Sch 5C, para 3(3)).

Accordingly, the Inland Revenue will not raise an assessment before the end of that three-year period in any case where the qualifying foreign employment condition is satisfied.

In this context, a person is taken to have disposed of his or her shares if and only if the disposal would have been a chargeable event if the person making the disposal had been UK-resident (TCGA 1992, Sch 5C, para 3(4)).

14.7.5 Loss of VCT status by the investor company

An investor with a minority interest may find it difficult to ensure that the investor company continues to qualify for VCT status. If the investor becomes aware that there is likely to be a breach, he or she should consider selling the shares so that there is enough cash to pay the tax on the deferred gain or making a further qualifying investment.

Another disadvantage of allowing a gain to crystallise other than on a disposal is that other reliefs are not available. For example, gift holdover relief **[see 23.2]** only applies where there is a disposal.

Example 14.6

Giambattista defers a chargeable gain of £80,000 by investing £80,000 in new ordinary shares of Vico Venture Capital Trust and claiming VCT investment relief. A year later Giambattista is warned that Vico's VCT status may soon become endangered because its investments may fail to meet the required percentages **[see 5.6]**. As a precaution, Giambattista transfers the shares to a discretionary trust, and elects to hold over the gain under TCGA 1992, s 260.

Using a discretionary trust in this way is no longer effective to hold over the gain after 9 December 2003, however, unless the settlor (Giambattista in this case) has no interest in the trust either at the time or subsequently, which is unlikely in these situations.

Of course, Giambattista would still have the option to defer the gain arising on the transfer into trust against a new VCT investment (before 6 April 2004) or an EIS investment made at any time between one year preceding the transfer and three years after the transfer, although he would have generated no new funds with which to make the investment.

14.7.6 Loss of investment relief in other circumstances

A deferred gain also crystallises if the VCT investment relief is reduced or withdrawn for reasons other than those specifically listed as chargeable events (TCGA 1992, Sch 5C, para 3(1)(g)). This may happen, for instance, because the investor obtains a 'linked loan' **[see 11.2]**.

14.7.7 Exception for death

Death is not a chargeable event, nor is anything that happens to the shares after death. Thus if what otherwise would be a chargeable event occurs on or after the death of the investor or of the investor's spouse (if the shares have been transferred within marriage to that spouse), it is not a chargeable event in relation to the shares (TCGA 1992, Sch 5C, para 3(5)).

Chapter 15

Reinvestment in EIS Companies

15.1 Introduction and background

15.1.1 Background to EIS deferral relief

The ability to defer chargeable gains by reinvesting into EIS companies has been available since 6 April 1998. As explained in **14.1.1**, EIS deferral relief underwent a major change in 1998, when the former reinvestment rollover relief, the previous mechanism for deferring gains, was abolished. As part of our general approach to this book, as explained in **Chapter 1**, we shall not deal here with the old reinvestment rollover relief, since it applies (to the extent that it still does at all) to shares issued before 6 April 1998 only.

15.1.2 Scope of this chapter

This chapter deals with the following topics:

(*a*) A summary of EIS deferral relief **[see 15.2]**
(*b*) Which gains can be deferred? **[see 15.3]**
(*c*) Who can claim EIS deferral relief? **[see 15.4]**
(*d*) What are qualifying investments? **[see 15.5]**
(*e*) How much of the gain can be deferred? **[see 15.6]**
(*f*) When and how does the gain crystallise? **[see 15.7 to 15.12]**
(*g*) The effect of company reconstructions **[see 15.13]**

15.2 A summary of EIS deferral relief

EIS deferral relief allows a chargeable gain made by an individual (and in certain circumstances by trustees – see **15.4.5**) to be deferred if, within the 'qualifying time', that individual ('the investor') makes a 'qualifying investment' (broadly, subscribes for shares that would be eligible for EIS investment relief, but on which the investor does not have actually to obtain EIS investment relief) **[see 15.5]**. The gain is deferred to the extent that it is matched by the qualifying investment. The qualifying investment must be made within a certain time preceding the accrual of the gain or within a certain time afterwards. The deferred gain crystallises (becomes taxable) when there is a 'chargeable event' in relation to the investment, but can be deferred again if matched with a further qualifying investment, and so on indefinitely **[see 15.6]**.

15.2.1 Deferred gains, indexation and taper relief

It is important to realise that EIS deferral relief, like the former VCT deferral relief but not like CGT rollover reliefs, does not provide for the deferred gain to be rolled over into the cost of the replacement asset (shares in EIS companies). Instead, it stands deferred unless and until a chargeable event occurs **[see 15.7]**, when it becomes immediately assessable in its original amount. There is thus no question of indexation or taper relief during the period of deferment. For the interaction of taper relief and the EIS reliefs generally, see **Chapter 23**.

15.2.2 Restricted periods

There is a multiplicity of periods during which certain events must occur or transactions must be undertaken and others must not occur or must not be undertaken. For the sake of convenience, they are defined here, except for the 'qualifying time' during which the investment must be made **[see 15.3.2]**.

The 'relevant period', which relates to investment-linked loans **[see 15.4.5]** and the grant of options **[see 15.12]** is the period beginning on the later of:

(*a*) the incorporation of the company and
(*b*) two years before the issue date of the shares

and ending immediately before the later of:

(*a*) the third anniversary of the issue date and
(*b*) the third anniversary of the date on which the qualifying trade begins

(TA 1988, s 312(1A)(a)) and TCGA 1992, Sch 5B, para 19(1)).

The 'period of restriction' is the period during which value must not be received by the investor **[see 15.8]**, and it is defined as the period that begins one year before the issue date and ends immediately before the later of:

(*a*) the third anniversary of the issue date and
(*b*) the third anniversary of the date on which the qualifying trade begins

(TCGA 1992, Sch 5B, para 19(1)).

Yet other periods applied to shares issued before 6 April 2000 and to events occurring before 7 March 2001.

15.3 Which gains can be deferred?

15.3.1 The type of gain eligible for deferment

There are three main types of gain that may be deferred:

(*a*) the chargeable gain arising on the disposal (after 28 November 1994) or deemed disposal of any asset;
(*b*) a gain that has already been deferred under either VCT deferral relief, EIS deferral relief or reinvestment rollover relief **[see 15.1.1]** and has now come back into charge whether because of a disposal or on the occurrence of some other chargeable event; and
(*c*) gain arising on a clawback of the former reinvestment rollover relief. The latest possible date on which such a clawback could have occurred is 5 April 2001. The latest date on which a qualifying investment could therefore have been made in order to defer the clawback charge is 5 April 2004

(TCGA 1992, Sch 5B, para 1(1)(a), (b)).

Gains that may arise (under TCGA 1992, s 116(10)(b)) as a result of a disposal of a qualifying corporate bond acquired as a result of a paper-for-paper exchange in a company reconstruction are also eligible gains for deferral relief (Revenue Interpretation RI 134, *Tax Bulletin,* Issue 20, December 1995). This interpretation was given for reinvestment rollover relief, but there is no reason why it should not be valid for EIS deferral relief also.

15.3.2 Period for making qualifying investments

The time allowed for making the qualifying investment on which the claim to defer the gain is based is known as the 'qualifying time'. That time is the period beginning one year before and ending *three* (note the contrast with VCT deferral relief) years after the gain arises (the date on which the gain arises is known as the 'accrual time').

The Inland Revenue has the power to allow an extension of the qualifying time to a point more than a year before the accrual time and to a point more than three years after the accrual time. This power, incidentally, may only be exercised at higher levels within the Inland Revenue, as it has not been delegated to area inspectors (Venture Capital Schemes Manual, para VCM 38030).

15.3.2.1 *The Inland Revenue's policy in considering extensions to the qualifying time*

The following extract from the Venture Capital Schemes Manual sets out the Inland Revenue's policy when considering requests to allow qualifying investments to be made outside the statutory time limits.

'The Board will extend the time limits where the claimant can show that he or she:

(*a*) had a firm intention to comply with the time limits but

(*b*) was prevented by some fact or circumstance beyond his or her control from complying and

(*c*) acted as soon as he or she reasonably could after ceasing to be so prevented.

It is a question of fact and degree and each case is considered on its own merits. Examples of circumstances outside the claimant's control might include death or a serious illness of a vital party at a crucial time, unsettled disputes or litigation or unexpected delay in receipt of disposal consideration.

A mere change of intention at a late stage or a shortage of funds arising out of the application of the disposal consideration to some purpose other than the subscription for [eligible EIS] shares will not normally be regarded as circumstances beyond the claimant's control.

No decision on a possible extension of the time limits can be made until the disposal has taken place, the [eligible EIS] shares have been issued and all other conditions of relief are satisfied.

If the [EIS] shares have been issued outside the statutory time limits and a request is made for an extension [the inspector] should explain the criteria set out above to the claimant so that [he or she] can demonstrate [his or her] case. [The inspector] should then make a report to CGT (Solihull) with [his or her] recommendation and the claimant's file.'

(para VCM 68060).

It should be noted that the 'years' referred to in the legislation are calendar years and not tax years **[see 15.3.3]**.

15.3.3 Limits on the gain deferred

There is no quantitative limit on the amount that the investor may invest in qualifying investments in any given tax year. The only monetary limit that may be imposed is that set by the gross asset test that the qualifying company must satisfy **[see 15.5.2]**.

Example 15.1

Paul disposes of a property on 24 June 2003, realising a gain of £1.2 million. He can defer the gain if he makes qualifying investments under the EIS or VCT deferral reliefs, as follows:

Tax year	*VCT deferral limit*	*EIS deferral limit*
2002–03*	£100,000	no limit
2003–04	£100,000	no limit
2004–05	not available	no limit
2005–06	not available	no limit
2006–07	not available	no limit**

*= the investment must not have been made before 24 June 2002

**= the investment must be made before 25 June 2006

15.3.4 Date of disposal

For a discussion of the effective date of disposal of an asset for CGT purposes, see **14.3.4**.

15.4 Entitlement to claim a deferment

15.4.1 Claimants

The investor claiming EIS deferral relief must be an individual (TCGA 1992, Sch 5B, para 1(1)(a)).

In certain circumstances, however, trustees may claim EIS deferral relief **[see 15.4.5]**.

15.4.1.1 *Nominees*

Since EIS deferral relief is part of the capital gains regime, it is also available where the shares in the qualifying investment are acquired not by the investor in person but by the investor's nominee (TCGA 1992, s 60).

15.4.1.2 *Partnerships*

If a partnership realises a gain on the disposal of an asset, the gain is attributed to each of the partners personally. This means that all or any of them can invest their part of the gain and claim EIS deferral relief.

However, it is the Inland Revenue's view that a partnership as an entity may not make a qualifying investment that would allow partners to claim EIS deferral relief. This is because EIS deferral relief is only available where there is a direct acquisition by an individual of the entirety of a number of eligible shares **[see 15.5.1]** and in a partnership, each of the partners holds a fractional share in the partnership's assets (TCGA 1992, Sch 5B, para 1(2)(a)).

15.4.2 UK residence

The investor must be resident or ordinarily resident in the UK both at the accrual time and at the time when he or she makes the qualifying investment (TCGA 1992, Sch 5B, para 1(1)(d)).

15.4.3 Dual residence

The investor is not treated as meeting the UK residence condition if:

(*a*) although resident or ordinarily resident in the UK at the time of the qualifying investment, he or she is regarded for the purposes of any double tax treaty as resident outside the UK; and (*b*) ignoring the capital gains exemption on EIS shares, the treaty would have the effect of relieving the investor of liability to tax in the UK on a gain that would arise on a disposal of the shares acquired in making the investment ('the acquired shares') immediately after their acquisition

(TCGA 1992, Sch 5B, para 1(4)).

This situation would arise where the investor was resident in the UK under UK domestic law (say, because he was physically present in the UK for more than 183 days in the tax year concerned) but also resident in some other jurisdiction under that jurisdiction's domestic law concerning residence. In such cases, if the other jurisdiction has a tax treaty with the UK, there will normally be a 'tie-breaker' article to determine for treaty purposes whether the investor is UK resident or resident in the other jurisdiction.

Tax treaties also contain provisions conferring the right to tax any particular type of income or capital gain to either or both treaty partners. In the case of capital gains made by a non-resident of the UK, the treaty could well provide that the gain be taxable only by the treaty partner. This rule has in mind the situation where the particular treaty concerned denies the UK the right to tax the gain arising on any disposal of the EIS shares acquired.

15.4.4 Active or passive investor

An individual who wishes to defer a gain may also want to be involved in the company in which he or she invests. This is feasible under the EIS deferral regime where the investor can be an employee or a paid director or even control the company, since there is no bar on investors who are 'connected' with the company. However, the investor must not receive 'value' (subject to the rules for replacement value) **[see further 15.8]**.

15.4.5 Trustees as investors

Trustees cannot claim EIS investment relief when acting as such (if they are individuals, they may of course do so in their personal capacities) but they may, in certain circumstances, claim EIS deferral relief.

In order for them to do so, the gain they are seeking to defer must arise on certain trust assets. Those trust assets must either be:

(*a*) where all the beneficiaries of the trust are individuals or charities, any property in a discretionary trust (and any other settled property in which the beneficiaries do not have an interest in possession) ('type-A assets'); or

(*b*) where any of the beneficiaries is an individual or a charity, any property in which the beneficiaries do have an interest in possession ('type-B assets')

(TCGA 1992, Sch 5B, para 17(1), (2), (8)).

An interest for a fixed term is not an interest in possession for this purpose.

Where the gain arises on type-A assets, the trustees will be entitled to claim deferral relief only if the acquired shares are also type-A assets immediately after the acquisition (TCGA 1992, Sch 5B, para 17(4)).

Similarly, where the gain that the trustees wish to defer is on a type-B asset, the trustees must invest in shares that become type-B assets (TCGA 1992, Sch 5B, para 17(5)).

If not all of the beneficiaries are individuals or charities at the accrual time, only the 'relevant proportion' of the gain qualifies for deferral relief. The relevant proportion is A/B, where A is the total trust income in which the beneficiaries who are individuals or charities have an interest and B is the total trust income (TCGA 1992, Sch 5B, para 17(6)). No deferral relief is available at all if the relevant proportion immediately after the qualifying investment is made is less than the relevant proportion at the accrual time, ie the effect of the qualifying investment must not be to dilute the interests in the trust property of beneficiaries who are individuals or charities (TCGA 1992, Sch 5B, para 17(5)(b)).

Where in the case of trust property in which any beneficiaries hold an interest in possession, there are any beneficiaries who hold interests that are not interests in possession (remaindermen, for example):

(*a*) the interests of the beneficiaries without interests in possession are treated as if they were a single interest in possession; and
(*b*) where all those beneficiaries are individuals or charities, the deemed single interest is treated as if held by an individual or charity; or
(*c*) where that is not the case, it is treated as if held by a person who is neither an individual nor a charity

(TCGA 1992, Sch 5B, para 17(7).

The rules on receipt of value and receipt of replacement value **[see 15.8 and 15.10]** apply to trustees as does the rule on investment-linked loans **[see 15.4.6]**.

15.4.6 The prohibition on investment-linked loans

This rule will be familiar from EIS investment relief **[see 7.3.4]**. Deferral relief is denied, or later withdrawn, if at any time in the 'relevant period' **[see 15.2.2]** the investor or an associate of the investor receives a loan that would not have been made at all or would not have been made on the same terms if the investor had not subscribed for the shares or been intending to do so. Making a loan includes the giving of credit or the assignment (in Scotland, assignation) of a debt due from the investor (TCGA 1992, Sch 5B, para 15). For a fuller discussion of investment-linked loans, see **7.3.4**).

15.4.7 The prohibition on pre-arranged exits

The investor cannot claim EIS deferral relief if when he or she makes the investment, there are arrangements in place at the time of the share issue or before the share issue but in connection with it with a view to:

(*a*) the repurchase, exchange or disposal of those shares or any other shares or securities in the company; or
(*b*) the cessation of any trade that is, will be or may be carried on by the company or by a person connected with the company; or
(*c*) the disposal of all or a substantial part of the assets of the company or of a person connected with the company; or
(*d*) the provision of partial or complete protection against the risks attached to making the investment (whether by a form of insurance, indemnity etc or otherwise)

(TCGA 1992, Sch 5B, para 11).

Normal arrangements for the winding-up of the company in the event of insolvency etc, of the kind that might be found in a company's Articles of Association are exempt from this rule.

The arrangements in (*a*) do not include arrangements to create a holding company to take over the investee company in the circumstances described in **15.13.3**.

The arrangements in (*d*) do not include arrangements which are confined to the provision of such protection against the risks arising in the course of carrying on its business as the company might be expected to provide in normal commercial circumstances (TCGA 1992, Sch 5B, para 11(4)).

'Arrangements' include any scheme, agreement or understanding, whether or not legally binding (TCGA 1992, Sch 5B, para 19(1)).

15.5 Qualifying investments

15.5.1 The meaning of 'qualifying investment'

The investor makes a qualifying EIS investment if:

(*a*) he or she subscribes for eligible shares in a 'qualifying company';
(*b*) the subscription is in cash and the EIS shares are fully paid up when issued (in both cases except to the extent that some shares are bonus shares);
(*c*) the shares are issued at the qualifying time;
(*d*) where the shares are issued before the accrual time, the investor still holds the shares at the accrual time;
(*e*) the subscription and the issue are made for bona fide commercial purposes and not as part of a tax avoidance scheme;
(*f*) all the shares comprised in the issue (not just the EIS shares), except for any bonus shares, are issued in order to raise money for a qualifying business activity;

(*g*) where the company is the parent company of a trading group, the company carrying on the qualifying business activity is either the parent company or a qualifying 90% subsidiary (the same rules about disregarding certain activities apply as for EIS investment relief – see **5.7.3.2**); and

(*h*) at least 80% of the money raised by the issue of the shares and any other eligible shares of the same class issued on the same day is employed in the trade within 12 months of the later of the issue date and the date on which the qualifying trade began, and the remaining 20% is employed in that way within 24 months of the later of the two dates

(TCGA 1992, Sch 5B, para 1(2)).

As regards points (*b*) and (*f*), the exception for bonus shares applies to shares issued after 16 March 2004 only. For earlier share issues, the inclusion of bonus shares in an issue would have disqualified the investment.

As regards point (*b*), shares issued after 16 March 2004 are not considered to be fully paid up if there is only an undertaking to pay cash to any person at some future date in respect of the acquisition (TCGA 1992, Sch 5B, para 1(5)). For earlier share issues, there was no specific reference to the disregard of future undertakings to pay that the payment be connected to the acquisition. At the same time, only undertakings to pay the company were disregarded. In essence therefore, for shares issued before 17 March 2004, an undertaking to pay a third person other than the company may, in theory, not be disregarded, nor may an undertaking to pay cash to the company in some other connection entirely.

In point (*g*), reference to a 'qualifying 90% subsidiary' should be read as a reference to a '90% subsidiary for shares issued before 17 March 2004. For such shares also, the rules about disregarding certain activities discussed in **5.7.3.2** do not include an ability to disregard the fact that the qualifying trade or business activity may have been carried on by a company other than the investee company and a subsidiary before either the investee company or a qualifying 90% subsidiary began to carry it on **[see 5.7.5.2]**.

As regards point (*h*), before 7 March 2001, only 12 months were allowed before all of the money raised had to have been employed for the purpose of the qualifying business activity.

'Eligible shares' are new ordinary shares that, throughout the period from their issue to the later of (*a*) the third anniversary of the issue and (*b*) the third anniversary of the date on which the qualifying trade began, carry no present or future preferential right to dividends or to a company's assets on its winding-up and no present or future right to be redeemed (TCGA 1992, Sch 5B, para 19(1); TA 1988, s 289(7)). For shares issued before 6 April 2000, the restricted period ran for five years from the later of the issue date and the commencement of the trade. Shares can cease to be eligible on the occurrence of a number of events.

For the meaning of 'qualifying business activity', see **5.7.5.1**; for 'parent company of a trading group', see **5.7.3.2**.

15.5.2 Qualifying companies

A 'qualifying company' is a qualifying company for the purposes of EIS investment relief **[see Chapters 5 and 6]**. Hence the limitation on investment provided by the gross assets test of TA 1988, s 293(6A).

15.5.3 Shares that can be acquired

As the investor is not restricted as to the amount that he or she can invest and does not have to obtain EIS investment relief on the acquired shares, the investor can:

(*a*) subscribe for 100% of the shares of a company;
(*b*) subscribe for further shares in a company in which he or she is a shareholder;
(*c*) subscribe for shares in a company owned by a relative; or
(*d*) set up a new company, which he or she would wholly own, either to acquire or to start a qualifying trade;
(*e*) subscribe for shares at different times and in different companies

as long as on each occasion the investee company is and remains a qualifying company for EIS purposes.

Example 15.2

On 3 December 2003 Rachel sells a portfolio of rented office blocks for £3 million realising a gain of £2 million. A year later she sets up a company to own and operate a sports injury clinic and subscribes £1.5 million for 100% of the ordinary share capital. On 1 December 2004 Rachel defers paying tax on £1.5 million of her gain on the grounds that she has made a qualifying investment. If Rachel makes further qualifying investments before 3 December 2006 of up to £500,000 she will be able to make a further claim for EIS deferral relief and obtain a repayment of the tax she has paid.

15.5.4 Shares that are excluded

The qualifying investment cannot be either of the following:

(*a*) shares in the same company, or in a company in the same group, as any shares that were the subject of the original disposal **[see 15.5.5]**; or
(*b*) shares in the same company as an earlier qualifying investment where some or all of the shares have been sold **[see 15.5.6]**.

15.5.5 Reinvestment in the same company

An investor is not regarded as having made a qualifying investment if the asset disposed of consisted of shares (or securities), and the investee company is either:

(*a*) the same company in which the shares subsisted; or

(*b*) a company that is, at the accrual time, or is, at the time of the investment, a member of the same group of companies as the company in which the shares subsisted

(TCGA 1992, Sch 5B, para 10(1)).

For disposals after 16 March 2004, there is a new definition of 'group' for this purpose. A group consists of a company and its 51% subsidiaries (TCGA 1992, Sch 5B, para 10(4)). For the meaning of '51% subsidiary', see **5.15.1**. For earlier disposals, there was no definition in TCGA 1992, Sch 5B of what was meant by a group; for most capital gains purposes, a group consists of a company and its 75% subsidiaries, with some exclusions and conditions (TCGA 1992, s 170(2)).

This will prevent a claim to EIS deferral relief where an individual sells shares in his or her company and later buys back shares in a subsidiary that the purchaser decides he does not want.

Example 15.3

Rudolph and Henry each own half the shares in Steiner Ltd, which has a 75% subsidiary, Sidgwick Ltd, the remaining shares being held by Claude. Following a dispute with Rudolph, Henry sells his shares in Steiner in May 2003 to Rudolph and realises a gain of £43,000. Six months later Henry subscribes for shares in Sidgwick for £60,000. Henry is unable to defer his gain because, at the time that it arose, Steiner and Sidgwick were part of a group.

15.5.6 Sale of shares in a qualifying company

There is a further situation where relief is denied. This is where the investor has previously acquired shares in the same company or group as a qualifying EIS deferral investment and has disposed of those shares before making the acquisition that is being considered (TCGA 1992, Sch 5B, para 10(2), (3)).

For shares issued after 16 March 2004, the same new definition of 'group' applies for this purpose as applies for reinvestment in **15.5.5** above. For earlier issues, recourse has probably had to be had to the TCGA 1992, s 170(2) definition.

Example 15.4

In May 2003 Francis subscribes for shares in Bradley Ltd for £14,000 and defers a £10,000 gain. He sells the shares in July 2004 and tax on the gain becomes payable. In September 2005 he sells a property and realises a gain of £22,000 that he wishes to defer by subscribing for further ordinary shares in Bradley. Such an acquisition would not qualify because of the previous share sale.

15.5.7 Cash consideration

The consideration given for the shares must be in cash (TCGA 1992, Sch 5B, para 1(5)).

However, it is not necessary for the actual proceeds from the sale of the asset to be invested; cash from another source can be used to subscribe for the shares.

Example 15.5

Jane, who has substantial savings, intends to use £40,000 from her building society account to subscribe for shares representing 50% of the share capital of an unquoted company in which her daughter is the other shareholder. Jane is planning to sell some of her quoted shares in order to realise a £40,000 gain and use the proceeds to purchase some other shares. She will then claim to defer the gain into the shares she subscribes for in her daughter's company.

15.6 Deferring gains

15.6.1 Introduction

A claim for EIS deferral relief may be made in respect of a gain arising on the disposal of an asset or on the crystallisation of a gain previously deferred under the EIS or VCT deferral reliefs (or indeed, until 5 April 2004, under the previous reinvestment rollover relief – see **15.3.1**). All of these gains will be referred to as the 'original gain' in this section.

15.6.2 The amount of the gain that can be deferred

The amount of the gain that can be deferred cannot be greater than either:

(*a*) the investor's unused qualifying expenditure; or
(*b*) the investor's unmatched original gain;

but subject to those limits any amount of expenditure specified in the claim may be set against the corresponding amount of the gain (TCGA 1992, Sch 5B, para 2(1)).

15.6.2.1 *What is meant by the chargeable gain?*

The gain to be matched is the gain as computed after deduction of indexation allowance (if any) and retirement relief (where the gain accrued before 6 April 2003) but before reduction by taper relief, loss relief or the annual exempt amount.

15.6.3 Unused qualifying expenditure

Qualifying expenditure is the amount subscribed by the investor for the shares acquired by him or her in making the qualifying investment. Where the investment is made before the accrual time, it represents the amount subscribed for the shares that the investor still holds (TCGA 1992, Sch 5B, paras 2(3)(a), 19(1)).

Qualifying expenditure is unused to the extent that it has not already been set for the purposes of EIS deferral relief against the whole or any part of a chargeable gain (TCGA 1992, Sch 5B, para 2(3)(b)).

15.6.4 The unmatched gain

The unmatched gain is that part of the original gain which has not already been deferred by making a qualifying VCT or EIS investment (TCGA 1992, Sch 5B, para 2(4)).

Example 15.6

Zhuangzi disposes of a property on 22 July 2003 and realises a gain of £155,000. In May 2004, he subscribes £90,000 for a qualifying investment in an EIS company. He claims EIS deferral relief on £90,000 of his gain. His unmatched gain after the investment is £65,000 and his unmatched expenditure is nil. If Zhuangzi were to make another qualifying investment before 22 July 2006 of, say, £70,000, he would have £70,000 of unmatched expenditure to set against the unmatched gain of £65,000. If he were then to make a claim for EIS deferral relief for all of the unmatched gain, he would be left with unmatched expenditure of £5,000.

15.6.5 Effect of deferral relief on the deferred gain

Where a successful claim to EIS deferral relief is made, that part of the gain that is deferred is deemed not to have accrued at the accrual time. Instead, it is deferred and brought back into charge on the occurrence of a chargeable event, such as a disposal of the acquired shares or a breach of the qualifying conditions (TCGA 1992, Sch 5B, para 2(2)).

15.7 Bringing gains back into charge

15.7.1 Introduction

A chargeable gain that has been deferred on making a successful claim for EIS deferral relief crystallises (is brought back into charge) on the occurrence of any of the following 'chargeable events':

(*a*) a disposal by the investor of the acquired shares at any time – where the shares have been transferred within marriage to the investor's spouse, the chargeable event is a disposal by the transferee spouse to a third party. For disposals of EIS shares, see **Chapter 18**;

(*b*) a cessation of UK residence by the investor before the 'termination date' for the shares or, where the acquired shares have been transferred within marriage to the investor's spouse, a cessation of UK residence by the transferee spouse before the 'termination date' for the shares **[see 15.7.4]**; or

(*c*) loss of eligibility status for the acquired shares.

The 'termination date' for the shares is the later of:

(*a*) the third anniversary of the issue date and

(*b*) the third anniversary of the date on which the qualifying trade commenced

(TCGA 1992, Sch 5C, paras 3(1), 19(1)).

15.7.2 Gain accruing on a chargeable event

When the first chargeable event in relation to the shares occurs, the deferred chargeable gain is treated as accruing at the time of that event. The amount of the chargeable gain is equal to so much of the deferred gain as is attributable to the shares in relation to which the chargeable event has occurred (TCGA 1992, Sch 5B, para 4(1)(b)).

If the chargeable event is not a disposal or is a disposal of all the acquired shares, the entire deferred gain crystallises. If the chargeable event is a disposal of some of the shares, then that proportion of the gain crystallises which corresponds to the proportion of shares disposed of (TCGA 1992, Sch 5B, para 4(6)).

Example 15.7

Sarah Michelle realises a gain of £80,000, which she defers by subscribing for 8,000 £10 shares in Sunnydale Ltd. Two years later, she sells 3,600 of the shares for £45,000 to fund a house purchase. The sale will bring

$$\frac{3{,}600}{8{,}000} \times £80{,}000 = £36{,}000$$

of the deferred gain into charge. This is, of course, in addition to any CGT liability on the disposal itself, plus any loss of EIS investment relief if it was obtained. Both the £36,000 gain and any gain on disposal can themselves be deferred by a suitable further EIS or VCT investment (but, in the case of a VCT investment only if the qualifying time includes a period before 6 April 2004 and the investment is in fact made before that date).

The remainder of the deferred gain, £44,000, will be brought into charge if a further chargeable event occurs.

15.7.2.1 *Gains matched with several acquisitions*

For the rules matching the gain to more than one issue of eligible shares and for identifying which shares out of a mixed holding are disposed of, see **Chapter 18**.

15.7.3 Persons chargeable on crystallisation

The deferred chargeable gain when it crystallises does not always accrue to the person who made the qualifying EIS investment. It could, for example, accrue to the spouse to whom the shares were transferred. The person chargeable could thus be:

(*a*) the person who makes the disposal;
(*b*) the person who becomes non-resident while holding the shares; or
(*c*) the person holding the shares when they cease to be eligible shares,

as the case may be (TCGA 1992, Sch 5B, para 5(1)).

Where:

(*a*) the person holding the shares at a particular time is the person to whom the chargeable gain accrues; and
(*b*) at that time, some of those shares are held by the investor and others are held by the investor's spouse or former spouse (to whom they were transferred during marriage);

the amount of the chargeable gain accruing is computed separately in relation to the investor and to the spouse, without reference to the shares held by the other (TCGA 1992, Sch 5, para 5(2)).

15.7.4 Cessation of UK residence

To make a successful claim for EIS deferral relief, the investor must be resident or ordinarily resident in the UK and not be a dual resident **[see 15.4.2 and 15.4.3]**. The entire deferred gain is brought into charge, however, if before the termination date **[see 15.2.2]**, the investor or the investor's spouse (as the case may be, if they have been transferred to that spouse) becomes non-resident (ie ceases to be both resident and ordinarily resident) while holding the shares (TCGA 1992, Sch 5B, para 3(1)(c), (d)).

15.7.4.1 *Working abroad temporarily*

There is an exception for employees seconded abroad or working abroad temporarily. The deferred gain does not crystallise if:

(*a*) the reason why the person in question has ceased to be UK resident is that he or she is working in an employment or office all the duties of which are performed outside the UK; and (*b*) the person becomes UK resident or ordinarily resident again within the period of three years from the time when he or she became non-resident, without meanwhile having disposed of any of the shares.

Accordingly, the deferred gain will not become assessable before the end of the three-year period in any case where the qualifying foreign employment condition is satisfied (TCGA 1992, Sch 5B, para 3(3)).

In this context, a person is taken to have disposed of his or her shares if and only if the disposal would have been a chargeable event if the person making the disposal had been UK resident (TCGA 1992, Sch 5B, para 3(4)).

15.7.5 Loss of eligibility by acquired shares

Any loss of qualifying status by the investee company will cause the acquired shares to lose their status as eligible shares, and in turn cause the entire gain to crystallise (TCGA 1992, Sch 5B, para 3(1)(e)).

Shares cease to be eligible shares if, within the period beginning with the issue of the shares and ending immediately before the 'termination date', they begin to carry preferential rights or they begin to be entitled to do so at some future time, or if they cease to be ordinary shares (TA 1988, s 289(7); TCGA 1992, Sch 5B, para 19(1)).

For shares issued before 6 April 2000, the restricted period is the period beginning with the issue of the shares and ending five years later.

For the 'termination date', see **15.7.1**.

Shares are treated as ceasing to be eligible shares in the following circumstances:

(*a*) the company ceases to be a qualifying company, ie if any of the conditions described in **Chapters 5** and **6** cease to be satisfied. The shares cease to be eligible shares on the date when the conditions cease to be satisfied;
(*b*) the company carrying on the qualifying activity (where it is not the parent company of a trading group) ceases within the relevant period to be a qualifying 90% subsidiary of the company that issued the shares. The shares cease to be eligible shares at the date of change;
(*c*) if it transpires that the money received for the shares (ignoring insignificant amounts) was not raised for the purposes of a qualifying business activity, the shares are treated as never having been eligible shares;
(*d*) the money received for the issue of the shares is not employed wholly for the purposes of a qualifying business activity within the time limits mentioned at **15.5.1**. If the claim for deferral relief is made after the end of the 12- or 24-month period (whichever is relevant), the shares are treated as never having been eligible shares; otherwise they cease to be eligible shares at the end of that 12- or 24-month period.

For the relevant period, see **15.2.2**.

As regards point (*b*), the reference to a 'qualifying 90% subsidiary' should be read, for shares issued before 17 March 2004, as a reference to a '90% subsidiary'.

The provisions described in (*a*)–(*d*) above only apply if either:

(1) the company has given notice of the circumstance concerned, or
(2) the Inland Revenue has given notice that it considers that the shares should not be, or should cease to be treated as, eligible shares.

(TCGA 1992, Sch 5B, para 1A).

There is a right of appeal against the Inland Revenue notice; if an appeal was made against a notice on the same issue regarding EIS income tax relief, a determination of that appeal is conclusive for the deferral relief provisions.

15.7.5.1 *Choices for the minority investor*

An investor with only a minority interest may find it difficult to ensure that the investee company continues to qualify for EIS status. Where the investor's capital is essential to the company, he or she may be able to obtain assurances that the directors will use their best endeavours to ensure that the company meet the conditions. If the investor becomes aware that there is likely to be a breach, he or she should consider selling the shares so that there is enough cash to pay the tax on the gain or make a further qualifying investment.

Another disadvantage of allowing a gain to crystallise other than on a disposal is that other capital gains tax reliefs are not available. For example, business-gift holdover relief **[see 23.2]** only applies where there is a disposal.

Example 15.8

Gorgias defers a chargeable gain of £205,000 by investing £205,000 in new ordinary shares in Leontini Ltd, a machine-manufacturing company, and successfully claiming EIS deferral relief. A year later, Leontini starts leasing as well as selling its machines. Before Leontini's leasing becomes a substantial activity, Gorgias transfers his shares to a discretionary trust and elects to hold over the gain under TCGA 1992, s 260. Note that where the transfer takes place after 9 December 2003, holdover relief under section 260 is available only if the trust is not, and will not become, a settlor-interested trust. Gorgias would therefore have to renounce any possible beneficial interest or accept potential liability to capital gains tax on the transfer.

15.7.6 Exception for death

Death is not a chargeable event, nor is anything that happens to the shares after death. Thus if what otherwise would be a chargeable event occurs on or after the death of the investor or of the investor's spouse (if the shares have been transferred within marriage to that spouse), it is not a chargeable event in relation to the shares (TCGA 1992, Sch 5B, para 3(5)).

15.8 The return of value

15.8.1 Introduction

If once the investor has acquired shares in a qualifying company and has claimed EIS deferral relief, the whole or any part of the value of that investment is returned to the investor, those shares will be treated as having ceased to be eligible shares, which in turn will lead to crystallisation of the entire deferred gain. If value is received before the shares are issued, they are treated as never having been eligible shares (TCGA 1992, Sch 5, para 13(1)). An exception is made, however, for receipts of insignificant value **[see 15.9]**.

15.8.2 Occasions on which value received

These provisions are virtually the same as the value-received rules for the purposes of EIS investment relief **[see 12.5]**. They include situations where the company enters into any of the following transactions:

(*a*) repays, redeems or repurchases any of its share capital or other securities belonging to the investor **[see 12.5.4]**;
(*b*) makes any payment to the investor in return for the investor's giving up his or her right to any of the company's share capital or any security on its cancellation or extinguishment;
(*c*) repays any debt owed to the investor under arrangements made in connection with the investment, other than a debt that was incurred by the company:
    (1) on or after the issue of the shares; and
    (2) was not the replacement of an earlier debt **[see 12.5.6]**;
(*d*) makes to the investor any payment for giving up his or her right to any debt on its extinguishment **[see 12.5.7]**;
(*e*) releases or waives any liability of the investor to the company or discharges, or undertakes to discharge, any liability of the investor to a third person **[see 12.5.8]**;
(*f*) makes a loan or advance to the investor, which remains outstanding in full or in part at the time of the acquisition – instances where the investor incurs any debt other than an ordinary trade debt to the company or where the investor's debt to a third party is assigned to the company count as making a loan **[see 12.5.9]**;
(*g*) provides a benefit or facility for the investor **[see 12.5.10]**;
(*h*) transfers an asset to the investor for no consideration or at an undervalue **[see 12.5.11]**;

(*i*) acquires an asset from the investor at an overvalue **[see 12.5.11]**;
(*j*) makes any other payment to the investor other than a qualifying payment **[see 12.5.12]**.

(TCGA 1992, Sch 5B, para 13(2), (3)).

15.8.2.1 *Associated and connected persons*

All references to the investor in the above list include references to an associate of the investor and all references to the company (ie the investee company) include references to a person (including a subsidiary) who is at any time in the 'relevant period' connected to the company. This is regardless of whether the connection exists at the time of the relevant transaction.

For the definitions of 'associate' and 'connected person', **see 7.3.4.1** and **5.1.6** respectively.

Also, any mention of payments or disposals to the investor include payments and disposals made to the investor indirectly or to his or her order or benefit. (TCGA 1992, Sch 5B, para 13(10)).

15.8.3 Repayment, redemption or repurchase of capital

There is no restriction on the type of share or security repayment etc of which will cause value to be received by the investor or the investor's associate. It includes, for example, the redemption of preference shares or debentures.

15.8.3.1 *Amount of value received*

The value received on the occasion of a repayment, repurchase or redemption is the greater of the amount received and the market value of the shares or securities concerned (TCGA 1992, Sch 5B, para 13A(1)(a)).

Example 15.9

In August 2003, Zeno defers a gain of £30,000 by investing £40,000 in Elea Ltd, in which he already holds £10,000 of redeemable preference shares. In November 2005, Elea redeems Zeno's preference shares for their market value of £1.30. Zeno is treated as receiving value of £13,000, and his ordinary shares in Elea cease to be eligible, meaning that the whole of his deferred gain of £30,000 becomes chargeable, not just £13,000 of it.

15.8.4 Repayment of the investor's loan

The investor's deferred gain will crystallise if any loan he or she has made to the company at any time before the acquisition of the shares is repaid during the period of restriction under any arrangement linked to that acquisition. If there is no such link between the acquisition and the repayment, there is no receipt of value for the purposes of EIS deferral relief, and, provided that the shares are issued after 16 March 2004, neither is there a loss of EIS investment relief if the investor has claimed it, either on those shares or any other shares he or she may have in the investee company. There is a similar rule for the purposes of EIS investment relief. For shares issued before 17 March 2004, however, there was an automatic loss of investment relief when a prior loan was repaid, whether or not the repayment was linked to the acquisition **[see 12.5.6]**.

15.8.5 Payment for giving up right to a debt

The investor is treated as receiving value if the company pays him or her (or an associate) for giving up his or her right to any debt on its extinguishment (TCGA 1992, Sch 5B, para 13(2)(c)). Debts that the investee company could discharge by making a 'qualifying payment' are excluded (TCGA 1992, Sch 5B, para 13(9)(a)). 'Qualifying payment' is defined in **15.8.10** below, but, broadly, these are ordinary trade debts, and debts the company owes in respect of reasonable remuneration, rent, interest etc payable to the investor.

15.8.6 Release of investor's liabilities

A company is treated as having released or waived a liability if the liability is not discharged within 12 months of the time when it ought to have been discharged (TCGA 1992, Sch 5B, para 13(8)).

If the liability is of a type that the company could discharge by making a 'qualifying payment' **[see 15.8.10]**, it is excluded from these rules and no value would be received on its release or waiver (TCGA 1992, Sch 5B, para 13(9)(a)).

15.8.7 Loans to investors

An investor who has subscribed for shares in a company and used the acquisition to defer a gain is not allowed to have indirect access to the investment moneys by borrowing from the company or by assigning to the company debts that he or she may have to third parties. Unless any such loans or debts have been fully paid before the investor subscribes for the shares, value is deemed to be received and the shares cease to be eligible (or are never eligible where the loan etc has already been incurred before the acquisition takes place) (TCGA 1992, Sch 5B, para 13(2)(e), (3)).

Example 15.10

On 1 January 2004, Emma borrows £6,000 from Much Ado Ltd, a company in which her father has a 25% stake, pending the settlement of a dispute with her former boyfriend. The loan is repayable in four equal instalments on 1 April, 1 July, 1 October and 1 January. On 22 July 2004, she realises a gain on some shares and three months later, is paid £15,000 in settlement of her dispute. However, instead of repaying the loan, she agrees to invest £10,000 in Much Ado, which is a qualifying company for EIS purposes. The investment takes place on 2 November 2004. Afraid that she will not have enough cash to pay her income tax and capital gains tax liability on 31 January 2005, she tries to claim EIS deferral relief on the gain (of £8,000). Her claim is refused because she still owes Much Ado the final instalment of the loan (£1,500).

15.8.8 The provision of benefits or facilities

This item has potentially a very wide scope indeed. Examples of benefits or facilities might be:

(*a*) the free use or use on favourable terms of property, equipment or cars;
(*b*) entitlement to discounts over and above those available to the public when purchasing the company's goods or services; or
(*c*) where the investee company enhances by its actions the value of an investment the investor may have in some other company.

There is no receipt of value where the benefit or facility is such that in the circumstances in which it is provided, a cash payment of the same value would have been a 'qualifying payment' (eg where it is provided as part of a director's reasonable remuneration) (TCGA 1992, Sch 5B, para 13(9)(b)).

15.8.9 Transfers of assets

This rule catches transactions in which the investor receives value either by transferring assets to the company for a consideration greater than their market value or conversely where the company transfers assets to the investor gratis or for a consideration of less than their market value. In both cases, the investor 'makes a profit' (TCGA 1992, Sch 5B, para 13(2)(g), (h)).

15.8.10 Payments other than qualifying payments

This is a sweeping-up item covering any other conceivable payments, but specifically excluding 'qualifying payments'. As has been mentioned, a qualifying payment is broadly one that the company might make in the ordinary course of business.

More precisely, a qualifying payment is any of the following:

(*a*) payment by any company of reasonable remuneration to the investor (or the investor's associate) for duties carried out as an officer or employee of that company or of a connected company;

(*b*) reimbursement of travelling and other expenses incurred wholly, necessarily and exclusively (and hence deductible from taxable earnings under ITEPA 2003, s 332) by the investor or the investor's associate as an officer or employee of the company or of a connected company;
(*c*) interest that represents no more than a reasonable commercial rate of return on money lent to the company or to a connected person;
(*d*) a dividend or distribution that represents no more than a normal return on the investment;
(*e*) a payment for goods at no more than market value;
(*f*) a payment for acquiring an asset of no more than its market value;
(*g*) a reasonable commercial rent for property occupied by the company or by a connected person;
(*h*) reasonable remuneration for professional or trade services; or
(*i*) discharge of an ordinary trade debt

(TCGA 1992, Sch 5B, para 13(7)).

15.8.10.1 *Meaning of 'ordinary trade debt'*

An ordinary trade debt is a debt for goods or services supplied in the ordinary course of trade or business, and where credit is given, it should not exceed six months and should be no longer than is normally given to the supplier's customers (TCGA 1992, Sch 5B, para 13(11)).

15.8.11 Purchase of shares etc by a connected person

The investor is also deemed to receive value where an individual who is a director or employee of the investee company or has an interest in it of 30% or more (ie an individual who is connected with the company under the definition in TA 1988, s 291 to the extent that he or she does not qualify for EIS investment relief) purchases any shares or securities in the company from the investor or the investor's associate, or makes a payment to the investor or an associate for giving up a right over any of the company's shares or securities (TCGA 1992, Sch 5B, para 13(5)).

15.8.12 Payments in a winding-up for shares issued before 7 March 2001

For shares issued before 7 March 2001, there was a further instance in which value was treated as received. This was where the investor or an associate received a payment or an asset in respect of his or her shares in the course of a winding-up or dissolution that did not cause the company to lose its qualifying status **[see 12.5.12.1]**.

15.8.13 No double charge on a share disposal

Where a chargeable event **[see 15.7.1]** occurs because there has been a share disposal, the investor is not also deemed to have received value from the company as a result (TCGA 1992, Sch 5B, para 13(6)).

15.8.14 Amount of value received

Although a receipt of value will cause the entire deferred gain to be brought back into charge (contrast the position with EIS investment relief), there are still provisions determining how much value is received in each case. These will be relevant when deciding whether the value can be disregarded as insignificant **[see 15.9]**.

Paragraph numbers in the left-hand column of the table below refer to the list of transactions representing receipt of value in **15.8.2**.

Transaction	*Amount of value received*
(*a*), (*b*), (*c*), (*d*)	The greater of (1) the amount received and (2) the market value of the shares, securities or debt
(*e*)	The amount of the liability
(*f*)	The outstanding balance of the loan or advance at the issue date
(*g*)	The cost to the company of providing the benefit or facility[1] less any consideration given by the investor
(*h*), (*i*)	The difference between the market value of the asset and any consideration given for it
(*j*)	The amount of the payment
Purchase by connected person of shares or securities etc **[see 15.8.11]**	The greater of (1) the amount received and (2) the market value of the shares or securities

Notes

1 For a discussion of what this means, see **12.5.10.2**.

(TCGA 1992, Sch 5B, para 13A(1)).

15.9 Exception for receipts of insignificant value

Where any receipt of value after 6 March 2001 is 'insignificant', it is disregarded (TCGA 1992, Sch 5B, para 13(1)).

Amounts are insignificant in all cases where they are no greater than £1,000. Amounts that are greater than £1,000 may still be insignificant if they are considered to be such relative to the individual's expenditure on the shares which has been used in the claim for deferral relief (TCGA 1992, Sch 5B, para 13A(3)).

For a discussion and criticism of the Inland Revenue's interpretation of this rule, which is repeated in para VCM 40300 of the Venture Capital Schemes Manual, see **12.6**.

There are provisions to ensure that no amount, however small, is insignificant if there are arrangements in place at any time in the 12 months preceding the share issue for the investor or an associate to receive or become entitled to receive any value during the period of restriction from the investee company or a connected person (TCGA 1992, Sch 5B, para 13A(4)). For this purpose, an associate of the investor is any person who is an associate at any time during the period of restriction, whether or not that person is an associate at the time the value is received (TCGA 1992, Sch 5B, para 13A(5)(a)).

What is more, to prevent a dripfeed of insignificant amounts, there is also a rule aggregating various receipts of value within the period of restriction. This rule provides that where an investor receives value and has previously received one or more insignificant amounts of value during the period of restriction, and the aggregate of those previous receipts and the latest receipt is not insignificant, the investor is treated as having received the aggregate amount at this latest time. Amounts that have previously been aggregated under this rule are disregarded (TCGA 1992, Sch 5B, para 13(1B)).

Example 15.11

On 2 February 2004, Alison subscribes £10,000 for 5,000 ordinary shares in Tara Ltd, which begins trading on 1 July 2004, and claims EIS deferral relief for a gain of £10,000 that she realised on 31 December 2003. During the course of 2006, she receives two items of equipment from the company, worth respectively £300 and £400, for which she pays a nominal £5 each. In May 2007, Tara gives her, free of charge, a second-hand laptop worth £750. The first two receipts were insignificant, but she is now treated as receiving value of (£300 + £400 + £750 – £10) = £1,440, causing the whole of the deferred gain to crystallise (in 2007–08). If the laptop had been transferred to her three months later, the period of restriction would have expired (on 30 June 2007) and the gain could have remained deferred.

Before 7 March 2001, no amount of value, however small, was disregarded.

15.10 The exception for return of replacement value

15.10.1 Introduction

A second exception that applies where value is received after 6 March 2001 is for occasions when the value given is returned or replaced (hence the name 'replacement value').

The exception applies where:

(*a*) the person from whom the value ('the original value') was received ('the original supplier') receives value in return ('the replacement value') from the person who received the original value ('the original recipient') by way of a 'qualifying receipt';

(*b*) the replacement value is at least equal to the original value; and

(*c*) the replacement value is given before or after the original value, subject to certain conditions **[see 15.10.2]**

(TCGA 1992, Sch 5B, para 13B(1)).

Where the exception applies, the receipt of the original value is disregarded and the deferred gain is not brought into charge.

A receipt is a qualifying receipt if it arises as a result of:

(*a*) any one, or any combination of, the following:

  (1) a payment (other than an 'excepted payment') by the original recipient to the original supplier;

  (2) the acquisition of an asset by the original recipient from the original supplier for a consideration exceeding market value;

  (3) the disposal of an asset by the original recipient to the original supplier for no consideration or for a consideration less than its market value;

  or

(*b*) where the receipt of the original value arose as a result of the release or waiver of any liability of the investor to the company or of an undertaking to discharge the investor's liability to a third party **[see 15.8.6]**, the reversal of that event; or

(*c*) where the receipt of the original value arose as a result of the purchase by a party connected to the company of any of the investor's share capital or securities or of the payment by such a connected person to the investor in return for the latter's giving up any right in relation to the company's capital or securities **[see 15.8.11]**, a repurchase by the original recipient of the shares or securities in question or the reacquisition by the original recipient of the right in question for consideration of not less than the market value of the shares, securities or right

(TCGA 1992, Sch 5B, para 13B(4)).

An 'excepted payment' (see point (*a*)(1) above) is broadly the type of payment disregarded as a receipt of value in the first place; namely:

(1) a payment for any goods, services or facilities provided, whether in the course of trade or otherwise, by the original supplier or any person who is an associate or connected with the original supplier at any time in the period of restriction, of an amount that is reasonable in relation to their market value;

(2) a payment of interest at no more than a reasonable commercial rate of return on a loan made to the original recipient or to a person who is an associate of the original recipient at any time in the period of restriction;

(3) a payment of no more than market value for the acquisition of an asset;

(4) a payment not exceeding a reasonable and commercial rent for property occupied by the original recipient or by any person who is an associate of the original recipient at any time during the period of restriction;
(5) a payment in discharge of an ordinary trade debt;
(6) a payment for any shares or securities of the company in any circumstances other than those in point (*a*)(2) above; or
(7) a repurchase or reacquisition within point (*c*) above

(TCGA 1992, Sch 5B, para 13B(5)).

15.10.2 Time restraints on a receipt of replacement value

The receipt of replacement value may take place either before or after the original receipt. However, certain time limits are put in place.

Where the replacement value is received before the original receipt, it must be provided within the period of restriction (ie no earlier than one year before the issue of the shares).

Where the replacement value is received after the original receipt, it must be provided as soon as is 'reasonably practicable in the circumstances'.

Where the original receipt of value is the subject of appeal proceedings, the replacement value must be provided within 60 days of the conclusion of the appeal.

Unless the replacement value is received within these time limits, it is disregarded and the original receipt of value stands, with the consequential crystallisation of the gain

(TCGA 1992, Sch 5B, para 13C(2)).

15.10.3 The amount of replacement value

The amount of the replacement value deemed to be received depends on the nature of the qualifying receipt.

Where the receipt is one of those enumerated in point (*a*) in **15.10.1**, the amount is the aggregate of the payment and the difference between the market value of any asset mentioned in point (*a*)(1) or (*a*)(2) and the consideration received.

Where the receipt is of the kind mentioned in point (*b*) in **15.10.1**, the amount of replacement value is equal to the amount of the original value.

Where the receipt is of the kind mentioned in point (*c*) in **15.10.1**, the amount of replacement value is the amount of consideration received by the original supplier (TCGA 1992, Sch 5B, para 13B(6)).

Unless the replacement value is at least equal to the original value, it is disregarded and does not prevent the crystallisation of the deferred gain caused by the receipt of the original value.

15.10.4 The effect of replacement value

Where replacement value is received and the conditions described in **15.10.1** and **15.10.2** are satisfied, the receipt of the original value is disregarded, and the deferred gain is not brought back into charge (TCGA 1992, Sch 5B, para 13B(1)).

However, if the replacement value is provided by a subscription for new shares by the investor or an associate, no EIS investment relief is granted for those shares or for any other shares in the same issue, nor is EIS deferral relief available for that subscription (TCGA 1992, Sch 5B, para 13C(4)).

15.11 Value received by other persons

15.11.1 Introduction

As with EIS investment relief, the rules on receipt of value for EIS deferral relief are widely drawn so as to treat the investor as having received value even where it is actually received by another shareholder entirely. Again, as with EIS investment relief latterly, these rules apply in limited situations only.

15.11.2 Repayment of capital to other shareholders

An investor who has deferred a gain can find that the gain crystallises if, at any time during the period of restriction **[see 15.2.2]**, the investee company or any subsidiary repays, redeems or repurchases the share capital of another shareholder or makes any payment to that person for giving up his right to capital on its cancellation or extinguishment (TCGA 1992, Sch 5B, para 14(1)). A 'subsidiary' here means any company that is a 51% subsidiary of the investee company at any time in the period of restriction, regardless of whether it is such a subsidiary at the time of the repayment, redemption, repurchase or payment (TCGA 1992, Sch 5B, para 14(7)).

There will be some 'other' shareholders to whom this rule does not extend. Essentially, the target is shareholders who personally do not stand to lose any venture capital relief themselves as a result of receiving the repayment. Payments to the following shareholders are therefore excluded from the ambit of this rule and will not cause the investor to lose his or her entitlement to the deferral relief:

(*a*) those (other investors) for whom the repayment is a chargeable event for the purposes of EIS deferral relief because it is a disposal of shares or securities;

(*b*) those (other investors) for whom the repayment is a chargeable event for the purposes of EIS deferral relief because that person receives value as a result;

(*c*) those who lose EIS investment relief as a result of the repayment because it is an early disposal of shares or a receipt of value; or
(*d*) those who lose CVS investment relief as a result of the repayment because it is an early disposal of shares or a receipt of value; or
(*e*) any of these who would have lost EIS deferral relief, EIS investment relief or CVS investment relief in these circumstances if the receipt had not been insignificant

(TCGA 1992, Sch 5B, para 14(3), (4)).

This rule differs from that applying to receipts by the investors themselves **[see 15.8.3]** in that it does not cover the purchase of shares by a person connected with the company for EIS purposes **[see 15.8.11]**. However, this rule is particularly harsh where the repayment occurs in a subsidiary of the investee company before it becomes such a subsidiary.

Example 15.12

Take the facts of Example 12.15. Garai Ltd raises £1 million of EIS capital on 1 April 2002. Daniel Ltd is a successful company in the same business, with a wholly owned dormant subsidiary, Deronda Ltd. In October 2004, proposals are brought forward for Garai to buy the shares in Daniel. It comes to light that in May 2003, Deronda had purchased some of its own shares for £100,000.

In this situation, not only would EIS shareholders in Garai stand to lose part of their investment relief because of Deronda's share purchase within the period of restriction (1 April 2001 to 31 March 2005) but any investors who had acquired shares in Garai in order to defer gains would also see their claims for deferral relief retroactively refused, whether or not they had received investment relief.

In such circumstances, it is even more imperative that the shares in Deronda be sold before Daniel is acquired.

15.11.2.1 *Effect of a repayment of share capital*

Where a repayment etc takes place in the circumstances described in **15.11.2**, and this event takes place before the shares involved in the claim for deferral relief are issued, the shares are treated as never having been eligible, so that no claim for deferral relief is permissible. If the fact only emerges after the claim has been allowed (as in Example 15.12), the claim must be withdrawn. Where (as is more likely, if due diligence is exercised before the acquisition) the repayment takes place after the issue, the shares are treated as ceasing to be eligible at that time, so the gain will crystallise at that point (TCGA 1992, Sch 5B, para 14(2)).

15.11.2.2 *Repayments received before 7 March 2001*

Where repayments were received before 7 March 2001, different restricted periods applied.

In respect of EIS shares issued after 5 April 2000 but before 7 March 2001, the restricted period (known then as 'the designated period') began a year earlier than the current 'period of restriction', ie two years before the issue date, but ended coterminously with the current period (ie immediately before the later of (*a*) the third anniversary of the issue date and (*b*) the third anniversary of the commencement of the qualifying trade).

For shares issued after 5 April 1998 but before 6 April 2000, there was yet a different restricted period (known as 'the seven-year period'). This was the period that began two years before the issue date and ended five years after the issue date.

Regardless of when the shares were issued, however, if the repayment falls after 6 March 2001, the period of restriction as currently defined applies.

15.11.3 Exceptions

There are three exceptions to the rule.

15.11.3.1 *Exception for minimum capital requirements*

The first exception is for payments that are made to satisfy Companies Act requirements. Where shares are issued in order to satisfy the minimum capital requirements for a public company under Companies Act 1985, s 117, and then redeemed within 12 months of issue, the redemption is ignored for these purposes (TCGA 1992, Sch 5B, para 14(5)).

15.11.3.2 *Insignificant repayments*

The second exception has applied since 7 March 2001 only (and in respect of shares issued on or after that date, whenever the repayment takes place). A repayment is disregarded where the greater of:

(*a*) the amount received by the other member and
(*b*) the market value immediately before the repayment is made of the shares to which it relates

is 'insignificant' in relation to the market value immediately after the repayment of the remaining issued share capital of the investee company (or of the subsidiary, where appropriate) (TCGA 1992, Sch 5B, para 14AA(1)). Here again, a 'subsidiary' is any company that is a 51% subsidiary of the investee company at any time in the period of restriction, regardless of whether it is such a subsidiary at the time of the repayment, redemption, repurchase or payment (TCGA 1992, Sch 5B, para 14(7)).

Again, no definition of 'insignificant' is given nor is there a monetary amount specified, as there is in relation to value received by investors **[see 15.9]**, but attention must again be drawn to the highly restrictive interpretation put on the term by the Inland Revenue (see Venture Capital Schemes Manual, para VCM 40780 and elsewhere) and the commentary in **12.6** as to the unlikelihood that this could have been the intention.

As with the rule in **15.9**, insignificant repayments are not disregarded where there are arrangements in place at any time in the 12 months preceding the share issue for the repayment to be made or for any person to become entitled to such a repayment (TCGA 1992, Sch 5B, para 14AA(4), (5)).

15.11.3.3 *Restriction on loss of EIS deferral relief where CVS relief lost*

Shares issued by an investee company between 1 April 2000 and 31 March 2010 may also be qualifying shares under the CVS. That scheme also contains rules **[see Chapter 13]** reducing or withdrawing investment relief on the receipt of value. In order to prevent a double loss of relief in a company that has both EIS and CVS investors, there is a rule restricting the loss of EIS deferral relief in such circumstances. It is exactly parallel to the rule restricting the loss of EIS investment relief in the same circumstances **[see 12.8.5.3]**.

More precisely, where:

(*a*) there is a repayment, redemption or repurchase of share capital from any other shareholder other than a CVS shareholder and the EIS investor(s) affected under the conditions described in **15.11.1** to **15.11.2**, such that the EIS investor(s) otherwise stand(s) to lose EIS deferral relief; and

(*b*) an amount of CVS investment relief has been lost by the CVS shareholder(s) as a result of the same repayment **[see 13.7.2.1]**

there is no loss of EIS deferral relief if the result of the formula X – 5Y, where X is the amount of the repayment and Y is the amount of CVS investment relief lost, is £1,000 or less (TCGA 1992, Sch 5B, para 14A(1)–(4)).

Example 15.13

The shareholdings in Fukien Ltd are distributed as follows:

Shareholder	*Shares*	*Amount subscribed*
Zhu Xi	5,000	£10,000
Wang Yangming	8,000	£16,000
Yu Yao plc	20,000	£35,000
Others	37,000	£59,000
Total	**70,000**	**£120,000**

Zhu Xi is an investor who has received EIS deferral relief of £2,000. Yu Yao plc is a CVS investor, which has received CVS investment relief of £7,000. The other shareholders also hold £10,000 of preference shares. Within the restricted periods for both the EIS shares and the CVS shares, those preference shares are redeemed for their market value at the time of £12,000. As a result, Yu Yao loses £12,000 × 20% = £2,400 of CVS investment relief and Zhu Xi stands to lose his EIS deferral relief.

The formula X – 5Y, however, yields the result £12,000 – £12,000 = £nil, which is not greater than £1,000. Therefore, the repayment is disregarded for EIS purposes, and Zhu Xi's gain remains deferred.

It will be quickly seen that, unless the CVS investor's investment relief was originally restricted because of an insufficient corporation tax liability (or for some other reason such as an earlier receipt of value), or is reduced rather than withdrawn, X will always equal 5Y and EIS deferral relief will not be lost.

As with the exceptions for insignificance **[see 15.9 and 15.11.3.2]**, this exception does not operate if, in the 12 months preceding the issue of the EIS shares, there were arrangements in place for a repayment to be made to a non-EIS, non-CVS shareholder by the investee company or by a subsidiary, or for any person to be entitled to such a repayment (TCGA 1992, Sch 5B, para 14A(4)–(6)).

'Subsidiary' again means a company that is a 51% subsidiary of the investee company at any time in the restricted period, regardless of whether it is such a subsidiary at the time of the repayment (TCGA 1992, Sch 5B, para 14(7), as amended by FA 2004, Sch 18, para 17(1) for repayments made after 16 March 2004; TCGA 1992, Sch 5B, para 14A(6)(a) for earlier repayments) or, indeed, at the time the arrangements are made (TCGA 1992, Sch 5B, para 14A(6)(b)).

Where the repayment is made after 6 March 2001, and whenever it is made in respect of shares issued after that date, the above rules come into play even when no CVS relief was actually lost because the amount of the repayment was insignificant.

15.12 The grant of options over the shares

Another event that will cause the withdrawal of EIS deferral relief is the grant during the *relevant period* (NB: not the period of restriction) by a third party of a put option (binding the grantor to buy shares) or by the investor company of a call option (binding the grantor to sell shares) over any of the acquired shares (TCGA 1992, Sch 5B, para 12(1)).

If the option is granted before the shares are issued, they are treated as never having been eligible shares, so deferral relief will not be available, or if it has been given, will be revoked. If the option is granted after the issue, the shares cease to be eligible when the grant takes place, and the deferred gain crystallises at that point (TCGA 1992, Sch 5B, para 12(2)).

15.13 Company reconstructions

15.13.1 Reorganisation of share capital

An investor who has claimed EIS deferral relief may hold shares in more than one of the following categories:

(*a*) shares to which both EIS deferral relief and EIS investment relief are attributable;
(*b*) shares to which EIS deferral relief but not EIS investment relief is attributable;
(*c*) shares to which EIS deferral relief is not attributable.

If there is a reorganisation of the company's capital affecting those shares, the provisions in TCGA 1992, s 127 (equating the new holding with the old holding) apply separately to each of these categories of shares; this means that shares in each category are treated as separate holdings and identified with separate new holdings. But if the reconstruction involves a rights issue of new shares in respect of a holding in category (*a*) or (*b*) and both old and new shares then qualify for EIS deferral relief, the investor is treated as having acquired the new shares at the time of the rights issue for the amount paid for the rights issue; this means that the old shares and the new shares are treated as separate holdings and the normal CGT provisions in TCGA 1992, ss 127–130 will not apply (TCGA 1992, Sch 5B, para 7).

Where there is a bonus issue of shares, the bonus shares are allocated pro rata among the categories concerned (Revenue Capital Gains Manual, CG 62936).

15.13.2 Other reconstructions and amalgamations

Where shares to which deferral relief is attributable are exchanged for shares in another company, the normal provisions treating the new shares as the same asset as the old shares (TCGA 1992, ss 135, 136) do not apply. This means that such a share exchange is a disposal and the deferred gain will be brought into charge (TCGA 1992, Sch 5B, para 9(1)).

This rule does not apply:

(*a*) where the company issuing the new shares is an EIS company (ie it has already issued eligible shares in respect of which it has issued certificates authorising EIS relief);
(*b*) the new shares are new ordinary shares carrying no present or future preferential rights to dividends or to a company's assets on a winding-up, and no present or future right to be redeemed; and
(*c*) the new shares are issued after the expiration of the relevant period for the original shares

(TCGA 1992, Sch 5B, para 9(2), (4)).

In such a case, the provisions of TCGA 1992, s 135 will operate to treat the new shares as the same asset as the old shares and the deferred gain will not be brought into charge at that time.

15.13.3 Acquisition by a new company

In addition, a share exchange will not constitute a disposal of the old shares where a new company acquires the investee company in the following circumstances:

(*a*) the new company has previously issued only subscriber shares;
(*b*) the new company acquires all the shares in the investee company;
(*c*) the consideration is wholly in shares of the new company;
(*d*) the consideration for the new shares consists wholly of the old shares of the corresponding description;
(*e*) new shares of each description are issued to the holders of the corresponding description of old shares in proportion to those holdings;
(*f*) before the issue of the new shares, the investee company has issued eligible shares and has issued a certificate that the shares qualified for EIS relief.

In those circumstances, TCGA 1992, s 127 applies to treat the takeover as not involving a disposal of the old shares, and deferral relief is then attributable to the new shares (TCGA 1992, Sch 5B, para 8(1), (2)).

The new shares are deemed to have been acquired by the investor at the time of, and for the consideration for, the old shares and the deferral claim is deemed to have been made in respect of the new shares (TCGA 1992, Sch 5B, para 8(3)).

The new company becomes responsible for providing the information that the old company would have been required to supply, and has the same right of appeal against any notice issued by the inspector to the effect that the shares have ceased to be eligible shares (TCGA 1992, Sch 5B, para 8(5)).

Chapter 16

Reinvestment in CVS Companies

16.1 Background and introduction

CVS deferral relief has been available since the introduction of the CVS on 6 April 2000. Like its companion deferral reliefs – for VCT deferral relief, see **Chapter 14**; for EIS deferral relief, see **Chapter 15** – it allows gains to be deferred against new investments in qualifying companies under the scheme. Unlike the other two, however, the CVS relief applies solely to gains arising on its own scheme shares. With that proviso, its rules are similar to those of the VCT deferral relief, without the complication attendant on the EIS version.

Note that VCT deferral relief has been withdrawn for shares issued after 5 April 2004 – see **14.3.2**.

16.1.1 Scope of this chapter

This chapter is concerned with the following topics:

(*a*) A summary of the CVS deferral relief **[see 16.2]**
(*b*) Which gains may be deferred? **[see 16.3]**
(*c*) Who can claim deferral relief? **[see 16.4]**
(*d*) What are qualifying investments? **[see 16.5]**
(*e*) How much of the gain can be deferred? **[see 16.6]**
(*f*) When does the gain crystallise? **[see 16.7]**

16.2 A summary of CVS deferral relief

A CVS investor company that realises a chargeable gain on a disposal of CVS shares that qualified for CVS investment relief not as yet withdrawn may defer some or all of that gain by making a 'qualifying investment' into further CVS shares within the 'qualifying time'. The gain is deferred to the extent that it is matched by the qualifying investment. The qualifying investment may be made within a specified period before the gain is realised as well as within a specified time afterwards. The deferred gain crystallises (becomes taxable) when there is a 'chargeable event' in relation to the investment, but can be deferred again if matched with a further qualifying investment, and so on indefinitely **[see 16.6]**.

16.2.1 Deferred gains and indexation

It is important to realise that CVS deferral relief is not like capital gains tax rollover reliefs in that the deferred gain is not rolled over into the cost of the replacement asset (CVS shares) but stands deferred unless and until a chargeable event occurs **[see 16.7]**, when it becomes immediately assessable in full or in part. There is thus no question of indexation during the period of deferment. For the interaction of VCT disposal reliefs and other capital gains and inheritance tax reliefs, see **Chapter 23**.

16.2.2 Restricted periods

The 'qualifying time' within which a qualifying investment must be made in relation to the deferrable gain is the period that begins one (calendar) year before the date on which the gain accrues ('the accrual time') and ends three (calendar) years after the accrual time (FA 2000, Sch 15, para 74(2)).

Another feature that marks the CVS relief as distinctive is that there is no provision in the legislation for discretionary powers for the Inland Revenue to allow extensions to the qualifying time.

There is no restriction, on the other hand, on the time within which a chargeable event can occur – the deferred gain can be made to crystallise at any time after the claim for deferral relief has been made.

16.3 Gains eligible for relief

There are two types of gain that are eligible for CVS deferral relief:

(*a*) gains on a disposal of shares to which CVS investment relief was attributable immediately before the disposal (ie shares on which investment relief was obtained and has not been withdrawn); and
(*b*) gains that have previously been deferred and have now crystallised

(FA 2000, Sch 15, para 73(1)(b)).

The investor company must have held the shares continuously since they were issued (FA 2000, Sch 15, para 73(3)).

16.4 Who may claim CVS deferral relief?

This question is relatively simple to answer. The only type of investor that can claim CVS deferral relief is a qualifying company for CVS purposes. See **5.17** for the conditions that must be satisfied by CVS investor companies.

16.5 Qualifying investments

16.5.1 What is meant by a qualifying investment

In order to make a successful claim for CVS deferral relief, the investor company must make a qualifying investment within the four-year 'qualifying time' **[see 16.2.2]**.

An investor company makes a qualifying investment if:

(*a*) it subscribes for shares qualifying for CVS investment relief;
(*b*) the shares are not issued by a 'prohibited company';
(*c*) the shares are issued to the investor company at a 'qualifying time' **[see 16.2.2]**;
(*d*) and where the shares were issued before the accrual time:
  (1) they must have been held continuously by the investor company since they were issued until the accrual time, and
  (2) investment relief must still be attributable to the shares at that time

(FA 2000, Sch 15, para 74(1)).

A 'prohibited company' is:

(*a*) the company whose shares are the subject of the disposal giving rise to the gain; or
(*b*) where the gain to be deferred is a crystallised gain, the company with respect to whose shares the chargeable event that led to the crystallisation has occurred; or
(*c*) a member of the same group as the company in (*a*) or (*b*) as the case may be. It need not be a member of that group both at the accrual time and on the issue date of the new shares, but it must be a member at least at one of those times. If it is not a member of the same group at either of those times, it is not a prohibited company

(FA 2000, Sch 15, para 74(2), (3)).

Example 16.1

Stoic Ltd is a CVS investor in Epicurean Ltd, in which it holds 100,000 ordinary shares. In June 2003, it disposes of 20,000 shares within the qualification period. As a result, it loses some CVS investment relief and realises a chargeable gain of £50,000. If Stoic wishes to defer this gain, it cannot do so by making further CVS investments in Epicurean, which is a prohibited company with respect to that gain. However, ten months later, in April 2004, Stoic invests £60,000 in CVS shares in Eleatic Ltd, for which it claims CVS investment relief and CVS deferral relief to cover the gain on the Epicurean shares. Eleatic must not be a member of the Epicurean group at this time nor must it have been a member of the Epicurean group in June 2003, when the original gain arose.

In November 2006, another shareholder in Eleatic receives value from the company, causing Stoic's deferred gain to crystallise. The prohibited company with respect to this gain is Eleatic. Any qualifying investment that Stoic wishes to make to defer this gain a second time cannot be in Eleatic nor in a member of the Eleatic group either in November 2006 when the chargeable event occurs or at the time of the new investment.

16.5.1.1 *Shares issued before the accrual time*

If the investment in respect of which deferral relief is claimed was made in the 12 months before the gain arose, the investor company must have held the acquired shares continuously from their issue date until the accrual time. However, there is no need for the entire holding of which those shares form part to have been retained. Some shares in the holding may be disposed of, according to the Inland Revenue, but it is only the remaining shares that may be used in a deferral claim (Venture Capital Schemes Manual, para VCM 57050).

16.6 Deferring gains

16.6.1 Introduction

A claim for CVS deferral relief may be made in respect of a gain arising on the disposal of CVS shares or on the crystallisation of a gain previously deferred under the scheme. Both of these gains will be referred to as the 'original gain' in this section.

16.6.2 The amount of the gain that can be deferred

The amount of the gain that can be deferred cannot be greater than either:

(*a*) the investor company's unused qualifying expenditure; or
(*b*) the investor company's unmatched original gain;

but subject to those limits any amount of expenditure specified in the claim may be set against the corresponding amount of the gain (FA 2000, Sch 15, para 76(1)).

16.6.2.1 *What is meant by the chargeable gain?*

The gain to be matched is the gain as computed after deduction of indexation allowance.

16.6.2.2 *Must the proceeds of the disposal be used?*

As with the VCT and EIS deferral reliefs, there is no requirement to apply the actual funds obtained by a disposal (where there is an actual disposal that gives rise to the deferrable gain) in making the investment. Entirely separate monies may be used.

16.6.3 Unused qualifying expenditure

Qualifying expenditure is the amount subscribed by the investor for the shares acquired by him in making the qualifying investment (FA 2000, Sch 15, para 76(3)(a)).

Qualifying expenditure is unused to the extent that it has not already been set for the purposes of CVS deferral relief against the whole or any part of a chargeable gain (FA 2000, Sch 15, para 76(3)(b)).

16.6.4 The unmatched gain

The unmatched gain is that part of the original gain which has not already been deferred by making a qualifying CVS investment (FA 2000, Sch 15, para 76(4)).

Example 16.2

Descartes Ltd disposes of CVS shares on 31 December 2003 and realises a gain of £155,000. In May 2004, it subscribes £90,000 for a qualifying investment in another CVS investee company. It claims CVS deferral relief on £90,000 of its gain. Its unmatched gain after the investment is £65,000 and its unmatched expenditure is nil. If Descartes were to make another qualifying investment before 31 December 2006 of, say, £70,000, it would have £70,000 of unmatched expenditure to set against the unmatched gain of £65,000. If it were then to make a claim for CVS deferral relief for all of the unmatched gain, it would be left with unmatched expenditure of £5,000.

16.6.5 Effect of deferral relief on the deferred gain

Where a successful claim to CVS deferral relief is made, that part of the gain that is deferred is deemed not to have accrued at the accrual time. Instead, it is deferred and brought back into charge (if at all) on the occurrence of a chargeable event, such as a disposal of the acquired shares or a breach of the qualifying conditions (FA 2000, Sch 15, para 76(2)).

There is therefore no question of indexation relief for the period during which the gain has been deferred.

16.6.6 Attribution of the deferred gain

The deferrable gain may be matched with any number of investments in any proportion the investor company chooses, as long as the investments are made within the qualifying time.

Example 16.3

Rationalist Ltd sells its CVS shares in Humanism Ltd on 1 February 2003, realising a chargeable gain of £100,000. It makes the following qualifying investments into CVS companies:

£20,000 in Scholasticism Ltd on 25 January 2002
£35,000 in Existentialism Ltd on 26 July 2003
£15,000 in Transcendentalism Ltd on 28 December 2004
£65,000 in Stoicism Ltd on 5 March 2005
£25,000 in Existentialism Ltd on 22 July 2006

The investment in Scholasticism and the second investment in Existentialism (22 July 2006) are outside the qualifying time (1 February 2002–31 January 2006), so Rationalist elects to match the gain with the following expenditure:

£65,000 against the £65,000 invested in Stoicism Ltd
£10,000 against the £15,000 invested in Transcendentalism Ltd
£25,000 against the £35,000 invested in Existentialism Ltd on 26 July 2003

There is no obligation to match the gain with the earliest (or indeed the latest) qualifying investment.

16.7 Bringing gains back into charge

16.7.1 Introduction

A chargeable gain that has been deferred on making a successful claim for CVS deferral relief crystallises (is brought back into charge) on the occurrence of a 'chargeable event'. A chargeable event can be either:

(*a*) a disposal by the investor company of the 'qualifying shares' at any time – for disposals of CVS shares, see **Chapter 19**; or
(*b*) any other event causing CVS investment relief to be reduced or withdrawn **[see Chapter 13]**

(FA 2000, Sch 15, para 78(1)).

16.7.2 Qualifying shares

A chargeable event is triggered not just by actions relating to the shares acquired on making the qualifying investment ('the acquired shares'), but also by actions relating to any bonus shares the investor company has since received relating to the acquired shares, and in certain circumstances, to replacement shares. This 'ensemble' of related shares is referred to as 'qualifying shares' in the legislation.

Bonus shares are qualifying shares if they are issued in respect of the acquired shares, are in the same company, of the same class and carry the same rights (FA 2000, Sch 15, para 75(2), (3)).

When there is a share exchange involving an issue of new shares in another company in exchange for the acquired shares, there is no disposal of the old shares if certain conditions are satisfied **[see 19.3.6.1]**. In such a case, the new shares are also treated as qualifying shares (FA 2000, Sch 15, para 75(4)).

16.7.3 Effect of a chargeable event

Once the first chargeable event occurs in relation to any qualifying shares, a chargeable gain is treated as accruing to the investor company at the time of the event. The amount of that gain is the proportion of the deferred gain that can be attributed to the shares in question. Attribution is done on a pro rata basis within a particular holding (FA 2000, Sch 15, para 79(1)–(3)).

Example 16.4

Take the facts of Example 16.3. Rationalist Ltd has deferred £65,000 of its £100,000 gain against its investment in Stoicism Ltd. If it subsequently disposes of half of its holding in Stoicism, half of the deferred gain matched with the Stoicism shares (ie £32,500) will be brought back into charge. At the same time, of course, Rationalist may have a chargeable gain on its disposal of those shares. Both that gain and the £32,500 of the deferred gain that has now crystallised may themselves be deferred by matching with qualifying investments.

The same rule applies where more than one gain has been deferred by being matched with the same qualifying investment.

Example 16.5

Colvin Ltd makes two disposals of CVS shares, realising gains of £50,000 ('the A gain') and £30,000 ('the B gain'), respectively. Both gains are deferred by matching them with a qualifying investment of £100,000 in 50,000 shares of Empedocles Ltd. If a chargeable event occurs with respect to 20,000 of the Empedocles shares, the amount of the A gain that crystallises is £20,000 ((20,000/50,000) × £50,000) and the amount of the B gain that crystallises is (20,000/50,000) × £30,000 = £12,000.

If only part of the deferred gain crystallises on the occasion of the first chargeable event, the balance remains subject to any future chargeable events in respect of the qualifying shares with which it is matched (FA 2000, Sch 15, para 79(2)(b)).

16.7.4 Non-resident investor companies

CVS investor companies need not be UK resident **[see 5.17.1.1]**. If a deferred gain has been realised by a non-resident company trading in the UK through a UK permanent establishment, so that the company is chargeable to corporation tax (under TCGA 1992, s 10B) on the business-related chargeable gains of that permanent establishment, and the gain then crystallises, it is covered by any exemption for gains conferred by a double tax treaty between the UK and the company's state of residence (FA 2000, Sch 15, para 79(5)).

Part 6

Disposing of Investments

Chapter 17

Disposal of VCT Shares

17.1 Introduction and background

17.1.1 Introduction

The three venture capital schemes reviewed in this book – the VCT scheme, the EIS and the CVS – are designed to give a range of tax reliefs to those individuals and companies prepared to put their capital at risk for a specified period. For all three schemes, although differently expressed and differently marked, that period is now at least three years. As a result, it is not surprising that where the investor disposes of some or all of his qualifying shares before the end of that period (such a disposal is called an 'early disposal' from now on in this book), all or part of the investment relief may be lost **[see Chapters 11 to 13]**. The effect for capital gains purposes is varied, however. Whereas an early disposal of VCT shares is free of capital gains tax consequences, a similar disposal of EIS or CVS shares gives rise to a 'double whammy' – not only is investment relief lost, but there may also be a capital gains liability for the investor. In every case, a disposal of shares, early or not, will cause a partial or total 'crystallisation' of gains deferred under any of the deferral reliefs **[see Chapters 14 to 16]**.

By the same token, each scheme also provides for a measure of capital gains relief when there is a disposal of shares once the restricted period has elapsed (in the case of the VCT scheme, a disposal at any time). These reliefs are called collectively in this book 'disposal reliefs' and such disposals are called 'later disposals'.

This chapter and **Chapters 18 and 19** will examine the consequences of share disposals separately for each scheme. Each chapter falls naturally into five parts. The first considers the tax treatment of disposals generally and their impact on investment relief. The second part deals with an early disposal of scheme shares at a gain; the third part considers the treatment of losses on an early disposal. The fourth part considers the tax treatment of a disposal at a gain of shares outside the restricted period, whereas the fifth part considers the treatment of losses on such a later disposal.

For the impact on an investor's capital gains tax or corporation tax liability of share disposals, see **Chapter 22**. For the interaction of these reliefs and charges with other tax provisions, see **Chapter 23**. For procedures for claiming relief and Inland Revenue procedures generally, see **Chapter 24**. For information requirements, see **Chapter 25**.

17.1.2 Scope of this chapter

This chapter examines the following areas:

(*a*) Remaining general introductory material **[see 17.1.3 to 17.1.5]**
(*b*) What constitutes a disposal **[see 17.2]**
(*c*) Company reorganisations **[see 17.3]**
(*d*) Identification rules **[see 17.4]**
(*e*) Gains on early disposals of VCT shares **[see 17.5]**
(*f*) Losses on early disposals of VCT shares **[see 17.6]**
(*g*) Gains on later disposals of VCT shares **[see 17.7]**
(*h*) Losses on later disposals of VCT shares **[see 17.8]**

17.1.3 Investor's restricted period for disposals

In the VCT scheme, the restricted period within which the investor may not dispose of his or her shares if investment relief is to be preserved, is the period beginning with the issue of the shares and ending three years later (TA 1988, Sch 15B, para 3(1)).

In the case of shares issued before 6 April 2000, the restricted period ended five years after the issue. Such periods can still be current for a short while yet, therefore, as the last date on which they can possibly end is no earlier than 5 April 2005.

Other restricted periods apply in the case of other events that may give rise to a loss of VCT investment relief – for instance, the receipt of a loan-linked investment **[see Chapter 11]**.

17.1.4 Crystallisation of deferred gains

A disposal of scheme shares matched with a gain under VCT deferral relief will also cause part or all of the deferred gain to crystallise **[see Chapter 14]**.

17.1.5 Eligible shares

Eligible shares are ordinary shares that carry no present or future preferential right to dividends or to a company's assets on its winding-up and no present or future right to be redeemed throughout the restricted period (TA 1988, Sch 15B, para 6(1)).

17.2 The disposal

17.2.1 Introduction

A disposal of VCT shares includes a sale, gift or exchange **[see 17.3]** and a part-disposal **[see 17.4]**. It also includes the disposal of an interest or right in or over the shares **[see 17.2.2]** (TA 1988, Sch 15B, para 6(3); TCGA 1992, s 21(2)(b)). For details of the interaction between the disposal of shares and business-gift holdover relief see **23.2**.

17.2.2 Options

The VCT scheme rules contain no special provision on options. It follows that the normal capital gains rules apply to both put and call options over VCT shares.

For capital gains tax purposes, if an option is exercised, the grant of the option and the transaction (in this case the sale of the shares) are treated as a single transaction. The amount paid for the grant of a call option (ie an option binding the grantor to sell shares) is treated as part of the consideration for the sale of the shares and the consideration for a put option (ie an option binding the grantor to buy shares) is deducted from the cost of acquisition (TCGA 1992, s 144(2)).

If the option is not exercised, the grant of the option is treated as the disposal of an asset separate from the shares, not as a part-disposal of the shares. As there is no cost of the new asset, the full amount received for granting the option is chargeable (TCGA 1992, s 144(1) and *Strange v Openshaw* [1983] STC 416).

17.2.3 Deemed disposal

Should the VCT lose its approval, other than in a case where it is treated as never having received approval **[see 24.4.4]**, for the purposes of withdrawing investment relief there is a deemed disposal of the VCT shares at market value immediately before the VCT approval is lost (TA 1988, Sch 15B, para 3(9)).

The effect of this for capital gains tax is that any accrued gain at the time of the deemed disposal would not be chargeable, any loss would not be an allowable loss and there would be an uplift of the base cost of the shares to market value. For an explanation of this, see **17.5** and **17.6**.

This deemed disposal does not constitute a chargeable event for VCT deferral relief **[see 14.7.1]**, but nevertheless any deferred gain still becomes chargeable at the time the VCT approval is lost (TCGA 1992, Sch 5C, para 3(6)).

17.2.4 Death

The transfer of a person's assets at death is not treated as a disposal for capital gains tax (TCGA 1992, s 62). Neither does the transfer of ownership of eligible shares cause either the VCT investment relief to be withdrawn or the gains deferred as a result of making VCT investments before 6 April 2004 to become chargeable. Furthermore, where there is a disposal of eligible shares after the investor's death, the VCT investment relief is not reduced or withdrawn and any deferred gains do not become chargeable. The person who inherits VCT shares benefits from the tax-free capital gains on his or her shares **[see 17.5 and 17.7]** and from tax-free dividends – distribution relief **[see 8.5]**.

17.2.5 Transfers to a spouse

Husband and wife are treated as separate persons for most purposes of income tax and capital gains tax. For example, each is entitled to make qualifying VCT investments up to an annual limit of £200,000.

A transfer of shares between a husband and wife who are living together does not cause the VCT reliefs to be withdrawn. What is more, the VCT capital gains tax exemption attaches to the shares and is not lost on a transfer between spouses.

There is no capital gains tax liability on a transfer between spouses (TCGA 1992, s 58(1)). There is also no clawback of the VCT reliefs when the shares are transferred by an investor to his or her spouse when they are living together (TA 1988, Sch 15B, para 3(5)). Instead, the transferee spouse stands in the shoes of the investor who made the initial claim to investment or deferral relief. The spouse can benefit from the capital gains tax exemption on a later sale or gift of the shares, provided that the investment relief has not been withdrawn.

17.2.6 Early disposals

If the transferee spouse disposes of the shares he or she has received within the restricted period, the normal rules for withdrawal of investment relief apply, except that the tax is recovered from the transferee spouse, not the original investor (TA 1988, Sch 15B, para 3(6)).

17.3 Company reorganisations

17.3.1 Introduction

Where there is a reorganisation of shares, such as a bonus or rights issue of shares or a qualifying share exchange, the normal rule for capital gains tax purposes is that there is deemed to be no disposal of the original shares or any acquisition of the new shares: the new holdings are treated as a single asset acquired at the time the original shares were acquired (TCGA 1992, s 127). This general rule is subject to certain amendments in the case of the VCT scheme (and indeed the EIS and CVS also).

17.3.2 Subdivision of shares

If a qualifying company decides to subdivide its shares, this would be treated as a reorganisation and not a disposal and acquisition. Provided that all of the shares after subdivision are eligible shares, the tax reliefs should be preserved.

17.3.3 Categories of share comprised in an investor's holding

Immediately before a reorganisation, a VCT investor's holding of shares in a VCT company will comprise one or more of the following categories:

(1) shares that are both eligible for VCT disposal relief and are 'VCT investment-relief shares';
(2) shares that are eligible for VCT disposal relief but are not VCT investment-relief shares;
(3) shares that are VCT investment-relief shares but are not eligible for VCT disposal relief;
(4) shares that are neither eligible for VCT disposal relief nor are they VCT investment-relief shares

(TCGA 1992, s 151B(3)).

17.3.3.1 *Shares that are eligible for VCT disposal relief*

These are at any time shares that are held by an investor who would be eligible for VCT disposal relief if he or she were to dispose of them at that time. For this purpose, the investor is assumed to be at least 18 years old, even if that is not in fact the case (TCGA 1992, s 151B(8)(a)). For what shares are eligible for VCT disposal relief, see **17.5**.

17.3.3.2 *VCT investment-relief shares*

These are shares in respect of which any person has been given, or is entitled to claim, VCT investment relief. Conversely, shares that are not VCT investment-relief shares are shares in respect of which no person has been given, and no person is entitled to claim, VCT investment relief. However, shares are also not VCT investment-relief shares once:

(*a*) any VCT investment relief given in respect of them has been lost (ie withdrawn totally or reduced); or
(*b*) a chargeable event for VCT deferral relief has occurred in respect of them; or
(*c*) the (previous) holder of them has died

(TCGA 1992, s 151B(8)(b)).

17.3.4 Separate identification following a reorganisation

In a reorganisation involving the exchange of new shares ('the new holding') for the investor's previous shares ('the old holding') the no-disposal rule of TCGA 1992, s 127 **[see 17.3.1]** is applied separately to each category of shares as listed in **17.3.3** so that each category is treated as a separate holding and identified separately with the corresponding category of new shares (TCGA 1992, s 151B(2)).

17.3.5 Reorganisation involving a rights issue

Where the reorganisation does not involve an exchange of shares but takes the form of a rights issue (ie there is an allotment of new shares for payment), the reorganisation rules of TCGA 1992, ss 127–130 do not apply if any of the old shares or any of the new shares (the rights issue) fall within any of the categories (1) to (3) in **17.3.3** (ie qualify for either VCT investment relief or VCT disposal relief) (TCGA 1992, s 151B(4)). As a consequence, the new shares (the rights issue) are not identified with the old shares, with all the capital gains tax consequences that follow. An immediate consequence for VCT purposes is that the rights acquisition counts towards the permitted maximum (£200,000) for the year.

17.3.6 Bonus issues

By contrast, where there is a bonus issue with respect to VCT shares, the bonus shares are treated as a single holding with the original shares, and a part-disposal of such a shareholding is treated accordingly.

17.3.7 Where new shares are not VCT shares

Where a scheme of company reconstruction takes place involving an exchange of shares or securities within the conditions set out in TCGA 1992, ss 135 and 136, the new holding is again identified with the old holding. However, if the old holding consists of shares in categories (1) or (2) in **17.3.3** – that is to say, shares that are eligible for VCT disposal relief and the new holding consists of securities or shares that are not ordinary shares in a VCT company – ss 135 and 136 are disapplied, so that there is no continuity and there is deemed to be a disposal of the old holding, for a consideration equal to the market value of the shares or securities obtained in exchange (the new holding) (TCGA 1992, s 151B(5)).

17.4 Part-disposals

17.4.1 Introduction

A disposal of qualifying shares would include a part-disposal of a larger holding of shares of the same class including bonus shares. The normal capital gains tax rules for matching disposals with acquisitions do not apply to VCT shares eligible for VCT disposal relief (TCGA 1992, s 151B(1)). Instead there are specific rules to determine which shares are being disposed of.

Shares in a company are not treated as being of the same class unless they would be so treated if dealt with on the Stock Exchange (TCGA 1992, s 108(1)).

17.4.2 Identifying disposals with acquisitions

When a disposal of shares in a VCT (ie a VCT investor company) takes place, it will often be necessary to identify which of them, if any, were acquired in excess of the permitted maximum or which are shares on which investment relief has been given and which are not. The rule in this situation is that shares acquired earlier are disposed of before shares acquired later (the first in, first out (FIFO) principle). If any shares were acquired before the investor company became a VCT, they are assumed to be disposed of in priority to the other shares (TCGA 1992, s 151A(5)). This rule preserves investment relief as long as possible, but accelerates any potential capital gains liability.

17.4.2.1 *Shares acquired on the same day*

Where shares were acquired on the same day, the FIFO rule is of no use; instead, disposals are matched with shares acquired in excess of the permitted maximum or shares on which relief has not been given in priority to those acquired within the permitted maximum or shares on which relief has been given.

This rule applies for the purpose of both:

(*a*) withdrawing investment relief (TA 1988, Sch 15B, para 3(8)(b)) and
(*b*) determining which shares qualify for disposal relief (TCGA 1992, s 151A(4)(b))

17.4.2.2 *Shares acquired on different days*

If shares acquired on different days have to be identified, the FIFO rule applies, also for the purpose of both:

(*a*) withdrawing investment relief (TA 1988, Sch 15B, para 3(8)(a)), and
(*b*) determining which shares qualify for disposal relief (TCGA 1992, s 151A(4)(a)).

Example 17.1

Julia makes the following acquisitions of shares in VCTs:

1 May 2004	Subscription for 60,000 shares in Notting VCT plc	£120,000
1 August 2004	Subscription for 30,000 shares in Hill VCT plc	£60,000
1 August 2004	Purchase of 40,000 shares in Notting VCT plc	£110,000

The acquisition on 1 May 2004 is within the permitted maximum. Of the acquisitions on 1 August 2004, the purchased shares do not qualify for investment relief but they are eligible for disposal relief. However, £90,000 is in excess of the permitted maximum. That excess is apportioned as between 60/170 (or £31,765) to the Hill shares and 110/170 (or £58,235) to the Notting shares. The number of shares corresponding to the excess are 15,882 in Hill and 40,000 × (58,235/110,000) = 21,177 in Notting.

On 1 July 2006, Julia sells 90,000 shares in Notting VCT plc for £136,000. The 90,000 shares sold are matched first with the 60,000 acquired on 1 May 2004 and then with 30,000 of the shares acquired on 1 August 2004. Of those 30,000 shares, 21,177 were acquired in excess of the permitted maximum, and hence have priority over the shares acquired within the permitted maximum. The complete identification of the disposal is thus:

60,000 acquired on 1 May 2004
21,177 'excess' acquired on 1 August 2004
8,823 'non-excess' acquired on 1 August 2004

Disposal relief **[see 17.5]** is available on the 60,000 acquired on 1 May 2004 and on 8,823 acquired on 1 August 2004. There will be a capital gains liability on the 21,177 'excess' shares.

As Julia has disposed of VCT shares within the restricted three-year period (which ends on 1 May 2006 for the Notting VCT issue), she faces a loss of investment relief.

17.4.2.3 *Shares acquired before 6 April 1998*

The special identification rules just described do not apply to VCT shares acquired before 6 April 1998 in excess of the permitted maximum or to shares acquired before that date when the company was not a VCT. Those shares are subject to the normal pooling rules applicable before that time – that is to say, they form part of the investor's 'section 104 pool'.

Because a five-year restricted period applied to those shares, the latest of which will not have expired before 6 April 2003, the rule is illustrated here.

Example 17.2

Abu Hamid has made the following acquisitions of ordinary shares, all in Ghazali plc, which gains VCT approval on 8 August 1997.

1	5 May 1996	15,000 shares for £16,500
2	10 September 1997	50,000 shares for £60,000
3	2 February 1998	60,000 shares for £78,000
4	26 July 1998	120,000 shares for £162,000

Purchase 1 was made while Ghazali was not a VCT and forms part of Abu Hamid's section 104 pool. Of purchases 2 and 3, 29,230 shares in purchase 3 (with a cost of 29,230 × £1.30 = £38,000) are treated as the excess beyond the permitted maximum. They also form part of the pool. The remaining shares (all of the 50,000 in purchase 2 and 30,770 of purchase 3) are eligible VCT shares, to which the special VCT identification rules apply. Of purchase 4, 45,926 shares at an apportioned cost of £62,000 (45,926 × £1.35) are in excess of the permitted maximum.

Abu Hamid therefore has five separate blocks of shares for capital gains tax purposes:

A The section 104 pool:

Date	*No of shares*	*Cost*	*Indexed cost*
5.5.96	15,000	£16,500	£16,500
Indexation (say)			£1,850
Subtotal	*15,000*	*£16,500*	*£18,350*
2.2.98	29,230	£38,000	£38,000
Indexation (say)			£1,750
Total	**44,230**	**£54,500**	**£58,100**

Indexation values are for illustrative purposes only. None of the pool shares qualifies for VCT disposal relief.

B 50,000 shares acquired on 10 September 1997
C 30,770 shares acquired on 2 February 1998
D 74,074 shares acquired on 26 July 1998
E 45,926 shares acquired on 26 July 1998

Blocks B, C and D qualify for VCT disposal relief; blocks A and E do not.

Suppose now that Abu Hamid disposes of 25,000 shares for £32,000 in January 2000. These are identified in the following order:

1: 15,000 acquired 5.5.96	(pre-VCT shares: TCGA 1992, s 151A(5))
2: 10,000 acquired 10.9.97	(FIFO: TCGA 1992, s 151A(4)(a))

The 15,000 pool shares have an unindexed acquisition cost of (15,000/44,230) × £54,500 = £18,483, and an indexation allowance of (15,000/44,230) × £3,600 = £1,221, giving an indexed total of £19,704. The proceeds are (15,000/25,000) × £32,000 = £19,200. Since an indexation allowance cannot be used to create a loss the chargeable gain will be reduced to nil.

The 10,000 shares acquired on 10 September 1997 have an unindexed acquisition cost of (10,000/50,000) × £60,000 = £12,000. They will have their own indexation allowance for the period 10.9.97 to 5.4.98. This gain (if any) does qualify for disposal relief.

For the application of taper relief to scheme disposals, see **Chapter 23**.

17.5 Gains on early disposals of VCT shares

17.5.1 Disposal relief

An investor who makes a 'qualifying disposal' of ordinary shares in a company that is a VCT both when the investor acquires the shares and when he or she disposes of them is exempt from capital gains tax on any gain arising from the disposal (TCGA 1992, s 151A(1)).

A 'qualifying disposal' is one made by an individual aged 18 or over of shares that:

(*a*) were not acquired in excess of the permitted maximum for any tax year; and
(*b*) were acquired for bona fide commercial purposes and not as part of a tax avoidance scheme

(TCGA 1992, s 151A(2)).

No other conditions are attached. It does not matter therefore whether:

(*a*) the VCT company loses its VCT status temporarily between the time of the acquisition and the time of the disposal;
(*b*) the shares were acquired by subscription, purchase, gift or inheritance;
(*c*) VCT investment relief was obtained on them or not;
(*d*) the disposal is an early disposal (within the three-year restricted period) or a later disposal;
(*e*) VCT investment relief has been lost or withdrawn in respect of the shares.

An early disposal will, of course, lead to a loss of VCT investment relief **[see Chapter 20]**.

For rules to identify what shares out of a mixed holding were acquired outside the permitted maximum, see **17.4**.

17.5.2 Non-qualifying disposals

On a non-qualifying disposal (say, of shares acquired in excess of the permitted maximum), disposal relief does not apply, and any gain would be taxable in the normal way.

17.6 Losses on early disposals of VCT shares

17.6.1 Non-recognition of losses

If a loss is incurred on a qualifying disposal **[see 17.5.1]**, the loss is not an allowable loss for CGT purposes (TCGA 1992, s 151A(1)). This is the quid pro quo for the exemption of gains, and is so whether or not the disposal is an early disposal.

17.6.2 Non-qualifying disposals

If the disposal is a non-qualifying disposal, say of shares acquired outside the permitted maximum, disposal relief does not apply, and any gain is taxable. By the same token, any loss will be allowable.

17.7 Gains on later disposals of VCT shares

17.7.1 Disposal relief

Provided that the conditions set out in **17.5.1** are satisfied, disposal relief (in the form of exemption) applies equally to disposals outside the restricted period as it does to disposals within the restricted period (TCGA 1992, s 151A(1)).

Example 17.3

Jean-Paul, who is 45, inherits VCT shares from his mother (who acquired them in 1996) in December 2002, when they are worth £14,000. Two years later, he sells them for £20,000. The company has retained its VCT status continuously since 1995. Jean-Paul's gain is exempt.

17.7.2 Non-qualifying disposals

If the disposal is a non-qualifying disposal, say of shares acquired before or while the company is not a VCT, disposal relief does not apply and the normal capital gains rules apply instead. The gain on any non-qualifying disposal will therefore be chargeable, as mitigated by indexation and taper reliefs, where appropriate.

17.8 Losses on later disposals

17.8.1 Non-recognition of losses

A loss realised on a qualifying disposal is not an allowable loss (TCGA 1992, s 151A(1)). If the disposal is not a qualifying disposal, the loss is an allowable loss, which may be set off against gains in the normal way.

Chapter 18

Disposal of EIS Shares

18.1 Introduction

As explained in **17.1.1**, this chapter, which discusses the capital gains consequences of disposals of EIS shares falls naturally into five parts. The first considers the tax treatment of disposals generally. The second part considers the tax treatment of a disposal at a gain of shares outside the restricted period; the third part considers the treatment of losses on such a later disposal. The fourth part deals with an early disposal of scheme shares at a gain and the fifth part considers the treatment of losses on an early disposal. In contrast to the VCT scheme, the EIS does not exempt early disposals of scheme shares.

For the impact on an investor's capital gains tax or corporation tax liability of share disposals, see **Chapter 22**. For the interaction of these reliefs and charges with other tax provisions, see **Chapter 23**. For procedures for claiming relief and Inland Revenue procedures generally, see **Chapter 24**. For information requirements, see **Chapter 25**.

18.1.1 Scope of this chapter

This chapter covers the following topics:

(*a*) Remaining general introductory material **[see 18.1.2 to 18.1.5]**
(*b*) What constitutes a disposal **[see 18.2]**
(*c*) Company reorganisations **[see 18.3]**
(*d*) Identification rules **[see 18.4]**
(*e*) Gains on later disposals of EIS shares **[see 18.5]**
(*f*) Losses on later disposals of EIS shares **[see 18.6]**
(*g*) Gains on early disposals of EIS shares **[see 18.7]**
(*h*) Losses on early disposals of EIS shares **[see 18.8]**

18.1.2 Investor's restricted periods for disposals

In the EIS scheme, the restricted period within which the investor may not dispose of his or her shares if investment relief is to be preserved is the 'relevant period'. This period begins on the later of (*a*) the incorporation of the company and (*b*) two years before the issue date, but what matters for disposal purposes is the end of the period (since the period cannot start before the shares are issued). The period ends immediately before a date known as the 'termination date'. The termination date is the later of (*a*) the third anniversary of the issue date and (*b*) the third anniversary of the date on which the qualifying trade began (TA 1988, s 312(1A)(a)). The same period applies to demarcate disposals qualifying for disposal relief (exemption) from earlier disposals that do not qualify for disposal relief (TCGA 1992, s 150A(2)).

Disposal relief therefore applies to disposals made on or after the termination date. Disposals made before the termination date do not qualify for disposal relief. The minimum length of this period is three years, and it will often be longer; its maximum length is five years.

In the case of shares issued before 6 April 2000, the termination date was invariably five years after the issue date. Its minimum length was thus five years and its maximum length, seven. Such periods will therefore not finally have expired until 6 April 2007.

18.1.3 Crystallisation of deferred gains

A disposal of EIS shares will cause gains deferred under EIS deferral relief to crystallise **[see Chapter 15]**.

18.1.4 EIS shares

In this chapter, the term 'EIS shares' or 'qualifying EIS shares' is used to denote shares to which EIS investment relief is attributable. Shares from which relief has been withdrawn are not EIS shares.

18.2 The disposal

18.2.1 Introduction

A disposal of EIS shares includes a sale, gift or exchange and a part-disposal **[see 18.4]**.

18.2.2 Options

The EIS rules relating to disposals for capital gains purposes contain no special provision for options (unlike the rules for disposals for investment relief purposes – see below). However, under those investment relief rules, both the grant by the investor of a call option and to the investor of a put option causes investment relief to be withdrawn if the grant takes place during the relevant period for the shares (TA 1988, s 299(5), (5A), (8)(b)). It follows that shares over which an option has been granted in these circumstances are no longer EIS shares and do not qualify for disposal relief once the call option is exercised, whether this happens before or after the termination date.

Subject to that, the normal capital gains rules must thus apply to both put and call options over EIS shares.

Those rules provide that if an option is exercised, the grant of the option and the transaction (in this case the sale of the shares) are treated as a single transaction. The amount paid for the grant of a call option (an option binding the grantor to sell) is treated as part of the consideration for the sale of the shares. The consideration for a put option (an option binding the grantor to buy) is deducted from the cost of acquisition (TCGA 1992, s 144(2)).

If the option is not exercised, the grant of the option is treated as the disposal of an asset separate from the shares, not as a part-disposal of the shares. As there is no cost of the new asset, the full amount received for granting the option is chargeable (TCGA 1992, s 144(1) and *Strange v Openshaw* [1983] STC 416).

For the treatment of options in relation to withdrawal of investment relief, see **20.5.2.3**.

18.2.3 Transfers to a spouse

Husband and wife are treated as separate persons for most purposes of income tax and capital gains tax. For example, each is entitled to make qualifying investments up to the annual limit of £200,000 for EIS relief purposes.

A transfer of shares between a husband and wife who are living together does not cause the EIS reliefs to be withdrawn. What is more, the EIS capital gain exemption attaches to the shares and is not lost on a transfer between spouses.

There is no capital gains tax liability on a transfer between spouses (TCGA 1992, s 58(1)). There is also no clawback of the EIS reliefs when the shares are transferred by an investor to his or her spouse when they are living together (TA 1988 s 304(1)). Instead the recipient stands in the shoes of the investor who made the original claim to investment relief or deferral relief. The spouse can benefit from the capital gains tax exemption on a later sale or gift of the shares, provided the investment relief has not been withdrawn.

18.2.3.1 *Early disposals*

If, before the termination date for the EIS share issue, a person who has received shares from his or her spouse disposes of the shares, the normal rules for withdrawal of investment relief apply except that the tax is recovered from the person who made the disposal, not the person who originally subscribed and received the tax relief (TA 1988, s 304(2)).

If the EIS investment relief was restricted when the shares were issued, the adjustment to the capital gains exemption **[see 18.5.2]** and the formula for withdrawal of relief **[see 18.8.5]** will apply to the person who makes the disposal (TCGA 1992, s 150A(3)).

Example 18.1

Marsilio subscribes £10,000 for 10,000 shares in Ficino Ltd in May 2002 and receives £2,000 EIS relief. In May 2003 he gifts half of his shares to his wife Rosanne. This gift would not cause a withdrawal of EIS relief. For capital gains tax purposes Marsilio is treated as having disposed of the shares for a consideration equal to their cost of £10,000.

In August 2004 Rosanne sells her shares at their market value for £12,000. There would be a withdrawal of all the EIS relief attributable to those shares amounting to £2,000 (£10,000 × 20%). The assessment would be raised on Rosanne. She would also have a chargeable gain, which may be covered by her annual exemption.

	£
Proceeds	12,000
Less acquisition cost	10,000
Chargeable gain (before taper relief)	2,000

18.2.4 Death of the investor

18.2.4.1 *Investment relief*

As the transfer of shares on death is not treated as a disposal, EIS investment relief is not withdrawn. The deceased's personal representatives and beneficiaries are free to deal with the EIS shares without affecting the deceased's investment relief. There is no requirement for them to retain the shares for the restricted period.

18.2.4.2 *Death during the four-month period*

Provided that the shares are issued before death, the fact that an investor dies before the EIS company has carried on its qualifying activities for four months **[see 12.7]** does not prevent EIS relief from being due for the tax year in which the share issue took place, even though the actual claim may not be made until some time after death. If, however, the company never carries on a qualifying trade, there is no relief available for any shareholder.

18.2.4.3 *Breach of conditions*

If an EIS company has carried on a qualifying trade for four months but breaches the EIS conditions after the investor's death, this will not affect the deceased's initial relief (TA 1988, s 307(3)).

Example 18.2

Guarino subscribes £10,000 for 10,000 shares in Carignano Ltd in May 2003 and receives EIS relief. Guarino dies in July 2004 and the company ceases trading in August 2004. The relief received by Guarino is not disturbed even though the company has not carried on a qualifying trade for three years and the other EIS shareholders' relief would be withdrawn.

18.2.4.4 *Capital gains and losses*

There can be no chargeable gains or allowable losses arising on death because the deceased is treated as not having disposed of the shares, even though the personal representative is deemed to have acquired the shares at market value (TCGA 1992, s 62(1)).

Example 18.3

Abarbanel subscribes £10,000 for ordinary shares in Dialogues Ltd in January 2002 and claims £2,000 EIS relief. He dies four years later when the shares are worth £9,000. Six months later the shares are sold by his personal representatives at their market value of £11,000. The EIS relief given would not be withdrawn and there would be no allowable capital loss at death. The capital gains computation for the personal representatives would be:

	£
Sale proceeds	11,000
Less probate value	9,000
Capital gain (before taper relief)	2,000

18.2.4.5 *Tax benefits of VCT and EIS shares*

It may be thought that the personal representative, the widow, widower or other beneficiary will, at a later date, be making the first disposal of the shares and can therefore obtain a tax-free gain. This is not the case; apart from shares received from a spouse **[see 18.2.3]** only a disposal by the individual who received the initial relief can benefit from the EIS capital gains exemption (TCGA 1992, s 150A(2)).

18.3 Company reorganisations

18.3.1 Introduction

Where there is a reorganisation of shares, such as a bonus or rights issue or a qualifying share exchange, the normal rule for capital gains tax is that there is deemed to be no disposal of the original shares or any acquisition of the new shares; the new holding is treated as a single asset acquired at the time the original holding was acquired (TCGA 1992, s 127). When it comes to EIS shares, however, just as for VCT shares **[see 17.3]**, this rule is modified.

18.3.2 Subdivision

If a qualifying EIS investee company decides to subdivide its shares, such a subdivision would be treated as a reorganisation and not a disposal and acquisition. Provided that all of the shares after the subdivision are eligible shares, the tax reliefs should be preserved.

18.3.3 Categories of share comprised in an investor's holding

Immediately before a reorganisation, an EIS investor's holding of shares in an EIS company will comprise one or more of the following categories:

(*a*) shares that are EIS shares and 'EIS deferral-relief shares';
(*b*) shares that are EIS shares but are not EIS deferral-relief shares;
(*c*) shares that are not EIS shares;

(TCGA 1992, s 150A(6)).

18.3.3.1 *EIS deferral-relief shares*

These are shares the investment in which has been matched to all or part of a chargeable gain under EIS deferral relief **[see Chapter 15]** and in respect of which there has not yet been a chargeable event **[see 15.7]**.

18.3.4 Separate identification following a reorganisation

In a reorganisation involving an exchange of shares in which the old holding comprises at least two of the three categories listed in **18.3.3**, each category is treated as a separate holding and identified separately with the corresponding category of new shares (TCGA 1992, s 150A(6)).

18.3.5 Reorganisation involving a rights issue

Where the reorganisation does not involve an exchange of shares, but takes the form of a rights issue (ie there is an allotment of new shares for payment), the reorganisation rules of TCGA 1992, ss 127–130 do not apply if any of the old shares or any of the new shares (the rights issue) fall within either category (*a*) or (*b*) in **18.3.3** (ie are EIS shares) (TCGA 1992, s 150A(7)). As a consequence, the new shares (the rights issue) are not identified with the old shares, and the new shares are treated as a separate acquisition. They thus count towards the investor's permitted maximum (£200,000) for the year. At the same time, they may qualify for EIS investment relief and EIS deferral relief if the normal qualifying conditions are satisfied.

18.3.6 Bonus issues

By contrast, where there is a bonus issue with respect to EIS shares, the bonus shares are treated as a single holding with the original shares, and a part-disposal of such a shareholding is treated accordingly.

18.3.7 Where new shares are not EIS shares

Where a scheme of company reconstruction takes place involving an exchange of shares or securities, and the old holding comprises EIS shares, there is normally deemed to be no continuity between the old holding and the new holding, even if the conditions set out in TCGA 1992, ss 135 and 136 (satisfaction of which allows for continuity for normal capital gains tax purposes) are otherwise fully satisfied (TCGA 1992, s 150A(8)). Instead, there is a disposal of the old holding, for a consideration equal to the market value of the shares or securities obtained in exchange (the new holding). Any subsequent disposal of the new shares will not qualify for EIS disposal relief.

Example 18.4

In July 2004, Juan Luís subscribes £100,000 for 50,000 shares in Vivés Ltd, which has been trading for a year previously and obtains EIS investment relief. Four years later, in July 2008, Adversus Ltd, which is not an EIS company, makes an offer for the Vivés shares. Juan Luís exchanges his shares for 25,000 Adversus shares, which have a market value of £125,000.

Juan Luís is treated as disposing of his Vivés shares for £125,000, but his gain qualifies for disposal relief as the exchange takes place after the termination date for the shares **[see 18.5]** and is therefore exempt from capital gains tax. His Adversus shares are treated as acquired for £125,000 in July 2008. They are not EIS shares and will not qualify for disposal relief.

However, if the exchange takes place after the relevant period for the old shares has expired (ie after the termination date), and the acquiring company is an EIS company, then there is after all deemed to be continuity, provided that several other conditions are satisfied also. Those conditions are that:

(*a*) the acquiring company has issued eligible shares at some previous time;

(*b*) the acquiring company has issued EIS tax relief certificates to investors **[see Chapter 25]** in respect of those issues; and

(*c*) the new holding consists of new ordinary shares carrying no present or future preferential right to dividends or to a company's assets on its winding-up, and no present or future right to be redeemed – this condition is the normal definition of 'eligible shares'

(TCGA 1992, s 150A(8A)–(8C)).

In the case of shares issued before 6 April 2000, the exchange had to take place more than five years after the issue date of the old shares.

Where these conditions are satisfied, there is deemed to be no disposal. The new shares are identified with the old shares, are deemed to have been acquired at the acquisition date of the old shares, at the same acquisition cost. A subsequent disposal of the new shares will qualify for EIS disposal relief under the normal conditions **[see 18.5]**.

18.3.8 Acquisition by a new company

Where a new company whose only issued share capital is represented by subscriber shares takes over an EIS company (the target company), acquiring all the shares and securities in the target company in exchange for an issue of shares and securities of its own of a corresponding description, and does so with Inland Revenue approval, the EIS investment relief attributable to the old shares transfers across to the new shares (TA 1988, s 304A – see **5.10.2**). It is important to ensure that before the issue of the new shares, the old company has issued eligible shares and has issued a certificate that those shares qualified for EIS investment relief (this, of course, requires the old company to have been trading for at least four months).

Again, there is continuity between the new and old holdings, and the new shares are deemed to have been acquired at the same cost and at the same time as the old shares (TCGA 1992, s 150A(8D)).

Example 18.5

In March 2002, Arthur subscribes £20,000 for shares in Paralipomena Ltd and obtains EIS investment relief. In June 2004, all the shares in Paralipomena Ltd are acquired by Reason Ltd in exchange for its own ordinary shares. Reason Ltd is a newly formed company whose only shares before it took over Paralipomena were subscriber shares. Arthur's investment relief is not withdrawn (TA 1988, s 304A applies); there is no capital gains tax disposal and he is deemed to have acquired the Reason shares in March 2002 and to have received EIS investment relief in respect of those shares.

In January 2006 (after the termination date, March 2005 for the Paralipomena shares), Schopenhauer Ltd acquires all the shares in Reason Ltd in exchange for its own shares. If Schopenhauer has previously issued EIS shares and if the new shares carry no preferential rights, Arthur will be treated as if he had acquired the Schopenhauer shares in March 2002. Again, there is no disposal, and any gain on the subsequent sale of the Schopenhauer shares will be exempt (disposal relief). But if Schopenhauer has not previously issued EIS shares, Arthur is treated as disposing of his Reason shares (again, the gain is exempt) and to have acquired the Schopenhauer shares at market value. They do not qualify for EIS disposal relief on a future disposal.

18.4 Matching disposals with acquisitions

18.4.1 Introduction

When a part-disposal is made out of a larger holding including EIS shares, the normal capital gains tax rules for matching disposals with acquisitions do not apply (TCGA 1992, s 150A(5)). Instead, there are specific rules to determine which shares are being disposed of.

18.4.2 Shares acquired on different days

The general rule is FIFO – first in, first out – so that earlier acquisitions are treated as being disposed of before later acquisitions (TCGA 1992, s 150A(4); TA 1988, s 299(6)).

18.4.3 Shares acquired on the same day

Where there is a need to distinguish between different acquisitions on the same day, the order of priority is:

(*a*) shares that are neither EIS shares nor EIS deferral-relief shares;
(*b*) shares that are not EIS shares but are EIS deferral-relief shares;
(*c*) shares that are EIS shares but are not EIS-deferral shares
(*d*) shares that are both EIS shares and EIS-deferral shares

(TCGA 1992, s 150A(4); TA 1988, s 299(6A)).

For the meaning of 'EIS shares', see **18.1.4** and for 'EIS deferral-relief shares', see **18.3.3.1**.

18.4.4 A single issue of EIS shares

On a part-disposal out of a single issue of EIS shares, the shares disposed of and the shares retained benefit from disposal relief (where available) equally until all of the shares have been disposed of or the investment relief attributable to the shares has been withdrawn, whichever is earlier.

18.4.5 EIS share acquisitions above the permitted maximum

Where EIS shares are subscribed for in excess of the £200,000 annual limit, the maximum investment relief is apportioned to each share acquired **[see 9.5]**. On a part-disposal, the investment relief attributable to each share is reduced pro rata.

18.4.6 Shares acquired before 6 April 1998

Different rules applied to shares acquired before 6 April 1998. Because the latest restricted periods for these shares did not finally expire before 6 April 2003, mention of the rules is made here.

EIS shares were not subject to pooling, but non-EIS shares were. The FIFO identification rule applied also to shares issued before 6 April 1998.

Example 18.6

Tara subscribes £30,000 for 20,000 new shares in an EIS company on 1 June 1996. They represent her only EIS investment in 1996–97, and she obtains full EIS investment relief of £6,000. On 15 January 1998, she buys a further 20,000 shares in the same company from another investor for £25,000. These shares are not EIS shares.

In January 2004, Tara sells 30,000 of the shares for £48,000.

Two separate holdings must be distinguished. The 20,000 shares acquired on 1 June 1996 are EIS shares, qualifying for disposal relief if sold after five years (ie after 1 June 2001). The second holding of shares, non-EIS shares, form part of the pool ('the section 104 holding') together with any other non-EIS shares of the same class in the same company acquired before 6 April 1998. Assume there are none.

The January 2004 disposal is identified first with the earlier acquisition, ie the 20,000 shares @ £1.50. The disposal proceeds for this part are (20,000/30,000) × £48,000 = £32,000. Since the disposal has taken place after the termination date for the shares (1 June 2001), this part of the gain (£2,000) qualifies for disposal relief (exemption).

The remaining 10,000 shares are identified with the 20,000 section 104 shares. This pool will include indexation allowance for the period from January to April 1998, say £50. The acquisition cost is therefore:

(10,000/20,000) × £25,000 = £12,500

The indexation allowance is (10,000/20,000) × £50 = £25.

The disposal proceeds attributable to this tranche of the gain are (£48,000 – £32,000) = £16,000.

Ignoring taper relief, this gain (£16,000 – £12,525) = £3,475, is chargeable.

18.5 Gains on later disposals of EIS shares

18.5.1 Disposal relief

18.5.1.1 *The basic rule*

Provided that the EIS investment relief attributable to the shares has not been withdrawn or reduced, a disposal of the shares after the end of the termination period **[see 18.1.2]** is exempt from capital gains tax (TCGA 1992, s 150A(2)).

Example 18.7

John subscribes £100,000 for ordinary shares in McTaggart Ltd on 9 August 2003 and receives EIS relief of £20,000. In March 2007 he sells the shares for £124,000. Ignoring taper relief, the computation is:

	£
Disposal proceeds	124,000
Less acquisition cost	100,000
Exempt gain	24,000

The termination date for the shares (assuming McTaggart's qualifying trade had already begun when the shares were issued) is 9 August 2006.

18.5.2 Restriction of the exemption

Where a disposal takes place of shares on which the investor's investment relief was initially restricted for some reason, there may also be a restriction on the amount of the gain that qualifies for exemption. There are three main reasons why EIS investment relief may be restricted at the time of the original subscription. They are:

(*a*) because the subscription is in excess of the permitted maximum; or
(*b*) because other shareholders have received value before the investor's subscription; or
(*c*) because the investor does not have sufficient income tax liability to absorb all of the available relief.

If reasons (*a*) or (*b*) are in point, or any other reason except (*c*), the exempt part of the gain on disposal of the shares is the fraction A/B where A is the amount of relief given and B is equal to the lower rate of tax (currently 20%) on the amount subscribed (TCGA 1992, s 150A(3)).

Example 18.8

Gangesa subscribes £10,000 for shares in Nyaya Ltd but because Nyaya had redeemed some of its shares a year earlier, he only receives EIS relief of £1,500 rather than the full £2,000. Six years later he sells his shares for £15,000. Ignoring taper relief, the gain is computed as follows:

	£
Sale proceeds	15,000
Less acquisition cost	10,000
Gain	5,000
Exempt gain £1,500/£2,000 × £5,000	£3,750
Chargeable gain	£1,250

Example 18.9

In June 2002 Maurice subscribed £200,000 for a single issue of eligible shares in Merleau Ltd and received restricted EIS investment relief of £30,000 (20% of £150,000). After three years he sells the shares for £250,000. Ignore taper relief.

	£
Sale proceeds	250,000
Less acquisition cost	200,000
	50,000
Exempt gain (30,000/40,000) × £50,000	£37,500
Chargeable gain	£12,500

18.5.2.1 *Insufficient income tax liability*

However, if the EIS investment relief was restricted because the investor's income tax liability was less than the full relief **[see 20.2.8]**, there is no restriction of the capital gains exemption on the shares (TCGA 1992, s 150A(3)(aa)).

18.5.3 Later restriction on receipt of value

There is a similar restricted capital gains tax exemption on the EIS shares where part of the investment relief attributable to the eligible shares has subsequently been withdrawn because the investor has received value before the termination date for the shares. Assuming that the shares are held beyond the termination date and other conditions are met, only part of any gain on their disposal is exempt. The exemption is restricted by excluding the proportion X/Y, where X is the relief withdrawn and Y is the relief originally given. The same rule applies where investment relief is reduced because other shareholders have received value **[see 12.5]** (TCGA 1992, s 150B(1)).

Example 18.10

Jennifer subscribes £100,000 for 100,000 ordinary shares in Pride Ltd in May 2003 and receives EIS initial relief of £20,000. Six months later she receives a

£10,000 loan from the company and £2,000 of her investment relief is withdrawn. In June 2006 she sells her shares for £145,000. Ignore taper relief.

	£
Sale proceeds	145,000
Less acquisition cost	100,000
Gain	45,000

Investment relief retained was £18,000 whereas the full initial relief was £20,000.

Gain as above	45,000
Restriction on exempt gain:	
(£2,000/£20,000 × £45,000	4,500
Exempt gain	40,500

18.5.4 Repeated receipts of value

Where value is received on more than one occasion before the disposal, the exempt gain is restricted by reference to the total amounts withdrawn (TCGA 1992, s 150B(4), (5)).

Example 18.11

Take the facts of Example 18.10, but suppose that, in addition to receiving value (the £10,000 loan) in November 2003, Jennifer also receives a £2,500 computer free of charge from Pride Ltd in February 2004. Investment relief of £500 (£2,500 @ 20%) is withdrawn.

The capital gains computation on the disposal by Jennifer of the shares in June 2006 (two weeks after the termination date) is now as follows, again ignoring taper relief:

	£
Sale proceeds	145,000
Acquisition cost	100,000
Gain	45,000
Less restriction on exempt gain:	5,625
(£2,500/£20,000) × £45,000	
Exempt gain	39,375
Chargeable gain (before taper relief)	5,625

18.5.5 Initial restriction and subsequent receipts of value

If the investor's investment relief is restricted initially, for example because the subscription for the shares exceeded the permitted maximum, and there is subsequently a receipt of value, the exempt gain is first restricted with reference to the initial restriction and then with reference to the value received (TCGA 1992, s 150B(3)).

Example 18.12

Cheryl subscribes £100,000 for 100,000 shares in Vera Ltd in November 2002. Because the subscription carries her over the permitted maximum for 2002–03, she receives investment relief of £15,000 instead of the full £20,000. Vera Ltd begins trading on 1 January 2003. In May 2005, Cheryl borrows £20,000 from Vera, and loses investment relief of £4,000 as a result. In February 2006, Cheryl sells all of her shares for £124,000.

Her capital gains computation is as follows (ignoring taper relief):

	£	£
Sale proceeds		124,000
Acquisition cost		100,000
Gain		24,000
Restriction on exempt gain (TCGA 1992, s 150A(3)): (£15,000/£20,000) × £24,000		18,000
Chargeable gain	6,000	
Restriction on exempt gain (TCGA 1992, s 150B(3)): (£4,000/£15,000) × £18,000	4,800	(4,800)
Exempt gain		**£13,200**
Chargeable gain	**£10,800**	

18.6 Losses on later disposals of EIS shares

18.6.1 Loss relief

In sharp contrast to the VCT scheme, the EIS recognises a loss on the later disposal of EIS shares even though the corresponding gain is exempt. However, in computing the loss, the EIS investment relief attributable to the shares and not withdrawn or reduced has to be deducted from the disposal proceeds. In some circumstances, this may convert a loss into a gain (TCGA 1992, s 150A(1)).

Example 18.13

After five years, Rachel sells the following shares at arm's length on which she had claimed 20% investment relief.

Company	*Relief*	*Cost*	*Cost net of tax relief*	*Proceeds of sale*	*Allowable loss*
		£	£	£	£
Mummy	EIS	100,000	80,000	nil	80,000
Imhotep	VCT	50,000	40,000	43,000	–
Osiris	VCT	60,000	48,000	40,000	–
Isis	EIS	25,000	20,000	15,000	5,000

Example 18.14

Frederick subscribes for 1,000 shares in Copleston Ltd on 1 May 2003 for £50,000 and obtains full EIS investment relief of £10,000. On 1 July 2006, when it is obvious the company is failing, Frederick sells the shares for £42,000, realising a gross loss of £8,000. The computation is as follows:

Disposal proceeds		£42,000
Less acquisition cost	£50,000	
Less investment relief	£10,000	
		£40,000
Gain (ignoring taper relief)		£2,000

The adjustment for investment relief has turned what was a monetary loss into a gain for capital gains purposes. However, since the disposal took place after the termination date (1 May 2006) for the shares, the gain qualifies for disposal relief, and is therefore exempt.

18.6.2 Relief for a capital loss

An allowable capital loss on EIS shares can be set against the investor's capital gains in the year of disposal or in subsequent years except where the disposal is to a connected person (TCGA 1992, s 18(3)).

18.6.3 Losses on disposals to connected persons

Where an individual makes a loss on a disposal of EIS shares to a connected person, the disposal is treated as not being a bargain made at arm's length, market value is substituted for the consideration and the capital loss (if there still be one) can only be relieved against a gain on a future disposal of an asset to that person.

Example 18.15

Jürgen subscribes £10,000 for ordinary shares in Heidelberg Ltd and claims EIS relief of £2,000. After the termination date, he sells his shares to his mother Marlene for £1,000 when the market value is £6,000. As this is treated as not a bargain at arm's length, the loss of £4,000 (£10,000–£6,000) can only be set against a gain arising from a disposal of an asset by Jürgen to Marlene.

18.6.4 Applying the loss against income

The investor who disposes of an EIS shareholding at arm's length for full consideration has the alternative of electing to set the allowable loss first against his or her taxable income in the year of disposal or the previous year. (TA 1988, ss 305A, 575(1)).

Where an investor loses his or her EIS investment at any time he or she can receive 52% of the investment back in the form of tax relief. In Example 18.13 on the Mummy investment Rachel would receive initial relief of 20% and 32% loss relief, assuming the £80,000 receives tax relief at 40%.

18.6.5 Part-disposals

Where there is a part-disposal of EIS shares, only the corresponding proportion of the investment relief is deducted from cost in calculating the allowable loss.

Example 18.16

Miranda subscribes £60,000 for 60,000 eligible shares in Blackadder Ltd and receives EIS relief of £12,000. After the termination date she sells 20,000 shares for £14,000.
The EIS relief attributable to the 20,000 shares is £4,000 (one-third of £12,000). As the shares are EIS shares Miranda will be entitled to a capital loss.

	£	£
Sale proceeds		14,000
Less acquisition cost	20,000	
Less EIS relief	4,000	16,000
Allowable capital loss		2,000

18.7 Gains on early disposals of EIS shares

18.7.1 Introduction

If a gain arises on the disposal of EIS shares before the termination date, all of the investment relief on those shares is withdrawn. This is the inevitable result of the formula prescribed by TA 1988, s 299(1), (2) for reducing the relief – see **20.5.2.6** for details.

On a part-disposal of the EIS shares, the earliest acquisition of shares is treated as having been disposed of first (TA 1988 s 299(6)).

18.7.2 No disposal relief

Since an early disposal of EIS shares leads to withdrawal of the investment relief, there is also a loss of disposal relief, since this applies only where investment relief has been given and not withdrawn in respect of the shares.

A gain on an early disposal will therefore be taxable in the normal way.

It is interesting that whereas later disposals benefit from both exemption of gains and recognition of losses, a double benefit, early disposals suffer a 'double whammy', in the form of loss of investment relief and a liability to tax on the gain.

Example 18.17

Jane subscribes £100,000 for 100,000 ordinary shares in Voice Ltd and claims £20,000 EIS investment relief. After a year she sells the shares for £110,000. Jane would have all her EIS investment relief withdrawn and she would pay tax on the chargeable gain in the normal way.

	£
Disposal proceeds	110,000
Less cost	100,000
Chargeable gain before taper relief	10,000

18.8 Losses on early disposals of EIS shares

18.8.1 Full withdrawal of EIS investment relief

If any of the conditions for the relief ceases to be satisfied and the EIS investment relief is fully withdrawn at or before the first disposal, the shares are no longer EIS shares and the normal capital gains tax rules apply. Where a capital loss is suffered, loss relief for shares in unquoted trading companies may be available if the conditions for that relief under TA 1988, ss 574–576 are met **[see 21.3]**.

18.8.2 Partial loss of investment relief

Where an investor makes an early disposal of his or her EIS shares in a bargain at arm's length there is a loss but not a withdrawal of the investment relief. The amount of relief lost is equal to tax at the lower rate for the year of the share issue multiplied by the proceeds received (TA 1988, s 299(1), (2)).

Example 18.18

After two years Rachel sells the following shares at arm's length on which she has claimed 20% investment relief.

Company	*Relief*	*Cost*	*Investment relief*	*Proceeds of sale*	*Loss of investment relief*
		£	£	£	£
Mummy	EIS	100,000	20,000	nil	nil
Imhotep	VCT	50,000	10,000	40,000	8,000
Osiris	VCT	60,000	12,000	40,000	8,000
Isis	EIS	25,000	5,000	15,000	3,000

Where any investment relief has been lost, the acquisition cost used to calculate the loss is only reduced by the investment relief that has been retained. There is no VCT loss relief **[see 17.8]** but loss relief is available on the early disposal of EIS shares as follows.

Example 18.19

Continuing Example 18.18, Rachel could claim the following allowable losses:

		(A) *Cost*	(B) *Reduced investment relief*	(C) *Proceeds of sale*	(C)−((A)−(B)) *Allowable loss*
		£	£	£	£
Mummy	EIS	100,000	20,000	nil	80,000
Isis	EIS	25,000	2,000	15,000	8,000

18.8.3 Bargains not at arm's length

If an investor disposes of EIS shares before the end of the termination date and in a bargain that is not at arm's length, all of the EIS investment relief attributable to those shares is withdrawn (TA 1988, s 299(1)(a)).

As a result, the shares are no longer EIS shares, and the normal capital gains rules apply. A loss on such a transaction would be allowable, but after the disposal proceeds were adjusted to market value (TCGA 1992, s 17(1)(a)).

18.8.4 Disposals to connected persons

The provisions for withdrawal of investment relief on an early disposal of EIS shares do not state that a disposal to a connected person will be treated as a transaction otherwise than by way of a bargain made at arm's length. However, as such a provision exists for capital gains tax purposes (TCGA 1992 s 18(2)) **[see 18.6.3]** it would be advisable to ensure, wherever possible, that the market value for shares is paid by connected persons. There are special rules for transfers between husband and wife **[see 18.2.3]**.

Example 18.20

Assume the facts in Example 18.15 except that Jürgen disposes of the shares after two years. In such a case, EIS relief of £2,000 would be withdrawn. The shares would no longer be EIS shares. He would have an allowable capital loss of £4,000 (£6,000 less £10,000) but restricted to an offset against a gain on a disposal of an asset to Marlene. Income tax loss relief **[see 18.6.4]** would not be available.

18.8.5 Reduced or restricted investment relief

The investment relief given is not always the full amount for a number of reasons. Furthermore, the relief may have been reduced during the ownership of the shares. They are nevertheless still EIS shares and the actual investment relief given or retained is used in the calculation of allowable losses.

Example 18.21

Renée originally receives EIS relief of £20,000 on her £100,000 subscription but £2,000 is withdrawn when she obtains a £10,000 loan from the company. Before the end of the termination period, she sells the shares for £62,000.

	£	£
Sale proceeds		62,000
Less acquisition cost	100,000	
Less EIS relief (£20,000–£2,000)	18,000	82,000
Allowable capital loss		20,000

18.8.6 Part-disposals where EIS investment relief was restricted

An adjustment to the formula for withdrawing relief is made where the amount of tax 'A' saved by the investor was less than the tax at the lower rate on the subscription ('B'). In such a case the amount or value of the relief to be withdrawn on a part-disposal of the shares is reduced by multiplying it by the fraction A/B (TA 1988, s 299(4)). This adjustment is also made when the investor receives value from the company within his or her relevant period **[see 20.5.2.6]**.

Example 18.22

Take the facts of Example 18.16 except that now assume that Miranda receives £6,000 EIS initial relief instead of £12,000. The relief attributable to the 20,000 shares she is selling is £2,000 (one-third of £6,000) and the maximum relief is £4,000 (£20,000 × 20%). The relief to be withdrawn is £1,400 (£2,000/£4,000 × £14,000 × 20%), being smaller than the attributable relief of £2,000. As the 20,000 shares are EIS shares Miranda will be entitled to a capital loss.

	£	£
Sale proceeds		14,000
Less acquisition cost	20,000	
Less EIS relief (£2,000–£1,400)	600	19,400
Allowable capital loss		5,400

Where an EIS company is taken over by another company, otherwise than in any case where the relief transfers across under TA 1988, s 304A **[see 18.3.8]**, the EIS company would cease to satisfy the no-control rule at the same time as the disposal by the individual investor.

In this situation, it is the Inland Revenue's practice to regard the disposal as occurring before the event that removes qualifying status from the EIS company, with the result that a disposal at a loss will cause the investment relief to be reduced rather than wholly withdrawn (Venture Capital Schemes Manual, para VCM 26010).

Chapter 19

Disposal of CVS Shares

19.1 Introduction

This chapter concludes our survey of the capital gains aspects of disposals of venture capital scheme shares by looking at the rules for the CVS. The chapter follows the format of the previous two chapters on the VCT scheme and the EIS. It too falls into five parts. The first considers the tax treatment of disposals generally. The second part considers the tax treatment of a disposal at a gain of shares outside the restricted period; the third part considers the treatment of losses on such a later disposal. The fourth part deals with an early disposal of scheme shares at a gain and the fifth part considers the treatment of losses on an early disposal. Unlike either the VCT scheme or the EIS, the CVS does not exempt a gain on a disposal at any time but offers loss relief in certain circumstances whatever the time of the disposal if some or all of the original investment relief is still attributable to the shares.

For the impact on an investor's chargeable gains or corporation tax liability of share disposals, see **Chapter 22**. For the interaction of these reliefs and charges with other tax provisions, see **Chapter 23**. For procedures for claiming relief and Inland Revenue procedures generally, see **Chapter 24**. For information requirements, see **Chapter 25**.

19.1.1 Scope of this chapter

This chapter covers the following topics:

(*a*) Remaining general introductory material **[see 19.1.2 to 19.1.4]**
(*b*) What constitutes a disposal **[see 19.2]**
(*c*) Company reorganisations **[see 19.3]**
(*d*) Identification rules **[see 19.4]**
(*e*) Gains on later disposals of CVS shares **[see 19.5]**
(*f*) Losses on later disposals of CVS shares **[see 19.6]**
(*g*) Gains on early disposals of CVS shares **[see 19.7]**
(*h*) Losses on early disposals of CVS shares **[see 19.8]**

19.1.2 Investor company's restricted period for disposals

In the CVS scheme, investment relief is withdrawn where the investor company disposes (or is deemed to dispose) of shares within the 'qualification period' for the shares. This is the period that begins on the issue date and ends immediately before the later of (*a*) the third anniversary of the issue date and (*b*) the third anniversary of the date on which the investee company (or a subsidiary) began its qualifying trade (FA 2000, Sch 15, para 3). A loss of investment relief has an impact on the capital gains computation.

Investment relief can also be reduced or withdrawn if the company investor (or in some circumstances, other shareholders) receive value during the 'period of restriction'. This is the period that begins one year before the issue date and ends at the end of the qualification period (FA 2000, Sch 15, para 48).

19.1.3 CVS shares

In this chapter, the term 'CVS shares' refers to shares on which CVS investment relief has been obtained and has not been withdrawn in full.

19.1.4 Shares held continuously

Conditions attaching to many of the rules described in this chapter depend on the continuous holding of the CVS shares by the investor company from the date of issue until the occurrence of the event concerned – a reorganisation or a disposal, for example.

The investor company is not regarded as having held shares continuously if during the period concerned any event has occurred on which TCGA 1992 deems there to have been a disposal and immediate reacquisition or on which the CVS rules deem there to have been a disposal (FA 2000, Sch 15, para 97).

19.2 The disposal

19.2.1 Meaning of 'disposal'

For the purposes of the CVS disposal rules, 'disposal' has the meaning given to it in the Taxation of Chargeable Gains Act 1992 (FA 2000, Sch 15, para 96(1)), subject to one exception.

A disposal therefore includes a part-disposal, the creation of an interest in or right over an asset (in this instance, shares), and the derivation of capital sums from shares without a corresponding acquisition by another party (TCGA 1992, ss 21, 22). It also includes receipt of a distribution on a winding-up, the extinction of the shares and their being the subject of a negligible-value claim (TCGA 1992, ss 23, 24).

There is one exception for CVS purposes from the normal capital gains rules. In some circumstances, where the capital gains rules would deem there to be no disposal of the old holding on a share exchange or company reconstruction, the CVS rules stipulate instead that there is a disposal (FA 2000, Sch 15, para 96(2)) **[see 19.3.6]**.

19.2.2 Options

Both the grant of a call option (binding the grantor to sell shares) by the investor company over CVS shares and the grant of a put option (binding the grantor to buy shares) to the investor company over CVS shares causes the investment relief to be withdrawn (FA 2000, Sch 15, para 59). As a result, when the option is exercised, the shares are not CVS shares and will not qualify for loss relief **[see 19.5]**.

If the options are exercised, the normal capital gains rules apply. Those rules provide that if an option is exercised, the grant of the option and the transaction (in this case the sale of the shares) are treated as a single transaction. The amount paid for the grant of a call option is treated as part of the consideration for the sale of the shares. The consideration for a put option is deducted from the cost of acquisition (TCGA 1992, s 144(2)).

If the option is not exercised, the grant of the option is treated as the disposal of an asset separate from the shares, not as a part-disposal of the shares. As there is no cost of the new asset, the full amount received for granting the option is chargeable (TCGA 1992, s 144(1)) and *Strange v Openshaw* [1983] STC 416).

See also, in relation to withdrawal of investment relief, **see 20.3.6.2**.

19.3 Company reorganisations

19.3.1 Introduction

As with the VCT scheme and the EIS, there are special rules in the CVS dealing with company reorganisations and reconstructions, which override the normal capital gains rules in specified circumstances. These are where:

(*a*) there is a reorganisation or reduction of the investee company's share capital involving the issue or exchange of qualifying corporate bonds (such that TCGA 1992, s 116 applies); or
(*b*) a reorganisation or reduction of the investee company's share capital such that the continuity (no-disposal) rule of TCGA 1992, s 127 applies, equating the new holding with the old holding; or
(*c*) a reorganisation involving a rights issue; or
(*d*) a scheme of reconstruction affecting an existing holding of CVS shares

(FA 2000, Sch 15, paras 80–88).

19.3.2 Reorganisations

Where immediately before a reorganisation, a CVS investor company holds shares of the same class which fall into more than one of the following categories:

(1) 'deferral shares';
(2) CVS shares that are not deferral shares but have been held continuously by the investor company since their issue;
(3) shares that are neither CVS shares nor deferral shares,

each category is treated as a separate holding and identified separately with the corresponding category of new shares (FA 2000, Sch 15, para 80).

19.3.2.1 *Meaning of 'deferral shares'*

'Deferral shares' means here CVS shares the investment in which has been used to defer a gain under CVS deferral relief **[see Chapter 16]**.

19.3.3 Rights issues

Where there is:

(*a*) a rights issue;
(*b*) new shares or debentures are allotted to shareholders in the company in proportion to their existing holdings;
(*c*) either the existing holding or the allotted shares are CVS shares;
(*d*) in the case of the original holding, those shares have been held continuously since their issue,

the new shares are treated as a separate holding acquired by the investor company at the time of the reorganisation for the amount paid and do not form part of the original holding (FA 2000, Sch 15, para 81(1), (3)).

19.3.4 Bonus issues

If the new allotted shares are bonus shares of the same class and carrying the same rights, the normal capital gains rules reassert themselves and the bonus shares are treated as comprised in the original holding, diluting the investment relief attributed to any particular share (FA 2000, Sch 15, para 81(1)(b)).

19.3.5 Qualifying corporate bonds

If the investing company has CVS shares that it has held continuously since their issue immediately before a reorganisation and the reorganisation involves the issue of qualifying corporate bonds, TCGA 1992, s 116(10) would normally deem there to be no disposal. However, this rule is overridden and the investor company in this situation is deemed to dispose of the CVS shares (FA 2000, Sch 15, para 81(2), (3)). This means that there is either a taxable gain (which may be deferred if there is a suitable reinvestment – see **Chapter 16**) or a loss, on which loss relief may be available **[see 19.6]**.

For the consequences for investment relief, see **20.6.3.3**.

19.3.6 Share exchange on a reconstruction

On a reconstruction involving the exchange of the investor's CVS shares for shares or debentures in another company, where:

(*a*) the old holding consists of, or includes, CVS shares held continuously by the investor company since their issue; and

(*b*) another company issues its shares or debentures ('the new shares') in exchange for those shares

the normal capital gains rules of TCGA 1992, ss 135 and 136 are disapplied and the old holding is treated as disposed of at the time of the reconstruction for a consideration equal to the market value of the new shares (FA 2000, Sch 15, para 82).

19.3.6.1 *Continuity on certain takeovers*

The rule in **19.3.6** is itself overridden in one particular set of circumstances. These involve a takeover of the CVS investee company by a new holding company. This is often in preparation for a flotation of the investee company. Where a specific set of conditions is satisfied, the new holding and the old holding are deemed to be one and the same and CVS relief is fully preserved.

The conditions may be summarised as follows.

(*a*) the only consideration for the old shares or securities is the issue of the new shares or securities;

(*b*) the new shares or securities are issued by a new company that has no issued shares or securities other than subscriber shares or new shares or securities previously issued as consideration for the old shares or securities;

(*c*) the consideration for the new shares or securities of each description consists wholly of old shares or securities of the same class with the same rights;

(*d*) the new shares or securities are issued in proportion to those they replace; and

(*e*) the Inland Revenue has given its prior approval before any exchange of shares or securities takes place

(FA 2000, Sch 15, para 83).

Where these conditions are satisfied, the exchange is not deemed to be a disposal of the old shares nor an acquisition of the new. Instead, there is continuity between the old and new holdings. Any CVS investment relief or CVS deferral relief attributable to the old shares is transferred to the new shares (FA 2000, Sch 15, paras 84, 85).

What is more, if the old shares that were subscribed for by the investor company have been held continuously by that company from the time they were issued to the time they are exchanged, the legislation specifically provides that the replacement shares take the place of the old shares in determining when and how much the investing company subscribed for the shares; when the shares were issued and whether they have been held continuously since then; when investment relief, or deferral relief, was claimed for the shares; and in which accounting period the investor company's corporation tax liability was reduced by investment relief and gains were deferred by the deferral relief. In addition, the replacement shares are deemed to meet the requirements of the CVS in relation to qualifying investee companies and qualifying investor companies. When considering the independence requirement **[see 5.15.1]** and the qualifying subsidiaries requirement **[see 5.16]**, the arrangements to exchange and any exchange itself are ignored. When determining whether the trading activities **[see 5.12.13]** requirement is met, the new company is deemed to meet it to the extent that the old company did and also for the period beginning on the date that the arrangements for the exchange first come into existence until the exchange happens and, further, until the old company ceases to meet that requirement (FA 2000, Sch 15, paras 86, 87).

19.4 Matching disposals with acquisitions

19.4.1 Introduction

Special identification rules apply to match disposals with acquisitions when there is a disposal out of a holding including CVS shares that have been held continuously by the investor company since the date of issue (FA 2000, Sch 15, para 93(1)).

19.4.2 Shares acquired on different days

The basic identification rule, as in the VCT scheme and the EIS, is FIFO (first in, first out) – disposals are deemed to be made out of earlier acquisitions in priority to later acquisitions (FA 2000, Sch 15, para 93(3)).

19.4.3 Shares acquired on the same day

Where there is need to distinguish between different acquisitions on the same day, CVS shares that have been held continuously by the investor company since their issue are treated as disposed of after any other shares (FA 2000, Sch 15, para 93(4)).

19.5 Gains on later disposals of CVS shares

A gain arising on a disposal of CVS shares outside the qualification period does not qualify for any form of disposal relief. The chargeable gain is computed according to normal capital gains rules, subject to the special identification rules discussed above.

Example 19.1

Baltasar Ltd subscribes £300,000 for 100,000 shares in Gracian Ltd in July 2003 and claims £60,000 in CVS investment relief. The qualification period for the shares ends in July 2006. In December 2008, Baltasar sells 60,000 of the shares for £220,000.

As the shares are sold outside the qualification period, there is no loss of investment relief. Baltasar's chargeable gain, computed as follows:

Sale proceeds		£220,000
Acqusition cost: 6/10 × £300,000	£180,000	
Indexation allowance (say)	£36,000	
		£216,000
Chargeable gain		£4,000

is liable to corporation tax in its accounting period ended 31 December 2008.

If Baltasar makes a further investment in CVS shares at any time between December 2007 and December 2011, it may elect to defer the gain under CVS deferral relief **[see Chapter 16]**.

19.5.1 Exemption for substantial shareholdings

If the investor company's shareholding in the investee company is 'substantial' (ie amounts to 10% or more), the gain may be exempt under the substantial-shareholdings exemption in TCGA 1992, Sch 7AC **[see 23.8]**.

19.6 Losses on later disposals of CVS shares

19.6.1 Introduction

A loss realised by a CVS investor company on a disposal of CVS shares may be set against its income chargeable to corporation tax (FA 2000, Sch 15, para 68). Provided that the conditions for loss relief are satisfied **[see 19.6.2]**, this applies whether or not the disposal takes place during the qualification period.

19.6.2 Conditions for loss relief

The conditions that must be satisfied for loss relief to be available are these:

(*a*) the CVS shares must have been held continuously by the investor company from the time they were issued to the time of disposal;
(*b*) the investment relief must not be withdrawn in full as a result of the disposal;
(*c*) the disposal itself must take one of the following forms:
  (1) a sale at arm's length for full consideration,
  (2) a distribution during the winding-up or dissolution of the investee company,
  (3) a deemed disposal on the making of a negligible-value claim under TCGA 1992, s 24(2),
  (4) a deemed disposal on the loss, extinction, destruction or dissipation of the shares; and
(*d*) there must be no breach of the anti-avoidance rules of FA 2000, Sch 15, para 71 **[see 19.6.2.1]**

(FA 2000, Sch 15, para 67).

The disposals listed at (1) to (4) are precisely those that are the only types of disposal that may be made during the qualification period that avoid a complete withdrawal of investment relief (FA 2000, Sch 15, para 46(2)), but the condition applies even if the disposal is made after the qualification period has expired.

19.6.2.1 *The anti-avoidance rules of para 71*

These rules apply in two different situations.

In a company reconstruction, CVS loss relief will be denied if the reconstruction is not carried out for bona fide commercial reasons or as part of a tax avoidance scheme (FA 2000, Sch 15, para 71(1)).

The second situation involves a modification of the value-shifting provisions of TCGA 1992, s 30. Where the loss has been artificially increased by a reduction in value of the shares accompanying the receipt of a benefit (not necessarily a tax-free benefit) by the investor company or any other person, CVS loss relief is denied (FA 2000, Sch 15, para 71(3)).

19.6.3 Computing the allowable loss

When computing the allowable loss under these rules, an adjustment is made for the investment relief that remains attributable to the shares immediately after the disposal. It is a condition for loss relief that an element of investment relief remain (see point (*b*) in **19.6.2**). The remaining investment relief attributable to the shares is deducted from the acquisition cost (thus reducing the loss) (FA 2000, Sch 15, para 94(1), (2)).

If this deduction converts the 'raw' loss into a gain, that gain is exempt (FA 2000, Sch 15, para 94(3)).

Example 19.2

Samuel Ltd makes the following arm's length transactions in Clarke Ltd:

1 June 2002	Subscription for 30,000 shares	£30,000
2 May 2003	Subscription for 80,000 shares	£85,000
11 November 2003	Purchase of 25,000 shares	£25,000
2 January 2005	Sale of 40,000 shares	£35,000
2 July 2006	Sale of 70,000 shares	£60,000

The investment relief obtained was £6,000 for the 1 June 2002 acquisition and £17,000 for the 2 May 2003 acquisition. Clarke Ltd has been trading since 2001.

Disposal of 2 January 2005

This is identified first with the 1 June 2002 acquisition (30,000) and then with part of the 2 May 2003 acquisition. Since the disposal takes place within the qualification period of both issues, investment relief is reduced in both cases, at 20% of the disposal proceeds. The computation is as follows:

Disposal proceeds	(30,000/40,000) × £35,000		£26,250
Acquisition cost:		£30,000	
Original investment relief	£6,000		
Relief lost on disposal:			
£26,250 × 20%	£5,250		
Relief retained		£750	
			£29,250
Relievable loss (A)			£3,000
Disposal proceeds	(10,000/40,000) × £35,000		£8,750
Acquisition cost:			
(10,000/80,000) × £85,000		£10,625	
Original investment relief:			
(10,000/80,000) × £17,000	£2,125		
Relief lost on disposal:			
£8,750 × 20%	£1,750		
Relief retained		£375	
			£10,250
Relievable loss (B)			£1,500
The total relievable loss (A) + (B) is thus			**£4,500**

Disposal of 2 July 2006

The shares disposed of are matched with the earliest remaining parcel of shares, which are the 70,000 remaining from the acquisition of 2 May 2003. The qualification period has elapsed, so there is no reduction in the investment relief on the disposal, and hence all of the investment relief is deducted from the acquisition cost in the loss computation.

Disposal proceeds			£60,000
Acquisition cost:			
	(70,000/80,000) × £85,000	£74,375	
Investment relief retained			
	(70,000/80,000) × £17,000	£14,875	£59,500
Adjusted gain			£500

This 'gain' is exempt.

19.6.4 Relieving losses

For the order of set-off of losses against income, **see 22.8**. Any part of the loss that is not set against the investor company's income under FA 2000, Sch 15, para 68 may be set off in the normal way against the investor company's chargeable gains or carried forward against the chargeable gains of subsequent accounting periods.

19.7 Gains on early disposals of CVS shares

Whether the disposal of the CVS shares occurs during the qualification period or after it has elapsed **[see 19.5]** makes no difference to the capital gains treatment of the disposal. Any gain arising on the disposal is chargeable to tax, subject to possible exemption under the substantial-shareholdings legislation of TCGA 1992, Sch 7AC **[see 23.8]**.

An early disposal will, of course, lead to a reduction or withdrawal of CVS investment relief **[see Chapter 13]**.

19.8 Losses on early disposals of CVS shares

A disposal of CVS shares during the qualification period may lead to a complete withdrawal of investment relief. If it does so, loss relief is not available for any capital loss incurred by the investor company on the disposal (FA 2000, Sch 15, para 67(1)(a)). If there is no withdrawal of investment relief, merely a reduction, loss relief will be available **[see 19.6]**, provided that the other conditions are satisfied.

Part 7

How the Reliefs Work

Chapter 20

Giving and Withdrawing Investment Relief

20.1 Introduction

Part 7 of this book, which this chapter introduces, looks at the mechanisms for giving and withdrawing the various reliefs described in Parts 1 to 6, and at how they interact with other tax reliefs. This chapter describes how the investment relief for each scheme is given, attributed and withdrawn, and the resulting effects of this on the investor's liability to income tax (for the VCT scheme and the EIS) or corporation tax (for the CVS). The qualifying conditions for the investment reliefs were described in Part 2 **[Chapters 5 to 7]**. The investment reliefs themselves were covered in Part 3 **[Chapters 8 to 10]**. The events giving rise to loss of the investment reliefs (partial or total) were described in Part 4 **[Chapters 11 to 13]**.

The interaction between the investment reliefs and other tax reliefs is described in **Chapter 21**. The mechanism for claiming relief or seeking clearances, and the Inland Revenue's procedures and information powers, are dealt with in Part 8 **[Chapters 24 and 25]**.

20.1.1 Scope of this chapter

This chapter examines the following areas:

(*a*) Giving effect to investment reliefs **[see 20.2 to 20.3]**
(*b*) How investment relief is reduced or withdrawn **[see 20.4 to 20.6]**
(*c*) Interest on unpaid and overpaid tax **[see 20.7]**

20.2 Investment relief for the VCT and EIS investor

20.2.1 Introduction

The investor who makes a qualifying investment in a VCT or EIS investee company **[see Chapters 5 to 9]**, forwards the necessary documents etc to the Inland Revenue **[see Chapter 24]**, and claims the relief in his or her self-assessment tax return, is entitled to relief in the form of a reduction in his or her liability to income tax in the maximum amount of 20% or 40% of the amount invested, but for no more than 20% or 40% of the annual permitted maximum for the tax year.

Relief is at the 20% rate for EIS investments and for VCT investments made before 6 April 2004 and after 5 April 2006. Relief is given at 40% for VCT investments made between 6 April 2004 and 5 April 2006.

20.2.2 The VCT permitted maximum

The annual permitted maximum investment in the VCT scheme is £200,000 (£100,000 before 2004–05) (TA 1988, Sch 15B, para 1(3)). For details of what happens when this limit is exceeded, see **8.6**.

20.2.3 The EIS permitted maximum

The annual permitted maximum investment in the EIS (on which investment relief may be claimed) is £200,000 (£150,000 before 2004–05) (TA 1988, s 290(2)).The limit is applied to amounts subscribed in any tax year, regardless of when the shares may be issued **[see further 20.2.7]**. For details of what happens when this limit is exceeded, see **9.5**.

20.2.4 Minimum investment

There is no prescribed minimum investment by an investor in a VCT investor company **[see 8.3.2]**.

In the EIS, however, unless the investor uses the medium of an approved EIS investment fund, the minimum subscription qualifying for relief is £500 in any one company in any one tax year. In the reverse of the rule for the maximum, what matters is issues made in any one year, regardless of the amount actually subscribed in that year.

Example 20.1

Gwyneth subscribes £400 for shares in Shakespeare Ltd on 1 April 2004; the shares are issued on 7 April 2004. She subscribes a further £400 in the same company on 1 October for an issue on the same date. Gwyneth qualifies for relief in respect of the £800 invested in Shakespeare's issues in 2004–05, even though she actually subscribed less than £500 in both 2004–05 and 2005–06.

It is also possible to subscribe more than one amount of less than £500 in a given tax year in respect of issues by the same company and qualify for relief, if the aggregate is £500 or more **[see 7.6.1.8]**.

20.2.5 The rate of relief

For the years 2004–05 and 2005–06, an individual making a qualifying VCT investment obtains relief at the higher rate of income tax (currently 40%) on the total subscribed for eligible shares in the tax year, or, if it is smaller, the amount that reduces his or her liability to income tax for that year to nil (TA 1988, Sch 15B, para 1(5); FA 2004, s 89(1)).

In previous years, and in years following 2005–06, relief was (or will be) given at the lower rate of income tax (currently 20%) rather than at the higher rate.

Relief for qualifying EIS investments is given at the lower rate of income tax. As with VCT investment relief, EIS investment relief in any tax year cannot exceed the individual's liability to income tax in that year (TA 1988, s 289A(2)).

For the order of set-off of various reliefs, see **20.2.8**.

20.2.6 Restriction of investment relief

Investment relief may need to be restricted because one or more qualifying conditions have been breached, for example:

(*a*) where qualifying investments exceed the annual permitted maximum;
(*b*) in the EIS only, where the company has redeemed some of its share capital in the year before the issue; or
(*c*) where the investor has insufficient tax liability to absorb the full amount of the relief **[see 20.2.8.]**.

20.2.7 Tax year in which relief is given

Relief is given for the tax year in which the shares are issued, regardless of when the subscription actually takes place (TA 1988, Sch 15B, para 1(1); TA 1988, s 289A(1)) **[see 8.4 and 9.4]**. For when shares are considered to be issued, see **8.1.6**.

Example 20.2

Isabelle subscribes £25,000 for 25,000 shares in Lacemaker Ltd on 28 March 2004 and £10,000 for 5,000 shares in H Gate Ltd on 6 April 2004. Both companies issued the relevant shares on 7 April 2004.

Isabelle receives relief for both investments in 2004–05, when the shares are issued.

Under the EIS, there are two exceptions to this rule:

(1) in certain cases where the investment is made through an approved EIS fund, the shares are treated as issued when the fund closes;
(2) one-half of all investments, subject to a total maximum of £25,000 made before 6 October in any tax year may be carried back to the previous tax

year. The relevant EIS shares are accordingly deemed to be issued in that year and relief is due in that year for the amount carried back **[see 9.4.1]**.

20.2.8 Computing the investor's liability to income tax

To give effect to VCT and EIS investment relief, one has to start by computing the investor's taxable income in the normal way, reducing it by allowances and deductions that reduce his or her total income. These include:

(*a*) the personal allowance and blind person's allowance;
(*b*) interest on qualifying loans (eg to invest in a partnership or employee-controlled company).

The next step is to calculate the investor's tax liability by reference to his or her taxable income. The amount of the liability is computed without taking into account any of the following:

(*a*) personal allowances given by way of a tax reduction (eg the married couple's allowance for persons aged 65 and over);
(*b*) qualifying maintenance payments;
(*c*) interest paid on a loan to secure a life annuity;
(*d*) double tax relief;
(*e*) basic rate tax deducted at source from various payments (eg personal pension payments)

(TA 1988, Sch 15B, para 1(6); TA 1988, s 289A(5)).

If the investor is entitled to both VCT and EIS investment relief in the same year, VCT relief has priority (TA 1988, Sch 15B, para 1(6)(a)).

Example 20.3

In 2004–05, Bertrand subscribes £50,000 for EIS shares and £10,000 for VCT shares. His other income consists of £70,000 as a partner in a firm of chartered surveyors and £6,800 (net) of bank and building society interest. He and his wife are under 65. He pays £5,850 a year (net) to a personal pension plan.

His income tax computation is as follows:

	£	£
Schedule D, Case I income		70,000
Deposit interest (£6,800 × 100/80)		8,500
Total income		78,500
Less personal pension payments (gross) (£5,850 × 100/78)	7,500	
personal allowance	4,745	
		12,245
Taxable income		66,255

	£	£
Income tax payable		
£2,020 @ 10%	202.00	
£29,380 @ 22%	6,463.60	
£34,855 @ 40%	13,942.00	
		20,607.60
Less VCT relief £10,000 @ 40%	4,000.00	
EIS relief £50,000 @ 20%	10,000.00	
		14,000.00
		6,607.60
Add basic-rate relief on pension payments: £7,500 @ 22%		1,650.00
Income tax liability		8,257.60

Example 20.4

On 1 May 2004, Amanda, who is 66, and whose pension is £22,500 a year, subscribes for 40,000 eligible £1 shares issued at par to raise money by Tigger VCT plc, an approved venture capital trust. Tigger makes no distribution in 2004–05. Amanda's other income for 2004–05 consists of dividends of £16,200 (net).

Amanda's income tax computation for 2004–05 is as follows:

	£	£
Pension		22,500
Dividends: £16,200 × 100/90		18,000
Total income		40,500
Less: personal allowance		6,830
Taxable income		33,670
Income tax payable:		
£2,020 @ 10%	202.00	
£13,650 @ 22%	3,003.00	
£15,730 @ 10% (Sch F ordinary rate)	1,573.00	
£2,490 @ 32.5% (Sch F higher rate)	809.25	
		5,587.25
Less VCT relief £40,000 @ 40% (restricted)		5,587.25
Income tax liability		0.00

Amanda's remaining £10,412.75 of VCT investment relief is lost because she has insufficient income tax liability and the excess cannot be carried back or forward. She will get a repayment of whatever PAYE tax was deducted from her pension, but no repayment of any dividend tax credits.

A reduction of the investment relief for this reason (insufficient liability) does not restrict the amount of a gain that can be deferred **[see 14.3.3, 15.3.3]** nor does it affect the EIS capital gains exemption on disposal **[see 18.5.2.1]**.

20.2.9 Adjustments to PAYE code

If a VCT or EIS investment is made early enough in the tax year and the investment relief is claimed promptly and accepted by the inspector, an investor can elect for his or her notice of coding to be changed (TA 1988, s 306(7)).

20.2.10 Postponement of tax

On making a claim for VCT or EIS investment relief, it is possible to postpone tax on the grounds that the investor is eligible for investment relief. Provided that the investor has submitted his or her tax relief certificate and it is accepted by the inspector, there should be no problem in postponing the tax (TA 1988, s 306(8)).

20.3 CVS investment relief in the hands of the investor

20.3.1 No limit

There is no minimum or maximum subscription for the CVS. Provided that all the qualifying conditions have been met, a company subscribing for CVS shares may receive as much investment relief in any particular accounting period as its liability to corporation tax can bear.

20.3.2 The rate and method of relief

CVS investment relief is available as a deduction from corporation tax chargeable on profits (not as a deduction in computing those profits). The amount of investment relief is the smallest of:

(*a*) 20% of the amount subscribed by the investor company for shares issued in the accounting period;
(*b*) the amount specified in the investor company's claim; and
(*c*) the investor company's liability to corporation tax

(FA 2000, Sch 15, para 39).

Example 20.5

Baconthorpe Ltd makes the following investments in CVS companies in its accounting period ended 31 March 2004:

£100,000 in John Ltd
£50,000 in Cambridge Ltd

Its taxable profits in the accounting period are £225,000. It has no associated companies.

Its corporation tax computation for the year ended 31 March 2004 is:

Taxable profits	£225,000
Corporation tax liability:	
£225,000 @ 19%	£42,750.00
Less CVS investment relief: £150,000 @ 20%	£30,000.00
Corporation tax payable	£12,750.00

It makes the same investments in the following accounting period, when its taxable profits fall to £140,000.

Baconthorpe's corporation tax computation for the year ended 31 March 2005 is:

Taxable profits	£140,000
Corporation tax liability:	
£140,000 @ 19%	£26,600.00
Less CVS investment relief:	
£150,000 @ 20%, restricted	£26,600.00
Corporation tax payable	0.00

The surplus investment relief, £3,400, may neither be carried forward nor back, and is lost.

20.3.3 Restriction of investment relief

There are other reasons why investment relief may be restricted, apart from an insufficient liability to corporation tax. For example, the investor company or other shareholders may have received value in the year preceding the issue of the shares **[see 13.4 to 13.7]**.

20.3.4 Accounting period in which relief is given

Investment relief is given in the accounting period in which the relevant shares are issued, regardless of when the subscription is made (FA 2000, Sch 15, para 39(1)). For when shares are considered to be issued, see **8.1.6**.

20.4 Loss of VCT investment relief

20.4.1 Loss of investment relief

VCT investment relief will be withdrawn or reduced if within three years of the issue of the VCT shares to the investor (five years for shares issued before 6 April 2000):

(*a*) there is a breach of the qualifying conditions; or
(*b*) there is a disposal of the VCT shares.

For the qualifying conditions, see **Chapters 5** to **7**. For the occasions for withdrawal, see **Chapter 11**. Essentially, if there is a breach of the qualifying conditions within three years of the issue date, investment relief is withdrawn. It is also withdrawn if the disposal does not take place at arm's length (TA 1988, Sch 15B, para 3(2)).

20.4.2 Disposals at arm's length

If there is an arm's length disposal, relief is reduced by 20% of the disposal proceeds. In fact, strictly speaking, it is reduced by an amount found by multiplying the disposal proceeds by the lower rate of income tax in force in the tax year in which the relief was *given* (TA 1988, Sch 15B, paras 3(3), (4); 4(2)). In other words, the reduction is related back to the year in which the relief was received. Accordingly, as relief is given at 40% in 2004–05 and 2005–06, it will be withdrawn at the 40% rate (FA 2004, s 89(2)). If the disposal proceeds are sufficiently large (equal to or greater than the amount subscribed, if there was no restriction of the investment relief initially), the relief is reduced to nil. This essentially happens whenever there is a paper gain on the shares.

Example 20.6

Roger subscribes £50,000 for 50,000 ordinary shares in Mirabilis VCT on 1 March 2004 and obtains investment relief of £10,000 for 2003–04. On 1 December 2004, he sells 30,000 of the shares at arm's length for £35,000. The whole of the investment relief of £6,000 obtained on those shares is withdrawn (the withdrawal, otherwise £7,000, is restricted to the relief obtained – (30,000/50,000) × £10,000). The withdrawal is related back to 2003–04. On 1 October 2005, Roger sells the remaining 20,000 shares at arm's length for £15,000 (effectively a loss). This time, the relief is reduced by £15,000 @ 20% = £3,000. This reduction too is related back to 2003–04, although the disposal takes place in 2005–06. From Roger's point of view, he has realised (£35,000 + £15,000) = £50,000, which is exactly what he invested. However, he has retained £1,000 of the investment relief.

20.4.3 Breach of qualifying conditions

Where provisional approval of a company **[see 24.2.4]** as a VCT is given under TA 1988, s 842AA(4), but the company fails to satisfy the qualifying conditions within the extended time allowed, the approval is treated as never having been given, and any investment relief given to an investor who subscribed for shares in that company is withdrawn retroactively (TA 1988, s 842AA(8)).

If approval of a company as a VCT is withdrawn for any other reason (a breach of the qualifying conditions), an investor who has received investment relief is deemed to have disposed of the shares immediately before the withdrawal takes effect other than by way of a bargain at arm's length (TA 1988, Sch 15B, para 3(9)). This means that if the withdrawal occurs within the restricted three-year period (five years for shares issued before 6 April 2000), the investor's relief is withdrawn, again retroactively.

20.4.4 Disposals not at arm's length

Where an investor makes an early disposal of his or her VCT shares which is not a bargain made at arm's length, the full investment relief is withdrawn (TA 1988, Sch 15B, para 3(2)). Where a loss arises on a disposal of VCT shares, loss relief is not available (TCGA 1992, s 151A(1)).

20.4.5 Identifying shares in a disposal

Whenever there is a disposal of some but not all shares in a holding, there has to be a method of identifying which shares are in question. The identification rules for the VCT scheme relating to the loss of investment relief are also applied for capital gains purposes and have been fully explained in **17.4**.

Essentially, the basic rule is that earlier acquisitions are disposed of in priority to later acquisitions (TA 1988, Sch 15B, para 3(8)(a)).

Example 20.7

David acquires 110,000 shares in Hartley VCT in November 2002 and May 2003 as follows, and claims investment relief of £21,000 (£105,000 × 20%). David then disposes of 80,000 shares in May 2005 for £90,000.

Month	*Year*	*Transaction*	*Shares*	*Cost*
			No	£
Nov	2002	Subscription	60,000	57,000
May	2003	Subscription	50,000	48,000

The disposal of 80,000 shares would be identified with the November 2002 subscription of 60,000 shares and 20,000 of the May 2003 subscription. Investment relief would be withdrawn of £15,240 made up of £11,400 (£57,000 × 20%) + £3,840 (20,000/50,000 × £48,000 × 20%).

20.4.6 Death of the investor

If an event occurs after an investor dies which, had he or she been alive, would have caused a loss of investment relief, the relief is not lost (TA 1988, Sch 15B, para 4(3)).

20.4.7 Withdrawal by assessment

Reduction or withdrawal of relief is carried out by means of a Schedule D, Case VI assessment for the year in which the relief was given (TA 1988, Sch 15B, para 4(1), (2)). In the equivalent situation for the EIS, the Inland Revenue's Venture Capital Schemes Manual mentions the inappropriateness of an assessment when the investor's self-assessment tax return is still capable of amendment **[see 20.5.5]**. The Manual is silent on this question when it comes to withdrawing VCT investment relief.

The assessment is merely a mechanism for reducing or withdrawing the relief and the investor cannot set off any existing unrelieved Schedule D, Case VI losses against it.

20.4.7.1 *Time limits for assessments*

Where approval of VCT status is withdrawn from a company, any assessments to charge tax as a consequence, including assessments on the investors (to withdraw their investment relief) may be made within three years of the date on which the Inland Revenue issues the notice withdrawing approval (TA 1988, s 842AA(10)).

20.5 Loss of EIS investment relief

20.5.1 Introduction

A reduction or withdrawal of EIS investment relief can be made where one of several events occurs. As a convenient aide-memoire, those events are set out below; for detailed treatment, see **Chapter 12**.

(*a*) The investor ceases to be a qualifying individual.
(*b*) The investor disposes of EIS shares.
(*c*) The investor receives value from the company.
(*d*) Value is received by other shareholders.
(*e*) The investor receives replacement capital.
(*f*) The investor receives a loan-linked investment.
(*g*) The company ceases to be a qualifying company.
(*h*) The shares cease to be eligible shares.
(*i*) Pre-existing arrangements are put into effect.

In cases (*a*), (*e*), (*f*), (*g*) and (*h*) and (*i*), investment relief is withdrawn. In cases (*b*), (*c*) and (*d*), the relief is reduced, and may be reduced to nil.

20.5.2 Early disposal of shares

20.5.2.1 *Introduction*

A disposal of EIS shares within the restricted period gives rise to a reduction of investment relief.

20.5.2.2 *Restricted period*

The period during which a disposal of shares leads to a reduction of investment relief is the 'relevant period', which is the period beginning with the issue of the shares (in this instance) and ending immediately before the later of (*a*) the third anniversary of the issue date and (*b*) the third anniversary of the date on which the qualifying trade began (TA 1988, ss 299(1), (8)(c); 312(1A)(*b*)). For shares issued before 6 April 2000, the period ended five years after the issue date.

20.5.2.3 *Put and call options*

A disposal of shares includes the grant of a call option by the investor, binding him or her to sell the shares (TA 1988, s 289(8)(b)). There is also a disposal when a third party grants a put option to the investor, entitling the investor to sell shares to that person.

The Inland Revenue's practice on put and call options was published in *Tax Bulletin*, Issue 15, February 1995, but has not been reproduced in the Venture Capital Schemes Manual. However, as the substantive legislation has not changed, it is worth quoting in full:

> 'If the option is a "put option" – that is, it gives the investor the right to compel some other person to buy the shares at some future date – the granting of the option has the result that no relief is due on the shares.
>
> If the option is a "call option" – that is, it gives some other person the right to buy the investor's shares at some future date – the position is as follows. Under Section 299(8)(b) ICTA 1988 . . . the grant of such an option is to be dealt with as a disposal of the shares. Accordingly, if the option is granted by way of a bargain at arm's length, under section 299(1) the relief given must be reduced by an amount equal to tax at the lower rate on the consideration received in return for granting the option (or by the amount of relief given if that is smaller). When the option is actually exercised there will of course be another disposal, and if that happens within the investor's . . . relevant period section 299(1) must again be applied.
>
> If the option is granted otherwise than by way of a bargain made at arm's length all relief given must be withdrawn. This will be the case if it is not a normal commercial transaction, in that for reasons of their own the parties are not trying to obtain the best deal for themselves in their particular circumstances.

Example

John owns shares in Mini Ltd on which EIS relief has been obtained. The relevant period will expire on 30 September 1999. On 31 March 1997 a company called Maxi Ltd buys most of the issued share capital of Mini Ltd. (This is shortly after the end of the company's own relevant period, so the rule about control by another company does not apply). At the same time Maxi Ltd pays John £1 for an option under which it will have the right to buy John's shares on 1 October 1999 for £8,000, which both parties reckon will approximate to their likely market value at that date. The 'disposal' on 31 March 1997 is thus at arm's length and in law John's relief falls to be reduced by 20% of £1 (but, of course, in practice no adjustment would be made). The full disposal of the shares will not take place until just after the end of the relevant period, so it will have no effect on the relief.

Suppose John is short of money and insists on receiving £1,000 in return for granting the option. Because he is effectively receiving part of the consideration early Maxi Ltd secures an adjustment to the proposed terms of the option such that the sale price is £6,900 only. Because the parties have each obtained the best deal they can for themselves, the transaction is still regarded as being made by way of a bargain made at arm's length, so John's relief is not lost altogether but is reduced by 20% of £1,000.'

The grant of a put option at any time in the relevant period causes the investment relief to be withdrawn (TA 1988, s 299(5)). The grant of a call option at any time in the relevant period causes the investment relief to be reduced or withdrawn (TA 1988, s 289(8)(b)).

20.5.2.4 *Share exchanges*

For the purposes of EIS investment relief, a disposal of EIS shares includes an exchange of shares that would not normally be a disposal for capital gains tax purposes (TA 1988, s 312(3)). The consideration for the disposal is the market value of the shares received. This will reduce or eliminate the individual's investment relief if the exchange occurs before the end of the relevant period **[see 18.7 and 18.8]**.

20.5.2.5 *Identifying shares in a disposal*

When it is necessary to identify which shares have been disposed of out of a holding, the rules for capital gains purposes are also applicable to income tax. These rules are fully explained in **18.4**.

Essentially, the basic rule is that earlier acquisitions are identified in priority to later acquisitions (TA 1988, s 299(6)). For the special rules distinguishing between different acquisitions on the same day, see **18.4.3**.

20.5.2.6 *The consequences of a disposal*

If the disposal is not by way of a bargain at arm's length, the investment relief is withdrawn (TA 1988, s 299(1)(a)). If the disposal is an arm's length bargain, investment relief is reduced by the smaller of:

(*a*) 20% (tax at the lower rate for the year in which the relief was given) on the disposal proceeds; and
(*b*) the relief attributable to the shares

(TA 1988, s 299(1), (2)).

Effectively, therefore, relief is withdrawn if the investor makes a paper profit on the transaction.

Example 20.8

Isaiah subscribes for 10,000 eligible shares in Wolfson Ltd on 1 December 2003 for £20,000 and claims EIS investment relief of £4,000 for 2003–04. On 1 July 2004, he sells those shares at arm's length for £15,000 (an effective loss of £5,000).

The relief is reduced by £15,000 @ 20% = £3,000 and the reduction has effect for 2003–04.

Isaiah has made a loss on disposal of the shares and may be able to claim loss relief **[see Chapter 18]**.

If the original investment relief was less than 20% of the investment, perhaps because the investor had exceeded the annual maximum, any relief to be withdrawn is restricted by A/B, where A is the amount of investment relief given and B the maximum that could have been given.

Example 20.9

Take the facts of Example 20.8, but assume that Isaiah's liability to income tax in 2003–04, as measured for EIS purposes, was £3,425. This would therefore have been the amount of EIS investment relief that he obtained for the £20,000 investment in Wolfson.

When he sells the shares for £15,000 in July 2004, the clawback (reduction) of investment relief will be similarly limited to:

£15,000 × 3,425/4,000 × 20% = £2,568.75

This amount will be assessable under Schedule D, Case VI for 2003–04.

Isaiah has made a loss on disposal of the shares and may be able to claim loss relief **[see Chapter 18]**.

An exchange of shares under a company reconstruction is a disposal and gives rise to a withdrawal or reduction of relief if it occurs within the relevant period, unless it is an Inland Revenue approved share-for-share exchange on a takeover of the investee company under TA 1988, s 304A **[see 15.10.2]**.

20.5.2.7 *Events after a disposal at a loss*

When an investor disposes of his or her entire holding of EIS shares, investment relief may not be withdrawn totally if the disposal is at a loss, as we have seen (eg in Example 20.8). In such cases, there is no further assessment on the investor for a subsequent event (such as a loss of qualifying status) unless the investor is connected with the company (TA 1988, s 307(4)). For the extended meaning of 'connected' for this purpose, see **7.6.2**.

Example 20.10

Avicebron subscribes £10,000 for 10,000 shares in Malaga Ltd on 1 July 2001 and receives EIS investment relief of £2,000. He sells the shares for £6,000 on 20 June 2003 (before the termination date, which is 1 July 2004) and is assessed to tax of £1,200 for 2001–02 to recover the appropriate amount of relief. On 1 September 2003, Malaga sells its qualifying trade, with the consequence that investment relief must be withdrawn from all EIS investors. However, unless Avicebron is connected with the company at this time, he will retain his £800 of relief.

If Malaga were, say, to employ Avicebron's daughter in August 2003, he would become connected with the company, and an assessment to recover his outstanding £800 of relief would be raised.

20.5.3 Later disposals of shares

Once the relevant period has elapsed, ie more than three years after the issue of the shares (or three years after the commencement of the qualifying trade, if later), there is no loss of investment relief on a disposal of EIS shares. There may be capital gains tax exemption on a gain, and relief for a loss **[see Chapter 18]**.

20.5.4 Death of the investor

If an event occurs after an investor dies which, had he or she been alive, would have caused a loss of investment relief, the relief is not lost (TA 1988, s 307(3)).

20.5.5 Assessments for withdrawing or reducing relief

The legislation provides that investment relief is to be withdrawn (where it is subsequently found not to have been due) by an assessment under Schedule D,

Case VI for the tax year in which the relief was given (TA 1988, s 307(1)). Unlike the VCT legislation (TA 1988, Sch 15B, para 4(2)), there is no mention of assessments to withdraw or reduce investment relief on a subsequent event, such as a disposal or receipt of value. Nevertheless, the practice is the same. The assessment may be made at any time within six years of the event causing the investor to lose entitlement to the relief (TA 1988, s 307(2)), subject to the usual extension to 20 years in the case of fraudulent or negligent conduct (TA 1988, s 307(5)).

This could represent a considerable extension on the normal six-year time limit (TMA 1970, s 34).

Example 20.11

Resolutus Ltd issues eligible shares on 1 April 2003, which qualify for the EIS, and starts its trade on 31 December 2003. On 3 March 2013 the Inland Revenue could raise assessments for 2002–03 withdrawing the EIS relief if it were established that in June 2006 (2006–07), which is during the company's relevant period (1 April 2003 to 30 December 2006) Resolutus controlled another company that was not its qualifying subsidiary.

The Inland Revenue's Venture Capital Schemes Manual has this to say in connection with withdrawing relief:

> 'Withdrawal of relief is appropriate only where the tax return on which it [presumably, the claim to relief] is made ceases to be capable of amendment. Where for any reason relief which is claimed would, if it had been obtained, have had to be withdrawn, the individual ceases to be eligible for relief . . . and the tax return needs to be amended accordingly. The same principle applies where the relief claimed requires to be reduced.'

(para VCM 26000)

20.5.5.1 *Investment relief carried back*

Where investment relief has been carried back to a previous tax year **[see 9.4.1]**, the assessment is raised for that tax year (when the shares are deemed to have been issued). The investor's tax liability for that year is increased by the relief originally given (TA 1988, s 307(1)).

20.6 Loss of CVS investment relief

20.6.1 Introduction

CVS investment relief may be reduced or withdrawn where:

(*a*) the investor company disposes of the shares during the 'qualification period';

(*b*) the investor company or connected persons receive value during the 'period of restriction';
(*c*) the investee company or its subsidiary repays, redeems or repurchases its share capital, or makes a payment to the shareholder for giving up rights to the share capital, during the 'period of restriction';
(*d*) an option is granted over the relevant shares during the 'qualification period';
(*e*) where it becomes apparent that the relief was never due.

20.6.2 Restricted periods

The qualification period is the period ending on the later of:

(*a*) the third anniversary of the issue date and
(*b*) the third anniversary of the date on which the qualifying trade began

(FA 2000, Sch 15, para 3).

The period of restriction is the period that begins one year before the issue of the shares and ends at the end of the qualification period (FA 2000, Sch 15, para 48).

20.6.3 Early disposals

Investment relief is withdrawn, or reduced, on the first disposal of any of the CVS shares by the investor company within the qualification period.

There is a disposal of the shares if there is a disposal under the normal rules for corporation tax on chargeable gains, and on certain exchanges of shares under a company reconstruction or amalgamation **[see 19.3.6]**. In determining whether or not the shares have been disposed of in cases where those shares form part of a larger holding of shares of the same class in the same company, it is necessary to consider the special share identification rules **[see 20.6.3.1]**.

Once it is established that there has been a disposal of CVS shares during the qualification period, it is necessary to consider the extent to which the relief is withdrawn or merely reduced. This depends, in the first instance, on the circumstances of the disposal. The relief is withdrawn in full where the disposal of the shares is *not* one of the following disposals:

(*a*) a sale at arm's length for full consideration;
(*b*) a distribution during the dissolution or winding-up of the investee company; or
(*c*) a deemed disposal where there is either an entire loss, destruction, dissipation or extinction claim under TCGA 1992, s 24(1) or a negligible value claim under TCGA 1992, s 24(2).

If the disposal is within one of those circumstances, the extent to which the relief is reduced or withdrawn depends on the relationship between the amount of the relief and the amount of the sale proceeds. If the relief attributable to those shares is greater than 20 per cent of the proceeds, the relief is reduced by the smaller of:

(1) the amount of relief attributable to the shares; and
(2) 20% of the amount or value of the proceeds.

Otherwise, the relief attributable to the shares is withdrawn in full.

Where the relief is to be reduced (not withdrawn), the amount of the reduction is restricted if the amount of the corporation tax relief on the shares was less than 20% of the amount subscribed; this would be the case where there was insufficient liability to corporation tax to enable the subscription to be relieved in full. In such a case, the amount of the reduction in relief is correspondingly restricted; ie the relief is reduced by:

$$20\% \text{ of the proceeds} \times \frac{A}{B}$$

where,
A = the amount of investment relief actually obtained; and
B = 20% of the amount subscribed for.

In calculating A, any reduction in the relief before the relief was obtained (eg by a prior receipt of value) is ignored, unless that earlier reduction was because of a reduction, or dilution, following a bonus share issue. (FA 2000, Sch 15, paras 46, 96).

Example 20.12

Dialectic Ltd subscribes for £80,000 worth of qualifying shares; however, it obtains investment relief of only £10,000 because that amount reduces its corporation tax liability to nil.

During the qualification period, Dialectic Ltd sells the relevant shares at arm's length for full consideration of £60,000. The amount by which the relief is reduced is equal to:

$$£12{,}000 \times \frac{10{,}000}{16{,}000} = £7{,}500$$

Had Dialectic Ltd instead sold the shares for £100,000, the relief attributable to the shares (£10,000) would not be greater than 20% of the proceeds (£100,000 × 20% = £20,000). Accordingly, the relief would be withdrawn in full.

As to the method of withdrawing the relief, **see 20.6.4** below.

20.6.3.1 *Identifying shares in a disposal*

Whenever there is a disposal of some but not all shares in a holding, there has to be a method of identifying which shares are in question. The identification rules for the CVS relating to the loss of investment relief are also those applied for the purposes of corporation tax on chargeable gains, and have been fully explained in **19.4**.

20.6.3.2 *Options*

As mentioned in **19.2.2**, the grant of either a put option or a call option causes the withdrawal of investment relief on those shares that would normally be treated as disposed of when the option is exercised (FA 2000, Sch 15, para 59).

20.6.3.3 *Company restructuring*

Where there is a deemed disposal of the old shares on a reorganisation **[see 19.3]**, investment relief will be reduced if the reorganisation takes place during the qualification period, as explained in **20.6.4**. When it takes place outside the qualification period, there is no reduction of the investment relief.

20.6.4 Assessments to withdraw relief

Investment relief that has been obtained but was either not due, or is withdrawn or reduced on one of the events described in **20.6.1** is clawed back by an assessment under Schedule D, Case VI in respect of the accounting period in which the relief was obtained (FA 2000, Sch 15, para 60(1)).

The Inland Revenue must raise the relevant assessment withdrawing the relief or give notice of withdrawal **[see Chapter 25]** to the investing company, in the case of value received, within six years of the end of the relevant accounting period. That accounting period is the later of the accounting period in which the money raised by the issue must be invested and the period in which the event occurs that causes the withdrawal. These time limits can be extended in the case of fraud or negligence (FA 2000, Sch 15, para 62).

20.7 Interest on unpaid and overpaid tax

20.7.1 Unpaid tax on withdrawal or reduction of VCT investment relief

The VCT legislation contains no special rules for interest on unpaid tax, so the general rules must apply. Where relief is withdrawn or reduced, the assessment is related back to the tax year in which the relief was given **[see 20.4]**, so interest will run from the 'relevant date' for tax in that year.

The relevant date for Schedule D, Case VI tax is 31 January of the tax year following. Therefore, the tax demanded by an assessment to withdraw relief for 2003–04 will become due and payable on 31 January 2005 (TMA 1970, s 86(6)).

Example 20.13

Take the facts of Example 20.6. Roger subscribes £50,000 for 50,000 ordinary shares in Mirabilis VCT on 1 March 2003 and obtains investment relief of £10,000 for 2002–03. On 1 December 2003, he sells 30,000 of the shares at arm's length for £35,000. The whole of the investment relief of £6,000 obtained on those shares is withdrawn (the withdrawal, otherwise £7,000, is restricted to the relief obtained – (30,000/50,000) × £10,000). The withdrawal is related back to 2002–03, and the interest runs from 31 January 2004, so no interest will be charged if Roger pays the tax assessed together with any balancing payment for 2002–03 in time. On 1 October 2004, Roger sells the remaining 20,000 shares at arm's length for £15,000 (effectively a loss). This time, the relief is reduced by £15,000 @ 20% = £3,000. This reduction too is related back to 2002–03, although the disposal takes place in 2004–05. Again, the interest runs from 31 January 2004 until the date of payment.

20.7.2 Interest on overdue tax pending a claim to EIS investment relief

If the tax liability against which EIS investment relief is given, gives rise to an interest charge, that charge runs up to the date when the tax is paid or the claim to relief is made, whichever is the earlier. This rule does not apply where tax on an assessment is due and payable after the making of an EIS relief claim. In such a case, when calculating interest on overdue tax, tax will be regarded as paid on the later of the date on which the EIS investment-relief claim is made and the due and payable date (TA 1988, s 306(9)).

20.7.3 Interest on overdue tax following loss of EIS investment relief

In contrast to the situation with the VCT scheme, there are special rules governing the date from which interest runs ('the relevant date') for the purpose of assessments to reduce or withdraw EIS investment relief.

The table below summarises these rules.

Event giving rise to loss of relief	*Relevant date for interest*
Failure by the investee company to spend the money raised for the purpose of a qualifying business activity within the time permitted	The date on which relief is granted

Event giving rise to loss of relief	*Relevant date for interest*
The discovery of a pre-arranged exit for the investor	The date on which relief is granted
The subscription proves to be part of a tax avoidance scheme	The date on which relief is granted
An early disposal of shares	The date of the disposal
The grant of an option over the shares	The date of grant
Receipt of a linked loan	The date on which the loan is made
The receipt of value	The date of the receipt
Cessation of qualifying conditions relating to the investor, the investee company or the trade	The date of the event causing the breach
Cessation by the active company of conduct of the trade	The date of cessation
Acquisition by the investee company representing replacement capital for the investor	The date of acquisition

(TA 1988, s 307(6))

The date on which relief is granted is the date on which the repayment of tax resulting from the claim to relief is made or the date on which the inspector issues a notice showing the amount of tax payable after allowing the relief (TA 1988, s 307(7)).

20.7.4 Interest on overdue corporation tax following loss of CVS relief

Corporation tax is normally due and payable on the day following the expiry of nine months after the end of the accounting period (unless the instalment basis applies) (TMA 1970, s 59D). When tax is overdue, interest is then due from the due and payable date until payment (TMA 1970, s 87A).

The CVS legislation, however, contains special rules for determining the due and payable date. When any of the following events occurs:

(*a*) failure by the investor company or investee company to meet the qualifying conditions;
(*b*) an early disposal of shares;
(*c*) the receipt of value by the investor company;
(*d*) the receipt of value by other shareholders;
(*e*) the grant of a put or call option over the shares,

the due and payable date is taken to be the date of the event, if this is later than the normal due and payable date (FA 2000, Sch 15, para 63).

Example 20.14

Tractatus Ltd invests £50,000 in CVS shares during its accounting period ended 31 March 2004, and receives investment relief of £10,000. On 1 January 2006, it sells the shares for £60,000. As a result, a Schedule D, Case VI assessment is raised for the accounting period to 31 March 2004 to withdraw the relief.

The normal due date for corporation tax for the accounting period to 31 March 2004 is 1 January 2005. However, since the disposal did not take place until 1 January 2006, interest begins to run from that date.

20.7.5 Repayment supplement for repayment following a claim for VCT investment relief

There are no special rules relating to repayments of tax overpaid as a result of a claim for VCT investment relief.

The general rule for repayments of tax is that interest runs from:

(*a*) the date the tax was paid, in the case of instalment payments, the balancing payment and tax not deducted at source;
(*b*) 31 January following the later tax year, in the case of a claim covering two years;
(*c*) 31 January of the tax year following that for which tax is deducted, in the case of tax deducted at source;
(*d*) the date of payment, where a penalty or surcharge has been paid;
(*e*) 31 January of the following tax year, where qualifying interest on a secured loan for a life annuity is paid

(TA 1988, s 824).

Where the repayment has to be attributed to more than one type of payment, the order of priority is:

(1) the balancing payment and other payments comprised in the final payment;
(2) (in two equal parts) to the instalment payments (the later payment first);
(3) income tax deducted at source (including PAYE).

20.7.6 Repayment supplement for repayment following claim for EIS investment relief

What has just been said in respect of VCT repayments applies also to the EIS.

20.7.7 Interest on overpaid tax following claim for CVS investment relief

As with the other two schemes, there are no special rules covering the repayment of tax following a claim to CVS investment relief.

Under the general rules, interest is normally payable from the later of the date of payment and the due and payable date, until the date of repayment (TA 1988, s 826).

Chapter 21

Overlaps with Other Investment Reliefs

21.1 Introduction

21.1.1 A range of measures

The EIS, CVS and the VCT scheme are not the only measures designed to assist those who are willing to invest in, or make loans to, unquoted trading companies. This chapter and **Chapter 23** contain a brief survey of those other reliefs and of the overlap between them and the venture capital schemes that are the subject of this book. This chapter will look at other investment reliefs; **Chapter 23** will survey the other capital gains and inheritance tax reliefs and their overlap with the disposal and loss reliefs afforded by the VCT scheme, the EIS and the CVS.

21.1.2 Scope of this chapter

This chapter deals with the following:

(*a*) The relief for losses on shares in unquoted trading companies under TA 1988, ss 574–576 **[see 21 to 21.7]**.
(*b*) Relief for loan interest **[see 21.8]**.

21.2 Losses on unquoted shares

21.2.1 Introduction

There is a long-standing relief that allows a loss on the disposal of ordinary shares in a qualifying unquoted trading company (such as EIS shares) to be set against a taxpayer's total income or gains. It can only be claimed by the individual investor who subscribed for the shares. The conditions for qualification have now been aligned closely with those of the EIS (TA 1988, ss 574–576). This relief is not available for losses on the disposal of VCT shares.

A similar relief applies to investment companies that make losses on disposing of unquoted trading company investments (TA 1988, s 573). It is possible for some CVS investor companies to claim this relief also, but the restriction of the CVS to companies carrying on 'non-financial activities' **[see 5.17.5]** will exclude many investment companies **[see 21.7.3]**.

21.2.2 Giving effect to the relief

If the conditions are met **[see 21.3]**, the individual can claim relief from income tax for the amount of the loss in the year in which the disposal occurs or in the previous year. The amount of relief cannot exceed the individual's taxable income. When an individual suffers such a loss in a tax year, he or she has 12 months from the 31 January next following that year to make a claim for income tax relief (TA 1988, s 574(1)).

To the extent that the loss has not been relieved against income in the year of the loss or in the previous year, it is allowable against capital gains in the year of disposal or in future years.

The loss is set against total income in priority to relief for any trading losses (TA 1988, s 574(2)).

21.2.3 EIS shares

On the disposal of EIS shares at a loss, the investor can claim to reduce his or her taxable income by the loss (TA 1988, s 305A), provided that certain of the conditions for the relief **[see 21.3]** are met. The loss can be set against any deferred gains that crystallise.

Example 21.1

Eucken subscribes £20,000 for shares in Jena Ltd, an EIS company, on 1 July 2003. On 31 January 2004, Eucken disposes of a property for £80,000 and defers £20,000 of the gain realised through his investment in Jena Ltd. In November 2004, Jena Ltd is put into liquidation for bona fide reasons.

Eucken's tax situation is as follows:

Realised value of shares	NIL
Gross investment in shares	£20,000
Less EIS investment relief (£20,000 × 20%)	£4,000
Less Loss relief (£16,000 × 40%)	£6,400
Net cost of investment (48% of the gross)	£9,600

The deferred gain of £20,000 would become chargeable in November 2004, and, in the absence of reliefs, tax on the gain would be payable on 31 January 2006. However, the amount of the loss (after taking into account any investment relief initially obtained) can be set against Eucken's *gains or taxable income* in the tax year in which the disposal takes place.

21.3 Conditions to be met by EIS shares

21.3.1 Subscription for ordinary shares

To claim this relief, the individual (from now on, 'the investor') must have subscribed for 'qualifying shares'. Qualifying shares are shares or stock forming part of the ordinary share capital of a 'qualifying trading company' (TA 1988, s 574(1)). Ordinary share capital is as defined in TA 1988, s 832 – all the issued share capital (whatever it may be called), other than capital the holders of which have a right to a dividend at a fixed rate but no other right to share in the profits of the company.

21.3.2 Qualifying disposals

The relief is available for a loss arising on four kinds of disposal:

(*a*) a bargain made at arm's length for full consideration;
(*b*) a distribution in the course of a dissolution or winding-up of the investee company;
(*c*) the entire loss, destruction, dissipation or extinction of the shares; and
(*d*) the deemed disposal stipulated by a negligible-value claim

(TA 1988, s 575(1)).

For disposals made before 6 April 2000, paragraph (*c*) disposals were excluded, but there was a more limited extra-statutory concession (D46) where a company without assets was dissolved and either no distribution was made during the winding-up or no final distribution was made.

An individual can claim the relief where the shares were originally subscribed for by his or her spouse and transferred during the lifetime of that spouse (TA 1988, s 574(3)(b)).

Example 21.2

Louise subscribes £10,000 for 10,000 shares in House of Eliot Ltd and claims £2,000 EIS relief. After two years she sells her shares to Stella for £1,000. Louise would have £200 of her EIS relief (£1,000 × 20%) clawed back and her allowable loss would be £7,200 (£10,000 – £1,800 – £1,000). She could either set her loss against her capital gains or claim to set it against her taxable income.

Example 21.3

Take the same facts as in Example 21.2 except that Stella is Louise's sister. As there is no presumption for EIS purposes that the sale to Stella is a bargain otherwise than at arm's length, Louise would not suffer a clawback of all her EIS relief, just of £200 as before. However, Stella is a connected person for capital gains tax and therefore the disposal will not be treated as a bargain made at arm's length. Accordingly the only relief for Louise's loss would be to reduce a gain on a further disposal to her sister.

21.3.3 Share exchanges etc

Where shares are exchanged within a company or between companies there are provisions that allow the exchange not to be treated as a disposal for capital gains tax. Where there is an exchange of shares of one company for another on a scheme of reconstruction under TCGA 1992, ss 135 and 136, but TCGA 1992, s 137 stipulates there to have been a disposal of the old shares (because, for instance, the reconstruction was not carried out for bona fide commercial reasons), no loss relief is available under these rules if the stipulated disposal gives rise to a loss (TA 1988, s 575(3)).

21.3.4 Value shifting

Where a person having control of a company exercises his control so that value passes out of shares belonging to him or to a connected person and into other shares, any loss on the disposal of his shares will not be an allowable loss. Similarly, if there is a scheme that involves the material reduction of the value of an asset together with the receipt of a tax-free benefit by a person, an allowable loss or capital gain on the disposal of that asset is calculated by making an adjustment to reflect the tax-free benefit (TCGA 1992, ss 29 and 30). Where a claim is made for loss relief under these rules, a value-shifting adjustment is made for any benefit received by the investor, whether tax free or not (TA 1988, s 576(2)).

21.4 Conditions to be met by non-EIS shares

21.4.1 Introduction

There are a number of other conditions that must be met if the disposal is of non-EIS shares. These conditions are borrowed from the EIS, with a few modifications.

21.4.2 Qualifying trading company

For the relief to be available for a loss on non-EIS shares, the investee company must be a 'qualifying trading company'.

A qualifying trading company is one that:

(*a*) is an 'eligible trading company' on the date of the disposal and has been such for a continuous period of six years up to the date of the disposal; or (*b*) ceased to be an eligible trading company not more than three years before the disposal but was such for a continuous period of six years until that time, and has not since that time been an 'excluded company', an investment company or a trading company that is not an eligible trading company; or

(*c*) is an eligible trading company on the date of the disposal and has been such for a shorter continuous period ending on that date and has not before the beginning of that period been an 'excluded company', an investment company or a trading company that is not an eligible trading company; or

(*d*) ceased to be an eligible trading company not more than three years before the disposal but was such for a continuous period of less than six years until that time, but has not before or since that time been an 'excluded company', an investment company or a trading company that is not an eligible trading company.

In every case the company must have carried on its business wholly or mainly in the UK throughout a 'relevant period', which is the period beginning on the later of (*a*) the incorporation of the company and (*b*) the date one year before the issue date of the shares, and ending on the date of disposal (TA 1988, s 576(4), (5)).

A company is an eligible trading company at any time when, or in any period throughout which, it would be a qualifying company for the EIS, as defined by TA 1988, s 293, with some minor modifications.

For shares issued after 6 March 2001, the company must be unquoted at the issue date and no arrangements may exist for that status to come to an end. For earlier shares, the company had also to be unquoted throughout the whole of the relevant period falling before 7 March 2001. There is no requirement for the company to remain unquoted. A winding-up does not prevent a company from being an eligible trading company, but only for so long as it continues trading (TA 1988, s 576(4)–(4B)).

An 'excluded company' is a company

(*a*) whose trade consists wholly or mainly of:
  (1) dealing in land,
  (2) dealing in commodities or futures, or
  (3) dealing in shares, securities or other financial instruments; or

(*b*) whose trade is not carried on on a commercial basis and in such a way that there is a reasonable expectation of profits; or

(*c*) is a holding company of a non-trading group; or

(*d*) is a building society or a registered industrial and provident society

(TA 1988, s 576(5)).

A trading company is a non-excluded company whose business consists wholly or mainly of the carrying on of a trade or trades or which is the holding company of a trading group.

An investment company is any company whose business consists wholly or mainly in the making of investments and the principal part of whose income is derived from that business, and for these purposes, it cannot be the holding company of a trading group (TA 1988, ss 576(5), 130).

A trading group is a group the business of whose members, taken together, consists wholly or mainly in the carrying on of a trade or trades, but any trade carried on by a subsidiary that is an excluded company is treated as not being a trade (TA 1988, s 576(5)).

21.4.3 Additional condition concerning share exchanges etc

Where there is a reorganisation or reduction of share capital, and TCGA 1992, s 127 provides for there to be no disposal of the old shares, loss relief is not available under these rules on a disposal of the new shares, unless it could have been given on a disposal of the old shares for full consideration at the time of the reorganisation, had the reorganisation been a chargeable occasion producing a loss. However, this condition need not be fulfilled if the investor gave new consideration for the new shares. In that case, the relief is limited to the amount of the new consideration taken into account as a deduction in computing the loss incurred on the disposal of the new shares (TA 1988, s 575(2)).

21.5 Identification of shares

Where a person holds shares of the same class, but only some of which qualify for this relief while the others do not because they were purchased, disposals are normally identified on a LIFO basis (ie later acquisitions are identified in priority to earlier acquisitions) (TA 1988, s 576(1)).

However, this rule is disapplied where the holding includes any of the following categories of share:

(*a*) BES shares in respect of which relief has been given and not withdrawn;
(*b*) EIS shares to which EIS investment relief is attributable; or
(*c*) EIS shares to which EIS deferral relief is attributable.

Where this is the case, identification takes place on a FIFO basis, as for EIS purposes, under TA 1988, s 299(6)–(6D) (TA 1988, s 576(1A), (1B)) **[see 18.4]**.

Where the holding includes CVS shares to which CVS investment relief is attributable, and they have been held continuously since acquisition, the identification rules for that relief are adopted instead (TA 1988, s 576(1C)).

21.6 Claims and relief

21.6.1 Claims

Claims to loss relief under these rules must be made no later than 12 months after the 31 January following the tax year in which the loss is incurred. If the loss is incurred in 2004–05, for example, the claim must be made no later than 31 January 2007 (TA 1988, s 574(1)).

21.6.2 Relief

The loss may be set off against income of the tax year in which the loss is incurred or against the income of the previous tax year (TA 1988, s 574(1)).

21.7 Investment companies and CVS investor companies

21.7.1 Introduction

Loss relief is also available for disposals made by investment companies. The companies concerned must have been investment companies for at least six years or for a shorter continuous period, provided that they had not previously been a trading company or an excluded company.

'Trading company' and 'excluded company' are as defined in **21.4.2**.

A further condition is that the investment company must not be associated with, or a member of the same group as, the qualifying trading company at any time in the period beginning with the date of subscription for the shares and ending with the date of the disposal (TA 1988, s 573(1)).

The investment company must make the claim to relief within two years of the end of the accounting period in which the loss is incurred. The loss may be set off against the income of the same accounting period or be carried back to accounting periods ending no earlier than 12 months before the beginning of the accounting period in which the loss is incurred (TA 1988, s 573(2), (3)).

21.7.2 Priority of CVS loss relief and loss relief under these rules

Where both reliefs may be claimed, CVS loss relief has priority (TA 1988, s 573(5); FA 2000, Sch 15, para 70).

21.7.3 How many companies qualify for both reliefs

As we have seen in **21.4.2**, an investment company is any company whose business consists wholly or mainly in the making of investments and the principal part of whose income is derived from that business, and for these purposes, it cannot be the holding company of a trading group (TA 1988, ss 576(5), 130).

A CVS investor company, on the other hand, must be a company that exists wholly for the purpose of carrying on one or more 'non-financial trades', which means that its activities must not consist wholly or substantially of financial activities, which include:

(*a*) banking;
(*b*) money-lending;
(*c*) debt-factoring;
(*d*) finance-leasing;
(*e*) hire-purchase financing;
(*f*) insurance;
(*g*) dealing in shares, securities, currency, debts, or other financial assets;
(*h*) dealing in commodity or financial futures or options.

[see 5.17.5].

As might be expected, a trade must be carried on on a commercial basis and with a view to the realisation of profits (FA 2000, Sch 15, para 11).

In considering whether non-financial trades are being carried on, the following activities may be disregarded:

(*a*) the holding and managing of property used by the company for one or more non-financial trades that it carries on; and
(*b*) the holding of shares to which CVS investment relief is attributable, unless the holding of these shares amounts to a substantial part of the company's business

A trading company cannot be an investment company, and vice versa. It is difficult to see, therefore, much of an overlap at all between the two reliefs.

21.8 Relief for loan interest

21.8.1 Income tax relief

An individual who takes out a qualifying loan can obtain a tax deduction at his or her highest tax rate for the interest paid. An example of a qualifying loan is a loan to invest in or lend money to a close trading company. A close company is a company under the control of five or fewer participators or under the control of its directors. A trading company for this purpose is a company that exists wholly or mainly to carry on a trade (TA 1988, ss 360, 360A, 363). This is the case even if the company has not yet set up or acquired the trade (*Lord v Tustain* [1993] STC 755).

21.8.2 Qualifying individual

To be eligible for this relief the individual must either:

(*a*) with his or her associates own more than 5% of the company's ordinary share capital; or
(*b*) own some shares and work for the greater part of his or her time in the management of the company's business.

Relief is not available for interest that has been paid on an overdraft; the debt must take the form of a loan.

21.8.3 Other qualifying loans

A further example of a qualifying loan is a loan taken out to acquire property that is to be let commercially. Interest on such loans is deductible under the rules for a 'Schedule A business'. These broadly follow the principles of Schedule D, Case I. An individual may consider this way of funding the acquisition of a building (factory, office etc) that will be leased to the unquoted trading company in which he or she has made an EIS investment.

21.8.4 Interaction with other reliefs

Interest relief is not available on a loan to acquire shares in a close company if the individual who acquires the shares or the individual's spouse claims EIS relief on those shares (TA 1988, s 360 (3A)).

Chapter 22

Giving and Withdrawing Capital Gains Reliefs

22.1 Introduction

This chapter is concerned with the mechanisms and computations involved in the giving and withdrawing of capital gains reliefs under the VCT scheme, the EIS and the CVS. The qualifying conditions for these reliefs were covered in Part 5 **[Chapters 14 to 16]** in the case of the deferral reliefs and in Part 6 **[Chapters 17 to 19]** in the case of the disposal and loss reliefs.

The procedures involved in seeking and obtaining the reliefs are described in **Chapter 24** and the various information requirements are covered in **Chapter 25**.

22.1.1 Scope of this chapter

This chapter covers the following topics:

(*a*) Giving effect to deferral reliefs **[see 22.2 to 22.5]**
(*b*) Giving effect to disposal and loss reliefs **[see 22.6 to 22.8]**
(*c*) Crystallisation of gains **[see 22.9]**
(*d*) Interest on unpaid and overpaid tax **[see 22.10]**

22.2 The VCT, EIS and CVS deferral reliefs

22.2.1 Introduction

VCT deferral relief (which is no longer available where the investment is made after 5 April 2004) allowed a chargeable gain made by the investor on the disposal of any asset to be deferred if he or she made an investment by subscribing for (broadly) VCT shares on which VCT investment relief was available and given. The investment had to be made within a year either side of the disposal giving rise to the gain, although the Inland Revenue had discretion to extend the period **[see Chapter 14]**.

EIS deferral relief allows a chargeable gain made by individuals (and in certain circumstances, trustees) on the disposal of any asset to be deferred if the individual or trustee ('the investor') makes an investment by subscribing for shares of an EIS company (the shares do not have to qualify for EIS investment relief). The investment must be made within a period beginning one year before the disposal that gave rise to the gain (or the crystallisation of a previously deferred gain) and ending three years after that disposal **[see Chapter 15]**.

CVS deferral relief works more narrowly, in that only gains made on the disposal of CVS shares may be deferred by investment into further CVS shares in an unconnected company. The investment must be made no more than one year before the disposal or no later than three years after it **[see Chapter 16]**.

22.3 Giving effect to VCT deferral relief

22.3.1 How much of the gain may be deferred?

The gain available for deferral relief was the gain after all available reliefs (including indexation allowance up to its April 1998 value and, before 6 April 2003, retirement relief) other than taper relief had been given **[see Chapter 23]**.

The gain had to be matched against qualifying VCT investments, which could not exceed £100,000 in any one tax year. The maximum gain that could be matched by investments in any one tax year was therefore £100,000 less any investments already matched with gains. Of course, investments in subsequent tax years, up to the end of the qualifying period, could be used to match the balance.

The investor did not have to claim the maximum amount.

22.3.2 The withdrawal of VCT deferral relief

VCT deferral relief is no longer available in respect of shares issued (and hence investments made) after 5 April 2004 (FA 2004, Sch 19, para 5, 7(1)).

However, since gains can be deferred by matching with investments made up to one year previously (TCGA 1992, Sch 5C, para 1(3)(a)), it will still be possible to defer gains accruing up to 5 April 2005, provided that there is a suitable qualifying investment made in the preceding 12 months.

Of course, the withdrawal of VCT deferral relief by means of new investments does not prevent the crystallisation, upon the occurrence of a chargeable event, of gains already deferred.

22.3.3 Claims procedure

Unless a claim for deferral relief is made, capital gains tax on a chargeable gain is due and payable on 31 January of the following tax year (TMA 1970, s 59B(4)). A claim to any form of relief against capital gains tax must, if at all possible, be made in the investor's self-assessment tax return (TMA 1970, s 42(2)). Only if the claim cannot be included in a return (or by amendment to a return) can it be made by other means. In such an event, in the absence of any statutory forms for claiming VCT deferral relief, the inspector should be contacted in writing with the details.

A claim for deferral relief must be made no later than the fifth anniversary of the 31 January following the tax year in which the later of the following events occurred:

(*a*) the disposal giving rise to the gain; and
(*b*) the issue of the shares in which the matching investment is made.

However, the investor cannot make the claim until VCT investment relief has been given in respect of the shares, which may not be until after the end of the tax year in which they are issued. There are opportunities to claim VCT investment relief at an earlier stage, if it is included in the PAYE code for the year or where the payments on account for the year are adjusted to include the investment relief.

Example 22.1

Joely sells an asset, realising a gain of £30,000, on 1 January 2003. Capital gains tax is due on 31 January 2004. She subscribes £20,000 for VCT shares, which are issued on 1 June 2003. Joely claims VCT investment relief shortly afterwards and this is reflected in her payments on account for 2003–04. Before 31 January 2004, she amends her 2002–03 self-assessment return to defer £20,000 of the 2002–03 gain by using the deferral relief relating to the VCT shares issued in 2003–04.

The capital gains tax due on 31 January 2004 can be reduced to take account of VCT deferral relief, as VCT investment relief has been reflected in the reduced payments on account for 2003–04.

22.4 Giving effect to EIS deferral relief

22.4.1 How much of the gain may be deferred?

The gain available for EIS deferral relief is the gain after all available reliefs (including indexation allowance up to its April 1998 value and, before 6 April 2003, retirement relief) other than taper relief have been given **[see Chapter 23]**.

The gain must be matched against qualifying investments in EIS companies, but because the acquired shares do not have to earn EIS investment relief, there is no maximum qualifying investment in any one tax year – the £200,000 upper limit for EIS investment relief does not apply.

22.4.2 Claims procedure

As stated in **22.3.2**, a claim to any form of relief against capital gains tax must, if at all possible, be made in the investor's self-assessment tax return (TMA 1970, s 42(2)). Only if the claim cannot be included in a return (or by amendment to a return) can it be made by other means. In such an event, in the absence of any statutory forms for claiming EIS deferral relief, the claim form attached to form EIS 3 **[see Chapter 24]** may be used for this purpose.

A claim for deferral relief must be made no later than the fifth anniversary of the 31 January following the tax year in which the shares are issued (Venture Capital Schemes Manual, para VCM 38100 – note the contrast with the limits for VCT deferral relief in **22.3.3**).

However, the investor cannot make the claim until the qualifying trade has been carried on for at least four months, although there is no need to wait for the granting of any EIS investment relief, as this is not a necessary precondition for the deferral relief. Indeed, as we have seen, EIS deferral relief may be claimed by investors who are not eligible to claim EIS investment relief on account of their being connected with the investee company.

22.5 Giving effect to CVS deferral relief

22.5.1 How much of the gain may be deferred?

The gain available for CVS deferral relief is the gain after all available reliefs (including indexation allowance) have been given **[see Chapter 23]**.

The gain must be matched against qualifying investments in CVS companies, and there is no maximum qualifying investment in any one accounting period.

The investor company does not have to claim the maximum amount.

22.5.2 Claims procedure

There is no prescribed procedure or pro forma for claiming the relief. In common with claims to all other reliefs related to corporation tax, therefore, a claim to CVS deferral relief must be made no later than six years after the end of the accounting period to which it relates (FA 1998, Sch 18, para 55), which will be the accounting period in which the gain arises. It is also the case that the claim must be made in the company's self-assessment corporation tax return or by amendment to that return, if at all possible (FA 1998, Sch 18, para 57(2)).

22.6 Giving effect to VCT and EIS disposal reliefs

Since these disposal reliefs take the form of an exemption, no claim or special procedure is necessary. Gains made on disposals that qualify for VCT or EIS disposal relief will not form part of the investor's chargeable gains for the tax year concerned.

22.7 Giving effect to EIS loss relief

22.7.1 Introduction

Losses on the disposal of EIS shares may either be used to offset the taxpayer's other gains in the same way as other capital losses, or be used in a claim for relief against income tax under TA 1988, s 574 as a loss on shares in unlisted trading companies **[see Chapter 21]**.

22.7.2 Claims procedure for section 574

A claim for a loss under TA 1988, s 574 must be made no later than the first anniversary of the 31 January in the tax year following that in which the lossmaking disposal occurs (TA 1988, s 574(1)). If the disposal takes place in 2004–05, for example, the claim must be made no later than 31 January 2007. As with all relief claims under self-assessment, they should if at all possible be made in the taxpayer's return or amended return. The due date for the tax return for 2004–05 is 31 January 2006, so the claim must be made before the expiry of the normal 12-month period for amendment of the return.

The Inland Revenue has the power to make any adjustment, assessment or discharge or repayment of tax needed to give effect to the relief (TA 1988, s 576(3)).

22.8 Giving effect to CVS loss relief

22.8.1 Introduction

A CVS investor company may claim to set a loss on the disposal of CVS shares **[see Chapter 19]** against its income of the accounting period in which the loss is incurred or the income of accounting periods in the preceding 12 months (FA 2000, Sch 15, para 68(1)). It must make such a claim no later than two years after the end of the accounting period in which the loss is incurred. The claim must be for the whole of the loss. The income against which the loss may be set is as computed before any deduction for charges on income or any other reduction or set-off. Later periods have priority over earlier periods. Where the claim involves more than one loss, it is the earlier loss that has priority (FA 2000, Sch 15, para 69(1)).

Example 22.2

Jaimini Ltd incurs two losses on CVS shares in its accounting period to 31 March 2005. As adjusted for retained investment relief, the losses are £10,000 (on a disposal made on 3 June 2004) and £45,000 (disposal date: 25 January 2005). Jaimini makes a claim for loss relief to set the losses against its income of the periods ended 31 March 2005 and 31 March 2004. Relief is given as follows:

Accounting period ending 31 March 2005	£
Income	30,000
Deduct CVS losses (£10,000 + £20,000)	30,000
Profits chargeable to corporation tax	nil

Accounting period ended 31 March 2004	£
Income	112,000
Deduct CVS loss carried back (£45,000 – £20,000)	25,000
Profits chargeable to corporation tax	87,000

No claim for loss relief may be made until the investee company or a subsidiary has been carrying on its qualifying trade for at least four months and a compliance certificate **[see Chapter 24]** has been obtained from the investee company.

Once a loss has been allowed under these rules, it may not be used in a claim under TA 1988, s 573 **[see 22.8.2]** nor to offset the company's chargeable gains (FA 2000, Sch 15, para 70(2)).

The Inland Revenue has the power to make any necessary adjustment to the company's liability to corporation tax to give effect to the claim (FA 2000, Sch 15, para 72).

22.8.2 Claims under TA 1988, s 573

If the CVS investor company also qualifies as an investment company **[see 21.7]**, it may claim under TA 1988, s 573 to set off the loss against its income of the same accounting period or carry it back to accounting periods in the previous 12 months. Given that the scope of the relief is no greater than under the CVS provisions, and the difficulties that a CVS investor company may have in qualifying as an investment company, it will rarely be worthwhile for those companies to make a claim under section 573, especially as the loss still has to be restricted for any retained investment relief.

However, where such a claim is contemplated, loss relief under the rules described in **22.8.1** has priority (TA 1988, s 573(4A)). A claim under section 573 must be made within two years of the end of the accounting period in which the loss is incurred (TA 1988, s 573(2)).

22.9 Crystallisation of gains

Gains deferred under any of the deferral reliefs will crystallise (come back into charge) on the occurrence of a 'chargeable event' **[see Chapters 14 to 16]**. When a gain crystallises, it becomes chargeable for the period in which the chargeable event occurs, not in the period in which it was originally derived. However, there is no extension of the holding period for taper relief or additional indexation allowance for the period between deferment and the occurrence of the chargeable event. These are frozen at the date of the original disposal.

The result may be that the tax actually payable by the investor is more than would originally have been paid – for example, a VCT investor who deferred a gain when his or her marginal rate of tax was 20% may find that the gain crystallises in a year when his or her marginal rate is 40%. The resulting disadvantage has to be weighed against the cashflow benefit in deferring the payment. By the same token, the gain may crystallise in a tax year or accounting period when the investor's marginal rate of tax is lower than it was at the time of deferment, so that a double advantage has been obtained. To the extent that the occurrence or not of a chargeable event is within the taxpayer's control, this is a point to be carefully monitored.

The investor is required to inform the Inland Revenue of any chargeable event **[see Chapter 25]**.

22.10 Interest on unpaid and overpaid tax

22.10.1 Interest on unpaid tax

As described in **22.9**, loss of deferral relief, leading to a crystallisation of the deferred gain, will not of itself give rise to any overdue tax, since the charge relates to the tax year or accounting period in which the event occurs. Of course, if the event is unreported or undetected until a time after the capital gains tax or corporation tax for the relevant tax year or period has become due and payable, interest will then be chargeable.

Capital gains tax is due and payable on the 31 January following the tax year in which the disposal giving rise to the gain takes place (TMA 1970, s 59B(4)). Corporation tax is due and payable nine months and one day after the end of the accounting period concerned (TMA 1970, s 59D(1)). 'Large' companies paying corporation tax in instalments will be charged interest if the amount of the instalment payment, even if made in time, is insufficient when the final liability to tax for that accounting period is established – instalments are based on the company's estimated liability for the current period, not on its agreed liability for a previous period.

The same considerations apply if a relief that has been claimed and given turns out not to have been due. The tax that was reduced or deferred becomes payable when it was originally payable, and interest will inevitably become chargeable. If the claim was made fraudulently or negligently, of course, penalties and other sanctions may be imposed.

22.10.2 Interest and repayment supplement on tax overpaid

There are no special rules relating to interest on repayments or reductions of tax following claims to disposal or deferral reliefs. The normal rules therefore apply **[see 20.7.5 to 20.7.7]**.

Chapter 23

Overlaps with Other Capital Gains Reliefs

23.1 Introduction

This chapter briefly examines other reliefs that could apply to capital gains and losses arising from disposals of scheme shares and looks at the interaction of those reliefs and the disposal, deferral and loss reliefs described in Parts 5 and 6 **[Chapters 14 to 19]**. In particular, it describes the complicated interaction between the capital gains taper-relief rules and the EIS.

23.1.1 Scope of this chapter

This chapter covers the following topics:

(*a*) The holdover relief for business gifts **[see 23.2]**
(*b*) The holdover relief for gifts on which IHT is chargeable **[see 23.3]**
(*c*) Choosing between the optional reliefs **[see 23.4]**
(*d*) The former retirement relief **[see 23.5]**
(*e*) Relief for unpaid loans and guarantees **[see 23.6]**
(*f*) Taper relief **[see 23.7]**
(*g*) Substantial-shareholdings relief **[see 23.8]**

23.2 Holdover relief for business gifts

23.2.1 Introduction

Under normal capital gains rules, a disposal includes a gift or a sale at an undervalue and capital gains tax applies in the normal way. In these situations, the consideration is deemed to be the market value of the asset being disposed of, and tax is charged accordingly. There are, however, two gift holdover reliefs, which allow the chargeable gain to be deferred and the transferee's base cost to be reduced by the deferred gain (TCGA 1992, ss 165(4), 260(3)). In both cases, the holdover relief does not apply where the transferee is not UK resident (TCGA 1992, ss 166, s 261). Neither of the reliefs applies to gifts of CVS shares, as the donor must either be an individual or a trustee (in the case of the latter relief). Neither does holdover relief apply if the *transferee* is a company.

23.2.2 Opting for holdover

Where an asset is to be gifted and the gift would give rise to a gain, it is necessary to weigh up the advantages and disadvantages of electing to hold over the gain. Relevant considerations include:

(*a*) the tax position of the donor and donee such as the availability of losses and annual exemptions;
(*b*) the donee's age, as there is no capital gains tax payable on death;
(*c*) the expectation that the rate of capital gains tax may be higher or lower in the future;
(*d*) the availability of the VCT or EIS deferral reliefs for both the donor and donee; and
(*e*) the amount of taper relief **[see 23.7]** accrued on the asset by the donor, which will be lost.

23.2.3 Gifts of business assets

Where an individual transfers a business asset by way of a disposal that does not represent a bargain at arm's length, a claim can be made to defer the gain made by the individual until the donee disposes of the asset (TCGA 1992, s 165). This relief, which can only be claimed by individuals, is available where the price paid by the recipient (if any) is at an undervalue, ie there is a gift element. The amount of gain deferred reduces the donor's chargeable gain and the base cost of the gifted asset for the purposes of calculating gains or losses on a future disposal by the donee (TCGA 1992, s 165(4)). Because it is the donee, and not the donor, who is liable for capital gains tax on a future disposal of the asset (and his acquisition cost is reduced), the consent of the donee is normally required.

23.2.4 Business assets

For this purpose, business assets include shares and securities in trading companies or holding companies of trading groups, in one of the following situations:

(*a*) where the shares and securities are not listed on a recognised stock exchange – it is acceptable for shares to be bought and sold under Rule 4.2 of the Alternative Investment Market (IR Press Release of 20 February 1995); or
(*b*) the company is the transferor's personal company.

(TCGA 1992, s 165(2)(b)).

A company is an individual's personal company if the individual is able to exercise at least 5% of the voting rights in it (TCGA 1992, s 165(8)(a)).

'Holding company', 'trading company' and 'trading group' are as defined for the purposes of taper relief in TCGA 1992, Sch A1 (TCGA 1992, s 165(8)(b)).

Example 23.1

David owns shares in an unquoted trading company which, if sold, would realise £18,000 and a gain of £10,000. The shares are business assets. David gifts the shares to his daughter Iris and they claim to hold over the gain. At the time of the gift, David would pay no tax on the gain and Iris would have a base cost for her shares of £8,000 (£18,000 less £10,000) on a future disposal.

Example 23.2

On 20 June 2000, Xenophanes gave some shares in the family trading company to his daughter Doris, at a time when the shares were worth £49,000. He had acquired them on incorporation in 1988 for £100. Xenophanes and Doris elect for his gain to be held over under TCGA 1992, s 165.

Xenophane's gain is as follows:

Market value	£49,000
Less Acquisition cost	£100
Gain	£48,900
Gain held over	£48,900
Chargeable gain	0

Doris's acquisition cost on a future disposal is conversely:

Acquisition at market value	£49,000
Less gain held over	£48,900
Revised acquisition cost	£100

It should be noted that Doris does not inherit Xenophane's period of accrual for taper relief purposes. The taper relief clock is reset each time a holdover election is made. For the interaction of taper relief and EIS, see **23.7**.

23.2.5 EIS shares

Where all or part of the gain on a disposal of EIS shares will be chargeable because:

(*a*) the EIS conditions have been breached within the relevant periods **[see 14.5.13]**; or
(*b*) the original EIS relief was restricted **[see 14.5.8]**

the investor could defer the non-exempt part of the gain by gifting the shares provided that they are still business assets **[see 23.2.4]**.

Example 23.3

Richard claimed EIS relief on his shares in Brampton Ltd but because the company redeemed another shareholder's preference shares, part of his EIS relief was withdrawn. A disposal of Richard's shares, which are business assets, would realise a chargeable gain of £10,000. Richard could gift them to his brother and claim to hold over the gain.

23.2.6 Withdrawal of holdover relief for transfers to settlor-interested trusts

Where the gift of business assets is made after 9 December 2003, it is no longer possible to claim holdover relief under TCGA 1992, s 165 (nor, indeed, under TCGA 1992, s 260 – see **23.3**) where the transferee is a settlor-interested trust, or where arrangements exist under which the trust may or will become a settlor-interested trust (TCGA 1992, ss 165(1), 169B).

Holdover relief for gifts of business assets is equally denied for gifts made after 9 December 2003 where the asset being transferred to a trust that is, or will or may become, a settlor-interested trust has been the subject of an earlier claim for holdover relief under either TCGA 1992, s 165 or TCGA 1992, s 260 **[see 23.3]**.

23.3 Holdover relief for gifts on which IHT is chargeable

At the date of the gift, the shares may not meet the definition of business assets **[see 23.2.4]**, because, for example, the company may no longer be trading. There is, however, another holdover relief for gifts of any type of asset (with specific exceptions), provided that the gift is an occasion of charge to inheritance tax, for example, where an asset is being transferred to the trustees of a discretionary trust (TCGA 1992, s 260). The rules apply to transfers by individuals and trustees and where the price (if any) paid by the transferee is at an undervalue, ie there is a gift element. The amount of gain deferred reduces the transferor's chargeable gain and the base cost of the gifted asset for the purposes of calculating gains or losses on a future disposal by the transferee (TCGA 1992, s 260(3)).

However, it is specifically provided that this relief is not available to defer:

(*a*) a gain frozen on a previous share exchange, which has become payable on the disposal of a qualifying corporate bond (TCGA 1992, s 260(6));
(*b*) a gain that was deferred on making a VCT or EIS investment and has become chargeable on a chargeable event (TCGA 1992, s 260(6A), (6B));

(*c*) where the gift is made after 9 December 2003 and to a trust in which the settlor has an interest ('a settlor-interested trust') or in respect of which arrangements exist under which the settlor will or may acquire an interest (TCGA 1992, ss 260(1), 169B); or

(*d*) where the gift is made after 9 December 2003 to a settlor-interested trust or a trust that may or will become a settlor-interested trust (because arrangements to that end are in place) and the asset concerned has been the subject of an earlier claim to holdover relief under either TCGA 1992, s 165 or TCGA 1992, s 260 (TCGA 1992, ss 260(1), 169B)

23.4 Choosing between the optional reliefs

Where an individual realises a gain on making a gift of any asset (including shares) consideration must be given as to whether, and if so how, to defer the gain. Assuming the necessary conditions can be met, it is a question of deciding whether to elect to use one of the two gift holdover reliefs **[see 23.2 and 23.3]**, or to invest an amount equivalent to the gain in a qualifying investment and claim EIS deferral relief.

It should be borne in mind that under the gift holdover reliefs, the deferred gain reduces the base cost of the asset given to the transferee (see Example 23.2). Under the EIS deferral relief (and, formerly, the VCT deferral relief also), the base cost of the shares subscribed for is not reduced, rather the earlier gain is 'frozen' and will crystallise on a chargeable event **[see 14.7 and 15.7]**. This is sometimes known as 'suspending' the gain or 'postponing' it. The base cost of the new asset is not affected.

Example 23.4

Jean, who is 64, wishes to give the following assets to her sons Thomas and George, her daughter Bette (all in their 40s) and her sister Mae aged 75 years.

Asset	*Market value*	*Chargeable Gain*
House (formerly rented) to Bette to be her main residence	£80,000	£15,000
Quoted shares to George	£25,000	£12,000
Trade patent to Thomas	£40,000	£8,000
Family company shares to Mae	£100,000	£40,000
Cottage to trustees of childrens' discretionary trust	£60,000	£20,000

No gift holdover relief is available for the gifts to Bette and George (as neither the house nor the quoted shares are business assets) but Jean's gains could be deferred by making EIS investments at least equal to the gain. It was also possible to defer the gain by making a qualifying VCT investment before 6 April 2004.

As most of the gain on the gift to Thomas would be covered by Jean's annual exemption it may be better not to hold over that particular gain. Thomas would then have a higher base cost on any future disposal.

The gift to Mae should be deferred using gift holdover relief as the gain would be exempt on Mae's death.

The gain on the gift to the trustees could be deferred by either using gift holdover relief under TCGA 1992, s 260 or by claiming EIS deferral relief after making qualifying investments. After 9 December 2003, holdover relief is only available for the gift of the cottage if Jean has no present interest in the children's trust and there are no arrangements for her to acquire an interest. What is more, if holdover relief is successfully claimed because these factors are absent, but Jean then acquires an interest in the trust or arrangements are put into place for her to acquire an interest and either the acquisition takes place or the arrangements are put into place at any time before the sixth anniversary of the end of the tax year in which she makes the gift, the holdover relief will be clawed back.

23.5 The former retirement relief

23.5.1 Introduction

Where an individual formerly disposed of shares in a trading company or the holding company of a trading group, which was his or her personal company and of which he or she was a full-time working officer or employee, the individual was entitled to retirement relief if certain conditions were met (TCGA 1992, s 163 (now repealed)). These shares could have been acquired as EIS investments.

Retirement relief was also available in cases where assets used in a business were disposed of, but this situation will not be considered further.

Retirement relief is no longer available for disposals made after 5 April 2003. However, because its demise is so recent, and it was mandatory where the prescribed conditions were met, we shall discuss it briefly here.

23.5.2 Qualifying individuals

At the time of the disposal of the shares the following conditions had to be met:

(*a*) The individual had either to be at least 50 years old or, if younger, be retiring through ill health.

(*b*) He or she had to be a full-time working officer or employee of the company (or of any other group or association member if the company was a member of a group or association).

(*c*) The company had to be a qualifying company.

Normally, if the conditions were met, retirement relief was given automatically. However, a claim had to be made where an individual was retiring at below the age of 50 through ill-health. By contrast the EIS deferral relief has to be claimed.

23.5.3 Qualifying companies

The qualifying company had to meet the following conditions:

(*a*) The shares had to be in the individual's personal company ie one in which he or she could exercise at least 5% of the voting rights.
(*b*) The company had either to be a trading company or a holding company of a trading group.

23.5.4 Period for conditions

The conditions for retirement relief had to be met for a minimum of one year immediately before the disposal of the shares but the maximum exemption was given if the conditions were met for ten years. Relief was given as a proportion of the maximum amount if the conditions were met for between one and ten years. For example, if they were met for seven years, 70% of the relief was given.

23.5.5 Retirement relief and EIS shares

Where all or part of the gain on EIS shares was not exempt under EIS loss relief – for example, where restricted EIS investment relief was originally given – **[see 18.5.5]** the gain could have been exempt under retirement relief if the conditions had been met.

Example 23.5

In May 1996 Owen, who is 49, subscribes £10,000 for shares in Catlin and Brittain Ltd and claims EIS relief. Owen has a 25% interest in the company, with Bernard, Owen's uncle, owning the other 75%. In June 1998 Bernard dies; Owen's father, Arthur, inherits Bernard's shares and Owen becomes a full-time working director. Owen loses his EIS relief as he then, with his associates, owns 100% of the company. If Owen sells his shares four years later (June 2002) realising a gain of £250,000, £40,000 of the gain will be tax free. The exemption will be £20,000 (£50,000 × 100% × 40%) plus £20,000 (50% of the excess of (£150,000 × 40% = £60,000) over £20,000).

Retirement relief was progressively withdrawn over a five-year period, and an earlier disposal would have attracted more relief (subject to a reduction in qualifying years).

23.5.6 Exchange of shares

Normally when shares are exchanged for other shares and securities, the exchange is not treated as a disposal for capital gains tax purposes. Any inherent gain is not taxed until there is a disposal of the shares received in the exchange. Where, at the time of the exchange, a shareholder was eligible for retirement relief, he would have done well to consider whether to elect for this treatment not to apply. These elections, made under TCGA 1992, Sch 6, para 2(1), had to be made no later than the first anniversary of the 31 January following the tax year in which the exchange took place. At the time of writing, such elections are therefore still possible for 2002–03 (final date 31 January 2005).

Example 23.6

Thomas, aged 46, makes a claim under EIS deferral relief to defer a gain of £40,000 by acquiring shares for £40,000 in Leviathan Ltd where he is a full-time working director. Ten years later, in June 2002, Leviathan is taken over by Malmesbury plc. Thomas receives shares equal to a 1% interest in Malmesbury and he becomes a consultant. Thomas can elect for the gain of £120,000 on his shares to be brought into charge as it would be reduced to £35,000 (£50,000 + ½ (£120,000 – £50,000) being exempt) by retirement relief. The remaining gain of £35,000 would be further reduced by taper relief, which, in June 2002, would have been available at 75%, leaving a chargeable gain of £8,750. On a later disposal of his shares in Malmesbury, Thomas would not be eligible for retirement relief at all, and 25% of any gain would remain in charge after the application of taper relief (the maximum amount of which is 75%).

23.5.7 Retirement relief and EIS relief

There were cases where the disposal of an asset on which a gain was realised met the conditions for retirement relief and this automatically exempted all of the gain. Where, however, only a proportion of a taxpayer's gains were eligible for retirement relief, a claim could be made to defer the remainder of the gain using VCT or EIS reliefs.

Example 23.7

Benedetto makes a gain of £370,000 in February 2003. As he has met the necessary conditions for at least ten years, retirement relief will exempt £125,000, ie £50,000 plus £75,000 being half of £150,000 (£200,000 – £50,000). He can claim to defer the non-exempt gain of £245,000 to the extent to which he makes qualifying VCT or EIS investments. The maximum annual investment in VCT shares was, of course, £100,000 for all the tax years in which the VCT investment could be made.

23.5.8 Interaction with gift holdover relief

Where an individual made a disposal by gifting a business asset and his or her gain was reduced by retirement relief, the remaining gain could and can be deferred by claiming gift holdover relief **[see 23.2]**.

23.6 Relief for unpaid loans and guarantees

23.6.1 Relief for loans to traders

If a loan has been made to an EIS or CVS company that is UK resident and all or part of the loan proves to be irrecoverable, tax relief may be available. Provided that certain conditions are met, the lender can claim an allowable loss for capital gains tax purposes equal to the irrecoverable amount, excluding unpaid interest (TCGA 1992, s 253). For losses suffered by guarantors see **23.6.4**.

The relief is not available where the loan is a 'debt on a security', which broadly means marketable loan stock.

23.6.2 Conditions for relief

Before the inspector agrees to the claim he must be satisfied that:

(*a*) the amount outstanding of the trading company's loan is irrecoverable;
(*b*) the claimant is the lender or has made a payment to the lender under the guarantee;
(*c*) he has not assigned his right to recover the amount paid; and
(*d*) the lender and borrower are not companies in the same group either at the time of the loan or subsequently (TCGA 1992, s 253(3)).

23.6.3 Year of the relief

The allowable loss is normally treated as incurred at the time the claim is made. It can, however, be related back to an earlier year if at that earlier time the loan was irrecoverable and the claim is made not later than two years after the end of that earlier tax year or accounting period (TCGA 1998, s 253(3A)). This may be worthwhile if different tax rates and exemptions applied.

Example 23.8

Anselm lends £30,000 to Aosta Ltd, an EIS company, in February 2002 but the company goes into liquidation in May 2004. It was established that Anselm's loan became irrecoverable in March 2004. Anselm could therefore claim for the loss to be set against his 2004–05 gains of £28,000 and the excess against his 2004–05 gains of £10,000. Any unused loss can automatically be carried forward to offset future gains.

23.6.4 Guarantees

A capital loss can be claimed by a person who makes a payment under a guarantee, where the loan was made to a UK resident trading company. Unlike the rules for loans to traders, under this provision the amount eligible for relief can include outstanding interest in respect of the trader's loan and this loan can be a debt on a security (TCGA 1992, s 253(4)). If the inspector agrees the claim, the allowable loss is treated as arising when the payment under the guarantee was made.

Example 23.9

In 2001 Aristippus agrees to act as guarantor when Cyrenaics Ltd, an EIS company of which he is a shareholder, obtains a £16,000 bank loan. The company goes into liquidation in May 2004 and Aristippus is required to pay the bank £9,000. He can make a claim for a capital loss of £9,000.

23.7 Taper relief and the disposal of EIS and VCT shares

23.7.1 Introduction

Taper relief was introduced from 6 April 1998 with the intention of simplifying the calculation of gains made by individuals, trustees and other persons not liable to corporation tax on gains. It replaced indexation relief (which is frozen at its April 1998 value for assets held at that time) and also retirement relief, which was gradually phased out, disappearing completely after 5 April 2003 **[see 23.4]**. It works by reducing the gain chargeable to tax by a percentage increasing with the period of ownership of the asset (measured from 6 April 1998) by the person making the disposal. Two different rates of taper relief apply, according to whether the asset is a 'business asset' or not. For disposals after 5 April 2002, the maximum taper (reduction) is 75%, available after two complete years of ownership. For 'non-business assets', the maximum taper is 40%, attained after ten years of complete ownership. Taper relief does not apply to losses.

23.7.2 Application of taper relief to EIS and VCT gains generally

A chargeable gain that is the subject of a claim for EIS or VCT deferral relief is calculated after deduction of indexation allowance (where appropriate) but before taper relief. This is because taper relief is a reduction in the amount on which capital gains tax is to be charged, applied to the total of chargeable gains over allowable losses for the year concerned (TCGA 1992, s 2A); indexation allowance is a factor in the computation of each chargeable gain. This gain is then 'frozen' or 'suspended'. Taper relief on the gain is calculated only in the tax year in which the gain crystallises.

When a deferred gain on the disposal of an asset is revived on the occasion of a chargeable event, taper relief is due for the period from the date of acquisition of that asset (or, if later, from 6 April 1998) to the date of disposal of that asset. Taper relief is not due for the period for which the gain is deferred, but only for the period of ownership by the disponer. Where the chargeable event is the disposal of the shares that have been matched with the gain, there will be a separate computation of the gain on the disposal of those shares; if that gain is not exempt, it will be reduced by taper relief.

Example 23.10

Helena disposes of a business asset (which she acquired on 20 May 1998) on 1 June 2001 and realises a gain (before taper relief) of £50,000, on which she claims deferral relief by virtue of a subscription on 1 August 2001 of £60,000 for £1 ordinary shares of Aspidistra Ltd. She also claims EIS income tax relief of £12,000 on this subscription. On 1 July 2003 Helena sells the shares in Aspidistra Ltd for £80,000.

The sale is a chargeable event in relation to the deferral relief, and the original frozen gain of £50,000 will be assessed for 2003–04. The qualifying holding period for taper relief for that gain is from 6 April 1998 to 1 June 2001. The assessment on the gain is £25,000 (£50,000 reduced by 50% taper relief).

The sale of the shares of Aspidistra Ltd takes place within three years of acquisition so that the EIS income tax relief of £12,000 is withdrawn. Assuming that the shares of Aspidistra Ltd qualify as a business asset for the purpose of taper relief, the gain on this second disposal is reduced by 50% (for one complete year of ownership).

23.7.3 Taper relief for serial EIS investments

Special rules regarding taper relief operate where:

(*a*) the investor disposes of shares (the original shares) in a company to which EIS deferral relief or EIS investment relief is attributable (company A) (see below);

(*b*) the shares in company A were issued after 5 April 1998 and disposed of after 5 April 1999;

(*c*) a chargeable gain (the original gain) arises on the disposal in (*a*), but all or part of that gain is deferred by matching it with a further qualifying investment in shares of another company (company B);

(*d*) a chargeable gain (the revived gain) arises on the subsequent disposal of all or part of the holding in company B which has been matched with the gain in (*c*)

(TCGA 1992, Sch 5BA, para 1).

If the gain on the sale of the shares in company B is again deferred by being matched with a further qualifying investment in company C, the original gain will not be revived until the disposal of the shares in company C, and so on.

EIS deferral relief is attributable to shares if the shares have been matched with a chargeable gain and there has been no chargeable event in relation to those shares (TCGA 1992, Sch 5B, para 19(2)). EIS investment relief is attributable to shares if it has been given in relation to those shares and not wholly withdrawn (TA 1988, s 289B).

'*Reinvestment shares*' are shares investment in which has been matched with all or part of a gain. '*Relevant reinvestment shares*' means those reinvestment shares whose disposal gives rise to a revived gain or that are shares in a chain of deferral-relief claims where the ultimate disposal gives rise to the revived gain (TCGA 1992, Sch 5BA, para 7).

The '*relevant disposal*' is the disposal of shares that have been matched with a chargeable gain and whose disposal is not the subject of a further deferral claim, ie the last in a series of reinvestments that are the subject of deferral relief (TCGA 1992, Sch 5BA, para (1)(c)).

Under these rules, the qualifying holding period for the original shares for the purposes of taper relief begins with the date of issue of the original shares and ends with the date of the relevant disposal (TCGA 1992, Sch 5BA, para 3(1)). For this purpose, a period within those dates does not count for taper relief purposes if:

(*a*) it is subject to the anti-avoidance provisions referred in TCGA 1992, Sch A1, para 2(4); or

(*b*) it is a period in which neither the original shares nor any relevant reinvestment shares were held (ie there is a gap between a disposal and an acquisition) (TCGA 1992, Sch 5BA, para 3(2), (4)).

The anti-avoidance provisions referred to in TCGA 1992, Sch A1, para 2(4) are, broadly, where the company is a close and 'inactive' company (TCGA 1992, Sch A1, para 11A); where there has been value shifting to enhance the value of the shares (TCGA 1992, Sch A1, para 12), and when there has been only limited exposure to fluctuations in value (TCGA 1992, Sch A1, para 10).

It has to be determined whether each successive holding of shares qualifies as a business asset for the purpose of taper relief. If the acquisition of the reinvestment shares precedes the disposal of the shares whose gain is matched with that reinvestment, the status of the holding for the overlap period is taken as that of the earlier holding. Thus if some of the investment shares were not held as business assets but some were, the eventual gain has to be treated as a 'mixed' asset (TCGA 1992, Sch 5BA, para 5).

If the revived gain is deferred by an investment in VCT shares (which must have been made before 6 April 2004) and VCT deferral relief is claimed, the qualifying holding period for these rules ends when the EIS shares are disposed of.

Example 23.11

Callista realises a gain of £270,000 (before taper relief) on 1 May 2003 on the disposal of a complete holding of shares in McBeal Ltd (an EIS company), for which she had subscribed on 1 May 2002 and in respect of which she had deferred a gain of £50,000 that would otherwise have accrued in 2000–01 on a disposal of quoted shares. The McBeal Ltd shares are a business asset throughout for taper relief purposes. Callista makes no other disposals in 2003–04. On 1 November 2004, she subscribes £210,000 for new ordinary shares in a new company, Ally Ltd. The investment is a qualifying investment for the purposes of EIS deferral relief (but not EIS investment relief) and a business asset for the purposes of taper relief. Callista makes a claim to defer the maximum £210,000 of the May 2003 gain against her investment in Ally Ltd.

The capital gains tax position for is 2003–4 is as follows.

	£
Gain on McBeal Ltd shares	270,000
Less deferred under EIS provisions	210,000
	60,000
Less taper relief £60,000 @ 50% (qualifying holding period 1.5.02–1.5.03 = 1 year)	30,000
	30,000
Previously deferred gain now chargeable	50,000
	80,000
Less annual exemption	7,900
Taxable gain 2003–04	£72,100

The taper-relief period for the first asset (the quoted shares – a non-EIS investment) ends on the date of disposal of that asset and does not fall to be extended under these provisions. No taper relief is due in this case as the asset is a non-business asset held for less than three years.

On 1 May 2008, Callista sells her holding of Ally Ltd shares for £500,000. She makes no other disposals in 2008–09. Her capital gains tax position for that year is as follows (assuming no change to the current rules).

Gain on Ally Ltd shares	£
Disposal proceeds	500,000
Less cost	210,000
	290,000
Less taper relief £290,000 @ 75% (qualifying holding period 1.11.04–1.5.08 = 3 years)	217,500
Gain	£72,500

Deferred gain brought into charge	£
Gain deferred	210,000
Less taper relief £210,000 @ 75%*	157,500
Gain	£52,500

*Qualifying holding period:	
1.5.02–1.5.03 = 1 year	
1.11.04–1.5.08 = 3.5 years	
Total = 4.5 years	
Number of whole years in qualifying holding period = 4	
Taxable gains 2008–09 (subject to annual exemption) (£72,500 + £52,500)	£125,000

23.8 Substantial-shareholdings relief

A company that disposes of shares forming part of a 'substantial shareholding' can, if certain conditions are satisfied, be entitled to exemption from corporation tax on chargeable gains in respect of that disposal. For a shareholding to be substantial, it must consist, broadly, of an interest of at least 10%. For the gain to be exempt, the investor company must have held that substantial shareholding for a continuous period of at least 12 months within the 24 months preceding the disposal. Additionally, the investor company must either be a trading company or a member of a trading group, whereas the investee company must be a trading company or the holding company of a trading group or subgroup.

In deciding whether there has been a disposal to which the exemption can apply, certain general capital gains rules that deem no disposal to have taken place are 'switched off'. Those rules are:

(*a*) TCGA 1992, s 116(10) – no disposal where the new holding on a company reorganisation consists of a qualifying corporate bond or bonds;
(*b*) TCGA 1992, s 127 – no disposal on a reorganisation; and
(*c*) TCGA 1992, s 192(2)(a) – no disposal on an exempt demerger

(TCGA 1992, Sch 7AC, para 4(1)).

The reason for this disapplication is to allow the substantial-shareholdings exemption to apply on a disposal that would otherwise be deemed not to have taken place in circumstances where the exemption would not apply on a disposal of the new holding.

However, this disapplication is itself switched off where the effect would be to cause CVS investment relief to be reduced or withdrawn under FA 2000, Sch 15, para 46, ie where the disposal would take place within the qualification period (TCGA 1992, Sch 7AC, para 4(2)). In other words, the rules in points (*a*) to (*c*) will apply where there would otherwise be a disposal of a substantial shareholding that would result in the loss of CVS investment relief.

If the reorganisation takes place outside the qualification period, there would be no reduction or withdrawal of investment relief under FA 2000, Sch 15, para 46, and hence the disapplication of the rules in points (*a*) to (*c*) in deciding whether there is a disposal for the purposes of the substantial-shareholdings exemption does still have force. Where the effect of this is that there is a disposal and that disposal qualifies for the exemption, the exemption is not nullified by the continuity rule on certain takeovers discussed in **19.3.6.1**. That rule, it will be recalled, provided that where there is a takeover of the investee company and certain conditions were satisfied, the new holding and old holding would nevertheless be deemed to be one, overriding the general rule that there is a disposal of the old holding on a reconstruction where that old holding includes CVS shares held continuously by the investor company since their issue (FA 2000, Sch 15, paras 83–85). Thus the CVS continuity rule yields to the substantial-shareholdings rule. When this happens, there is no transfer of the CVS investment relief to the new holding, as there is now deemed to be a disposal after all (TCGA 1992, Sch 7AC, para 4(4)).

Other occasions on which the CVS rules themselves disapply both the rule in point (*a*) **[see 19.3.5]** and the rule in paragraph (*b*) **[see 19.3.3]** are not affected.

For a potential problem with applicability of CVS relief where a shareholding is a substantial shareholding, see **5.17.6**.

Part 8

Administration

Chapter 24

Claims, Approval and Clearances

24.1 Introduction

The Parts 1 to 7 of this book have concentrated on the qualifying conditions for tax relief under the three venture capital schemes covered, how the tax reliefs work and how they interact with other provisions of the tax code. Part 8 concentrates on procedures and administration. This chapter looks in detail at how to obtain approval and clearances from the Inland Revenue and how to go about claiming the various reliefs. **Chapter 25** will set out the information requirements and powers of the Inland Revenue in relation to the schemes.

24.1.1 Scope of this chapter

This chapter covers the following topics:

(*a*) Obtaining VCT approval from the Inland Revenue **[see 24.2]**
(*b*) Monitoring of VCT status **[see 24.3]**
(*c*) Withdrawal of VCT approval **[see 24.4]**
(*d*) Tax-relief certificates for VCT investors **[see 24.5]**
(*e*) Informal VCT and EIS clearance of investments **[see 24.6]**
(*f*) The EIS four-month period **[see 24.7]**
(*g*) Tax-relief certificates for EIS investments **[see 24.8]**
(*h*) Obtaining CVS approval from the Inland Revenue **[see 24.9]**
(*i*) Clearance certificates for CVS investors **[see 24.10]**

24.2 Obtaining approval for a VCT

24.2.1 Introduction

A venture capital trust (VCT) is an investment trust company that is approved by the Inland Revenue. To keep its approved status it must continue to meet certain conditions. This section describes how a company obtains VCT approval and the ongoing conditions that it will then have to meet. References will be made to the VCT Regulations 1995 (SI 1995/1979), as amended.

Where an investee company decides it wishes to offer potential shareholders VCT relief, it can ascertain from the Inland Revenue that it and its trade would qualify. There is a provisional clearance procedure for VCT investment, which is described below.

24.2.2 Eligible shares

Reference will be made in this chapter, as it has been in other chapters, to eligible shares. These are ordinary shares that do not carry:

(*a*) any present or future preferential rights to dividends or to a company's assets on its winding-up; or
(*b*) any present or future right to be redeemed

(TA 1988, s 289(7) and s 842AA (14)).

24.2.3 Continuing to meet the conditions

Even where the VCT conditions have been met in relation to a company's most recent accounting period, full approval will not be given unless the Inland Revenue is satisfied that the conditions will continue to be met in the next accounting period, ie the current period in which approval is applied for (TA 1988, s 842AA(3)).

24.2.4 Provisional VCT approval

As noted previously **[see 5.6.3]**, a VCT that does not yet satisfy all the criteria for full approval may apply for provisional approval.

The Inland Revenue will not give provisional approval before the company has a source of income and an accounting period has started. Assuming this has occurred, provisional clearance can be obtained. However, this approval will only be given if the Inland Revenue is satisfied on three points.

First, that the company will meet the conditions set out in **24.2.4.1** by its second accounting period, by which is meant the accounting period following that in which the application is made (TA 1988, s 842AA(4)(a)). Secondly, that the conditions relating to qualifying holdings **[see 5.6.2.6 and 5.6.2.8]** will be met within the three-year initial period **[see 24.2.4.2]**. Thirdly, in the case of every condition that the Inland Revenue is satisfied will be met in a subsequent accounting period, that the conditions once met, will continue to be met thereafter (TA 1988, s 842AA(4)(c)).

24.2.4.1 *Second accounting period*

The company must meet the following conditions in relation to either its accounting period that is current when the application is made, or its next accounting period (TA 1988, s 842AA(4)(a)). The conditions that have to be met by the second accounting period are as follows:

(*a*) The company's shares must be quoted **[see 5.6.2]**.
(*b*) Its income must be wholly or mainly from shares and securities **[see 5.6.2.5]**.
(*c*) There must be no more than 15% of the VCT's investments in one company or group of companies **[see 5.6.2.9]**.
(*d*) The company must not retain more than 15% of its income **[see 5.6.2.13]**.

24.2.4.2 *Three-year initial period*

Where the company has not yet met the 70% and 30% qualifying holding tests **[see 5.6.2.6 and 5.6.2.8]**, the Inland Revenue must be satisfied that those conditions will be met in relation to an accounting period of the company beginning no more than three years after the time when it gives provisional approval or, if earlier, when the approval takes effect (TA 1988, s 842AA(4)(b)).

Accounting periods cannot be longer than 12 months for tax purposes but can be shorter. Care needs to be taken not inadvertently to shorten the initial period by the choice of accounting date.

24.2.5 Application procedure

Application for full or provisional VCT approval should be made by letter to Inland Revenue, Savings and Pension Schemes (VCT Scheme-Technical), in Bootle (for the address, see **Appendix 5**). There is no form to fill in. It is expected that the Inland Revenue will be able to deal with the application within 28 days and its approval will have immediate effect.

24.2.5.1 *Information required for provisional approval*

The company's letter applying for provisional VCT approval should be accompanied by the following:

(*a*) details of the company such as its incorporation date, place of incorporation, registered office, tax office and tax reference number;
(*b*) its memorandum and Articles of Association and details of any proposed changes;
(*c*) a draft of the prospectus or similar document that it intends to issue;
(*d*) a copy of the detailed proposed application to the Stock Exchange for listing or details of its listing;
(*e*) an outline of its investment strategy or business plan including its distribution policy – this should include a timetable showing when the company is likely to meet the relevant conditions **[see 24.2.4]**;

(*f*) the company's latest accounts, if any, or a current statement of affairs or balance sheet;
(*g*) a declaration by the company that to the best of its knowledge and belief the conditions for full approval will be met within the prescribed periods **[see 24.2.4]** and that the particulars given are true and correct

(SI 1995/1979, reg 3(4)).

24.2.5.2 *Application for full approval*

If the application is for full approval, it must contain:

(*a*) details of the company's Stock Exchange listing;
(*b*) a copy of the company's latest accounts;
(*c*) a copy of the current Memorandum and Articles of Association and details of any proposed changes;
(*d*) a report containing details demonstrating that the company met the qualifying conditions in relation to its last complete accounting period; and
(*e*) the address of the company's registered office, its tax office and tax reference number.

The company must also declare that, to the best of its knowledge and belief:

(*a*) the conditions for approval were met in relation to its last complete accounting period;
(*b*) the conditions will be met in relation to the current accounting period; and
(*c*) the particulars given are true and correct

(SI 1995/1979, reg 3(3)).

24.2.5.3 *Signatures*

A company's application for VCT approval must be signed by the company secretary or by a director of the company (SI 1995/1979, reg 3(5)).

Companies intending to seek provisional approval as a VCT may make an informal application in advance, before submitting a formal application after their first accounting period has begun. They should approach the Savings and Pension Schemes (SPS) office at Bootle; in its response, the SPS will indicate whether approval is likely to be granted when the formal application is made (Venture Capital Schemes Manual, para VCM 60340).

24.2.6 Notice of provisional approval

The Inland Revenue will issue a notice of approval in writing, which will specify the following:

(*a*) the date on which the approval is given;
(*b*) the date from which the approval takes effect, if different **[see 24.2.7]**;
(*c*) any conditions of approval

(SI 1995/1979, reg 4).

The Inland Revenue has the power to set out a timetable for applicants to meet the conditions and set any other conditions. It will only do so where it appears that a particular applicant will not routinely proceed with its plan to meet the conditions (see the Venture Capital Schemes Manual, para VCM 60350). Once the conditions are met the VCT is approved, and it does not have to apply again for full approval.

24.2.7 Effective date of approval

VCT approval by the Revenue is effective from the date specified in the approval notice. This can be a date before or after the approval was given. However, it cannot be earlier than the time when the application for approval was made (TA 1988, s 842AA(1)).

The effective approval date determines when the three-year initial period starts and ends **[see 24.2.4.2]**.

24.2.8 Refusal to grant VCT status

If the Inland Revenue is not satisfied with the information provided and the assurances given, it will usually ask for further information or ask the company to modify its proposal. Assuming that having done this the Inland Revenue decides to refuse VCT status it must do so in writing, specifying the reasons for refusal and stating that the company has a 30-day period within which to appeal (SI 1995/1979, regs 5 and 7).

24.2.9 Appeals against decisions

The company may appeal to the Special Commissioners in connection with any of the following:

(*a*) any conditions included in the provisional approval **[see 24.2.6]**;
(*b*) any refusal to grant approval to the company **[see 24.2.8]**;
(*c*) the withdrawal of VCT approval **[see 24.4.3]**.

The appeal must be made in writing to the Inland Revenue within 30 days of the date of the notice in question. On appeal, the notice will be confirmed or quashed or, if it concerned provisional approval conditions, the Commissioners may vary any of the conditions. If the Commissioners allow an appeal against a refusal of approval, they must specify the date from which the approval is to have effect (SI 1995/1979, reg 7).

24.3 Monitoring of VCT status

24.3.1 Introduction

The Inland Revenue will monitor the company's provisional VCT status and where necessary will withdraw it **[see 24.4]**. The provisional approval will continue as long as the conditions are met. It will not be replaced by a formal approval or an annual approval as is the case with other investment trusts.

24.3.2 Sources of information

The Inland Revenue will have access to the following sources of information:

(*a*) reports from the inspectors dealing with the investee companies **[see 24.3.3]**;
(*b*) the VCT's accounts and investment returns **[see 24.3.5]**;
(*c*) inspection of the VCT's records **[see 24.3.8]**.

24.3.3 Qualifying companies

The inspector dealing with the tax affairs of the investee companies making up the VCT's qualifying holdings will be asked to report annually to the SPS on their qualifying status. The report will usually be made when each company's accounts are submitted, but each inspector will be encouraged to report any qualifying-status problems that have come to his notice as they occur during the year.

24.3.4 VCT timetable

In the initial three-year period, a VCT that has provisional approval will need to adhere to a timetable as to when it should reach its targets for qualifying holdings during and at the end of that period **[see 24.2.4.2]**.

24.3.5 Investment return for a specified period

A VCT (or a company that has been a VCT) must send to the Inland Revenue an investment return for a specified period that is the shortest of the following:

(*a*) an accounting period of the VCT;
(*b*) a period beginning on the date from which its approval was effective and ending on an accounting date of the VCT;

(*c*) a period beginning at the start of a VCT's accounting period and ending on the day it ceased to be approved

(SI 1995/1979, reg 22(2)).

24.3.5.1 *Contents of the investment return*

The VCT's investment return must include a certificate regarding its status **[see 24.3.5.2]**, a declaration **[see 24.3.5.3]**, and the following information:

(*a*) the value **[see 5.6.2.11]** of each of its investments at the beginning of the specified period;
(*b*) in respect of any new investment made by the VCT during the specified period:
 (1) the date on which the investment was made, and
 (2) the value of that investment, together with any revaluation of existing investments required as a result (this will usually be where the new shares are added to an existing holding and the value per share increases);
(*c*) in relation to each investment, whether or not it is a qualifying holding;
(*d*) in relation to each qualifying holding:
 (1) the name of the company in which the investment has been made, and
 (2) the address of the investee company's registered or principal office;
(*e*) in relation to each disposal of an investment by the VCT during the specified period:
 (1) the name of the company in which the investment was held,
 (2) the address of that company's registered or principal office,
 (3) the date of the disposal, and
 (4) the value, immediately afterwards, of the remainder of any holding from which the disposal will be made (eg where the value per share has fallen)

(SI 1995/1979, reg 22(4)).

A company is an individual's personal company if the individual is able to exercise at least 5% of the voting rights in it (TCGA 1992, s 165(8)(a)).

'Holding company', 'trading company' and 'trading group' are as defined for the purposes of taper relief in TCGA 1992, Sch A1 (TCGA 1992, s 165(8)(b)).

24.3.5.2 *Certificate regarding VCT status*

In the investment return the company will certify one of the following:

(*a*) where the VCT has been given full approval or has been given provisional approval three years or more before the beginning of the specified period, that it has satisfied all the conditions;

(*b*) where the VCT has been given provisional approval less than three years before the start of the specified period, that it has satisfied the conditions that are required to be met by its second accounting period **[see 24.2.4.1]** together with any other conditions attached to the provisional approval throughout the specified period; or
(*c*) that it has ceased to be approved

(SI 1995/1979, reg 22(5)).

24.3.5.3 *The declaration*

This is a declaration, in such form as the Inland Revenue may specify or approve, that the particulars contained in the investment return are to the best of the company's knowledge and belief, true and correct. The declaration must be signed on behalf of the company by the company secretary or one of its directors (SI 1995/1979, reg 22(6), (7)).

24.3.6 Return of investors' subscriptions

VCTs must also make a return for each tax year (including the year in which approval ceases), containing particulars of amounts subscribed by investors for eligible shares.

The return must contain in respect of each investor:

(*a*) the investor's full name;
(*b*) the investor's permanent residential address, including postcode;
(*c*) the investor's date of birth;
(*d*) the investor's national insurance number (if he or she has one);
(*e*) the amount paid for eligible shares subscribed for in the year; and
(*f*) the date on which the amount(s) was (were) paid

(SI 1995/1979, reg 21A).

24.3.7 Records to be kept by a VCT

A VCT must at all times during its 'relevant period' keep sufficient accounts, records and other information to enable the requirements of VCT approval, including the investee companies' qualifying status and the Regulations, to be satisfied. For this purpose the relevant period is one of the following:

(*a*) in the case of a VCT that is no longer approved, the period of six years from the date when approval ceased;
(*b*) in any other case, the period of six years from the end of the period of account or year to which the accounts, records and information relate, whichever is the longer

(SI 1995/1979, reg 23).

24.3.8 Inspection of records

The Inland Revenue can require a VCT or any person who holds or has held its shares, to make certain information available for inspection by one of its officers within a specified period of not less than 14 days. The officer may inspect the accounts, records and other information that the VCT has in its possession or is under its control, provided that it is a reasonable request to establish whether the VCT conditions have been met. Where records are computerised, the Inland Revenue officer must be provided with all the necessary facilities for inspecting them (SI 1995/1979, reg 25).

24.4 Withdrawal of VCT approval

24.4.1 Notice of breach of conditions

A VCT that has been given full approval is required to notify the Inland Revenue if it has breached the VCT conditions (SI 1995/1979, reg 8).

24.4.2 Grounds for withdrawal

The Inland Revenue may withdraw approval at any time if it appears to it that there are reasonable grounds for believing the existence of any of the following:

(*a*) a resolution that has been passed or a petition that has been presented to wind up the company (SI 1995/1979, reg 8(1)(b) and (2)(d));
(*b*) non-fulfilment of the conditions at the time of the approval (TA 1988, s 842AA (6)(a));
(*c*) where the VCT met the conditions and received full approval, a subsequent failure to meet the conditions (SI 1995/1979, reg 8(1)(a));
(*d*) where provisional approval was given **[see 24.2.4]**:
  (1) failure to meet any of the conditions that the Inland Revenue was satisfied would be met in the second accounting period or within the initial three-year period (SI 1995/1979, reg 8(2)(a)) (TA 1988, s 842AA(6)(b)),
  (2) a breach of one or more of the conditions set out in the notice of provisional approval **[see 24.2.6]** (SI 1995/1979, reg 8(2)(b)),
  (3) a failure by the VCT to meet some other condition after fulfilling the conditions to be met during the second accounting period and the three-year initial period (SI 1995/1979, reg 8(2)(c)), or
  (4) a failure or pending failure by the VCT during its latest complete accounting period or its current period to meet a condition, the failure of which was not allowed for at the time of approval (TA 1988, s 842AA (6)(d)).

24.4.3 Notice of withdrawal

If VCT approval is to be withdrawn, the Inland Revenue will serve a notice in writing withdrawing the approval. The notice will specify:

(*a*) the date from which the withdrawal of approval takes place, which may be the date of the notice or an earlier date; and
(*b*) the reasons for the Inland Revenue's withdrawal of approval

(TA 1988, s 842AA (7) and SI 1995/1979, reg 6).

The VCT can appeal against the decision **[see 24.2.9]**.

24.4.3.1 *Earlier withdrawal date*

A notice withdrawing approval may specify a time that is before the time when the notice is given. This earlier withdrawal date is effective for the purposes of the capital gains exemptions (TCGA 1992, s 100) for the company and its investors. However, the date must not be earlier than the beginning of the accounting period in which the company failed to fulfil the conditions specified by the Inland Revenue in the withdrawal notice (TA 1988, s 842AA(9)).

24.4.4 Approval deemed never to have been given

If, in the case of a provisional approval, the approval is withdrawn at a time before all the conditions have been fulfilled with respect to that company in relation either to:

(*a*) a complete accounting period of 12 months; or
(*b*) successive complete accounting periods constituting a continuous period of 12 months or more

the withdrawal has effect as if provisional approval had never been given (TA 1988, s 842AA(8)). This will lead to the raising of assessments on the company for corporation tax on capital gains unless the company could obtain approval as an investment trust.

24.4.5 Effect on VCT shareholders

Where VCT approval is lost in circumstances where it is treated as never having been given **[see 24.4.4]**, unless the company could obtain approval as an investment trust, any gains on the disposal of the shares would be taxable and any losses on the shares would be allowable losses.

Where full VCT approval is obtained and then subsequently lost, the shares are deemed to have been sold and reacquired at market value immediately before the loss of approval. Gains on the shares at that time would therefore be exempt, losses would not be allowable and the base cost of the shares would be uplifted to market value (TCGA 1992, s 151B(6)).

24.5 Tax-relief certificates for VCT investors

24.5.1 VCT certificates

If an investor who owns eligible shares **[see 7.3.2]** in an approved VCT makes a request for a tax-relief certificate, the VCT must provide it within 30 days. The VCT does not have to seek authorisation from the Inland Revenue before issuing the certificate as is the case with EIS tax-relief certificates. The VCT must keep a record of every certificate that it issues (SI 1995/1979, reg 9). The VCT should issue these certificates as a matter of course. Without one, an investor cannot verify that tax relief has been properly obtained **[see 24.5.3]**.

24.5.2 Contents and form of the certificate

Although the certificates do not have to be in any standard form, any certificate issued by a VCT must contain the following information:

(*a*) the name of the investor and his or her permanent address including post-code;
(*b*) the date on which the eligible shares were issued to him or her;
(*c*) the amount payable in respect of those shares and the date on which the amount is payable; and
(*d*) the amount paid in respect of those shares and the date on which it was paid

(SI 1995/1979, reg 9(2)).

The certificate will make the following statements:

(*a*) that eligible shares have been issued to the investor;
(*b*) that to the best of the VCT's knowledge and belief the shares were both subscribed for and issued for bona fide commercial purposes and not as part of a scheme or arrangement the main purpose of which, or one of the main purposes of which, was the avoidance of tax; and
(*c*) that to the best of the VCT's knowledge and belief the shares were not issued to an investor who is not entitled to relief because he or she has received a loan that is linked to his or her investment **[see 7.3.4]**.

(SI 1995/1979, reg 9(3)).

24.5.3 Claiming investment relief

Like other claims under self-assessment, a claim for VCT investment relief must be made in the investor's self-assessment return or amended return, if at all possible. However, a claim for a particular tax year may not be made until after the tax year has elapsed, since it takes the form of a reduction in tax payable and ranks after certain other reliefs and allowances, so cannot be quantified any earlier **[see 20.2.8]** (TMA 1970, s 42(1A)). An exception is made for claims for the relief to be given through an adjustment to the investor's PAYE coding (TMA 1970, s 42(3)). Only if it is too late to claim through a return or amended return, should the investor write directly to his or her tax office to claim the relief. In that case, it is probably necessary to enclose the tax-relief certificate, but otherwise, when the claim is made through the investor's return, the inspector will normally not require to see the certificate, unless he or she has reason to doubt the validity of the claim (Venture Capital Schemes Manual, para VCM 64050).

Claims can be made to reduce the investor's payments on account of the current tax year in the normal way. If the claim proves to be excessive, interest will be charged from the due dates.

A claim for relief may not be made later than the fifth anniversary of the 31 January following the tax year to which the relief relates (TMA 1970, s 43).

24.5.4 Claiming VCT deferral relief

[See 22.3.2].

24.6 Informal VCT and EIS clearance of investments

24.6.1 Introduction

When a VCT identifies an unquoted company in which to invest some of its funds, it will need to seek the Inland Revenue's opinion as to whether the proposed investment would qualify. Similarly, when an investment is about to be made under the EIS, the Inland Revenue's opinion should be sought. Where a VCT wishes to invest in a company alongside a business angel it is important to ensure that the company meets the conditions for both VCT and EIS purposes. Matters that apply to both VCT and EIS clearances are dealt with at **24.6.2** to **24.6.7**. Additional matters that only affect EIS issues are set out in **24.6.8** and **24.6.9** and those that only affect VCT issues can be found at **24.6.10**.

24.6.2 An informal opinion

Neither the VCT nor the EIS legislation or regulations provide for an advance clearance procedure. In both cases, however, it is the Inland Revenue's practice to provide an informal clearance before the shares are issued.

All applications for informal clearances and opinions relating to any of the three schemes should now be addressed not to the company's tax office but to the Inland Revenue's Small Companies Enterprise Centre (SCEC). The headquarters of the SCEC is in Cardiff, at:

TIDO
Tŷ Glas Road
Llanishen
Cardiff
CF14 5ZG
tel: 0292 032 7400; fax: 0292 032 7938;
e-mail: enterprise.centre@ir.gsi.gov.uk

The SCEC also has regional offices in Dundee and Maidstone.

The SCEC deals with:

(*a*) enquiries from companies about the conditions of the VCT scheme, the EIS and the CVS;
(*b*) requests from companies for advance clearance that they will meet the requirements for any of the three schemes; and
(*c*) the corporation tax liability of companies using any of the three schemes for the restricted periods during which the requirements of the various schemes need to be met

However, the following matters should not be referred to the SCEC:

(*a*) claims to relief under any of the three schemes – these remain the responsibility of the investor's tax office; and
(*b*) applications for approval of VCTs – as we have seen, these are dealt with by the SPS in Bootle

(Venture Capital Schemes Manual, paras VCM 10050, VCM 10060).

An application for informal clearance should be made by, or on behalf of, the directors of the investee company by contacting the SCEC.

24.6.3 Timeliness of applications

It is recommended that the SCEC be given at least three weeks to deal with an application for informal clearance. The SCEC is a specialist unit, experienced in dealing with such applications, although it has been in existence only since September 2000, and has been dealing with CVS applications only since April 2002. However, it also deals with companies operating EMI schemes, and its workload at any one time may be considerable.

Although the application should not be submitted at the last minute, there is very little point in submitting it before important matters have been decided. The SCEC will not be very pleased if the company goes back to it several times with additional information and a request for a letter saying that it is still of the opinion that the company should qualify.

If, on the other hand, only one informal clearance application is made and then the information changes considerably, the investors will have relied on a worthless informal clearance.

24.6.4 The importance of simplicity

The proposal should be kept as simple as possible. If it is difficult to understand, the SCEC is less likely to deal with it promptly and if the project is complicated, a full explanation should be given as to why certain features are necessary.

24.6.5 Value of the informal clearance

The SCEC's opinion will be based on the information provided to it, which should be accurate and complete. If the company's directors or advisers are aware of a potential problem area, for example, an unusual trading activity, this should be drawn to the SCEC's attention in the informal clearance application. If this is not done, the clearance will be worthless.

24.6.5.1 *The MFK Underwriting case*

The decision in *R v IRC, ex p MFK Underwriting Agents Ltd* [1989] STC 873 concerned a taxpayer who relied on statements made by the Inland Revenue. In that case it was held that the Inland Revenue would only be bound by its statements if the taxpayer:

(*a*) gave full details of the specific transaction on which he sought the Inland Revenue's ruling;
(*b*) indicated the ruling sought and made it plain that a fully considered ruling was sought;
(*c*) indicated the use he intended to make of any ruling given; and
(*d*) the ruling or statement made was clear, unambiguous and devoid of qualification.

24.6.5.2 *The Matrix Securities case*

The case of *Matrix-Securities Ltd v IRC* [1994] STC 272 concerned a prospectus offering the public an opportunity to invest in property in Docklands. The sponsor's solicitors obtained provisional clearance from a local inspector that enterprise zone capital allowances would be available to investors. When the prospectus came to the notice of the Inland Revenue's Financial Institutions Division (FID) it withdrew the clearance. The sponsor seeking to rely on the *MFK Underwriting* case **[see 24.6.5.1]** asked for a judicial review on the grounds that the withdrawal of the Inland Revenue's clearance was unfair and amounted to an abuse of its power. The House of Lords and the lower courts found for the Inland Revenue. On 6 May 1993 the Inland Revenue had written to the Enterprise Zone Property Unit Trust Association to say that any scheme involving a put option needed to be cleared by the FID. The sponsor was a member of that association and yet had sought clearance at a local level although it had suggested to the inspector that he might wish to consult the FID. It was also said that there was a failure to make a full disclosure of all the facts to the inspector and that he was put under pressure to give a quick answer.

If the courts had decided against the Inland Revenue, there might not have been a VCT, EIS or CVS provisional clearance procedure. As the decision was in the Inland Revenue's favour these procedures continue. However, it should be borne in mind that the Inland Revenue can revoke provisional clearances where the information provided is not set out clearly and accurately.

24.6.5.3 *Inland Revenue view on informal clearances*

This is what the Inland Revenue's own guidance to staff has to say on the approach towards informal clearance applications relating to the EIS.

> 'Companies which are hoping to attract subscriptions under the EIS are encouraged to seek an assurance from the Revenue, in advance of inviting applications for shares, to the effect that it is accepted that the conditions of the scheme will be satisfied . . .
>
> Requests can be dealt with only if they come from the company's secretary or directors or from some other person authorised by them to negotiate with the Revenue on their behalf. The rules of confidentiality apply, and potential investors making enquiries about a company should address those enquiries to the company itself.
>
> It is not necessary for the request to identify the intending subscribers, and no assurance as to the availability of relief to a particular subscriber can be given either to the company or to the subscriber in question . . .
>
> . . . the Revenue is normally bound by any assurance given, provided the information supplied was correct and complete at the time it was given and has not been superseded by subsequent events. It is therefore important, in order to avoid misunderstanding, that all information supplied is given in writing. For the same reason, it is also important that requests should be considered very carefully, in the light of both the information supplied and information available on the tax files of the company and any subsidiaries, before any decision is made. Companies seeking an assurance therefore need to allow adequate time for the Revenue to consider the request properly.
>
> Any assurance supplied to a company can only be given on the basis of the information provided. The inspector is under no obligation to check the accuracy of that information. However, it is important that any obvious gaps in the information should be filled and any apparent contradictions explained.

The response to a request for an assurance will take the form of a statement as to whether, on the basis of the information provided, the Revenue would be able to issue certificates under section 306(2) [EIS 2 certificates] in respect of the shares to be issued, following receipt of a form EIS 1 satisfactorily completed.

In some cases there will be a clear possibility that the company will at some future time within the three-year period . . . cease to satisfy one of the conditions (for example, excluded activities which the company intends to carry on might come to be a substantial part of its trade . . .). Any assurance given in such a case will need to be expressed as being subject to the proviso that the condition in question is satisfied throughout, and may incorporate an explanation as to how it is proposed to apply the test in question (for example, how it is proposed to decide whether the excluded activities make up a substantial part of the trade).

Where a company supplies valuations or forecasts responsibility for their accuracy lies with the company.

Where an assurance is given and shares are issued in reliance on it the company will need to take care that the conditions relating to the company and its trade are complied with throughout the three-year period related to the shares.

Where the inspector is unable to give a favourable response to a request for an assurance, a brief explanation of the reason will be given. But it is entirely the company's responsibility to decide what amendment, if any, it should make to its proposals.'

(Venture Capital Schemes Manual, paras VCM 21030–21040)

Advice regarding informal clearances for the VCT scheme is similar:

'A company which has been offered, or is hoping to be offered, funding by a VCT may seek assurances from the Revenue that following the issue of a holding to the VCT that holding will be regarded as part of [the VCT's] qualifying holdings. It may also seek an assurance that all or some of the shares to be issued will be eligible shares.

In some cases, particularly where the purpose of the VCT's investment is to fund a management buy-out or buy-in, inspectors may be approached by a third party, perhaps in advance of the incorporation of the company to be invested in. While there is no objection to any specific causes of concern about the potential application of TA 1988, Sch 28B being discussed with a third party at this stage (or indeed, at any stage, provided the right of the company to have its affairs dealt with in confidence is respected), it should be made clear that no actual assurance can be given to any person other than the company, when formed, or its authorised representative. Similarly, a company whose business is to be bought by another company with money raised from a VCT is entitled to expect that the Revenue will not discuss its affairs with any third party.

It is for the company to decide what information it wishes to put forward with a view to obtaining the assurances it is seeking. It may choose to supply only primary facts or it may prefer to give its own conclusions in broad statements (such as 'the trade will be a qualifying trade'). However, [the inspector] should not give any assurance that the company will satisfy the requirements unless the information supplied includes all the following:

(*a*) a copy of the latest available accounts for the company, and for any subsidiary company;
(*b*) details of all trading or other activities to be carried on by the company and any subsidiary;
(*c*) details of the approximate sum the company hopes to raise, and how it (or its subsidiary) intends to use the money;
(*d*) an up-to-date copy of the memorandum and articles of association of the company and of any subsidiary, and details of any changes to be made;
(*e*) (where an investment by a particular VCT is in prospect) details of any subscription agreement or other side-agreement to be entered into by the company and the VCT

. . .

The response to a request for an assurance will take the form of a statement as to whether, on the basis of the information provided, the inspector is satisfied that following the issue of the holding that holding will comply with the requirements of TA 1988, Sch 28B (and, where applicable, that the shares to be issued will be eligible shares) . . .

In some cases whether a requirement needs to be satisfied may depend on when the VCT originally raised the money which it is investing. Where appropriate, an assurance should be given in such a case subject to the proviso that the money to be invested is money which the VCT raised before the date in question. If the VCT requests confirmation that its view on that matter is accepted, it should be invited to contact SPS (VCT Schemes – Technical).'

(Venture Capital Schemes Manual, paras VCM 62500–62520)

24.6.6 Basic information to be supplied

It is important to make the application for informal clearance comprehensive. It saves everyone's time if all the relevant information is supplied at the outset and the SCEC is asked to comment on possible areas of difficulty.

Assume when contacting the SCEC that it requires the following information:

(*a*) the company's date and country of incorporation, registered number and registered office;
(*b*) details of the company's present and proposed authorised and issued share capital;
(*c*) details of any share options that have been or will be granted, together with copies of the share-option agreements;
(*d*) the names of the directors, including proposed directors;
(*e*) details of the company's loan capital immediately following the share issue;
(*f*) a description of the company's and/or its subsidiaries' present and proposed activities or trades;

(*g*) the tax references of any companies with which the company has, or will have, a close business relationship;
(*h*) details of how and when the proceeds of the share issue will be used;
(*i*) a copy of the latest audited accounts, if there are any;
(*j*) a copy of the company's Memorandum and Articles of Association (including particulars of any changes to be made to facilitate the issue);
(*k*) details of any side agreements between shareholders or others which might affect their rights or regulate the company's affairs such as a shareholders' agreement or a subscription agreement – if there are no side agreements there should be a statement to that effect; and
(*l*) a near-complete draft of any memorandum or prospectus that the investee company intends to issue to prospective investors.

24.6.7 Cash flow and profit projections

Depending on the circumstances, it may be prudent to provide the SCEC with cash flow and profit projections to demonstrate the following:

(*a*) that the intention is that the funds from the share issue will be employed in the trade within the first 24 months; and
(*b*) that the company's income from any prohibited activities **[see 6.5]** will not be substantial.

24.6.8 Further points relevant to EIS issues

An EIS company has to carry on a trade or other qualifying activities for four months before an application can be made for tax-relief certificates **[see 24.8]**. When applying for informal clearance the company should indicate when it started or intends to start trading.

As all EIS shares must be fully paid up at the date of issue and the company must not have repaid any of its capital in the last 12 months, and there should be a statement to that effect.

The informal clearance is not an opportunity to obtain any comfort from the Inland Revenue regarding the eligibility of any of the individual investors, for example, as to whether remuneration for a paid director is reasonable.

Although a claim can be made for EIS relief without first having obtained EIS informal clearance, it is essential for commercial reasons to obtain clearance if the public is going to be asked to subscribe for shares.

24.6.9 Small EIS investments

If in the case of a small EIS investment, the individuals are determined to invest whether or not EIS tax relief is available, there is the option of going ahead without an informal clearance. After the share issue, an application can be made for tax-relief certificates on form EIS 1. If, at that stage, the inspector refuses to authorise the issue of certificates, the company can appeal to the Commissioners **[see 24.8.5]**.

24.6.10 Further points relevant to VCT issues

A VCT clearance should set out the package of investments that it is proposed will be made, indicating the terms of any preference shares and loans to the company.

In the case of an investment into an existing company a balance sheet should be drawn up immediately before the investment to ensure that the value of gross assets immediately before the investment does not exceed £15 million and the value immediately afterwards does not exceed £16 million **[see 5.3.6]**.

Example 24.1

A proposed investment of £1 million by Croce VCT should qualify, if the gross assets of Aosta Ltd at 10 December 2003 prior to investment by Croce VCT were valued as follows:

	Balance sheet Values £000
Buildings at cost	10,500
Machinery	500
Vehicles	1,800
Current Assets	2,000
Total Assets	14,800

If the buildings were valued at £10.8 million the proposed investment would not qualify.

24.6.11 Provisional clearance refused

If the SCEC has any doubts that the company will qualify, it will decline to give clearance and spell out its doubts in full. The SCEC has a responsibility to potential investors as they are likely to decide whether or not to invest in the company on the basis of what it says. If it is of the opinion that the proposed investment would not qualify, there is no right of appeal. What therefore can be done?

If it is thought that the SCEC is justified in taking its stance, the proposed investment may have to be abandoned. If, however, it has indicated what it finds objectionable, it might be persuaded to think again if adjustments are made to the proposals. Beware of changing a project to get within the VCT or EIS rules where this does not make commercial sense. In such a case it is often better for the investee company to pursue another source of finance. If it is not clear whether SCEC is correct to refuse the clearance it would be worth taking expert advice on whether to accept its answer.

24.7 EIS four-month period

24.7.1 Meeting the condition

The procedure for obtaining tax-relief certificates for EIS investors does not normally start until the company has issued the EIS shares and either the company or one of its subsidiaries has carried on the qualifying activities for four months (TA 1988, s 289A(7)).

Assuming the trade or the research and development has been carried on for four months, form EIS 1 can be submitted. The inspector will, however, need to satisfy himself that all the conditions for the relief which relate to the company appear to be satisfied (TA 1988, s 289A (6)). A company that is preparing to trade has two years from the date of the EIS share issue to start its qualifying trade **[see 6.2.1]**.

24.7.2 Where a company is wound up

In order to claim EIS relief a company would normally have to carry on its qualifying trade for four months. However, an exception is made where the company or subsidiary is wound up or dissolved. A condition of this exception is that the winding-up or dissolution must be for bona fide commercial reasons and not be part of a tax avoidance scheme TA 1988, 289A (8)).

24.8 Tax-relief certificates for EIS investors

24.8.1 Submission of form EIS 1

To obtain tax-relief certificates for the shareholders, form EIS 1 must be submitted by the company stating that it has and will be able to satisfy the conditions of the EIS (TA 1988, s 306(3)). The form EIS 1 can be submitted when the company has completed its four-month qualifying period (TA 1988, s 289A(7)). If the money raised is for more than one company in the group, for example, for the EIS company and two of its UK subsidiaries, it is the Inland Revenue's view that form EIS 1 cannot be submitted until all the companies have been trading for four months (Venture Capital Schemes Manual, para VCM 21050). Form EIS 1 can be obtained from the company's inspector.

A company must send in a form EIS 1 for EIS shares no later than two years after the end of the tax year in which the shares were issued or, if the company's four months, trading ended after the end of that tax year, no later than two years after the end of that period. This time limit is not affected by the deeming of shares to be issued in earlier years for purposes of the carry-back relief (TA 1988, s 306(3A)). Form EIS 1 is reproduced in **Appendix 6**.

24.8.2 Information required

The company must complete a separate form EIS 1 for each date on which EIS shares are issued. The information to be provided on the EIS 1 is as follows:

(*a*) the company's reference number at the SCEC office where its affairs are being dealt with – if there is no such number, because, for example, no informal clearance has been sought, see below;

(*b*) the company's name, address of the registered office, date of incorporation and company registration number;

(*c*) a brief description of the trade or business, for example, 'ship chartering' or 'house building';

(*d*) the date the trade or activity started – check to see whether this agrees with the date given on the Inland Revenue form CT 41G (Notification of a new company). If it does not, give an explanation in the covering letter;

(*e*) the names and addresses of the EIS shareholders, the number and description of shares issued to them and the amount subscribed in most cases there is too little room for this information on the form, it is therefore usually provided on a schedule headed with the date the shares were issued, which is sent as an attachment to the EIS 1. If the shares are held in the name of a nominee company, this should be stated as follows:
'XY Nominees Ltd (see list of the beneficial owners attached)';

(*f*) the issued share capital of the company immediately after the issue of the EIS shares – each class of share needs to be described separately, stating the number of shares issued and the total amount subscribed. Non-EIS shares should be included, even where they have been issued otherwise than for cash and further details given in the covering letter;

(*g*) the loan capital immediately after the EIS issue, showing the amount, nature of loan and name and address of the lender – note that there is a wide meaning given to loan capital but it excludes bank overdrafts;

(*h*) details of shares (EIS and non-EIS) already issued to the EIS shareholders before the share issue that is the subject of the EIS 1 – if there are many shareholders in this category, or if shareholders have had shares issued on several occasions, it is advisable to attach a separate schedule;

(*i*) details of changes in the company's share capital between the date of the EIS share issue that is the subject of the EIS 1 and the date of signing the declaration on the form – this would include further share issues and any redemption of shares;

(*j*) details of value received by shareholders **[see Chapter 12]** from the company or any subsidiary in the shareholder's relevant period;

(*k*) an indication as to whether the EIS capital was raised for a trade or research and development to be carried on by the EIS company and/or by a subsidiary;

(*l*) details of all companies that have been subsidiaries at any time since the issue of the EIS shares that are the subject of the EIS 1;

(*m*) at the end of the EIS 1 there is a declaration that, to the best of the company's knowledge and belief, it meets the conditions for the relief, so far as they apply in relation to the company and its activities, and has done so at all times since the beginning of the relevant period.

Having completed and signed form EIS 1, the company should send it with a covering letter to the SCEC office dealing with the company's affairs. If there is as yet no such office, the form should be sent to SCEC headquarters. For the address, and the role of the SCEC, see **24.6.2**.

Form EIS 1 should be completed and signed by the company secretary or a director acting in the capacity of the company secretary. If the company is in liquidation it is completed by the liquidator.

24.8.3 Penalties

Where a company has made statements on the EIS 1 either fraudulently or negligently, it is liable to a penalty not exceeding £3,000 (TA 1988, s 306(6)).

24.8.4 Inland Revenue procedure on receipt of the EIS 1

This is best described in the Inland Revenue's own guidance.

> 'A company cannot be authorised to issue certificates to its investors [EIS 3 certificates] unless it has submitted a statement on form EIS 1 . . . and the inspector is satisfied that:
>
> (*a*) all the information given on form EIS 1 is correct and
> (*b*) there is no reason not to accept the declaration given on the form.
>
> If so satisfied, the inspector must give the authorisation even if it appears that none of the subscribers listed will be able to obtain relief (see *Wild v Cannavan* (1997) 70 TC 554). It is therefore not necessary to consider the identity of the subscribers at this stage.
>
> In examining the statement the inspector will consider whether any of the information supplied at any 'advance assurance' stage has proved inaccurate, and will explore any matters about which unsupported statements were originally accepted. Where only draft documents were previously seen (for example, a draft prospectus) the final document will be obtained and examined. If the company did not seek an assurance in advance, all the items [to be supplied with the application for informal clearance] will now need to be supplied.
>
> As with the giving of advance assurances, the Revenue is normally bound by a decision to authorise relief, so the company's statement will be considered very carefully and any necessary clarification obtained before a decision is made . . .

If form EIS 1 shows that any of the listed subscribers, or any associate of such a person, has received value the implications of this for the availability of relief need to be considered. In any case where the amount of income tax relief which might be claimed by any subscriber will be affected the inspector and the company should agree the amount to be recorded on the form EIS 3 to be issued to that subscriber.

If satisfied that everything on the form is correct the inspector will authorise the company to issue certificates to those subscribers who have requested them . . .

If, after obtaining all necessary information, the inspector decides that not everything on the form EIS 1 is correct, a formal refusal to authorise the issue of certificates to the subscribers will be sent. The refusal will normally be in the following form:

"The company's statement on form EIS 1 relating to the share issue made on [date] and dated [date form duly signed] has been duly considered and I hereby give notice of my decision as follows: authority to issue certificates under section 306(2), Income and Corporation Taxes Act 1988 is refused. The grounds of this decision are that the statement is not correct in the following respect[s]: [specify] . . ." '

(Venture Capital Schemes Manual, paras VCM 21060–21080)

24.8.5 Appeals against refusal to authorise certificates

If after the company has submitted an EIS 1 and has provided the inspector with any further information, he then refuses to authorise the issue of form EIS 2, (refusal will take the form described in **24.8.4**) this refusal is a decision refusing a claim by the company (TA 1988, s 306(10)). The company can therefore appeal to the Commissioners of Inland Revenue. Its right to do so is made explicit in the SCEC's letter of refusal.

24.8.6 Form EIS 2

If, on the other hand, the inspector is satisfied that a company qualifies under the EIS, he will complete and sign an EIS 2, which is the authority for the company to issue to each shareholder a tax-relief certificate – Form EIS 3 (TA 1988, s 306(4)).

24.8.7 Contents of Form EIS 3

Form EIS 3 is in two parts. Part 1 is in the form of a declaration by the company secretary or one of the directors of the company or a liquidator, that the EIS conditions, as far as they relate to the company and its activities, are satisfied. It includes the following:

(*a*) the subscriber's name and address with post code;
(*b*) a description of the shares issued;
(*c*) the company's name and tax reference number;
(*d*) the date the certificate was authorised;
(*e*) the address of the registered office of the company;
(*f*) the signature of the company secretary, director or liquidator.

The second part of the EIS 3 is a claim for relief by the investor and includes the following:

(*a*) the name and reference number of the investor's tax district;
(*b*) a declaration that:
   (1) the investor subscribed for the shares on his or her own behalf, or alternatively, the name and address of the person who subscribed as the investor's nominee,
   (2) the investor's subscription was not for the avoidance of tax,
   (3) the investor is not 'connected with the company' **[see 7.6.2]**,
   (4) the investor is not disqualified because of the replacement capital provisions **[see 7.6.4]**,
   (5) the investor has not received any value from the company **[see Chapter 12]** or if he or she has received value, the amount of that value;
(*c*) the investor's claim for investment relief in the tax year in which the shares were issued and/or the previous year **[see 9.4]**.

The EIS 3 is then signed and dated by the investor or, if the investor has died, by his or her personal representative, and sent to the tax office dealing with the investor's affairs.

24.8.8 Form EIS 5

Where a person invests in EIS companies through an approved EIS fund **[see 7.6.5]**, the fund manager receives the EIS 3s and sends each investor a form EIS 5, which is a summary of the information from several EIS 3s (TA 1988, s 311(4)). Part of the EIS 5 is similar to part 2 of the EIS 3 and enables the investor to claim his or her EIS relief.

In addition, the manager of an approved EIS fund is required to make a return to the inspector within the time specified on the notice of the holdings of eligible shares shown on certificates issued by it during a particular year (TA 1988, s 311(5)).

24.8.9 Penalties

Where a company has issued a form EIS 3 without authority or has made fraudulent or negligent statements on form EIS 1 or part 1 of form EIS 3, it is liable to a penalty not exceeding £3,000 (TA 1988, s 306(6)). There is no similar penalty for form EIS 5 (TA 1988, s 311 (6)).

Where an investor makes a fraudulent or negligent VCT or EIS claim he or she is liable to a penalty equal to the correct tax payable less the amount paid (TMA 1970, s 95).

24.8.10 Claiming EIS investment relief

A claim for EIS investment relief must be made by the investor no later than the fifth anniversary of the 31 January following the tax year for which the claim is made (TA 1988, s 306(1)(b)). As with all claims under self-assessment, it must be made, if at all possible, in the investor's self-assessment tax return or amended return. The required details in respect of each holding of shares should be copied from the EIS 3 (or EIS 5, for fund investors) into the space reserved at the end of the return for further information.

Investors making repayment returns (on forms R40) may use that form to make a claim.

Where it is too late for the return to be amended, and in the case of investors who do not make self-assessment returns, the investor should write claiming relief – the Inland Revenue prefers these 'stand-alone' claims to be made using the claim section of form EIS 3 (or EIS 5, as appropriate).

A claim does not become final, and relief is not finally confirmed, until the tax return on which it is made (subject to the above) is no longer legally capable of amendment. However, a measure of relief can be obtained 'in-year' by requesting an adjustment to the investor's PAYE code number (where he or she has one) or by claiming a reduction in payments on account for the year.

24.8.10.1 *Extension of time limit*

The time limit in **24.8.10** is extended where the relief can be given in an assessment that is made in order to make good tax lost as a result of fraudulent or negligent conduct (TMA 1970, s 36(3)).

Following a 'discovery' assessment under TMA 1970, s 29, a claim that would otherwise be out of time may be made no later than 12 months from the end of the tax year in which the assessment is made (TMA 1970, s 43A (2)).

24.8.11 Revenue procedure on checking claims

The Inland Revenue's internal instructions on receiving claims for investment relief are as follows:

The inspector will be expected to consider the following matters:

(*a*) Was the investor employed by the company or was the investor a paid director of the company at any time within the two years before the share issue? If so, the matter should be reported to the SCEC inspector who authorised the issue of the EIS 3 forms for him or her to decide whether the investor is a qualifying individual.

(*b*) Will the relief fall within the maximum allowed (now £200,000) for the year in question?

(*c*) Where the investor is making a carry-back claim, were the relevant shares issued before 6 October and will the total for the previous year fall within the permitted maximum for that year?

(*d*) Does the amount on which relief is claimed tally with the amount shown on part 1 of the EIS 3, and is the claim for the correct year?

(*e*) If part 1 of EIS 3 shows that any value has been received, has the amount on which relief is claimed been taken into account?

Where the investment on which relief is claimed exceeds £10,000, the papers are normally reviewed by higher line management before approval

(Venture Capital Schemes Manual, para VCM 25490)

When an EIS claim has been accepted the following action is taken:

(*a*) Form EIS 4 is completed in duplicate and the top copy sent to the inspector dealing with the company so that he or she will have a record of the relief given and be able to identify false certificates.

(*b*) A photocopy of part 2 of the EIS 3 or EIS 5 is sent to the Economics and Statistics Office under cover of form EIS 9.

(*c*) A permanent note of the shares on which relief is being given, the amount of the subscription and the amount on which the relief is given, is made on the front of the folder EIS 8, which holds the papers relating to claims for relief. This enables staff, *inter alia*, to determine the capital gains tax consequences when the shares are disposed of

(Venture Capital Schemes Manual, para VCM 25500).

The inspector at the SCEC who receives the form EIS 4 will check in every case that the name of the investor and the amount invested tallies with the information given on form EIS 1. The inspector will also consider whether the investor is entitled to claim the relief obtained. This involves consideration of all the circumstances surrounding the share issue. Is there, for example, some indication that the subscription may not have been for bona fide commercial reasons? This might be suggested by an excessive premium or the fact that the company appears to be 'hopelessly insolvent'. Exceptionally, according to the Manual, there may be evidence that the investor had received a loan or had an option to sell the shares (Venture Capital Schemes Manual, para VCM 21090).

24.9 The approval procedure for the CVS

24.9.1 Introduction

A company hoping to attract CVS investment may apply to the Inland Revenue for an advance clearance before issuing shares (FA 2000, Sch 15, para 89(1)). Applications should be sent to the Small Companies Enterprise Centre (SCEC – **see 24.6.2**) at Cardiff. Note that, in contrast to the VCT scheme and the EIS, this process is statutory.

24.9.2 Information and applications

The advance clearance notice will state that the Inland Revenue is (or will be) satisfied that the requirements for qualifying investee companies and qualifying investments **[see 5.12 to 5.17]** are met. It will be given on the basis of the particulars, assurances and statements of intent given by the investee company (FA 2000, Sch 15, para 89(2), (3)).

The application for advance clearance must contain the particulars, undertakings and declarations required by the Inland Revenue, and disclose all material facts and circumstances (FA 2000, Sch 15, para 89(4)). Inland Revenue Statement of Practice SP 1/00 states that the application should include the following:

(*a*) the name of the company's tax office and the tax reference (or the address of its registered office if it is newly formed and the tax office is not yet known);
(*b*) the latest financial statements, and details of any material events subsequent to the accounts;
(*c*) any document to be made available to prospective investors;
(*d*) a draft copy of any subscription agreements;
(*e*) as regards the issuing company, confirmation that the requirements relating to unquoted status, independence, individual owners, partnerships and joint ventures are met – sufficient information must be supplied to determine whether subsidiaries will be qualifying subsidiaries and whether the gross assets test will be satisfied, and there must be a description of each activity comprised in a trade carried on by the company;
(*f*) details as to the number, nominal value, rights and price of the shares to be issued to investors seeking investment relief;
(*g*) details as to the activity for which the money raised will be used and confirmation that it will be carried on wholly or mainly in the UK; and
(*h*) undertakings that the money will be used within the set time, that corporate investors seeking investment relief are subscribing in cash, that the share issue is for commercial reasons and not for tax avoidance purposes, and that there are no guaranteed exit arrangements etc.

The Inland Revenue must respond to the application within 30 days of receiving it. During this period, it may issue an advance clearance notice, a notice requiring further information (an 'information notice'), or notify the applicant of its refusal to issue the notice (FA 2000, Sch 15, paras 90(1)(2), 91(1)).

If the shares are issued before the advance clearance notice is given, the Inland Revenue does not have to proceed with the application (FA 2000, Sch 15, para 91(3)).

24.9.3 Information notices

Any information notice issued by the Inland Revenue will specify the time limit for providing additional information, which must not be less than 30 days. If the applicant misses that deadline the Inland Revenue need not proceed with the application (FA 2000, Sch 15, para 90(2), (3)).

Within 30 days of the receipt of all the information required by the information notice, the Inland Revenue must either issue the advance clearance notice or notify the applicant of its refusal to do so. Where the Inland Revenue has issued more than one information notice in respect of an application, that 30-day time limit runs from the receipt of information required by the last information notice that was issued (FA 2000, Sch 15, para 91(1), (2)).

24.9.4 Appeals

If the Inland Revenue refuses to issue the advance clearance notice or does not meet the deadline for a reply, the investee company may require the Inland Revenue to pass the application, information notices and replies thereto to the Special Commissioners for their review. Where the Special Commissioners notify their satisfaction as to the details covered by an advance clearance notice, that notification has the same effect as an advance clearance notice (FA 2000, Sch 15, para 91(4), (5)).

24.9.5 Effect of advance clearances

Once a clearance is given, the requirements to which it relates are treated as satisfied. However, if there is anything less than full and accurate disclosure of material facts and circumstances or the applicant, or its subsidiaries, fails to live up to its assurances, or statements of intent, the advance clearance notice is void (FA 2000, Sch 15, para 92).

24.10 Clearance certificates for CVS investors

24.10.1 Claiming investment relief

In brief, the statutory procedure for claiming CVS investment relief is as follows:

(*a*) the investee company supplies the Inland Revenue with a compliance statement, which gives details about the preconditions of the relief in so far as they do not relate to the investor company;
(*b*) if the Inland Revenue is satisfied with that statement, it issues the investee company with a blank compliance certificate;
(*c*) the investee company completes the compliance certificate, which it then sends to the investor company;
(*d*) if the investor company considers itself to be a qualifying investor company under the CVS rules, it claims investment relief on its self-assessment tax return.

24.10.2 Investing company's entitlement to claim

The investor company may claim the relief if it is under the impression that the requirements for the relief are satisfied. However, a claim for relief cannot be made unless two additional preconditions are satisfied:

(*a*) the funded trade must have been carried on by the investee company or its subsidiary for at least four months (disregarding any time spent preparing to carry on that trade);
(*b*) the investor company must have received a compliance certificate (CVS 3) from the investee company.

The funded trade, referred to in (*a*) above, is the trade that meets the requirement as to the use of the money raised **[see 5.12.4]** in respect of the relevant issue of shares. A claim for relief may be made if the funded trade has not been carried on for four months if this is because the trading company is wound up or dissolved, or is in administration or receivership. This is provided that the winding-up etc was for genuine commercial reasons, and was not part of a scheme or arrangement **[see 5.17.7]** with a main purpose to avoid tax.

The investee company can only provide the investor company with a compliance certificate if it has authority from the Inland Revenue to do so. In order to obtain the Inland Revenue's authority, the investee company must send a compliance statement to the SCEC (FA 2000, Sch 15, paras 40, 41(2), (3)).

24.10.3 Time limits

There is no specific time limit for claiming CVS investment relief. Accordingly, the general time limit for making claims applies, whereby claims must be made within six years of the end of the accounting period to which the relief relates (FA 1998, Sch 18, para 55).

A claim cannot be made by the investor company before it delivers a company tax return for the period to which the claim relates. The investor company cannot apply to postpone paying tax pending an appeal on the grounds that a claim for investment relief will be made; in other words, it has to make a claim for the relief before it can apply to postpone paying the tax as a result of the relief claimed (FA 1998, Sch 18, para 9; FA 2000, Sch 15, para 40(7), Sch 16, para 5(1), (3)).

24.10.4 Compliance statements

The compliance statement states that the preconditions for investment relief, in so far as they do not relate to the investor company, are satisfied and have been since the shares were issued.

The statement is made on a form CVS 1, available from the Inland Revenue's Corporate Venturing Scheme Unit at Somerset House **[see 24.10.8]** or from the Small Company Enterprise Centre (SCEC). The CVS 1 may be submitted no earlier than the later of (*a*) four months after the funded trade has begun and (*b*) the date on which the shares are issued. It must be submitted no later than the later of (*a*) two years after the end of the accounting period in which the issue took place and (*b*) the second anniversary of the beginning of the funded trade.

The statement must contain any additional information reasonably required by the Inland Revenue, a declaration that it is correct to the best of the investee company's knowledge and belief, and any other declarations that the Inland Revenue reasonably requires.

24.10.5 Compliance certificates

Once it has had the opportunity to examine the CVS 1, the Inland Revenue (in the person of the SCEC) will, if it is satisfied, issue the investee company with authority to issue a compliance certificate (form CVS 3) to investors. The CVS 3 (analogous to EIS 3) certifies that, from the investee company's point of view, the requirements for investment relief are for the time being met in relation to the shares.

24.10.6 Refusal and appeal

If, after having examined the CVS 1 and the company's tax file, the SCEC refuses to authorise the investee company to issue the CVS 3, it must inform the company of this and its reasons in writing. The company has the right to appeal, within 30 days, to the Commissioners (FA 2000, Sch 15, para 43).

24.10.7 Penalties

A company that issues a compliance certificate (CVS 3) without authority, or fraudulently or negligently, is liable to a penalty of up to £3,000 (FA 2000, Sch 15, para 44).

24.10.8 Informal approaches by investor companies

There is no advance clearance procedure for investor companies, but if they have any queries concerning interpretation of the CVS rules, they are welcome to approach the Corporate Venturing Scheme Unit, located at:

New Wing
Somerset House
Strand
LONDON
WC2R 1LB
telephone: 020 7438 4485

Chapter 25

Information Powers and Requirements

25.1 Introduction

This chapter concludes the survey in Part 8 of administration and procedures by looking at the information powers and requirements of the Inland Revenue in administering the available tax reliefs, and on its obligations to provide information. For the information that needs to be supplied in claiming relief and seeking advance clearances etc, see **Chapter 24**.

25.1.1 Scope of this chapter

This chapter covers the following areas:

(*a*) Information requirements relating to the VCT scheme **[see 25.2]**
(*b*) Information requirements relating to the EIS **[see 25.3]**
(*c*) Information requirements relating to the CVS **[see 25.4]**

25.2 Information requirements relating to the VCT scheme

25.2.1 Events causing investment relief to be lost

Investors who have received VCT investment relief are obliged to notify the Inland Revenue within 60 days of becoming aware of the occurrence of any event that gives rise to a reduction or withdrawal of that relief (TA 1988, Sch 15B, para 5(1)).

If the inspector has reason to believe that an investor has not let the Inland Revenue know of such an event when he or she ought to have done, the inspector has the power to issue a notice to that investor, requiring him or her to supply whatever information is specified in the notice, which it is reasonable for the Inland Revenue to require. The investor must be allowed no less than 60 days in which to comply (TA 1988, Sch 15B, para 5(2)).

25.2.2 Refusal and withdrawal of approval

The Inland Revenue's refusal to approve a company's application for VCT status must be given in writing, be dated, and contain the reasons for refusal. The company has the right to appeal to the Special Commissioners (SI 1995/1979, reg 4).

Subsequent to approval, if the Inland Revenue decides to withdraw its approval, it must again do so in writing; give the date from which the withdrawal has effect; and give its reasons. The company again has the right to appeal to the Special Commissioners (SI 1995/1979, reg 5).

For details of the application process, see **24.2.**

25.2.3 Notices and returns

For the information and returns that the company needs to supply, see **24.2.5.2.**

25.2.4 General information power

The Inland Revenue has the right to demand of any company that is or has been a VCT and of any person who holds or has held shares in an existing or former VCT to provide it with any information that it might reasonably require for the purposes of the VCT scheme. The company or person must have at least 14 days to comply (SI 1995/1979, reg 24).

The Inland Revenue also has the power to require those companies or persons to make available for inspection any accounts, records or other information in their possession or under their control. The information specified must be no more than is reasonable for the purposes of the VCT scheme. Where the records are contained on a computer, facilities for obtaining that information should be made available to the Inland Revenue officer making the inspection (SI 1995/1979, reg 25).

25.3 Information requirements relating to the EIS

25.3.1 Introduction

Because the EIS reliefs are dependent on the satisfaction of specified conditions throughout an extended period of time, it is necessary for the Inland Revenue to be informed either about any changed circumstances that might cause investment relief to be withdrawn **[see Chapter 12]** or about a chargeable event for deferral relief **[see Chapter 15]**. An investor who has obtained relief and a company that has issued EIS shares are required to notify the inspector of any such changed circumstances or chargeable event. To supplement this provision, the inspector is empowered to obtain information if he or she has reason to believe that relief should be withdrawn or a chargeable event has occurred.

25.3.2 Information to be supplied by the investor

If an investor becomes aware that any of the following events has occurred which gives rise to withdrawal of investment relief, he or she must within 60 days notify the inspector in writing:

(*a*) the investor's ceasing to be a qualifying individual, for example, by becoming connected with the company **[see 7.6]**;
(*b*) a disposal of the investor's shares or the grant of an option to dispose of them **[see 18.1.2]**;
(*c*) receipt of a loan linked to the issue of the shares **[see 7.3.4]**;
(*d*) receipt by the investor of value from the company **[see 12.5]**.

Notification must also be given where a receipt of value would have given rise to withdrawal of relief but for the 'replacement value' provisions **[see 12.7]**. In all cases a notice under this provision should include details of the replacement value received (or expected to be received) where this is within the knowledge of the person giving the notice. (TA 1988, s 310(1)(2A)).

In relation to deferral relief, if an investor who has claimed relief becomes aware that any of the following events has occurred, he or she must similarly notify the inspector in writing within 60 days:

(*a*) the investor disposes of any of the eligible shares (other than to a spouse) before the termination date in relation to those shares;
(*b*) the investor becomes non-resident in the UK before the termination date in relation to those shares;
(*c*) the shares cease to be eligible shares because:
    (1) an option has been granted in respect of the shares **[see 18.2.2]**,
    (2) the investor has received value from the company **[see 12.5]**, or
    (3) the investor has received an investment-linked loan **[see 7.34]**; or
(*d*) the shares would have ceased to be eligible shares as a result of the receipt of value from the company but for the 'replacement value' rules **[see 12.7]** – in this case, the notice must include particulars of the replacement value

(TCGA 1992, Sch 5B, para 16(1), (2A), (3A)).

25.3.3 Information to be supplied by the company or a connected person

If the company, or any connected person (within TA 1988, s 839) who has knowledge of the matter, becomes aware that any of the following events has occurred which gives rise to withdrawal of investment relief, the inspector must be notified in writing within 60 days:

(*a*) the money raised has not been used for the purpose of a qualifying business activity within the time limits **[see 5.7.5 above]**;
(*b*) the company ceases to be a qualifying company **[see 5.7]**;

(*c*) an investor or a non-EIS member receives value from the company **[see 12.5 to 12.9]**;
(*d*) the company acquires a trade or a company by way of replacement capital **[see 7.6.4]**;
(*f*) the active company ceases to carry on a qualifying trade or ceases to be a 90% subsidiary **[Chapter 6 and 5.11.1]**.

Notification must also be given where a receipt of value after 6 March 2001 would have given rise to withdrawal of relief but for the replacement-value provisions **[see 12.7]**. In all cases a notice under this provision should include details of the replacement value received (or expected to be received) where this is within the knowledge of the person giving the notice. (TA 1988, s 310(2), (2A), (3)).

In relation to deferral relief, the company, or any connected person who has knowledge of the matter, must within 60 days of any of the following events (or within 60 days of the person's coming to know of it) notify the inspector in writing. The events are those where:

(*a*) the company ceases to be a qualifying company, ie ceases to satisfy the conditions described in **5.7**;
(*b*) the subsidiary carrying on the qualifying business activity ceases to be a 90% subsidiary **[see 5.11.1 above]**;
(*c*) an investor (or associate) receives value from the company **[see 12.5]**;
(*d*) another shareholder receives value from the company **[see 12.8]**;
(*e*) the money raised by the share issue is not used for the purpose of a qualifying business activity within the prescribed time limits **[see 5.11.1]**.

In the case of (*c*) above, where replacement value has been received, the notice must include particulars of that replacement value. (TCGA 1992, Sch 5B, para 16(2), (2A), (3A), (4), (4A); FA 2001, Sch 15, paras 28, 35(2), (3), (5), 40).

25.3.4 The Inland Revenue's request for information

In relation to investment relief or deferral relief, if the inspector has reason to believe that:

(1) a person has not given a notice of changed circumstances which he or she is required to give **[see 25.3.2 and 25.3.3]**;
(2) a person has given or received value after 6 March 2001 which, but for the fact that the amount was an amount of insignificant value, would have triggered a requirement to give a notice; or
(3) a person has made or received any repayment etc of share capital after 6 March 2001 which, but for the fact that it was an insignificant repayment **[see 12.6]**, would have triggered a requirement to give a notice,

he or she may issue a notice to that person to furnish him or her within a specified time (not less than 60 days) with such information relating to the changed circumstances as the inspector may reasonably require.

If the inspector has reason to believe that relief has been claimed where there is a scheme or arrangement that would deny relief in one of the following circumstances, he or she may issue a notice to the investor, the company, a person controlling the company or connected with the company and a spouse to whom the investor may have transferred shares. The notice may require a declaration in writing as to whether such a scheme or arrangement exists or has existed and information that the inspector may reasonably require and which the addressee has or can reasonably obtain.

In relation to investment relief, the schemes or arrangements concerned relate to:

(*a*) the issue of shares under a non-commercial arrangement to avoid tax **[see 7.1.6.9]**;
(*b*) subscription for shares under a reciprocal arrangement **[see 7.6.1.4]**;
(*c*) arrangements for the company to control another company (other than a qualifying subsidiary) or to be controlled by another company **[see 5.10]**;
(*d*) pre-arranged exits **[see 7.6.1.5]**;
(*e*) reduction of the company's interest in any of its subsidiaries below 75% **[see 5.1.11]**.

In relation to deferral relief, the schemes or arrangements concerned relate to:

(1) the issue of shares under a non-commercial arrangement to avoid tax **[see 15.5.1]**;
(2) arrangements for the company to control another company (other than a qualifying subsidiary) or to be controlled by another company **[see 5.10]**;
(3) pre-arranged exits **[see 15.4.7]**;
(4) reduction of the company's interest in any of its subsidiaries below 75% **[see 5.1.11]**.

Where any person receives from the company a payment or asset that may constitute value received (in relation to investment relief see **12.5** to **12.9**, and for deferral relief see **7.20** and **15.8** to **15.11**), the inspector may require that person to state whether the payment was received on behalf of another person, and if so to give the name and address of that other person.

Where a company has issued shares that have qualified for EIS investment relief or deferral relief, any person who holds or has held shares in that company may be required to state whether the shares were held on behalf of another person, and if so to give the name and address of that other person.

The inspector may disclose to a company that EIS investment relief or deferral relief has been given or claimed in respect of particular shares (TA 1988, s 310(4)–(9); TCGA 1992, Sch 5B, para 16(5)–(10)).

25.3.5 Penalties

Any person who is required to give notice of an event listed above who fails to do so is liable to a penalty not exceeding £300, and if the failure continues after the penalty is imposed, to a further penalty not exceeding £60 for each day on which the failure continues. A similar penalty is imposed for failure to supply information in reply to an inspector's notice under these provisions.

A person who fraudulently or negligently supplies incorrect information in reply to an inspector's request under these provisions is liable to a penalty not exceeding £3,000.

An EIS investor who fraudulently or negligently makes an incorrect claim for EIS relief is liable to a penalty not exceeding the difference between the amount of tax paid and the amount that would have been paid if a correct claim had been made (TMA 1970, ss 95, 98(1), (2)).

25.4 Information requirements relating to the CVS

25.4.1 Notices relating to withdrawal of relief

Where CVS investment relief needs to be reduced or withdrawn, notices must be issued where the reason for the withdrawal is because:

(*a*) the investee company proves not to be a qualifying investee company in relation to the shares in question; or
(*b*) the general requirements as to the investment itself (in FA 2000, Sch 15, Part IV – see **5.17**) are not satisfied; or
(*c*) value is received by the investing company or other persons.

In these circumstances, either the investee company or the Inland Revenue must give notice. In the case of the investee company, the notice must comply with the requirements set out in **25.4.3**. In the case of the Inland Revenue, it must specify the grounds for the withdrawal or reduction in a notice to the investee company and, in the case of a receipt of value, to the investor company.

25.4.2 Information to be provided by the investor company

The investor company must give the Inland Revenue notice if any of the following three events happens:

(*a*) anything happens to disqualify the investor company **[see 5.17]**;
(*b*) there is any receipt of value causing a withdrawal or reduction of relief **[see 13.4 to 13.7]**; or
(*c*) there is a grant of any put or call option causing a withdrawal or reduction of relief **[see 13.8]**.

The notice must give details of the event. If the event is the receipt of value and the investor company knows of any replacement value, received or expected, the notice must also give those details.

Normally the notice must be given within 60 days of the event or, when relevant, within 60 days of the date on which the investor company became aware that a connected person had received value. However, when the relevant event is the investor's failure to qualify for relief because a connected person received value and that occurred before the share issue then the time limit is 60 days after the investee company or the investor company becomes aware of that receipt (FA 2000, Sch 15, para 64).

25.4.3 Information to be provided by the investee company

The investee company, having provided a compliance statement, must give the Inland Revenue notice if any of three events happens:

(*a*) anything happens to disqualify the investee company **[see 5.12 to 5.16]**;
(*b*) the general requirements as to the investment itself **[see 5.12 and 5.14]** are not met; or
(*c*) there is any receipt of value by the investor company or other person **[see 13.4 to 13.7]**.

Any person connected with the investee company and who has knowledge of these events must also give notice of the details.

The notice must give details of the event. If the event is the receipt of value and the person giving the notice knows of any replacement value, received or expected, the notice must also give those details.

Normally the notice must be given within 60 days of the event or no more than 60 days after the investee company becomes aware that either it fails the individual-owner test or a connected person has received value. In the case of a person connected with the issuing company, the 60 days runs from the date of that person's first knowledge of the event. However, when the relevant event is a receipt of value then, if both the event and the knowledge of the person responsible for giving the notice pre-date the issue, the time limit is 60 days after the issue (FA 2000, Sch 15 para 65).

25.4.4 Information required by the Inland Revenue

In certain circumstances, the Inland Revenue may require the relevant person to provide certain information. The information is whatever the Inland Revenue reasonably requires. It may set a time limit of no less than 60 days for the provision of the information.

The circumstances are that the Inland Revenue has reason to believe that the company or another person satisfies one of two conditions. The first is that it has not given notice as required under the rules set out above. The second is that the company or person has given or received value that would have triggered an obligation to give notice had it not been of an insignificant amount **[see 13.7.4]** (FA 2000, Sch 15, para 66).

25.4.5 Penalties

Penalties may be imposed up to £3,000 under TMA 1970, s 98 if the information requirements are not satisfied.

25.4.6 Interest on withdrawn relief

Interest is due on any assessment for withdrawn relief under TMA 1970, s 87A from the due and payable date for the tax assessed or, if later, the date of the relevant event. The relevant events are failing to satisfy the requirements as to qualifying investor companies or qualifying investee companies; disposing of the shares; the receipt of value by the investor or other persons and the grant of put or call options (FA 2000, Sch 15, para 63).

Part 9

Practical Matters

Chapter 26

Small Private Schemes

26.1 Introduction

This final Part of the book is dedicated to exploring different ways of applying the venture capital schemes to practical business situations, particularly those facing growing and family businesses.

This chapter explores the possibility of investment by a small group of private investors, and also goes through the legal and administrative formalities of forming a company; **Chapter 27** discusses the public prospectus route for attracting a large number of outside investors, while **Chapter 28** concentrates on the other end of the process – how best to extract one's investment once (it is to be hoped) it has borne fruit.

Instead of investing through prospectus issues **[see Chapter 27]**, individuals may wish to invest in small private schemes with members of their family, friends or business colleagues.

This chapter describes how the EIS reliefs can be used by a small group of individuals to start, expand or rescue a business. Although most of the chapters in this book are relevant to the small private issue, the opportunity will be taken here to emphasise certain of the rules that are particularly important to the small issue.

26.1.1 Professional advisers

As the EIS rules are so complicated, the best course of action is to engage professional advisers to help set up the company and to advise the directors during the investment period on how to prevent withdrawal of the reliefs. In the case of EIS relief the directors can also obtain provisional clearance that the proposals satisfy the necessary conditions for the relief to be granted.

It is, nevertheless, understandable that where the proposed investment is say, £50,000 or less, the founders will want to do as much of the work themselves in order to reduce the professional fees. The contents of this book should go some way towards helping the directors of these very small companies to obtain and keep the tax reliefs.

26.1.2 Scope of this chapter

After defining some of the technical terms that are fundamental to the schemes, this chapter examines the following:

(*a*) The meaning of 'associates' **[see 26.2]**
(*b*) EIS reliefs in outline **[see 26.3]**
(*c*) The EIS deferral relief in outline **[see 26.4]**
(*d*) How the EIS investment and deferral reliefs compare **[see 26.5]**
(*e*) What is involved in setting up a company **[see 26.6]**
(*f*) The share issue **[see 26.7]**
(*g*) The directors' responsibilities **[see 26.8]**
(*h*) How to avoid losing the reliefs **[see 26.9]**

26.1.3 The EIS company's 'relevant period'

Most conditions relating to the EIS investee company need to remain satisfied throughout what is known as the 'relevant period'. For companies, this period begins with the date on which the shares are issued ('the issue date') and ends immediately before the 'termination date'. The termination date is the later of:

(*a*) the third anniversary of the issue date and
(*b*) the third anniversary of the date on which the qualifying trade begins

(TA 1988, s 312(1A)(b)).

See further **Chapter 5**. Other periods that may apply will be defined as they are mentioned.

26.1.4 The EIS investor's 'relevant period'

As we have seen from **Chapter 7** and *passim*, various different restricted periods apply to the investor. However, if in the rest of this chapter we refer to the investor's 'relevant period', this is the period that begins on the earlier of:

(*a*) the date of the company's incorporation and
(*b*) the date two years before the share issue

and ends immediately before the termination date **[see 26.1.3]** (TA 1988, s 312(1A)(a)). **[see further Chapter 7]**.

Other periods that may apply will be defined as they are mentioned.

26.1.5 Eligible shares

The investor must acquire eligible shares in an EIS qualifying company. Eligible shares are ordinary shares that carry no present or future preferential right to dividends or to a company's assets on its winding-up and no present or future right to be redeemed (TA 1988, s 289(7)).

26.1.6 Qualifying companies

Most unquoted companies that are carrying on, or are preparing to carry on, a trade, should be qualifying companies for EIS investment relief purposes. The company must either exist to carry on a qualifying trade or be the parent company of a trading group. During its relevant period, the company must not be controlled by another company or control another company unless the latter company is a qualifying subsidiary. There are also certain prohibited activities that it must not carry on to any substantial extent **[see Chapters 5 and 6]**.

26.2 Associates

26.2.1 Introduction

Where there is a small private issue it is important to understand that often the conditions for the relief apply not only to the investor but to his or her associates. In general terms, associates of an EIS investor are his or her close relatives, business partners and certain trustees and beneficiaries (TA 1988, s 312(1) and 417(3), (4)).

26.2.2 Relatives

Husbands and wives are associates for EIS purposes even if they are separated. Other relatives who are associates are children, grandchildren and great-grandchildren, parents, grandparents and great-grandparents. Relatives who are not treated as associates under the EIS are brothers, sisters, nephews, nieces, uncles, aunts, cousins, stepchildren and other relatives acquired by marriage (TA 1988, s 417(3)(a)).

26.2.3 Partners

A business partner is an associate (TA 1988, s 417(3)(a)). Whether a person is a partner depends on all the facts. A partnership is the relationship which subsists between persons carrying on a business in common with a view to profits (Partnership Act 1890, s 1). A person (which includes a company) is likely to be treated as a partner if he is:

(*a*) a member of the partnership by name (named on letterheads etc);
(*b*) entitled to a profit share;
(*c*) assessed to tax under Schedule D as part of the partnership, ie from the same tax reference number.

An individual is not normally treated as a partner if he or she is assessed to tax on earnings from employment (the former Schedule E), and tax is deducted under PAYE.

Individuals who are merely directors and shareholders of the same company are not partners.

A life partner, as opposed to a business partner, is not an associate as such.

26.2.4 Joint owners of property

Individuals who simply own property as an investment, share profits and losses equally and are assessed to tax under Schedule A or Schedule D, Case VI should not be treated as partners. However, if these individuals enter into a partnership agreement, agree to develop the property for sale, and use headed paper describing themselves as partners, these would be strong indications that they had entered into a partnership.

26.2.5 Trustees of related settlements

An associate of the EIS investor would be any trustee of a related settlement (TA 1988, s 417 (3)(b)). This would be a settlement where the investor or any relative (living or dead) was the settlor. For example, an EIS investor who settles property on a charitable trust would be an associate of its trustees.

A settlement includes any disposition, trust, covenant, agreement, arrangement or transfer of assets. A person is deemed to have made a settlement if he or she has made or entered into the settlement directly or indirectly, and if he or she has provided or undertaken to provide funds directly or indirectly for the purpose of the settlement, or has made with any other person a reciprocal arrangement for that other person to make or enter into the settlement (TA 1988, s 660 G(1), (2)).

26.2.6 Other trustees and personal representatives

An EIS investor is an associate of any trustees or personal representatives, if he or she is interested in any shares or obligations of a company which are subject to a trust or are part of a deceased person's estate. The EIS investor is interested in the shares if he or she is a beneficiary of the trust or the estate, a trustee, executor or administrator. This is a complex area where many of the terms used are open to interpretation. It is advisable for an EIS investor not to act as a personal representative of a deceased shareholder of the EIS company.

Furthermore, where a company accepts the duties as trustee and executor, care must be taken that a qualifying company (for VCT or EIS purposes) does not come under the control of that company **[see 7.5]**.

26.3 EIS relief

26.3.1 Four tax reliefs

EIS relief consists of four separate tax reliefs:

(*a*) investment relief against income tax on the amount subscribed for the shares **[see Chapter 9]**;

(*b*) deferral relief for gains arising on the disposal of another asset **[see Chapter 15]**;

(*c*) disposal relief by way of exemption for capital gains arising on the disposal of EIS shares after the termination date **[see Chapter 18]**; and

(*d*) loss relief on the disposal of EIS shares at any time by way of set-off against capital gains or taxable income **[see 18.6, 18.8 and 21.3]**.

26.3.2 EIS investment relief

Qualifying individuals **[see Chapter 7]** can obtain income tax relief on the amount subscribed for their shares. The initial relief is equal to 20% of the amount subscribed with a minimum subscription of £500 per company and a maximum subscription of £200,000 per individual per tax year (£150,000 for tax years before 2004–05). Husband and wife can each subscribe and claim investment relief on £200,000. The individual's tax liability for the year in which the shares are issued will be reduced by the EIS relief. However, a claim can be made to carry back to the previous tax year up to £25,000 of the subscription on qualifying investments made in the first six months of the tax year **[see 9.4.1]**. The investment relief is the subject of **Chapter 9**.

26.3.3 EIS deferral relief

To the extent that an individual subscribes wholly in cash for eligible shares in a qualifying company, he or she is able to defer gains arising on the disposal of any asset or on the occurrence of a 'chargeable event' causing an already deferred gain under these rules or under VCT deferral relief **[see Chapter 14]** to crystallise. Qualifying companies are broadly those that qualify for the purposes of EIS investment relief **[see Chapters 5 and 6]** but the difference between the rules for EIS deferral relief and investment relief are significant. They are broadly that:

(*a*) eligible shares for EIS deferral relief need not have received nor indeed qualify for EIS investment relief;
(*b*) the individual investor can be connected to the company;
(*c*) EIS deferral relief is available to trustees, whereas EIS investment relief is not.

See further **Chapter 15**.

26.3.4 EIS disposal relief

If the EIS conditions are met until the termination date **[see 26.1.3]** has elapsed, on the first disposal of the shares at any time thereafter, any capital gain is tax free. This is particularly attractive for the small EIS company where some individuals may well want to keep their shares for longer than the minimum three years.

26.3.5 EIS loss relief

If a loss is suffered on EIS shares at any time, the loss is an allowable loss and attracts income tax or capital gains tax relief **[see 18.6, 18.8 and 21.3]**.

26.3.6 Qualifying investors

In general terms, for an individual ('the investor') to qualify for investment relief and disposal relief under the EIS he or she must not, during the relevant period, be connected with the company **[see 7.6.2]**. An exception is made for EIS deferral relief, where there is no bar on connection. One of the ways in which an investor can become connected with the company is by being entitled to an interest of more than 30% in the company **[see 7.6.3]**. This is why it is often four individuals who set up a small EIS company, each owning 25% of the shares. For the 30% test the holdings of associates such as husband and wife are added together.

If an investor's EIS relief is to be preserved, he or she must meet the conditions of the scheme throughout a period of broadly at least five years **[see 26.1.3]**. This means that during that time he or she must not become connected with the company, receive value from the company **[see Chapter 12]** or dispose of the shares **[see Chapter 18]**.

Example 26.1

Acceptable share structures for small EIS investments where investment relief is claimed

The proprietor and EIS investors

	£000	*%*	*EIS?*
Bertrand	70	70	No
David	20	20	Yes
Thomas	10	10	Yes
	100	100	

Family members

	£000	*%*	*EIS*
George	20	10	Yes
Nicole (George's wife)	30	15	No*
Freddie	30	15	Yes
Kate (Freddie's wife)	30	15	Yes
Roger (Freddie's brother)	30	15	Yes
Vanessa (Nicole's mother)	40	20	Yes
Natasha (George's cousin)	20	10	Yes
	200	100	

* Nicole, with associates George and Vanessa, owns 45% of the share capital

26.3.7 Mix of loans and shares

There can be benefits in investing in an EIS company using a mix of loans and shares. Four people can obtain a 25% interest in a new company by subscribing as little as £500 each and providing, say, £9,500 by way of loans. This is particularly suitable where the company could be cash-rich within its relevant period. It is important to ensure that loans to the company are made after the EIS shares have been issued so that the value-received rules **[see 12.5.6]** do not apply when the loans are repaid.

The benefits are as follows:

(*a*) The CGT exemption is no less valuable if the shares are sold after the termination date at a gain.
(*b*) Most of the cash can be withdrawn if it is not needed in the company without having to wait for the termination date.
(*c*) There is less chance of having surplus cash and being forced to spend it on trading assets or paying a dividend.
(*d*) If the company fails, there will be a smaller loss on the shares to be set against the investor's income but the capital loss relief on loans to traders (TCGA 1992, s 253) should apply **[see 23.6]**.
(*e*) If the investor borrows to make a loan to the close company, income tax relief is likely to be available on the loan interest (TA 1988, s 360) **[see 21.8]**.

There are three potential disadvantages:

(*a*) Investment relief on subscriptions applies only to the £500 **[see 26.3.2]**.
(*b*) It is necessary to ensure that the loans are repaid evenly to avoid breaching the 30% limit **[see 7.6.3.3]**.
(*c*) There may be commercial reasons for wanting a larger share capital.

26.3.8 EIS provisional clearance

EIS provisional clearance is not essential but it is advisable. It is a request for the inspector to give an opinion as to whether the company and its trade or activity will qualify.

EIS provisional clearance applications should be sent to:

Small Company Enterprise Centre
TIDO
Tŷ Glas
Llanishen
Cardiff
CF14 5ZG

The staff at this centre will then forward the clearance to one of the Small Companies Enterprise Centre (SCEC) offices at Cardiff, Dundee or Maidstone, which are specialist units dealing, *inter alia*, with clearance applications for the EIS and the VCT scheme. For full details, see **24.6.2**. For the addresses of the SCEC offices, see **Appendix 5**.

It is important to give the SCEC sufficient time to consider the application. The recommended time is a minimum of three weeks; most applications are dealt with within 15 to 20 working days **[see 24.6.3]**.

26.3.9 Tax relief certificates

The company cannot obtain tax relief certificates for EIS investors until after it has issued the shares and has been carrying on the qualifying trade for four months **[see 24.7]**. There are no certificates or forms for claiming the EIS deferral relief. The claim should, if possible, be included in the investor's self-assessment tax return. Failing that, the investor could simply write to the inspector dealing with his or her affairs and give details of the gain and investment and claim to defer all or part of the gain, perhaps using the claim form attached to the EIS 3 certificate.

26.4 Further notes on EIS deferral relief

26.4.1 A résumé of EIS deferral relief

EIS deferral relief is available to individuals and trustees **[see 15.4]** who subscribe for eligible shares **[see 15.5.1]** in qualifying companies **[see 15.5.2]** up to one year before or up to three years after realising a gain **[see 15.3.2]**. The only tax benefit of the deferral relief is the ability to defer gains on other assets. However, it is the most generous of the three deferral reliefs described in Part 5 and is the only deferral relief that is available to trustees.

26.4.2 Persons who can claim the relief

Only claimants who are resident or ordinarily resident in the UK and not dually resident, both at the time they realise the gain and when they subscribe for the shares in the qualifying company, can claim the relief. It does not matter whether the individual has a UK domicile or not **[see 15.4.2]**.

The investor can either be a passive investor or be actively involved in the company's business, in which case he or she can be an employee or paid director or even control the company.

26.4.3 Traps for the unwary

There are many conditions to be met by the company and the investor (broadly, these are the EIS conditions generally) and they can easily trap the unwary. There are also anti-avoidance provisions **[see 15.4.6 and 15.4.7]** which, if they apply, will treat the gain as never having been deferred, which could leave the investor with a tax bill at a time when he or she is out of time for making another qualifying investment.

26.4.4 Inland Revenue clearance

As is the case with investment relief, deferral relief also has a provisional clearance procedure that can be used before making an investment **[see 26.3.8]**. Also, Chapter 4 of IR Booklet IR137, on the EIS, contains notes on deferral relief.

Chapter 15 of this book describes EIS deferral relief in more detail.

26.5 Comparison of the EIS investment and deferral reliefs

26.5.1 Advantages of EIS investment relief

The EIS investor:

(*a*) can obtain investment relief against income tax of 20% on his or her share subscription;
(*b*) obtains an exemption from capital gains tax on his or her EIS shares on a disposal after the termination date;
(*c*) need not be resident or ordinarily resident in the UK to claim investment relief, except where he or she wishes to defer a gain;
(*d*) can obtain provisional clearance before acquiring the shares; and
(*e*) will automatically qualify for EIS deferral relief.

26.5.2 Advantages of EIS deferral relief

The shares acquired by the investor need not have any investment relief attributable to them. The deferral-relief investor:

(*a*) has no monetary limit on the gains that can be deferred or the consideration paid for the shares in the qualifying investment (EIS investment relief imposes a £200,000 annual limit);
(*b*) can own 100% of the qualifying investment (EIS investment relief has a 30% limit);
(*c*) can be an employee of the company provided that the remuneration received is reasonable for the duties performed (EIS investment relief is not available to employees);
(*d*) can receive payments from the company for services that include management and secretarial services (not acceptable for EIS investment relief);
(*e*) can obtain relief even if the company acquires assets or a trade that belongs to a company in which that person and others owned a controlling interest ('replacement capital') (not acceptable for EIS investment relief).

26.6 Setting up a private company

26.6.1 Introduction

It is not essential to set up a new company in order to obtain EIS investment or deferral relief. If the plan is to raise capital for an existing business there is no need to read this section.

26.6.2 Business plans

To obtain EIS investment for a company, it is advisable for the founders to prepare a business plan that gives potential investors information about:

(*a*) who will manage the company, their experience and track record;
(*b*) the market for the company's product or service;
(*c*) the cash and profit projections for the company;
(*d*) if a trade is to be bought, details of the acquisition;
(*e*) details of any property that will be owned (purchased or built) by the company;
(*f*) the minimum and maximum amount of funds required and how they will be used; and
(*g*) how shareholders will be able to realise their investment after the termination date (a minimum of three years), for example, by liquidating the company.

If the founder is raising less than, say, £100,000 from a few people who know him or her, the business plan might be relatively short. If the scheme is more ambitious and more shareholders are involved, the plan needs to be more comprehensive. Some matters to be found in a business plan, such as directors' duties, how the proceeds of the share issue will be spent, the exit route etc, can also be included in a shareholders' agreement **[see 26.6.13]**.

26.6.3 Company law

The rules concerning setting up companies are governed by the Companies Act 1985 as amended, and the records are kept by the Registrar of Companies (the Registrar) whose address is shown in **Appendix 5**. There are various forms that need to be completed and sent to the Registrar. These can be obtained from law stationers. It is an offence for a company not to obey company law and fines are payable at the time of default and in some cases there is a daily default fine (CA 1985, Sch 24).

26.6.4 What kind of company?

For most private issues a private limited company is suitable. Public limited companies are described in **27.2.4.** A company comes into existence on the day its certificate of incorporation is issued by the Registrar. A private company can start its business immediately after incorporation.

26.6.5 Off-the-shelf companies

Rather than go to the trouble of forming a company, it is usually better to buy an 'off-the-shelf' company from company formation agents. The agents will have incorporated the company and any one of them will act as the first shareholder as well as the first-named director and company secretary. They will have produced a standard Memorandum of Association and set of Articles of Association. The directors and company secretary of the new company need to send the following particulars to the formation agents:

(*a*) a completed form 288a, which the new directors sign to say that they consent to act, and which gives their full names, addresses, nationalities and a list of any other directorships;
(*b*) the address of the registered office **[see 26.6.7]**;
(*c*) the company's name, if this is to be changed.

The agents then change the name and address of the registered office, notify the Registrar that they have resigned and a new director and company secretary have consented to act (CA 1985, s 288).

At this stage the directors of the new company receive from the formation agent:

(*a*) a stock transfer form in respect of the subscriber share;
(*b*) letters of resignation of the first director and company secretary;
(*c*) the Memorandum of Association **[see 26.6.8]** and Articles of Association **[see 26.6.9]**;
(*d*) form G 224 to notify the Registrar of the accounting reference date **[see 26.8.5]**;
(*e*) the registers in which must be recorded details of the members **[see 26.7.3]**, directors and company secretaries, directors' interests in the company's shares and debentures, and the charges over company property;
(*f*) the minutes of the first directors' meeting; and
(*g*) blank share certificates.

It is important when buying a company to ensure that the objects of the company as set out in its Memorandum of Association **[see 26.6.8]**, are suitable for the type of business that is to be carried on. In a standard Memorandum of Association it is usual for the main object to be described as a 'general commercial company' although this can be amended to provide for a more specific description of the company's business.

26.6.6 Registration – the place and number

The certificate of incorporation of the new company will show its registered number and the place of incorporation, for example, England and Wales, Scotland etc. All companies are required to show their registered number, place of registration and the registered office address on their business letters and order forms (CA 1985, s 351).

26.6.7 Company's registered office

Every company must have a registered office to which communications and notices can be sent. Details of any changes must be sent to the Registrar on form 287 within 14 days of the change. It is not sufficient merely to show the change on the next annual return **[see 26.8.7]**. Any change of registered office takes effect upon being registered by the Registrar (CA 1985, s 287).

26.6.8 Memorandum of Association

A private company's Memorandum of Association includes:

(*a*) the name of the company;
(*b*) a statement that the company is registered with limited liability;
(*c*) the country where the registered office is situated;
(*d*) the objects of the company, ie what business and transactions it has the power to carry out; and
(*e*) the amount of its authorised share capital and its division into a number of shares of a fixed amount.

26.6.9 Articles of Association

A company's Articles of Association (Articles) govern the day-to-day administration of the company's affairs. If its Articles are not registered, Table A, the model Articles for companies limited by shares, will apply (CA 1985, s 8).

Examples of the areas that are covered in the Articles are:

(*a*) the transfer of shares;
(*b*) rights attaching to shares;
(*c*) borrowing powers;
(*d*) proceedings of directors;
(*e*) authority to allot shares; and
(*f*) shareholders' meetings.

It is usual for an EIS company to include in its Articles a provision prohibiting the transfer of shares during the company's relevant period **[see 26.1.3]**, if this would result in the company coming under the control of another company **[see 5.10]**.

26.6.10 Company name

Every company must show its full registered name legibly on its letterheads, notices and official publications, cheques, invoices, receipts, e-mails etc (CA 1985, s 349). If the company has one or more places of business it must paint or affix its name outside these places (CA 1985, s 348).

A company purchased off-the-shelf will often have an unsuitable name but it can change its name by special resolution **[see 26.8.3]** (CA 1985, s 28). The resolution must be sent to the Registrar with a registration fee of £10.

26.6.11 Directors

It is only necessary to have one director for a private limited company (CA 1985, s 282 (3)) but most companies find it useful to have two or three directors so that each can take responsibility for a different aspect of the business, for example, finance, sales etc. EIS shareholders can be unpaid directors or even paid directors if they meet certain conditions **[see 7.6.2.9 and 7.6.2.11]**.

It is usual for one of the directors to be the chairman of the board. He or she would be responsible for calling and chairing the directors' meetings.

The managing director is the person who executes the policies that have been agreed by the board. The finance director supervises the company's accounting procedures and the preparation of its annual accounts. He or she would normally be the person who arranges finance for the company, and would ensure that income is received on a timely basis and that the company pays its expenses.

If any new directors are appointed they must complete form 288a and send it to the Registrar.

The terms of the directors' appointment should be agreed from the outset, covering such matters as when their position will be reviewed, what expenses they can claim, what powers they will have, and whether and when they may draw directors' remuneration.

Every company must either state the names of all directors, or none (ie it cannot be selective) on all company business letters (CA 1985, s 305).

26.6.12 Company secretary

It is necessary to have a company secretary, who could be one of the directors (although not a sole director), to be responsible for keeping the company's statutory books. These include the members' register and the board meeting minutes book. The company secretary is responsible for making the company's annual return **[see 26.8.7]**. The company's solicitor or accountant will usually advise on company law matters including how the various forms should be prepared.

The company secretary, even if he or she is also a director, has to complete and sign a separate form 288a.

26.6.13 Shareholders' agreement

With small EIS companies it is advisable to have a solicitor draw up a shareholders' agreement in order to avoid any misunderstanding regarding the purpose of the share issue, the directors' roles and proposed exit routes after the termination date has elapsed. **See Appendix 1** for an outline of a shareholders' agreement.

26.6.14 Share capital

An off-the-shelf company will have an authorised share capital and usually one issued share known as a subscriber share. This share is first issued to the company formation agent and then transferred to the new owners of the company.

If the subscriber share(s) is or are transferred to individuals who wish to claim EIS relief, this does not mean that the 30% rule is breached, provided that at that time no preparatory trading activities have been begun **[see 7.6.3.2]**.

The company's authorised share capital can be increased, provided that there are the necessary powers in the company's Articles and an ordinary resolution **[see 26.8.3]** is passed in a general meeting (CA 1985, s 121). A copy of the resolution must be sent to the Registrar with form 123 within 15 days of its adoption (CA 1985, s 123).

26.7 The share issue

26.7.1 Issuing a memorandum

A private company cannot offer its shares to the public but only to persons who have expressed an interest in subscribing for shares in the company. If details of the proposed share issue are to be set out in a memorandum for colleagues and friends who have shown an interest, each copy should be numbered and addressed clearly to a particular person. The document should include a disclaimer along the following lines:

> 'This document is not a public offering of securities and is sent for the attention only of the addressee named at the top of the page for his private and personal attention. The addressee must treat this document and the information contained in it with the utmost confidence and must not circulate it or permit it to be circulated to any other person. The sole purpose of this document is to assist the recipient in deciding whether to proceed with presenting a formal offer for a shareholding.'

It is advisable to ask a solicitor to express an opinion as to whether the final draft of the document is acceptable before sending it out.

26.7.2 Issuing the shares

There is no minimum issued or paid-up capital for a private company. The simplest situation would be to issue, for cash, the required number of £1 ordinary shares at par value, ie £1. Each person who wishes to subscribe for shares in the company should fill in an application form so that it is clear that he or she is investing in, rather than lending money to, the company.

Once the money is banked it is necessary to call a board meeting to allot the shares. The details should then be written in the members' register. Only if the entry has been made in the register has the process of issuing shares been completed **[see 8.1.6]**. It is very important that this be done by 5 April or 5 October so that tax relief can be obtained in the appropriate tax year.

26.7.3 Register of members

Every company must keep a register of members that contains the:

(*a*) name and address of each shareholder;
(*b*) date on which that person was registered as a member;
(*c*) date that person ceased to be a member;
(*d*) number of shares held and the amount subscribed

(CA 1985, s 352).

26.7.4 Company seal

Companies may choose whether or not they have a seal.

26.7.5 Last-minute changes

Where there are only a few subscribers, it is important to ensure that cheques are cashed and shares are ready to be issued on the agreed date. It is too easy for one person to drop out at the last moment and cause another person's interest to exceed 30% **[see 7.6.3]**. Note that breaching the 30% limit does not matter if only EIS deferral relief is to be claimed.

Furthermore, share issues should not be planned too near the end of the tax year because a delay of a day could have the result that shares are issued in the 'wrong' tax year.

The company secretary would normally write up the members' register and write out the share certificates. The certificates should be signed by two directors, or one director and the company secretary, and sent to the shareholders. If it is a requirement of the Articles of Association, the certificates should first be sealed with the company seal **[see 26.7.4]**.

26.8 Directors' responsibilities

26.8.1 Annual general meeting (AGM)

Shareholders exercise control through voting at meetings. Assuming that there is only one class of share, a private company will have two types of general meeting.

The first is the AGM, at which the company's audited accounts (where an audit is necessary or has been performed) are presented to members, where the directors recommend dividends, and the auditors' fees and directors' fees are presented for approval.

The general rule is that every company should hold an AGM each calendar year and there should not be more than 15 months between AGMs. So long as a company holds its first AGM within 18 months of its incorporation, it need not hold one in the year of its incorporation or in the following year (CA 1985, s 366).

However, a private company can elect by 'elective resolution' to dispense with the holding of an AGM that is not yet due (CA 1985, ss 366A and 379A). At least 21 days' notice must be given of an AGM (CA 1985, s 369).

26.8.2 Extraordinary general meeting (EGM)

An EGM is any meeting other than the AGM. Usually the company's Articles provide for an EGM to be called at the directors' discretion or at the request of members. At least 14 days' notice must be given of an EGM (CA 1985, s 369).

26.8.3 Resolutions

An ordinary resolution is passed if there is a simple majority of those who vote on the issue.

An extraordinary resolution is one that is passed if no less than 75% of the company's members at a general meeting vote in favour of it.

A special resolution is one that is voted for by no less than 75% of members at a general meeting, where 21 days' notice has been given of the meeting and the notice stated that the resolution would be a special resolution (CA 1985, s 378). In certain circumstances less than 21 days' notice can be given.

26.8.4 Annual financial statements

Every company must maintain accounting records comprehensive enough to disclose, with reasonable accuracy, the financial position of the company at any time. The financial statements (accounts) must consist of:

(*a*) a profit and loss account;
(*b*) a balance sheet;
(*c*) a statement of total recognised gains and losses where appropriate;
(*d*) a cash flow statement where the company exceeds a certain size;
(*e*) an auditor's report where necessary; and
(*f*) a directors' report (CA 1985, s 234).

A new company's first period of account begins on the date of its incorporation and must be for a period of more than six months but not more than 18 months (CA 1985, s 224). Only one director need sign the balance sheet (CA 1985, s 233).

The financial statements of a private company must be filed with the Registrar within 10 months of the end of the financial year or, in the case of a newly incorporated company, within 10 months of the anniversary of its date of incorporation, whichever is earlier. Every balance sheet of a company and every copy that is laid before the company in general meeting or delivered to the Registrar must be signed on behalf of the board by a director.

The company's directors are each personally liable for filing the directors' report and financial statements. Failure to file is a criminal offence and it can lead to the striking-off of the company. There are additional penalties where a private company is late in filing its financial statements. These are £100 up to three months late, £250 up to six months late, £500 up to 12 months late and £1,000 more than 12 months late. Late filing of the corporation tax return gives rise to further penalties.

Although for company law purposes a private company has to preserve its accounting records for three years, for tax purposes the records need to be kept for six years.

26.8.5 Accounting reference date

Every newly formed company may notify the Registrar on form 225 of the date on which its period of account will end. This is known as the company's accounting reference date (ARD). If the company does not notify the Registrar on form 225 within nine months of incorporation, the ARD will be the last day of the month in which the anniversary of its incorporation falls (CA 1985, s 224).

26.8.6 Directors' report

The directors' report must present a fair view of the development of the company's business during the financial year ended with the balance sheet date. It must state, *inter alia*, if there are to be any dividends or transfers of profits to reserves. The report must be signed by a director or the company secretary (CA 1985, s 234A).

26.8.7 The annual return

Every company is required to make an annual return to the Registrar at least once a year. It should contain the following details:

(*a*) the address of the company's registered office;
(*b*) the company's principal business activities;
(*c*) the address where the register of members and the register of debenture holders are kept, if this is not the registered office;
(*d*) details of the company's issued share capital;
(*e*) details of the members of the company and the shares (or stock if relevant) that they hold – this must be submitted every three years and details of changes in membership and shareholdings are required in the intermediate years; and
(*f*) particulars of the directors and the company secretary.

The annual return must be made up to a date not later than the company's return date, that is:

(*a*) the anniversary of the company's incorporation; or
(*b*) if the company's last properly delivered return was made up to a different date, the anniversary of that date;

and be delivered to the Registrar within 28 days of the date to which it is made up with a cheque for £15.

26.9 Avoiding a clawback of relief

26.9.1 Introduction

The withdrawal of relief is discussed in detail in **Chapters 12** (investment relief) and **Part 5** (deferral relief). There are, however, certain situations that are more likely to occur with small private issues than with prospectus issues.

26.9.2 Payments to directors

As a general rule, if a director is claiming EIS investment or deferral relief, he or she must not receive any payment from the company unless the payment is of a kind that is specifically listed in the legislation **[see 7.6.2.9 and 15.8.10]**. Directors who are not connected with the company (in the case of investment relief) and directors generally in the case of deferral relief may receive reasonable remuneration **[see 7.6.2.11]**. Particular care needs to be taken with these conditions as even a £1 payment to an unpaid director or any excessive remuneration to a paid director could cause all his or her tax reliefs to be withdrawn.

Directors may receive expenses wholly, exclusively and necessarily incurred in carrying out their duties. This is not a loophole to be exploited. It is a very difficult area of tax law and one should err on the side of non-payment. For example, payment should never be made for the cost of travelling from home to work as a director's duties do not commence until he or she reaches his or her place of work.

26.9.3 Investors' loans

One of the most common problems concerns individuals who make or have made loans to the qualifying company. Neither EIS investment nor EIS deferral relief is available where loans are converted into ordinary shares. Furthermore, any loan that is in existence before the investment cannot be repaid within the period of restriction without forfeiting all or part of the relief, except in respect of shares issued after 16 March 2004 (see below). It is necessary to look at the balance sheet at the date of the investment. The amount of a director's loan to the company at that date should be frozen until the termination date in the case of shares issued before 17 March 2004. The reason given is that these schemes were designed to encourage additional capital not the replacement of loans with equity **[see 12.5.6]**. Where loans are made after the eligible shares have been issued, care must be taken in the case of investment relief that the 30% test **[see 7.6.3]** is not breached.

However, the harshness of this rule has been recognised and it has been significantly relaxed. For shares issued after 16 March 2004, the repayment of short-term loans no longer denies EIS relief if the lender subscribes for shares in the next 12 months, provided that the repayment is not made in connection with arrangements for the acquisition of the shares. For example, an individual who has advanced funds to the company to enable it to pay wages or a creditor and is then repaid when the company has sufficient liquid funds is not now denied EIS relief.

26.9.4 Directors' services

Similar caution is required where a director provides the company with services. It should not, for example, be a problem if the director is a professional person such as a lawyer, who charges fees in connection with the conveyance of properties. But any fee that is excessive is likely to be challenged by the inspector on the grounds that it is not 'reasonable and necessary remuneration' **[see 7.6.2.11 and 15.8.10]**.

26.9.5 Properties purchased from EIS shareholders

With small EIS companies it is not uncommon for the company to wish to purchase a property from either an EIS investor or his or her associate, or from a construction company controlled by the investor and associates. Care must be taken to check the effect of such a transaction before deciding to go ahead.

A property should not be purchased from a director or his or her associate. This is because the director or the associate(s) would be receiving a payment from the company that is not a qualifying payment. In such a case all of the investor's EIS investment relief would be withdrawn and his or her deferred gains would crystallise.

If neither the vendor nor the vendor's associate is a director but merely a shareholder, there are two other potential problems. The first relates to the EIS replacement-capital provisions **[see 7.6.4]**. These could be relevant if, for example, the property is a factory that has been used for a similar business which the investor, with others, controlled.

It is also necessary to consider whether value has been received, to establish whether the company is directly or indirectly:

(*a*) providing a benefit or facility **[see 12.5.10]**; or
(*b*) acquiring an asset from the investor for consideration exceeding its market value **[see 12.5.11]**.

26.9.6 Properties purchased from non-EIS shareholders

Assuming a shareholder does not want EIS relief, he or she could transfer property owned privately to the company. This should not adversely affect any EIS shareholders. Although it is normally still advisable for other reasons, it is no longer necessary for the purchase to be at market value. Relief is no longer lost when 'value' is received by other shareholders, except in the form of a repayment of capital **[see 12.9]**.

Chapter 27

Public Offers

27.1 Introduction

This chapter looks at the work and considerations necessary before, during and after the issuing of a public prospectus and is aimed at companies seeking venture capital investment from a wider circle of potential investors. It applies equally to EIS, VCT and CVS investment. The second part of the chapter looks at public offers from the investor's point of view. This is of little relevance to the VCT scheme as the investment in investee companies is undertaken under the direction of professional fund managers.

27.1.1 Scope of this chapter

The first part of this chapter considers the following aspects of prospectus issues from the point of view of those who wish to raise venture scheme capital:

(*a*) The company law requirements **[see 27.2]**
(*b*) The work to be carried out before preparing a prospectus **[see 27.3]**
(*c*) The preparation of the prospectus **[see 27.4]**
(*d*) Post-prospectus activities **[see 27.5]**

The second part of the chapter looks at prospectuses from the EIS investor's point of view **[see 27.6]**.

27.1.2 Public offers

VCT shares – ie shares in the VCTs (the investor companies) themselves – are offered to the public by means of a prospectus. As VCTs are quoted companies, the Listing Rules of the UK Listing Authority will set out the information that has to be included in the prospectus.

Approved and unapproved EIS funds and EIS companies that are public limited companies, can also offer their shares to the public. Where such companies are quoted on the Alternative Investment Market (AIM), the issuers will need to comply with the AIM Rules, which will include the requirements of the Public Offers of Securities Regulations 1995 (POS 1995).

The remainder of this chapter deals with the situation where shares are offered to the public by companies that are not quoted on AIM or the main market. This can be done in one of two ways:

(*a*) the issue of a prospectus by a single company; or
(*b*) a multi-company prospectus.

27.1.3 Approved EIS funds

In the case of an approved EIS fund, the fund manager issues a prospectus. With the money received from subscribers the manager subscribes for shares on the individuals' behalf. The managers effectively retain control over the portfolio for the period of the fund's life, which is normally three to seven years so that the managers can make an orderly divestment of the shares. The managers are empowered to agree to reconstructions and amalgamations as well as to the sale of the investments.

If an investor subscribes through an approved EIS fund, there are some relaxations in the EIS rules, as follows:

(*a*) the £500 lower limit on the amount that an individual must subscribe for shares in a company to qualify for investment relief does not apply where the investment in that company is made on the individual's behalf by the manager of an approved fund; and
(*b*) the investor can obtain tax relief on his or her entire investment in the fund in the tax year in which the fund closes, ie provided that all the necessary conditions are satisfied, all shares acquired through the fund are treated as if they had been issued on the date the fund closes. This contrasts with the position of investors in unapproved funds, who obtain tax relief on their share of the investments made by the fund only at the time the fund itself makes those investments.

Due to the restrictions placed on approved EIS funds, for example, the necessity of investing at least 90% of the capital raised within six months of closure **[see 27.1.4]**, such funds have been little used and do not provide any real competition for VCTs.

27.1.4 Conditions to be met by an approved EIS fund

An approved EIS fund must meet certain conditions; for example, the managers cannot start making investments until after the fund closes, and at least 90% of the funds raised must be invested in new shares in qualifying companies within six months of the date of closure. The Inland Revenue has issued guidelines regarding the approval of EIS funds, which prospective fund managers may obtain by writing to Inland Revenue, Business Tax (EIS), at Room 4W5, 22 Kingsway, London WC2B 6NR, or by ringing 020 7438 4485.

27.1.5 Unapproved EIS funds and schemes

The managers of an unapproved EIS fund or managed EIS scheme will have made a decision not to seek the Inland Revenue's approval because they do not wish to be bound by the conditions set out by the Inland Revenue. As in the case of an approved EIS fund, however, the manager subscribes for EIS shares on the individual's behalf and effectively retains control over the portfolio for the period of the fund's life.

It should be borne in mind that investors in an unapproved fund do not enjoy the benefits described in **7.6.5**.

27.2 Company law requirements

27.2.1 Offering shares to the public

Offering shares to the public is governed by POS 1995 **[see 27.1.2]**.

Only an authorised person under the Financial Services and Markets Act 2000 can carry on investment business (FSMA 2000, s 19). Where an authorised person is issuing a prospectus to raise capital for a company, he is carrying on investment business and must abide by the rules of his self-regulatory organisation (SRO), which are derived from the rules originally issued by the Securities and Investment Board (now the Financial Services Authority – FSA).

A company seeking to raise capital for itself (an unsponsored issue, see **27.3.5**) is not carrying on investment business.

27.2.2 Approval of advertisements

An invitation or inducement to engage in investment activity may only be communicated by a person authorised under FSMA 2000, unless the content of the communication is approved by an authorised person. Although the prospectus itself is governed by POS 1995, any other advertisement, for example a covering letter, whether for a sponsored or unsponsored issue, must be approved.

27.2.3 FSA marketing rules

The FSA has marketing recommendations for EIS public issues, which are as follows:

(*a*) It is necessary to ensure that no statement in an advertisement is misleading, that the authorised person has written evidence of facts contained in advertisements and that a 'health warning' is incorporated.

(*b*) Projections are generally not allowed although there is provision to grant waivers on a case-by-case basis.
(*c*) Approved EIS funds are in the same regime as unit trusts with regard to a cooling-off period for investors. This means that applications received direct from the investors do not require a seven-day cooling-off period.

27.2.4 Public limited companies

If shares are to be offered to the public it is necessary for the company to be a public limited company (plc). For new companies the solicitors may form a company or buy an off-the-shelf company from formation agents **[see 11.6.5]**. In some circumstances a private company might consider re-registering as a plc before issuing a prospectus. However, a private company cannot re-register if it has a deficit on its profit and loss account.

The main differences between a private limited company and a public limited company are as follows:

	plc	*Ltd*
Shares can be issued to public	Yes	No
Minimum number of directors	Two	One
Trading can start after incorporation	No	Yes
Minimum issued/paid up capital	Yes	No
Small or medium-sized companies need not file full accounts or consolidated accounts	No	Yes
Valuation report required for non-cash assets from subscribers	Yes	No
Redemption or repurchase of shares out of capital	No	Yes
Rules on serious loss of capital	Yes	No

27.2.5 Trading certificate

Before a plc can commence business or borrow money it must obtain a trading certificate from the Registrar of Companies (the Registrar), whose address is shown in **Appendix 5**. If this is not done, the company and any officer in default is liable to a fine.

The application for a trading certificate must include a declaration confirming the following:

(*a*) the nominal value of the issued share capital – his must not be less than the authorised minimum, which is currently £50,000 (CA 1985, s 118);

(*b*) the paid-up share capital at the date of application – the minimum paid-up capital is one-quarter of the nominal value of the issued share capital plus the whole of any premium payable (CA 1985, s 101);
(*c*) the actual or estimated amount of the company's preliminary expenses and the persons who have paid or will pay the expenses; and
(*d*) the amount or benefit that has or will be paid to any promoter of the company and the consideration given for the payment or benefit (CA 1985, s 117).

27.2.6 Directors and company secretary

A plc is required to have at least two directors, and its company secretary must be suitably qualified (CA 1985, ss 282 and 286).

27.2.7 Financial statements

A public company must lay its financial statements before the members and deliver them to the Registrar within seven months of the end of the accounting reference period (CA 1985, s 244).

27.3 Pre-prospectus activities

27.3.1 The business plan

If a decision is made by certain individuals (the founders) to raise capital from the public, it will be necessary to prepare a business plan. The preparation of the business plan usually concentrates the minds of the founders and may lead to their abandoning the prospectus route in favour of another source of finance. It is better that they have second thoughts at this stage before heavy costs are incurred.

A business plan should address the following questions:

(*a*) What is the maximum amount sought and what is the minimum amount required for the project to be viable?
(*b*) What is the business and its strategy?
(*c*) Who will manage the business?
(*d*) Why should anyone invest in this particular company?
(*e*) What is the exit route for investors?

27.3.2 Appointment of advisers

If it is decided to go ahead, the founders of the proposed company should appoint the advisers for the prospectus issue. It is essential to engage firms to be the solicitors to the offer and reporting accountants to the offer.

Consideration should also be given to appointing marketing and public relations advisers.

As a prospectus is a public document it is important to have advisers who are experienced in this kind of work.

27.3.3 Should the issue be sponsored?

Sponsored prospectus issues usually, but not always, raise more money than unsponsored issues and usually result in higher issue costs. Before making this decision it is worth looking at what a sponsor offers and comparing the success of issues that were sponsored with those that were not.

27.3.4 What is the role of a sponsor?

In the case of VCTs, matters concerning the identification and evaluation of the possible investee companies will be done by the VCT managers. For EIS prospectuses it will be part of the sponsor's role:

(*a*) Before the prospectus is issued:
  (1) to identify those projects that are both marketable and likely to produce a good return to shareholders over the next three years;
  (2) to investigate the track record of any existing business and the potential for the proposed business, to assess the opportunities for future growth;
  (3) to establish whether the management has a strong personal commitment to succeed and has the ability to manage a public company;
  (4) to enquire into the background of the management to uncover any past poor performance, litigation, involvement with failed companies etc;
  (5) to consider whether the structure and activities of the proposed company or companies will mean that they are qualifying companies;
  (6) to negotiate with the founders the subscription price for the shares;
  (7) to ensure that a VCT has applied to the Inland Revenue for VCT approval; and
  (8) to ensure that an EIS company has obtained provisional or advance clearance before issuing the prospectus.

(*b*) At the time of the prospectus:
  (1) to be involved in drafting the prospectus, to ensure that it is attractive but is not misleading;
  (2) to ensure that the minimum subscription is adequate and to consider whether loan finance is needed;
  (3) to promote the company through intermediaries and other contacts in order to raise the finance; and
  (4) to oversee any advertising or public relations activities.

(*c*) After the prospectus has been issued:
   (1) to check that the shares are issued in a timely and orderly way;
   (2) to ensure that where an EIS company has not started its qualifying activities, that they are started promptly;
   (3) to oversee the issue of the shareholders' tax certificates;
   (4) to monitor the company's performance and adherence to VCT and EIS rules both through the Offer for Subscription agreement and by having a director of the sponsoring company on the board of the investee companies;
   (5) to ensure that the shareholders receive half-yearly unaudited reports as well as annual audited reports and accounts in good time;
   (6) to act as financial adviser to the company, which may need further equity or loan capital; and
   (7) to plan for and implement an exit route for EIS shareholders.

27.3.5 Unsponsored EIS issues

In the past where there have been unsponsored issues, many of the activities normally carried out by the sponsor have been divided between the solicitors to the offer, the reporting accountants, the directors and the public relations organisation, if any. However, there was often no:

(*a*) independent investigation or evaluation of the directors; or
(*b*) independent evaluation of the project beyond that carried out by the reporting accountants, for example, as to the adequacy of the minimum subscription; or
(*c*) director on the board who was specifically looking after the interests of the EIS shareholders.

It is arguable whether a director appointed by a sponsor is the best person to represent the interests of the shareholders, as the interests of the sponsor and those of the shareholders will sometimes conflict.

Directors of unsponsored issues usually emphasise how they reduce issue costs because of their 'hands-on approach' and therefore maximise the amount of the proceeds of the share issue that will be used in the business. When it comes to exit routes, they argue that a City specialist is required rather than the sponsor of the original issue.

Unsponsored issues will usually succeed if the founders:

(*a*) have good contacts;
(*b*) have a good track record, preferably managing EIS companies; and
(*c*) are able to market the prospectus by giving presentations to intermediaries and potential investors.

27.4 The prospectus

27.4.1 Contents of the prospectus

The contents of the prospectus are governed by POS 1995 and FSMA 2000. The latter requires specific statements to be made prominently, which warn the investor about the risks of investing in unquoted shares and tell him to seek appropriate independent advice. There is now a general disclosure obligation, so that a prospectus must contain all such information as investors would reasonably require, and reasonably expect to find there, for the purpose of making an informed assessment of:

(*a*) the assets and liabilities, financial position, profits and losses, and prospects of the company issuing the shares; and
(*b*) the rights attaching to those shares (POS 1995, reg 9).

The following information is usually included in the prospectus:

(*a*) details of the shares offered and the minimum subscription;
(*b*) background to the issue, the business and strategy;
(*c*) details of the directors, the managers and the company's advisers;
(*d*) benefits and risks to the investors;
(*e*) a summary of the VCT and EIS legislation as appropriate;
(*f*) statutory and general information; and
(*g*) application form and procedure.

27.4.2 Details of shares offered

In the prospectus there must be full details of the shares being offered. The information required includes the following:

(*a*) the number, description, and par value of the shares being offered and the issue price;
(*b*) the purpose for which the shares are being issued;
(*c*) when the subscription lists open and close;
(*d*) the amount of the minimum subscription (if any) and whether or not it is underwritten; and
(*e*) the total proceeds that it is expected will be raised by the offer and the expected net proceeds, after deduction of the expenses of the offer.

Shares in a new company may be offered at a premium. The reason for this is that for accounting purposes the issue costs can be set against the share premium. If this is done, the company's profit and loss account balance will more accurately reflect the results of the business.

27.4.3 Underwriting

Consideration should be given as to whether all or part of the minimum subscription should be underwritten for a fee. Alternatively, there might be irrevocable commitments from interested investors, details of which will appear in the prospectus. Another possibility is initially to restrict the circulation of the prospectus to interested investors and then re-issue the prospectus to the public when the minimum subscription has been raised.

27.4.4 Background, business and strategy

The prospectus should contain a full description of the project and the reasons why capital is required. The company should describe how its business strategy is different from that of other companies.

27.4.5 Directors, management team and advisers

There should be a paragraph providing details of each director and his or her roles in the company. The aim is to assure the potential investor that the company, and in the case of VCTs the underlying investments, will be managed by and advised by people with the relevant skills, experience and track record. Often a well-respected public figure is asked to be the company's chairman in order to give the company a seal of approval.

27.4.6 Benefits and risks to investors

As well as describing the appropriate tax relief that should be available to investors there should be an indication of when tax relief is likely to be available. The prospectus may state whether or not it is the intention to pay dividends during the investment period and will usually indicate what exit routes are likely at the end of that period **[see Chapter 28]**.

The prospectus should contain a list of risk factors so that the investor is aware of what can go wrong.

27.4.7 The accountants' report

A prospectus must contain either a statement from a firm of accountants (the accountants' report) which reports on the company's profits, losses, assets and liabilities and dividends paid or the previous three years' audited accounts (POS 1995, Sch 1, para 45).

For a new company, the accountants' report will state that the company has not started its business or made up its accounts and has not declared or paid any dividends.

27.4.8 Approval and clearances

A VCT company must apply to the Inland Revenue for conditional approval and would include such a statement in its prospectus.

It has become normal practice for EIS company prospectuses to state that the Inland Revenue has given provisional clearance. Application to the Inland Revenue for provisional EIS clearance should be made about three weeks before the launch date, by which time most decisions concerning the prospectus have been made.

27.4.9 Statutory and general information

At the back of a prospectus (usually in small print) can be found the section headed 'Statutory and General Information'. As the name suggests, this section contains information that is required by statute, which includes the following:

(*a*) disclosures as to the company's authorised, issued and paid-up share capital;
(*b*) the rights of different classes of shares;
(*c*) the amount paid or payable by the company in commission for procuring subscriptions;
(*d*) the amount of any preliminary expenses and the persons to whom these are payable unless the company has been in existence for more than two years;
(*e*) the minimum subscription;
(*f*) the aggregate of remuneration and benefits-in-kind paid to the directors in the last financial year, along with an estimate of what these will be in the current year;
(*g*) the interests of each director in the share capital of the issuer, distinguishing between beneficial and non-beneficial holdings;
(*h*) the consents of those who have agreed to the publication of their letters or reports in the prospectus;
(*i*) documents that have been delivered to the Registrar;
(*j*) documents that can be inspected and where they can be inspected; and
(*k*) a statement as to whether the company is engaged in any litigation.

27.4.10 Minimum subscription

A decision will have been made as to the amount that would need to be raised to make it worthwhile going ahead with the project. The amount of the minimum subscription must be stated in the prospectus. This amount must be broken down into:

(*a*) the price of any property to be taken from the proceeds;
(*b*) any preliminary expenses payable by the issuer and any commission payable;

(*c*) any borrowings that will be repaid; and
(*d*) working capital.

Additionally, the prospectus should detail any amounts to be paid in respect of the matters mentioned above, otherwise than out of the issue proceeds, and state from which sources the amounts will be provided.

If the minimum subscription is not raised within 40 days of the opening of the subscription lists, the investors must have their cheques returned (CA 1985, s 83).

27.4.11 Offer for Subscription agreement

The prospectus will usually set out the main points of the Offer for Subscription agreement, which is an agreement between the company, its directors and the sponsor. It will usually contain details of:

(*a*) commissions payable to the sponsor and intermediaries for raising the capital;
(*b*) fees to be paid to the sponsor for acting as financial adviser and for providing the services of a director;
(*c*) share options to be granted to the sponsor;
(*d*) warranties and indemnities given by the company to the sponsor on behalf of itself and the investors:
  (1) to ensure compliance with the VCT or EIS requirements,
  (2) to produce regular management accounts and other information about the company's performance, and
  (3) to seek shareholders' approval for all major transactions.

27.4.12 Application form and procedure

Preceding the application form is usually a section stating the minimum amount of shares that an individual can apply for and the conditions and procedure for dealing with the application. The company will usually reserve the right to:

(*a*) extend the period for which the subscription lists remain open;
(*b*) present all cheques on receipt and retain documents until cheques are cleared;
(*c*) reject applications; and
(*d*) retain interest on the money held pending the issue of shares or return.

27.4.13 Verification

All statements in the prospectus, whether of fact or of opinion, have to be verified. For example, if there is a photograph of what is held out to be one of the company's warehouses someone would have to verify this. Statements of fact must be true and statements of opinion must be reasonable and based upon knowledge held by the directors. Finally, no material facts should be omitted which would make a statement of fact or opinion misleading.

27.5 Post-prospectus activities

27.5.1 Lodging the prospectus

A copy of the final version of the prospectus is lodged with the Registrar. If the Registrar refuses to register the prospectus it cannot be circulated until the matter is resolved.

27.5.2 Marketing the prospectus

Copies of the prospectus are sent to intermediaries or to those individuals who have previously invested under the VCT scheme or the EIS. It is possible to buy lists of the names and addresses of such people.

27.5.3 Commission

Many investments are made by clients of intermediaries and a commission is paid to the intermediary for the introduction. Rates of commission are usually between 2% and 3% of the subscription.

27.5.4 Issue of the shares

Applications for shares are normally processed by the sponsor, a bank or a firm of registrars. Once the minimum subscription has been reached the shares are issued. The board minute and the form 88(2) should be sent to the Registrar.

27.5.5 Tax certificates for the investors

After the EIS share issue, and after the company has traded for four months, the company should apply to its inspector for the EIS tax-relief certificates for the investors. Following a subscription for VCT shares, investors must apply to the VCT in question for their tax-relief certificates.

27.6 Choosing an investment

27.6.1 Investment policy

It cannot be over-emphasised that any investment should be judged on its merits and if there are tax reliefs these should be seen as a bonus. The normal investment criteria should apply. Only capital that is not required for a minimum of three and a maximum of closer to seven years should be committed and, where possible, this should be spread over several companies in order to reduce the risk of losing the investment.

27.6.2 Commentary on EIS offers

There are magazines, such as *Tax Efficient Review* and *The Tax Shelter Report*, which analyse and comment on tax-based investments. As well as keeping the investor up to date with what is currently on offer, these magazines report on existing EIS and VCT companies. Newspapers and journals such as *Investors Chronicle* and *Money Management* are likely to list what prospectuses are available. The EIS Association, which represents professional advisers of companies using the EIS, is able to provide information to investors, companies and financial advisers about the scheme. Also, the British Venture Capital Association lists many business introduction services in a free publication entitled *Sources of Business Angel Capital*. See **Appendix 5** for addresses.

27.6.3 Areas of investment

Public prospectuses have traditionally given investors the following choices:

(*a*) companies with high risk and unlimited growth potential, usually with no clearly defined exit route;
(*b*) companies with an exit route and a limited specified return; and
(*c*) approved and unapproved EIS funds.

27.6.4 Costs of raising the capital

When looking at prospectuses, it is important to calculate the cost of raising the capital. With an unsponsored issue the cost will vary according to the amount raised as there are fixed elements, such as the costs of writing, designing, reporting on, verifying, printing and distributing the prospectus, and variable elements such as intermediaries' commission. The percentage cost at the minimum subscription level could be in the region of 20% to 25% and at the top end, between 7% and 8%. The sponsored issues usually state that the sponsor will take, say, 6% of the amounts raised, from which all issue costs will be paid, and make an annual management charge. From the investors' point of view, if less than the maximum amount is raised, the sponsored issue will normally result in low issue costs but if the maximum is reached, the unsponsored issue could have the lower costs.

It is necessary to check how much of the amount paid to an EIS fund will be used to pay a fee to the managers for identifying the investments. It should be borne in mind that the investor does not receive tax relief on the management fee as it does not represent an amount subscribed for shares. The managers may instead of, or as well as, charging the investor a management fee, charge each qualifying company for raising the capital.

VCT tax relief is based on the amount paid for the VCT shares but high issue costs reduce the amount the VCT has to invest.

27.6.5 Ongoing costs

Sponsors and directors may decide to take a bigger risk with regard to covering issue costs provided that they can be remunerated for managing the company and/or be granted options to purchase shares at a price that is below market value. The options can usually only be exercised if specified targets are reached.

27.6.6 Return on the investment

The returns from making an EIS or VCT investment can be attractive provided that the individual pays UK tax. Because of the investment relief, the individual who invests £10,000 should get a reasonable return even if there is only a small increase in the value of the shares.

% return on net EIS investment after 5 years

	Nil	*10%*	*20%*
	(£)	(£)	(£)
Proceeds	10,000	11,000	12,000
Less net cost of investment	8,000	8,000	8,000
Increase	2,000	3,000	4,000
Return on net investment	25%	37.5%	50%

27.6.7 The managers

It is important for investors to ensure that their investment is in the hands of experienced management. It is also preferable for the directors to make a financial commitment alongside the investors, so that they are less inclined to walk away from the project when problems arise.

27.6.8 Whether to borrow to invest

There are arguments in favour of the individual's taking out borrowings to make the investment because it may result in a greater return and tax advantages. However, interest rates seem likely to rise in the immediate future and assets such as property may not appreciate at the same rate. It is also important to ensure that any loan is not provided on terms that are linked to the investment **[see 7.6.1.7]**.

27.6.9 Dual pricing

Dual pricing is the offering of new shares at two or more prices within a 12-month period. This is done:

(*a*) to encourage early investment so that:
   (1) the minimum subscription is achieved,
   (2) an EIS company can start its qualifying activities, which will bring forward the receipt of the tax-relief certificates; and

(*b*) to encourage support from investors who have invested in a sister company, ie a company operated on similar lines by substantially the same management.

An investor who takes his cash off deposit at an early stage in order to invest and runs the risk of providing the company's seed capital, will expect to pay less for his or her shares than those who invest later. It is therefore important that the number of shares on offer at the lower price be limited.

Example 27.1

Wittgenstein & Heidegger plc offered its 50p ordinary shares to the public on 28 August 2003 as follows: for subscriptions received by 3 October 2003 the share price is 95p a share, after which it increases to £1. If Ludwig subscribes on 1 September and the issue is fully subscribed by 3 October, neither Ludwig nor any other shareholder will have benefited by the lower price.

27.6.10 Monitoring the company's qualifying status

If the investor is to keep his or her tax relief, it is necessary for the VCT or EIS company to meet the appropriate scheme conditions not only when the shares are issued but also for the relevant restricted period, which will not be less than three years. Before investing it is important to ascertain whether those responsible for managing the investment have experience of keeping within the scheme rules. If they do not, they should consider engaging the services of an independent monitor who has that experience.

The risk that the relief may be withdrawn is greatest where the investors claiming tax relief, or the VCT, have a minority holding and do not have a representative on the board.

Chapter 28

Exit Routes

28.1 Introduction

28.1.1 Predicting the company's progress

To retain VCT or CVS relief, the shares must be held for at least three years and for EIS relief, for a period that is at least three years and often longer. But at the end of the investment period the circumstances may be such that those who wish to dispose of their shares will either not be able to do so or will have to accept a low price for their shares. No one can accurately predict the state of the economy, how markets will change etc.

28.1.2 Realising the investment

Although no one can predict whether the price paid for the shares will be exceeded in three or more years' time, VCT shares do have the advantage of being quoted on the Stock Exchange. A similar advantage applies if the EIS or CVS shares are dealt in on the Alternative Investment Market (AIM).

However, there is unlikely to be a market for most EIS and CVS shares when the investor wishes to sell them. This is a problem that needs to be addressed at the time the company is offering its shares. To reassure the potential investors, the directors, fund managers and sponsors are likely to say that they will use their best endeavours to find a way for shareholders to realise their investments after, say, three years. Usually the choice of exit routes is set out in any offer document with an indication of the route most favoured by the directors.

Where an investment is made in a family company, particularly by a working director, the exit route is less likely to be a problem.

28.1.3 Scope of this chapter

This chapter will consider the following ways in which shareholders can dispose of their investments after three or so years:

(*a*) Through a market for the shares **[see 28.2]**
(*b*) By a sale of assets and voluntary liquidation of the company **[see 28.3]**
(*c*) By a sale of the company's shares **[see 28.4]**
(*d*) By a purchase of its own shares by the company **[see 28.5]**
(*e*) By a gift of the shares to relatives or to charities **[see 28.6]**

28.1.4 Deferred gains

When there is a disposal of shares in a qualifying investment, any gains that were deferred on other assets, at the time of the investment, become chargeable (TCGA 1992, Sch 5B, para 3(1), Sch 5C, para 3(1)).

28.2 A market for the shares

28.2.1 Investors' choice

A market for the company's shares, either through a full listing on a stock exchange or by trading on AIM, is the route many shareholders would prefer. It gives the investor a choice as to whether to realise a tax-free gain after three or so years or to wait until later, knowing that any gain that is accumulating is tax free. It is particularly suitable for partial realisations or where a company has made several share issues so that there are various dates when shareholders can sell their shares without losing their investment relief.

28.2.2 Advantages and disadvantages

In addition to the opportunity for shareholders to realise their investment, the main benefits of a quotation are that:

(*a*) it enables a market value to be established for the shares, and this value will increase because the shares are marketable;
(*b*) the status of the company is enhanced; and
(*c*) new shares can be issued to the public in order to make trading acquisitions or to repay borrowings.

However, it must be borne in mind that:

(*a*) the directors are likely to be subjected to increased pressure to improve the company's profits and dividends;
(*b*) the company can be more vulnerable to an unwelcome takeover bid; and
(*c*) there are high costs involved in obtaining a full listing and in meeting the reporting requirements of a listed company. The cost of joining AIM is less expensive.

28.2.3 Capital gains exemption

As a general rule the capital gains tax exemption on EIS shares ends when a shareholder exchanges his shares for new shares in another company **[see 18.3]**. However, there are provisions in all three schemes to allow relief to be preserved on the occasion of certain takeovers and mergers carried out for bona fide commercial reasons.

Example 28.1

Immanuel subscribed for EIS shares in Critique Ltd. After three years Kant plc offers ordinary shares in itself as consideration for the entire share capital of Critique. If Critique's shareholders accept the offer, Immanuel's gain at that date, of say £8,000, would be exempt (although any deferred gains will be brought into charge). He would acquire the shares in Kant at market value and any subsequent gain on those shares would be taxable. If, however, Kant had been an EIS company, and the new shares were new ordinary shares carrying no preferential rights, then the deferred gains would not crystallise, and Immanuel's future gain on the Kant shares would also be exempt.

28.3 Sale of assets and voluntary liquidation

28.3.1 Introduction

There are provisions in the EIS legislation to deny tax relief if, at the outset, arrangements exist for the subsequent disposal of the EIS shares, or for the cessation of the investee company's trade, or for a disposal of the company's assets **[see 7.6.1.5]**. However, a subsequent decision by the investor to dispose of his or her shares following the end of his or her 'relevant period' should not affect the investor's EIS reliefs.

28.3.2 Sale as a going concern

If a voluntary liquidation of a qualifying company is contemplated there is the problem of whether the business can be sold as a going concern. If it cannot, and only individual assets can be sold, the value of the company's goodwill will be lost.

28.3.3 Corporation tax on sale of assets

It should also be borne in mind that the company, when it sells its assets such as goodwill, property and plant, will pay corporation tax on any gain realised in excess of the indexed price paid for the assets as well as tax on any capital allowance balancing charges. Rollover reliefs exist, however, for these classes of asset (in the case of plant, only for fixed plant), and in the case of goodwill under the new regime for intangible assets, where applicable.

28.3.4 Whether to pay a dividend before liquidation

If the company has cash and distributable profits, the question arises as to whether to pay a dividend before liquidation. For VCT investments this may be suitable as both the dividend and any gain realised on the shares after three years will be tax free.

In the case of an EIS investment, a gain on the shares after three years would be tax free but not a dividend, so it will usually be preferable not to pay a dividend before liquidation.

28.3.5 Voluntary winding-up

There are basically two ways for a company to wind up voluntarily:

(*a*) the company can resolve by special resolution that it be wound up voluntarily; or

(*b*) the company can resolve by extraordinary resolution that it cannot, by reason of its liabilities, continue its business, and that it is advisable to wind up (Insolvency Act 1986, s 84).

If it is resolved to wind up the company and the directors make a statutory declaration that the creditors can be paid, this is known as a members' voluntary winding-up. If no declaration is made, there is a creditors' voluntary winding-up.

28.4 Sale of shares

28.4.1 Introduction

The sale of an EIS company's shares after three years is a very likely exit route for the investors. However, at the time at which an individual subscribes for shares in the EIS company, there must be no arrangements with a view to the subsequent disposal of the shares **[see 7.6.1.5]**. Also it must be borne in mind that there can be no arrangements during the company's relevant period, whereby another company could control the EIS company.

28.4.2 Sale of EIS shares to EBT trustees

There may be scope for the investors to sell their shares to the trustees of an employee benefit trust, which may provide a market for the shares.

28.5 Purchase of own shares

28.5.1 Introduction

An exit route that may be a viable option is for the qualifying company to buy back its own shares. Of course, this can only be undertaken outside the 'restricted period' applying to all EIS investors. In addition to the tax position (which is outlined below), it will be necessary to take advice on the company law implications before undertaking a buy-back of shares.

28.5.2 Income payment

When a company repurchases its own shares, an investor who is an individual may be treated for tax purposes as having received income or capital.

An income payment is taxed in the same way as a dividend. The taxable amount is a sum equal to the difference between the amount the company is paying for each share and the amount originally subscribed. The shareholder will receive a notional tax credit, but is liable to any higher-rate tax. Alternatively, provided that certain conditions are met, the share repurchase may be treated as a capital payment **[see 28.5.3]**.

A shareholder in a VCT company would be treated as having received an income payment because the VCT cannot meet the conditions in **28.5.4** and **28.5.5**.

Example 28.2

Alison invests £50,000 for a 30% interest in Abigail Ltd and claims £10,000 EIS relief. After five years the company agrees to buy in her shares for £49,000. As the amount she will receive does not exceed the amount she subscribed, Alison will not have to pay tax on the share purchase.

28.5.3 Capital receipt

Where the shares have appreciated, an EIS shareholder will have a tax-free gain on his or her disposal, provided that all the necessary conditions are satisfied. The shareholder would therefore want his or her receipt from the company to be treated as capital rather than income. For a shareholder to be treated as having a capital receipt when the EIS company buys in his or her shares, certain conditions **[see 28.5.4 to 28.5.8]** must be met by him or her and the company.

28.5.4 Unquoted shares

For the payment to be treated as capital the qualifying company must be an unquoted trading company or the holding company of a trading group at the time of the purchase (TA 1988, s 219). For this purpose, a company whose shares are dealt in on AIM is treated as unquoted.

28.5.5 Benefits the trade

Assuming the EIS company is carrying on a trade at the time, it will need to demonstrate to the inspector that the purchase of its own shares is for the benefit of its trade or the trade of one of its 75% subsidiaries.

28.5.6 No tax avoidance

A further condition is that one of the main purposes of the transaction must not be to enable the shareholders to participate in the company's profits without receiving a dividend; or to avoid tax (TA 1988, s 219(1)). The Inland Revenue accepts as a reason for the purchase the fact that outside investors wish to realise their investment.

28.5.7 Conditions for the investor

The main conditions to be met by the investor are that he or she must have owned the shares for five years before the purchase and must be resident and ordinarily resident in the UK in the year of assessment in which the purchase is made (TA 1988, s 220(1), (5)). There are anti-avoidance provisions, which basically prevent investors from selling shares while remaining connected with the company.

Example 28.3

Philo subscribes £50,000 for 50,000 shares in Alexandria Ltd, becomes an unpaid director and claims £10,000 EIS relief. After five years, there is a dispute over the future of the company. It is decided that Philo should resign as a director and that the company should purchase three-quarters of his shares for £55,000. It is likely that the conditions will be met and Philo will receive a tax-free capital payment from the company.

28.5.8 Clearance

There is a clearance procedure to establish whether the Inland Revenue will treat the amount received by the investor for his or her shares as capital or income (TA 1988, s 225).

28.6 Gifts of shares

28.6.1 Introduction

After a VCT or EIS investor has received investment relief **[see Chapter 7]** and held the shares for three years, he or she may lose interest in holding the shares, particularly if any gain on the shares is not likely to materialise in the near future. It may in such circumstances be worth considering gifting the shares to a relative, such as a son or daughter, or to a charity.

28.6.2 Capital gains tax

For capital gains tax purposes a gift of any asset is a disposal at market value. However, if EIS investment relief was given on the shares and not withdrawn, the gain on the first disposal of the shares after three years is tax free. If the investment relief is restricted or withdrawn, any gain arising on the disposal of EIS qualifying shares may be deferred using the gift holdover provisions **[see 23.2]**. In any event, in the case of a gift to charities, which include such bodies as universities and the British Museum, the deemed consideration ensures that no gain or loss arises (TCGA 1992, s 257).

28.6.3 Inheritance tax

Where an individual makes a gift, his or her estate is reduced and this has inheritance tax (IHT) implications. No IHT is payable on an outright gift if the donor survives for seven years (IHTA 1984, s 3A), or on gifts to charities (IHTA 1984, s 23). However, IHT is payable where an asset is gifted into a discretionary trust and on the value of a person's estate at death. Where IHT is payable, the value of what leaves a person's estate has to be ascertained and discounts can be applied to that value if certain conditions are met.

28.6.4 Business property relief

Shares in a trading company attract 100% business property relief (IHTA 1984, s 104) if, at the time of the transfer, the shares were unquoted and the shareholder had owned the shares for two years. For this purpose, shares that are traded on AIM are treated as unquoted (IR Press Release of 21 February 1995).

Example 28.4

In 2001 Philostratus subscribes £100,000 for 25% of the ordinary shares in Heroicon Ltd and claims £20,000 EIS relief. After three years, he gives them to his daughter Rachel. As they are EIS shares the capital gain on the disposal is tax free. The conditions for 100% business property relief are also met. Therefore, even if Philostratus does not survive for seven years following the gift, and Rachel still owns the shares at the time of his death, the value of the shares transferred from his estate would be reduced to nil and no IHT would be payable on the gift.

28.6.5 Stamp duty

There is no stamp duty payable on a gift of shares.

Appendix 1

Contents of a Shareholders' Agreement for EIS companies

The following list of contents is not meant to be comprehensive but will give the reader some idea of the matters that might be covered in a shareholders' agreement.

1 *Date Agreement is signed*

2 *Parties to the Agreement*

The company, the founders (if any) and the shareholders. The full names, addresses and amounts to be subscribed are usually in a Schedule attached to the agreement.

3 *Company Details*

Details are given about the company, eg incorporation date, registered number, etc. There is a statement that the company intends to be a qualifying company for the purposes of investors claiming EIS relief and a description of the business it intends to carry on.

4 *The Subscription*

This section states that the shareholders shall subscribe for the shares at a certain price and by a certain time and that the company will issue the shares. This provision might be conditional on:

* the investment of a minimum amount by shareholders generally or by the founders;
* entering into a purchase contract;
* the obtaining of a provisional EIS clearance from the Inland Revenue; and
* the passing of certain resolutions such as increasing the authorised share capital; and adopting new Articles of Association.

If this provision is conditional there would be further provisions that state what happens if the conditions are not fulfilled.

5 *Directors and Management*

There would be statements as to how directors will be appointed, removed, remunerated and of their titles and responsibilities.

6 *Advisers*

Details are given of the company's accountants, solicitors and bankers.

7 *EIS Conditions*

The company and the shareholders usually agree to use their best endeavours to ensure that the company stays within the EIS rules.

8 *Transfers of Shares*

There are usually provisions restricting transfers of shares, so that, for example, the company does not come under the control of another company.

9 *Matters Requiring Consent*

There is often a list of transactions requiring shareholders' consent.

10 *Termination of Agreement*

The period of the agreement is stated together with a list of events that would cause the agreement to terminate.

11 *Exit Route*

It is usual to state in the shareholders' agreement intention regarding any exit route. This may be in general or in specific terms, for example:

'Within six months of the fifth anniversary of this agreement a general meeting of the shareholders will be convened and the advice of the company's tax and legal advisers shall be sought.'

'In the event that the company has not been sold by the time of the annual general meeting at which the accounts for the year to . . . (third year) are approved, the Board of Directors will be irrevocably authorised to dispose of any remaining interests in the company's property and a general meeting will be held to resolve to put the company into members' voluntary liquidation.'

Specific statements must be voided if any investors are claiming EIS relief as these will be viewed as arrangements for the disposal of the shares (see **7.6.5.1**).

12 *General*

There are often miscellaneous provisions stating, for example, that:

* the agreement does not amount to a partnership;
* if there is a dispute over the interpretation of the agreement the point will be referred to an expert;
* if the agreement conflicts with the Articles of Association, the agreement will prevail.

Appendix 2

Checklist for directors of a VCT or EIS investee company

References to 'the company' are to a company which has received or will receive investment from a VCT or from EIS investors. References to 'Shares' are to shares which have attracted or will attract VCT or EIS relief. Where necessary the words 'company' and 'shares' are qualified, eg EIS shares.

1 *Before or at the time of the share issue*

(a) Ensure that professional advice is taken before offering any shares to other people (see **26.7.1** and **27.2.1**) Understand your responsibilities regarding the contents of any offer document (see **27.4.13**) and your ongoing responsibilities (see **26.8**).

(b) Do not accept subscriptions for shares which would mean that the company would exceed the £16 million gross assets test immediately after the issue (see **5.8.2**).

(c) Ensure that shares are not issued which could result in:

  * the acquisition by an individual who intends to claim EIS relief of an interest greater than 30% (see **7.6.3**);
  * the acquisition by a company (or a company and a person connected with it) of an interest greater than 50% (see **5.10.1**) in the company. This could arise where another company agrees to underwrite the minimum subscription (see **5.1.9.5**).

(d) Ensure that the shares are in fact issued on the proposed date (see **8.1.5** and **14.3.2**).

(e) If there is a prospectus issue, be aware of the date that is 40 days after the subscription lists open. If the minimum subscription has not been reached by that date, subscriptions must be sent back (see **27.4.10**).

2 *The first two years*

(a) Ensure that the share proceeds are used for a qualifying purpose (see **5.7.3**).

(b) Be aware of the following dates:

  * When the company started its trade or qualifying activities (see **6.8**).

* When the EIS four-month trading period ends and application can be made for EIS investors' tax-relief certificates (see **24.7**). Start preparing information for Form EIS 1 a week ahead of the submission date.
* The second anniversary of the share issue or the start of the trade if later. Ensure that the proceeds of the VCT or EIS share issue are employed by the company within that 24-month period (see **6.2.5**).

(c) Where capital has been raised for a UK trade, do not let its use for overseas activities exceed 50% of the total activities (see **6.4**).
(d) Ensure that the company starts its trade within two years of the share issue (see **6.8.1**).

3 *The company's relevant period*

(a) Be aware of when the company's relevant period ends (see **5.1.2** and **5.1.3**).
(b) Do not allow the company to come under the control of another company or enter into any arrangements whereby control could pass to another company at any time:

* Do not allow shares to be issued to a company if, together with persons connected with that company, your company could come under its control (see **5.1.8**).
* Take care if corporate shareholders are to be given special rights. They could become entitled to more than 50% of the company's income or assets in a winding-up (see **5.1.9** and **5.1.10**).
* Do not forget that granting an option to acquire the company's shares, albeit contingent, could result in control of the company (see **5.1.9.7**).
* Consider carefully any agreement with another company to see whether the Inland Revenue could contend that it is an arrangement to allow control of the EIS company to pass to the other company (see **5.1.7**).
* Consider carefully any loans the company obtains (see **5.1.9**).

(c) Do not set up a subsidiary or gain control of another company during your company's relevant period which will not be a qualifying subsidiary:

* Do not allow the company to control another company unless it owns more than 50% of that company's shares, votes etc (90% if that company is to use any of the proceeds of the VCT/EIS share issue for its trade.
* Do not allow the company to grant options to shareholders of another company, agreeing to buy their shares (see **5.1.7**).

(d) Do not allow the company or any of its subsidiaries to make investments (see **6.2.6**).
(e) Ensure that the company or its qualifying 90% subsidiary carries on a qualifying trade throughout its relevant period:

* Do not let the company or any of its subsidiaries carry on non-qualifying activities. Check to see if the aggregate of the company's income

from non-qualifying activities (such as rent or interest) would exceed 20% of its total income (see **5.2.3.2**).

* Do not allow the company to stop trading before starting another qualifying trade (see **6.9.1**).

(f) Monitor and plan to use any large cash balances the company may have to avoid their being treated as investments (see **6.2.9**).

(g) Do produce good management accounts for the company and review them regularly in order to monitor (e) and (f) above.

(h) If it appears that the appointment of a receiver is imminent, take action to protect the EIS shareholders' tax relief (see **6.9.5**).

4 *The first three to five years*

(a) Be aware of the conditions that must be met by the investors in their restricted periods (see **Chapter 7**).

(b) Be aware of the date when the shareholders can sell their shares without losing their initial relief. If the shares were issued at different times there would be several such dates.

(c) Do not take over a business controlled by a group of persons that includes any of the company's EIS shareholders (see **7.6.4**).

(d) Do not allow an EIS company to repay or redeem any share capital or give value or provide benefits to any of its shareholders (see **12.5.4** and **12.8.2**).

(e) If there is an EIS shareholder who is also a loan creditor consider the effect on him if the company repays its borrowings (see **7.6.3.3** and **12.5.9**).

(f) If you are claiming EIS relief (for EIS as an unpaid director) ensure that you only receive payments that are permitted (see **7.6.2.9**).

(g) If you are claiming EIS and are being paid for your services to the company, ensure you understand what is meant by 'reasonable remuneration' (see **7.6.2.11**).

Appendix 3

Checklist for VCT or EIS investors

References to 'shares' are to shares that have attracted or will attract VCT or EIS relief. Similarly, references to 'the company' are to a company that has received or will receive a VCT or EIS investment. If the rule relates only to one of the reliefs or where otherwise necessary the word 'company' or 'shares' will be qualified, eg EIS company.

1 *Before the share issue*

(a) If there is a shareholders' agreement (see **Appendix 1**) ensure that you read it carefully and agree with its contents.
(b) Do not obtain a loan the terms of which are linked to your investment (see **11.2** and **12.4**).
(c) Decide whether you wish the shares to be issued in your name or in the name of a nominee (see **8.2.6**).
(d) Check that your proposed investment will not exceed the VCT or EIS total investment limits of £200,000 in a tax year (see **7.5** and **7.6.1.8**).
(e) Check to see if you have sufficient income tax liability in the tax year in which the shares will be issued to benefit from the VCT or EIS investment relief (see **9.3.3** and **20.2.8**).
(f) If you expect to claim EIS investment relief, ensure that you are not connected with the company (see **7.6.2.1**).
(g) Check that the EIS company has received provisional clearance from the Inland Revenue that the company and its trade qualify (see **24.6**).
(h) Be aware of the rules regarding your UK-residence status if you are claiming deferral relief if your tax status is likely to change in the next three to five years (see **7.6.1.1** and **15.7.4**).
(i) Ensure that the company's directors undertake that they will endeavour to keep the company within the qualifying conditions for the required period (see **Appendix 1**).

2 *During the company's relevant period*

(a) If directors of an EIS company announce that they are proposing changes to:

* how the share proceeds will be employed;
* the type of trade carried on;
* the way in which the trade is carried on;

ask whether directors have taken advice as to whether the EIS conditions will still be met.

(b) Make sure that the directors of the company keep you informed as to its progress and send you copies of the company's annual report and accounts.

(c) Do not allow an EIS company to redeem any of your shares or give you value or provide you with any benefits (see **Chapter 12**).

3 *If the company is in financial difficulties*

(a) If there is a danger that the company might cease to trade before it has carried on a qualifying trade for the required period put pressure on the directors to take action (see **6.9.1**).

(b) If the share become of negligible value make a loss-relief claim (see **20.6.3**).

(c) If the company is to be taken over, check to see whether it can be done in such a manner as to cause the minimum impact on your EIS relief (see **28.2.3**).

Appendix 4

Recognised Stock Exchanges

The following exchanges are recognised stock exchanges under TA 1988, s 841.

List of Stock Exchanges designated as 'recognised stock exchanges' by Order of the Board under Section 841(1)(b) ICTA 1988 as at current date; and date of recognition.

The Athens Stock Exchange	14 Jun 1993
The Australian Stock Exchange and any of its stock exchange subsidiaries	22 Sep 1988
The Cayman Islands Stock Exchange	4 Mar 2004
The Colombo Stock Exchange	21 Feb 1972
The Copenhagen Stock Exchange	22 Oct 1970
The Helsinki Stock Exchange	22 Oct 1970
The Johannesburg Stock Exchange	22 Oct 1970
The Korea Stock Exchange	10 Oct 1994
The Kuala Lumpur Stock Exchange	10 Oct 1994
The Mexico Stock Exchange	10 Oct 1994
The New Zealand Stock Exchange	22 Sep 1988
The Rio De Janeiro Stock Exchange	17 Aug 1995
The Sao Paulo Stock Exchange	11 Dec 1995
The Singapore Stock Exchange	30 Jun 1977
The Stockholm Stock Exchange	18 Jul 1985
The Stock Exchange of Thailand	10 Oct 1994
The Swiss Stock Exchange	12 May 1997

Any stock exchange in the following countries which is a stock exchange within the meaning of the law of the particular country relating to stock exchanges (or as specified below):

Austria	22 Oct 1970
Belgium	22 Oct 1970
Canada – Any stock exchange prescribed for the purposes of the Canadian Income Tax Act	22 Oct 1970

France	22 Oct 1970
Germany	5 Aug 1971
Guernsey	10 Dec 2002
Hong Kong – Any stock exchange which is recognised under Section 2A(1) of the Hong Kong Companies Ordinance	26 Feb 1971
Italy	3 May 1972
Ireland (Republic of)	22 Oct 1970
Japan	22 Oct 1970
Luxembourg	21 Feb 1972
Netherlands	22 Oct 1970
Norway	22 Oct 1970
Portugal	21 Feb 1972
Spain	5 Aug 1971
USA – Any exchange registered with the Securities and Exchange Commission of the United States as a National securities exchange	22 Oct 1970
USA – The NASDAQ Stock Market as maintained through the facilities of the National Association of Securities Dealers, Inc and its subsidiaries	10 Mar 1992

Appendix 5

Useful addresses

Small Company Enterprise Centre (SCEC) contact details

All VCT, EIS and CVS clearances should be sent to the following address:

Small Company Enterprise Centre
TIDO
Tŷ Glas
Llanishen
Cardiff
CF14 5ZG

Tel: 0292 032 7400
Fax: 0292 032 7398
E-mail enterprise.centre@ir.gsi.gov.uk

The staff at this centre will allocate the clearance to one of the SCECs listed below for consideration by an inspector of taxes:

Small Company Enterprise Centre Cardiff
Tŷ Glas
Llanishen
Cardiff
CF14 5ZG

Small Company Enterprise Centre Dundee
Caledonian House
Greenmarket
Dundee
Tayside
DD1 4XQ

Small Company Enterprise Centre Dundee
Medvale House
Mote Road
Maidstone
Kent
ME15 6AF

Association of Investment Trust Companies
Durrant House
8–13 Chiswell Street
London
EC1Y 4YY
0207 282 5555

British Venture Capital Association (BVCA)
Tower 3
3 Clements Inn
London
WC2A 2A2
0207 025 2950

EISA, Enterprise Investment Scheme Association
c/o Tylers Croft
Hitchen Hatch Lane
Sevenoaks
Kent
TN13 3AY
www.eisa.org.uk
01732 465828

Inland Revenue
Information Centre
South-West Wing
Bush House
Strand
London WC2B 4RD
0207 438 7772

Inland Revenue
Small Company Enterprise Centre
Tŷ Glas Road
Llanishen
Cardiff
CF14 5ZG
0292 032 7400

Inland Revenue
Capital and Savings
Sapphire House
550 Streetsbrook Road
Solihull
B91 1QU
0121 713 4617 (Venture Capital Trusts)

The Patent Office
Concept House
Cardiff Road
Newport
Gwent
NP10 8QQ
01633 81400

Registrar of Companies

England and Wales
Companies House
Crown Way, Maindy
Cardiff
CF4 3UZ
0870 333 3636
enquiries@companieshouse.gov.uk
www.companieshouse.gov.uk

Northern Ireland
Companies Registry
64 Chichester Street
Belfast
BT1 4JX
0289 023 4488

Scotland
Companies House
37 Castle Terrace
Edinburgh
EH1 2EB
0870 333 3636

Small Firms Centre
Dial 100 and ask for
Freefone Enterprise

Appendix 6

IR forms

Inland Revenue

Enterprise Investment Scheme-Company Statement

(for use where the shares are issued after 6 March 2001)

There is a time limit for submitting this form - ***see Note 1 on page 4 for details.***

Please use CAPITAL LETTERS or typescript to complete this form.

To ______ *See Note 1* Reference ______

Company details

Name of company issuing shares ______

Address of registered office ______ Postcode ______

Date of incorporation / / ______ Company Registration number ______

1 The following subscribers have asked the company to issue certificates on forms EIS3 in respect of shares which it issued to them on / / *see Note 3*

Full names and addresses of the subscribers (*see Note 3*)	Description of shares, and nominal value of each share	Number of shares issued	Amount subscribed £
	Totals		

2 All shares of the class described at **1** above, which were issued on the date shown above, were issued to raise money for a qualifying business activity consisting of

'✓'

☐ a trade, or preparation for a trade, of ______

☐ research and development, intended to lead to a trade of ______

carried on, or intended to be carried on, by

☐ the company, or

☐ a subsidiary company named ______

The trade, or research and development, mentioned above commenced on / /

EIS1(2001)(Substitute)(LexisNexis UK) 1 BS8/01

3 The issued share capital of the company immediately after the issue of the shares shown at **1** was

Description of shares, and nominal value of each share	Total number of issued shares	Amount of share capital £

4 The loan capital (*see Note 4*) of the company immediately after the issue of the shares was

Name of holder or lender	Nature of loan capital	Amount £

5 The subscribers listed at **1** also held the following share capital at the date given at **1**

Full name of the holder	Description of each class of share held and nominal value of each share	Number of shares held

6 There have been the following changes relating to the company's issued share capital and loan capital since the issue of the shares listed at **1**

7 In the period beginning one year before the date shown at **1** and ending on the date of the Declaration on page 3, value has been received (*see Note 5*) by persons from the company or any person connected with the company as shown below

Date	Name of person receiving value	Nature of value received	Amount of value received £
/ /			
/ /			
/ /			

8 In the period beginning one year before the date shown at **1** and ending on the date of the declaration on page 3, the company or a subsidiary has repaid, redeemed or repurchased share capital as follows

Date	Name of holder of shares	Amount paid £
/ /		
/ /		
/ /		

9 Details of all companies which have been subsidiaries of the company, or controlled by the company, at any time since the date shown at **1** are as follows

Date it became a subsidiary	Name of company	Nature of business
/ /		
/ /		
/ /		

2

Declaration

I declare that:

- the trade (or research and development) mentioned at 2 has been carried on for four months (or was carried on until the date when the company commenced winding up)
- the shares listed at 1 were issued wholly for cash, which was fully paid by the time of their issue
- they are ordinary shares which have not, at any time since their issue, carried any preferential right to dividends or to the company's assets on a winding up, or any right to be redeemed
- they were issued for bona fide commercial purposes and not as part of a scheme or arrangement, a main purpose of which was the avoidance of tax
- there are no arrangements relating to the shares within Section 299B or paragraph II, Schedule 5B, TCGA 1992
- the money raised by the issue of all shares of the class described at 1 which were issued on the date shown at 1 has been, or will be, employed for the purpose of the business activity mentioned at 2 . Of that money at least 80% has been or will be employed by the time specified in Section 289(3), and any money remaining within the following 12 months
- immediately before the issue of the shares the value of the gross assets of the company and its subsidiaries did not exceed £15,000,000, and immediately after the issue that value did not exceed £16,000,000 (see Note 6)
- at the date shown at 1 the company was an unquoted company (see Note 6) and there were no arrangements for it to cease to be an unquoted company
- from the date shown at 1 to the date of this Declaration (or, if the company is now in liquidation, to the date when the winding up commenced)
  - the business activity mentioned at 2 has been carried on wholly or mainly in the United Kingdom
  - the company has **either** existed for the purpose given in Section 293(2)(a) **or** been the parent company of a trading group
  - where the business activity mentioned at 2 is carried on by a subsidiary, that subsidiary has satisfied the requirements of Section 289(1A)
  - the company has not
    a) had a 51% subsidiary (see Note 6) or controlled (or, together with any other person connected with it, controlled) another company except in so far as the conditions on Section 308 have been satisfied
    b) been a 51% subsidiary of another company or been controlled by another company (or by another company and any person connected with that other conpany)

  and there have been no arrangements whereby either of these could cease to be the case
- the company intends that all the conditions of the scheme relating to the company and the shares will continue to be satisfied until three years after the date shown at 1 or, where the money was raised for a trade not yet commenced, after the date of commencement (see Note 7)
- to the best of the company's knowledge and belief the information given on this form is correct.

Signature	Date
	/ /
Capacity in which signed	
	(see Note 2)

3

Notes

All statutory references made in this form are references to Part VII, Chapter III, Income and Corporation Taxes Act, 1988 as revised by Finance Act 1994 and subsequently amended, except where otherwise indicated.

1 If the company's tax affairs are already dealt with at an office of the Small Company Enterprise Centre, please send this form to that office. Otherwise, please send it to

Small Company Enterprise Centre,
TIDO,
Ty Glas,
Cardiff CF14 5ZG

and in a covering letter state the name and reference of the Inland Revenue office which currently deals with the company.

The form should not be submitted until the trade (or research and development) mentioned at 2 has been carried on for four months. But it must be submitted within

- two years after the completion of that four month period, or
- two years after the end of the tax year of assessment in which the shares were issued, **whichever is the later.**

2 This form may be signed by the secretary of the company issuing the shares or any person authorised by the company or, if the company is in liquidation, by the liquidator.
If a company furnishes a false statement it is liable to a penalty not exceeding £3,000.

3 The date when shares are issued is the date when the subscriber's title to them becomes complete. This cannot be before the date when the ownership of the shares is recorded in the company's Register of Members.

Where certificates are requested in respect of shares issued on different dates or shares of a different class, a separate statement must be supplied in respect of each date or class.

Where the shares are registered in the name of someone other than the subscriber please also state the name and address of that person.

4 Loan capital for this purpose includes the items at Section 291B(7) except a bank overdraft as in Section 291B(9). Where the holder or lender is known to be a nominee, this fact should be stated. If known, the name and address of the beneficial owner of the loan capital should be stated.

5 The circumstances in which value is received by a person, and how the amount of that value is computed, are as set out in Sections 300-301A, and 303, and in paragraphs 13- 13C, Schedule 5B, TCGA 1992. 'Insignificant' amounts must be included. If replacement value has been received, please supply details in a covering letter.

6 For the meaning of:

- 51% subsidiary - see Sections 312(1) and 838
- gross assets - see Statement of Practice 2/00
- person connected with - see Sections 312(2) and 839
- unquoted company - see Section 312(1) to (1E)
- parent company of a trading group - see Section 293(3A).
- value received - see Section 300-301A, and paragraphs 13-13C, Schedule 5B, TC6A 1992

7 The company is obliged to notify the Inspector within 60 days if any event occurs as a result of which the Declaration on page 3 could no longer be made. (Section 310 and paragraph 16, Schedule 5B, TCGA 1992).

For official use

A copy of this form has been sent to Analysis and Research Initials [ ] Date [/ /]

Inland Revenue

Certificate and Claim to Relief

Enterprise Investment Scheme

Part 1 Certificate

A certificate may not be issued to a subscriber on this form unless its issue has been authorised by the Inland Revenue. To obtain authorisation, the company must provide the Inland Revenue with details of the subscription on form *EIS1*.

This certificate is to be signed by the company secretary or by any person authorised by it, or in the case of a company in liquidation, by the liquidator.

A company giving a certificate fraudulently, or negligently, or issuing a certificate without the authority of the Inland Revenue, is liable to a penalty of up to £3,000.

Separate certificates are required for eligible shares issued on different dates.

To: *(enter full name and address of person who subscribed for eligible shares)*

Postcode

The following eligible shares were subscribed for by you and issued as directed by you

Description of shares	Nominal value of each share	Number of shares issued	Amount subscribed £	Date of issue of the shares

I certify that the conditions of the scheme, other than those which you have to satisfy, are satisfied in relation to these shares.

The relevant period related to these shares will end in / /

You have received value from the company or a subsidiary amounting to £
(See page 2 for the effect of this on your tax relief).

The issue of this certificate was authorised by Inland Revenue office

Reference number

Signature Date / /

Capacity in which signed

Company name and registered office address

Postcode

Please keep this certificate. If you claim relief, you may be asked to produce it.

EIS3(2000) (Substitute)(LexisNexis UK) 1 BMSD 5/00

Notes for claiming tax relief

You may wish to claim -

- **income tax relief** on the amounts you subscribed for the shares, or
- **deferral relief,** which enables you to defer a chargeable gain which you have reinvested in these shares, or
- **both.**

A claim to income tax relief should normally be made on your Tax Return. But in some circumstances (explained in the notes later) you should use the claim form provided on page 3.

A claim to deferral relief should be made using the claim form provided on page 3.

Rules relating to both reliefs

You are not eligible for either relief if -

- you subscribed for the shares as part of a scheme or arrangement aimed at avoiding tax
- you receive a loan which would not have been made, or would not have been made on the same terms, were it not for the investment in the shares
- you have an option under which you can sell the shares.

If you have received value from the company (see page 1) you are not eligible to claim deferral relief, and the amount on which you can claim income tax relief must be restricted by the amount received.

If any of the above should take place before the end of the 'relevant period', or if you dispose of any of the shares within that period, whether by way of sale, gift or exchange, relief which you have obtained may need to be withdrawn or reduced. If any such event occurs you must report it to your Inland Revenue office within 60 days. The date when the relevant period ends is shown on page 1.

Rules relating to income tax relief only

You are not eligible for the relief if

- you are, or have been, 'connected with the company' (see sections 291 - 291B), **unless** you qualify for relief under Section 291A(4) **or**
- you are disqualified by the rules relating to replacement capital as a previous owner of the company's business.

No relief is due if your subscriptions for shares in the company issued in the year total less than £500. And there is a limit of £150,000 on the **total** amount on which you can obtain the relief for any one tax year.

The relief is normally due for the tax year (ending on 5 April) in which the shares are issued. (You can find the date of issue in Part 1 of this form). But in the case of shares issued between 6 April and 5 October inclusive, you can claim the relief as if some of the shares had been issued in the previous year. (You may wish to do this if you do not have sufficient tax liability for the year of issue to make full use of the relief). The number of shares you can have treated in this way is limited to half the number issued to you in the year, and relief on no more than £25,000 out of the **total** amount on which you are entitled to claim the relief for the year can be allowed in this way.

Statutory references

Except where otherwise indicated, all statutory references in this form are to Part VII, Chapter III of the Income and Corporation Taxes Act 1988 as revised by Finance Act 1994 and subsequently amended.

2

Part 2 Claim forms

To: ______ **Inland Revenue office**

My reference number is ______

My National Insurance number is ______

The claim(s) below relate to a subscription of £ ______ for shares in

______ issued on / /

Declaration

I hold an EIS certificate in respect of these shares whose issue was authorised by

______ Inland Revenue office under reference ______

I claim relief as shown below. The particulars given in this claim are correct to the best of my knowledge and belief.

Signature ______ Date / /

Full name and address in CAPITAL letters

Postcode

Claim to EIS Income Tax relief *(please read the notes on page 4 before deciding whether to complete this part of the form)*

'✓' as appropriate

- I wish relief to be allowed in my PAYE coding. ☐
- I claim relief against a payment on account of my tax bill for the current year. ☐
- I am claiming relief for a year for which I have already sent in a Tax Return. ☐

The amount on which I claim relief is *(Enter year)*

£ ______ for the year ended 5 April ______ being the year in which the shares were issued.

£ ______ for the year ended 5 April ______ being the previous year (*see page* 2).

Claim to EIS deferral relief *(see the notes on page 4)*

The chargeable gains against which I claim the relief are -

Asset disposed of	Date of disposal	Chargeable gain	Gain to be deferred

3

Notes

Income Tax relief

1 **If your shares were issued in the current tax year,** you can claim relief for that year now:
- if you pay tax under PAYE
- if you have made, or are making, a payment on account of your tax bill for the year.

Complete the claim form overleaf, then tear off this page and send it to your Inland Revenue office.

Remember that if you are sent a Tax Return after the end of the year, you will also have to enter details of the claim on that Return.

2 **If you want to claim relief for a previous tax year and you have already sent in your Tax Return for that year,** complete the claim form overleaf, then tear off this page and send it to your Inland Revenue office.

3 **In all other circumstances, do not complete this form,** but
- keep it carefully until you receive your Tax Return
- in the appropriate box on the Tax Return, enter the **total** subscriptions on which you are claiming relief
- in the large box reserved for 'additional information' at the end of the Tax Return, enter
  - the name of the company invested in
  - the amount of the subscription qualifying for relief
  - the date of issue of the shares
  - the name of the Inland Revenue office authorising the issue of the certificate on Part 1 of this form, and its reference.

Deferral Relief

1 If your chargeable gain accrues in the current tax year and the shares were issued either in the current tax year, or in a previous year, complete the claim form provided and send it with your Tax Return to your Inland Revenue office after the end of the tax year.

Remember that you will still need to enter the relevant chargeable gain(s) details on page CG1 (or pages CG2 and CG3 if appropriate) of the Capital Gains pages (see the Notes on Capital Gains).

2 If your chargeable gain accrued in a previous tax year, complete the form provided and send it to your Inland Revenue office, with your Tax Return if not already submitted.

Again, remember to enter the chargeable gain(s) details on the appropriate Capital Gains page if submitting your claim with a Tax Return.

Both Income Tax Relief and Deferral Relief

If you wish to claim both income tax relief and deferral relief on the same acquisition of shares, follow the notes on income tax relief in the first instance. Keep a copy of your claim form for your deferral relief claim if it is to be sent at a later date in accordance with the notes on deferral relief.

Inland Revenue

Corporate Venturing Scheme Compliance Statement

There is a time limit for submitting this form - ***see Note 1 on page 4 for details.***

Please use CAPITAL LETTERS or typescript to complete this form.

To **Small Companies Enterprise Centre**
TIDO, Ty Glas,
Llanishen, Cardiff, CF14 5ZG

CVS Unit reference (*if applicable*) ______________________

Name of company issuing shares ______________________

Address of registered office ______________________

Postcode ______________________

Date of incorporation ___ / ___ / ___ Company Registration number ______________________

Inland Revenue office dealing with the company ______________________ Reference ______________________

1 The following subscribers have asked the company to issue certificates on forms CVS3 in respect of shares which it issued to them on ___ / ___ / ___ *see Note 3*

Names and addresses of the subscribers (*see Note 3*)	Description of shares, and nominal value of each share	Number of shares issued	Amount subscribed £
Please use a separate schedule if there is not enough space.	**Totals**		

2 All shares of the class described at **1** above which were issued on the date shown above were issued to raise money for a qualifying business activity consisting of

√

☐ a trade, or preparation for a trade, of ______________________

☐ research and development, intended to lead to a trade of ______________________

carried on, or intended to be carried on, by

☐ the company, or

☐ a subsidiary company named ______________________

Trading (or research and development) commenced on ___ / ___ / ___

CVS1 (Substitute)(LexisNexis)

1

3 Immediately after the issue of the shares shown at **1**, the issued share capital of the company was

Description of shares, and nominal value of each share	Total number of issued shares	Amount of share capital £

4 Immediately after the issue of the shares, the company had the following loan capital (*see Note 4*) carrying a right to conversion into shares

Name of holder or lender	Nature of loan capital	Amount £

5 The subscribers listed at **1** also held the following share capital at the date given at **1**

Name of the holder	Description of each class of share held and nominal value of each share	Number of shares held

6 There have been the following changes relating to the company's issued share capital and loan capital since the issue of the shares listed at **1** and the date of the Declaration on page 3

7 In the period beginning one year before the date shown at **1** and ending on the date of the Declaration on page 3, value has been received (*see Note 5*) by persons from the company or any person connected with the company (*see Note 6*) as shown below

Date	Name of person receiving value	Nature of value received	Amount of value received £
/ /			
/ /			
/ /			

8 In the period beginning one year before the date shown at **1** and ending on the date of the Declaration on page 3, the company or a subsidiary has repaid, redeemed or repurchased share capital as follows

Date	Name of holder of shares	Amount paid £
/ /		
/ /		
/ /		

9 Details of all companies which have been subsidiaries of the company, or controlled by the company (*see Note 6*), at any time since the issue of the shares listed at **1** are as follows

Name of company	Date it became a subsidiary	Nature of business
	/ /	
	/ /	
	/ /	

Declaration

I declare that:

- the trade (or research and development) mentioned at **2** (page 1) has been carried on for four months (or was carried on until the date when the company commenced winding up or went into receivership)
- the shares listed at **1**

  - were issued wholly for cash, which was fully paid by the time of their issue

  - are ordinary shares which have not, at any time since their issue, carried any preferential right to dividends or to the company's assets on a winding up, or any right to be redeemed

  - were issued for bona fide commercial purposes and not as part of a scheme or arrangement, a main purpose of which was the avoidance of tax

- there are no arrangements relating to the shares within paragraph 37
- the money raised by the issue of all shares of the class described at **1** which were issued on the date shown at **1** has been, or will be, employed for the purpose of the business activity mentioned at **2** and within the time allowed (*see Note 7*)
- immediately before the issue of the shares the value of the gross assets of the company and its subsidiaries did not exceed £15,000,000, and immediately after the issue that value did not exceed £16,000,000
- at the date shown at **1** the company was an unquoted company and there were no arrangements for it to cease to be an unquoted company
- from the date shown at **1** to the date of this Declaration (or, if the company is now in liquidation or receivership to the date when the winding up or receivership commenced)

  - the activity mentioned at **2** has been carried on wholly or mainly in the United Kingdom

  - the company has **either** existed for the purpose given in paragraph 23(2) **or** satisfied the conditions of paragraph 23(3)

  - the company and its subsidiaries have satisfied the partnerships and joint ventures requirement in paragraph 19

  - at least 20% of the ordinary share capital has been beneficially owned by independent individuals as defined in paragraph 18(2)

  - the company has not

  a) had a subsidiary or controlled (or, together with any other person connected with it, controlled) another company (*see Note 6*) except in so far as the conditions of paragraph 20 have been satisfied

  b) been controlled by another company (or by another company and any person connected with that other company) (*see Note 6*)

  and there have been no arrangements whereby either of these could cease to be the case

- the company intends that all the conditions of the scheme relating to the company and the shares will continue to be satisfied until the end of the qualification period (*see Notes 6 and 8*)
- to the best of the company's knowledge and belief the information given on this form is correct.

Signature ______________________ Date ___/___/___

Capacity in which signed ______________________

(*see Note 2*)

3

Notes

References in this form to paragraphs are to paragraphs of Schedule 15, Finance Act 2000. Other statutory references are references to Income and Corporation Taxes Act, 1988 as amended by subsequent Finance Acts.

1 This form should not be submitted until the trade or research and development for which the money was raised has been carried on for four months. But it must be submitted within

- two years after the completion of that four month period, or
- two years after the end of the accounting period in which the shares were issued, **whichever is the later.**

2 This form may be signed by the secretary of the company issuing the shares or any person authorised by the company. If a company makes a false statement it is liable to a penalty not exceeding £3,000.

3 Where certificates are requested in respect of shares issued on different dates, or shares of different classes, a separate compliance statement must be supplied in respect of each issue.

Where the shares are registered in the name of someone other than the subscriber please also state the name and address of that person.

4 Loan capital for this purpose includes the items at paragraph 7(3) except a bank overdraft as in paragraph 7(4). Where the holder or lender is known to be a nominee, this fact should be stated. If known, the name and address of the beneficial owner of the loan capital should be stated.

5 The circumstances in which value is received, and how the amount of that value is computed, are as set out in paragraphs 47 - 52. 'Insignificant' amounts must be included. If the company has received any replacement value as set out in paragraph 54 details may be supplied in a covering letter.

6 For the meaning of:

- controlled - see Section 840
- ordinary share capital - see Section 832(1)
- person connected with - see paragraph 102(3) and Section 839
- qualification period - see paragraph 3
- unquoted company - see paragraph 16.

7 Of the money raised, at least 80% has to be spent within 12 months of the shares being issued, and any money remaining must be spent within the following 12 months.

8 The company is obliged to notify the Inspector within 60 days if any event occurs within the qualification period as a result of which the Declaration on page 3 could no longer be made (paragraph 65).

4

Index

A

Accountancy services, 6.5.10
Accounting reference date, 26.8.5
Addresses,
  useful, App.5
AIM, 1.8
Alternative investment market (AIM), 1.8
Annual general meeting (AGM), 26.8.1
Annual return, 26.8.7
Anti-avoidance,
  corporate venturing scheme (CVS), 5.17.7
  CVS disposal relief, 19.6.2.1
  enterprise investment scheme (EIS), 7.6.1.9
  provisions, 1.5
  VCT investment relief, 7.3.3
Approval,
  corporate venturing scheme (CVS), 24.9–24.9.5
  venture capital trust (VCT) scheme, 1.2.2, 2.2–2.2.4, 24.2–24.2.9
    appeals, 24.2.9
    application for full approval, 24.2.5.2
    application procedure, 24.2.5–24.2.9
    continuing to meet conditions, 24.2.3
    effective date of approval, 24.2.7
    eligible shares, 24.2.2
    generally, 24.2.1
    information required for provisional approval, 24.2.5.1
    notice of provisional approval, 24.2.6
    provisional approval, 24.2.4–24.2.4.2
    refusal to grant VCT status, 24.2.8
    second accounting period, 24.2.4.1
    three-year initial period, 24.2.4.2
    withdrawal, 24.4–24.4.5
Arrangements,
  corporate venturing scheme (CVS), 5.1.6
  enterprise investment scheme (EIS), 5.1.7
  qualifying companies, 5.1.7
  venture capital trust (VCT) scheme, 5.1.7
Articles of association, 26.6.9
Associated persons,
  EIS deferral relief, 15.8.2.1
Associates,
  corporate venturing scheme (CVS), 5.17.2
  meaning, 7.3.4.1, 7.6.2.3
  small private schemes, 26.2–26.2.6
    joint ownership, 26.2.4
    partners, 26.2.3
    personal representatives, 26.2.6
    relatives, 26.2.2
    trustees of related settlements, 26.2.5

B

Banking, 6.5.5
BES, 1.1.2, 1.3.1, 1.6, 3.1.1
Bona fide contingencies,
  control, 5.1.9.7
Bonus issue,
  CVS disposal relief, 19.3.4
  EIS disposal relief, 18.3.6
  VCT disposal relief, 17.3.6
British Venture Capital Association, 27.6.2
BSS, 1.1.2, 1.6, 3.1.1
Business angels, 7.6.2.11
  enterprise investment scheme (EIS), 3.2.1
Business expansion scheme (BES), 1.1.2, 1.3.1, 1.6, 3.1.1
Business plans, 26.6.2, 27.3.1
Business start-up scheme, 1.1.2, 1.6, 3.1.1

C

Capital gains,
  relief, *see* Deferral relief
  venture capital trust (VCT) scheme, 2.2.4
Capital gains tax,
  venture capital trust (VCT) scheme, 2.3.2
Certificates,
  corporate venturing scheme (CVS), 24.10–24.10.8
    appeal, 24.10.6
    claiming investment relief, 24.10.1
    compliance certificates, 24.10.5
    compliance statements, 24.10.4
    informal approaches, 24.10.8

Certificates – *contd*
corporate venturing scheme (CVS) – *contd*
investing company's entitlement to claim, 24.10.2
penalties, 24.10.7
refusal, 24.10.6
time limits, 24.10.3
enterprise investment scheme (EIS), 3.2.1, 24.7–24.7.2, 24.8–24.8.11
appeals against refusal to authorise certificates, 24.8.5
checking claims, 24.8.11
Form EIS 1, 24.8.1
Form EIS 2, 24.8.6
Form EIS 3, 24.8.7
Form EIS 5, 24.8.8
information required, 24.8.2
penalties, 24.8.3, 24.8.9
submission of form EIS 1, 24.8.1
small private schemes, 26.3.9
venture capital trust (VCT) scheme, 24.3.5.2, 24.5–24.5.4
claiming investment relief, 24.5.3
contents, 24.5.2
form, 24.5.2
Clawback of relief, 26.9–26.9.6
Close company, 2.2.1
Commodities, dealing in, 6.5.3
Company,
accounting reference date, 26.8.5
annual general meeting (AGM), 26.8.1
annual return, 26.8.7
formation, *see* Formation of private company
reorganisations, *see* Company reorganisations
resolutions, 26.8.3
share issue, 26.7–26.7.5
Company reorganisations,
CVS disposal relief, 19.3–19.3.6.1
bonus issues, 19.3.4
deferral shares, 19.3.2.1
qualifying corporate bonds, 19.3.5
reconstructions, 19.3.6
reorganisations, 19.3.2
rights issue, 19.3.3
takeovers, 19.3.6.1
EIS disposal relief, 18.3–18.3.7
bonus issue, 18.3.6
categories of share, 18.3.3
rights issue, 18.3.5
separate identification, 18.3.4
subdivision, 18.3.2
rights issue, 19.3.3
VCT disposal relief, 17.3–17.3.7
bonus issue, 17.3.6
categories of share, 17.3.3
investment-relief shares, 17.3.3.2
new shares not VCT shares, where, 17.3.7
rights issue, 17.3.5
Company reorganisations – *contd*
VCT disposal relief – *contd*
separate identification following, 17.3.4
shares eligible for relief, 17.3.3.1
subdivision of shares, 17.3.2
Company secretary, 7.6.2.5, 26.6.12, 27.2.6
Connected persons,
corporate venturing scheme (CVS), 5.1.6
EIS deferral relief, 15.8.2.1
EIS disposal relief, 18.6.3, 18.8.4
EIS investment relief, 12.5.3.1
enterprise investment scheme (EIS), 5.1.6, 7.6.2–7.6.2.10
ability to control the company or a subsidiary, 7.6.3.5
approved EIS funds, 7.6.5
associate, meaning of, 7.6.2.3, 7.6.2.8, 7.6.2.3
business angels, 7.6.2.11
company secretaries, 7.6.2.5
director, meaning of, 7.6.2.7
directors' companies, 7.6.2.10
employees, 7.6.2.4
generally, 7.6.2.1
individuals with a significant interest in the company, 7.6.3–7.6.3.5
loan capital, 7.6.3.3
ownership of a trade, 7.6.4.2
partners, 7.6.2.4
preliminary definition of connection, 7.6.2.2
replacement capital, 7.6.4–7.6.4.2
subscriber shares, 7.6.3.2
subsidiary, meaning of, 7.6.2.6
unpaid directors, 7.6.2.9
example, 5.1.6
meaning, 5.1.6
qualifying companies, 5.1.6
venture capital trust (VCT) scheme, 5.1.6
Control,
associated, 5.1.9.2
bona fide contingencies, 5.1.9.7
broader definition, 5.1.9–5.1.9.8
corporate venturing scheme (CVS), 5.1.8, 5.1.9–5.1.10
CVS investee company, 5.15.1
definition,
broad, 5.1.9–5.1.9.8
narrow, 5.1.10
enterprise investment scheme (EIS), 5.1.8, 5.1.9–5.1.10
entitlement to acquire, 5.1.9.1
management company, 5.1.9.8
narrow definition, 5.1.10
nominees, 5.1.9.2
participators, 5.1.9.3
qualifying companies, 5.1.8, 5.1.9–5.1.10
shares charged against loans, 5.1.9.6
undertakings, 5.1.9.5
underwriting, 5.1.9.5

Control – *contd*
  VCT investee companies, 5.4–5.4.6
    convertible shares and securities, 5.4.6
    fixed-rate preference shareholders, 5.4.3
    generally, 5.4.1
    loan creditors, 5.4.4
    meaning of control, 5.4.2
    restructuring of company, 5.4.5
  venture capital organisations, 5.1.9.4
  venture capital trust (VCT) scheme, 5.1.8, 5.1.9–5.1.10
Convertible shares and securities, 5.4.6
Corporate venturing scheme (CVS), 1.1.1, 4.1–4.2.3
  aim, 1.1.2, 1.4.1
  approval, 24.9–24.9.5
  arrangements, 5.1.6
  associates, 5.17.2
  background, 1.1.2
  certificates, 24.10–24.10.8
    appeal, 24.10.6
    claiming investment relief, 24.10.1
    compliance certificates, 24.10.5
    compliance statements, 24.10.4
    investing company's entitlement to claim, 24.10.2
    penalties, 24.10.7
    refusal, 24.10.6
    time limits, 24.10.3
  clearance certificates, 24.10–24.10.8
  connected persons, 5.1.6
  control, *see* Control
  employment of funds in a given way, 5.2.5–5.2.5.9
    example, 5.2.5
    first period, 5.2.5.2
    intermediate rules, 5.2.5.4–5.2.5.8
    joint ventures, 5.2.5.4
    newest rules, 5.2.5.1
    old rules, 5.2.5.9
    partnerships, 5.2.5.4
    previous traders, 5.2.5.4
    second period, 5.2.5.3
  expiry, 1.1.2
  generally, 24.9.1
    advance clearances, 24.9.5
    appeals, 24.9.4
    applications, 24.9.2
    information, 24.9.2
    information notices, 24.9.3
  independence requirement, 5.1.8
  information powers,
    interest on withdrawn relief, 25.4.6
    investee company, information provided by, 25.4.3
    investor company providing information, 25.4.2
    notices relating to withdrawal of relief, 25.4.1

Corporate venturing scheme (CVS) – *contd*
  information powers – *contd*
    penalties, 25.4.5
    required by revenue, information, 25.4.4
  Inland Revenue booklet, 1.5
  introduction, 1.1.2, 1.4.1, 1.6, 4.1
  investee company, 4.2.2, 5.12–5.12.6.4
    administration, 5.12.3.1
    cease trading, arrangements to, 5.12.6.2
    control, 5.15.1
    disposal, 5.12.6.1
    disposal of assets, arrangements for, 5.12.6.3
    employment of funds in a given way, 5.12.4
    exchange, 5.12.6.1
    general rule, 5.12.1
    gross-assets limit, 5.13.2
    independence requirement, 5.15.1
    individual-owners requirement, 5.12.5
    insuring against loss, arrangements for, 5.12.6.4
    limits of investment, 5.13–5.13.2
    liquidation, 5.12.3.1
    maximum investment, 5.13.1
    partnerships, 5.12.3.2
    pre-arranged exits, 5.12.6–5.12.6.4
    qualifying subsidiaries, 5.16–5.16.7
    receivership, 5.12.3.1
    repurchase arrangements, 5.12.6.1
    share capital, 5.14–5.14.2
    trading requirements, 5.12.3
    unquoted requirement, 5.12.2
  investor company, 4.2.1, 5.17–5.17.7
    chargeable assets, 5.17.6
    control, prohibition of, 5.17.4
    financial activities, prohibition of, 5.17.5
    general rule, 5.17.1
    material interest, prohibition of, 5.17.2
    reciprocal arrangements, prohibition of, 5.17.3
    residence, 5.17.1.1
    tax avoidance, 5.17.7
  joint ventures, 5.2.5.4
  loss relief, 22.8–22.8.2
  outline, 4.2
  partnerships, 5.2.5.4
  qualifying companies,
    and see Qualifying companies
    arrangements, 5.1.7
    conditions, 5.2.1–5.2.5.6
    connected persons, 5.1.6
    control, *see* Control
    controlled company, 5.5
    independence requirement, 5.1.8
    investee company, 5.12–5.12.6.4
    investor company, 5.17–5.17.7
    periods of restriction, 5.1.4
    qualification period, 5.1.4
    qualifying purpose, 5.2.3–5.2.3.2

Corporate venturing scheme (CVS) – *contd*
qualifying companies – *contd*
qualifying trade, 5.2.4
unquoted, 5.2.2
qualifying purpose, 5.2.3–5.2.3.2
commencement of trade within 24 months, 5.2.4
employment of funds in a given way, 5.2.5–5.2.5.9
mainly trading, 5.2.3.2
parent company of a trading group, 5.2.3.2
purpose for which company exists, 5.2.3.1
qualifying subsidiaries, 5.2.3.2
qualifying shares, 4.2
qualifying subsidiaries, 5.2.3.2, 5.16–5.16.7
dormant subsidiaries, 5.16.5
generally, 5.16.1
property management, 5.16.4.1, 5.16.4
qualifying 90subsidiaries, 5.16.1.1
sale of subsidiary, 5.16.7
sub-subsidiaries, 5.16.2
trading or wholly or mainly abroad, 5.16.3
winding up subsidiary, 5.16.6
relief, *see* CVS deferral relief; CVS disposal relief; CVS investment relief
restructuring company, 4.2.3
share capital, 5.14–5.14.2
use, 4.2
Corporation tax,
venture capital trust (VCT) scheme, 2.4
CVS, *see* Corporate venturing scheme (CVS)
CVS deferral relief, 1.4.2, 4.2, 16.1–16.7.4, 22.2.1
background, 16.1
bringing gains back into charge, 16.7–16.7.4
chargeable event, 16.7.1
effect on a chargeable event, 16.7.3
non-resident investor companies, 16.7.4
qualifying shares, 16.7.2
chargeable event, 16.2
claimants, 16.4
claims procedure, 22.5.2
crystallisation of deferred gain, 16.2, 22.9
deferred gains, 16.2.1
deferring gains, 16.6–16.6.6
amount of gain that can be deferred, 16.6.2
attribution of deferred gain, 16.6.6
chargeable gain, 16.6.2.1
effect of deferral relief on, 16.6.5
unmatched gain, 16.6.4
unused qualifying expenditure, 16.6.3
using proceedings of sale, 16.6.2.2
eligible gains, 16.3
giving effect to, 22.5–22.5.2
claims procedure, 22.5.2
how much of gain deferred, 22.5.1

CVS deferral relief – *contd*
indexation, 16.2.1
interest,
overpaid tax, 22.10.2
unpaid tax, 22.10.1
introduction, 16.1
qualifying investment, 16.2, 16.5–16.5.1.1
meaning, 16.5.1
prohibited company, 16.5.1
shares issued before accrual time, 16.5.1.1
qualifying time, 16.2
restricted periods, 16.2.2
summary, 16.2
CVS disposal relief, 19.1–19.8
bonus issues, 19.3.4
company reorganisations, 19.3–19.3.6.1
bonus issues, 19.3.4
qualifying corporate bonds, 19.3.5
reorganisations, 19.3.2
takeovers, 19.3.6.1
continuously, shares held, 19.1.4
CVS shares, 19.1.3
disposal,
meaning, 19.2.1
options, 19.2.2
gains,
early disposals of CVS shares, 19.7
later disposals of CVS shares, 19.5–19.5.1
losses,
early disposals of CVS shares, 19.8
later disposals of CVS shares, 19.6–19.6.3
anti-avoidance rules, 19.6.2.1
computing allowable loss, 19.6.3
conditions for loss relief, 19.6.2
relieving losses, 19.6.4
matching disposals with acquisitions, 19.4–19.4.3
different days, shares acquired on, 19.4.2
same day, shares acquired on, 19.4.3
options, 19.2.2
qualifying corporate bonds, 19.3.5
reconstructions, 19.3.6
restricted periods for disposal, investor company's, 19.1.2
substantial shareholdings, 19.5.1
CVS investment relief, 1.4.2, 4.2, 10.1–10.4.1
accounting period in which relief given, 20.3.4
amount, 10.3–10.3.3
attribution of relief, 10.3.3
fixed rate, relief at, 10.3.2
no limit on subscription, 10.3.1
assessments to withdraw relief, 20.6.4
carry-back not available, 10.4.1
deferred shares, 10.1.2
early disposals, 20.6.3
eligible shares, 10.1.2

CVS investment relief – *contd*
entitlement, 10.2–10.2.4
bona fide commercial subscription, 10.2.4
companies, 10.2.1
period of restriction, 10.2.3
qualification period, 10.2.3
residence, 10.2.2
fully paid-up shares, 10.1.3
interest,
overdue corporation tax, 20.7.4
overpaid tax, 20.7.7
losing, 13.1–13.8.1, 20.6–20.6.4
assessments to withdraw relief, 20.6.4
breach of qualifying conditions, 13.3.1, 13.3
early disposals, 20.6.3–20.6.3.3
insignificant value, receipts of, 13.5
interest on overdue corporation tax, 20.7.4
occasions giving rise to loss, 13.2, 13.2.1, 20.6.1
options granted over shares, 13.8–13.8–1
put options, 13.8.1
receipt of value, 13.4–13.4.3
replacement value, return of, 13.6–13.6.5
restricted periods, 13.2.1, 20.6.2
shareholders, value received by, 13.7–13.7.5
maximum limit, 20.3.1
method of relief, 20.3.2
ordinary shares, 10.1.2
pre-emption rights, 10.1.2
qualification period, 10.1.2, 10.2.3
qualifying investment, 10.1
rate of relief, 20.3.2
receipt of value, 13.4–13.4.3
replacement value, return of, 13.6–13.6.5
amount of replacement value, 13.6.5
duration of qualifying receipt, 13.6.2
effect of replacement value, 13.6.6
excepted payment, 13.6.3
time restraints, 13.6.4
residence, 10.2.2
restriction, 20.3.3
shareholders, value received by, 13.7–13.7.5
company law requirements, 13.7.5
effect of repayment, 13.7.3
insignificant value received, 13.7.4
more than one investor, loss of relief by, 13.7.3.1
repayment of capital to other shareholders, 13.7.2, 13.7.2.1
when relief is given, 10.4.1, 10.4
CVS relief,
See also CVS deferral relief; CVS investment relief
loss relief, 1.4.2, 4.2
restricting, 4.2.3
types of relief, 1.4.2
withdrawal, 1.5, 4.2.3

D

Death,
EIS deferral relief, 15.7.6
EIS disposal relief,
breach of conditions, 18.2.4.3
capital gains and losses, 18.2.4.4
four-month period, 18.2.4.2
investment relief, 18.2.4.1
tax benefits, 18.2.4.5
EIS investment relief, 20.5.4
VCT deferral relief, 14.7.7
VCT disposal relief, 17.2.4
VCT investment relief, 20.4.6
Deferral relief, *see* CVS deferral relief; EIS deferral relief; VCT deferral relief
Directors,
accounting reference date, 26.8.5
annual financial statements, 26.8.4
annual general meeting (AGM), 26.8.1
annual return, 26.8.7
checklist, App.2
companies, directors', 7.6.2.10
extraordinary general meeting (EGM), 26.8.2
formation of private company, 26.6.11
meaning, 7.6.2.7
payments to, 26.9.2
public offer of securities, 27.2.6
resolutions, 26.8.3
responsibilities, 26.8–26.8.7
services, 26.9.4
Disposal at arm's length,
VCT investment relief, 20.4.2
Disposal relief, *see* CVS disposal relief; EIS disposal relief; VCT disposal relief
Distribution of capital gains,
venture capital trust (VCT) scheme, 2.2.4
Distribution relief, *see* VCT distribution relief
Dividends,
venture capital trust (VCT) scheme, 2.2.3, 2.4

E

EIS Association, 27.6.2
EIS deferral relief, 1.3.2, 1.6, 3.2.1, 15.1–15.13.3, 22.2.1
associated persons, 15.8.2.1
background, 15.1.1
bringing gains back into charge, 15.7–15.7.6
cessation of UK residence, 15.7.4
chargeable events, 15.7.1
death, exception for, 15.7.6
gain accruing on a chargeable event, 15.7.2
loss of eligibility by acquired shares, 15.7.5
minority investors, 15.7.5.1

EIS deferral relief – *contd*
bringing gains back into charge – *contd*
persons chargeable on crystallisation, 15.7.3
several acquisitions, gains matched with, 15.7.2.1
temporarily working abroad, 15.7.4.1
cessation of UK residence, 15.7.4
claimants, 15.4.1–15.4.1.2
nominees, 15.4.1.1
partnerships, 15.4.1.2
connected persons, 15.8.2.1
crystallisation of deferred gain, 15.2, 22.9
death, exception for, 15.7.6
deferred gains, 15.2.1
date of disposal, 15.3.4
extensions to the qualifying time, 15.3.2.1
Inland Revenue policy, 15.3.2.1
limits, 15.3.3
period for making qualifying investments, 15.3.2–15.3.2.1
type of gain eligible for deferrment, 15.3.1
deferring gains, 15.6–15.6.5
amount of gain that can be deferred, 15.6.2
effect on deferred gain, 15.6.5
unmatched gain, 15.6.4
unused qualifying expenditure, 15.6.3
dual residence, 15.4.3
entitlement to claim deferrment, 15.4–15.4.7
active investor, 15.4.4
claimants, 15.4.1–15.4.1.2
dual residence, 15.4.3
investment-linked loans, 15.4.6
nominees, 15.4.1.1
partnerships, 15.4.1.2
passive investor, 15.4.4
pre-arranged exits, 15.4.7
residence, 15.4.2
trustees as investors, 15.4.5
giving effect to, 22.4–22.4.2
claims procedure, 22.4.2
how much of gain deferred, 22.4.1
indexation, 15.2.1
insignificant value, exception for receipts of, 15.9
interest,
overpaid tax, 22.10.2
unpaid tax, 22.10.1
investment-linked loans, 15.4.6
loans to investors, 15.8.7
nominees, 15.4.1.1
options over shares, grant of, 15.12
partnerships, 15.4.1.2
payment for giving up right to debt, 15.8.5
pre-arranged exits, 15.4.7
qualifying companies, 15.5.2
qualifying investment, 15.2, 15.5–15.5.7
cash consideration, 15.5.7

EIS deferral relief – *contd*
qualifying investment – *contd*
meaning, 15.5.1
qualifying companies, 15.5.2
reinvestment in same company, 15.5.5
sale of shares in qualifying company, 15.5.6
shares that are excluded, 15.5.4
shares that can be acquired, 15.5.3
qualifying time, 15.2, 15.2.2
reconstructions, 15.13–15.13.3
acquisition by a new company, 15.13.3
amalgamations, 15.13.2
reorganisation of share capital, 15.13.1
redemption of capital, 15.8.3, 15.8.3.1
release of investor's liabilities, 15.8.6
relevant period, 15.2.2
repayment of capital, 15.8.3, 15.8.3.1
repayment of investor's loan, 15.8.4
repurchase of capital, 15.8.3, 15.8.3.1
residence, 15.4.2, 15.4.3
cessation of UK residence, 15.7.4
temporarily working abroad, 15.7.4.1
restricted periods, 15.2.2
return of replacement value, 15.10–15.10.4
amount of replacement value, 15.10.3
effect of replacement value, 15.10.4
excepted payment, 15.10.1
time restraints, 15.10.2
return of value, 15.8–15.8.14
amount of value received, 15.8.14
associated persons, 15.8.2.1
benefits or facilities, provision of, 15.8.8
connected persons, 15.8.2.1
loans to investors, 15.8.7
no double charge on share disposal, 15.8.13
occasions on which value received, 15.8.2
ordinary trade debt, meaning of, 15.8.10.1
payment for giving up right to debt, 15.8.5
payments other than qualifying payments, 15.8.10–15.8.10.1
purchase of shares by connected person, 15.8.11
redemption of capital, 15.8.3, 15.8.3.1
release of investor's liabilities, 15.8.6
repayment of capital, 15.8.3, 15.8.3.1
repayment of investor's loan, 15.8.4
repurchase of capital, 15.8.3, 15.8.3.1
share disposal, 15.8.13
transfer of assets, 15.8.9
winding up, 15.8.12
share disposal, 15.8.13
small private schemes, 26.3.3, 26.4–26.4.4
advantages, 26.5.2
summary, 15.2–15.2.2
taper relief, 15.2.1
trustees as investors, 15.4.5

EIS deferral relief – *contd*
value received by other persons, 15.11–15.11.3.3
CVS relief lost, where, 15.11.3.3
effect of repayment of share capital, 15.11.2.1
exceptions, 15.11.3–15.11.3.3
insignificant repayments, 15.11.3.2
minimum capital requirements, 15.11.3.1
repayment of capital to other shareholders, 15.11.2
repayments received before 7 March 2001, 15.11.2.2
EIS disposal relief, 1.3.2, 3.2.1, 18.1–18.8.6
bonus issue, 18.3.6
company reorganisations, 18.3–18.3.7
bonus issue, 18.3.6
categories of share, 18.3.3
EIS deferral relief shares, 18.3.3.1
new shares not EIS shares, 18.3.7
rights issue, 18.3.5
separate identification, 18.3.4
subdivision, 18.3.2
connected persons, 18.6.3, 18.8.4
crystallisation of deferred gains, 18.1.3
death of investor, 18.2.4–18.2.4.5
breach of conditions, 18.2.4.3
capital gains and losses, 18.2.4.4
during four-month period, death, 18.2.4.2
investment relief, 18.2.4.1
tax benefits, 18.2.4.5
disposal, 18.2–18.2.4.5
early disposals, 18.2.3.1
options, 18.2.2
spouse, transfers to, 18.2.3
early disposals, 18.2.3.1
EIS shares, 18.1.4
gains on early disposals of EIS shares, 18.7–18.7.2
gains on later disposals of EIS shares, 18.5–18.5.5
basic rule, 18.5.1.1
initial restriction and subsequent receipts of value, 18.5.5
insufficient income tax liability, 18.5.2.1
later restriction on receipt of value, 18.5.3
repeated receipts of value, 18.5.4
restriction of the exemption, 18.5.2
giving effect to, 22.6
losses on early disposals of EIS shares, 18.8–18.8.6
bargains not at arm's length, 18.8.3
disposals to connected persons, 18.8.4
full withdrawal of EIS investment relief, 18.8.1
part-disposals, 18.8.6
partial loss of investment relief, 18.8.2
reduced or restricted investment relief, 18.8.5
EIS disposal relief – *contd*
losses on later disposals of EIS shares, 18.6–18.6.5
applying loss against income, 18.6.4
capital loss relief, 18.6.2
connected persons, disposals to, 18.6.3
loss relief, 18.6.1
part-disposals, 18.6.5
matching disposals with acquisitions, 18.4–18.4.6
acquisitions above permitted maximum, 18.4.5
different days, shares acquired on, 18.4.2
pre-6 April 1998 acquisition of shares, 18.4.6
same day, shares acquired on, 18.4.3
single issue of EIS shares, 18.4.4
options, 18.2.2
restricted periods for disposal, investor's, 18.1.2
rights issue, 18.3.5
spouse, transfers to, 18.2.3
EIS investment relief, 1.3.2, 3.2.1, 9.1–9.1.6
amount, 9.3–9.3.5
annual limit, 9.3.1
attribution of relief to shares, 9.3.5
lower rate of tax, relief at, 9.3.3
minimum investment, 9.3.2
restriction of investment relief, 9.3.4
approved EIS funds, investment through, 9.4.2, 9.4.2.1
benefits or facilities, provision of, 12.5.10–12.5.10.2
bona fide commercial subscription, 9.2.7
breach of qualifying conditions, 12.3–12.3.2
carry-back, 9.4.1
claiming relief, 20.2.1, 24.8.10–24.8.10.1
computing investor's liability to tax, 20.2.8
connected persons, 12.5.3.1
death of investor, 20.5.4
documentations, 20.2.1
early disposal of shares, 20.5.2–20.5.2.7
eligible shares, 9.1.2
entitlement, 9.2–9.2–8
bona fide commercial subscription, 9.2.7
individuals, 9.2.1
joint ownership, 9.2.6
loan-linked investments, 9.2.8
nominees, 9.2.6
period of restriction, 9.2.3
residence, 9.2.2
several share issues, 9.2.4
subscription for shares, 9.2.5
exceeding investment limit, 9.5
general rules, 9.1
interest on overdue tax, 20.7.2, 20.7.3
issue of shares, 9.1.5
joint ownership, 9.2.6
later disposal of shares, 20.5.3

EIS investment relief – *contd*
loan-linked investments, 9.2.8, 12.4–12.4.2
consequences of receiving, 12.4.2
restricted period, 12.4.1
losing, 12.1–12.10.2, 20.5–20.5.5.1
assessments for withdrawing or reducing relief, 20.5.5
breach of qualifying conditions, 12.3–12.3.2
carry back of investment relief, 20.5.5.1
CVS relief lost, where, 12.8.5.3
death of investor, 20.5.4
early disposal of shares, 20.5.2–20.5.2.7
insignificant value, exception for, 12.6
later disposal of shares, 20.5.3
loan-linked investments, 12.4–12.4.2
occasions giving rise to loss, 12.2–12.10, 20.5.1
receipt of value 12.5–12.5.6.2,,
see also receipt of value *below*
replacement value, exception for, 12.7–12.7.4
restricted periods, 12.2.1, 12.3.1, 12.4.1
value received by other shareholders, 12.8–12.8.5.3
minimum investment, 20.2.4
nominees, 9.2.6
ordinary shares, 9.1.4
PAYE code adjustment, 20.2.9
permitted maximum, 20.2.2
postponement of tax, 20.2.10
pre-emption rights, 9.1.3
qualifying company, 9.1
rate of relief, 20.2.5
receipt of value, 12.5–12.5.6.2
amount of value received, 12.5.5.1, 12.5.6.1
assets, transfers of, 12.5.11–12.5.11.2
associates, 12.5.3.1
benefits or facilities, provision of, 12.5.10–12.5.10.2
connected persons, 12.5.3.1
debt, payment for giving up right to, 12.5.7–12.5.7.3
former rules, 12.9–12.9.2
loan sandwich, 12.5.6.2
loans to investors, 12.5.9
meaning of value, 12.5.3
payments from company, 12.5.12.2
purchase of shares or securities by connected person, 12.5.5–12.5.6.1
purpose of rules, 12.5.1
redemption of shares/securities, 12.5.4–12.5.4.1
release of investor's liabilities, 12.5.8, 12.5.8.1
repayment of investor's loan, 12.5.6–12.5.6.2
repayment of shares/securities, 12.5.4–12.5.4.1

EIS investment relief – *contd*
receipt of value – *contd*
replacement capital, 12.10–12.10.2
repurchase of shares/securities, 12.5.4–12.5.4.1
restricted period, 12.5.2
when received, 12.5.3
winding-up, payments on a, 12.5.12.1
repayment supplement, 20.7.6
residence, 9.2.2
restriction, 20.2.6
small private schemes, 26.3.2
advantages, 26.5.1
subscription for shares, 9.2.5
tax year in which relief given, 20.2.7
value received by other shareholders, 12.8–12.8.2.5
exceptions to rule, 12.8.5–12.8.5.3
insignificant requirements, 12.8.5.2
loss relief by more than one investor, 12.8.4
minimum capital requirements, 12.8.5.1
more than one investor, loss of relief, 12.8.4
repayment of capital to other shareholders, 12.8.2
repayment of share capital, 12.8.3
when relief is given, 9.4–9.4.2.1
EIS relief, 3.1.2
see also Enterprise investment scheme (EIS)
certificate, 3.2.1
deferral relief, 1.3.2, 1.6, 3.2.1
disposal relief, 1.3.2, 3.2.1
investment relief, 1.3.2, 3.2.1
loss relief, 1.3.2, 3.2.1
origins, 3.1.1
types of relief, 1.3.2, 3.2.1
withdrawal, 1.5
EIS scheme, *see* Enterprise investment scheme (EIS)
Eligible shares,
CVS investment relief, 10.1.2
EIS investment relief, 9.1.2
enterprise investment scheme (EIS), 3.2.1
VCT investment relief, 7.3.1, 7.3.2, 8.1, 8.1.2
venture capital trust (VCT) scheme, 2.2.1
Enterprise capital funds,
introduction, 1.7
Enterprise investment scheme (EIS), 1.1.1, 3.1–3.2.1
advance opinion from Revenue, 3.2.1
aim, 1.3.1
arrangements, 5.1.7
background, 3.1.1
business angels, 3.2.1
CBI Report (1999), 1.5
certificates, 24.8–24.8.11
appeals against refusal to authorise certificates, 24.8.5

Enterprise investment scheme (EIS) – *contd*
certificates – *contd*
Form EIS 2, 24.8.6
Form EIS 3, 24.8.7
Form EIS 5, 24.8.8
information required, 24.8.2
Inland Revenue procedure on receipt of EIS 1, 24.8.4
penalties, 24.8.9, 24.8.3
submission of form EIS 1, 24.8.1
conditions, 3.2.1
connected persons, 5.1.6, 7.6.2–7.6.2.10
ability to control the company or a subsidiary, 7.6.3.5
approved EIS funds, 7.6.5
associate, meaning of, 7.6.2.8, 7.6.2.3
business angels, 7.6.2.11
company secretaries, 7.6.2.5
director, meaning of, 7.6.2.7
directors' companies, 7.6.2.10
employees, 7.6.2.4
generally, 7.6.2.1
individuals with a significant interest in the company, 7.6.3–7.6.3.5
loan capital, 7.6.3.3
ownership of a trade, 7.6.4.2
partners, 7.6.2.4
preliminary definition of connection, 7.6.2.2
replacement capital, 7.6.4–7.6.4.2
subscriber shares, 7.6.3.2
subsidiary, meaning of, 7.6.2.6
unpaid directors, 7.6.2.9
control, *see* Control
eligible shares, 3.2.1
four-month period, 24.7–24.7.2
gross-asset value, 3.2.1
historical background, 1.1.2
informal clearance 24.6–24.6.11,,
see also Informal and VCT and EIS clearance
information powers, 25.3–25.3.5
penalties, 25.3.5
request for information, 25.3.4
supplied by company, information, 25.3.3
supplied by investor, information, 25.3.2
Inland Revenue booklet, 1.5
introduction, 1.3.1, 1.6, 3.1.1
investee companies, 5.7–5.7.6.4
employment of funds in a given way, 5.7.5–5.7.5.3
generally, 5.7.1
gross assets test, 5.8.2
limits of investment, 5.8–5.8.2
maximum investment, 5.8.1
pre-arranged exits, 5.7.6–5.7.6.4
qualifying purpose, 5.7.3–5.7.3.2
unquoted requirement, 5.7.2
investment fund, 3.2.1
limit on amount of investment, 3.2.1

Enterprise investment scheme (EIS) – *contd*
loss relief, 22.7.1–22.7.2
nature, 3.1.2, 3.2.1
outline, 3.2.1
purpose, 1.1.2
qualifying companies, 5.10–5.10.2
and see Qualifying companies
arrangements, 5.1.7
connected persons, 5.1.6
control, *see* Control
employment of funds in a given way, 5.7.5–5.7.5.3
gross assets test, 5.8.2
independence requirement, 5.10.1
investee companies, 5.7–5.7.6.4
limits of investment, 5.8–5.8.2
maximum investment, 5.8.1
periods of restriction, 5.1.3
pre-arranged exits, 5.7.6–5.7.6.4
qualifying purpose, 5.7.3–5.7.3.2
qualifying subsidiaries, *see* Qualifying subsidiaries
relevant date, 5.1.3
relevant period, 5.1.3
takeover of qualifying company, 5.10.2
termination date, 5.1.3
three-year period, 5.1.3
qualifying investors, 7.6–7.6.5
connected persons 7.6.2–7.6.2.10,,
see also Connected persons
general rules, 7.6.1
guaranteed exit arrangements, 7.6.1.5
joint names, shares in, 7.6.1.2
loan-linked investments, 7.6.1.7
maximum subscriptions, 7.6.1.8
minimum subscriptions, 7.6.1.8
outside investors, 7.6.1.3
reciprocal arrangements, 7.6.1.4
residence, 7.6.1.1
restriction, period of, 7.6.1.6
tax avoidance, 7.6.1.9
qualifying purpose, 5.7.3–5.7.3.2
commencement of trade within 24 months, 5.7.4
employment of funds in a certain way required, 5.7.5–5.7.5.2
generally, 5.7.3.1
parent company of trading group, 5.7.3.2
qualifying business activity, 5.7.5.1, 5.7.5.2
qualifying subsidiaries, 5.11–5.11.8
administration, 5.11.5.3
disposal of subsidiary, 5.11.6
dormant subsidiaries, 5.11.5.2
general rule, 5.11.1
option to acquire shares, 5.11.7
post-16 March 2004 share issue, 5.11.2–5.11.2.2
pre-17 March 2004 share issue, 5.11.3
property management, 5.11.5.1

Enterprise investment scheme (EIS) – *contd*
qualifying subsidiaries – *contd*
receivership, 5.11.5.3
sub-subsidiaries, 5.11.4
subscription for shares in subsidiary, 5.11.8
trading wholly or mainly abroad, 5.11.5
winding up, 5.11.5.3
qualifying trades, 3.2.1
qualifying companies, 3.2.1
reform proposals, 1.5
relief, *see* EIS deferral relief; EIS disposal relief; EIS investment relief
replacement capital, 7.6.4–7.6.4.2
residence, 7.6.1.1
shareholder's agreement, App.1
Treasury review, 1.7
venture capital scheme compared, 5.18
Entrepreneurs' rollover relief, 1.6, 14.1.1
Exit routes, 28.1–28.6.5
capital gains exemption, 28.2.3
deferred gains, 28.1.4
gifts of shares, 28.6–28.6.5
business property relief, 28.6.4
capital gains tax, 28.6.2
inheritance tax, 28.6.3
stamp duty, 28.6.5
liquidation,
dividend payment before, 28.3.4
voluntary winding up, 28.3.5
market for shares, 28.2–28.2.3
predicting progress of company, 28.1.1
purchase of own shares, 28.5–28.5.8
benefits the trade, 28.5.5
capital receipt, 28.5.3
clearance, 28.5.8
conditions for investor, 28.5.7
income payment, 28.5.2
no tax avoidance, 28.5.6
unquoted shares, 28.5.4
realizing investment, 28.1.2
sale of assets,
corporation tax, 28.3.3
going concern, sale as, 28.3.2
sale of shares, 28.4–28.4.2
trustees, to, 28.4.2
venture capital trust (VCT) scheme, 2.2.3
Extraordinary general meeting (EGM), 26.8.2

F

Farming, 6.5.11
Film production, 6.5.8.2.1
Financial statements,
public offers, 27.2.7
Forestry, 6.5.12
Formation of private company, 26.6–26.6.14
articles of association, 26.6.9
business plans, 26.6.2
company law, 26.6.3

Formation of private company – *contd*
company secretary, 26.6.12
company's registered office, 26.6.7
directors, 26.6.11
memorandum of association, 26.6.8
name of company, 26.6.10
off-the-shelf companies, 26.6.5
registration, 26.6.6
share capital, 26.6.14
share issue, 26.7.5
shareholders' agreement, 26.6.13
type of company, 26.6.4

G

General meetings,
annual, 26.8.1
extraordinary, 26.8.2
Generally,
corporate venturing scheme (CVS), 24.9.1
advance clearances, 24.9.5
appeals, 24.9.4
applications, 24.9.2
information, 24.9.2
information notices, 24.9.3
Gross assets test,
CVS investee company, 5.13.2
EIS investee company, 5.8.2
VCT investee company, 5.3.5
Groups of companies,
qualifying trades, 6.4.3
Guest houses, 6.5.13

H

Holdover relief,
business gifts,
business assets, 23.2.4
EIS shares, 23.2.5
generally, 23.2.1
meaning, 23.2.3
option for holdover, 23.2.2
settlor-interested trusts, transfers to, 23.2.6
choosing between optional reliefs, 23.4
IHT chargeable, gifts on which, 23.3
Hotels, 6.5.13

I

Indexation,
CVS deferral relief, 16.2.1
EIS deferral relief, 15.2.1
VCT deferral relief, 14.2.1
Informal VCT and EIS clearance, 24.6–24.6.11
basic information, 24.6.6
cash flow, 24.6.7
further points, 24.6.10, 24.6.8
generally, 24.6.1
informal opinion, 24.6.2

Informal VCT and EIS clearance – *contd*
Inland Revenue view, 24.5.6.3
Matrix case, 24.6.5.2
MFK Underwriting case, 24.6.5.1
profit projections, 24.6.7
refusal of provisional clearance, 24.6.11
simplicity, importance of, 24.6.4
small EIS investments, 24.6.9
timeliness of applications, 24.6.3
value, 24.6.5
Information powers,
corporate venturing scheme (CVS),
interest on withdrawn relief, 25.4.6
investor company providing information, 25.4.2
notices relating to withdrawal of relief, 25.4.1
penalties, 25.4.5
required by revenue, information, 25.4.4
enterprise investment scheme (EIS), 25.3–25.3.5
connected person, information supplied by, 25.3.3
penalties, 25.3.5
request for information, 25.3.4
supplied by company, information, 25.3.3
supplied by investor, information, 25.3.2
venture capital trust (VCT) scheme,
event causing investment relief to be lost, 25.2.1
general information power, 25.2.4
notices, 24.5.2, 25.2.3
refusal of approval, 25.2.2
returns, 24.5.2, 25.2.3
withdrawal of approval, 25.2.2
Inland Revenue,
booklets, 1.5
forms, App.6
information powers, *see* Information powers
statements of practice, 1.1.1
Venture Capital Schemes Manual, *see* Venture Capital Schemes Manual
Insurance, 6.5.5
Intellectual property, 6.5.8–6.5.8.2.1
Investee company,
corporate venturing scheme (CVS),
administration, 5.12.3.1
cease trading, arrangements to, 5.12.6.2
disposal, 5.12.6.1
disposal of assets, arrangements for, 5.12.6.3
employment of funds in a given way, 5.12.4
exchange, 5.12.6.1
gross-assets limit, 5.13.2
individual-owners requirement, 5.12.5
insuring against loss, arrangements for, 5.12.6.4
limits of investment, 5.13–5.13.2
liquidation, 5.12.3.1
Investee company – *contd*
corporate venturing scheme (CVS) – *contd*
maximum investment, 5.13.1
partnerships, 5.12.3.2
pre-arranged exits, 5.12.6–5.12.6.4
receivership, 5.12.3.1
repurchase arrangements, 5.12.6.1
trading requirements, 5.12.3
Investment companies,
loss relief, 21.7–21.7.3
Investment relief, *see* CVT investment relief; EIS investment relief; VCT investment relief
Investment trusts,
venture capital trusts compared, 2.2.4
Investor company,
corporate venturing scheme (CVS),
material interest, prohibition of, 5.17.2
residence, 5.17.1.1
Investors,
checklist, App.3
Issue of shares,
VCT investment relief, 8.1.5

J

Joint ownership,
EIS investment relief, 9.2.6
VCT investment relief, 8.2.6
Joint ventures,
corporate venturing scheme (CVS), 5.2.5.4
definition, 5.3.4
meaning, 5.3.4
venture capital trust (VCT) scheme, 5.3.4

L

Legal services, 6.5.10
Licence fees, 6.5.9, 6.5.9.1, 6.6.7
Loan-linked investments,
EIS investment relief, 9.2.8, 12.4–12.4.2
consequences of receiving a linked loan, 12.4.2
restricted period, 12.4.1
enterprise investment scheme (EIS), 7.6.1.7
VCT investment relief, 7.3.4, 7.3.4.1, 8.2.8
consequences of receiving linked loan, 11.2.3
restricted period, 11.2.2
venture capital trust (VCT) scheme, 7.3.4, 7.3.4.1
Loans,
interest relief, 21.8–21.8.4
investors', 26.9.3
traders, to, 23.6.1–23.6.4
Losing,
VCT investment relief, 20.4.2
Loss relief,
CVS relief, 1.4.2, 4.2
EIS relief, 1.3.2, 3.2.1

M

Management company,
 control, 5.1.9.8
Market gardening, 6.5.11
Memorandum of association, 26.6.8

N

Nominees,
 control, 5.1.9.2
 EIS deferral relief, 15.4.1.1
 EIS investment relief, 9.2.6
 VCT investment relief, 8.2.6
Nursing homes, 6.5.14

O

Off-the-shelf companies, 26.6.5
Official listing, 1.8
 VCT investee company, 5.6.2.1
 venture capital trust (VCT) scheme, 2.1.2, 2.2.1
Oil exploration and extraction, 6.7
Oil rigs, 6.5.6.5
Options,
 call, 13.8.1
 EIS deferral relief, 15.12
 EIS disposal relief, 18.2.2
 losing CVS investment relief, 13.8.1
 put, 13.8.1
 VCT disposal relief, 17.2.2
Ordinary shares,
 CVS investment relief, 10.1.2
 EIS investment relief, 9.1.4
 VCT investment relief, 8.1.4

P

Participators,
 control, 5.1.9.3
 definition, 5.1.9.3
Partnerships,
 corporate venturing scheme (CVS), 5.2.5.4
 EIS deferral relief, 15.4.1.2
PAYE code adjustment,
 EIS investment relief, 20.2.9
 VCT investment relief, 20.2.9
Personal representatives, 26.2.6
Pleasure craft, 6.5.6.5
Pre-emption rights,
 CVS investment relief, 10.1.2
 EIS investment relief, 9.1.3
 VCT investment relief, 8.1.3
Public offers, 27.1–27.6.10
 approved EIS funds, 27.1.3
  conditions, 27.1.4
 business plans, 27.3.1
 choosing investment,
  areas of investment, 27.6.3

Public offers – *contd*
 choosing investment – *contd*
  borrow or invest, whether to, 27.6.8
  costs of raising capital, 27.6.4
  dual pricing, 27.6.9
  EIS offers, 27.6.2
  managers, 27.6.7
  monitoring qualifying status, 27.6.10
  ongoing costs, 27.6.5
  policy, 27.6.1
  return on investment, 27.6.6
 company law,
  advertisements, 27.2.2
  company secretary, 27.2.6
  directors, 27.2.6
  marketing rules, 27.2.3
  offering shares to the public, 27.2.1
  public limited companies, 27.2.4
  trading certificate, 27.2.5
 financial statements, 27.2.7
 generally, 27.1.2
 post-prospectus activities,
  commission, 27.5.3
  issue of shares, 27.5.4
  lodging prospectus, 27.5.2
  marketing prospectus, 27.5.2
  tax certificates, 27.5.5
 pre-prospectus activities, 27.3–27.3.5
  appointment of advisers, 27.3.2
  business plans, 27.3.1
  sponsoring issue, 27.3.3, 27.3.4
  unsponsored EIS issues, 27.3.5
 prospectus, 27.4–27.4.13
  accountant's report, 27.4.7
  advisers, 27.4.5
  application form, 27.4.12
  approval, 27.4.8
  background, 27.4.4
  benefits, 27.4.6
  business strategy, 27.4.4
  clearances, 27.4.8
  contents, 27.4.1
  details of shares offered, 27.4.2
  directors, 27.4.5
  general information, 27.4.9
  lodging, 27.5.1
  management team, 27.4.5
  marketing, 27.5.2
  minimum subscription, 27.4.10
  offer for subscription agreement, 27.4.11
  procedure, 27.4.12
  risks, 27.4.6
  statutory information, 27.4.9
  underwriting, 27.4.3
  verification, 27.4.13
 unapproved EIS funds and schemes, 27.1.5
Put options, 13.8.1

Q

Qualifying companies, 5.1–5.18
  arrangements, 5.1.7
  connected persons, 5.1.6
  control, *see* Control
  corporate venturing scheme (CVS),
    arrangements, 5.1.7
    conditions, 5.2.1–5.2.5.6
    connected persons, 5.1.6
    control, *see* Control
    controlled company, 5.5
    independence requirement, 5.1.8
    investee company, 5.12–5.12.6.4
    investor company, 5.17–5.17.7
    periods of restriction, 5.1.4
    qualification period, 5.1.4
    qualifying purpose, 5.2.3–5.2.3.2
    qualifying trade, 5.2.4
    unquoted, 5.2.2
  definition, 5.1.1
  differences between schemes, 5.1.1
  EIS deferral relief, 15.5.2
  eligible shares, 5.9.1
  enterprise investment scheme (EIS), 3.2.1, 5.10–5.10.2
    arrangements, 5.1.7
    connected persons, 5.1.6
    control, *see* Control
    employment of funds in a given way, 5.7.5–5.7.5.3
    independence requirement, 5.10.1
    investee companies, 5.7–5.7.6.4
    limits of investment, 5.8–5.8.2
    maximum investment, 5.8.1
    periods of restriction, 5.1.3
    pre-arranged exits, 5.7.6–5.7.6.4
    qualifying purpose, 5.7.3–5.7.3.2
    qualifying subsidiaries, 5.11–5.11.8
    relevant date, 5.1.3
    relevant period, 5.1.3
    takeover of qualifying company, 5.10.2
    termination date, 5.1.3
  periods of restriction,
    CVS companies, 5.1.4
    EIS company, 5.1.3
    VCT company, 5.1.2
  residence, 5.1.5
  share capital, 5.9–5.9.2, 5.14–5.14.2
    eligible shares, 5.9.1
    fully paid-up shares, 5.9.2, 5.14.2
    qualifying shares, 5.14.1
  VCT deferral relief, 14.5.2
  venture capital trust (VCT) scheme, 1.2.2
    arrangements, 5.1.7
    connected persons, 5.1.6
    control, *see* Control
    fragmentation of activities, 5.3.3
    gross asset limit, 5.3.5
    investee company, 5.3–5.3.5, 5.4–5.4.6

Qualifying companies – *contd*
  venture capital trust (VCT) scheme – *contd*
    investor companies, 5.6–5.6.3
    maximum investment, 5.3.1
    periods of restriction, 5.1.2
    qualifying subsidiaries, 5.5–5.5.8
    VCT money raised, 5.3.2
Qualifying conditions, *see* Qualifying companies; Qualifying investors; Qualifying trades
Qualifying holdings,
  venture capital trust (VCT) scheme, 2.2.1
Qualifying investment,
  CVS deferral relief, 16.2, 16.5–16.5.1.1
    meaning, 16.5.1
    prohibited company, 16.5.1
  EIS deferral relief, 15.5–15.5.7
    cash consideration, 15.5.7
    meaning, 15.5.1
    qualifying companies, 15.5.2
    reinvestment in same company, 15.5.5
    sale of shares in qualifying company, 15.5.6
    shares that are excluded, 15.5.4
    shares that can be acquired, 15.5.3
  VCT deferral relief, 14.2
    meaning, 14.5.1
    period for making qualifying investment, 14.3.2
    qualifying companies, 14.5.2
Qualifying investors, 7.1–7.6.5
  distribution relief,
    VCT investors, 7.4
  enterprise investment scheme (EIS), 7.6–7.6.5
    connected persons 7.6.2–7.6.2.10,, *see also* Connected persons
      general rules, 7.6.1
      guaranteed exit arrangements, 7.6.1.5
      joint names, shares in, 7.6.1.2
      loan-linked investments, 7.6.1.7
      maximum subscriptions, 7.6.1.8
      minimum subscriptions, 7.6.1.8
      outside investors, 7.6.1.3
      reciprocal arrangements, 7.6.1.4
      residence, 7.6.1.1
      restriction, period of, 7.6.1.6
      tax avoidance, 7.6.1.9
  generally, 7.1
  investment relief, *see* Investment relief
  loan-linked investments,
    enterprise investment scheme (EIS), 7.6.1.7
    venture capital trust (VCT) scheme, 7.3.4.1, 7.3.4
  residence,
    enterprise investment scheme (EIS), 7.6.1.1
  venture capital trust (VCT) scheme,
    distribution relief, 7.4

Qualifying investors – *contd*
venture capital trust (VCT) scheme – *contd*
investment relief, *see* Investment relief
loan-linked investments, 7.3.4, 7.3.4.1
maximum investment in a VCT, 7.5
Qualifying purpose,
corporate venturing scheme (CVS),
commencement of trade within 24 months, 5.2.4
employment of funds in a given way, 5.2.5–5.2.5.9
mainly trading, 5.2.3.2
parent company of a trading group, 5.2.3.2
purpose for which company exists, 5.2.3.1
qualifying subsidiaries, 5.2.3.2
enterprise investment scheme (EIS), 5.7.3–5.7.3.2
commencement of trade within 24 months, 5.7.4
employment of funds in a certain way required, 5.7.5–5.7.5.2
generally, 5.7.3.1
parent company of trading group, 5.7.3.2
qualifying business activity, 5.7.5.1, 5.7.5.2
Qualifying shares,
corporate venturing scheme (CVS), 4.2
Qualifying subsidiaries,
corporate venturing scheme (CVS), 5.2.3.2, 5.16–5.16.7
dormant subsidiaries, 5.16.5
generally, 5.16.1
property management, 5.16.4, 5.16.4.1, 5.16.4
qualifying 90subsidiaries, 5.16.1.1
sale of subsidiary, 5.16.7
sub-subsidiaries, 5.16.2
trading or wholly or mainly abroad, 5.16.3
winding up subsidiary, 5.16.6
enterprise investment scheme (EIS), 5.11–5.11.8
administration, 5.11.5.3
disposal of subsidiary, 5.11.6
dormant subsidiaries, 5.11.5.2
general rule, 5.11.1
option to acquire shares, 5.11.7
post-16 March 2004 share issue, 5.11.2–5.11.2.2
pre-17 March 2004 share issue, 5.11.3
property management, 5.11.5.1
receivership, 5.11.5.3
sub-subsidiaries, 5.11.4
subscription for shares in subsidiary, 5.11.8
trading wholly or mainly abroad, 5.11.5
winding up, 5.11.5.3

Qualifying subsidiaries – *contd*
venture capital trust (VCT) scheme, 5.5–5.5.9
activities, 5.5.5–5.5.5.2
property management, 5.5.5.1
dormant subsidiaries, 5.5.5.2
general rule, 5.5.1
options to acquire shares, 5.5.8
post-16 March issue of shares/securities, 5.5.2–5.5.2.2
pre-17 March issue of shares/securities, 5.5.3
relevant qualifying subsidiaries, 5.5.2.2
sale of subsidiary, 5.5.7
sub-subsidiaries, 5.5.4
subscription for shares, 5.5.9
winding up, 5.5.6
Qualifying trades, 6.1–6.9.7
carrying on qualifying trade, 6.3–6.3.13
case law on meaning of trade, 6.3.3
deemed trades, 6.3.9
definition of trade, 6.3.2
difficult areas, 6.3.10
frequency of transaction, 6.3.7
general rule, 6.3.1
management agreements, 6.3.12
marketable assets, 6.3.8
method of finance, 6.3.4
motive for acquisition, 6.3.4
nature of assets, 6.3.5
partnerships, 6.3.13
period of ownership, 6.3.6
reason for the sale, 6.3.6
sub-contracting, 6.3.11
cessation, 6.9–6.9.7
appointment of receiver to realise assets, 6.9.4
breach of conditions, 6.9.1
disposal to preserve tax relief, 6.9.5
events subsequent to disposal, 6.9.7
proceeds from liquidation, 6.9.6
winding up company, 6.9.2
commercial basis, trade conducted on, 6.1.4
enterprise investment scheme (EIS), 3.2.1
excluded activities,
accountancy services, 6.5.10
banking, 6.5.5
commodities, dealing in, 6.5.3
farming, 6.5.11
film production, 6.5.8.2.1
financial activities, 6.5.5
forestry, 6.5.12
guest houses, 6.5.13
hotels, 6.5.13
insurance, 6.5.5
intellectual property, 6.5.8–6.5.8.2.1
land, dealing in, 6.5.2
leasing, 6.5.7
legal services, 6.5.10
letting assets on hire, 6.5.7

Qualifying trades – *contd*
excluded activities – *contd*
licence fees, 6.5.9–6.5.9.1
list of, 6.5.1
market gardening, 6.5.11
nursing homes, 6.5.14
providing services to excluded trades, 6.5.15–6.5.15.2
residential care homes, 6.5.14
royalties, 6.5.8–6.5.8.2.1
shipping 6.5.6–6.5.6.8,,
see also Shipping
timber production, 6.5.12
upkeep of property, 6.5.9.1
wholesale and retail distribution, 6.5.4–6.5.4.4
groups of companies, 6.4.3
non-qualifying activities, starting, 6.8.3
notification periods, 6.1.3–6.1.3.3
CVS companies, 6.1.3.3
EIS companies, 6.1.3.2
VCT companies, 6.1.3.1
oil exploration and extraction, 6.7
periods of notification, 6.1.3–6.1.3.3
CVS companies, 6.1.3.3
EIS companies, 6.1.3.2
VCT companies, 6.1.3.1
providing services to excluded trades, 6.5.15–6.5.15.2
research and development, 6.6–6.6.7
2000 definition, 6.6.4
activities normally constituting, 6.6.4.1
activities normally excluded, 6.6.4.2
applied research, 6.6.3.2
development, 6.6.3.3
DTI guidelines, 6.6.3.4
generally, 6.6.1
immediately, requirement to start, 6.6.6
licence fees, 6.6.7
meaning, 6.6.2
new definition, 6.6.3
old definition, 6.6.4
pure or basic research, 6.6.3.1
royalties, 6.6.7
sub-contractors, 6.6.5
starting trade, 6.8–6.8.3
how soon need trade start, 6.8.1
non-qualifying activities, starting, 6.8.3
when does trade start, 6.8.2
types of trades, 6.1.1
use of money raised, 6.2–6.2.9
cash deposits, 6.2.9
deciding how much to raise, 6.2.8
employment of funds, 6.2.5
how funds are used, 6.2.3
investments, 6.2.6
management buy-outs, 6.2.4
management charges, 6.2.7
parent companies, 6.2.7
qualifying non-trade activities, 6.2.2

Qualifying trades – *contd*
use of money raised – *contd*
to carry on a trade, 6.2.1
wholly of mainly in UK, trade carried on, 6.4–6.4.3
criteria, 6.4.2
groups of companies, 6.4.3
Quoted investment trusts,
venture capital trust (VCT) scheme, 1.2.2

R

Rate of relief,
CVS investment relief, 20.3.2
EIS investment relief, 20.2.5
VCT investment relief, 20.2.5
Reconstructions,
CVS disposal relief, 19.3.6
EIS deferral relief, 15.13–15.13.3
VCT investment relief, 8.6.3
Records,
venture capital trust (VCT) scheme, 24.3.7
inspection, 24.3.8
Reinvestment relief, *see* CVS deferral relief; EIS deferral relief; VCT deferral relief
Reinvestment rollover relief (RIR), 14.1.1, 15.1.1
Research and development,
qualifying trades, 6.6–6.6.7
activities normally constituting, 6.6.4.1
activities normally excluded, 6.6.4.2
development, 6.6.3.3
DTI guidelines, 6.6.3.4
generally, 6.6.1
licence fees, 6.6.7
meaning, 6.6.2
new definition, 6.6.3
old definition, 6.6.4
pure or basic research, 6.6.3.1
royalties, 6.6.7
Residence,
CVS investment relief, 10.2.2
EIS deferral relief, 15.4.2, 15.4.3
cessation of UK residence, 15.7.4
temporarily working abroad, 15.7.4.1
EIS investment relief, 9.2.2
enterprise investment scheme (EIS), 7.6.1.1
qualifying companies, 5.1.5
VCT deferral relief, 14.4.2, 14.4.3
cessation of UK residence, 14.7.4–14.7.4.1
working abroad temporarily, 14.7.4.1
VCT investment relief, 8.2.2
venture capital trust (VCT) scheme, 2.2.2, 2.2.4, 2.2.2
Residential care homes, 6.5.14
Restructuring company,
corporate venturing scheme (CVS), 4.2.3
Retirement relief,
EIS relief, 23.5.7

Retirement relief – *contd*
EIS shares, 23.5.5
generally, 23.5.1
gift holdover relief, interaction with, 23.5.8
period for conditions, 23.5.4
qualifying companies, 23.5.3
qualifying individuals, 23.5.2
share exchange, 23.5.6
Rights issue,
company reorganisations, 19.3.3
EIS disposal relief, 18.3.5
VCT disposal relief, 17.3.5
RIR relief, 1.6
Rollover relief on reinvestment, 1.6
Royalties, 6.5.8–6.5.8.2.1, 6.6.7

S

SBIC, 1.7
Share capital,
CVS investee company, 5.14–5.14.2
issue of shares, 26.7–26.7.5
qualifying companies, 5.9–5.9.2
eligible shares, 5.9.1
fully paid-up shares, 5.9.2
Share exchange,
VCT investment relief, 8.6.3
Shipping,
charter conditions, 6.5.6.7
oil rigs, 6.5.6.5
permissible ship chartering, 6.5.6.4
pleasure craft, 6.5.6.5
ship chartering, 6.5.6–6.5.6.2
spot market, 6.5.6.2, 6.5.6.3
time charter, 6.5.6.1, 6.5.6.3
trading wholly or mainly in the UK, 6.5.6.8
UK registration of ship, 6.5.6.6
voyage charter, 6.5.6.2, 6.5.6.3
Small business investment company (SBIC), 1.7
Small businesses,
needs of, 1.7
small business investment company (SBIC), 1.7
United States, 1.7
Small private schemes, 26.1–26.9.6
see also Company; Directors
associates, 26.2–26.2.6
joint ownership, 26.2.4
partners, 26.2.3
personal representatives, 26.2.6
relatives, 26.2.2
trustees of related settlements, 26.2.5
certificates, 26.3.9
EIS company,
mix of loans and shares, 26.3.7
provisional clearance, 26.3.8
qualifying investors, 26.3.6
relevant period, 26.1.3

Small private schemes – *contd*
EIS deferral relief, 26.3.3, 26.4–26.4.4
advantages, 26.5.2
EIS disposal relief, 26.3.4
EIS investment relief, 26.3.2
advantages, 26.5.1
EIS investor's relevant period, 26.1.4
EIS loss relief, 26.3.5
eligible shares, 26.1.5
investors' loans, 26.9.3
payments to directors, 26.9.2
professional advisers, 26.1.1
property purchase,
EIS shareholders, 26.9.5
non-EIS shareholders, 26.9.6
qualifying companies, 26.1.6
qualifying investors, 26.3.6
setting up a private company 26.6–26.6.14,, *see also* Formation of private company
Spouse, transfers to,
EIS disposal relief, 18.2.3
VCT disposal relief, 17.2.5
Subscription for shares,
EIS investment relief, 9.2.5
VCT investment relief, 8.2.5
Substantial shareholdings relief, 23.8

T

Taper relief,
EIS deferral relief, 15.2.1
EIS gains, 23.7.2
EIS investments, 23.7.3
introduction, 23.7.1
VCT deferral relief, 14.2.1
VCT shares, 23.7.3
Timber production, 6.5.12

U

Undertakings,
control, 5.1.9.5
Underwriting,
control, 5.1.9.5
United States,
small business investment company (SBIC), 1.7
small businesses, 1.7
Unlisted Securities Market (USM), 1.8
Unquoted companies,
investment in, 1.9
Unquoted shares,
losses on, 21.2.1–21.2.3
claims, 21.6.1
EIS shares, 21.2.3, 21.3–21.3.4, 22.7.1–22.7.2
giving effect to relief, 21.2.2
identification of shares, 21.5
non-EIS shares, 21.4–21.4.3
ordinary shares, 21.3.1

Unquoted shares – *contd*
losses on – *contd*
qualifying disposals, 21.3.2
qualifying shares, 21.3.1
qualifying trading company, 21.4.2
relief, 21.6.2
share exchanges, 21.3.3, 21.4.3
value shifting, 21.3.4
tax advantages, 1.8.1
USM, 1.8

V

Valuation,
VCT investee company shares, 5.6.2.11, 5.6.2.12
VCT deferral relief, 1.2.3, 1.6, 2.3.2, 14.1–14.7.7, 22.2.1
background, 14.1.1
cessation of UK residence, 14.7.4–14.7.4.1
chargeable event, 14.2
chargeable gain, 14.6.2.1
claimants, 14.4.1
crystallisation of gains, 14.7–14.7.7, 22.9
cessation of UK residence, 14.7.4–14.7.4.1
chargeable events, 14.7.1
gain accruing on a chargeable event, 14.7.2
person chargeable on crystallisation, 14.7.3
date of disposal, 14.3.5
death, exception for, 14.7.7
deferred gains, 14.2.1
deferring gains, 14.6–14.6.4
amount of gain deferred, 14.6.2
chargeable gain, 14.6.2.1
expenditure on which investment relief is given, 14.6.5
unmatched gain, 14.6.4
unused qualifying expenditure, 14.6.3
discretionary trusts, 14.7.5
dual residence, 14.4.3
eligible gain, 14.3.1
entitlement to claim deferment, 14.4–14.4.3
claimants, 14.4.1
dual residence, 14.4.3
UK residence, 14.4.2
giving effect to, 22.3–22.3.2
claims procedure, 22.3.3
how much of gain deferred, 22.3.1
withdrawal of relief, 22.3.2
historical development, 14.1.1
how much of gain deferred, 22.3.1
indexation, 14.2.1
limits on gain deferred, 14.3.4
loss of investment relief, 14.7.6
loss of status by investee company, 14.7.5
period for making qualifying investments, 14.3.2

VCT deferral relief – *contd*
qualifying companies, 14.5.2
qualifying investment, 14.2, 14.5.2
meaning, 14.5.1
period for making, 14.3.2
qualifying companies, 14.5.2
residence, 14.4.2, 14.4.3
cessation of UK residence, 14.7.4–14.7.4.1
working abroad temporarily, 14.7.4.1
summary, 14.2, 14.2.1
taper relief, 14.2.1
window, deferral relief, 14.3.3
withdrawal, 22.3.2
VCT disposal relief, 1.2.3, 17.1–17.8.1
bonus issue, 17.3.6
company reorganisations, 17.3–17.3.7
bonus issue, 17.3.6
categories of share, 17.3.3
investment-relief shares, 17.3.3.2
new shares not VCT shares, where, 17.3.7
rights issue, 17.3.5
separate identification following, 17.3.4
shares eligible for relief, 17.3.3.1
subdivision of shares, 17.3.2
crystallisation of deferred gains, 17.1.4
death, 17.2.4
disposal, 17.2–17.2.6
death, 17.2.4
deemed disposal, 17.2.3
early disposals, 17.2.6
options, 17.2.2
spouse, transfers to, 17.2.5
early disposal, 17.1.1, 17.2.6
disposal relief, 17.5.1
gains, 17.5–17.5.2
losses, 17.6–17.6.2
non-qualifying disposals, 17.5.2, 17.6.2
non-recognition of losses, 17.6.1
eligible shares, 17.1.5
giving effect to, 22.6
later disposals, 17.1.1
disposal relief, 17.7.1
gains, 17.7–17.7.2
losses, 17.8.1
non-qualifying disposals, 17.7.2
non-recognition of losses, 17.8.1
options, 17.2.2
part disposals, 17.4–17.4.2.3
identifying disposals with acquisitions, 17.4.2
shares acquired before 6 April 1998, 17.4.2.3
shares acquired on different days, 17.4.2.2
shares acquired on same day, 17.4.2.1
purpose, 17.1.1
restricted periods for disposals, 17.1.3
rights issue, 17.3.5
spouse, transfers to, 17.2.5

VCT distribution relief, 1.2.3, 2.3.2, 7.5, 8.5–8.5.4
  permitted maximum, 8.5.4
  qualifying conditions, 8.5.2
  relevant distributions, 8.5.3
VCT investment relief, 1.2.3, 2.3.2, 7.3–7.3.4.1, 8.1–8.6.3
  £200,000 limit, investment exceeding, 8.6–8.6.3
  amount, 8.3–8.3.4
    annual limit, 8.3.1
    attribution of VCT initial relief to shares, 8.3.4
    lower rate of tax, relief at, 8.3.3
    minimum investment, 8.3.2
  assessment, withdrawal by, 20.4.7, 20.4.7.1
  associates, 7.3.4.1
  availability, 8.1
  bona fide commercial subscription, 8.2.7
  breach of qualifying conditions, 11.3–11.3.2, 20.4.3
  claiming relief, 20.2.1, 24.5.3
  computing investor's liability to income tax, 20.2.8
  conditions, 7.3.1
  death of investor, 20.4.6
  disposal at arm's length, 20.4.2
  disposal not at arm's length, 20.4.4
  documentation, 20.2.1
  eligible shares, 7.3.1, 7.3.2, 8.1, 8.1.2
  entitlement, 8.2–8.2.8
    bona fide commercial subscription, 8.2.7
    individuals, 8.2.1
    joint ownership, 8.2.6
    loan-linked investments, 8.2.8
    more than one share issue, 8.2.4
    nominees, 8.2.6
    period of restriction for individuals, 8.2.3
    residence, 8.2.2
    subscription for shares, 8.2.5
  identifying shares in a disposal, 20.4.5
  interest, 20.7.1
  issue of shares, 8.1.5
  joint ownership, 8.2.6
  loan-linked investments, 7.3.4, 7.3.4.1, 8.2.8
    consequences of receiving linked loan, 11.2.3
    restricted period, 11.2.2
  losing, 11.1–11.3.2, 20.4–20.4.7.1
    assessment, withdrawal by, 20.4.7, 20.4.7.1
    breach of qualifying conditions, 11.3–11.3.2, 20.4.3
    death of investor, 20.4.6
    disposal at arm's length, 20.4.2
    disposal not at arm's length, 20.4.4
    identifying shares in a disposal, 20.4.5
    linked loan, receipt of, 11.2–11.2.3
    occasions for loss of relief, 11.1.3, 20.4.1
    restricted period, 11.2.2
    unpaid tax, 20.7.1
VCT investment relief – *contd*
  minimum investment, 20.2.4
  nominees, 8.2.6
  ordinary shares, 8.1.4
  overdue tax, 20.7.2
  PAYE code adjustment, 20.2.9
  permitted maximum, 20.2.2
  postponement of tax, 20.2.10
  pre-emption rights, 8.1.3
  prohibition of tax avoidance, 7.3.3
  rate of relief, 20.2.5
  reconstructions, 8.6.3
  repayment supplements, 20.7.5
  residence, 8.2.2
  restriction, 20.2.6
  share exchange, 8.6.3
  subscription for shares, 8.2.5
  tax avoidance, prohibition, 7.3.3
  tax year in which relief given, 20.2.7
  unpaid tax, 20.7.2
  when relief is given, 8.4
VCT relief, 2.1
  see also VCT deferral relief; VCT disposal relief; VCT distribution relief; VCT investment relief; Venture capital trust (VCT) scheme
  rate, 2.1.3
  types of relief, 1.2.3, 2.3.2
  withdrawal, 1.5
VCT scheme, *see* Venture capital trust (VCT) scheme
Venture Capital Schemes Manual,
  extracts, 1.1.1
Venture capital trust (VCT) scheme, 1.1.1, 2.1–2.4
  advantages, 1.1.2
  approval, 1.2.2, 2.2–2.2.4, 24.2–24.2.9
    appeals, 24.2.9
    application for full approval, 24.2.5.2
    application procedure, 24.2.5–24.2.9
    continuing to meet conditions, 24.2.3
    effective date of approval, 24.2.7
    eligible shares, 24.2.2
    generally, 24.2.1
    information required for provisional approval, 24.2.5.1
    notice of provisional approval, 24.2.6
    provisional approval, 24.2.4–24.2.4.2
    refusal to grant VCT status, 24.2.8
    second accounting period, 24.2.4.1
    signatures, 24.2.5.3
    three-year initial period, 24.2.4.2
    withdrawal, 24.4–24.4.5
  arrangements, 5.1.7
  benefits, 2.3.2, 2.3.1
  cancellation of approval, 2.2.1
  capital gains, 2.2.4
  capital gains tax, 2.3.2
  certificates, 24.3.5.2, 24.5–24.5.4
    claiming investment relief, 24.5.3

Venture capital trust (VCT) scheme – *contd*
certificates – *contd*
contents, 24.5.2
form, 24.5.2
conditions for approval, 1.2.2, 2.2–2.2.4, 2.6
eligible shares, 2.2.1
exit route, 2.2.3
failure to meet, 2.2.1
listed shares, 2.2.1
provisional approach, 2.2.1
qualifying holdings, 2.2.1
residence, 2.2.2
shares, 2.2.1
connected persons, 5.1.6
control, *see* Control
corporation tax, 2.4
deferrment relief, 2.3.2
distribution of capital gains, 2.2.4
distribution relief, 2.3.2
dividends, 2.2.3, 2.4
eligible shares, 2.2.1
enterprise investment scheme compared, 5.18
exit route, 2.2.3
fragmentation of activities, 5.3.3
informal clearance 24.6–24.6.11,,
see also Informal VCT and EIS clearance
information powers,
event causing investment relief to be lost, 25.2.1
general information power, 25.2.4
notices, 25.2.3
refusal of approval, 25.2.2
returns, 24.5.2, 25.2.3
withdrawal of approval, 25.2.2
Inland Revenue booklet, 1.5
introduction, 1.1.2, 1.2.1, 2.1
investee company, 5.3–5.3.5, 5.4–5.4.6
15test, 5.6.2.9
fragmentation of activities, 5.3.3
gradual fulfillment of conditions, 5.6.3
income retention, 5.6.2.13
investment limits, 5.3.1–5.3.5
investments, 5.6.2.2
maximum investment, 5.3.1
minimum eligible share content, 5.6.2.14
modified valuation, 5.6.2.12
non-qualifying holdings, 5.6.2.7
proportion of qualifying holdings, 5.6.2.6
qualifying subsidiaries, *see* Qualifying subsidiaries
securities, 5.6.2.4
share exchanges, 5.6.2.10
shares, 5.6.2.3
valuation, 5.6.2.11, 5.6.2.12
VCT money raised, 5.3.2
wholly or mainly, 5.6.2.5
investment limits,
fragmentation of activities, 5.3.3
gross asset limit, 5.3.5

Venture capital trust (VCT) scheme – *contd*
investment limits – *contd*
joint ventures, 5.3.4
maximum investment, 5.3.1
VCT money raised, 5.3.2
investment trusts compared, 2.2.4
investor company,
conditions for approval, 5.6.2–5.6.2.14
listing requirements, 5.6.2.1
official listing, 5.6.2.1
joint ventures, 5.3.4
monitoring status, 24.3–24.3.8
certificate, 24.3.5.2
investment return for a specified period, 24.3.5–24.3.5.3
qualifying companies, 24.3.3
sources of information, 24.3.2
VCT timetable, 24.3.3
nature, 2.1.2
official listing, 2.1.2, 2.2.1
operation, 2.1
PEP for unquoted investments, 2.1.3
qualifying companies, 1.2.2
and see Qualifying companies
arrangements, 5.1.7
connected persons, 5.1.6
control, *see* Control
fragmentation of activities, 5.3.3
gross asset limit, 5.3.5
investee company, 5.3–5.3.5, 5.4–5.4.6
investor companies, 5.6–5.6.3
maximum investment, 5.3.1
periods of restriction, 5.1.2
qualifying subsidiaries, 5.5–5.5.8
VCT money raised, 5.3.2
qualifying holdings, 2.2.1
qualifying investors,
distribution relief, 7.4
investment relief, *see* Investment relief
maximum investment in a VCT, 7.5
qualifying subsidiaries, 5.5–5.5.9
activities, 5.5.5–5.5.5.2
property management, 5.5.5.1
dormant subsidiaries, 5.5.5.2
general rule, 5.5.1
options to acquire shares, 5.5.8
post-16 March issue of shares/securities, 5.5.2–5.5.2.2
pre-17 March issue of shares/securities, 5.5.3
relevant qualifying subsidiaries, 5.5.2.2
sale of subsidiary, 5.5.7
sub-subsidiaries, 5.5.4
subscription for shares, 5.5.9
winding up, 5.5.6
quoted investment trusts, 1.2.2
records, 24.3.7
inspection, 24.3.8
reinvestment, *see* VCT deferral relief

Venture capital trust (VCT) scheme – *contd*
relief, *see* VCT deferral relief; VCT disposal relief; VCT distribution relief; VCT investment relief
residence, 2.2.2, 2.2.4, 2.2.2, 2.2.4
return of investors' subscriptions, 24.3.6
tax advantages, 2.3.2
withdrawal of approval, 24.4–24.4.5
approval date deemed never to have been given, 24.4.4
earlier withdrawal date, 24.4.3.1

Venture capital trust (VCT) scheme – *contd*
withdrawal of approval – *contd*
effect on VCT shareholders, 24.4.5
grounds for withdrawal, 24.4.2
notice of breach of conditions, 24.4.1
notice of withdrawal, 24.4.3

W

Wholesale and retail distribution, 6.5.4–6.5.4.4